D0352322

Indonesian Living Standards

Before and After the Financial Crisis

The RAND Corporation is a nonprofit research organization providing objective analysis and effective solutions that address the challenges facing the public and private sectors around the world.

RAND publications do not necessarily reflect the opinions of its research clients and sponsors. "RAND" is a registered trademark.

This product is part of the RAND Corporation's monograph series. RAND monographs present major research findings. All RAND monographs undergo rigorous peer review to ensure high standards for research quality and objectivity.

The **Institute of Southeast Asian Studies (ISEAS)** was established as an autonomous organization in 1968. It is a regional centre dedicated to the study of socio-political, security and economic trends and developments in Southeast Asia and its wider geostrategic and economic environment.

The Institute's research programmes are the Regional Economic Studies (RES, including ASEAN and APEC), Regional Strategic and Political Studies (RSPS), and Regional Social and Cultural Studies (RSCS).

The Institute is governed by a twenty-two-member Board of Trustees comprising nominees from the Singapore Government, the National University of Singapore, the Chambers of Commerce, and professional and civic organizations. An Executive Committee oversees day-to-day operations; it is chaired by the Director, the Institute's chief academic and administrative officer.

Indonesian Living Standards

Before and After the Financial Crisis

John Strauss • Kathleen Beegle • Agus Dwiyanto • Yulia Herawati
Daan Pattinasarany • Elan Satriawan • Bondan Sikoki
Sukamdi • Firman Witoelar

RAND CORPORATION
LABOR AND POPULATION
Center for the Study of the Family in Economic Development

INSTITUTE OF SOUTHEAST ASIAN STUDIES
Singapore

UNIVERSITY OF GADJAH MADA
Yogyakarta

First published in Singapore in 2004 by
Institute of Southeast Asian Studies
30 Heng Mui Keng Terrace
Pasir Panjang
Singapore 119614

E-mail: publish@iseas.edu.sg
Website: http://bookshop.iseas.edu.sg

First published in the United States of America in 2004 by
RAND Corporation
1700 Main Street, P.O. Box 2138
Santa Monica, CA 90407-2138
USA

To order through RAND Corporation or to obtain additional information, contact Distribution Services: Tel: 310-451-7002; Fax: 310-451-6915; E-mail: order@rand.org

All rights reserved. No part of this publication may be reproduced, stored in a retrieval system, or transmitted in any form or by any means, electronic, mechanical, photocopying, recording or otherwise, without the prior permission of the Institute of Southeast Asian Studies and RAND Corporation.

© 2004 RAND Corporation

The responsibility for facts and opinions in this publication rests exclusively with the authors and their interpretations do not necessarily reflect the views or the policy of the Institute, RAND Corporation or their supporters.

ISEAS Library Cataloguing-in-Publication Data

Indonesian living standards before and after the financial crisis / John Strauss ... [et al.].

1. Cost and standard of living—Indonesia.
2. Wages—Indonesia.
3. Poverty—Indonesia.
4. Education—Indonesia.
5. Public health—Indonesia.
6. Birth control—Indonesia.
7. Household surveys—Indonesia.

I. Strauss, John, 1951-

HD7055 I412 2004

ISBN 981-230-168-2 (ISEAS, Singapore)
ISBN 0-8330-3558-4 (RAND Corporation)

Cover design by Stephen Bloodsworth, RAND Corporation
Typeset by Superskill Graphics Pte Ltd
Printed in Singapore by Seng Lee Press Pte Ltd

Contents

List of Figures

List of Tables

Acknowledgements

The authors would like to thank the following staff for their very important assistance in creating tables and figures: Tubagus Choesni, Endang Ediastuti, Anis Khairinnisa, Umi Listyaningsih, Wenti Marina Minza, Muhammad Nuh, Agus Joko Pitoyo, Pungpond Rukumnuaykit, Henry Sembiring and Sukamtiningsih.

The authors would also like to thank Jean-Yves Duclos, Kai Kaiser and Jack Molyneaux for very helpful discussions early in the drafting process and thanks to Tubagus Choesni, Molyneaux and the RAND Data Core for aid in obtaining the BPS data.

Thanks also to the participants of a workshop held in Yogyakarta on 2–3 July 2002, at which the first draft was extensively discussed and many suggestions made that were incorporated into the revisions. In addition to the authors, attendees included: Irwan Abdullah, I Gusti Ngurah Agung, Stuart Callison, Muhadjir Darwin, Faturochman, Johar, Kai Kaiser, Yeremias T. Keban, Soewarta Kosen, Bevaola Kusumasari, Imran Lubis, Amelia Maika, Jack Molyneaux, Mubyarto, Ali Gufron Mukti, Sri Purwatiningsih, Sri Kusumastuti Rahayu, Mohammad Rum Ali, and Suyanto.

Thanks, too, to the following persons for helpful comments: T. Paul Schultz, Vivi Alatas, Aris Ananta and Ben Olken.

Funding for work on this report comes from a Partnership on Economic Growth (PEG) Linkage Grant to RAND and the Center for Population and Policy Studies, University of Gadjah Mada, from the United States Agency for International Development (USAID), Jakarta Mission: "Policy Analysis and Capacity Building Using the Indonesia Family Life Surveys", grant number 497-G-00-01-0028-00. Support for Beegle's time came from the World Bank. These are the views of the authors and should not be attributed to USAID or the World Bank.

IFLS3 was funded by the US National Institute of Aging (NIA) and the National Institute of Child Health and Human Development (NICHD) under grants 1R01AG17637 and 1R01HD38484. IFLS2 was funded by NIA, NICHD, USAID, The Futures Group (POLICY Project), Hewlett Foundation, International Food Policy Research Institute, John Snow International (OMNI Project), and the World Health Organization.

IFLS3 fieldwork was headed by John Strauss and Agus Dwiyanto, Principal Investigators, and Kathleen Beegle and Bondan Sikoki, co-Principal Investigators. Victoria Beard was a co-Principal Investigator in the early stages of the project. Fieldwork was co-ordinated by the Center for Population and Policy Studies, University of Gadjah Mada, Agus Dwiyanto, Director; with Bondan Sikoki as Field Director; Elan Satriawan, Associate Director; Cecep Sumantri, head of fieldwork for the household questionnaire, Yulia Herawati, head of fieldwork for the community and facility questionnaires; and Iip Rifai, head and chief programmer for data entry. Overall programming was headed by Roald Euller, assisted by Afshin Rastegar and Chi San. Faturochman, David Kurth and Tukiran made important contributions to instrument development, as well as to other aspects of the fieldwork.

IFLS2 fieldwork was headed by Elizabeth Frankenberg and Duncan Thomas, Principal Investigators. Fieldwork was co-ordinated by Lembaga Demografi, University of Indonesia, Haidy Pasay, Director; with Bondan Sikoki as Field Director. Wayan Suriastini made important contributions to the household fieldwork, Muda Saputra directed the community and facility fieldwork, and Sutji Rochani directed data entry. Programming for data entry was co-ordinated by Trevor Croft of Macro International with Hendratno. Overall programming was co-ordinated by Sue Pollich.

List of Authors

John Strauss	Department of Economics, Michigan State University, East Lansing, Michigan
Kathleen Beegle	World Bank, Washington D.C.
Agus Dwiyanto	Center for Population and Policy Studies, University of Gadjah Mada, Yogyakarta, Indonesia
Yulia Herawati	World Bank, Jakarta, Indonesia
Daan Pattinasarany	Department of Economics, Michigan State University, East Lansing, Michigan
Elan Satriawan	Center for Population and Policy Studies, University of Gadjah Mada, Yogyakarta, Indonesia
Bondan Sikoki	RAND, Santa Monica, California
Sukamdi	Center for Population and Policy Studies, University of Gadjah Mada, Yogyakarta, Indonesia
Firman Witoelar	Department of Economics, Michigan State University, East Lansing, Michigan

1

The Financial Crisis in Indonesia

The Asian financial crisis in 1997 and 1998 was a serious blow to what had been a 30-year period of rapid growth in East and Southeast Asia (see World Bank 1998, for one of many discussions of the crisis in Asia). During this period before this crisis, massive improvements occurred in many dimensions of the living standards of these populations (World Bank 1997). In Indonesia, real per capita GDP rose four-fold between 1965 and 1995, with an annual growth rate averaging 4.5% until the 1990s, when it rose to almost 5.5% (World Bank 1997). The poverty headcount rate declined from over 40% in 1976 to just under 18% by 1996. Infant mortality fell from 118 per thousand live births in 1970 to 46 in 1997 (World Bank 1997, Central Bureau of Statistics et al. 1998). Primary school enrolments rose from 75% in 1970 to universal enrolment by 1995 and secondary enrolment rates from 13% to 55% over the same period (World Bank 1997). The total fertility rate fell from 5.6 in 1971 to 2.8 in 1997 (Central Bureau of Statistics et al. 1998).

In April 1997, the financial crisis began to be felt in the Southeast Asia region, although the major impact did not hit Indonesia until December 1997 and January 1998. Real GDP declined 13% in 1998, stayed constant in 1999 and finally began growing in 2000, by 4.5%. Different sectors of the economy were affected quite differently. Macroeconomic data from the Central Bureau of Statistics (BPS) shows that the decline in GDP in 1998 hit investment levels very hard. Real gross domestic fixed investment fell in 1998 by 35.5%. For the household sector, much of the impact was due to rapid and large swings in prices, which largely resulted from exchange rate volatility. Figure 1.1 shows the movement of the monthly rupiah-US dollar exchange rate over this period. One can see a depreciation of the rupiah starting in August, but with a massive decline starting in

January 1998 and appreciating substantially after September 1998, but slowly depreciating once again starting at the end of 1999, through 2000.

The exchange rate depreciation was a key part of the crisis because the relative prices of tradable goods increased, especially of foodstuffs. Figure 1.2 shows estimates from Kaiser et al. (2001) of the monthly food price index for rural and urban areas of Indonesia from January 1997 to March 2000. Starting in January 1998 and continuing through March 1999, nominal food prices exploded, going up three-fold, with most of the increase coming by September 1998. While non-food prices also increased, there was a sharp rise in the relative price of food through early 1999. Arguably any major impact during this period felt by Indonesians, except those at the top of the income distribution, occurred because of the massive increase in food prices. The food share (excluding tobacco and alcohol) of the typical Indonesian's household budget is approximately 50% in urban

FIGURE 1.1
Timing of the IFLS and the Rp/USD Exchange Rate

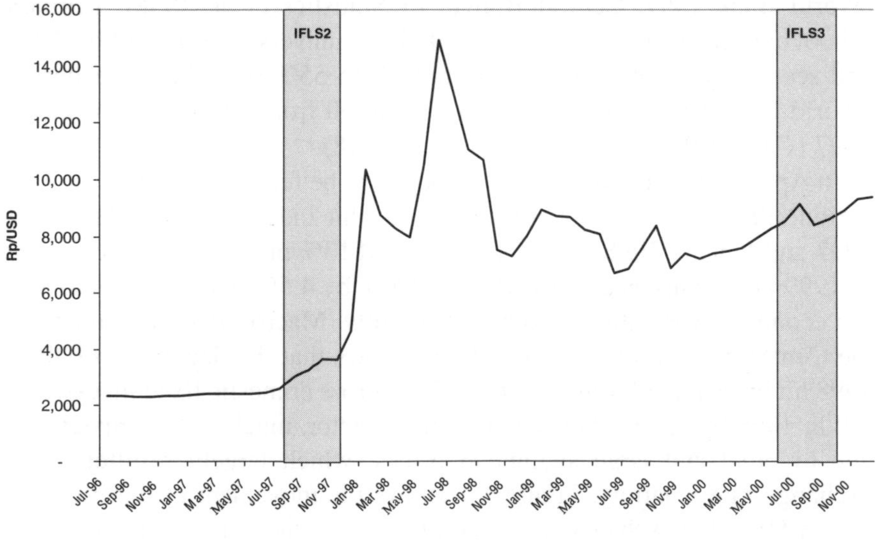
16,000
14,000
12,000
10,000
8,000
6,000
4,000
2,000
-
Rp/USD
IFLS2
IFLS3
Jul-96
Sep-96
Nov-96
Jan-97
Mar-97
May-97
Jul-97
Sep-97
Nov-97
Jan-98
Mar-98
May-98
Jul-98
Sep-98
Nov-98
Jan-99
Mar-99
May-99
Jul-99
Sep-99
Nov-99
Jan-00
Mar-00
May-00
Jul-00
Sep-00
Nov-00

Source: Pacific Exchange Rate Service, http://pacific.commerce.ubc.ca.xr/.

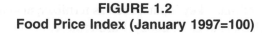

FIGURE 1.2
Food Price Index (January 1997=100)

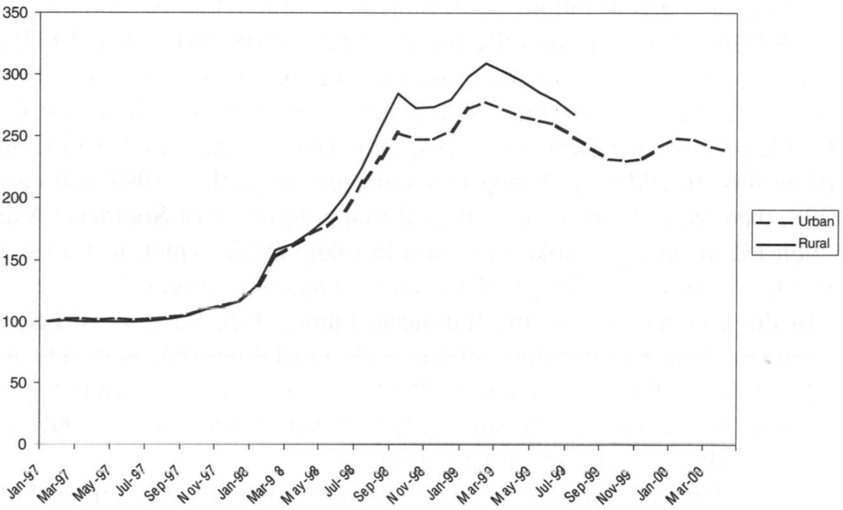
350
300
250
200
150
100
50
0
Urban
Rural
Jan-97
Mar-97
May-97
Jul-97
Sep-97
Nov-97
Jan-98
Mar-98
May-98
Jul-98
Sep-98
Nov-98
Jan-99
Mar-99
May-99
Jul-99
Sep-99
Nov-99
Jan-00
Mar-00

Source: Kaiser, Choesni, Gertler, Levine, Molyneaux (2001), "The Cost of Living Over Time and Space in Indonesia".

areas and 57% in rural regions. Among the poor, of course, food shares are even higher.

The large increases in relative food prices by itself resulted in a fall of real incomes for net food purchasers (most of the Indonesian population), while net food producers were helped. Of course there were many other changes that occurred during the crisis period, which had additional, sometimes differing, impacts on household welfare. For instance, nominal wages also rose during this period. This ameliorated the impact of food price increases for those who rely on market wages, but only very slightly since the increase in nominal wages was considerably less than the increase in food and non-food prices, hence real wages declined. With these kinds of economic shocks, one would expect to find serious welfare consequences on individuals.

Within the household sector, it is likely that different groups of people were affected rather differently. For instance, farmers who are net sellers of foodstuffs may have seen their real incomes rise over this period (although prices of many key inputs, such as fertilizer, also increased, they did so by less; Bresciano et al. 2002). Furthermore, in late 1997 and early 1998, there was a serious rural crisis caused by a major drought, especially in the eastern parts of Indonesia. National rice production fell roughly 4% in 1997 from 1996 and was 9% lower in 1998 (Fox 2002). The 1997/98 drought helped to push up rice prices during that period over and above that due to the exchange rate. As a result, compared to 1997, farmers in 2000, especially in eastern provinces, may have had increased crop yields and profits. In addition, during this same period, in late 1997 and early 1998, there were serious forest fires throughout much of Southeast Asia, which led to serious smoke pollution in many areas, which in turn may have led to serious health problems and decreases in productivity.[1]

In this chapter, we use the Indonesia Family Life Surveys (IFLS) to examine different dimensions of the welfare of Indonesians during the crisis. Waves of IFLS span the period of the 1998 crisis, as shown in Figure 1.1. The second wave of the survey, IFLS2, was fielded in late 1997 and the third full wave, IFLS3, in late 2000.

IFLS allows a comprehensive examination of individual, household and community welfare. Data is gathered on household expenditures, allowing one to examine what happened to real expenditures and to poverty. IFLS also contains information on many other topics that are of central interest in the assessment of welfare changes. There is an especially rich set of data regarding wages, employment, and health; also detailed information is collected pertaining to schooling, family planning, and receipt of central government sponsored (JPS), and other, social safety-net programmes. In addition, IFLS includes an extremely rich set of data at the community level and for individual health and school facilities, so that we can also track the availability and quality of services, both publicly and privately provided. Related to this, we have in 2000 some baseline information regarding decentralization. Moreover, since IFLS is a panel survey it is possible to analyse changes for specific communities, households and individuals.

With this data one has the unique opportunity to investigate the medium-term impacts of the crisis on health and other measures of welfare. These results can then be compared to an analysis of very short-term crisis impacts documented by Frankenberg et al. (1999), who analysed changes between IFLS2 and a special 25% sub-sample, IFLS2+, that was fielded in late 1998.

We start in Chapter 2 with a description of IFLS and its sampling of households and individuals. We provide evidence on how characteristics of IFLS2 and IFLS3 compare to those of large-scale representative household surveys fielded in the same years. Chapter 3 describes the levels of real per capita expenditure and the incidence of poverty of individuals in the IFLS sample in 1997 and 2000.[2] Chapter 4 discusses results pertaining to subjective measures of welfare fielded in IFLS3 that assess respondents' perception of their welfare in the current year and just before the crisis began in 1997. These subjective measures are analysed and compared with more standard, objective measures of per capita expenditures. Chapter 5 focuses on labour markets, discussing changes in real wages and employment, overall and by market and self-employment. We also present evidence on the incidence of child labour. Chapter 6 begins an analysis of a series of important non-income measures of welfare, by examining child school enrolments in 1997 and 2000 and the quality and cost of schooling services as reported by schools surveyed in IFLS3. Chapter 7 provides details of different dimensions of child and adult health outcomes over this period and Chapter 8 examines health utilization patterns in 1997 and 2000. Chapter 9 provides a complementary perspective from the point of view of health facilities: examining changes in availability, quality and cost of services offered. Chapters 10 and 11 examine family planning usage by couples (Chapter 10), and services offered at the community level (Chapter 11). Chapter 12 discusses the set of special safety-net programmes (JPS) established by the central government after the crisis began. We present evidence regarding their incidence, amounts and on how well they were targeted to poor households. Chapter 13 presents baseline evidence relevant to the new decentralization laws, regarding how much budgetary and decision-making control was exercised by local governments and facilities over their programmes and policies at the time IFLS3 was fielded in late 2000. Chapter 14 concludes.

Notes

1. See Sastry (2002) for an analysis of the health impacts of smoke in Malaysia
2. In this chapter, we measure poverty using information on household consumption expenditures (and not income). This has become standard in low-income settings, where income is difficult to measure and has an important seasonal component.

2

IFLS Description and Representativeness

SELECTION OF HOUSEHOLDS

IFLS1

The first wave of IFLS was fielded in the second half of 1993, between August and January 1994.[1] Over 30,000 individuals in 7,224 households were sampled. The IFLS1 sampling scheme was stratified on provinces and rural-urban areas within provinces. Enumeration areas (EAs) were randomly sampled within these strata, and households within enumeration areas. The sampling frame came from the Central Bureau of Statistics and was the same used by the 1993 SUSENAS. Provinces were selected to maximize representation of the population, capture the cultural and socioeconomic diversity of Indonesia, and be cost-effective given the size of the country and its transportation and telecommunications limitations in 1993. The resulting sample spanned 13 provinces on Java, Sumatra, Bali, Kalimantan, Sulawesi and Nusa Tenggara.[2]

Some 321 EAs in the 13 provinces were randomly sampled, over-sampling urban EAs and EAs in smaller provinces in order to facilitate rural-urban and Java–non-Java comparisons. The communities selected by province and urban/rural area are listed in Appendix Table 2.1.

From each urban EA, 20 households were selected randomly, while 30 households were randomly chosen from each rural EA. This strategy minimized expensive travel between rural EAs and reduced intra-cluster correlation across urban households, which tend to be more similar than rural households. A household was defined as a group of people whose members reside in the same dwelling and share food from the same cooking pot (the standard Central Bureau of Statistics definition).

In the IFLS1, a total of 7,730 households were selected as the original target sample. Of these households, 7,224 (93%) were interviewed. Of the 7% of households that were never interviewed, approximately 2% refused and 5% were never found.

IFLS2

Main fieldwork for IFLS2 took place between June and November 1997, just before the worst of the financial crisis hit Indonesia.[3] The months were chosen in order to correspond to the seasonal timing of IFLS1. The goal of IFLS2 was to resurvey all the IFLS1 households. Approximately 10–15% of households had moved from their original location and were followed. Moreover, IFLS2 added almost 900 households by tracking individuals who "split-off" from the original households.

If an entire household, or a targeted individual(s) moved, then they were tracked as long as they still resided in any one of the 13 IFLS provinces, irrespective of whether they moved across those provinces. Individuals who split off into new households were targeted for tracking provided they were a "main respondent" in 1993 (which means that they were administered one or more individual questionnaires), or if they were born before 1968 (that is they were 26 years and older in 1993). Not all individuals were tracked in order to control costs.

The total number of households contacted in IFLS2 was 7,629, of which 6,752 were panel households and 877 were split-off households (see Appendix Table 2.2).[4] This represents a completion rate of 94.3% for the IFLS1 households that were still alive. One reason for this high rate of retention was the effort to follow households that moved from their original housing structure. Fully 11% of the panel households reinterviewed in the IFLS2 had moved out of their previous dwelling. About one-half of these households were found in relatively close proximity to their IFLS1 location (local movers). The other half were "long-distance" tracking cases who had moved to a different sub-district, district, or province (Thomas, Frankenberg and Smith 2001).

IFLS2+

IFLS2+ was fielded in the second half of 1998 in order to gauge the immediate impact of the Asian financial crisis that had hit Indonesia starting in January 1998. Since time was short and resources limited, a scaled-down survey was fielded, while retaining the representativeness of IFLS2 as much as possible. A 25% sub-sample of the IFLS households was taken from 7 of the 13 provinces that IFLS covers.[5] Within those, 80 enumeration areas were purposively selected in order to match the full IFLS sample. As in IFLS2, all households that moved since the previous interview to any IFLS province were tracked. In addition, new households (split-offs) were added to the sample, using the same criteria as in IFLS2 for tracking individuals who had moved out of the IFLS household.

IFLS3

Main fieldwork for IFLS3 went on from June through November, 2000.[6] The sampling approach in IFLS3 was to recontact all original IFLS1 households, plus split-off households from both IFLS2 and IFLS2+. As in 1997 and 1998, households that moved were followed, provided that they still lived in one the 13 provinces covered by IFLS, or in Riau.[7] Likewise, individuals who moved out of their IFLS households were followed. Over 10,500 households were contacted (Appendix Table 2.2), containing over 43,600 individuals. Of these households, there were 2,648 new split-off households. A 94.8% recontact rate was achieved of all "target" households (original IFLS1 households and split-offs from IFLS2 and IFLS2+) still living, which includes 6,796 original 1993 households, or 95.2% of those still living (Appendix Table 2.2).

The rules for following individuals who moved out of an IFLS household were expanded in IFLS3. These rules included tracking the following:

- 1993 main respondents;
- 1993 household members born before 1968;
- individuals born since 1993 in original 1993 households;
- individuals born after 1988 if they were resident in an original household in 1993;
- 1993 household members who were born between 1968 and 1988 if they were interviewed in 1997.
- 20% random sample of 1993 household members who were born between 1968 and 1988 if they were not interviewed in 1997.

The motivation behind this strategy was to be able to follow small children in panel households (children five years and under in 1993 and children born subsequently to 1993), and to follow at least a subset of young adults, born between 1968 and 1988. This strategy was designed to keep the sample, once weighted, closely representative of the original 1993 sample.

SELECTION OF RESPONDENTS WITHIN HOUSEHOLDS

IFLS1

In IFLS, household members are asked to provide in-depth individual information on a broad range of substantive areas, such as on labour market outcomes, health, marriage, and fertility. In IFLS1, not all household members were interviewed with individual books, for cost reasons.[8] Those that were interviewed are referred to as main respondents. However, even if the person was not a main respondent (not administered an individual book), we still know a lot of information about them from the household sections, the difference is in the degree of detail.

IFLS2

In IFLS2, in original 1993 households re-contacted in 1997, individual interviews were conducted with all current members who were found, regardless of whether they were household members in 1993, main respondents, or new members. Among the split-off households, all tracked individuals were interviewed (that is those who were 1993 main respondents, or who were born before 1968), plus their spouses, and biological children.

IFLS2+

In IFLS2+, the same rules used in IFLS2 were applied. In original IFLS1 households, all current members were interviewed individually. One difference was that all current members of split-off households were also interviewed individually, not just a subset.

IFLS3

For IFLS3, as in IFLS2, individual interviews were conducted with all current members of original 1993 households, that is all current residents who could be contacted in the household, were interviewed. For split-off households (whether a split-off from 1997, 1998 or new in 2000) the selection rule was broadened from IFLS2 to include any individuals who had lived in a 1993 household, whether or not they had been targeted to be tracked; plus their spouses and biological children.

SELECTION OF FACILITIES

The health facilities surveyed in IFLS are designed to be from a probabilistic sample of facilities that serve households in the community. The sample is drawn from a list of facilities known by household respondents. Thus the health facilities can include those that are located outside the community, which distinguishes the IFLS sampling strategy from others commonly used, such as by the Demographic and Health Surveys, where the facility closest to the community (as reported by community leaders) is interviewed. Moreover, some facilities serve more than one IFLS community. The sampling frame is different for each of the 312 communities of IFLS and for each of the three strata of health facilities: *puskesmas* and *puskesmas pembantu* (or *pustu*), *posyandu* and private facilities.[9] Private facilities include private clinics, doctors, nurses and paramedics, and midwives. For each strata and within each of the 312 communities, the facilities reported as known in the household questionnaire are arrayed by the number of times they are mentioned. Health facilities are then chosen randomly up to a set limit, with the most frequently reported facility always being chosen.

Schools are sampled in the same way, except that the list of schools comes from households who have children currently enrolled and includes only those that are actually being used. The schools sample has three strata: primary, junior secondary and senior secondary levels.

Appendix Table 2.3 shows the distribution of sampled facilities in 1997 and 2000. As can be seen, the fraction of *puskesmas* went up slightly in 2000, compared to *puskesmas pembantu*. Within private facilities, the fraction of private physicians and nurses dropped slightly while midwives increased. For schools, there were very few compositional changes between IFLS2 and IFLS3.

COMPARISON OF IFLS SAMPLE COMPOSITION WITH SUSENAS

IFLS 2 and 3 are designed to stay representative of the original 1993 IFLS1 households. While IFLS1 is representative within strata (province and rural/urban area), as mentioned, urban areas and small provinces were oversampled. Hence for statistics to be representative of the overall 13 provinces, the data should be weighted to reflect the oversampling. In addition, by 1997 or 2000 it may be that the IFLS sample lost representativeness of the population then residing in the 13 provinces. To make the IFLS samples representative of the more general population, we calculate separate weights for 1997 and 2000, for households and for individuals, to be applied to each of those years. These weights are used throughout this analysis. The weights are designed to match the IFLS2 and IFLS3 sample proportions of households and individuals in 1997 and 2000 to the sample proportions in the SUSENAS Core Surveys for the same years. The SUSENAS Core surveys are national in scope, probabilistic surveys fielded by the Central Bureau of Statistics (BPS), and usually contain up to 150,000 households. We match the IFLS samples to SUSENAS using the household population weights reported in SUSENAS to calculate the SUSENAS proportions. In doing so, we only use data from the same 13 provinces that IFLS covers. For the household weights, we match by province and urban/rural area within province. For the individual weights we add detailed age groups by gender to the province/urban-rural cells.[10]

In Appendix Tables 2.4 and 2.5 we compare some basic individual characteristics. Relative proportions by gender and age are reported in Appendix Table 2.4, and province and urban-rural proportions in Appendix Table 2.5. The proportions are very close for the weighted IFLS2 and the 1997 SUSENAS, and the weighted IFLS3 and the 2000 SUSENAS. This simply reflects our weighting scheme.[11] The unweighted IFLS frequencies are surprisingly close to the weighted SUSENAS ones. One can see that IFLS does indeed oversample in urban areas and in some provinces.

One factor important in influencing many of our outcomes is education of adults in the household. Appendix Table 2.6 compares levels of schooling for men and women over 20 years and by urban/rural residence. The weighted (and unweighted) IFLS2 shows a slightly higher fraction of those with no and less than primary schooling than SUSENAS, while SUSENAS has commensurately higher fractions reporting completed primary and junior secondary school. The fractions of those completing secondary school or higher are close. Most of the differences in schooling levels are among rural residents. The comparisons of education in the 2000 data are quite similar, except that the differences in the no-schooling group are smaller and there is a slightly higher fraction in IFLS3 who have completed secondary school or beyond than in SUSENAS.

In Appendix Table 2.7 we report various household characteristics. Average household size is smaller in both SUSENAS than in IFLS, although the difference in 2000 is small. The average age of the household head is slightly higher in IFLS2 than the 1997 SUSENAS, although in 2000 the ages are almost identical. Comparisons of schooling of the household head is very similar to schooling comparisons for all individuals. Finally, a larger fraction of heads are reported to be women in IFLS.

Notes

[1] See Frankenberg and Karoly (1995) for complete documentation of IFLS1.

[2] The provinces are four from Sumatra (North Sumatra, West Sumatra, South Sumatra, and Lampung), all five of the Javanese provinces (DKI Jakarta, West Java, Central Java, DI Yogyakarta, and East Java), and four from the remaining major island groups (Bali, West Nusa Tenggara, South Kalimantan, and South Sulawesi).

[3] See Frankenberg and Thomas (2000) for full documentation of IFLS2. IFLS1 and 2 data and documentation are publicly available at www.rand.org/labor/FLS/IFLS.

[4] This includes 10 households that merged with other IFLS1 households. There are separate questionnaires for 6,742 panel households in IFLS2.

[5] The provinces were Central Java, Jakarta, North Sumatra, South Kalimantan, South Sumatra, West Java and West Nusa Tenggara.

[6] The IFLS3 data used in this report is preliminary. The data will be released publicly, hopefully by the end of 2003. It will be available at the same RAND website as IFLS1 and 2 (see Note 3 above).

[7] There were also a small number of households who were followed in Southeast Sulawesi and Central and East Kalimantan because their locations were assessed to be near the borders of IFLS provinces and thus within cost-effective reach of enumerators. For purposes of analysis, they have been reclassified to the nearby IFLS provinces.

[8] See Frankenberg and Karoly (1995) for a discussion of the IFLS1 selection procedures.

[9] IFLS includes 321 enumeration areas which constitute 312 communities because 9 are so close that they share the same infrastructure.

[10] The age groups (in years) used are: 0–4 , 5–9, 10–14, 15–19, 20–24, 25–29, 30–39, 40–49, 50–64, and 65 and over. In order to keep cell sizes large enough to be meaningful, we aggregate North and West Sumatra into one region and do likewise for South Sumatra and Lampung, Central Java and Yogyakarta, Bali and West Nusa Tenggara, and South Kalimantan and South Sulawesi.

[11] Any differences reflect our aggregation, discussed in Note 10 above.

APPENDIX TABLE 2.1
Number of Communities in IFLS

		Number of Communities
Urban		
	Province	
	North Sumatra	16
	West Sumatra	6
	South Sumatra	8
	Lampung	3
	Jakarta	36
	West Java	30
	Central Java	18
	Yogyakarta	13
	East Java	23
	Bali	7
	West Nusa Tenggara	6
	South Kalimantan	6
	South Sulawesi	8
	All IFLS provinces	180
Rural		
	Province	
	North Sumatra	10
	West Sumatra	8
	South Sumatra	7
	Lampung	8
	Jakarta	–
	West Java	21
	Central Java	18
	Yogyakarta	6
	East Java	22
	Bali	7
	West Nusa Tenggara	10
	South Kalimantan	7
	South Sulawesi	8
	All IFLS provinces	132
Total IFLS		312

Source: IFLS1.

APPENDIX TABLE 2.2
Household Recontact Rates

Number of Households	IFLS1	All Members Died	IFLS2 Households Contacted	Recontact Rate (%)	IFLS3 Target Households	All Members Died	IFLS3 Households Contacted	Recontact Rate (%)
IFLS1 households	7,224	69	6,752	94.3	7,155	32	6,768	95.0
IFLS2 split-off households	–	–	877	–	877	2	817	93.4
IFLS2+ split-off households	–	–	–	–	338	0	308	91.1
IFLS3 target households	–	–	–	–	8,370	34	7,893	94.7
IFLS3 split-off households	–	–	–	–	–	–	2,648	–
Total households contacted	7,224	69	7,629			34	10,541	

Source: IFLS2 and IFLS3.

Recontact rates are conditional on at least some household members living. Households that recombined into other households are included in the number of households contacted. IFLS3 target households are IFLS1 households, IFLS2 split-off households and IFLS2+ split-off households

APPENDIX TABLE 2.3
Type of Public and Private Facilities and Schools
(In percent)

	1997	2000
Public Facilities		
– *Puskesmas*	61.4	65.9
– *Puskesmas Pembantu*	37.9	34.1
– Don't know	0.7	0.0
Number of Observations	920	944
Private Facilites		
– Private physician	28.5	25.4
– Clinic	8.0	11.3
– Midwife	28.6	29.4
– Paramedic/Nurse	25.5	24.4
– Village midwife	7.3	9.5
– Don't know	2.1	0.1
Number of observations	1,852	1,904
Schools		
– Primary, public	33.0	32.2
– Primary, private	5.1	5.8
– Junior high, public	23.1	23.5
– Junior high, private	14.3	14.1
– Senior high, public	12.0	11.6
– Senior high, private	12.4	12.8
Number of observations	2,525	2,530

Source: IFLS2 and IFLS3.

APPENDIX TABLE 2.4
Age/Gender Characteristics of IFLS and SUSENAS: 1997 and 2000

Percentages of Men and Women

	Susenas 1997 weighted	IFLS 1997 weighted	IFLS 1997 unweighted	Susenas 2000 weighted	IFLS 2000 weighted	IFLS 2000 unweighted
Men	49.6	49.6	48.3	50.0	50.0	48.8
Women	50.4	50.4	51.7	50.0	50.0	51.2
Total	100.0	100.0	100.0	100.0	100.0	100.0
Number of observations	609,782	33,934	33,934	584,675	43,649	43,649

Percentages of Individuals in Age Groups, Men and Women

	Susenas 1997 weighted		IFLS 1997 weighted		IFLS 1997 unweighted		Susenas 2000 weighted		IFLS 2000 weighted		IFLS 2000 unweighted	
	Men	Women	Men	Women	Men	Women	Men	Women	Men	Women	Men	Women
0–59 months	9.2	8.7	9.2	8.7	9.7	9.0	8.7	8.3	8.7	8.3	10.6	9.7
5–9 years	11.1	10.4	11.1	10.3	11.2	9.9	10.4	9.8	10.4	9.8	9.9	8.9
10–14 years	12.4	11.4	12.4	11.4	12.5	11.5	10.8	10.1	10.8	10.1	10.3	9.4
15–19 years	10.7	10.3	10.7	10.3	11.8	11.1	10.9	10.2	11.0	10.2	11.0	11.4
20–24 years	8.0	9.1	8.1	9.1	7.4	7.8	8.7	8.9	8.7	9.0	9.5	10.0
25–29 years	8.0	8.9	8.0	8.9	7.3	7.7	8.3	9.0	8.3	9.1	8.7	8.3
30–34 years	7.4	8.0	7.5	8.3	7.2	7.9	7.6	7.9	8.2	8.2	7.7	7.5
35–39 years	7.5	7.7	7.4	7.4	6.9	7.2	7.5	7.9	6.9	7.7	6.5	7.0
40–44 years	6.4	5.9	6.0	6.1	5.7	6.1	6.6	6.4	6.7	6.2	5.9	5.9
45–49 years	4.9	4.6	5.2	4.3	4.9	4.3	5.6	5.1	5.5	5.3	4.8	4.9
50–54 years	4.1	4.2	3.5	3.8	3.7	4.1	4.0	4.4	3.9	3.6	3.6	3.5
55–59 years	3.1	3.2	3.6	3.7	3.6	4.1	3.3	3.4	3.5	3.9	3.3	3.6
60+ years	7.2	7.7	7.3	7.6	8.2	9.2	7.6	8.5	7.4	8.6	8.1	9.6
All age groups	100.0	100.0	100.0	100.0	100.0	100.0	100.0	100.0	100.0	100.0	100.0	100.0

Source: SUSENAS 1997, SUSENAS 2000, IFLS2, IFLS3.

APPENDIX TABLE 2.5
Location Characteristics of IFLS and SUSENAS: 1997 and 2000

Percentages of Individuals in Urban and Rural Areas, Men and Women

	Susenas 1997 weighted		IFLS 1997 weighted		IFLS 1997 unweighted		Susenas 2000 weighted		IFLS 2000 weighted		IFLS 2000 unweighted	
	Men	Women	Men	Women	Men	Women	Men	Women	Men	Women	Men	Women
Urban	39.2	39.3	40.2	40.3	47.3	47.6	44.1	44.4	45.4	45.1	48.7	48.8
Rural	60.8	60.7	59.8	59.7	52.7	52.4	55.9	55.6	55.6	54.9	51.3	51.2
Total	100.0	100.0	100.0	100.0	100.0	100.0	100.0	100.0	100.0	100.0	100.0	100.0

Percentages of Individuals by Provinces, Men and Women

	Susenas 1997 weighted		IFLS 1997 weighted		IFLS 1997 unweighted		Susenas 2000 weighted		IFLS 2000 weighted		IFLS 2000 unweighted	
	Men	Women	Men	Women	Men	Women	Men	Women	Men	Women	Men	Women
North Sumatra	6.9	6.9	5.4	5.3	7.7	7.3	6.9	6.8	5.0	5.0	7.2	7.0
West Sumatra	2.6	2.8	4.1	4.2	5.4	5.5	2.5	2.6	3.9	3.9	5.1	5.2
South Sumatra	4.6	4.5	4.9	4.8	5.3	4.8	4.6	4.6	4.9	4.7	5.6	5.2
Lampung	4.3	4.1	4.2	4.0	4.3	3.9	4.1	3.8	3.6	3.4	4.0	3.8
DKI Jakarta	5.8	5.6	5.9	5.7	9.5	9.1	5.0	5.0	5.5	5.5	8.8	8.6
West Java	25.0	24.1	24.9	23.9	17.4	16.5	26.3	25.4	26.8	25.8	18.3	17.5
Central Java	18.2	18.3	14.1	14.3	12.0	13.0	18.2	18.5	14.2	14.5	12.0	12.5
Yogyakarta	1.8	1.8	5.5	5.5	5.3	5.6	1.8	1.9	5.5	5.5	4.9	5.1
East Java	20.5	21.2	20.6	21.4	12.9	13.5	20.2	20.9	20.4	21.1	13.3	13.9
Bali	1.8	1.8	1.7	1.7	4.5	4.5	1.9	1.9	1.8	1.8	4.5	4.6
West Nusa Tenggara	2.2	2.4	2.3	2.5	6.1	6.6	2.2	2.3	2.3	2.3	6.2	6.5
South Kalimantan	1.8	1.8	2.8	2.8	4.2	4.0	1.8	1.3	3.0	2.9	4.5	4.3
South Sulawesi	4.6	4.8	3.6	3.9	5.4	5.6	4.5	4.7	3.3	3.6	5.6	5.9
Total	100.0	100.0	100.0	100.0	100.0	100.0	100.0	100.0	100.0	100.0	100.0	100.0

Source: SUSENAS 1997, SUSENAS 2000, IFLS 2, and IFLS3.

APPENDIX TABLE 2.6
Completed Education of 20 Year Olds and Above in IFLS and SUSENAS: 1997 and 2000

	Susenas 1997 weighted		IFLS 1997 weighted		IFLS 1997 unweighted		Susenas 2000 weighted		IFLS 2000 weighted		IFLS 2000 unweighted	
	Men	Women	Men	Women	Men	Women	Men	Women	Men	Women	Men	Women
Total												
Highest education level completed (percent)												
No schooling	8.6	19.6	13.6	26.7	13.3	27.6	7.9	18	9.8	21	9.9	21.6
Some primary school	20	22.2	21.1	20.5	20.9	20.5	18.1	20.8	18.5	20.6	18	20
Completed primary school	32.4	30.4	27.2	25.4	26	23.5	31.7	30.6	27.1	25.2	25.9	23.8
Completed junior HS	13.4	10.5	12	9.4	12	9.7	14.3	11.4	13.6	10.7	13.7	11
Completed senior HS	20.9	14.4	20.4	14.9	21.5	15.4	22.8	15.7	22.3	16.3	23.4	17.3
Completed Academy	2.2	1.6	2.6	1.5	2.9	1.7	2.1	1.8	4.1	3.3	4.2	3.5
Completed university	2.5	1.3	3.1	1.6	3.5	1.7	3.1	1.8	4.6	2.8	4.8	2.8
Number of observations	168,879	182,251	9,537	10,127	9,006	10,256	170,308	180,810	12,680	13,243	11,930	13,006
Urban												
Highest education level completed (percent)												
No schooling	3.7	10.7	6.1	14.9	6.9	17.8	3.6	10.7	4.2	12.73	4.8	14
Some primary school	10.7	14.8	13.1	14.9	14.1	16.4	10.3	14.4	11.5	15.1	11.7	15.5
Completed primary school	23.9	26.7	22.9	24.3	22.9	23.2	24.4	26.9	21.2	22.3	21.3	21.3
Completed junior HS	17.1	15.7	14.9	13.7	14.6	13.1	16.7	14.9	15.5	13.7	15.3	13.5
Completed senior HS	35.6	26.3	32	25.1	30.6	23.1	35.7	26.5	33	25.3	32.6	25.4
Completed Academy	4.2	3.2	5.2	3.4	5	3.2	3.6	3.2	6.7	5.7	6.5	5.5
Completed university	5	2.7	5.9	3.6	5.9	3.2	5.8	3.4	8	5.2	7.9	4.8
Number of observations	64,652	69,139	3,957	4,142	4,395	5,003	74,090	78,517	5,875	6,096	5,934	6,542
Rural												
Highest education level completed (percent)												
No schooling	11.9	25.4	19	34.9	19.3	36.9	11.4	23.9	14.7	28.1	14.9	29.4
Some primary school	26.4	27.2	26.9	24.3	27.3	24.4	24.7	26	24.6	25.3	24.4	24.5
Completed primary school	38.2	32.9	30.3	26.1	28.9	23.8	37.8	33.7	32.2	27.6	30.6	26.3
Completed junior HS	10.8	7.1	9.9	6.3	9.6	6.4	12.2	8.4	11.9	8.3	12.1	8.5
Completed senior HS	11	6.5	12.1	7.8	12.9	8	12.1	6.9	13.1	8.5	14.2	9.2
Completed Academy	0.9	0.6	0.8	0.3	0.8	0.3	1	0.7	1.9	1.4	2	1.4
Completed university	0.7	0.4	1	0.3	1.1	0.3	0.8	0.4	1.6	0.8	1.7	0.8
Number of observations	104,227	113,112	5,580	5,985	4,611	5,253	96,218	102,293	6,804	7,148	5,996	6,464

Source: SUSENAS 1997, SUSENAS 2000, IFLS2, and IFLS3.

APPENDIX TABLE 2.7
Household Comparisons of IFLS and SUSENAS: 1997 and 2000

	Susenas 1997 weighted	IFLS 1997 weighted	IFLS 1997 unweighted	Susenas 2000 weighted	IFLS 2000 weighted	IFLS 2000 unweighted
Average household size	4.1	4.4	4.5	4.0	4.1	4.2
Average # of children 0–4.9 years	0.4	0.4	0.4	0.3	0.4	0.4
Average # of children 5–14.9 years	0.9	1.0	1.0	0.8	0.8	0.8
Average # of adult 15–59.9 years	2.5	2.6	2.6	2.5	2.6	2.6
Average # of adult 60+ years	0.3	0.4	0.4	0.3	0.4	0.4
% male headed households	86.8	82.0	82.5	86.2	82.2	82.5
Average age of household head	45.1	47.5	47.3	45.8	45.3	45.2
Education of household head						
% with no schooling	13.7	20.9	20.4	13.2	15.1	15.5
% with some primary school	23.9	24.7	24.3	22.4	22.1	21.7
% completed primary school	32.0	25.9	25.0	31.5	26.2	25.2
% completed junior high school	11.4	10.0	10.5	11.9	11.9	12.3
% completed senior high school	15.2	14.4	15.3	16.5	17.3	17.9
% completed academy	1.9	1.6	1.8	1.9	3.6	3.5
% completed university	2.0	2.4	2.8	2.6	3.7	3.8
% households in urban areas	39.0	39.0	45.9	44.0	44.0	48.0
Number of households	146,351	7,622	7,619	144,058	10,435	10,435

Source: SUSENAS 1997, SUSENAS 2000, IFLS2, and IFLS3.

3

Levels of Poverty and Per Capita Expenditure

A person is deemed to be living in poverty if the real per capita expenditure (*pce*) of the household that they live in is below the poverty line. In this section we report results on the incidence of poverty. For descriptive statistics, we use household data, weighted by household size.[1] This method will account for the fact that poor households tend to have more children than non-poor households. In addition, we also present results for different demographic groups (by age and gender).[2] This implicitly assumes total household expenditure is equally distributed among all individuals within households, which we believe is likely not the case. Nevertheless, it is unavoidable since our basis for measuring poverty is collected at the household-level and it is of interest to examine poverty rates for different demographic groups in the population.

Assignment of poverty status requires data on real per capita expenditure (*pce*) and poverty lines. We construct measures of nominal *pce* for 1997 and 2000, and deflate to December 2000 rupiah in Jakarta by using price deflators that we construct from detailed price and budget share data. We use existing data on poverty lines, also deflated to December 2000 Jakarta values. Details are described in Appendix 3A.

In our measures of poverty rates, we include all individuals found living in the interviewed households, whether or not the persons were selected to be interviewed individually (see the discussion of the selection process for individual interviews, in Chapter 2). We separately calculate headcount measures of poverty for children under age 15 and adults over 15. We break down children into age groups of 0–59 months and 5–14 years. We disaggregate adults into prime-aged, 15–59 and elderly, 60 and over. Standard errors are adjusted for clustering at the enumeration area.[3]

In Table 3.1, the 1997 headcount measure is 17.7%, just above the 15.7% reported by Pradhan et al. (2001) for February 1996.[4] Not

TABLE 3.1
Percent of Individuals Living in Poverty: IFLS, 1997 and 2000

	National			Urban			Rural		
	1997	2000	Difference	1997	2000	Difference	1997	2000	Difference
All individuals	17.7	15.9	–1.8	13.8	11.7	–2.1	20.4	19.3	–1.1
	(0.97)	(0.68)	(1.19)	(1.25)	(0.94)	(1.56)	(1.37)	(0.94)	(1.66)
No. of individuals	[33,441]	[42,733]		[15,770]	[20,732]		[17,671]	[22,001]	
No. of households	[7,518]	[10,223]		[3,433]	[4,905]		[4,085]	[5,318]	
Adults, aged 15+ years	16.1	14.4	–1.6	12.8	10.6	–2.3	18.4	17.7	–0.7
	(0.87)	(0.63)	(1.08)	(1.20)	(0.85)	(1.47)	(1.22)	(0.87)	(1.50)
No. of individuals	[22,756]	[30,096]		[11,226]	[15,194]		[11,530]	[14,902]	
Adults, aged 15–59 years	15.9	14.1	–1.8	12.7	10.2	–2.4	18.3	17.5	–0.8
	(0.88)	(0.62)	(1.08)	(1.21)	(0.83)	(1.46)	(1.25)	(0.86)	(1.52)
No. of individuals	[19,856]	[26,355]		[9,978]	[13,572]		[9,878]	[12,783]	
Adults, aged 60+years	17.2	16.6	–0.7	14.2	13.2	–1.0	19.0	18.8	–0.2
	(1.11)	(1.03)	(1.52)	(1.55)	(1.50)	(2.15)	(1.50)	(1.40)	(2.05)
No. of individuals	[2,900]	[3,741]		[1,248]	[1,622]		[1,652]	[2,119]	
Children, aged 0–14 years	21.2	19.4	–1.8	16.0	14.6	–1.3	24.2	22.6	–1.6
	(1.26)	(0.91)	(1.55)	(1.50)	(1.29)	(1.98)	(1.75)	(1.21)	(2.13)
No. of individuals	[10,685]	[12,637]		[4,544]	[5,538]		[6,141]	[7,099]	
Children, aged 0–59 months	22.5	19.0	–3.5 *	17.0	14.5	–2.6	25.7	22.3	–3.4
	(1.39)	(0.96)	(1.69)	(1.88)	(1.38)	(2.33)	(1.88)	(1.30)	(2.28)
No. of individuals	[3,127]	[4,394]		[1,340]	[2,002]		[1,787]	[2,392]	
Children, aged 5–14 years	20.7	19.6	–1.1	15.5	14.7	–0.8	23.6	22.7	–0.9
	(1.29)	(0.98)	(1.62)	(1.52)	(1.38)	(2.05)	(1.79)	(1.31)	(2.22)
No. of individuals	[7,558]	[8,243]		[3,204]	[3,536]		[4,354]	[4,707]	

Source: IFLS2 and IFLS3.
Estimates are from household data weighted using household sampling weights multiplied by number of household members in each respective age group. Standard errors (in parentheses) are robust to clustering at the community level. Significance at 5% (*) and 1% (**) are indicated.

surprisingly, poverty rates for children are higher than for the aggregate population, since poorer households tend to have more children than do the non-poor. Also the adults in these households may be younger, with less labour market experience, also leading to lower incomes and *pce*. The difference in this case is large, 21% of all children and 23% of children under 5 years were poor in late 1997, as against 16% of prime-aged adults. Headcount rates for the elderly are not very different than rates for other adults, which may reflect a high degree of the elderly living with their adult children. In urban areas the poverty-rate differential between the elderly and prime-aged adults is slightly larger, which probably reflects that an elderly person is more likely to be living apart from their children if they live in an urban area. Headcount rates are higher in rural areas: 20.4% in rural areas for all individuals, as against 13.8% in urban areas in 1997.

What is perhaps surprising is that the headcount rate actually decreased slightly by late 2000, to 15.9% for all individuals, and to 19.4% for children. Neither decline is statistically significant at 10% or lower levels, although the decline for children under 5 years is at the 5% level. Measures of the poverty gap and squared poverty gap also show small, but not statistically significant, declines between 1997 and 2000 (see Tables 3.5a, b).[5, 6] Independent estimates of poverty throughout the crisis period show consistent findings. Using SUSENAS data and the same poverty lines that we use, Pradhan et al. (2001) and Alatas (2002) find that poverty rates climbed from 15.7% in February 1996 to 27.1% by February 1999, falling to 15.2% by February 2000.[7]

Other studies have shown a large increase in poverty from 1997 to 1998 or early 1999, however comparing the various estimates is difficult because of differences in methods used to construct deflators and differences in poverty lines used to calculate headcount rates. Frankenberg et al. (1999), using the prior BPS poverty line as their anchor, estimated poverty at 11% in late 1997 (using IFLS2) rising to 19.9% by late 1998 (using IFLS2+), a 10% rise in the headcount, similar to the rise found by Pradhan et al. using different poverty lines. Other studies reported by Suryahadi et al. (2000) show a fall in poverty rates by as much as 5% (or half of the increase) from February to August 1999 using a smaller, or mini-, SUSENAS survey fielded in August 1999.

The sharp increase in poverty from 1997 until February 1999 and then a decline through early 2000 is consistent with the movements in the food price index over the same period, shown in Figure 1.2. It is also consistent with the limited GNP growth that occurred during 2000. This suggests the enormous importance that food prices, especially rice, play in determining levels of expenditure (see Alatas 2002, for a more formal simulation of this point). However, households are not passive in response to sharp changes in their environment, changes in behaviour are also greatly responsible for the recovery that has occurred.

Table 3.2 demonstrates why rice prices can play an important role in changing real incomes, at least for consumers. Here we present budget shares of rice and all foods not including tobacco and alcohol (including consumption of foods grown at home). The mean food share barely changed over the entire sample, although it did rise for urban and non-poor individuals. On one level this could be interpreted as indicating a decline in welfare of these groups, although evidence on *pce* reported below belies this interpretation except for the very top of the distribution. The mean rice share was nearly 14% in 1997 and fell to 11.6% in 2000, a significant decline. Rice shares declined for all the groups we examined: urban and rural, poor and non-poor. The decline in rice shares evidently represents a behavioural change by households in their consumption patterns, plausibly in response to the relative rise in rice prices, although we don't show that rigorously. The levels of rice share are especially high for the poor and in rural areas, 21% and 17% respectively. This underlines the importance of rice price as a determinant of well-being of the poor.

Of course for agricultural households, who both produce and consume rice, it is not the rice share of the budget, but the net demand of rice that is relevant to whether real incomes will decline or rise as the relative price of rice rises (Singh et al. 1986). Those rice farmers who are net sellers of rice will have favourable real income effects (all else equal) from a relative price increase. We do not have data in IFLS that can distinguish net sellers from net buyers. Many rice farmers will be net buyers of rice, especially if they own only a small amount of land, as most Indonesian farmers do. A study of income among farmers between 1995 and 1999 shows that larger landowners derive a larger fraction of their income from farming than do smallholders, who rely much more on non-farm income sources. Between 1995 and 1999, farmers, especially large farmers, experienced an *increase* in income (Bresciani et al. 2002). To the extent that higher rice prices were capitalized into land prices, this differential effect by land size was enhanced. Hence the rapid changes in relative prices hit different parts of the population in different ways.

The extremely rapid changes in poverty demonstrates the importance of frequent collection of data in order to assess the full dynamic impacts of macroeconomic changes.

TABLE 3.2
Rice and Food Shares 1997 and 2000
(In percent)

		1997	2000	Change	
All					
	Rice	13.9	11.6	–2.3	**
		(0.37)	(0.26)	(0.45)	
	Food	52.8	53.7	0.9	
		(0.49)	(0.36)	(0.61)	
	No. of individuals	[33,441]	[42,733]		
	No. of households	[7,518]	[10,223]		
Rural					
	Rice	16.7	13.9	–2.8	**
		(0.48)	(0.34)	(0.59)	
	Food	56.8	57.0	0.3	
		(0.58)	(0.42)	(0.72)	
	No. of individuals	[17,671]	[22,001]		
Urban					
	Rice	9.7	8.7	–1.0	**
		(0.36)	(0.28)	(0.46)	
	Food	46.9	49.4	2.4	**
		(0.58)	(0.47)	(0.75)	
	No. of individuals	[15,770]	[20,732]		
Poor					
	Rice	21.4	18.0	–3.4	**
		(0.81)	(0.56)	(0.99)	
	Food	58.3	57.8	–0.5	
		(0.75)	(0.58)	(0.95)	
	No. of individuals	[5,568]	[6,473]		
Non-poor					
	Rice	12.3	10.4	–1.9	**
		(0.29)	(0.24)	(0.37)	
	Food	51.6	52.9	1.3	**
		(0.49)	(0.37)	(0.61)	
	No. of individuals	[27,873]	[36,260]		

Source: IFLS2 and IFLS3.

Food does not include alcohol and tobacco. Estimates are from household data weighted using household sampling weights multiplied by the number of household members. Standard errors (in parentheses) are robust to clustering at the community level. Significance at 5% (*) and 1% (**) indicated.

By comparing the years 1997 and 2000, as we do in this report, we propose to measure the medium-run measure of the impact of the crisis. However this may not provide the best medium-run measure of the impact. Rather one could compare the 2000 results with the level of poverty (or other dimensions of welfare) that would have been expected in 2000 had the crisis not occurred (for instance, Smith et al. 2002, analyse changes in wages and employment from 1993 to 1998 using this approach). This is difficult, requiring strong assumptions about what would have occurred over time, and certainly would require using data from pre-crisis years (IFLS1 for instance). This is left to future work.

One key factor that helps to explain the slight improvement in poverty rates in the IFLS sample is the splitting-off of households. Table 3.3 shows poverty levels of individuals from two types of households. In 2000, the sample includes individuals in new split-off households, that can be linked to an origin 1997 household.[8] The poverty rates in 2000 for these persons can be compared to the 1997 poverty rates of all people who lived in the 1997 origin households. Poverty rates in 2000 in these split-off households are far lower than they are in their 1997 origin households. About 21% of individuals in 1997 origin households are poor, as compared to just under 13% in the 2000 split-off households.[9] For children under 5 years the rates are lower by roughly half! On the other hand, poverty in 1997 in the households that these split-off individuals come from is higher than overall poverty in 1997. We can conclude that split-off households do not occur randomly. Evidently there are forces which lead younger, better educated youth to leave their poor origin households, forming new households in which their real *pce* is subsequently higher (see Witoelar 2002, who tests whether these split-off and origin households should be treated as one extended household, rejecting that hypothesis). Clearly this pattern needs to be examined more closely in future work.

Means and medians of real per capita expenditure (*pce*), overall and by rural/urban residence, are reported in Table 3.4 for all individuals and the poor and non-poor separately. All values are deflated to December 2000 rupiah values and to Jakarta as the base region (see Appendix 3.A). As one can observe, median *pce*s increased by a small amount, 4.5%, to just over Rp 200,000, but mean *pce*s fell by roughly 11.5%, to Rp 292,000; a fall which is statistically significant at almost 5%. Among urban residents mean *pce* fell by nearly 20% (significant at 5%), compared to a 5.5% decrease (not significant at any standard level) among rural residents.

As can be seen in the poor–non-poor breakdowns, the reason for the decline in the mean is a large downwards shift in the upper tail of the *pce*

TABLE 3.3
Percent of Individuals Living in Poverty for Those Who Live in Split-off Households in 2000: IFLS, 1997 and 2000

	National			Urban			Rural		
	1997	2000	Difference	1997	2000	Difference	1997	2000	Difference
All individuals	21.4	12.7	–8.7 **	16.3	8.7	–7.5 **	24.9	16.2	–8.7 **
	(1.63)	(1.19)	(2.02)	(2.22)	(1.62)	(2.75)	(2.29)	(1.73)	(2.87)
No. of individuals	[8,805]	[6,453]		[4,201]	[3,344]		[4,604]	[3,109]	
No. of households	[1,545]	[1,839]		[714]	[995]		[831]	[844]	
Adults, aged 15+ years	19.3	11.5	–7.8 **	14.8	7.9	–7.0 **	22.8	14.9	–7.9 **
	(1.44)	(1.16)	(1.85)	(2.02)	(1.59)	(2.57)	(2.05)	(1.68)	(2.65)
No. of individuals	[6,280]	[4,797]		[3,186]	[2,566]		[3,094]	[2,231]	
Adults, aged 15–59 years	19.3	11.1	–8.2 **	15.0	8.0	–7.0 **	22.7	14.1	–8.6 **
	(1.50)	(1.17)	(1.90)	(2.14)	(1.66)	(2.71)	(2.12)	(1.66)	(2.69)
No. of individuals	[5,653]	[4,471]		[2,873]	[2,427]		[2,780]	[2,044]	
Adults, aged 60+years	19.1	16.8	–2.3	13.5	5.3	–8.3 **	23.8	23.4	–0.4
	(2.10)	(2.74)	(3.46)	(2.32)	(2.09)	(3.12)	(3.34)	(3.97)	(5.19)
No. of individuals	[627]	[326]		[313]	[139]		[314]	[187]	
Children, aged 0–14 years	26.4	16.0	–10.4 **	20.9	11.8	–9.1 **	29.3	19.1	–10.2 **
	(2.26)	(1.71)	(2.83)	(3.13)	(2.52)	(4.02)	(3.00)	(2.35)	(3.81)
No. of individuals	[2,525]	[1,656]		[1,015]	[778]		[1,510]	[878]	
Children, aged 0–59 months	29.7	14.8	–14.8 **	–14.8	9.6	–15.3 **	32.3	18.9	–13.4 **
	(2.81)	(1.70)	(3.28)	(4.31)	(2.43)	(4.95)	(3.68)	(2.40)	(4.39
No. of individuals	[699]	[859]		[293]	[406]		[406]	[453]	
Children, aged 5–14 years	25.1	17.2	–7.9 **	19.1	14.1	–5.0	28.1	19.3	–8.8 *
	(2.25)	(2.31)	(3.23)	(2.97)	(3.37)	(4.49)	(3.01)	(3.16)	(4.36)
No. of individuals	[1,826]	[797]		[722]	[372]		[1,104]	[425]	

Source: IFLS2 and IFLS3.

Estimates are from household data weighted using household sampling weights multiplied by number of household members in each respective age group. Standard errors (in parentheses) are robust to clustering at the community level. Significance at 5% (*) and 1% (**) are indicated.

TABLE 3.4
Real Per Capita Expenditures: IFLS, 1997 and 2000

	National			Urban			Rural		
	1997	2000	Difference	1997	2000	Difference	1997	2000	Difference
All individuals									
Mean	330,766	292,258	–38,508	440,400	355,189	–85,211 *	256,736	242,703	–14,033
Standard error	(18,868)	(5,895)	(19,767)	(40,406)	(10,278)	(41,693)	(13,611)	(4,948)	(14,483)
Median	194,351	203,068	8,717	233,917	240,881	6,965	176,188	180,911	4,723
Number of individuals	[33,441]	[42,733]		[15,770]	[20,732]		[17,671]	[22,001]	
Number of households	[7,518]	[10,223]		[3,433]	[4,905]		[4,085]	[5,318]	
Poor individuals									
Mean	78,392	81,544	3,151 *	81,046	83,366	2,321	77,185	80,675	3,490
Standard error	(1,144)	(859)	(1,431)	(1,383)	(1,324)	(1,915)	(1,495)	(1,094)	(1,852)
Median	82,089	84,591	2,501	82,766	85,455	2,689	81,409	84,511	3,102
Number of individuals	[5,568]	[6,473]		[1,938]	[2,224]		[3,630]	[4,249]	
Non-poor individuals									
Mean	385,142	332,154	–52,988 *	497,731	391,088	–106,544 *	302,767	281,376	–21,391
Standard error	(22,259)	(6,119)	(23,085)	(45,796)	(10,130)	(46,903)	(16,267)	(5,289)	(17,105)
Median	227,373	233,211	5,838	266,150	267,926	1,776	206,554	210,758	4,203
Number of observations	[27,873]	[36,260]		[13,832]	[18,508]		[14,401]	[17,752]	

Source: IFLS2 and IFLS3.

Per capita expenditures are deflated to December 2000 prices with Jakarta prices as the base. Estimates are from household data weighted using household sampling weights multiplied by number of household members. Standard errors (in parentheses) are robust to clustering at the community level. Significance at 5% (*) and 1% (**) are indicated.

distribution. When the data is disaggregated by poor–non-poor status, we see that mean *pce* actually increased by 4.5% among the poor, consistent with the small drop in poverty that we see. Median *pce* went up almost the same, 3.8%. Among the non-poor, mean *pce* dropped sharply among urban households; nearly 22%, with a much smaller decline among rural households, 7%. Median *pce* stayed virtually constant among the urban non-poor, while barely increasing, by 2%, among the rural non-poor. This difference between mean and medians for the non-poor indicates that it is among urban high income individuals that incomes declined the most, though still to high levels. This is very similar to the result observed by Frankenberg et al. (1999) for the change between 1997 and 1998. What is different here is that the lower and middle parts of the distribution have improved relative to 1998.

Focusing on the complete distribution of *pce* in the upper panel of Figure 3.1, we plot the poverty incidence curves for 1997 and 2000.[10] The poverty incidence curves are the cumulative distribution functions for *pce* and hence measure the incidence of poverty at any value of the poverty line (Ravallion 1994). They have the advantage of showing the entire distribution of *pce* and not being tied down to a particular poverty line, or set of lines. One can see that at low and moderate levels of *pce*, the 2000 curves lies below the 1997 curves. There is a crossing point at almost 525 thousand rupiah, above which the 1997 curve lies below.

In the lower panel of Figure 3.1 we focus on the lower and middle parts of the distributions, by plotting just those parts.[11] We can see more clearly now that the 2000 distribution lies below that for 1997, suggesting that there is less poverty in 2000 regardless where the poverty line is set. Following the poverty literature (for instance, Atkinson 1987), we can examine whether one curve first-order stochastically dominates the other at points below some maximum plausible poverty line. This is a statistical test of the null hypothesis that below the cut-off point, the poverty rates associated with one year are statistically larger/smaller than the poverty rates for the other year, for any poverty line chosen below the cut-off point. We set the cut-off at Rp 150,000, which is substantially above all of the province-urban/rural poverty lines, which range from Rp 75,000 in rural Central Java, to nearly Rp 108,000 in Jakarta, in December 2000 values.

In this case, if we have first-order stochastic dominance, then for any poverty line at or below Rp 150,000, the headcount, poverty gap and squared poverty gap measures rate will be lower for the curve that lies beneath the other at all points less than Rp 150,000. If the curves cross in this range one can also check for higher-order stochastic dominance.

FIGURE 3.1
Poverty Incidence Curves : 1997 and 2000

Poverty Incidence Curves

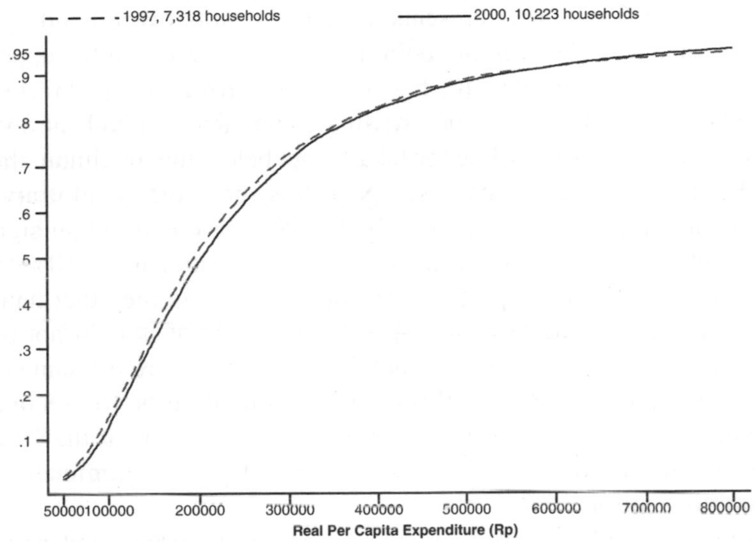
1997, 7,318 households
2000, 10,223 households
.95
.9
.8
.7
.6
.5
.4
.3
.2
.1
50000
100000
200000
300000
400000
500000
600000
700000
800000
Real Per Capita Expenditure (Rp)

Lower Tail of Poverty Incidence Curves

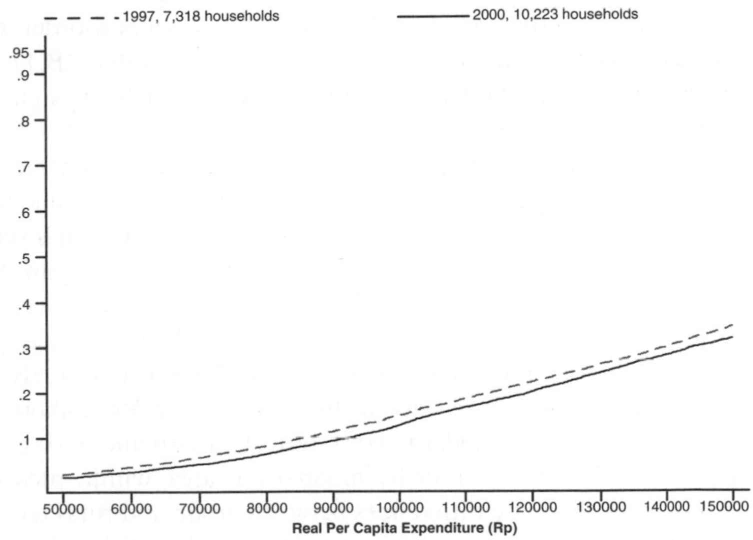
1997, 7,318 households
2000, 10,223 households
.95
.9
.8
.7
.6
.5
.4
.3
.2
.1
50000
60000
70000
80000
90000
100000
110000
120000
130000
140000
150000
Real Per Capita Expenditure (Rp)

Source: IFLS2 and IFLS3.

Observations were weighted using household sampling weights multiplied by the number of household members.

Second-order dominance is especially useful if first-order dominance is not met. If a curve dominates another at Order 2, then for any poverty line chosen, the poverty gap and squared poverty gap measures will be lower for the distribution that dominates (Atkinson 1987).[12]

Appendix Table 3B.1 presents these test results overall and by urban/rural residence. The crossing point for the two curves (in the upper panel of Figure 3.1), Rp 594,440, has a standard error of Rp 237,180. Two standard errors less than the crossing point, Rp 120,000, is above the December 2000 poverty line for Jakarta, but below the maximum threshold of Rp 150,000 that we have set. Now this threshold is arbitrary, so by selecting a threshold lower than Rp 120,000 we could obtain significant first-order stochastic dominance at the 5% level, and at the 10% level we achieve it even using Rp 150,000 as our cut-off. On the other hand, tests of differences in the ordinates at different levels of *pce* do not result in rejection of the null hypothesis that the distributions are the same over the range from Rp 60,000 to Rp 150,000. Similar tests for second-order dominance do reject that the distributions are the same at the 10% level. So one can say that there is weak evidence of poverty dominance by the 2000 distribution.

Figure 3.2 plots poverty incidence curves of urban and rural areas separately. The 2000 curves again lie underneath the 1997 curves over the relevant range for both urban and rural areas. However dominance tests show a lack of significance of both first- and second-order poverty dominance in both rural and urban areas (Appendix Table 3B.1). This is consistent with the mean urban and rural headcounts not being significantly different between the two years.

The results so far are aggregated across province and other characteristics. In Tables 3.5a and 3.5b we present estimates for three commonly used measures of poverty for each rural and urban area within each province: the headcount, the poverty gap and the squared poverty gap.[13] These results clearly show enormous provincial heterogeneity in movements of poverty, and therefore *pce*, between 1997 and 2000. In urban areas, poverty declined in 5 out of 7 provinces and in 7 out of 12 rural areas. Only a small number of these changes are statistically significant at 5%, although more are at 10%. The large standard errors reflect in part increasingly small sample sizes when we stratify by urban–rural area within province. In some provinces there are differences between urban and rural areas, such as in Central Java, where poverty increased in rural areas but decreased in urban locations. In some areas, such as rural West Nusa Tenggara, the increase in poverty is very large, while in others such as rural South Sumatra, the decline is large, although from very high levels. Notice too

FIGURE 3.2
Poverty Incidence Curves in Urban and Rural Areas : 1997 and 2000

Urban

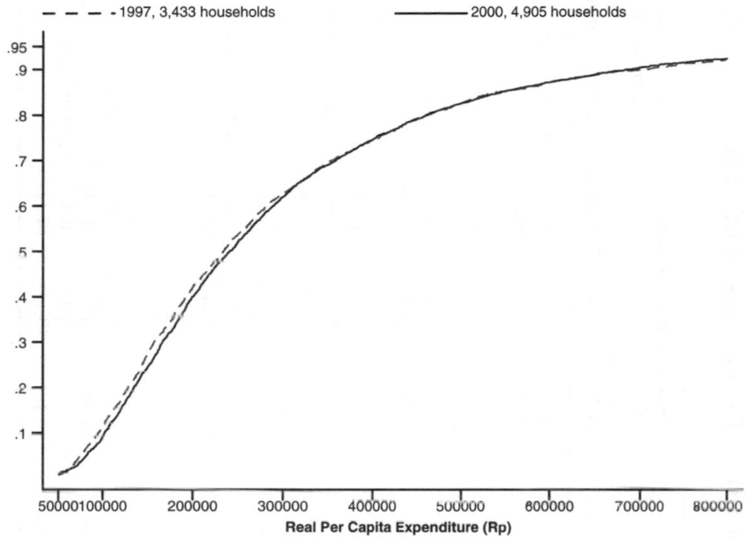
1997, 3,433 households
2000, 4,905 households
.95
.9
.8
.7
.6
.5
.4
.3
.2
.1
50000
100000
200000
300000
400000
500000
600000
700000
800000
Real Per Capita Expenditure (Rp)

Rural

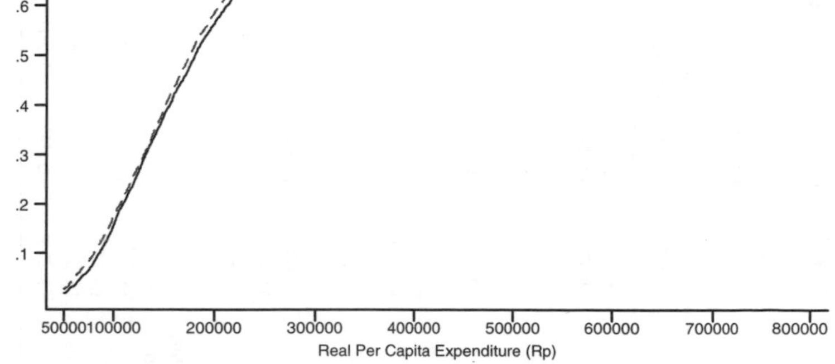
1997, 4,085 households
2000, 5,318 households
.95
.9
.8
.7
.6
.5
.4
.3
.2
.1
50000
100000
200000
300000
400000
500000
600000
700000
800000
Real Per Capita Expenditure (Rp)

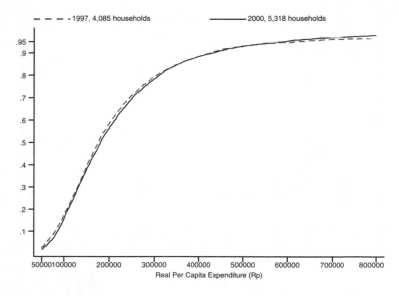

Source: IFLS2 and IFLS3.
Observations were weighted using household sampling weights multiplied by the number of household members.

TABLE 3.5a
Foster–Greer–Thorbecke Poverty Indices for Urban Residences: IFLS, 1997 and 2000

	Headcount			Poverty Gap			Squared Poverty Gap			Number of Individuals		Number of Households	
	1997	2000	Difference	1997	2000	Difference	1997	2000	Difference	1997	2000	1997	2000
North Sumatra	5.2	6.2	1.0	0.7	1.4	0.7	0.1	0.6	0.4	1,410	1,663	297	366
	(1.37)	(1.72)	(2.20)	(0.22)	(0.52)	(0.56)	(0.06)	(0.24)	(0.25)				
West Sumatra	–	–	–	–	–	–	–	–	–				
South Sumatra	–	–	–	–	–	–	–	–	–				
Lampung	–	–	–	–	–	–	–	–	–				
Jakarta	6.2	6.6	0.4	1.4	1.6	0.3	0.4	0.6	0.2	2,988	3,674	619	833
	(1.52)	(1.36)	(2.04)	(0.34)	(0.37)	(0.50)	(0.12)	(0.15)	(0.19)				
West Java	13.8	13.5	–0.3	3.3	2.9	–0.4	1.1	1.0	–0.1	2,716	3,831	584	930
	(2.83)	(2.27)	(3.62)	(0.78)	(0.60)	(0.98)	(0.33)	(0.27)	(0.43)				
Central Java	20.2	14.3	–5.9	5.3	3.6	–1.7	2.0	1.4	–0.6	1,711	2,130	382	519
	(3.57)	(2.68)	(4.47)	(1.28)	(0.98)	(1.61)	(0.58)	(0.46)	(0.74)				
Yogyakarta	11.7	11.2	–0.4	2.5	2.4	–0.2	0.8	0.8	0.0	1,149	1,336	294	376
	(2.03)	(2.68)	(3.36)	(0.46)	(0.72)	(0.86)	(0.20)	(0.28)	(0.34)				
East Java	21.3	13.6	–7.8 *	5.5	2.9	–2.6 *	2.1	0.9	–1.2	1,805	2,330	431	611
	(2.92)	(1.74)	(3.40)	(1.09)	(0.62)	(1.26)	(0.57)	(0.26)	(0.63)				
Bali	–	–	–	–	–	–	–	–	–				
West Nusa Tenggara	–	–	–	–	–	–	–	–	–				
South Kalimantan	–	–	–	–	–	–	–	–	–				
South Sulawesi	21.3	16.1	–5.3	6.7	4.1	–2.5	3.1	1.5	–1.6	750	1,371	157	269
	(5.14)	(2.78)	(5.84)	(2.08)	(0.88)	(2.26)	(1.08)	(0.37)	(1.14)				
All IFLS Provinces	13.8	11.7	–2.1	3.4	2.6	–0.8	1.3	0.9	–0.3	15,770	20,732	3,433	4,905
	(1.25)	(0.94)	(1.56)	(0.39)	(0.28)	(0.48)	(0.18)	(0.13)	(0.22)				

Source: IFLS2 and IFLS3.

Dash (–) indicates that the estimates are not reported due to small cell size. Estimates are from household data weighted using household sampling weights multiplied by the number of household members. Standard errors (in parentheses) are robust to clustering at the community level.

TABLE 3.5b
Foster–Greer–Thorbecke Poverty Indices for Rural Residences: IFLS, 1997 and 2000

	Headcount			Poverty Gap			Squared Poverty Gap			Number of Individuals		Number of Households	
	1997	2000	Difference	1997	2000	Difference	1997	2000	Difference	1997	2000	1997	2000
North Sumatra	23.9	19.7	–4.2	5.8	6.5	0.7	2.1	3.5	1.4	1,064	1,277	230	295
	(5.06)	(4.97)	(7.09)	(1.41)	(3.05)	(3.36)	(0.53)	(2.28)	(2.34)				
West Sumatra	10.6	10.8	0.3	3.6	2.5	–1.1	1.7	0.8	–0.9	1,146	1,494	241	323
	(6.44)	(3.54)	(7.35)	(2.59)	(0.83)	(2.73)	(1.37)	(0.27)	(1.40)				
South Sumatra	37.4	23.3	–14.1 *	13.7	6.1	–7.6 **	6.6	2.2	–4.4 **	1,029	1,448	222	317
	(6.09)	(3.45)	(7.00)	(2.68)	(0.88)	(2.82)	(1.41)	(0.41)	(1.47)				
Lampung	28.3	18.9	-9.5	8.1	5.1	–3.0	3.3	2.1	–1.3	1,108	1,285	240	306
	(3.66)	(3.86)	(5.32)	(1.77)	(1.35)	(2.23)	(1.00)	(0.58)	(1.15)				
West Java	14.1	18.7	4.6	3.1	4.3	1.2	1.2	1.6	0.5	2,953	3,797	658	917
	(2.24)	(1.91)	(2.95)	(0.63)	(0.55)	(0.84)	(0.31)	(0.26)	(0.41)				
Central Java	13.9	17.2	3.2	3.3	4.0	0.7	1.2	1.4	0.2	2,502	3,024	608	766
	(1.94)	(2.26)	(2.98)	(0.66)	(0.79)	(1.03)	(0.31)	(0.39)	(0.50)				
Yogyakarta	12.6	14.6	2.0	2.8	3.3	0.5	0.9	1.2	0.3	690	809	188	221
	(2.55)	(3.44)	(4.28)	(0.93)	(1.08)	(1.43)	(0.35)	(0.54)	(0.64)				
East Java	24.6	20.4	–4.2	7.7	5.3	–2.4	3.4	2.1	–1.3	2,656	3,534	681	883
	(3.25)	(1.59)	(3.62)	(1.72)	(0.59)	(1.82)	(1.04)	(0.31)	(1.08)				
Bali	22.1	15.9	–6.3	6.4	3.5	–2.9	2.8	1.6	–1.2	935	1,146	224	286
	(6.59)	(4.52)	(7.99)	(2.41)	(1.67)	(2.93)	(1.15)	(0.91)	(1.46)				
West Nusa Tenggara	19.4	31.3	11.9 *	4.7	7.8	3.1 *	1.6	2.8	1.2 *	1,669	1,994	353	477
	(3.64)	(3.13)	(4.80)	(1.13)	(0.66)	(1.31)	(0.42)	(0.28)	(0.51)				
South Kalimantan	18.0	10.5	–7.5	4.5	2.9	–1.5	1.8	1.2	–0.6	812	1,105	207	293
	(4.53)	(3.30)	(5.61)	(1.35)	(1.33)	(1.89)	(0.72)	(0.69)	(1.00)				
South Sulawesi	33.9	24.7	–9.1	11.5	6.2	–5.3	5.3	2.3	–3.0	1,107	1,088	233	234
	(6.66)	(4.81)	(8.22)	–3.0	–1.3	–3.2	–1.7	–0.6	–1.8				
All IFLS Provinces	20.4	19.3	–1.1	5.8	4.8	–0.9	2.4	1.9	–0.5	17,671	22,001	4,085	5,318
	(1.37)	(0.94)	(1.66)	(0.59)	(0.34)	(0.68)	(0.33)	(0.20)	(0.38)				

Source: IFLS2 and IFLS3.

Estimates are from household data weighted using household sampling weights multiplied by the number of household members. Standard errors (in parentheses) are robust to clustering at the community level.

the decline in rural poverty in South Kalimantan, South Sulawesi, North and South Sumatra and Lampung. These provinces were hit harder by the 1997 drought than others covered by IFLS (Fox 2002), and all of these provinces were affected by the smoke from the massive forest fires. Both drought and smoke would have caused lower farm outputs and incomes in 1997.

Levels of poverty are higher, often much so, in rural areas. Across provinces, rural areas in West and Central Java, Yogyakarta, plus rural West Sumatra, have lower poverty rates. In urban areas, Jakarta and cities in North Sumatra have less poverty.

Finally, to get an idea of how poverty in 1997 and 2000 varies over several economic, demographic and location characteristics taken together, we estimate a linear probability model (that is an OLS regression) of a binary indicator of the individual being in poverty, pooling the years (Table 3.6).[14] Columns 1 and 2 present results for all individuals, Columns 3 and 4 for adults, and Columns 5 and 6 for children. We include dummy variables for province, with Jakarta as the base province, and another for rural areas. We include a linear spline for age, which we use throughout the report unless otherwise specified. A linear spline allows for the regression line to have different slopes for different groups of the independent variable. We define our age groups as 0 to 59 months, 5 years to 14 years, 15 to 29 years, 30 to 59 years, and 60 years and older, requiring the line segments to join at the dividing points. We also add dummy variables for the level of education of the head of household (with additional controls for the few cases in which that information is missing), with no education as the base category and some primary (1–5 years), completed primary and/or some junior secondary (6–8 years), completed junior secondary and/or some senior secondary (9–11 years), and completed senior secondary or more (12 and more years) as the categories. We adjust the age splines as appropriate for adults and children. We replace the household head's schooling dummies with own schooling dummies in the regressions for adults and with mother's and father's schooling dummies in the regressions for children. In the case of parents, we create the education variables for those parents who are household members at the time of the survey. We create dummy variables (not reported) if the parental schooling variables are missing, either because the parent is not a household member, or because the data is missing. All covariates are interacted with a 2000 dummy variable.

Columns 1, 3 and 5 of Table 3.6 present the coefficients for 1997, while Columns 2, 4 and 6 show the *change* in each coefficient for 2000. As is

TABLE 3.6
Poverty: Linear Probability Models for 1997 and 2000

	All Individuals		Adults		Children	
	1997	Change in 2000	1997	Change in 2000	1997	Change in 2000
Age (spline, × 10^{-3}):						
0–59 months	–0.145	0.179				
	(0.50)	(0.50)				
5–14 years	–0.419 **	0.093				
	(5.32)	(0.89)				
15–59 years	–0.075 **	–0.008				
	(4.99)	(0.39)				
60+ years	0.050	0.069				
	(0.80)	(0.85)				
Age (spline, × 10^{-3}):						
15–29 years			–0.216 **	0.059		
			(3.14)	(0.63)		
30–59 years			–0.224 **	0.023		
			(5.72)	(0.49)		
60+ years			0.035	0.055		
			(0.51)	(0.62)		
Age (spline, × 10^{-3}):						
0–17 months					0.426	0.305
					(0.19)	(0.11)
18–35 months					–0.379	–0.279
					(0.24)	(0.14)
36–59 months					–0.919	0.217
					(1.15)	(0.21)
5–14 years					–0.629 **	0.202
					(5.32)	(1.28)
Female (× 10^{-2})	–0.026	0.003	–2.111 **	0.455	–0.091	0.022
	(0.08)	(0.01)	(4.79)	(0.86)	(0.11)	(0.02)

continued on next page

TABLE 3.6 – cont'd

	All Individuals		Adults		Children	
	1997	Change in 2000	1997	Change in 2000	1997	Change in 2000
Household head's / own education:						
1–5 years	–0.027	–0.017	–0.045 *	0.011		
	(1.16)	(0.54)	(2.57)	(0.53)		
6–8 years	–0.140 **	0.025	–0.117 **	0.021		
	(6.25)	(0.84)	(6.27)	(0.96)		
9–11 years	–0.170 **	–0.003	–0.184 **	0.028		
	(6.81)	(0.09)	(8.86)	(1.11)		
12+ years	–0.246 **	0.018	–0.232 **	0.031		
	(11.41)	(0.62)	(11.10)	(1.19)		
Mother's education if in household						
1–5 years					–0.048	0.026
					(1.47)	(0.60)
6–8 years					–0.117 **	0.027
					(3.58)	(0.63)
9–11 years					–0.168 **	0.036
					(4.81)	(0.78)
12+ years					–0.197 **	0.013
					(5.79)	(0.28)
Father's education if in household education,						
1–5 years					–0.042	–0.014
					(1.25)	(0.28)
6–8 years					–0.104 **	0.009
					(3.09)	(0.17)
9–11 years					–0.132 **	–0.012
					(3.79)	(0.23)
12+ years					–0.175 **	–0.010
					(5.50)	(0.19)
Rural ($\times 10^{-2}$)	–0.891	2.094	–1.311	3.262	–0.521	0.609
	(0.53)	(0.99)	(0.83)	(1.66)	(0.25)	(0.22)

North Sumatra	0.065	–0.028	0.056 *	–0.034	0.074	–0.022
	(1.89)	(0.62)	(2.06)	(0.94)	(1.49)	(0.35)
West Sumatra	–0.007	0.003	0.011	–0.012	–0.020	0.013
	(0.16)	(0.07)	(0.28)	(0.26)	(0.38)	(0.22)
South Sumatra	0.194 **	–0.131 *	0.187 **	–0.135 *	0.181 **	–0.122
	(3.87)	(2.23)	(3.79)	(2.40)	(3.58)	(1.94)
Lampung	0.114 **	–0.081	0.120 **	–0.083	0.112 *	–0.090
	(2.72)	(1.52)	(2.91)	(1.60)	(2.34)	(1.41)
West Java	0.045	0.017	0.049 *	0.002	0.030	0.035
	(1.91)	(0.54)	(2.29)	(0.09)	(0.97)	(0.87)
Central Java	0.050 *	–0.007	0.057 *	–0.010	0.046	–0.010
	(2.03)	(0.21)	(2.56)	(0.34)	(1.37)	(0.23)
Yogyakarta	0.056 **	–0.007	0.065 **	–0.013	0.060	–0.002
	(2.68)	(0.20)	(3.26)	(0.41)	(1.75)	(0.04)
East Java	0.127 **	–0.068 *	0.133 **	–0.074 *	0.127 **	–0.056
	(4.99)	(2.19)	(5.62)	(2.57)	(3.76)	(1.31)
Bali	0.123 **	–0.073	0.124 **	–0.089	0.090	–0.029
	(2.62)	(1.33)	(2.69)	(1.70)	(1.82)	(0.47)
West Nusa Tenggara	0.062	0.069	0.061 *	0.052	0.043	0.111
	(1.89)	(1.58)	(2.11)	(1.32)	(0.97)	(1.89)
South Kalimantan	0.050	–0.066	0.050	–0.073	0.025	–0.068
	(1.39)	(1.41)	(1.59)	(1.75)	(0.49)	(1.07)
South Sulawesi	0.182 **	–0.101	0.184 **	–0.105 *	0.214 **	–0.102
	(3.80)	(1.70)	(4.51)	(2.04)	(3.28)	(1.31)
Constant	0.270 **	–0.011	0.306 **	–0.031	0.369 **	–0.010
	(9.12)	(0.29)	(10.10)	(0.77)	(6.36)	(0.13)
F-test (p-values)						
Interaction variables	0.0347		0.0458		0.6139	
Education variables	0.0000		0.0000		0.0000	
Number of observations	76,174		52,852		23,322	
R-squared	0.07		0.05		0.08	

Source: IFLS2 and IFLS3.

Dummy variables for household head's education are used in all individuals specification. Dummy variables for own education are used in adults specification. Dummy variable for missing household head's education, for missing own education and for missing parental education or parent not in household are included in the regressions but not reported in the table. The omitted category for education is no schooling, and for province is Jakarta. Estimates were weighted using individual sampling weights. Standard errors are robust to clustering at the community level and to heteroskedasticity. Absolute t-statistics are in parentheses with significance at 5% (*) and 1% (**) indicated.

expected, higher schooling of the household head lowers the probability of being in poverty in both years. The impact of the household head's schooling is non-linear. Some primary schooling does little to lower poverty incidence, but completion of primary schooling is associated with a 14% drop in the probability of being poor, compared to individuals in households whose heads have no schooling. Completing senior secondary school or higher by the head results in a poverty rate 25% lower than the base of no schooling. These effects are much the same in 2000 as in 1997. These are very large effects given the mean rates we see in Table 3.1. For adults and children the schooling effects are correspondingly as large.

Adult women are less likely to be living in a poor household in 1997, although the magnitude declines by 2000. There is no difference between boys and girls in the likelihood of living in a poor household in either year. Poverty was higher in 1997 in South Sumatra, Lampung, East Java, Bali, and South Sulawesi, compared to Jakarta. By 2000, relative rates of poverty had declined in some of these provinces, but vastly increased in West Nusa Tenggara.

DYNAMICS OF POVERTY AND PCE

One issue that we can examine in IFLS that cannot be analysed with SUSENAS, or other repeated cross section data, is the change in poverty status of individuals. Table 3.7 presents a simple poverty transition matrix using those individuals who were in both IFLS2 and 3.[15] The results show substantial movement in and out of poverty. Over half of those in poverty in 1997 were not poor by 2000. On the other hand, almost 55% of the poor in 2000 were not poor in 1997. It is well known that poverty rates vary over time and that flows into and out of poverty are high (see for instance Baulch and Hoddinott 2000). This evidence is further demonstration of that fact. The flows into and out of poverty are similar in urban and rural areas.

In Table 3.8 we build on Table 3.7 by estimating a multinomial logit model of poverty transition for all individuals, using the same sample as in the transition matrix. We define four categories: being in poverty in both years (the base), in poverty in 1997 but not in 2000, in poverty in 2000 but not in 1997, and not in poverty either year. Relative risk ratios are reported instead of coefficients. These show the impact of covariates on the probability of one state occurring, such as being non-poor in both years, relative to the omitted state, being poor in both years. A relative risk ratio less than one means that a higher level of the covariate, say education,

TABLE 3.7
In- and Out-of-Poverty Transition Matrix: IFLS, 1997 and 2000
(In percent)

	2000								
	National			Urban			Rural		
1997	In Poverty	Out of Poverty	Total	In Poverty	Out of Poverty	Total	In Poverty	Out of Poverty	Total
In Poverty	7.2	10.1	17.3	5.8	7.5	13.3	8.1	11.9	20.0
	(0.50)	(0.64)	(0.97)	(0.69)	(0.69)	(1.23)	(0.68)	(0.93)	(1.37)
	[2,075]	[2,854]	[4,929]	[713]	[979]	[1,692]	[1,362]	[1,875]	[3,237]
Out of poverty	8.7	74.0	82.7	6.5	80.2	86.7	10.1	69.9	80.0
	(0.45)	(1.11)	(0.97)	(0.61)	(1.54)	(1.23)	(0.61)	(1.49)	(1.37)
	[2,485]	[22,207]	[24,692]	[839]	[11,200]	[12,039]	[1,646]	[11,007]	[12,653]
Total	15.9	84.1	100.0	12.3	87.7	100.0	18.2	81.8	100.0
	(0.72)	(0.72)	–	(1.06)	(1.06)	–	(0.94)	(0.94)	–
	[4,560]	[25,061]	[29,621]	[1,552]	[12,179]	[13,731]	[3,008]	[12,882]	[15,890]

Source: IFLS2 and IFLS3.
Estimates were weighted using individual sampling weights. Standard errors (in parentheses) are robust to clustering at the community level. Number of observations are in brackets.

TABLE 3.8
Poverty Transitions for All Individuals, 1997 and 2000
Multinomial Logit Models: Risk Ratios Relative to being Poor in both 1997 and 2000

	Poor in 1997 Not poor in 2000	Not poor in 1997 Poor in 2000	Not poor in 1997 Not poor in 2000
Age in 1997 (spline):			
0–59 months	0.992 **	0.995	0.996
	(3.11)	(1.56)	(1.58)
5–14 years	1.005 **	1.004 **	1.006 **
	(5.26)	(4.55)	(9.52)
15–59 years	1.000	1.000	1.000 *
	(1.91)	(1.19)	(2.27)
60+ years	1.000	1.002 *	1.000
	(0.48)	(2.20)	(0.58)
Female	1.077	1.077	1.034
	(1.36)	(1.44)	(0.78)
Household head's education:			
1–5 years	0.966	1.054	1.133
	(0.19)	(0.25)	(0.78)
6–8 years	0.875	2.032 **	2.356 **
	(0.67)	(3.19)	(5.01)
9–11 years	1.417	3.053 **	5.016 **
	(0.97)	(3.17)	(4.92)
12+ years	2.594	4.952 **	27.582 **
	(1.96)	(3.37)	(7.87)
Rural in 1997	1.213	1.545 **	1.187
	(1.44)	(2.62)	(1.01)
North Sumatra in 1997	2.388	1.260	0.660
	(1.67)	(0.42)	(0.77)
West Sumatra in 1997	1.262	1.136	1.160
	(0.52)	(0.22)	(0.18)

South Sumatra in 1997	1.506	0.398	0.212	**
	(0.93)	(1.81)	(3.21)	
Lampung in 1997	1.859	0.682	0.395	
	(1.28)	(0.72)	(1.79)	
West Java in 1997	1.459	1.366	0.533	
	(0.93)	(0.72)	(1.60)	
Central Java in 1997	1.440	0.953	0.536	
	(0.88)	(0.11)	(1.62)	
Yogyakarta in 1997	2.264	1.596	0.692	
	(1.66)	(1.13)	(0.84)	
East Java in 1997	1.551	0.541	0.318	**
	(1.06)	(1.01)	(3.02)	
Bali in 1997	1.907	0.737	0.346	
	(1.14)	(0.46)	(1.86)	
West Nusa Tenggara in 1997	0.785	1.222	0.298	**
	(0.56)	(0.41)	(3.01)	
South Kalimantan in 1997	2.410	0.799	0.763	
	(1.82)	(0.36)	(0.48)	
South Sulawesi in 1997	1.437	0.489	0.227	**
	(0.83)	(1.48)	(3.22)	
F-test (p-values)				
Education variables	0.0000			
X^2	852.45			
Log (Likelihood)	0.0000			
Pseudo R-squared	0.08			
Number of observations	29,621			

Source: IFLS2 and IFLS3.

Dummy variable for missing household head's education is included in the regressions but not reported in the table. The omitted category for education is no schooling, and for province is Jakarta. Estimates were weighted using individual sampling weights. Standard errors are robust to clustering at the community level and to heteroscedasticity Absolute t-statistics are in parentheses with significance at 5% (*) and 1% (**) indicated.

leads to a lower probability for being in the particular state (say non-poor in both years), relative to the odds of being in the base state (being poor in both years). A risk ratio greater than one means that higher values of the covariate leads to a higher probability of being in the particular state, relative to the likelihood of being in the base state.

Dummies for education of the head of household have positive, significant effects in keeping one out of poverty in both years relative to being in poverty in both years. It is also associated with a higher probability of being poor only in 2000 than being poor in both years, but the magnitude of the effects is smaller. Furthermore the effects of schooling are non-linear, with some primary schooling not having much impact, but secondary or more having a very large impact on not being poor either year (27 times more likely).

Among the regional effects, people in South Sumatra, Lampung, East Java, West Nusa Tenggara and South Sulawesi are more likely to be in poverty in both years relative to being poor in neither, as compared to people living in Jakarta.

We also estimate multinomial logits for adults and children separately. In the case of adults, we use own schooling dummies instead of schooling of the household head and for children, we use schooling dummies of the mother and the father if they are in the household. Results are presented in Appendix Tables 3C.1 and 3C.2. The own schooling and mother's and father's schooling effects are quite similar to that of the head. Similar to the results on being in poverty, women are 18% more likely to be living in households that are not in poverty in either year, compared to households in poverty in both years, than are men. We see no difference in the poverty transitions between boys and girls.

In Figure 3.3 we take a different approach and plot the smoothed real log *pce* of individuals in the 2000 survey against their log *pce* in 1997, again using a sample of persons who were in both waves.[16] A 45° line is plotted to make the graph easier to interpret. Points on the 45° line indicate that log *pce* was identical in the two years. Points above the 45° line indicate that log *pce* in 1997 was lower than in 2000 and visa versa.

As can be seen, the line has a flatter slope than the 45° line (an OLS regression estimates the slope to be 0.48), meaning that if log *pce* is very low in 1997, it rose in 2000, and if it was high in 1997, it fell in 2000. The point at which the smoothed real log *pce* line crosses the 45° line is at the 58th percentile of 1997 log *pce*. This means that the poorest 58% of IFLS individuals in 1997 on average had increases in their real *pce* in 2000, while the richest 42% on average saw declines in their *pce*.

FIGURE 3.3
Log Per Capita Expenditure 1997 and 2000 for Panel Individuals

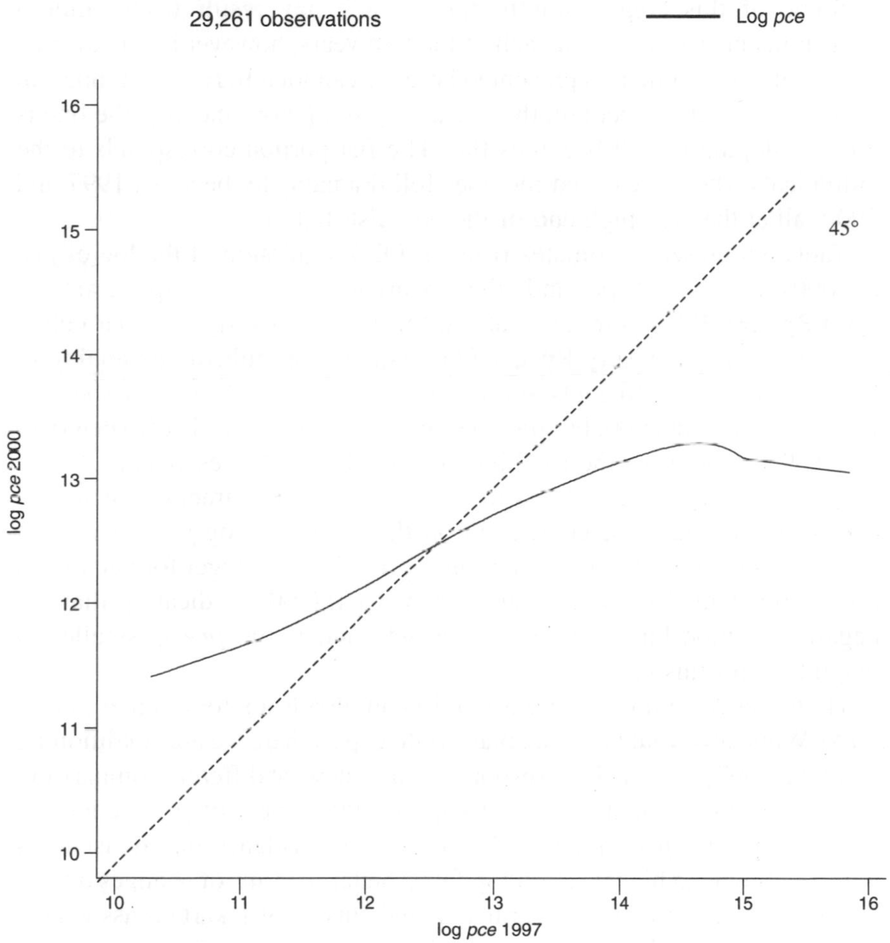
29,261 observations
Log pce
45°
log pce 2000
16
15
14
13
12
11
10
10
11
12
13
14
15
16
log pce 1997

Source: IFLS2 and IFLS3.
Lowess, bandwith=0.7

Appendix Figure 3.1 disaggregates these panel individuals by rural and urban residence in 1997. The shapes of the smoothed lines are similar to that for all persons in Figure 3.3. The crossing point with the 45° line for the urban sample is at the 61st percentile of the respective 1997 urban *pce* distribution and for the rural sample at the 57th percentile of the rural distribution. The slope of the curve for rural individuals is flatter (0.41 vs. 0.51 for the urban sample), reflecting the greater variability in rural incomes and expenditures.

Some of this "regression to the mean" may result from random measurement error in *pce* in each of the two years, however it may also be real; from the information presented here we cannot tell. However, one can also see that at the upper tail, there is a very sharp non-linearity, the line is upward sloping until it becomes flat. The flat portion corresponds to the individuals whose measured incomes fell dramatically between 1997 and 2000, all at the very high end of the *pce* distribution.

Table 3.9 presents estimates from an OLS regression of the log of *pce* in 2000 on log of 1997 *pce* and other covariates. Log *pce* is a spline around (log) Rp 150,000, a point 50% above the Jakarta poverty line, but below the median *pce* of nearly Rp 200,000. This is the multivariate analog to Figure 3.3. The coefficients show that higher *pce* in 1997 is associated with higher *pce* in 2000, but the coefficients are less than 1; between 0.45 and 0.39 depending on the 1997 level of *pce*. This indicates that the change in log *pce* is negatively related to the initial level (subtract one from the coefficient to obtain the coefficient on the change in log *pce*), the result seen in Figure 3.3. The coefficient on log 1997 *pce* is larger for persons in households with 1997 *pce* smaller than Rp 150,000, indicating that the negative relationship between *pce* growth and initial *pce* is smaller in magnitude for this group.

Higher education of the household head also leads to a higher *pce* in 2000. While this would be what one would expect, here we are conditioning on initial 1997 *pce*, which corresponds to a somewhat different comparison. It is much less clear that controlling for 1997 levels of *pce*, schooling would help raise *pce* in 2000. This is indirect evidence that households with heads having higher schooling fared better in terms of changes during these three years. Living in a rural area and outside of Jakarta is associated with lower *pce* in 2000, even controlling for *pce* in 1997. It is possible, however, that the significant impacts of head's schooling and place of residence in 1997 reflect non-linearities in the impact of 1997 *pce* that are not being captured by the spline specification.

One important qualification on these results is that the coefficients may be biased because of measurement error in 1997 *pce*. Random measurement error would bias the coefficient on log of 1997 *pce* towards zero. Common measurement error with *pce* in 2000 would bias the coefficient upwards. In results not shown, we have used two-stage least squares (2SLS) to estimate this equation for all individuals, using household non-land productive assets in 1997, its square and the value of household land owned as

TABLE 3.9
Log of Per Capita Expenditure 2000

	All Individuals	Adults	Children
Age (spline, × 10^{-3}):			
0–59 months	–0.656		
	(1.63)		
5–14 years	0.981 **		
	(7.47)		
15–59 years	0.026		
	(1.02)		
60+ years	–0.132		
	(1.15)		
Age (spline, × 10^{-3}):			
15–29 years		–0.149	
		(1.26)	
30–59 years		0.443 **	
		(7.40)	
60+ years		–0.285 *	
		(2.34)	
Age (spline, × 10^{-3}):			
0–17 months			3.963
			(1.21)
18–35 months			0.315
			(0.14)
36–59 months			–1.658
			(1.44)
5–14 years			1.539 **
			(7.53)
Female (× 10^{-2})	0.009	3.038 **	1.009
	(0.02)	(4.46)	(0.87)
Household head's/ own education:			
1–5 years	0.000	0.015	
	(0.02)	(0.82)	
6–8 years	0.058 *	0.111 **	
	(2.10)	(4.79)	
9–11 years	0.155 **	0.229 **	
	(4.72)	(8.89)	
12+ years	0.348 **	0.398 **	
	(12.14)	(15.94)	
Mother's education if in household:			
1–5 years			–0.053
			(1.47)
6–8 years			0.028
			(0.83)
9–11 years			0.126 **
			(2.79)
12+ years			0.296 **
			(7.05)
Father's education if in household:			
1–5 years			0.009
			(0.18)
6–8 years			0.054
			(1.15)

continued on next page

TABLE 3.9 – cont'd

	All Individuals		Adults		Children	
9–11 years					0.055	
					(1.10)	
12+ years					0.205	**
					(4.32)	
log 1997 *pce* : 0– log Rp 150,000	0.447	**	0.445	**	0.458	**
	(11.67)		(11.95)		(10.67)	
> log Rp 150,000	0.389	**	0.393	**	0.353	**
	(14.40)		(14.08)		(11.86)	
Rural ($\times 10^{-2}$)	–0.057	*	–0.040		–0.033	
	(2.52)		(1.82)		(1.33)	
North Sumatra	–0.122	*	–0.083		–0.173	*
	(2.15)		(1.61)		(2.44)	
West Sumatra	–0.056		–0.085		–0.062	
	(1.08)		(1.77)		(1.16)	
South Sumatra	–0.080		–0.068		–0.062	
	(1.52)		(1.35)		(1.04)	
Lampung	–0.130	*	–0.115	*	–0.134	*
	(2.28)		(2.06)		(1.99)	
West Java	–0.200	**	–0.184	**	–0.210	**
	(4.78)		(4.46)		(4.31)	
Central Java	–0.144	**	–0.147	**	–0.132	**
	(3.39)		(3.47)		(2.67)	
Yogyakarta	–0.102	*	–0.118	*	–0.121	
	(2.06)		(2.57)		(1.90)	
East Java	–0.123	**	–0.131	**	–0.109	*
	(2.98)		(3.22)		(2.14)	
Bali	–0.073		–0.054		–0.072	
	(1.19)		(0.88)		(1.12)	
West Nusa Tenggara	–0.328	**	–0.300	**	–0.351	**
	(6.02)		(5.63)		(5.38)	
South Kalimantan	–0.097	*	–0.086		–0.055	
	(2.03)		(1.86)		(0.91)	
South Sulawesi	–0.130	*	–0.142	**	–0.128	
	(2.40)		(2.76)		(1.96)	
Constant	6.842	**	6.860	**	6.589	**
	(15.09)		(15.41)		(12.67)	
F–test (p–values)						
Education variables	0.0000		0.0000		0.0000	
Expenditure variables	0.0000		0.0000		0.0000	
Number of observations	29621		19684		9937	
R–squared	0.31		0.30		0.33	

Source: IFLS2 and IFLS3.

Dummy variables for household head's education are used in all individuals specification. Dummy variables for own education are used in adults specification. Dummy variable for missing household head's education, for missing own education and for missing parental education or parent not in household are included in the regressions but not reported in the table. The omitted category for education is no schooling, and for province is Jakarta. Estimates were weighted using individual sampling weights. Standard errors are robust to clustering at the community level and to heteroscedasticity. Absolute t–statistics are in parentheses with significance at 5% (*) and 1% (**) indicated.

instruments for 1997 *pce*. Providing that any measurement error in the asset variables is uncorrelated with measurement error in *pce*, the 2SLS estimates will be consistent.[17]

The results are telling, the coefficient of log 1997 *pce* does indeed rise, to 0.91, with a standard error of 0.073. This means that the degree of mean reversion in *pce* is small, most of what had been estimated was due to measurement error. In turn this implies that there is a great deal of constancy in *pce* over time. Consistent with this interpretation, the coefficients on education of the household head are now both individually and jointly insignificant, once estimated by 2SLS.

SUMMARY

Over the three-year period from the second half of 1997 to the second half of 2000, poverty rates declined slightly, but not significantly, from 17.7% to 15.9%, although there are differences across provinces and between rural and urban areas. Considering the large and significant increase in poverty, to 27%, that occurred between 1997 and late 1998, this finding suggests a marked recovery in poverty since 1998. Large increases in relative rice prices played a large role in inducing the increase from 1997 to 1998, and declines afterwards helped to spawn the later decline in poverty rates. The fact that budget shares of rice among the poor are large, around 20%, is a major reason for this.

Corresponding to the movements in poverty, *pce* rose for much of the population. Median incomes increased by about 5.5% nationally. Among the poor, median *pce* went up 3.5% and for the non-poor, 3.2%. This increase in median *pce* occurred in both urban and rural areas. Mean *pce*, however, moved very differently. Overall, mean *pce* fell 12% from 1997 to 2000. Among the poor, mean *pce* actually rose, similar to the median, but among the non-poor it declined by 14%. In urban areas, mean incomes of the non-poor fell by even more, 22%. The different movements in mean and median *pce* for these different groups occurred because it was the top of the income distribution that had the largest percent decline in *pce*, while for lower and middle income Indonesians, we find an increase in *pce* from 1997 to 2000.

Using the panel aspect of IFLS, we can examine the change in poverty status of households and individuals therein between 1997 and 2000. Among individuals interviewed in both years, we find considerable movement into and out of poverty. Over half of those in poverty in 1997 are not in 2000 and over half of those in poverty in 2000 were not in 1997. This is a large movement in and out of poverty and is consistent with what is observed in many other low income economies. If we look at *pce* changes by *pce* in 1997, we find a consistent pattern. Those who started with low incomes in 1997 were likely to have had their *pce* rise by 2000, while those with higher *pce* in 1997 were more likely to suffer a fall by 2000.

We examine the correlates of poverty and income levels and changes. Consistent with what is universally found, we find that education is significantly correlated with *pce* and, thus, of being out of poverty. We also find that higher education is associated with moving out of poverty from 1997 to 2000 and with staying out of poverty in both years. Living in a rural area is a correlate of higher poverty, as in most low income economies, although interestingly, it is not related to movements into and out of poverty.

Notes

1 We actually use the product of household size and the household sampling weight, to also allow us to generalize at the population level. This is a common method to calculate poverty rates (see for instance, Deaton and Tarozzi 2000).

2 In this case we weight by the product of the number of individuals in the household in the particular demographic group by the household sampling weight.

3 This corrects for the fact that because clusters (or enumeration areas) are chosen randomly and then households chosen within clusters, the households within clusters are not statistically independent, as assumed when standard errors are normally calculated.

4 This difference may be due to a decline in economic conditions due to a combination of the 1997 draught (which began in mid-1997) and early effects from the economic crisis.

5 The poverty gap index measures the amount of money, per capita in the population, required to bring up the incomes of all of the poor to the poverty line, expressed as a percent of the poverty line.

6 The squared poverty gap, which squares the differential of the percent gap that each poor person's *pce* is below the poverty line, measures the distribution among the poor as well as the gap. For two populations with the same poverty gap, the one with the more unequal distribution among the poor will have the larger squared poverty gap. These are all special cases of the Foster, Greer, Thorbecke (FGT) class of poverty measures (see Foster et al. 1984).

7 The 2000 SUSENAS Core has a considerably shorter expenditure module than the modules used for the 1999 and 1996 estimates, which may understate the level of poverty in 2000 compared to what one might find with a longer form expenditure questionnaire. Alatas and Pradhan adjust their 2000 poverty estimates for the difference in consumption of the poor between the long and short forms.

8 1,839 out of the 2,645 new split-off households in 2000 can be matched.

9 Non-split-off households that can be matched from 1997 and 2000 exhibit constant poverty rates.

10 All curves are estimated using as weights, the product of household size with the household sampling weights.

11 We also use a lower cut-off point of Rp 50,000, which corresponds to approximately the 1st percentile, in order to remove any influence of outliers.

12 As is well known, first-order dominance implies second-order and higher-order dominance, though the reverse is not true (Atkinson 1987).

13 We only report data for province-rural/urban combination if the sample size of households within the cell is above 200.

14 We use linear probability models (LPMs) throughout this paper. LPMs consistently estimate the marginal effects of covariates on the probability that the dependent variable is one. LPMs tend to be somewhat more robust to distributional assumptions than probit or logit estimates, which are inconsistent when the distributional assumptions underlying them are violated. While LPMs have their weaknesses, which are well-known, they are simple and easy to interpret. Standard errors of LPM models are heteroskedastic, but we correct for this by calculating heteroskedastic-robust standard errors, and correcting for clustering at the enumeration area. The correction for clustering at the enumeration area allows general correlation of errors between individuals within an enumeration area. This also allows for a general correlation between error terms of individuals in the same household and thus adjusts the standard errors for the fact that individuals within households are not independent observations. Indeed, allowing clustering at the enumeration area rather than household results in more conservative standard errors.

15 We use 1997 individual weights, and location to adjust standard errors for clustering at the enumeration area.

16 This is estimated using locally weighted smoothed scatterplots (LOWESS), with a bandwidth of .7. Individual sampling weights were used.

17 There is an issue of endogeneity of 1997 *pce*, which may bias the coefficients. In this version we do not try to correct for this.

APPENDIX 3A

Calculation of Deflators and Poverty Lines

PCE is calculated using all consumption expenditures, including durables, as it was in Frankenberg et al. (1999).[1] We create our own deflators using disaggregated consumption value indices at the five-digit level, computed by BPS, separate for urban and rural areas.[2] In the case of urban areas, BPS collects and reports price information monthly in 43 cities, of which 34 are represented in the IFLS sample. For rural areas, prices are collected monthly at the district level, but reported at the province level.

We form Tornquist indices separately for urban and rural prices using the 34 cities covered in IFLS data as the level of aggregation for urban indices and the 13 IFLS provinces as the level of aggregation for the rural indices. We use consumption shares from the 1996 and 1999 SUSENAS consumption modules as weights for the price increases from the consumer price index (cpi) data.[3, 4] By considering consumption shares from both years, the Tornquist index allows for the fact that households will substitute away from expensive items, such as rice, towards cheaper ones as relative prices change. This substitution will mitigate the welfare impact of price changes that should in principle be accounted for in a cost of living index. Other indices such as Laspeyres do not account for such substitution.

Using SUSENAS share weights has an advantage over BPS procedures, at least for their urban price indices, because in calculating mean urban shares, BPS weights household shares using weights formed from total household expenditure and are not adjusted for household size.[5] This results in rich households getting a very high weight compared to poor households, which would not be the case if household size was used instead (Deaton and Grosh 2000, note that this is a common problem in many countries). The particular problem this causes in Indonesia over this time period is that the food share BPS uses is very low, 38% on average over all urban areas, compared to a share of 55% found in the 1996 SUSENAS module (both shares being for the same year) or 53% in IFLS (Table 3.2). In addition, food price inflation was higher over the period 1997–2000 than non-food inflation, so that a lower food share will understate inflation, and thus overstate real income growth over this period. Obviously this will overstate any recovery in *pce* levels.[6]

We apply the price deflators to *pce*s to calculate real values using December 2000 as the base.[7] Urban households are assigned a cpi for the nearest city from the BPS list and rural households are assigned a cpi based on their province of residence. To account for cost of living differences between provinces and rural and urban areas within each province, we use the deflator (with Jakarta as the base) that is implicit in the constructed poverty lines for each province-urban/rural combination from a study by Pradhan et al. (2001).

Poverty lines in Indonesia are controversial. BPS calculates poverty lines that are designed to reflect the total expenditure required to purchase a diet consisting of 2,100 calories per day (using the so-called "food-energy intake" method). Ravallion and Bindani (1994) among others have argued that the urban/rural gaps in the BPS poverty lines, nearly 25%, are too large compared to real cost-of-living differences. They, and other analysts, have suggested alternative poverty lines.

We follow a recent study by Pradhan et al. (2001) which suggests a set of province by rural/urban poverty lines based on the 1999 SUSENAS module. They use a fixed national food basket that will generate a caloric intake of 2,100 per person per day, and price that basket using regional prices, making adjustments for the fact that richer households will shift into more expensive sources of calories. These food poverty lines are then scaled-up to account for non-food expenditures to arrive at a set of poverty lines by province and rural/urban area within province. Their poverty lines have the advantage that the urban-rural differential is only approximately 11%, in contrast to the BPS derived lines. These lines are then converted to December 2000 values using our province-specific urban/rural deflators. From this we take the ratio of a poverty line valued in December 2000 rupiah, say in rural Lampung, to that in Jakarta, and divide all real expenditures in rural Lampung by this amount to finally arrive at a real expenditure valued at Jakarta prices.[8] These are the real expenditures used in this analysis. From these, poverty status can be determined by comparing to the Jakarta poverty line.

Notes

1 Housing rental expenditures for owner/occupiers is taken from a question that asks the respondent, usually the head male, to estimate the market rental value of the house. Of course in areas in which rental markets are thin, it is not clear how reliable these self-assessments are. On the other hand, estimating a housing rental value using hedonic regression techniques with a very small sample of renters is unlikely to be better.

2 These consumption value indices are the current month values of a baseline quantity level, which may differ by province and urban and rural area. The urban indices use baseline quantities taken from a 1996

consumer expenditure survey done specially to calculate weights for the cpi. This survey is fielded once a decade. The rural baseline quantities are taken from the 1993 SUSENAS consumption module. These consumption value indices can be aggregated to any level desired, and then ratios taken across different months to obtain a percent increase in price, or group price.

In the BPS rural price index series, housing rental is not covered, although it is in the urban price index. Rather than drop housing from the cpi calculations, we assume that the percent change in the consumption value indices for rural housing within a province is equal to the average percent change in cities within that province. We then weight these by the province rural housing shares when forming the rural price indices.

3 The Tornquist formula applied to our case is:

$$\log cpi_T = \sum_i 0.5(w_{i,1999} + w_{i,1996}) * \log (p_{i,1} / p_{i,0})$$

where $w_{i,1999}$ is the budget share of commodity i in 1999, taken from SUSENAS; $w_{i,1996}$ is the budget share in the base period, 1996; $p_{i,1}$ and $p_{i,0}$ are the prices of commodity I in periods 1 and 0 (in our case period 1 will correspond to Dec 2000 and period 0 to the month and year of interview of the household).

4 This required that we match a list of commodities from the urban price indices to separate lists from both the 1996 and 1999 SUSENAS (the two SUSENAS have different commodity code numbers) and conduct an analogous procedure for the rural price indices. Correspondences worked out by Kai Kaiser, Tubagus Choesni and Jack Molyneaux (Kaiser et al. 2001) proved very valuable in helping us do this, although we re-did the exercise and made a number of changes.

Other studies have used the quantities in the SUSENAS to form unit prices (see, for example, Friedman and Levinsohn 2001). For us this is not appropriate since we need prices deflators for months and years not covered by the SUSENAS. IFLS is not a very good source for prices for the purpose of constructing "cpis". Unit prices are not available in the household expenditure module because quantities are not collected. While some price information is collected in the household questionnaire and separately in the community questionnaire, from local markets; there are only a limited number of commodities available, and so we do not use them.

5 For rural shares it is not clear whether expenditure-based or population-based weights were used by BPS.

6 On the other hand, the BPS consumer expenditure survey collects expenditures for a far more disaggregated commodity list than does the SUSENAS module (which is the longer form of the two SUSENAS consumption surveys). It is especially more detailed on the non-food side. Having less detail on non-foods is thought to lead to serious underestimates of non-food consumption and thus an overstatement of food shares (Deaton and Grosh 2000).

7 The mean rupiah-US$ exchange rate in December 2000 was Rp 9,400.

8 We prefer using the Pradhan et al. (2001) data to deflate regional prices into Jakarta equivalents because of the problems that would have been incurred using the BPS cpi data. In order to make this calculation properly, one wants a fixed quantity bundle, priced at different regional prices, as Pradhan et al. (2001) did in their study (using quantity and unit value data from the 1999 SUSENAS). However combining the urban and rural cpi series, which are quite different, it is very difficult to find a set of common quantities that are representative of a large fraction of expenditures, to value in this way.

APPENDIX FIGURE 3.1
Log Per Capita Expenditure 1997 and 2000 for Panel Individuals in Urban and Rural Areas

Urban

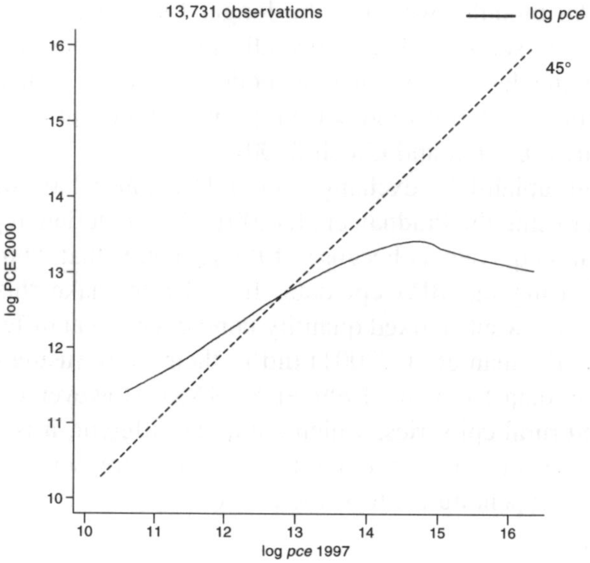
13,731 observations
log pce
45°
log PCE 2000
16
15
14
13
12
11
10
10
11
12
13
14
15
16
log pce 1997

Rural

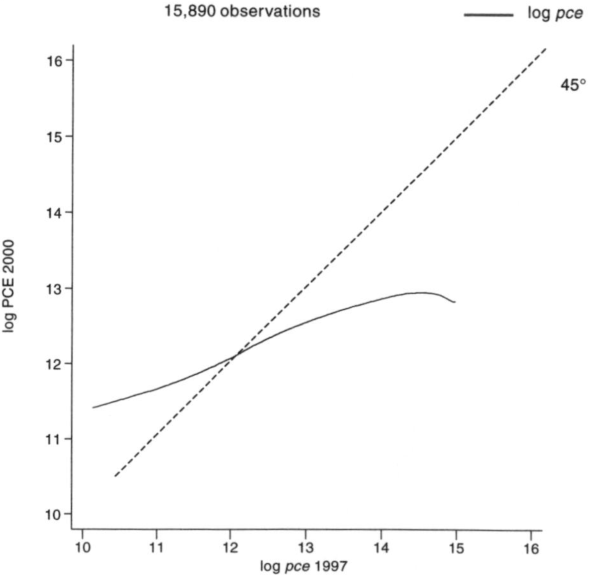
15,890 observations
log pce
45°
log PCE 2000
16
15
14
13
12
11
10
10
11
12
13
14
15
16
log pce 1997

Source: IFLS2 and IFLS3.
Lowess, bandwith=0.7.

APPENDIX TABLE 3A.1
Poverty Lines
(Monthly Rupiah Per Capita)

Province	February 1999		December 2000	
	Urban	Rural	Urban	Rural
North Sumatra	83,462	74,460	83,662	81,043
West Sumatra	85,361	78,499	87,377	79,035
South Sumatra	85,579	79,962	84,141	78,994
Lampung	88,877	78,637	89,820	79,180
Jakarta	102,814	–	107,766	–
West Java	94,405	86,024	95,594	85,351
Central Java	85,009	78,461	85,111	75,351
Yogyakarta	92,644	83,304	92,086	77,094
East Java	85,024	80,020	84,480	80,752
Bali	97,794	94,405	102,020	95,007
West Nusa Tenggara	87,783	84,718	85,282	87,832
South Kalimantan	86,921	82,932	89,769	77,716
South Sulawesi	84,561	74,376	87,361	82,259

February 1999 figures are from Pradhan et al. (2000). December 2000 figures are computed by applying the deflators calculated by authors as described in the text.

APPENDIX 3B

Tests of Stochastic Dominance

Several methods exist in the literature to statistically test for stochastic dominance. For first-order dominance, the Kolmorgorov-Smirnov test examines the maximum distance between two poverty incidence curves, but has notoriously low statistical power, and what power it does have is greatest in the centre of the distribution, whereas for our purposes we are most interested in the lower tail.

Recently Davidson and Duclos (2000) have derived under general conditions, the asymptotic distributions (which turn out to be Gaussian) for testing stochastic dominance of orders 1, 2 and 3 between two distributions. There are at least two distinct ways one can go about this using their results. If the two curves cross at least once, Davidson and Duclos derive the asymptotic distribution for the crossing points. With this, one can calculate a standard error for the crossing point and compute the lower end point of a confidence interval around that point.

For example, suppose that the *pce* curves in 1997 and 2000 cross at Rp 250,000, with the 1997 curve lying above the 2000 curve at all lower values of *pce* than Rp 250,000, so that this represents the first crossing point. Now suppose that the standard error of the crossing point is Rp 35,000. Then two standard errors less than the crossing point is Rp 180,000 Since this is above the maximum poverty line, or threshold, of Rp 150,000, one can conclude with 97.5% confidence that the crossing point is above Rp 150,000. Below that point, the 2000 distribution dominates the 1997 distribution. As shown in Chapter 3, in some cases it turns out to be possible to make such a statement. If, however, the point of two standard errors below the first crossing point is less than the threshold, say it is Rp 80,000, then we would not reject non-dominance below the threshold. Or if the first crossing point is below the threshold, we would also not reject the null hypothesis of non-dominance.

If the two curves do not cross, then obviously one cannot employ the strategy outlined above. In this case the Davidson-Duclos results suffer a disadvantage, but can still be used. They provide the asymptotic distributions needed to calculate the standard errors for the vertical difference between the two curves (cumulative distribution functions if we are examining first-order stochastic dominance) at any point in the distribution. For first-order dominance, we are looking at differences in the curves. Intuitively, at a point, say Rp 200,000 if we are analysing monthly *pce*, the vertical ordinate of the curve is the percentile of the distribution, say 60th in 1997.

So the vertical difference between two curves at a point such as Rp 200,000 tells us the difference in the percentiles that Rp 200,000 corresponds to the two distributions being compared. Davidson-Duclos have been able to derive the standard errors of such differences, enabling one to test the null hypothesis that the differences are zero. If the vertical differences between the curves are significant at every point beneath the threshold (or the maximum plausible threshold), then one could conclude that the curve underneath dominates the curve above. The problem, of course, is that there are an infinite number of points to test. Davidson and Duclos advocate testing at many points in the relevant range and if one can reject equality of the distributions at all points, then to conclude that the lower one dominates. While this strategy is not perfect, it seems better than not testing at all, and so we employ it.[1]

Appendix Table 3B.1 presents these test results for all individuals. The crossing point of Rp 594,440 has a large standard error of Rp 237,180, so that two standard errors less than the crossing point is only Rp 130,000. While this is more than the poverty line we use for Jakarta, it is less than the maximum line of Rp 150,000 that we set out. This suggests that we do not have first-order dominance, at the 5% level, by the 2000 distribution, in the relevant range. However taking a 10% confidence interval we do have first-order dominance. Tests of differences in the ordinates at different levels of *pce* also fail to result in rejection of the null hypothesis that the distributions are the same over the range from Rp 60,000 to Rp 150,000, although second-order dominance of the 2000 over the 1997 distribution is significant at the 10% level.

Note

1 Duclos distributes a program titled Distributive Analysis/Analyse Distributive (DAD), which can make these, and many other, poverty and inequality-related calculations; we used Version 4.2. See Duclos et al. (2002) at www.ecn.ulaval.ca/~jyves. For the poverty incidence curve tests, all test statistics are calculated using the product of household size and household sampling weights as the weight. For tests in later sections using individual data, individual sampling weights are used. In all cases, clustering at the enumeration area is accounted for.

APPENDIX TABLE 3B.1
Real Per Capita Expenditure 2000 and 1997: Test for Stochastic Dominance

	First crossing point and the difference between curves (2000–1997)											
	National				Urban				Rural			
	First-Order Dominance	Standard Error	Second-Order Dominance	Standard Error	First-Order Dominance	Standard Error	Second-Order Dominance	Standard Error	First-Order Dominance	Standard Error	Second-Order Dominance	Standard Error
First crossing point	594,440	(237,180)	–	–	497,322	(66,603)	–	–	535,812	(178,159)	–	–
Points of testing												
60,000	–0.011	(0.006)	–165	(101.8)	–0.003	(0.005)	–92	(71.2)	–0.016	(0.009)	–195	(165.2)
70,000	–0.015	(0.007)	–292	(161.8)	–0.010	(0.007)	–142	(124.5)	–0.016	(0.011)	–359	(258.3)
80,000	–0.018	(0.008)	–469	(233.5)	–0.015	(0.010)	–280	(199.9)	–0.018	(0.012)	–544	(367.1)
90,000	–0.021	(0.010)	–658	(314.7)	–0.019	(0.019)	–448	(297.0)	–0.019	(0.014)	–723	(486.6)
100,000	–0.023	(0.011)	–881	(408.1)	–0.021	(0.014)	–664	(412.4)	–0.020	(0.016)	–914	(621.4)
110,000	–0.019	(0.012)	–1,073	(511.0)	–0.022	(0.017)	–877	(546.5)	–0.012	(0.017)	–1,045	(766.6)
120,000	–0.022	(0.014)	–1,283	(626.9)	–0.018	(0.018)	–1,105	(702.4)	–0.019	(0.019)	–1,189	(927.2)
130,000	–0.019	(0.015)	–1,476	(756.3)	–0.025	(0.020)	–1,324	(878.7)	–0.008	(0.020)	–1,303	(1104.7)
140,000	–0.017	(0.015)	–1,646	(893.0)	–0.018	(0.021)	–1,524	(1070.1)	–0.010	(0.020)	–1,380	(1288.2)
150,000	–0.026	(0.016)	–1,859	(1036.3)	–0.029	(0.023)	–1,757	(1273.4)	–0.015	(0.021)	–1,502	(1477.4)
Number of individuals												
1997	33,441		33,441		15,770		15,770		17,671		17,671	
2000	42,733		42,733		20,732		20,732		22,001		22,001	
Number of households												
1997	7,518		7,518		3,433		3,433		4,085		4,085	
2000	10,223		10,223		4,905		4,905		5,318		5,318	

Source: IFLS2 and IFLS3.

Dash (–) indicates that the curves do not cross. Formulae for standard errors are from Russel Davidson and Jean-Yves Duclos (2000), "Statistical Inference for Stochastic Dominance and for the Measurement of Poverty and Inequality", *Econometrica* v86 n6. Computation for the table above was performed using "DAD: A Software for Distributive Analysis/Analyse Distributive", version 4.2, copyrighted by Jean-Yves Duclos, Abdelkrim Araar, and Carl Fortin. Estimates were weighted using household sampling weights multiplied by the number of household member. Standard errors (in parentheses) are robust to clustering at the community level.

APPENDIX TABLE 3C.1
Poverty Transitions for All Adults, 1997 and 2000
Multinomial Logit Models: Risk Ratios Relative to Being Poor in both 1997 and 2000

		Poor in 1997 Not poor in 2000	Not poor in 1997 Poor in 2000	Not poor in 1997 Not poor in 2000
Age in 1997 (spline):	15–29 years	1.000	1.001	1.002 **
		(0.31)	(0.56)	(2.61)
	30–59 years	1.000	1.000	1.002 **
		(0.37)	(0.13)	(5.21)
	60+ years	0.999	1.002	0.999
		(0.95)	(1.71)	(1.13)
Female (× 10^{-2})	1.007	1.052	1.180 **	
		(0.11)	(0.77)	(3.09)
Education:	1–5 years	0.865	1.017	1.248
		(1.11)	(0.11)	(1.88)
	6–8 years	1.056	1.385 *	2.562 **
		(0.37)	(2.10)	(7.89)
	9–11 years	1.751 **	2.305 **	6.757 **
		(2.86)	(4.26)	(11.09)
	12+ years	1.644 *	1.701	13.472 **
		(2.02)	(1.87)	(11.56)
Rural in 1997		1.218	1.467 *	1.238
		(1.38)	(2.37)	(1.25)
North Sumatra in 1997		2.654	1.076	0.777
		(1.85)	(0.13)	(0.46)
West Sumatra in 1997		0.840	0.673	0.744
		(0.41)	(0.74)	(0.40)
South Sumatra in 1997		1.472	0.335 *	0.202 **
		(0.96)	(2.10)	(3.42)
Lampung in 1997		1.885	0.511	0.337 *
		(1.40)	(1.26)	(2.03)

continued on next page

APPENDIX TABLE 3C.1 – cont'd

	Poor in 1997 Not poor in 2000	Not poor in 1997 Poor in 2000	Not poor in 1997 Not poor in 2000
West Java in 1997	1.357	0.997	0.467
	(0.80)	(0.01)	(1.95)
Central Java in 1997	1.352	0.750	0.442 *
	(0.78)	(0.65)	(2.13)
Yogyakarta 1997	1.924	1.236	0.534
	(1.42)	(0.46)	(1.43)
East Java in 1997	1.497	0.507	0.273 **
	(1.04)	(1.56)	(3.42)
Bali in 1997	1.780	0.514	0.312 *
	(1.07)	(1.03)	(2.09)
West Nusa Tenggara in 1997	0.936	0.948	0.313 **
	(0.16)	(0.11)	(2.92)
South Kalimantan in 1997	2.737 *	0.675	0.778
	(2.08)	(0.64)	(0.45)
South Sulawesi in 1997	1.495	0.343 *	0.202 **
	(0.97)	(2.22)	(3.63)
F-test (p-values)			
Education variables	0.0000		
X^2	806.38		
Log (Likelihood)	0.0000		
Pseudo R-squared	0.06		
Number of observations	19,684		

Source: IFLS2 and IFLS3.

Dummy variable for missing education is included in the regressions but not reported in the table. The omitted category for education is no schooling, and for province is Jakarta. Estimates were weighted using individual sampling weights. Standard errors are robust to clustering at the community level and to heteroscedasticity. Absolute t-statistics are in parentheses with significance at 5% (*) and 1% (**) indicated.

APPENDIX TABLE 3C.2
Poverty Transitions for All Children, 1997 and 2000
Multinomial Logit Models: Risk Ratios Relative to being Poor in both 1997 and 2000

	Poor in 1997 Not poor in 2000	Not poor in 1997 Poor in 2000	No6 poor in 1997 Not poor in 2000
Age in 1997 (spline):			
0–17 months	1.001	0.974	1.001
	(0.05)	(1.02)	(0.07)
18–35 months	0.990	0.989	1.000
	(0.70)	(0.67)	(0.04)
36-59 months	0.990	1.008	1.000
	(1.31)	(0.86)	(0.07)
5–14 years	1.005 **	1.003	1.008 **
	(3.75)	(1.75)	(7.11)
Female	1.233 *	1.198	1.130
	(2.15)	(1.84)	(1.48)
Mother's education if in household:			
1–5 years	0.711	1.037	1.068
	(1.61)	(0.16)	(0.38)
6–8 years	0.701	0.926	1.810 **
	(1.49)	(0.34)	(3.12)
9–11 years	1.502	1.756	4.685 **
	(1.05)	(1.54)	(5.15)
12+ years	2.413	1.595	11.510 **
	(1.57)	(0.82)	(4.85)
Father's education if in household:			
1–5 years	1.259	1.207	1.400
	(0.93)	(0.58)	(1.63)
6–8 years	1.496	2.093 *	2.193 **
	(1.45)	(2.47)	(3.39)
9–11 years	2.785 **	3.573 **	4.237 **
	(2.83)	(3.15)	(4.34)
12+ years	1.981	2.741 *	6.204 **
	(1.54)	(2.21)	(5.25)
Rural in 1997	1.482 *	1.453	1.331
	(2.51)	(1.88)	(1.48)

continued on next page

APPENDIX TABLE 3C.2 – cont'd

	Poor in 1997 Not poor in 2000	Not poor in 1997 Poor in 2000	No6 poor in 1997 Not poor in 2000
North Sumatra in 1997	2.099	2.282	0.667
	(1.29)	(1.32)	(0.72)
West Sumatra in 1997	1.982	3.266	1.988
	(1.22)	(1.61)	(0.75)
South Sumatra in 1997	1.381	0.684	0.295 *
	(0.59)	(0.66)	(2.48)
Lampung in 1997	1.814	1.140	0.526
	(1.03)	(0.21)	(1.20)
West Java in 1997	1.555	2.601	0.714
	(0.89)	(1.80)	(0.79)
Central Java in 1997	1.543	1.514	0.730
	(0.85)	(0.78)	(0.76)
Yogyakarta in 1997	2.424	3.078	0.773
	(1.48)	(1.85)	(0.50)
East Java in 1997	1.522	1.032	0.400 *
	(0.83)	(0.06)	(2.25)
Bali in 1997	2.039	1.690	0.565
	(1.06)	(0.64)	(0.93)
West Nusa Tenggara in 1997	0.578	2.120	0.365 *
	(1.03)	(1.30)	(2.32)
South Kalimantan in 1997	2.066	1.336	1.059
	(1.37)	(0.40)	(0.10)
South Sulawesi in 1997	1.327	0.918	0.239 **
	(0.53)	(0.14)	(2.79)
F-test (p-values):			
Education variables	0.0000		
X^2	642.74		
Log (Likelihood)	0.0000		
Pseudo R-squared	0.09		
Number of observations	9,937		

Source: IFLS2 and IFLS3.
Dummy variables for missing parental education are included in the regressions but not reported in the table. The omitted category for education is no schooling, and for province is Jakarta. Estimates were weighted using individual sampling weights. Standard errors are robust to clustering at the community level and to heteroscedasticity. Absolute t-statistics are in parentheses with significance at 5% (*) and 1% (**) indicated.

4

Individual Subjective Standards of Living and the Crisis

Analysis of welfare status is dominated by the use of objective measures of well-being, particularly so among economists. There are good reasons for this. However other social scientists are more willing to use subjective measures and there is a very small amount of such use among economists (see for example, Kapteyn et al. 1988, for a survey). Recently there has been renewed interest by economists in subjective measures (Lokshin and Ravallion 2000, for instance, examine subjective welfare in the context of the Russian economic crisis).

This chapter looks at how individuals subjectively evaluate their welfare status. It is composed of two parts. In the first part, we examine adults' perception toward their welfare status or standard of living in 1997 and 2000. This is obtained in IFLS3 from asking respondents to assess their current welfare status and their welfare status in 1997. The retrospective year was chosen to be just before the financial crisis. IFLS3 followed the Russia Longitudinal Monitoring Survey (RLMS) in asking respondents to imagine a ladder with six rungs, on which the poorest people were on the first rung and the richest on the sixth, and to place themselves on this ladder. Six rungs were used because during pre-testing it was found that when using nine, as in the Russia LSS survey, the bottom and top rungs were rarely used, and when only five rungs were used, a very large fraction, choose rung 3, the middle rung. The second part of the IFLS3 subjective questions included adults' assessment of specific aspects of the quality of life for themselves and their children, in 2000. Here respondents were asked to report the quality of life relative to their needs for specific aspects of living, using three responses: less than adequate, more than adequate or just adequate. The aspects of quality of life consist of general quality of life, food consumption, healthcare, and, for children only, education. Since this is a new module and the properties of these subjective questions are little known, we explore in a simple regression setting, how the answers to the ladder question compare with the correlates of poverty, as measured in Chapter 3, and *pce*.

In general, as shown in Table 4.1, most individuals' subjective standard of living did not change in 2000 compared to 1997. The cross-tabulation

TABLE 4.1
Distribution of Individual's Perception of Standard of Living, 1997 and 2000

	Standard of living just before economic crisis occurred (1997)						
Standard of living today (2000)	**1 (Poorest)**	**2**	**3**	**4**	**5**	**6 (Richest)**	**Total**
1 (Poorest)	3.7 (0.22)	0.8 (0.08)	0.3 (0.04)	0.0 (0.01)	0.0 (0.01)	0.0 (0.01)	4.8 (0.26)
2	1.2 (0.09)	15.6 (0.56)	3.2 (0.16)	0.3 (0.04)	0.0 (0.01)	0.0 (0.01)	20.3 (0.61)
3	0.4 (0.05)	6.4 (0.29)	42.9 (0.64)	6.5 (0.27)	0.4 (0.04)	0.0 (0.01)	56.5 (0.57)
4	0.0 (0.01)	0.4 (0.05)	3.5 (0.17)	11.5 (0.43)	1.4 (0.10)	0.0 (0.01)	17.0 (0.51)
5	0.0 (0.01)	0.0 (0.01)	0.1 (0.02)	0.4 (0.05)	0.5 (0.05)	0.0 (0.01)	1.0 (0.08)
6 (Richest)	0.0 (0.01)	0.0 (0.01)	0.0 (0.01)	0.0 (0.02)	0.1 (0.02)	0.2 (0.03)	0.3 (0.05)
Total	5.2 (0.26)	23.3 (0.58)	50.0 (0.57)	18.8 (0.54)	2.4 (0.14)	0.3 (0.04)	100.0 –

Source: IFLS3.
Number of observations = 25,215. Respondents are asked to imagine six steps of standard of living, from the poorest (1) to the richest (6), and on which step they perceive themselves within those standards. Estimates were weighted using individual sampling weights. Standard errors (in parentheses) are robust to clustering at the community level.

in Table 4.1 shows the respondents have a strong tendency to place themselves on the same rung each year. In addition, it is clear that there is an enormous amount of heaping at the third rung, in the middle of the distribution. This represents a disadvantage in using such a measure because it will have only limited discriminatory powers. To the extent that off-diagonal elements of the matrix are present, it is the case that the movement is towards the middle of the distribution; a regression to the mean that we also saw in Table 3.7 for poverty transitions, when poverty was classified by *pce*. So, for example, those who are Rung 2 in 1997 are more likely to place themselves on Rung 3 in 2000 than on Rung 1. Those on Rung 4 in 1997 are much more likely to be on Rung 3 in 2000 than on Rung 5. Those on Rung 3 in 1997 have roughly equal probabilities of being on Rung 2 or Rung 4 in 2000.

Similarly, Table 4.2, which is derived from Table 4.1, shows that roughly 75% of adults report no change in their standard of living. For those who do report a change, worsening and improving standards are equally probable. This is the case for rural and urban residents and by gender. Hence these subjective welfare results are similar to the *pce* and poverty results in showing not much change in welfare between 1997 and 2000, with what movement that was taking place being a regression to the mean.

TABLE 4.2
Individual's Perception of Standard of Living, 1997 and 2000

	Total	Urban	Rural	Male	Female
Worsening	13.1	14.7	11.7	14.3	11.9
	(0.40)	(0.59)	(0.54)	(0.48)	(0.44)
No change	74.4	73.0	75.6	73.2	75.5
	(0.64)	(0.84)	(0.94)	(0.71)	(0.69)
Improving	12.5	12.3	12.7	12.5	12.6
	(0.47)	(0.57)	(0.72)	(0.54)	(0.51)
Number of observations	25,215	12,524	12,691	11,960	13,255

Source: IFLS3.
Estimates are derived from Table 4.1. Estimates were weighted using individual sampling weights. Standard errors (in parentheses) are robust to clustering at the community level.

TABLE 4.3
Individual's Perception of Quality of Life, 2000

	Total			Urban			Rural		
	Less than adequate	Adequate	More than adequate	Less Than adequate	Adequate	More than adequate	Less than adequate	Adequate	More than adequate
All individuals									
General standard of living	16.1	69.4	14.5	13.4	70.9	15.7	18.4	68.2	13.4
	(0.50)	(0.67)	(0.65)	(0.53)	(0.81)	(0.83)	(0.79)	(1.03)	(0.97)
Food consumption	9.3	74.1	16.6	6.5	75.4	18.1	11.7	73.0	15.3
	(0.42)	(0.71)	(0.72)	(0.38)	(0.89)	(0.94)	(0.66)	(1.05)	(1.06)
Healthcare	11.0	85.0	4.0	8.3	87.3	4.3	13.3	82.9	3.8
	(0.47)	(0.51)	(0.24)	(0.40)	(0.46)	(0.33)	(0.76)	(0.81)	(0.33)
Number of observations		25,208			12,522			12,686	
Individuals with children residing in household									
Children's standard of living	12.8	74.1	13.1	9.9	74.7	15.4	14.9	73.6	11.5
	(0.58)	(0.76)	(0.69)	(0.57)	(0.98)	(0.98)	(0.87)	(1.08)	(0.92)
Children's food consumption	8.4	76.9	14.7	5.8	77.3	17.0	10.3	76.6	13.1
	(0.51)	(0.74)	(0.72)	(0.43)	(1.05)	(1.03)	(0.78)	(1.02)	(0.96)
Children's healthcare	6.3	89.6	4.1	4.0	91.2	4.8	8.0	88.5	3.6
	(0.48)	(0.54)	(0.31)	(0.39)	(0.58)	(0.45)	(0.75)	(0.81)	(0.41)
Number of observations		11,225			5,086			6,139	
Children's education	12.0	76.9	11.1	8.6	78.3	13.1	14.5	75.9	9.7
	(0.58)	(0.73)	(0.61)	(0.60)	(0.93)	(0.86)	(0.85)	(1.03)	(0.82)
Number of observations		9,483			4,330			5,153	

Source: IFLS3.

Respondents are asked about their life conditions, food consumption, healthcare as well as their children's. Estimates were weighted using individual sampling weights. Standard errors (in parentheses) are robust to clustering at the community level.

On adults' perception of specific dimensions of their quality of life, Table 4.3 indicates that 70% or more report adequate standards of living. People are even more satisfied with their level of food consumption and healthcare. This tendency can also be observed if rural and urban are separated. The same tendency can be applied when individuals with children report for their children's standard of living, food consumption, healthcare and education. Table 4.3 also shows that adults who do not report "just adequate" satisfaction with their quality of life, are evenly divided between reporting less-than-adequate quality of life compared to more-than-adequate levels.

We have not yet addressed the central question of how useful these subjective measures are. A full exploration of this question with the IFLS data is left for future research, but to get a glimpse, we regress the subjective score, first on the same covariates that were used to predict the poverty status of adults, and then including a spline in log of *pce* (Table 4.4). The results are somewhat encouraging. The effects of covariates are consistent with the results for *pce*.

Own education is a very strong predictor of higher subjective status. *PCE* is also significantly related to higher subjective status, especially so among those with *pce* below Rp 150,000. Because these questions were asked of individual adults, one can ask whether different types of people tend to answer differently. Some very interesting results emerge. Women are likely to put themselves nearly one rung higher compared to men. Young adults (15–19 years) tend to put themselves on lower rungs, although after adolescence, age has a positive effect on subjective well-being until one gets to the elderly, for whom age has a negative impact. Being in a rural area is associated with being on a lower rung, but when *pce* is controlled for, rural–urban area differences decline. Finally, people living in Central and East Java and in South Kalimantan assess their welfare to be higher than those living in Jakarta. Those in North Sumatra and West Nusa Tenggara assess their condition to be worse, although those differences shrink once *pce* is controlled.

SUMMARY

We supplement our quantification of poverty and *pce* with data on subjective evaluations of welfare. This analysis provides a consistent picture to that of *pce* in that the two measures are positively correlated. In addition, people who were low in their self-ranking in 1997 were more likely to say their ranking improved in 2000 than to say it worsened. Conversely for those who said they were better off in 1997, it is much more likely that their self-assessed situation worsened in 2000 than improved. However, the subjective measures are not able to discriminate very well, in that a very high fraction of people put themselves in the middle of the distribution and for changes, there is a lot of inertia at that point.

TABLE 4.4
Linear Regression Models of Subjective Well-being

		Without log PCE	With log PCE
Age (spline, × 10^{-3}):	15–19 years	–3.505 **	–2.899 **
		(6.55)	(5.70)
	20–29 years	0.510 **	0.340 **
		(5.15)	(3.53)
	30–59 years	0.657 **	0.418 *
		(3.35)	(2.16)
	60+ years	–0.222 *	–0.242 *
		(2.16)	(2.43)
Female (× 10^{-1})		0.922 **	0.781 **
		(9.03)	(7.42)
Education:	1–5 years	0.170 **	0.147 **
		(6.87)	(6.16)
	6–8 years	0.315 **	0.257 **
		(11.67)	(9.76)
	9–11 years	0.464 **	0.363 **
		(14.96)	(12.13)
	12+ years	0.664 **	0.485 **
		(20.36)	(15.75)
log *pce* (spline):	0- log Rp 150,000		0.323 **
			(9.96)
	> log Rp 150,000		0.198 **
			(16.25)
Rural (× 10^{-1})		–0.500 *	–0.321
		(2.36)	(1.63)
North Sumatra		–0.168 **	–0.122 *
		(2.95)	(2.36)
West Sumatra		–0.105	–0.083
		(1.79)	(1.59)
South Sumatra		–0.046	0.001
		(0.99)	(0.02)

continued on next page

TABLE 4.4 – cont'd

	Without log PCE	With log PCE
Lampung	–0.043	0.016
	(0.99)	(0.42)
West Java	–0.004	0.038
	(0.11)	(1.28)
Central Java	0.103 **	0.151 **
	(2.91)	(4.82)
Yogyakarta	–0.032	0.016
	(0.72)	(0.40)
East Java	0.082 *	0.140 **
	(2.57)	(4.93)
Bali	0.015	0.053
	(0.29)	(1.32)
West Nusa Tenggara	–0.149 **	–0.071
	(3.42)	(1.67)
South Kalimantan	0.171 **	0.203 **
	(4.02)	(5.65)
South Sulawesi	–0.039	0.033
	(0.98)	(0.86)
Constant	3.241 **	–0.754
	(26.62)	(1.87)
F-test (p-values):		
Education variables	0.0000	0.0000
Expenditure variables	–	0.0000
Number of observations	25,215	25,215
R-squared	0.08	0.11

Source: IFLS3.

The dependent variable is ordinal scaled from 1 to 6 with 1 being poorest and 6 being richest as displayed in Table 4.1 and defined in the text. Dummy variables for missing education and for missing per capita expenditures are included in the regressions but not reported in the table. The omitted category for education is no schooling, and for province is Jakarta. Estimates were weighted using individual sampling weights. Standard errors are robust to clustering at the community level and to heteroscedasticity. Absolute t-statistics are in parentheses with significance at 5% (*) and 1% (**) indicated.

5

Employment and Wages

In this chapter, we review a range of dimensions of employment for the adult population (15–75 years) including levels of employment, hours spent working, transitions in employment status, the distribution of workers between formal and informal sectors of the economy and the level and distribution of wages. Correlates of employment, transitions, and wage changes are also examined. Finally, this chapter concludes by presenting information on child labour.

EMPLOYMENT

Several studies have explored changes in employment patterns in Indonesia associated with the financial crisis in 1998 (see for example, Frankenberg et al. 1999, Smith et al. 2002, and Thomas et al. 2000) drawing on data from the IFLS (1997 and 1998) as well as the annual Indonesian labour force survey, SAKERNAS. These studies highlight various mechanisms that would lead to changes in the labour market due to the crisis, and, therefore, changes in employment characteristics. As interest rates rose and the rupiah collapsed, many employers laid off workers or went out of business. Meanwhile, if nominal incomes were not increasing as fast as prices, then real incomes would decline. At the same time, relative prices for non-tradeables — many of which are services — declined as the exchange rate depreciated. Employment and earnings in these non-tradeable sectors have likely fallen as well. To the extent that displaced workers from construction, manufacturing, and service industries could not afford to remain completely unemployed for an extended period of time, they may have taken up less formal jobs. In rural areas, the *El Nino* condition of 1997 and early 1998 and the associated drought and fires depressed rice production in 1997 by about 4% and by more in 1998 (Fox 2002). These dynamics suggest both that employment patterns in rural areas will differ between 1997 and 1998, independently of the crisis. What is unclear is whether changes in the characteristics of employment observed from 1997 to 1998 were temporary or reflect more permanent adjustments. As an extension of the previous work focusing on 1997 to 1998, this section explores labour market patterns over the medium-term, from 1997 to 2000.

Table 5.1 presents some basic employment characteristics by gender, for any work (either wage-employed, self-employed or employed unpaid family labour) and work with pay (wage-employed or self-employed) for the two cross-sections of IFLS data. Results for men are presented in the upper panel of Table 5.1. Most employed men are working for pay; only a small fraction of men did not receive pay in either year (about 5% of all men). For both categories of employment, the proportion of men working has increased significantly across years, including the proportion of men working as unpaid family labour. These aggregates mask considerably changes in employment rates for men by age. The proportion of men 15–24 years old working has risen significantly by 12% from 49% to 61%. Most, but not all, of this increase is from working for pay which rose by 7%. The oldest men (65–75) had the next largest increase in employment rates, from 63% to 67%, although this increase is not statistically significant. Men in the middle age categories had much smaller changes or no change in employment rates.

The second part of Table 5.1 presents comparable estimates for women. Employment rates for women were considerably lower than that for men in both 1997 and 2000. But the gap has shrunk because the increase in the proportion of women working from 1997 to 2000 grew by more than that of men. Employment rates rose from about 45% to 57%. This increase is partially, but not completely, a result of more women working for pay where employment rates rose from 37% to 42%. Thus, the increase in employment as unpaid family labour contributed to the overall increase in employment rates among women. While the increase in (paid and unpaid) employment rates is distributed across the entire age range of women — and is significant for all age groups — the increases are largest for women ages 35–54.

Parallel with the increase in employment rates, there has been a significant increase in the incidence of multiple job-holding between 1997 and 2000. Among men, the proportion of respondents with an additional (secondary) job has risen from 14% to 24%; for women, the increase is from 5% to 10%.

Another dimension of work that may have changed since 1997 is the number of hours worked. In the IFLS, we find no change in the number of

TABLE 5.1
Employment Characteristics, Adults 15–75

	Paid or Unpaid			Paid		
	1997	**2000**	**Change**	**1997**	**2000**	**Change**
MEN						
Employment rate: Overall	79.4	83.6	4.2 **	74.5	77.0	2.5 **
	(0.65)	(0.52)	(0.55)	(0.65)	(0.53)	(0.57)
Employment rate: Ages 15–24	48.7	61.3	11.6 **	39.4	46.3	7.0 **
	(1.57)	(1.25)	(1.51)	(1.46)	(1.26)	(1.37)
Employment rate: Ages 25–34	92.6	94.6	2.0 **	87.1	89.7	2.6 **
	(0.60)	(0.47)	(0.66)	(0.95)	(0.70)	(0.98)
Employment rate: Ages 35–44	97.4	96.7	–0.8	96.2	94.8	–1.4
	(0.43)	(0.41)	(0.56)	(0.51)	(0.52)	(0.71)
Employment rate: Ages 45–54	95.6	96.8	1.1	94.4	94.5	0.1
	(0.67)	(0.49)	(0.79)	(0.75)	(0.65)	(0.90)
Employment rate: Ages 55–64	79.9	83.1	3.2	77.6	79.5	1.8
	(1.56)	(1.57)	(1.60)	(1.53)	(1.62)	(1.66)
Employment rate: Ages 65–75	62.8	67.4	4.6	60.4	62.8	2.5
	(2.57)	(1.94)	(2.70)	(2.46)	(1.96)	(2.69)
Percent with an additional job	14.1	23.8	9.7 **	–	–	–
	(0.67)	(0.83)	(0.79)	–	–	–
Hours last week: main job if any	39.1	38.9	–0.3	–	–	–
	(0.50)	(0.42)	(0.45)	–	–	–
Hours last week: secondary jobs if any	19.0	15.8	–3.2 **	–	–	–
	(0.61)	(0.44)	(0.75)	–	–	–
Hours last week: all jobs if any	42.5	43.4	0.8	–	–	–
	(0.47)	(0.39)	(0.61)	–	–	–
Number of observations	9,819	12,457		9,819	12,457	

WOMEN						
Employment rate: Overall	45.4	56.6	11.1 **	36.7	42.2	5.5 **
	(1.12)	(0.88)	(0.99)	0.93	0.77	0.76
Employment rate: Ages 15–24	31.0	39.0	8.0 **	24.4	26.5	2.2
	(1.37)	(1.14)	(1.41)	(1.26)	(1.02)	(1.22)
Employment rate: Ages 25–34	48.0	58.6	10.6 **	40.6	45.0	4.4 *
	(1.54)	(1.16)	(1.53)	(1.44)	(1.11)	(1.32)
Employment rate: Ages 35–44	59.8	72.2	12.5 **	48.2	56.9	8.7 **
	(1.70)	(1.20)	(1.65)	(1.60)	(1.28)	(1.48)
Employment rate: Ages 45–54	55.4	71.5	16.1 **	43.6	53.7	10.1 **
	(1.99)	(1.71)	(2.06)	(1.80)	(1.69)	(1.83)
Employment rate: Ages 55–64	47.2	58.6	11.4 **	37.1	41.6	4.5
	(2.02)	(2.00)	(2.04)	(1.69)	(1.81)	(1.91)
Employment rate: Ages 65–75	28.8	39.3	10.5 **	22.7	27.4	4.7
	(2.16)	(2.26)	(2.41)	(1.97)	(1.92)	(2.32)
Percent with an additional job	4.5	9.5	5.0 **	–	–	–
	(0.34)	(0.50)	(0.50)	–	–	–
Hours last week: main job if any	35.3	35.2	–0.2	–	–	–
	(0.71)	(0.57)	(0.62)	–	–	–
Hours last week: secondary job if any	15.4	14.3	–1.16	–	–	–
	(1.01)	(0.56)	(1.15)	–	–	–
Hours last week: all jobs if any	36.8	37.6	0.7	–	–	–
	(0.71)	(0.56)	(0.91)	–	–	–
Number of observations	11,033	13,523		11,033	13,523	

Source: IFLS2 and IFLS3.
Estimates were weighted using individual sampling weights. Standard errors (in parentheses) are robust to clustering at the community level. Significance at 5% (*) and 1% (**) indicated.

hours worked last week on the main job or in total. The number of hours for the main job remained steady at 39 hours for men and 35 hours for women. Hours in secondary jobs were lower for men, declining from 19 hours per week on average to about 16.

Turning to the sector of employment (Table 5.2), we explore the changes by gender in the distribution of workers across the four main sectors (private employee, government employee, self-employed, and unpaid family labour). The distribution of working men across sectors has changed little. Private employment and self-employment are the dominant categories, each representing about 42–43% of working men in both years. There has been a small decline in the share of self-employment with a shift to the category of unpaid family labour which rose from 6% of working men in 1997 to 8% in 2000. Among women, on the other hand, we find a larger increase in the proportion who are reported as unpaid family labour which comes from a significant decline in shares among the other three categories. In 1997, 19% of working women classified themselves as unpaid family labour; by 2000, nearly 26% of working women were in this category.

TABLE 5.2
Distribution of Employment by Sector, Adults 15–75
(in percent)

	Men			Women		
	1997	**2000**	**Change**	**1997**	**2000**	**Change**
Employee, Private	42.8	43.0	0.3	34.5	32.2	–2.4
	(1.37)	(1.17)	(0.79)	(1.56)	(1.32)	(0.88)
Employee, Government	8.3	7.4	–0.9	6.0	5.1	–0.9
	(0.52)	(0.43)	(0.32)	(0.49)	(0.37)	(0.32)
Self-employed	42.7	41.6	–1.1	40.2	37.3	–2.9 *
	(1.18)	(0.98)	(0.77)	(1.11)	(0.91)	(0.97)
Unpaid Family Labour	6.1	7.9	1.8 *	19.2	25.5	6.2 **
	(0.62)	(0.52)	(0.52)	(1.40)	(1.29)	(1.00)
Number of observations	7,603	10,284		5,084	7,454	

Source: IFLS2 and IFLS3.

Estimates were weighted using individual sampling weights. Standard errors (in parentheses) are robust to clustering at the community level. Significance at 5% (*) and 1% (**) indicated.

Table 5.3 presents multivariate correlates of whether a respondent was working for pay in 1997 and 2000. For men and women, we estimate linear probability models of working for pay as a function of education, age and residence at the time of the survey.[1] For men, nine or more years of education is associated with lower probability of working for pay in 1997 and 2000. For women, nine to eleven years of education is associated with a lower probability of working for pay, while 12 or more years in school is positively associated with working for pay in both years. The first eight years of education have an insignificant relationship for both genders across both years. As men and women age, they are increasingly likely to work for pay, but only until age 55 when we see a negative impact of age on the likelihood of working for pay. By 2000, for men 25–55, the age-work relationship is flatter, whereas the association between work and aging for women 25–55 gets stronger. In any case, work is most responsive to aging in the youngest bracket (under 25 years old).

Rural residence is not associated with working for pay for men. However, women who reside in rural areas are less likely to be working for pay in 1997 and 2000 than their urban counterparts. Turning to province of residence, our excluded category is Jakarta. In 1997, men in East, West and Central Java were more likely to be working for pay than their counterparts in Jakarta. By 2000, this difference is gone. The same pattern is observed among men in Bali, West Nusa Tenggara and South Kalimantan. Among women, those residing in Lampung and South Sulawesi were less likely to be working for pay in both years than their counterparts in Jakarta. Whereas women in Yogyakarta were more like to be working in both years. For some provinces, we do see differences across regions and years. In Central Java and Bali women were more likely to be working for pay in 1997 than women in Jakarta but this difference is significantly lower by 2000.

Table 5.4 exploits the panel dimensions of the IFLS and focuses on transitions into and out of employment by age group and gender. The sample is restricted to individuals interviewed in both years and for their main job in each year. Our measure of transition is based on employment status at the time of the survey. This does not measure being employed in the same job, but rather being employed in some capacity at the time of both interviews. Moreover, this table does not measure turnover between jobs or from/to employment overall in the three years.

The youngest group of men have the highest rates of transitions in work status. Nearly one-fifth of men 22–24 in 1997 moved from unemployed in 1997 to employed by 2000. The oldest group of men (55–64) had the next highest rate of transition. Eight percent of these men became employed

TABLE 5.3
Working for Pay (Employee or Self-employed), Adults 15–75, Linear Probability Models

	Men		Women	
	1997	Change in 2000	1997	Change in 2000
Age (spline) <25	0.086**	–0.0002	0.030 **	0.003
	(40.63)	(0.06)	(12.31)	(0.98)
25–55	0.006**	–0.002 *	0.003 **	0.001
	(9.34)	(2.34)	(4.39)	(1.73)
>55	–0.007**	0.0002	–0.004 **	–0.001
	(12.01)	(0.29)	(6.61)	(0.88)
Education : 1–5 years	0.009	0.018	0.025	–0.033
	(0.56)	(0.84)	(1.25)	(1.24)
6–8 years	0.007	0.005	–0.012	–0.028
	(0.45)	(0.23)	(0.54)	(0.90)
9–11 years	–0.071**	0.039	–0.050 *	–0.027
	(3.76)	(1.54)	(2.07)	(0.81)
12+ years	–0.067**	0.006	0.100 **	–0.053
	(3.97)	(0.27)	(4.11)	(1.63)
Rural	–0.003	0.010	–0.064 **	0.014
	(0.29)	(0.63)	(4.00)	(0.68)
North Sumatra	–0.008	–0.017	–0.056	0.009
	(0.32)	(0.54)	(1.58)	(0.18)
West Sumatra	0.018	–0.013	0.054	–0.059
	(0.72)	(0.39)	(1.60)	(1.28)
South Sumatra	0.001	–0.032	–0.065	–0.056
	(0.03)	(0.85)	(1.77)	(1.14)
Lampung	–0.003	–0.0003	–0.108 **	–0.019
	(0.12)	(0.01)	(2.70)	(0.36)
West Java	0.049*	–0.059 *	–0.017	–0.045
	(2.43)	(2.26)	(0.60)	(1.26)
Central Java	0.056*	–0.054	0.139 **	–0.90 *
	(2.42)	(1.82)	(4.55)	(2.19)
Yogyakarta	0.037	–0.062	0.156 **	–0.086
	(1.39)	(1.83)	(3.80)	(1.65)
East Java	0.047*	–0.046	0.025	–0.026
	(2.20)	(1.63)	(0.83)	(0.68)
Bali	0.078**	–0.059	0.147 **	–0.108 *
	(3.26)	(1.87)	(3.56)	(2.10)
West Nusa Tenggara	0.067**	–0.059	0.030	–0.068
	(2.69)	(1.72)	(0.72)	(1.22)
South Kalimantan	0.084**	–0.063	0.006	–0.086
	(2.93)	(1.68)	(0.12)	(1.49)
South Sulawesi	–0.031	–0.031	–0.094 *	–0.059
	(1.12)	(0.88)	(2.42)	(1.16)
Constant	–1.258**	0.076	–0.333 **	–0.114
	(24.03)	(1.08)	(5.57)	(1.21)

continued on next page

TABLE 5.3 – cont'd

	Men		Women	
	1997	Change in 2000	1997	Change in 2000
F-test (p–values):				
Interaction variables	0.0001		0.0019	
Education variables	0.0000		0.0000	
Number of observations	22,276		24,556	
R-squared	0.33		0.09	

Source: IFLS2 and IFLS3.
Dummy variable for missing education is included in the regressions but not reported in the table. The omitted category for education is no schooling, and for province is Jakarta. Estimates were weighted using individual sampling weights. Standard errors are robust to clustering at the community level and to heteroscedasticity. Absolute t-statistics are in parentheses with significance at 5% (*) and 1% (**) indicated.

TABLE 5.4
Transitions in Work (Employee/Self-employed/ Unpaid Family Labour) by Gender and Age (in percent)

	Work both years	No work in either year	Get Job	Lose Job
Men (N= 6,336)				
Age 22–24 in 1997	74.6	4.1	18.9	2.4
	(2.14)	(0.81)	(2.00)	(0.66)
Age 25–34 in 1997	90.4	1.8	5.1	2.7
	(0.74)	(0.33)	(0.51)	(0.41)
Age 35–44 in 1997	95.8	0.1	1.7	1.8
	(0.56)	(0.22)	(0.40)	(0.34)
Age 45–54 in 1997	94.1	1.15	2.6	2.1
	(0.74)	(0.32)	(0.53)	(0.42)
Age 55–64 in 1997	73.1	10.2	8.1	8.7
	(1.92)	(1.2)	(1.0)	(1.0)
Women (N= 7,415)				
Age 22–24 in 1997	30.5	30.1	26.3	13.1
	(2.21)	(2.17)	(2.21)	(1.54)
Age 25–34 in 1997	41.1	27.5	23.9	7.5
	(1.58)	(1.40)	(1.23)	(0.67)
Age 35–44 in 1997	53.2	18.7	20.1	7.1
	(1.70)	(1.28)	(1.42)	(0.65)
Age 45–54 in 1997	48.0	22.5	21.6	7.9
	(2.05)	(1.68)	(1.55)	(0.83)
Age 55–64 in 1997	40.0	35.1	15.6	9.4
	(2.08)	(2.03)	(1.30)	(0.95)

Source: IFLS2 and IFLS3.
Sample are panel respondents. Estimates were weighted using individual sampling weights. Standard errors (in parentheses) are robust to clustering at the community level.

and 9% became unemployed from 1997 to 2000. Men 55–64 had the highest rate of unemployment in both years (10%). Among women, we observe much larger rates of transition, from unemployed to employed (reflected in Table 5.1 also among the cross-section samples). More than one-fifth of women under 55 years secured a job from 1997 to 2000. The oldest group of women (55–64) had the lowest rate of transition into working (16%). For all age categories, rates of losing a job for women were considerably lower (around 10%) than rates of getting a job. The oldest women had the highest rates of unemployment in both years (35%), followed by the women under 35 where about 28% were not employed in both years.

Table 5.5 extends Table 5.4 by breaking employment into four sectors. Among men, we observe the largest transitions between self-employment and private employment (non-government). About one tenth of privately employed men in 1997 are self-employed in 2000. This decline is partially

TABLE 5.5
Transitions in Work by Sector and Gender, Adults 15–75
(In percent)

1997:	Not Working	Self-employed	Government	Private Market	Unpaid Family Worker	Total
Men (N=6,336)						
2000:						
Not Working	2.7	1.2	0.2	1.5	0.1	5.9
Self-employed	2.2	32.9	0.7	10.1	1.8	47.7
Government	0.2	0.4	6.9	0.7	0.0	8.2
Private Sector	2.2	6.1	1.1	24.9	0.7	35.0
Unpaid Family Worker	0.6	1.2	0.1	0.8	0.7	3.3
Total	7.9	41.8	9.0	38.0	3.3	100.0
Women (N=7,415)						
2000:						
Not Working	25.5	3.3	0.2	2.9	1.9	33.7
Self-employed	8.5	15.2	0.1	2.2	2.3	28.4
Government	0.1	0.1	3.0	0.4	0.0	3.7
Private Market	5.7	1.3	0.3	9.2	0.5	17.0
Unpaid Family Worker	7.5	3.1	0.0	1.2	5.4	17.2
Total	47.4	23.0	3.7	15.9	10.0	100.0

Source: IFLS2 and IFLS3.
Sample are panel respondents. Estimates were weighted using individual sampling weights. Standard errors (in parentheses) are robust to clustering at the community level.

made up in movements to private employment from self-employment, but not fully. By 2000, private employment as a share of working men is 3% lower (falling from 38% to 35%). Self-employment represents a higher share of working men in 2000 compared to 1997 (48% and 42% respectively).

Among women, we observe the most transition from not working to working (self-employment, unpaid family labour or private employment). In 1997, 47% of women were not employed. Almost half of these women were working by 2000. We see this increase manifest itself in an increase in women reporting being self-employed (up from 23% in 1997 to 28% in 2000) and working as unpaid family labour (10% in 1997 to 17% in 2000). The increase in private employment from 1997 to 2000 is much smaller (16% to 17% respectively).

Using the panel of respondents, we can study the correlates of those that make employment transitions from 1997 to 2000. Tables 5.6 and 5.7 present multivariate correlates of the risk of moving from not working in both years to getting a job, losing a job and working in both years, for men

TABLE 5.6
Transitions in Work, Men 15–75
Multinomial Logit Models: Risk Ratios Relative to Not Working in Either Year

		Not Working in 1997 Working in 2000	Working in 1997 Not Working in 2000	Working in Both Years
Both Years				
Age in 1997 (spline):	<25	1.421	2.048	2.857**
		(1.22)	(1.83)	(4.27)
	25–55	0.939**	1.012	1.004
		(2.70)	(0.56)	(0.20)
	>55	0.929**	0.962**	0.896**
		(9.59)	(4.91)	(17.14)
Education in 1997:	1–5 years	0.729	0.734	0.657
		(1.03)	(0.94)	(1.59)
	6–8 years	0.677	0.634	0.634
		(1.16)	(1.40)	(1.71)
	9–11 years	0.713	0.579	0.479*
		(0.90)	(1.23)	(2.17)
	12+ years	0.509	0.486	0.401**
		(1.91)	(1.90)	(3.08)

continued on next page

TABLE 5.6 – cont'd

	Not Working in 1997 Working in 2000	Working in 1997 Not Working in 2000	Working in Both Years
Rural in 1997	2.116**	2.084**	3.140**
	(3.46)	(3.60)	(6.69)
North Sumatra in 1997	1.067	1.298	1.612
	(0.14)	(0.52)	(1.05)
West Sumatra in 1997	0.432*	1.251	0.715
	(2.09)	(0.63)	(0.93)
South Sumatra in 1997	0.891	0.731	1.501
	(0.24)	(0.65)	(1.12)
Lampung in 1997	1.152	0.668	1.604
	(0.27)	(0.60)	(1.36)
West Java in 1997	0.739	0.908	1.182
	(1.07)	(0.33)	(0.67)
Central Java in 1997	0.641	1.183	2.875**
	(1.11)	(0.50)	(3.60)
Yogyakarta in 1997	1.11	0.698	3.195**
	(0.27)	(0.87)	(4.23)
East Java in 1997	1.400	1.340	2.816**
	(1.03)	(0.85)	(3.42)
Bali in 1997	0.372*	1.137	1.026
	(2.34)	(0.35)	(0.08)
West Nusa Tenggara in 1997	0.490	1.322	1.909
	(1.47)	(0.65)	(1.50)
South Kalimantan in 1997	1.239	1.394	2.283
	(0.39)	(0.51)	(1.83)
South Sulawesi in 1997	1.319	0.696	1.104
	(0.69)	(0.67)	(0.27)
X^2	1051.08		
Log (Likelihood)	0.0000		
Pseudo R-squared	0.15		
F-test (p-values):			
Education variables	0.2923		
Number of observations	6,845		

Source: IFLS2 and IFLS3.

Workers include employees, self-employed, and unpaid family labour. Dummy variable for missing education is included in the regressions but not reported in the table. The omitted category for education is no schooling, and for province is Jakarta. Estimates were weighted using individual sampling weights. Standard errors are robust to clustering at the community level and to heteroscedasticity. Absolute t-statistics are in parentheses with significance at 5% (*) and 1% (**) indicated.

TABLE 5.7
Transitions in Work, Women 15–75
Multinomial Logit Models: Risk Ratios Relative to Not Working in Either Year

	Not Working in 1997 Working in 2000	Working in 1997 Not Working in 2000	Working in Both Years
Both Years			
Age in 1997 (spline):<25	1.137	0.970	1.363**
	(0.90)	(0.18)	(2.59)
25–55	0.992	1.000	1.022**
	(1.47)	(0.04)	(4.60)
>55	0.952**	0.976**	0.959**
	(12.63)	(5.20)	(13.18)
Education in 1997: 1–5 years	0.799	0.714*	1.019
	(1.60)	(2.32)	(0.18)
6–8 years	0.572**	0.553**	0.719**
	(3.56)	(3.62)	(2.52)
9–11 years	0.402**	0.677	0.549**
	(5.01)	(1.95)	(3.96)
12+ years	0.609**	0.882	1.364*
	(2.85)	(0.65)	(2.12)
Rural in 1997	2.033**	1.237	1.621**
	(6.05)	(1.55)	(4.11)
North Sumatra in 1997	1.659*	1.453	1.712
	(2.19)	(1.21)	(1.92)
West Sumatra in 1997	1.482	2.708**	1.456
	(1.70)	(3.55)	(1.80)
South Sumatra in 1997	1.313	1.079	1.173
	(0.93)	(0.22)	(0.57)
Lampung in 1997	1.878	1.645	1.850*
	(1.90)	(1.56)	(2.14)
West Java in 1997	0.970	1.086	0.683*
	(0.17)	(0.36)	(2.31)
Central Java in 1997	1.168	3.005**	3.153**
	(0.78)	(4.59)	(5.61)
Yogyakarta in 1997	2.140**	2.957**	5.965**
	(3.65)	(4.59)	(7.37)
East Java in 1997	1.503*	1.625*	1.532*
	(2.21)	(2.04)	(2.46)
Bali in 1997	0.889	4.614**	2.381**
	(0.33)	(5.93)	(4.70)
West Nusa Tenggara in 1997	0.874	2.665**	2.453**
	(0.57)	(3.11)	(4.47)
South Kalimantan in 1997	1.095	2.125**	2.066**
	(0.36)	(3.00)	(3.59)
South Sulawesi in 1997	0.697	0.623	0.343**
	(1.40)	(1.61)	(4.36)

continued on next page

TABLE 5.7 – cont'd

	Not Working in 1997 Working in 2000	Working in 1997 Not Working in 2000	Working in Both Years
X^2	861.62		
Log (Likelihood)	0.0000		
Pseudo R-squared	6.69		
F-test (p-values):			
Education variables	0.0000		
Number of observations	8,003		

Source: IFLS2 and IFLS3.
Workers include employees, self-employed, and unpaid family labour. Dummy variable for missing education is included in the regressions but not reported in the table The omitted category for education is no schooling, and for province is Jakarta. Estimates were weighted using individual sampling weights. Standard errors are robust to clustering at the community level and to heteroscedasticity. Absolute t-statistics are in parentheses with significance at 5% (*) and 1% (**) indicated.

and women respectively. Education, age, and residence are included as co-variates. Appendix Tables 5.1 and 5.2 present comparable results where work is restricted to work for pay (employee or self-employed, excluding unpaid family labour).

For men (Table 5.6), additional years of education from completed junior secondary onward are associated with a decreased chance of working in both years relative to working in neither. For young men, age is not associated with getting a job, but is associated with a higher risk of being employed in both years compared to employed in neither. Men over 55 are more likely to be working in neither year compared to getting a job, losing a job or being employed in both years. Men in rural areas have a much higher degree of churning in the labour market. Relative to remaining out of the workforce in both years, urban men are less likely to get a job, less likely to lose a job and less likely to be working in both years. That is, men in urban areas have a much higher chance of not working in either 1997 and 2000 than do men in rural areas. Turning to province indicators, respondents in West Sumatra and Bali have a lower chance of getting work relative to staying unemployed. For Central Java, Yogyakarta, and East Java, we observe significantly higher chance of being employed in both years relative to being unemployed in both, as compared to men in Jakarta.

Among women (Table 5.7), we find that higher schooling from completed primary onward is associated with a lower chance of gaining employment relative to not working in both years. This effect is largest for completed and post secondary schooling. Among the oldest group of women (over 55), aging is associated with lower chances of transitions or working in both years compared to not working in both years. For the younger age groups (15–55), aging is associated with increasing likelihood of being employed in both years. As opposed to our finding for urban men, urban women have a significantly higher chance of getting a job, losing work or working in both years than do women in rural areas. Women residing in North Sumatra, Yogyakarta and East Java have a higher chance of getting work relative to staying unemployed compared to women in Jakarta. For West Sumatra, Central Java, Yogyakarta, East Java, Bali, West Nusa Tenggara and South Kalimantan, we observe significantly higher chance of moving into unemployment versus being unemployed in both years, as compared to women in Jakarta. However, except for West Sumatra, these women are also more likely to be employed in both years than unemployed in both.

WAGES

Turning from employment rates, the IFLS data also includes information on wages for employees (in the public and private sectors) as well as earnings for the self-employed.[2] Hourly wage rates are computed on the basis of monthly earnings (net earnings in the case of self-employed) divided by hours (reported for the last week*4.33), for the main job. These wages are deflated to December 2000 so as to be in real terms. Statistics on median real wages are presented in Tables 5.8–5.10. Medians are used to reduce the influence of outliers. Overall, wage rates are higher for men than women in both years and, by gender, higher in urban areas. From 1997 to 2000, there has been a decline in real wage rates. The absolute decline in median wages was larger for men (Rp 69/hour) than women (Rp 56/hour). However, hourly earnings for women fell by a slightly larger percentage than the decline among men (5% decline for women and 4% decline for men) because men earn more. Workers in urban areas experienced larger declines than rural workers, among both men and women. Men in urban areas experienced a 7% decline whereas rural male workers had almost no change in real wages. Women in urban areas were earning almost 11% less in 2000 compared to a 3% decline for women in rural areas.

The decline in wages from 1997 to 2000 in Table 5.8 is smaller than the decline reported in Frankenberg et al. (1999) for 1997 to 1998. This suggests that wages have partially recovered from their drastic reduction

TABLE 5.8
Median Real Hourly Wages Among Self-employed and Employees, Adults 15–75

	1997	2000	Change	% Change
Men				
All	1,785	1,716	–69	–3.9
Number of observations	[5,870]	[7,991]		
Urban	2,108	1,957	–151	–7.2
Number of observations	[2,978]	[4,227]		
Rural	1,546	1,527	–19	–1.2
Number of observations	[2,892]	[3,764]		
Women				
All	1,093	1,037	–56	–5.1
Number of observations	[3,489]	[4,959]		
Urban	1,434	1,283	–151	–10.5
Number of observations	[1,914]	[2,788]		
Rural	895	865	–30	–3.4
Number of observations	[1,575]	[2,171]		

Source: IFLS2 and IFLS3.
Values are in real terms set to December 2000. Estimates were weighted using individual sampling weights.

TABLE 5.9
Median Real Hourly Wages by Type of Work, Adults 15–75

	1997	2000	Change	% Change
Employee, Private				
All	1,484	1,314	–173	–11.6
Number of observations	[4,307]	[6,237]		
Urban	1,668	1,492	–178	–10.7
Number of observations	[2,636]	[3,817]		
Rural	1,274	1,143	–132	–10.3
Number of observations	[1,671]	[2,420]		
Employee, Government				
All	4,005	4,339	334	8.3
Number of observations	[1,014]	[1,140]		
Urban	3,823	4,278	455	11.9
Number of observations	[669]	[754]		
Rural	4,230	4,621	391	9.2
Number of observations	[345]	[386]		
Self-employed				
All	1,280	1,411	131	10.2
Number of observations	[4,038]	[5,572]		
Urban	1,623	1,624	1	0.0
Number of observations	[1,587]	[2,444]		
Rural	1,150	1,286	136	11.8
Number of observations	[2,451]	[3,128]		

Source: IFLS2 and IFLS3.
Values are in real terms set to December 2000. Estimates were weighted using individual sampling weights.

TABLE 5.10
Median Real Hourly Wages by Education and Age

	1997	2000	Change	% Change
Less than completed primary				
Age 22–24	1,039	1,024	–15	–1.4
Age 25–34	1,179	1,030	–149	–12.6
Age 35–54	1,122	1,030	–92	–8.2
Age 55–75	812	859	47	5.8
Completed primary				
Age 22–24	1,150	1,149	–1	–0.0
Age 25–34	1,271	1,201	–70	–5.5
Age 35–54	1,468	1,370	–98	–6.7
Age 55–75	1,209	1,244	35	2.9
Some/Completed Secondary				
Age 22–24	1,694	1,453	–241	–14.2
Age 25–34	2,044	1,762	–282	–13.8
Age 35–54	2,951	2,661	–290	–9.8
Age 55–75	2,761	2,244	–517	–18.7
More than secondary				
Age 22–24	3,004	2,151	–853	–28.4
Age 25–34	3,888	3,450	–438	–11.3
Age 35–54	5,509	5,861	352	6.4
Age 55–75	7,972	6,423	–1549	–19.4

Source: IFLS2 and IFLS3.
Values are in real terms set to December 2000. Estimates were weighted using individual sampling weights.

immediately following the crisis. Moreover, while median wages have declined, recall that household real per capita expenditure changed very little at the median from 1997 to 2000. However, given the increase in employment rates (as well as higher prevalence of secondary jobs in 2000), in order to compare labour earnings with household expenditure, labour earnings should be computed at a household level which is not done here.

Table 5.9 demonstrates that the decline in wages has been concentrated among private-sector employees. This may reflect in part the large decline in private sector investment that took place during the financial crisis. In fact, real wages increased for both government employees and for the self-employed from 1997 to 2000. In both years, government workers were earning substantially more than private employees or self-employed workers (although note that these results do not control for worker characteristics such as age, education and residence).

Moving beyond medians, the cumulative density functions for wages by gender and sector are shown in Figures 5.1 and 5.2. Appendix Table 5.3 presents results from tests for stochastic dominance between the two distributions in these four graphs. The difference in the distribution of wages for male market workers is striking. The 2000 curve is below the 1997 curve (and this difference is significant), indicating a worsening from 1997 to 2000 in market sector wages for men. By contrast, the distribution of wages for self-employed men shows an increase in real wages from 1997 to 2000, consistent with the overall median results in Table 5.9.

Among women (Figure 5.2), we see a worsening of the distribution of earnings for market workers but it is not as striking as the shift we observed for men. For most of the distribution (below about 8 on the log wage scale), there has been a worsening of wages for women in market work (first-order dominance results are in Appendix Table 5.3). Results for women in self-employment are more mixed, as the distributions cross or overlap in parts. However, at the top portion of the distribution, there does appear to be a worsening in earnings from 1997 to 2000.

Table 5.10 presents wage results for age and education categories. As we would expect, wage rates are highest among workers with more than secondary education. Within education groups, wages are generally increasing in age for those below 55 but not for the least educated. Generally, workers with higher education had larger declines in real wages from 1997 to 2000 in terms of absolute declines of the median level and percent change. However, these results are not consistently observed. For example, median wages rose for workers 35–54 with more than secondary education. The group that had the largest percent change was young adults (22–24) with more than secondary education, who had a decline of 28% in real wages (Rp 853/hour).

Table 5.11 presents simple multivariate regressions of the change in (log) wages from 1997 to 2000. It is conditional on being employed for pay in both years and does not attempt to address selectivity issues. (Wages below Rp 30/hour are included and bottom coded to 30, including reports of zero earnings.) Regressions are estimated separately for men and women, and with and without baseline (1997) (log) wages. Among men, education and age are not statistically associated with the change in wages without including baseline wages. However, once we include baseline wages, we find that having at least nine years of education is associated with an increase in wages from 1997 to 2000. Aging is associated with an *increase* in wages for men aged 25–55. Working in rural areas is not associated with a difference in the decline of wages relative to urban

FIGURE 5.1
CDF of Market and Self-employment Log Wages in 1997 and 2000 for Men

Market

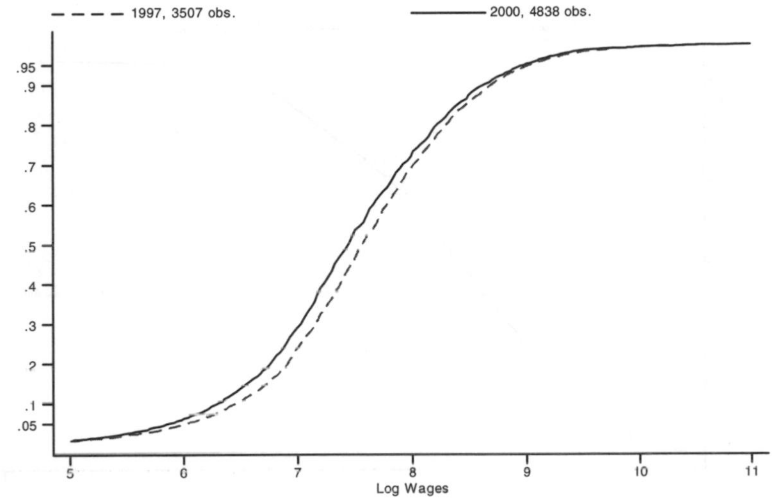
1997, 3507 obs.
2000, 4838 obs.
.95
.9
.8
.7
.6
.5
.4
.3
.2
.1
.05
5
6
7
8
9
10
11
Log Wages

Self-employment

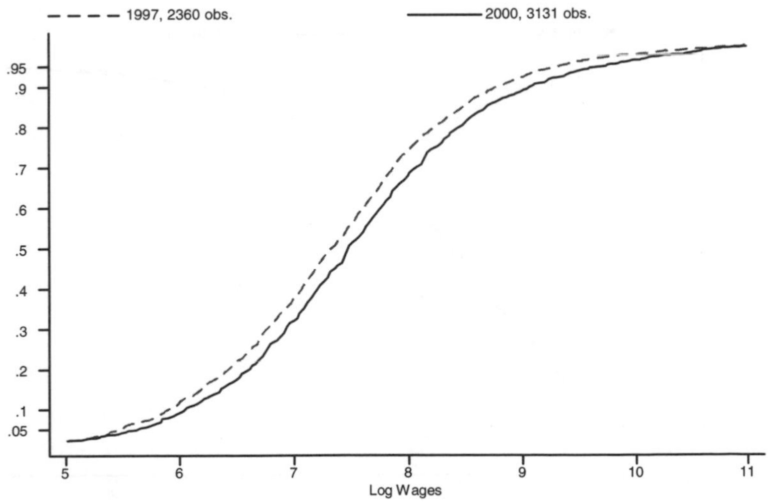
1997, 2360 obs.
2000, 3131 obs.
.95
.9
.8
.7
.6
.5
.4
.3
.2
.1
.05
5
6
7
8
9
10
11
Log Wages

Source: IFLS2 and IFLS3.
Observations were weighted using individual sampling weights.

FIGURE 5.2
CDF of Market and Self-employment Log Wages in 1997 and 2000 for Women

Market

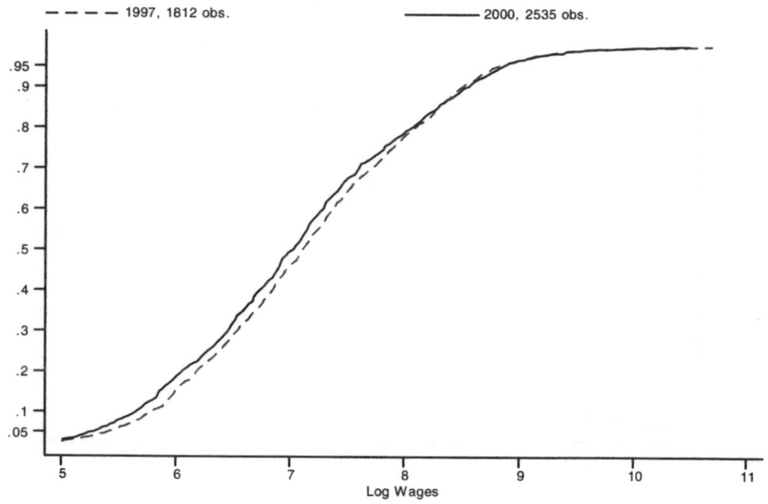
1997, 1812 obs.
2000, 2535 obs.
.95
.9
.8
.7
.6
.5
.4
.3
.2
.1
.05
5
6
7
8
9
10
11
Log Wages

Self-employment

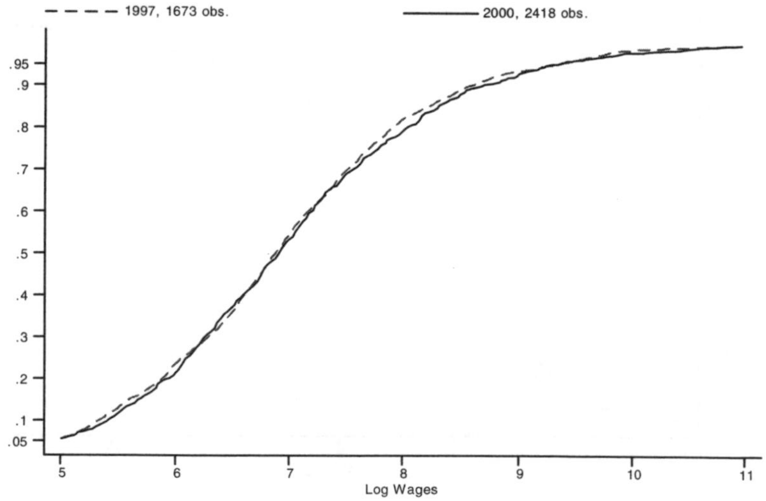
1997, 1673 obs.
2000, 2418 obs.
.95
.9
.8
.7
.6
.5
.4
.3
.2
.1
.05
5
6
7
8
9
10
11
Log Wages

Source: IFLS2 and IFLS3.
Observations were weighted using individual sampling weights.

TABLE 5.11
Change in Log Wages (2000 wage – 1997 wage), Adults 15–75, Linear Probability Models

		Men		Women	
		Excluding 1997 wages	Including 1997 wages	Excluding 1997 wages	Including 1997 wages
Age in 1997 (spline):	<25	–0.005	0.019	–0.010	0.015
		(0.37)	(1.69)	(0.41)	(0.78)
	25–55	0.003	0.010**	0.0005	0.010*
		(1.30)	(5.06)	(0.12)	(3.31)
	>55	–0.00003	–0.003	0.002	0.003
		(0.01)	(1.19)	(0.48)	(0.91)
Education in 1997:	1–5 years	–0.073	0.012	0.070	0.207**
		(0.69)	(0.13)	(0.70)	(2.59)
	6–8 years	–0.060	0.127	0.015	0.296**
		(0.59)	(1.44)	(0.14)	(3.19)
	9–11 years	–0.189	0.209*	–0.055	0.434**
		(1.82)	(2.27)	(0.44)	(3.91)
	12+ years	0.006	0.617**	0.168	1.099**
		(0.06)	(7.08)	(1.69)	(10.68)
Log Wages in 1997		–	–0.659**	–	–0.660**
			(31.39)		(21.73)
Rural in 1997		0.016	–0.0004	–0.028	–0.048
		(0.35)	(0.01)	(0.44)	(0.80)
North Sumatra in 1997		0.089	0.013	0.119	–0.025
		(1.12)	(0.19)	(1.04)	(0.25)
West Sumatra in 1997		0.048	0.079	–0.108	–0.166
		(0.35)	(0.75)	(0.77)	(1.33)
South Sumatra in 1997		0.236	0.022	0.436*	0.219
		(1.88)	(0.23)	(2.56)	(1.70)

continued on next page

TABLE 5.11 – cont'd

	Men		Women	
	Excluding 1997 wages	**Including 1997 wages**	**Excluding 1997 wages**	**Including 1997 wages**
Lampung in 1997	0.589**	0.081	0.410*	0.074
	(3.92)	(0.91)	(2.25)	(0.48)
West Java in 1997	0.090	0.012	0.092	–0.072
	(1.26)	(0.19)	(0.94)	(0.79)
Central Java in 1997	0.341**	–0.013	0.270**	–0.165
	(4.31)	(0.20)	(2.61)	(1.72)
Yogyakarta in 1997	–0.047	–0.340**	0.152	–0.227
	(0.62)	(5.19)	(1.31)	(1.92)
East Java in 1997	0.109	–0.127	0.017	–0.298**
	(1.41)	(1.99)	(0.17)	(3.05)
Bali in 1997	0.119	–0.121	0.236	0.077
	(1.21)	(1.48)	(1.69)	(0.55)
West Nusa Tenggara in 1997	0.005	–0.156	–0.006	–0.186
	(0.05)	(1.71)	(0.04)	(1.24)
South Kalimantan in 1997	0.406**	0.303**	–0.027	–0.040
	(4.39)	(3.82)	(0.21)	(0.34)
South Sulawesi in 1997	0.397**	0.102	0.556**	0.156
	(3.80)	(1.02)	(4.61)	(0.94)
Constant	0.008	4.224**	–0.021	3.876**
	(0.02)	(14.34)	(0.04)	(8.66)
F-test (p-values):				
Education variables	0.0305	0.0000	0.0720	0.0000
Number of observations	4,259	4,259	2,198	2,198
R-squared	0.021	0.314	0.017	0.332

Source: IFLS2 and IFLS3.
Dummy variable for missing education is included in the regressions but not reported in the table. The omitted category for education is no schooling, and for province is Jakarta. Estimates were weighted using individual sampling weights. Standard errors are robust to clustering at the community level and to heteroscedasticity. Absolute t-statistics are in parentheses with significance at 5% (*) and 1% (**) indicated.

workers, regardless of the inclusion of baseline wages. Men in Lampung, Central Java, South Kalimantan, and South Sulawesi experienced wage increases relative to men working in Jakarta, but, except for South Kalimantan, these increases disappear once baseline wages are included. Those with higher wages in 1997 had larger declines in wages between 1997 and 2000.

Among women, similar to men, we find that education is associated with increased wages when we control for baseline wages only, though for women the increase is significant for all levels of education. Conditional on 1997 wage, age is associated with wage increases for women 25–55. Also similar to the finding for men, women working in rural areas had similar declines in wages to urban workers. Likewise, women with higher wages in 1997 had larger declines in wages between 1997 and 2000. Women residing in South Sumatra, Lampung and Central Java had wage increases relative to counterparts in Jakarta, but only before we control for baseline wages. Once we control for baseline wages, we observe larger declines in wages for women in Yogyakarta and East Java relative to Jakarta for working women.

CHILD LABOUR

Child labour exists in Indonesia, as it does in other poor countries. The reasons for it are well known (see Basu 1999 for a recent survey), having to do with poverty and the high associated opportunity costs of sending children to school rather than working. Table 5.12 displays the main activities for boys and girls by age. The "other" category represents staying at home without household responsibilities, housekeeping or chronically sick. That is the most important activity for children under age 7. School attendance is clearly the main activity for children over 6. Even at age 14, work is the main activity for only 9% of children.

However, these very low percentages hide the extent of child labour, because for many children who work, work is not their major activity, and yet time is put in, which may conflict with schooling activities. Table 5.13 shows current (in the previous month from the date of interview), and ever, participation rates for any work activity: wage work or work for a family business (including as unpaid family workers). This corresponds closely to the International Labour Organization (ILO) definition of participation, but is narrow in that unpaid work on housekeeping activities is not included.

Current participation rates climb strongly with age, rising from under 2% for 5–9 year olds as a group, to 25.5% for 14 year olds. There are large

TABLE 5.12
Main Activities of Children
(As % of Total Number of Children in Each Age Group)

Age	Girls				Boys				Girls+Boys			
	Work/Help Earning Income	Attend School	House Keeping	Other	Work/Help Earning Income	Attend School	House Keeping	Other	Work/Help Earning Income	Attend School	House Keeping	Other
5	0.00	52.17	0.08	47.74	0.00	50.17	0.00	49.83	0.00	51.08	0.04	48.88
	(0.00)	(3.30)	(0.08)	(3.30)	(0.00)	(3.17)	(0.00)	(3.17)	(0.00)	(2.55)	(0.04)	(2.55)
6	0.76	77.75	0.00	21.49	0.39	74.55	0.00	25.07	0.58	76.23	0.00	23.19
	(0.44)	(2.44)	(0.00)	(2.47)	(0.39)	(2.82)	(0.00)	(2.80)	(0.29)	(2.02)	(0.00)	(2.03)
7	0.00	90.92	0.42	8.66	0.17	87.60	0.00	12.23	0.09	89.13	0.20	10.58
	(0.00)	(1.59)	(0.30)	(1.57)	(0.18)	(1.98)	(0.00)	(1.97)	(0.09)	(1.43)	(0.14)	(1.42)
8	0.07	94.93	0.32	4.68	0.73	93.19	0.24	5.84	0.40	94.05	0.28	5.26
	(0.07)	(1.14)	(0.32)	(1.09)	(0.46)	(1.33)	(0.18)	(1.26)	(0.23)	(0.93)	(0.18)	(0.90)
9	0.37	93.24	0.17	6.22	0.66	90.78	0.00	8.56	0.52	91.98	0.08	7.42
	(0.37)	(1.54)	(0.17)	(1.50)	(0.48)	(1.83)	(0.00)	(1.79)	(0.30)	(1.25)	(0.08)	(1.23)
10	0.95	91.09	0.31	7.65	0.51	94.89	0.06	4.54	0.72	93.06	0.18	6.04
	(0.54)	(1.70)	(0.30)	(1.64)	(0.30)	(1.08)	(0.06)	(1.02)	(0.30)	(0.97)	(0.15)	(0.94)
11	1.23	90.81	0.00	7.95	0.96	91.61	0.00	7.43	1.09	91.24	0.00	7.68
	(0.59)	(1.69)	(0.00)	(1.55)	(0.45)	(1.73)	(0.00)	(1.67)	(0.36)	(1.33)	(0.00)	(1.22)
12	1.48	86.19	0.31	12.01	2.46	87.47	0.73	9.34	1.98	86.85	0.53	10.65
	(0.81)	(2.36)	(0.24)	(2.11)	(0.89)	(1.95)	(0.43)	(1.64)	(0.60)	(1.61)	(0.25)	(1.41)
13	2.72	82.92	0.87	13.50	3.52	84.65	0.21	11.61	3.14	83.82	0.52	12.51
	(1.08)	(2.12)	(0.44)	(1.91)	(1.10)	(2.01)	(0.21)	(1.64)	(0.83)	(1.59)	(0.24)	(1.31)
14	10.39	73.10	2.19	14.33	7.61	78.89	0.33	13.17	9.00	75.98	1.26	13.75
	(1.67)	(2.48)	(0.70)	(1.96)	(1.34)	(2.15)	(0.33)	(1.77)	(1.09)	(1.85)	(0.39)	(1.49)
Total	1.92	83.50	0.49	14.09	1.72	83.51	0.15	14.61	1.82	83.51	0.32	14.36
	(0.26)	(0.94)	(0.11)	(0.89)	(0.25)	(1.08)	(0.08)	(0.99)	(0.18)	(0.91)	(0.07)	(0.85)

Source: IFLS3.

Work/help earning income includes job searching. Other includes stay at home, housekeeping, sick and retired. Estimates were weighted using individual sampling weights. Standard errors (in parentheses) are robust to clustering at the community level.

TABLE 5.13
Children Current and Ever Work Participation Rates by Age
(in percent)

	Current Participation									Ever Worked								
	Work for Either Wages or Family Business			Work for Wages			Work for Family Business			Work for Either Wages or Family Business			Work for Wages			Work for Family Business		
Age	Boys	Girls	Total	Boys	Girls	Total	Boys	Girls	Total	Boys	Girls	Total	Boys	Girls	Total	Boys	Girls	Total
5	0.6	0.4	0.5	0.0	0.2	0.1	0.6	0.2	0.4	0.6	0.4	0.5	0.0	0.2	0.1	0.6	0.2	0.4
	(0.41)	(0.28)	(0.26)	0.00	(0.18)	(0.08)	(0.41)	(0.21)	(0.24)	(0.41)	(0.28)	(0.26)	0.00	(0.18)	(0.08)	(0.41)	(0.21)	(0.24)
6	0.6	1.0	0.8	0.0	0.0	0.0	0.6	1.0	0.8	0.6	1.3	1.0	0.0	0.0	0.0	0.6	1.3	1.0
	(0.52)	(0.52)	(0.37)	0.00	0.00	0.00	(0.52)	(0.52)	(0.37)	(0.52)	(0.59)	(0.39)	0.00	0.00	0.00	(0.52)	(0.59)	(0.39)
7	1.5	1.3	1.4	0.0	0.2	0.1	1.5	1.3	1.4	1.5	1.5	1.5	0.0	0.2	0.1	1.5	1.5	1.5
	(0.57)	(0.58)	(0.40)	0.00	(0.16)	(0.07)	(0.57)	(0.58)	(0.40)	(0.57)	(0.63)	(0.42)	0.00	(0.16)	(0.07)	(0.57)	(0.63)	(0.42)
8	2.0	2.1	2.0	0.0	0.4	0.2	2.0	1.9	2.0	2.2	2.7	2.5	0.2	0.7	0.4	2.1	2.3	2.2
	(0.77)	(0.68)	(0.52)	0.00	(0.29)	(0.14)	(0.77)	(0.67)	(0.51)	(0.79)	(0.81)	(0.57)	(0.16)	(0.38)	(0.21)	(0.78)	(0.75)	(0.54)
9	3.3	4.7	4.0	0.6	0.4	0.5	3.0	4.7	3.8	4.8	6.1	5.4	1.0	0.6	0.8	4.2	5.8	5.0
	(0.94)	(1.13)	(0.74)	(0.46)	(0.40)	(0.30)	(0.91)	(1.13)	(0.71)	(1.25)	(1.28)	(0.93)	(0.79)	(0.47)	(0.46)	(1.05)	(1.26)	(0.85)
10	7.9	6.1	7.0	2.3	0.7	1.5	6.3	5.7	6.0	8.4	6.7	7.6	2.5	0.7	1.6	6.9	6.4	6.7
	(1.48)	(1.33)	(1.11)	(0.79)	(0.44)	(0.46)	(1.27)	(1.30)	(1.05)	(1.52)	(1.38)	(1.14)	(0.82)	(0.44)	(0.47)	(1.32)	(1.35)	(1.07)
11	7.8	10.3	9.0	1.6	2.7	2.1	6.7	8.6	7.6	8.9	10.9	9.8	1.7	2.8	2.2	8.2	9.0	8.6
	(1.47)	(1.74)	(1.19)	(0.64)	(0.86)	(0.58)	(1.37)	(1.62)	(1.12)	(1.63)	(1.77)	(1.25)	(0.64)	(0.88)	(0.58)	(1.58)	(1.66)	(1.21)
12	14.5	15.6	15.0	2.3	1.9	2.1	13.0	14.2	13.6	17.3	17.3	17.3	3.5	3.1	3.3	15.1	16.1	15.6
	(2.15)	(2.35)	(1.71)	(0.84)	(0.73)	(0.56)	(2.08)	(2.28)	(1.65)	(2.28)	(2.42)	(1.79)	(1.06)	(1.06)	(0.74)	(2.20)	(2.35)	(1.72)
13	16.3	17.8	17.0	4.1	3.5	3.8	13.5	14.6	14.0	20.5	19.5	20.0	5.8	4.7	5.2	18.1	16.2	17.2
	(2.01)	(2.33)	(1.55)	(1.10)	(1.13)	(0.77)	(1.84)	(2.09)	(1.43)	(2.31)	(2.41)	(1.69)	(1.40)	(1.30)	(0.93)	(2.24)	(2.18)	(1.57)

continued on next page

TABLE 5.13 – cont'd

	Current Participation									Ever Worked								
	Work for Either Wages or Family Business			Work for Wages			Work for Family Business			Work for Either Wages or Family Business			Work for Wages			Work for Family Business		
Age	Boys	Girls	Total	Boys	Girls	Total	Boys	Girls	Total	Boys	Girls	Total	Boys	Girls	Total	Boys	Girls	Total
14	26.7	24.3	25.5	7.3	11.5	9.4	21.0	14.9	17.9	29.8	27.2	28.5	10.3	12.7	11.5	23.7	18.4	21.0
	(2.64)	(2.25)	(1.80)	(1.58)	(1.72)	(1.10)	(2.29)	(1.90)	(1.61)	(2.79)	(2.43)	(1.90)	(1.78)	(1.79)	(1.17)	(2.50)	(2.15)	(1.78)
5–9	1.6	1.9	1.8	0.1	0.2	0.2	1.6	1.9	1.7	2.0	2.4	2.2	0.2	0.3	0.3	1.8	2.3	2.0
	(0.29)	(0.34)	(0.24)	(0.09)	(0.11)	(0.07)	(0.29)	(0.33)	(0.23)	(0.35)	(0.39)	(0.28)	(0.16)	(0.13)	(0.11)	(0.32)	(0.38)	(0.26)
10–14	14.5	14.8	14.7	3.5	4.1	3.8	12.0	11.6	11.8	16.8	16.4	16.6	4.7	4.9	4.8	14.2	13.2	13.7
	(1.06)	(1.20)	(0.94)	(0.49)	(0.53)	(0.38)	(0.95)	(1.09)	(0.84)	(1.15)	(1.31)	(1.00)	(0.57)	(0.59)	(0.43)	(1.06)	(1.20)	(0.93)
5–14	8.1	8.5	8.3	1.8	2.2	2.0	6.8	6.8	6.8	9.4	9.5	9.5	2.5	2.6	2.6	8.1	7.8	7.9
	(0.58)	(0.65)	(0.52)	(0.25)	(0.27)	(0.20)	(0.53)	(0.59)	(0.47)	(0.65)	(0.73)	(0.57)	(0.30)	(0.31)	(0.23)	(0.60)	(0.67)	(0.53)
Number of observations	3,854	3,696	7,550	3,854	3,696	7,550	3,854	3,696	7,550	3,854	3,696	7,550	3,854	3,696	7,550	3,854	3,696	7,550

Source: IFLS3.
Current participation is based on whether or not the child worked in last month. Estimates were weighted using individual sampling weights. Standard errors (in parentheses) are robust to clustering at the community level.

jumps in the percent working between ages 10 and 14 years. For 10–14 year olds as a group, the overall participation rate is 14.7%. This compares to an average from ILO data, across Asian countries, of 12.8% in 1995, a rate half that in Africa (see Basu 1999). Most of this participation is work on the family business; market wage work is unusual for children, with only 3.8% of 10–14 year olds participating. Participation rates are quite comparable between boys and girls.

Since children may go into and out of the labour market, current participation will underestimate the incidence of child labour. Ever participation rates are a little higher than current participation, with increasing differences for older ages. Almost 29% of 14 year olds have worked at one time. Again, working for the family business is far more common than market wage work.

Table 5.14 shows average hours of work in the past week, for those children who are currently working in either wage or family business work. Because the cell sizes by year are small, we aggregate into 5–9 and 10–14 years. Children aged 10–14 work on average 19.5 hours per week. Not surprisingly, younger children work fewer hours per week, an average of just below 13 hours per week. Of the work time for 10–14 year olds, about 60% is time spent on family businesses, the rest being on wage work. This work time is time that cannot be spent at school or on school work.

TABLE 5.14
Average Hours Worked Per Week for Children Age 5–14 Who Worked

	Average Total Hours Worked per Week			Average Hours Worked per Week for Wages			Average Hours Worked per Week for Family Business		
Age	Boys	Girls	Total	Boys	Girls	Total	Boys	Girls	Total
5–9	15.8	10.4	12.9	1.0	0.2	0.6	14.8	10.1	12.3
	(4.43)	(1.78)	(2.27)	(0.70)	(0.13)	(0.34)	(4.44)	(1.81)	(2.25)
10–14	18.4	20.6	19.5	7.1	7.9	7.5	11.3	12.7	12.0
	(1.52)	(1.61)	(1.11)	(1.34)	(1.30)	(0.91)	(0.90)	(1.27)	(0.80)
5–14	18.1	19.5	18.8	6.5	7.1	6.8	11.7	12.4	12.1
	(1.48)	(1.43)	(1.05)	(1.22)	(1.16)	(0.83)	(0.93)	(1.14)	(0.77)
Number of observations	292	297	589	292	297	589	292	297	589

Source: IFLS3.

Estimates were weighted using individual sampling weights. Standard errors (in parentheses) are robust to clustering at the community level.

When we compare current participation rates for 10–14 year olds by poor-non-poor status, urban versus rural residence, and farm versus non-farm household (Table 5.15), we find little difference by poverty status, but substantially higher rates for working on family businesses in rural areas and in farm households. Much of this difference surely reflects children working on their family farm. This in turn reflects a demand for child family labour on the farm, perhaps because their opportunity costs are low compared to what it would cost (including supervision costs) to hire adult labour for the same tasks. For wage work there is very little difference between rural and urban, or farm and non-farm children.

Linear probability models for current participation in any work, wage work or for family businesses are presented in Table 5.16 for boys and girls aged 10–14. Of course, there are very strong age effects, with older children being more likely to work. Interestingly *pce* does not have a significant impact on the probability of wage work, however higher *pce* among those above Rp 150,000 is associated with a *higher* likelihood of boys working for the family business. This may result from households with higher *pce* being more likely to have family businesses. For any work and work on the family business, there exists strong parental education effects. Father's schooling is associated with significantly lower participation rates for boys, but not for girls. Higher mother's education reduces the probability of boys working by 0.8% per year of mother's schooling. The impact on girls working is larger, 1.1% lower probability of working per year of mother's schooling. Thus girls of mothers with completed primary schooling will on average be less likely to work by 6.6% than a girl of a mother with no schooling. Compared to average participation rates of 14.5% for this age group, this is a large impact.

For work on family businesses, there is a large effect for boys residing in a farm household and for both girls and boys residing in a rural household. Boys who are in rural, farm households have a 13% higher probability of working for the family business than do urban boys, an almost 8% difference for girls. These results suggest that for work on family businesses, the bulk of child work, it is the demand for labour, largely on farms, that is the driving force. The lack of importance of *pce* within rural areas and across farm households is striking. In addition, regulatory approaches are unlikely to have much impact given the importance of labour demand.

TABLE 5.15
Percentage of Children Age 10–14 Currently Working by Residence, Per Capita Expenditure, and Type of Household

	Work for Either Wage or Family Business			Work for Family Business			Work for Wages		
	Boys	Girls	Total	Boys	Girls	Total	Boys	Girls	Total
Residence									
Urban	9.3	10.8	10.0	6.9	7.1	7.0	2.8	4.0	3.4
	(1.25)	(1.25)	(0.94)	(1.06)	(1.04)	(0.83)	(0.68)	(0.79)	(0.52)
Rural	18.0	17.8	17.9	15.3	14.7	15.1	4.0	4.3	4.1
	(1.52)	(1.80)	(1.38)	(1.40)	(1.65)	(1.25)	(0.69)	(0.73)	(0.54)
Per Capita Expenditure									
Poor	13.0	14.7	13.8	10.2	9.8	10.0	3.3	5.4	4.3
	(1.99)	(2.29)	(1.72)	(1.84)	(1.93)	(1.57)	(1.00)	(1.37)	(0.87)
Non-poor	14.9	14.9	14.9	12.4	12.0	12.2	3.6	3.8	3.7
	(1.15)	(1.37)	(1.01)	(1.03)	(1.27)	(0.92)	(0.54)	(0.58)	(0.42)
Household Type									
Non-farm HH	9.8	11.6	10.7	6.6	8.1	7.4	3.8	3.9	3.9
	(1.09)	(1.32)	(0.95)	(0.88)	(1.12)	(0.79)	(0.69)	(0.63)	(0.48)
Farm HH	20.7	19.4	20.1	19.1	16.2	17.7	3.1	4.5	3.8
	(1.75)	(1.85)	(1.49)	(1.71)	(1.76)	(1.41)	(0.68)	(0.90)	(0.55)
Number of observations	1,955	1,867	3,822	1,955	1,867	3,822	1,955	1,867	3,822

Source: IFLS3.
Estimates were weighted using individual sampling weights. Standard errors (in parentheses) are robust to clustering at the community level.

TABLE 5.16
Linear Probability Models of Current Work Participation for Children Age 10–14

	Work for Either Wages or Family Business		Work for Wages		Work for Family Business	
	Boys	Girls	Boys	Girls	Boys	Girls
Age	0.042 **	0.038 **	0.012 **	0.022 **	0.033 **	0.019 **
	(7.60)	(7.44)	(3.20)	(5.61)	(6.93)	(4.35)
Mother's education if in household (years)	–0.008 *	–0.011 **	–0.002	–0.004 **	–0.005	–0.009 **
	(2.48)	(3.68)	(1.42)	(2.63)	(1.89)	(2.95)
Father's education if in household (years)	–0.008 **	–0.001	–0.001	0.001	–0.007 **	–0.000
	(3.11)	(0.29)	0.017	(0.64)	(2.99)	(0.02)
log *pce* (spline) : 0 – log Rp 150,000	0.022	0.021	(1.00)	–0.020	0.016	0.043
	(0.64)	(0.62)	–0.010	(0.92)	(0.49)	(1.40)
> log Rp 150,000	0.044 *	0.036	(1.02)	0.007	0.055 **	0.032
	(2.03)	(1.60)	(1.12)	(0.54)	(2.60)	(1.63)
Farm household	0.071 **	0.024	–0.020 *	–0.000	0.096 **	0.030
	(3.72)	(1.03)	(1.97)	(0.01)	(5.18)	(1.45)
Rural	0.038	0.032	0.011	–0.007	0.034	0.047 *
	(1.92)	(1.36)	(0.97)	(0.55)	(1.90)	(2.30)
North Sumatra	0.002	0.019	–0.040	–0.023	0.029	0.038
	(0.03)	(0.38)	(1.26)	(1.00)	(0.62)	(0.76)
West Sumatra	–0.066	–0.007	–0.002	–0.011	–0.043	0.000
	(1.01)	(0.15)	(0.06)	(0.45)	(0.88)	(0.00)
South Sumatra	–0.047	–0.024	–0.011	–0.014	–0.044	–0.007
	(0.80)	(0.48)	(0.30)	(0.45)	(1.05)	(0.17)
Lampung	–0.112	–0.009	–0.025	–0.019	–0.094	0.023
	(1.80)	(0.19)	(0.65)	(0.72)	(1.93)	(0.55)

West Java	–0.073	–0.067	–0.031	–0.003	–0.054	–0.059 *
	(1.33)	(1.88)	(0.93)	(0.14)	(1.51)	(2.10)
Central Java	–0.049	0.039	–0.039	0.023	–0.014	0.023
	(0.82)	(0.75)	(1.19)	(0.95)	(0.32)	(0.52)
Yogyakarta	0.050	0.182 **	–0.033	0.028	0.084	0.162 **
	(0.79)	(3.59)	(1.03)	(0.86)	(1.71)	(3.27)
East Java	–0.028	–0.004	–0.019	–0.009	0.003	0.009
	(0.48)	(0.10)	(0.56)	(0.42)	(0.06)	(0.25)
Bali	–0.052	0.029	–0.033	0.049	–0.031	0.003
	(0.85)	(0.60)	(1.02)	(1.37)	(0.69)	(0.08)
West Nusa Tenggara	–0.065	–0.047	–0.008	–0.018	–0.063	–0.031
	(1.08)	(1.09)	(0.23)	(0.63)	(1.59)	(0.88)
South Kalimantan	0.065	–0.067	–0.000	–0.003	0.049	–0.073
	(0.87)	(1.44)	(0.00)	(0.10)	(0.88)	(1.96)
South Sulawesi	0.044	0.014	0.046	0.001	–0.005	0.023
	(0.66)	(0.29)	(1.02)	(0.03)	(0.11)	(0.52)
Constant	–0.578	–0.549	–0.265	0.014	–0.461	–0.637
	(1.45)	(1.36)	(1.35)	(0.05)	(1.21)	(1.78)
F-test (p-values):						
Education variables	0.0000	0.0001	0.0223	0.0226	0.0000	0.0021
Expenditure variables	0.0424	0.2004	0.4543	0.6101	0.0070	0.0758
Number of observations	1,955	1,867	1,955	1,867	1,955	1,867
R-squared	0.10	0.08	0.03	0.05	0.10	0.07

Source: IFLS3.

Observations are children age 10–14 who worked last month. The omitted category for province is Jakarta. Estimates were weighted using individual sampling weights. Standard errors are robust to clustering at the community level and to heteroscedasticity. Absolute t-statistics are in parentheses with significance at 5% (*) and 1% (**) indicated.

SUMMARY

Between 1997 and 2000 we find some significant changes in labour market outcomes among adults interviewed in IFLS. Employment rates rose slightly for men between 1997 and 2000 (from 79% to 84%), but women had a much larger rise, from 45% to 57%. About half the rise for both men and women was in paid work and the other half as unpaid family workers in family businesses. As a fraction of overall employment, unpaid work in family businesses increased dramatically among women to 25%. In addition, there was a rise for both men and women in the fraction that had a second or third job, to almost 25% of men and 10% of women. However, total hours worked on all jobs did not change significantly. Consequently there was a rise in the number of total hours worked, though there were no changes in the hours worked on the primary job.

Other studies have shown that between 1997 and 1998 there was a dramatic fall in wages, of up to 35% in urban areas. By 2000 there was a dramatic recovery overall, but very uneven across sectors. Wages among private sector employees are still 10% below their level in 1997, but this still represents a large increase from the levels of late 1998. Among government employees, however, wages increased by roughly 10% over 1997 levels. Among the self-employed, wages rebounded to their 1997 levels in urban areas and grew by nearly 12% over 1997 levels in rural areas.

Among children aged 10–14, the employment rate was 14.5% in 2000. Most of this entails working for family businesses, especially farm work in rural areas. We find no difference in employment rates between boys and girls and low household income is not correlated with child labour. Among those 10–14 who work, hours worked average about 20 hours per week. Yet even for those who work, the main activity listed for most is attending school, so that work and school are not mutually exclusive activities.

Notes

1 As for the poverty regressions, for age we use splines. Educational categories are modelled using dummies, also as in the poverty regressions, with groups defined as: 1–5, 6–8, 9–11, 12+ years.

2 This discussion does not focus on minimum wages which apply to formal sector employment. See SMERU Team (2001) for a review and analysis of minimum wages and employment effects in Indonesia. Prior

to 2001, regional minimum wages were established by decree issued by the Minister of Manpower. Starting in 2001, the power to set minimum wages has been transferred to heads of provinces, cities and districts. For reference, the minimum wage in 2000 for the greater Jakarta area was Rp 286,000 per month (just under Rp 1,700 per hour for full-time employment).

APPENDIX TABLE 5.1
Transitions in Work for Pay, Men 15–75
Multinomial Logit Models: Risk Ratios Relative to Not Working in Either Year

		Not Working in 1997 Working in 2000	Working in 1997 Not Working in 2000	Work Both Years
Age in 1997 (spline)	<25	1.482	1.457	2.228**
		(1.98)	(1.44)	(4.42)
	25–55	0.957*	1.042*	1.044**
		(2.36)	(2.30)	(2.78)
	>55	0.944**	0.974**	0.924**
		(8.22)	(3.60)	(12.53)
Education in 1997:	1–5 years	0.845	0.854	0.930
		(0.65)	(0.59)	(0.34)
	6–8 years	0.929	0.841	0.923
		(0.24)	(0.62)	(0.32)
	9–11 years	0.973	0.859	0.802
		(0.08)	(0.43)	(0.73)
	12+ years	0.683	0.639	0.673
		(1.13)	(1.35)	(1.50)
Rural in 1997		2.011**	1.489*	1.699**
		(3.62)	(2.29)	(3.53)
North Sumatra in 1997		0.998	0.959	1.201
		(0.00)	(0.11)	(0.54)
West Sumatra in 1997		0.571	1.238	0.855
		(1.43)	(0.58)	(0.49)
South Sumatra in 1997		1.390	1.144	1.596
		(0.77)	(0.27)	(1.35)

Lampung in 1997	0.981	0.522	1.121
	(0.05)	(1.47)	(0.35)
West Java in 1997	0.660	1.110	1.244
	(1.51)	(0.39)	(0.98)
Central Java in 1997	0.810	1.021	1.726*
	(0.58)	(0.06)	(2.13)
Yogyakarta in 1997	0.999	1.181	1.809*
	(0.00)	(0.58)	(2.37)
East Java in 1997	0.740	1.040	1.375
	(1.05)	(0.13)	(1.20)
Bali in 1997	0.410*	1.185	1.237
	(2.37)	(0.48)	(0.79)
West Nusa Tenggara in 1997	0.818	0.948	1.676
	(0.53)	(0.13)	(1.69)
South Kalimantan in 1997	0.973	1.162	1.882
	(0.06)	(0.31)	(1.75)
South Sulawesi in 1997	0.819	0.692	0.806
	(0.43)	(1.00)	(0.62)
X^2	817.78		
Log (Likelihood)	0.0000		
Pseudo R-squared	0.0987		
F-test (p-values): Education variables	0.8500		
Number of observations	6,845		

Source: IFLS2 and IFLS3. Workers include employees, self-employed, and unpaid family labour. Dummy variable for missing education is included in the regressions but not reported in the table. The omitted category for education is no schooling, and for province is Jakarta. Estimates were weighted using individual sampling weights. Standard errors are robust to clustering at the community level and to heteroscedasticity. Absolute t-statistics are in parentheses with significance at 5% (*) and 1% (**) indicated.

APPENDIX TABLE 5.2
Transitions in Work for Pay, Women 15–75
Multinomial Logit Models: Risk Ratios Relative to Not Working in Either Year

		Not Working in 1997 Working in 2000	Working in 1997 Not Working in 2000	Work Both Years
Age in 1997 (spline)	<25	1.164	1.238	1.408 **
		(1.10)	(1.29)	(3.01)
	25–55	0.988 *	1.005	1.015 **
		(2.44)	(0.74)	(3.85)
	>55	0.967 **	0.985 **	0.971 **
		(8.42)	(3.11)	(8.04)
Education in 1997:	1–5 years	0.950	0.882	1.119
		(0.43)	(1.03)	(1.01)
	6–8 years	0.687 **	0.733 *	0.824
		(2.88)	(2.22)	(1.41)
	9–11 years	0.603 **	0.881	0.758
		(3.14)	(0.71)	(1.88)
	12+ years	0.861	1.129	1.982 **
		(0.99)	(0.71)	(4.94)
Rural in 1997		1.023	0.973	0.726 **
		(0.23)	(0.22)	(3.25)
North Sumatra in 1997		1.410	0.955	1.042
		(1.69)	(0.17)	(0.17)
West Sumatra in 1997		1.650 *	2.222 **	1.605 *
		(2.38)	(3.57)	(2.22)
South Sumatra in 1997		0.724	0.975	0.638
		(1.36)	(0.09)	(1.98)

Lampung in 1997	0.883	0.779	0.611
	(0.52)	(0.80)	(1.74)
West Java in 1997	0.984	1.112	0.873
	(0.09)	(0.51)	(0.84)
Central Java in 1997	1.251	2.443 **	2.386 **
	(1.02)	(4.32)	(4.81)
Yogyakarta in 1997	1.374	2.852 **	2.706 **
	(1.69)	(3.49)	(4.93)
East Java in 1997	1.260	1.417	1.429 *
	(1.28)	(1.55)	(2.12)
Bali in 1997	1.482	2.969 **	2.517 **
	(1.65)	(3.76)	(3.93)
West Nusa Tenggara in 1997	0.833	1.107	1.412
	(0.76)	(0.38)	(1.38)
South Kalimantan in 1997	0.787	1.523	0.963
	(1.05)	(1.16)	(0.15)
South Sulawesi in 1997	0.645 *	0.662	0.562 **
	(2.02)	(1.48)	(2.60)
X^2	703.78		
Log (Likelihood)	0.0000		
Pseudo R-squared	0.0373		
F-test (p-values): Education variables	0.0000		
Number of observations	8,003		

Source: IFLS2 and IFLS3. Workers include employees, self-employed, and unpaid family labour. Dummy variable for missing education is included in the regressions but not reported in the table. The omitted category for education is no schooling, and for province is Jakarta. Estimates were weighted using individual sampling weights. Standard errors are robust to clustering at the community level and to heteroscedasticity. Absolute t-statistics are in parentheses with significance at 5% (*) and 1% (**) indicated.

APPENDIX TABLE 5.3
Log of Market and Self-employment Wages: Test for Stochastic Dominance

	First crossing point and the difference between curves (2000–1997)							
	Male				Female			
	First-Order Dominance	Standard Errors	Second-Order Dominance	Standard Errors	First-Order Dominance	Standard Errors	Second-Order Dominance	Standard Errors
Market wage								
First crossing point	–	–	–	–	8.345	(0.226)	–	–
Points of testing								
6.0	0.013	(0.007)	0.007	(0.005)	0.033	(0.017)	0.023	(0.014)
6.5	0.034	(0.010)	0.018	(0.008)	0.031	(0.025)	0.037	(0.022)
7.0	0.052	(0.010)	0.040	(0.013)	0.034	(0.029)	0.055	(0.034)
7.5	0.070	(0.019)	0.071	(0.020)	0.032	(0.025)	0.072	(0.044)
8.0	0.033	(0.017)	0.095	(0.027)	0.008	(0.019)	0.083	(0.051)
8.5	0.017	(0.010)	0.106	(0.032)	–0.007	(0.012)	0.085	(0.056)
9.0	0.005	(0.006)	0.111	(0.035)	–0.001	(0.006)	0.082	(0.058)
9.5	0.005	(0.003)	0.114	(0.036)	–0.002	(0.003)	0.082	(0.059)
10.0	0.001	(0.002)	0.114	(0.036)	0.002	(0.002)	0.082	(0.059)
Number of observations								
1997	3,507		3,507		1,812		1,812	
2000	4,838		4,838		2,535		2,535	

Self-employment wage								
First crossing point	5.013	(0.351)	5.23	(1.346)	6.223	(0.230)	–	–
Points of testing								
6.0	–0.028	(0.013)	–0.010	(0.010)	–0.022	(0.019)	–0.014	(0.017)
6.5	–0.043	(0.018)	–0.027	(0.017)	0.011	(0.021)	–0.013	(0.025)
7.0	–0.054	(0.021)	–0.051	(0.026)	–0.011	(0.022)	–0.014	(0.033)
7.5	–0.048	(0.021)	–0.080	(0.034)	–0.007	(0.019)	–0.017	(0.041)
8.0	–0.061	(0.016)	–0.108	(0.041)	–0.029	(0.016)	–0.026	(0.047)
8.5	–0.044	(0.013)	–0.134	(0.047)	–0.008	(0.012)	–0.034	(0.052)
9.0	–0.032	(0.010)	–0.153	(0.050)	–0.006	(0.010)	–0.040	(0.055)
9.5	–0.023	(0.008)	–0.167	(0.052)	–0.002	(0.007)	–0.040	(0.057)
10.0	–0.015	(0.006)	–0.177	(0.054)	–0.006	(0.005)	–0.043	(0.058)
Number of observations								
1997	2,360		2,360		1,673		1,673	
2000	3,131		3,131		2,418		2,418	

Source: IFLS 2 and IFLS 3.

Note: Dash (–) indicates that the curves do not cross. Formulae for the standard deviation are from Russel Davidson and Jean-Yves Duclos (2000), "Statistical Inference for Stochastic Dominance and for the Measurement of Poverty and Inequality", *Econometrica* v86 n6. Computation for the table above was performed using "DAD: A Software for Distributive Analysis/Analyse Distributive", version 4.2, copyrighted by Jean-Yves Duclos, Abdelkrim Araar, and Carl Fortin. Standard errors are robust to clustering at the community level. Estimates were weighted using individual sampling weights.

6

Education

In this section we explore changes in the characteristics of education from the demand side, including enrolment rates, hours in school, school expenditure patterns and assistance to students (scholarships). The correlates of enrolment and expenditure are also explored. We focus primarily on three age groups, based on the target ages for the three levels of school in Indonesia: 7–12 years, 13–15 and 16–18 (corresponding to primary, junior secondary and senior secondary levels). The section concludes with a brief description of some characteristics of schools surveyed as part of the IFLS.

EDUCATION UTILIZATION

Current enrolment refers to the person's enrolment status at the time of the interview. The IFLS2 interview took place during the early part of the 1997/98 school year. The IFLS3 interviews started earlier in the summer than the 1997 interviews. Thus, some households may have been interviewed at the end of the 1999/2000 school year. For consistency in definition, enrolment statistics for IFLS3 households interviewed before 15 July 2000 are not used in this section.

Table 6.1 presents the results for non-enrolment across age groups and by gender, expenditure group (where poor are individuals in households with monthly per capita expenditure below the poverty line) and residence. Overall, as children age, non-enrolment rates increase. Likewise, children in poorer or rural household are less likely to be enrolled. Looking at changes in enrolment between years, for primary school-aged children we observe a decline, though not significant, in non-enrolment rates (i.e., increase in enrolment) for boys and girls. This decline in enrolment for children 7–12 years is significant among poorer children, but not among urban children. This indicates that the gaps in enrolment by wealth have shrunk for the youngest children. In 1997, non-enrolment for children in

TABLE 6.1
Percentage of Children Not Currently Enrolled

	Children 7–12			Children 13–15			Children 16–18		
	1997	2000	Change	1997	2000	Change	1997	2000	Change
Gender									
– Boys	6.2	4.3	–1.9	20.9	20.3	–0.7	48.7	50.9	2.2
	(0.89)	(0.72)	(1.15)	(1.57)	(1.53)	(2.26)	(2.21)	(1.91)	(2.92)
– Girls	4.9	3.4	–1.6	22.5	23.6	1.0	53.1	53.4	0.3
	(0.83)	(0.51)	(0.98)	(1.79)	(1.74)	(2.49)	(2.07)	(1.89)	(2.81)
pce									
– Poor	12.8	6.2	–6.5 *	38.3	34.9	–3.9	65.1	66.4	1.4
	(2.67)	(1.11)	(2.89)	(2.90)	(3.00)	(4.18)	(4.42)	(3.61)	(5.71)
– Non-poor	3.7	3.3	–0.5	18.2	19.3	1.1	48.1	49.5	1.4
	(0.46)	(0.50)	(0.68)	(1.41)	(1.38)	(1.97)	(1.69)	(1.64)	(2.35)
Residence									
– Urban	2.2	1.6	–0.6	12.5	15.2	2.6	39.0	40.9	1.9
	(0.47)	(0.35)	(0.59)	(1.17)	(1.49)	(1.90)	(2.11)	(1.78)	(2.76)
– Rural	7.5	5.4	–2.1	27.7	27.2	–0.5	60.8	62.3	1.5
	(1.14)	(0.86)	(1.43)	(2.10)	(2.07)	(2.95)	(2.30)	(2.18)	(3.17)
Number of observations	4,411	4,421		2,564	2,342		2,383	2,697	

Source: IFLS2 and IFLS3.
Estimates were weighted using individual sampling weights. Standard errors (in parentheses) are robust to clustering at the community level.
Significance at 5% (*) and 1% (**) indicated.

poorer households was 13% and declined to 6% by 2000. By comparison, for children in non-poor households, non-enrolment did not change (4% and 3% in 1997 and 2000 respectively). Comparing these results with patterns from 1997 to 1998 (see Frankenberg et al. 1999, and Thomas et al. 2001) they suggest that enrolment rates recovered from the 1998 decline, and for primary school-aged children, actually rose above rates in 1997. This is consistent with findings from the SUSENAS survey (see Pradhan and Sparrow 2000). In addition to enrolment, the choice of school (public, private religious, and private non-religious) is also of interest. These results are reported in Appendix Table 6.1 for all children enrolled. We find little change from 1997 to 2000 in the distribution of students across these three school types. Older children are more likely to be enrolled in private schools, both religious and non-religious.

Tables 6.2–6.4 explore the correlates of enrolment, for each age group and by gender, in a multivariate framework. For per capita expenditure, we use splines, as we do for age, allowing log *pce* to have different effects if it is below or above the log of Rp 150,000.

Our review begins with primary school-aged children, 7–12 years, whose enrolment rates are quite high (above 90%). Thus, we see little variation in our outcome in Table 6.2. Therefore, it is not surprising that few of the co-variates are significantly associated with enrolment. Among the youngest children, higher *pce* in 1997 was associated with significantly higher enrolment probabilities, but only for values of *pce* below the median. This suggests that for the poor, *pce* matters. However, by 2000, the advantage associated with higher *pce* has reduced considerably. The reduced impact of *pce* in 2000 is consistent with the elimination of entrance fees by many public primary schools that occurred between 1997 and 2000 (see below). Young children with better educated parents are more likely to be enrolled. For girls, the impact of father's education goes away in 2000. Both boys and girls in rural areas are less likely to be enrolled. Generally, the province indicators are not significant except for Central Java for boys. Young boys in Central Java have significantly higher enrolment rates than their counterparts in Jakarta for both years, although only significantly so in 1997. The overall F-test indicates that the pattern between the co-variates and enrolment did not change significantly from 1997 to 2000.

Among children 13–15 (Table 6.3), age for boys and girls is associated with lower enrolment in 1997. For boys, by 2000, this association is even larger. For both boys and girls, higher *pce* is associated with greater enrolment rates but again only for increases for low income households (below Rp 150,000/month). The coefficients of *pce* are higher for junior secondary school enrolments than for primary school. This may result

TABLE 6.2
School Enrolment: Linear Probability Models Boys and Girls, 7–12 Years

	Boys		Girls	
	1997	Change in 2000	1997	Change in 2000
Age	0.005	–0.004	0.002	–0.007
	(1.09)	(0.70)	(0.47)	(1.48)
Mother's education if in hh (years × 10^{-1})	0.068**	–0.025	0.028*	0.001
	(3.69)	(1.03)	(1.99)	(0.05)
Father's education if in hh (years × 10^{-1})	0.025	0.008	0.045**	–0.046*
	(1.93)	(0.44)	(2.99)	(2.26)
log *pce* (spline): 0 – log Rp 150,000	0.126**	–0.086*	0.102	–0.084
	(3.34)	(2.04)	(1.93)	(1.46)
> log Rp 150,000	–0.006	–0.002	–0.010	0.016
	(0.64)	(0.13)	(0.75)	(1.10)
Rural	–0.026*	0.004	–0.021	–0.013
	(2.22)	(0.26)	(2.02)*	(0.95)
North Sumatra	0.009	0.048	–0.016	0.042
	(0.37)	(1.54)	(0.78)	(1.64)
West Sumatra	0.006	0.057	0.006	–0.007
	(0.18)	(1.53)	(0.36)	(0.29)
South Sumatra	0.001	–0.008	0.003	0.017
	(0.02)	(0.15)	(0.14)	(0.57)
Lampung	0.048	–0.003	0.011	0.014
	(1.63)	(0.08)	(0.38)	(0.42)
West Java	–0.009	0.025	–0.016	0.008
	(0.39)	(0.81)	(1.17)	(0.41)
Central Java	0.042*	0.028	0.014	–0.001
	(1.97)	(0.97)	(1.01)	(0.04)
Yogyakarta	0.027	0.017	0.009	–0.002
	(1.32)	(0.59)	(0.58)	(0.11)
East Java	0.011	0.020	–0.020	0.023
	(0.41)	(0.56)	(0.96)	(0.81)
Bali	0.019	0.003	–0.060	0.053
	(0.72)	(0.09)	(1.04)	(0.80)
West Nusa Tenggara	0.032	–0.010	–0.011	0.039
	(1.15)	(0.23)	(0.53)	(1.41)
South Kalimantan	–0.026	0.044	–0.005	0.043
	(0.54)	(0.76)	(0.19)	(1.31)
South Sulawesi	–0.032	0.018	–0.026	0.054
	(0.86)	(0.39)	(0.91)	(1.62)
Constant	–0.617	1.044*	–0.278	1.082
	(1.35)	(2.03)	(0.44)	(1.58)
F-test (p-values):				
Interaction variables	0.569		0.243	
Education variables	0.000		0.000	
Expenditure variables	0.001		0.184	
Number of observations	4,528		4,304	
R-squared	0.07		0.05	

Source: IFLS2 and IFLS3.

Dummy variable for missing parental education or parent not in household is included in the regressions but not reported in the table. The omitted category for province is Jakarta. Estimates were weighted using individual sampling weights. Standard errors are robust to clustering at the community level and to heteroscedasticity. Absolute t-statistics are in parentheses with significance at 5% (*) and 1% (**) indicated.

TABLE 6.3
School Enrolment: Linear Probability Models
Boys and Girls, 13–15 Years

	Boys		Girls	
	1997	Change in 2000	1997	Change in 2000
Age	–0.060**	–0.044*	–0.079**	0.008
	(4.67)	(2.32)	(5.82)	(0.39)
Mother's education if in hh (years × 10^{-1})	0.158**	–0.050	0.182**	–0.026
	(3.74)	(0.90)	(4.55)	(0.45)
Father's education if in hh (years × 10^{-1})	0.118**	0.025	0.097**	0.030
	(3.55)	(0.52)	(2.80)	(0.57)
log *pce* (spline): 0 – log Rp 150,000	0.151**	0.042	0.244**	–0.098
	(2.88)	(0.48)	(4.91)	(1.38)
> log Rp 150,000	–0.001	0.010	0.010	–0.024
	(0.03)	(0.29)	(0.50)	(0.68)
Rural	–0.117**	0.056	–0.076**	0.002
	(4.26)	(1.44)	(2.77)	(0.04)
North Sumatra	0.061	0.023	0.129**	0.069
	(1.13)	(0.28)	(2.93)	(0.99)
West Sumatra	0.129	–0.062	0.113*	0.018
	(2.43)*	(0.71)	(2.25)	(0.24)
South Sumatra	0.030	–0.069	–0.052	0.092
	(0.50)	(0.65)	(0.74)	(0.90)
Lampung	0.185**	–0.077	0.078	0.060
	(3.36)	(0.81)	(1.08)	(0.63)
West Java	–0.045	0.051	–0.071	0.063
	(1.06)	(0.72)	(1.59)	(0.88)
Central Java	0.017	0.026	0.108*	–0.016
	(0.31)	(0.32)	(2.41)	(0.23)
Yogyakarta	0.151**	–0.043	0.195**	0.056
	(3.82)	(0.64)	(4.19)	(0.82)
East Java	0.049	0.036	0.085*	0.027
	(1.10)	(0.47)	(1.96)	(0.38)
Bali	0.085	0.010	0.068	–0.061
	(1.50)	(0.11)	(1.09)	(0.61)
West Nusa Tenggara	–0.057	0.092	0.051	0.046
	(0.83)	(0.94)	(0.79)	(0.51)
South Kalimantan	–0.027	–0.138	0.097	–0.104
	(0.44)	(1.18)	(1.29)	(0.85)
South Sulawesi	–0.065	0.006	0.012	0.003
	(1.20)	(0.06)	(0.16)	(0.02)
Constant	–0.193	0.071	–1.079	1.001
	(0.29)	(0.07)	(1.74)	(1.16)
F-test (p-values):				
Interaction variables	0.092		0.672	
Education variables	0.000		0.000	
Expenditure variables	0.001		0.000	
Number of observations	2447		2459	
R-squared	0.18		0.19	

Source: IFLS2 and IFLS3.
Dummy variable for missing parental education or parent not in household is included in the regressions but not reported in the table. The omitted category for province is Jakarta. Estimates were weighted using individual sampling weights. Standard errors are robust to clustering at the community level and to heteroscedasticity. Absolute t-statistics are in parentheses with significance at 5% (*) and 1% (**) indicated.

TABLE 6.4
School Enrolment: Linear Probability Models
Boys and Girls, 16–18 Years

	Boys		Girls	
	1997	Change in 2000	1997	Change in 2000
Age	–0.099**	–0.001	–0.079**	–0.036
	(5.34)	(0.06)	(5.03)	(1.56)
Mother's education if in hh (years × 10^{-1})	0.269**	–0.074	0.271**	–0.006
	(4.90)	(0.96)	(4.95)	(0.08)
Father's education if in hh (years × 10^{-1})	0.141**	0.058	0.187**	–0.001
	(2.72)	(0.80)	(3.32)	(0.02)
log *pce* (spline): 0 – log Rp 150,000	–0.004	0.206	0.206**	–0.231*
	(0.04)	(1.92)	(3.36)	(2.07)
> log Rp 150,000	0.100**	–0.038	0.001	0.036
	(4.08)	(1.03)	(0.05)	(0.97)
Rural	0.117**	–0.061	–0.171**	0.034
	(2.70)	(1.15)	(5.30)	(0.72)
North Sumatra	0.049	0.124	0.160*	0.135
	(0.79)	(1.22)	(2.34)	(1.39)
West Sumatra	0.185*	0.050	0.275**	0.020
	(2.10)	(0.41)	(3.00)	(0.17)
South Sumatra	0.107	–0.017	0.076	–0.078
	(1.27)	(0.15)	(0.87)	(0.72)
Lampung	0.116	0.004	0.068	0.104
	(1.55)	(0.03)	(0.92)	(0.97)
West Java	0.005	0.066	–0.013	0.039
	(0.07)	(0.71)	(0.22)	(0.46)
Central Java	–0.022	0.141	0.096	0.032
	(0.32)	(1.44)	(1.41)	(0.38)
Yogyakarta	0.224**	0.139	0.336**	–0.082
	(3.31)	(1.37)	(4.64)	(0.83)
East Java	0.051	0.136	0.042	0.103
	(0.69)	(1.32)	(0.68)	(1.27)
Bali	0.076	0.132	0.145	–0.001
	(0.65)	(0.87)	(1.48)	(0.01)
West Nusa Tenggara	0.045	0.108	0.079	0.072
	(0.56)	(0.95)	(0.86)	(0.64)
South Kalimantan	–0.058	0.161	–0.009	0.045
	(0.70)	(1.38)	(0.11)	(0.42)
South Sulawesi	0.117	–0.073	0.021	–0.035
	(1.04)	(0.54)	(0.26)	(0.34)
Constant	2.064	–2.475	–0.705	3.243*
	(1.96)	(1.93)	(0.92)	(2.55)
F-test (p-values):				
Interaction variables	0.509		0.280	
Education variables	0.000		0.000	
Expenditure variables	0.000		0.009	
Number of observations	2438		2642	
R-squared	0.20		0.25	

Source: IFLS2 and IFLS3.
Dummy variable for missing parental education or parent not in household is included in the regressions but not reported in the table. The omitted category for province is Jakarta. Estimates were weighted using individual sampling weights. Standard errors are robust to clustering at the community level and to heteroscedasticity. Absolute t-statistics are in parentheses with significance at 5% (*) and 1% (**) indicated.

from the opportunity costs being higher for attending junior secondary school, or the fees being higher, or both. Mother's and father's education are significantly associated with higher enrolment in both years for boys and girls, controlling for *pce*. Their estimated impacts are also higher for junior secondary than for primary school. Rural boys and girls are less likely to be enrolled in both years than urban children 13–15. Among the set of province indicators, West Sumatra and Yogyakarta are associated with higher enrolment in both years for boys and girls. Lampung is associated with higher enrolment for boys, whereas North Sumatra, Central Java and East Java are associated with higher enrolment for girls in both years.

For children 16–18 (Table 6.4), we find that increasing *pce* for low income households is associated with higher enrolment for girls in 1997, but by 2000 this relationship is gone. For boys, *pce* for higher income households is associated with higher enrolment in both years. On the other hand, *pce* below Rp 150,000 was not associated with higher enrolment of boys in 1997 but is associated with higher enrolment in 2000. Again, as was the case for children 13–15, parental education is associated with higher enrolment in both years for boys and girls 16–18, with mother's education having a larger effect on both boys and girls than father's schooling. The magnitudes of the parental schooling co-efficients are higher for senior secondary than junior secondary or primary school, probably for reasons alluded to earlier. Rural residents have lower enrolment probabilities. Age is again negatively associated with enrolment rates across both genders and years. Children in West Sumatra and Yogyakarta have higher enrolment rates than children in Jakarta. Girls 16–18 in North Sumatra also had higher rates of enrolment in both years.

While we might not observe significant changes in enrolment rates (with the exception of increases for the youngest children from poor households), other characteristics of school are of interest. Table 6.5 presents results on hours in school in the last week among those enrolled for 2000 by gender and by residence and wealth (hours in school is not available for 1997). The average number of hours in school is practically identical across all sub-groups, about 24.

In addition to collecting information on enrolment, the education module also collects information on school expenditure for the current month and the previous school year. In Table 6.6 we review the expenditure in the previous school year for both IFLS rounds. The nine education expenditure categories are collapsed into four categories representing school fees, supplies, transport and miscellaneous, and other expenses.

TABLE 6.5
Hours in School Last Week, Among Those Currently in School

	Boys	Girls
Residence		
– Urban	25.5	24.7
	(0.53)	(0.53)
– Rural	23.7	24.2
	(0.52)	(0.60)
pce		
– Poor	23.6	23.3
	(0.59)	(0.65)
– Non-poor	24.6	24.7
	(0.42)	(0.44)
Number of observations	3,626	3,509

Source: IFLS3.
Sample includes primary and secondary students aged 5–19; excludes students in post-secondary school. Estimates were weighted using individual sampling weights. Standard errors (in parentheses) are robust to clustering at the community level

All amounts have been converted to real values (December 2000). In general, real education expenditures for urban students are higher than for rural students, particularly for fees and transport/misc. For supplies, the differences between urban and rural students are considerably smaller. Comparing changes across years, we find that real expenditures on fees and supplies declined significantly for both urban and rural students. However, this decrease in expenditure is partially offset by an increase in expenditure for transport and other miscellaneous items. Thus, although total expenditures for both urban and rural children do decrease, the decline is not statistically significant.

Table 6.7 presents results for the correlates of school expenditure for students 15–19. Using *pce* as a proxy for income, the first two columns in Table 6.7 present the income elasticity of education expenditure with no additional co-variates. In the second pair of columns, we include indicators of residence. In 1997, without controlling for location, the income elasticity of school expenditure was 0.41; and slightly higher in 2000. (For comparison, Pradhan 2001 finds an income elasticity of 0.50 for expenditure from July–December 1997 using 1998 SUSENAS data.) With controls for

TABLE 6.6
School Expenditures in Rupiah by Category, Students 15–19 Years

	Urban			Rural		
	1996/1997 School Year	1999/2000 School Year	Change	1996/1997 School Year	1999/2000 School Year	Change
Fees (school registration fee, other scheduled fee, and exam fee)	505,901	439,152	–66,749	328,233	266,912	–61,321*
	(24,042)	(28,160)	(37,027)	(15,785)	(19,40)	(24,810)
	[344,922]	[299,786]	[-45,136]	[173,086]	[229,596]	[56,510]
Supplies (books, writing supplies, uniforms, and sports)	179,439	152,262	–27,177**	195,894	149,028	–46,866**
	(6,433)	(5,993)	(8,792)	(9,922)	(6,554)	(11,891)
	[133,258]	[109,516]	[–23,742]	[107,523]	[132,635]	[25,112]
Transport/Misc. (transportation, housing and food, and special courses)	710,981	777,681	66,701	553,268	553,263	–4
	(32,863)	(33,136)	(46,669)	(52,910)	(25,214)	(58,611)
	[492,554]	[594,582]	[102,028]	[430,093]	[338,767]	[–91,326]
Other	5,185	10,688	5,503	2,763	10,967	8,205*
	(1,452)	(2,290)	(2,711)	(1,238)	(3,411)	(3,629)
	[0]	[0]	[0]	[0]	[0]	[0]
Number of observations	1,055	1,111		784	760	

Source: IFLS2 and IFLS3.

Excludes students in post-secondary school. Values are in real Rupiah set to December 2000. Medians are in brackets. Standard errors are in parentheses. Significance at 5% (*) and 1% (**) indicated.

TABLE 6.7
School Expenditure Models, Students 15–19 Years

	1997	Change in 2000	1997	Change in 2000
log *pce*	0.409**	0.023	0.355**	0.025
	(10.14)	(0.42)	(10.14)	(0.52)
Rural			–0.183**	–0.041
			(3.57)	(0.57)
North Sumatra			–0.289**	–0.024
			(3.10)	(0.19)
West Sumatra			–0.343*	0.234
			(2.85)	(1.61)
South Sumatra			–0.633**	0.309*
			(5.42)	(2.03)
Lampung			–0.755**	0.236
			(6.06)	(1.25)
West Java			–0.018	–0.045
			(0.23)	(0.44)
Central Java			–0.125	–0.001
			(1.44)	(0.07)
Yogyakarta			–0.138	–0.094
			(1.32)	(0.67)
East Java			–0.187*	–0.051
			(2.22)	(0.44)
Bali			–0.307**	0.245*
			(3.41)	(1.96)
West Nusa Tenggara			–0.493**	–0.204
			(3.74)	(1.33)
South Kalimantan			–0.792**	0.308
			(7.04)	(1.84)
South Sulawesi			–0.417**	–0.190
			(3.51)	(1.25)
Constant	8.650**	–0.269	9.637**	–0.307
	(17.05)	(0.39)	(21.68)	(0.49)
F-test (p-values):				
Interaction variables	0.8072		0.0222	
Observations	3,697		3,697	
R-squared	0.13		0.22	

Source: IFLS2 and IFLS3.
There are 13 observations with total expenditure of zero, these are excluded from the regressions. Dummy variable for missing parental education or parent not in household is included in the regressions but not reported in the table. The omitted category for province is Jakarta. Estimates were weighted using individual sampling weights. Standard errors are robust to clustering at the community level and to heteroscedasticity. Absolute t-statistics are in parentheses with significance at 5% (*) and 1% (**) indicated.

residence, the elasticity falls to 0.36 in 1997 (again, slightly higher in 2000), but remains significant in both years. Rural students spend less than urban students. Students in all provinces except for West Java had significantly lower school expenditures compared to students in Jakarta.

Results for receipt of assistance for school expenditures in the current school years 2000/2001 are presented in Table 6.8. Keep in mind that the survey was conducted in the beginning of the 2000/2001 school year so take-up rates are likely to be higher for the school year by the end of the school year (June 2001). Any source of assistance is reported in Table 6.8 as well as assistance from a government source (which would include, but is not limited to, the JPS programme).[1] Among the youngest children, a larger share of female students received scholarships (where any type of aid is 4.3% and government aid is 3.1%) than boys (3.6% and 2.3%

TABLE 6.8
Receipt of Assistance for School Among Enrolled Students, School Year 2000/2001

	Children 7–12		Children 13–15		Children 16–18	
	Any aid	Any aid from govt	Any aid	Any aid from govt	Any aid	Any aid from govt
Gender						
– Boys	3.6	2.3	8.8	6.6	2.3	2.0
	(0.50)	(0.39)	(1.12)	(1.01)	(0.76)	(0.73)
– Girls	4.3	3.1	10.2	8.2	2.9	1.7
	(0.58)	(0.49)	(1.26)	(1.16)	(0.74)	(0.55)
pce						
– Poor	4.9	3.4	12.3	8.2	4.1	2.7
	(1.02)	(0.76)	(2.29)	(1.90)	(2.43)	(2.00)
– Non-poor	3.7	2.4	9.0	7.2	2.4	1.7
	(0.41)	(0.35)	(0.94)	(0.85)	(0.54)	(0.47)
Residence						
– Urban	4.2	2.8	6.7	3.9	2.5	1.6
	(0.58)	(0.53)	(1.05)	(0.85)	(0.65)	(0.56)
– Rural	3.7	2.5	12.0	10.4	2.7	2.1
	(0.55)	(0.42)	(1.34)	(1.26)	(0.89)	(0.79)
Number of observations	3,850		1,567		1,032	

Source: IFLS3.

Estimates were weighted using individual sampling weights. Standard errors (in parentheses) are robust to clustering at the community level.

respectively). This is also true for girls 13–15. In every year, students from poorer households had higher incidence of scholarship than students from wealthier households. Not all, but the majority of assistance is from government sources. Children 13–15 had the highest incidence of assistance. About one-tenth of students in junior secondary were receiving some assistance. Nine percent of boys 13–15 and 10% of girls 13–15 were receiving assistance from any source. Assistance rates are lowest among senior secondary students, where less than 3% report getting any assistance in the 2000/2001 school year.

SCHOOL QUALITY AND FEES

Complementary to examining patterns of school enrolment and fees by individuals from the household survey, it is also possible to examine the characteristics of schools from the education facility survey.[2] Although we observe little changes in enrolment rates and the sample was re-drawn in both years based on the reports of schools in the household survey, it is nevertheless possible that the quality and other characteristics of school services has changed from 1997 to 2000.

The sample of schools in the IFLS2 and IFLS3 can be divided by public/private across three levels (Appendix Table 2.3). The proportion of private schools sampled in each level is constant in both years for all levels. About 15% of sampled primary schools, 38% of junior secondary and 50% of senior secondary schools are private. The fraction of schools with a religious orientation is also fairly constant across both years (Table 6.9). Among the public schools, less than 5% of primary schools, and 10% of junior and senior secondary schools have a religious orientation (almost all of which are Islamic). Among private schools, the fraction with a religious orientation falls by level: 87% private primary schools, 67% private junior secondary and about half of private senior secondary schools have a religious orientation. The majority of private schools with a religious orientation are Islamic. Christian private schools are the second largest category of religion. Few are Hindu or Buddhist.

Table 6.10 displays the number of students enrolled per grade (not class) for primary schools. Public primary schools had an average enrolment of 32–40 students per grade. Private primary schools in the IFLS sample are larger with a higher number of students enrolled at each grade, around 49–57. With the exception of Grade 2 in public schools, there are no significant changes in the number of students enrolled at either public or private primary schools. These numbers are consistent with the findings in

TABLE 6.9
Religious Orientation of Schools
(In percent)

	Primary School						Junior Secondary School						Senior Secondary School					
	Public			Private			Public			Private			Public			Private		
	1997	2000	Change	1997	2000	Change	1997	2000	Change	1997	2000	Change	1997	2000	Change	1997	2000	Change
No religious orientation	96.5	98.5	2.0 *	13.2	13.7	0.5	88.3	87.5	–0.8	34.3	32.5	–1.8	88.8	92.2	3.3	48.9	55.9	7.0
	(0.66)	(0.41)	(0.78)	(3.50)	(3.18)	(4.73)	(1.24)	(1.25)	(1.76)	(2.58)	(2.58)	(3.65)	(1.85)	(1.53)	(2.40)	(3.04)	(2.86)	(4.17)
Religious orientation:																		
– Islam	3.5	1.5	–2.0 *	58.1	66.4	8.3	11.7	12.3	0.7	55.2	53.8	–1.5	11.2	7.8	–3.3	41.9	35.2	–6.7
	(0.66)	(0.41)	(0.78)	(5.05)	(4.39)	(6.69)	(1.24)	(1.24)	(1.75)	(2.75)	(2.96)	(4.04)	(1.85)	(1.53)	(2.40)	(2.93)	(2.93)	(4.15)
– Catholic	0.0	0.0	0.0	18.6	13.0	–5.6	0.0	0.0	0.0	4.7	8.1	3.4	0.0	0.0	0.0	4.2	3.1	–1.1
	–	–	–	(3.87)	(3.15)	(4.98)	–	–	–	(1.09)	(1.56)	(1.90)	–	–	–	(1.12)	(0.95)	(1.47)
– Protestant	0.0	0.0	0.0	7.0	5.5	–1.5	0.0	0.2	0.2	4.7	5.3	0.6	0.0	0.0	0.0	4.2	5.6	1.4
	–	–	–	(2.23)	(1.85)	(2.89)	–	(0.17)	(0.17)	(1.21)	(1.14)	(1.66)	–	–	–	(1.28)	(1.31)	(1.83)
– Budha	0.0	0.0	0.0	3.1	1.4	–1.7	0.0	0.0	0.0	0.6	0.3	–0.3	0.0	0.0	0.0	0.6	0.3	–0.3
	–	–	–	(1.51)	(0.97)	(1.80)	–	–	–	(0.39)	(0.28)	(0.48)	–	–	–	(0.45)	(0.31)	(0.55)
– Hindu	0.0	0.0	0.0	0.0	0.0	0.0	0.0	0.0	0.0	0.6	0.0	–0.6	0.0	0.0	0.0	0.3	0.0	–0.3
	–	–	–	–	–	–	–	–	–	(0.39)	–	(0.39)	–	–	–	(0.32)	–	(0.32)
Number of observations	834	815		129	146		583	592		362	357		304	293		313	324	

Source: IFLS2 and IFLS3.

Standard errors (in parentheses) are robust to clustering at the community level. Significance at 5% (*) and 1% (**) indicated.

TABLE 6.10
Enrolment Rates and Student/Teacher Ratio: Primary Schools

	Public			Private		
	1997	**2000**	**Change**	**1997**	**2000**	**Change**
Enrolment Rates						
– Grade 1	37.6	39.8	2.3	56.3	53.5	–2.8
	(1.05)	(1.11)	(1.53)	(4.57)	(4.91)	(6.71)
– Grade 2	35.8	39.0	3.2 *	52.7	50.0	–2.7
	(0.98)	(1.12)	(1.49)	(4.24)	(4.63)	(6.28)
– Grade 3	34.8	36.7	1.9	51.7	51.5	–0.1
	(0.91)	(1.03)	(1.37)	(4.26)	(4.74)	(6.38)
– Grade 4	34.4	35.5	1.2	52.2	49.6	–2.6
	(0.89)	(0.97)	(1.32)	(4.30)	(4.54)	(6.25)
– Grade 5	33.9	34.0	0.2	50.7	48.9	–1.8
	(0.87)	(0.91)	(1.26)	(4.01)	(4.88)	(6.32)
– Grade 6	32.4	32.6	0.2	49.8	48.8	–1.0
	(0.87)	(0.82)	(1.19)	(4.04)	(5.00)	(6.43)
Number of observations	831	815		129	146	
Student/Teacher Ratio						
– Grade 1	18.1	17.7	–0.3	23.3	21.1	–2.2
	(0.72)	(0.66)	(0.98)	(1.97)	(1.30)	(2.36)
– Grade 2	16.9	17.3	0.3	20.5	19.4	–1.1
	(0.64)	(0.67)	(0.93)	(1.50)	(1.27)	(1.97)
– Grade 3	15.8	15.9	0.1	17.5	17.4	–0.2
	(0.56)	(0.61)	(0.83)	(1.24)	(1.07)	(1.64)
– Grade 4	15.0	14.6	–0.4	15.4	15.3	0.0
	(0.51)	(0.54)	(0.75)	(1.16)	(1.17)	(1.64)
– Grade 5	14.6	13.7	–0.9	14.1	14.6	0.5
	(0.48)	(0.48)	(0.68)	(1.11)	(1.10)	(1.56)
– Grade 6	14.1	13.1	–1.0	13.5	14.4	0.8
	(0.50)	(0.45)	(0.67)	(1.07)	(1.09)	(1.53)
Number of observations	799	814		119	146	

Source: IFLS2 and IFLS3.

Enrolment rates refer to the number of students per school enrolled in a particular grade. Standard errors (in parentheses) are robust to clustering at the community level. Significance at 5% (*) and 1% (**) indicated.

Filmer and Suwaryani (2001). Student–teacher ratios at the primary level grades are similar in public and private schools. This is consistent with the larger overall enrolment at private primary schools because private primary schools reported having more classes (2–3) than public primary schools (on average 1). Student–teacher ratios did not change significantly across years for any grade at the primary level.

Table 6.11 shows the number of students enrolled per grade at junior secondary schools. Schools sizes are considerable larger among secondary schools than primary schools. Moreover, unlike the pattern in primary schools, public schools have significantly more students at each grade than private schools. Public junior secondary school schools reported about 225–250 student per grade, while private secondary schools just had about 100–125 students per grade. There is no significant change in enrolment

TABLE 6.11
Enrolment Rates and Student/Teacher Ratio: Junior Secondary Schools

	Public			Private		
	1997	**2000**	**Change**	**1997**	**2000**	**Change**
Enrolment Rates						
– Grade 7	251.3	245.6	–5.8	101.1	109.0	7.9
	(7.31)	(5.72)	(9.28)	(4.67)	(5.81)	(7.45)
– Grade 8	234.8	235.9	1.1	125.8	102.5	–23.3
	(6.41)	(5.76)	(8.62)	(24.42)	(5.51)	(25.03)
– Grade 9	226.3	228.2	1.9	100.0	96.7	–3.3
	(6.55)	(5.87)	(8.79)	(4.65)	(4.87)	(6.74)
Number of observations	582	590		359	355	
Student/Teacher Ratio						
– Grade 7	14.4	14.6	0.2	7.0	8.4	1.3 **
	(0.40)	(0.37)	(0.55)	(0.28)	(0.42)	(0.51)
– Grade 8	13.3	14.0	0.7	8.8	8.0	–0.8
	(0.33)	(0.38)	(0.50)	(1.83)	(0.44)	(1.89)
– Grade 9	12.9	13.6	0.7	6.8	7.5	0.7
	(0.34)	(0.35)	(0.49)	(0.27)	(0.39)	(0.47)
Number of observations	564	586		340	355	

Source: IFLS2 and IFLS3.
Enrolment rates refer to the number of students per school enrolled in a particular grade. Standard errors (in parentheses) are robust to clustering at the community level. Significance at 5% (*) and 1% (**) indicated.

for any of the grades. Student–teacher ratios at public junior secondary schools are about double the ratio in private schools. With the exception of Grade 7 in private junior secondary schools, these ratios did not change significantly across the years.

Enrolment figures for senior secondary schools are reported in Table 6.12. As we observe for junior secondary, we find that enrolment levels are significantly higher at public than private schools. Although there are no changes from 1997 to 2000 in enrolment, we observe a significant increase in the number of students enrolled in Grade 12 for both public and private senior secondary schools. Likewise, student–teacher ratios are much higher in public senior secondary schools than private ones. Also, the enrolment increases in Grade 12 appear to spillover into significant increases in student–teacher ratios for both public and private schools.

TABLE 6.12
Enrolment Rates and Student/Teacher Ratio: Senior Secondary Schools

	Public			Private		
	1997	**2000**	**Change**	**1997**	**2000**	**Change**
Enrolment Rates						
– Grade 10	251.3	253.5	2.3	176.8	189.4	12.6
	(6.84)	(6.24)	(9.26)	(9.78)	(9.32)	(13.51)
– Grade 11	229.2	236.8	7.7	158.4	170.5	12.1
	(6.60)	(6.25)	(9.09)	(8.76)	(8.00)	(11.86)
– Grade 12	213.0	241.9	29.0 **	137.8	170.4	32.7 **
	(6.61)	(6.94)	(9.58)	(8.05)	(8.14)	(11.45)
Number of observations	303	291		310	323	
Student/Teacher Ratio						
– Grade 10	12.7	13.3	0.6	9.6	10.9	1.3
	(0.33)	(0.47)	(0.57)	(0.49)	(0.49)	(0.70)
– Grade 11	11.3	12.3	1.0	8.3	10.0	1.7 **
	(0.32)	(0.42)	(0.52)	(0.40)	(0.47)	(0.62)
– Grade 12	10.8	12.7	1.9 **	7.6	10.1	2.6 **
	(0.35)	(0.44)	(0.56)	(0.40)	(0.46)	(0.61)
Number of observations	292	288		292	322	

Source: IFLS2 and IFLS3.
Enrolment rates refer to the number of students per school enrolled in a particular grade. Standard errors (in parentheses) are robust to clustering at the community level. Significance at 5% (*) and 1% (**) indicated.

IFLS interviews one mathematics teacher and one teacher of Bahasa Indonesia per school. Table 6.13 shows background characteristics of the mathematics teachers.[3] Average years of schooling rises with level of school. Teachers in private primary and junior secondary schools are more likely to have completed senior secondary school than public school teachers, a difference that disappears for senior secondary school teachers. Interestingly, between 1997 and 2000 there was a sharp increase in the proportion of primary school teachers in public schools, who had completed senior secondary school; private school primary teachers also had an increase in this proportion, but smaller and not statistically significant. Teaching experience is higher for primary school teachers than junior or senior secondary school teachers. Experience tends to be higher among public school teachers compared to private schools.

A large fraction of teachers have second jobs, the fraction rising with level of school. Among public school primary teachers between 15–20% have second jobs, but for public senior secondary school teachers, this proportion is 30%. In private schools, it is even more likely that teachers have second jobs, as high as 67% among teachers in senior secondary schools. This is reflected in the hours that teachers spend in school. Among primary school teachers, average hours are over 30 hours per week, but as low as 20–25 hours for teachers in senior secondary schools. Presumably one reason for such a high prevalence of second jobs is the wage scale, but there may be other reasons as well.

In Table 6.14 we report some measures of physical infrastructure of schools: whether the school has electricity and whether there are water leakage or flooding problems during the rainy season. Higher level schools are more likely to have electricity. Private primary schools are considerably more likely to be electrified, while the reverse is true for junior secondary schools. Electrification rates are about equal between private and public schools at the senior secondary level. Water leakage during rainy season is a considerable problem among public primary schools, less so among private schools. The public–private differences are much smaller for junior and senior secondary schools.

Tables 6.15–6.17 report the prevalence of charges at each school level for various items. The charge categories are divided into three groups: charges for new students, charges for continuing students and charges for all students. The EBTANAS fee includes the EBTA fee. If fees reflect in part school quality, then we would expect private schools to be more likely to charge fees than public schools, given the quality differences we find.

TABLE 6.13
Teacher Characteristics: Mathematics

	Primary School						Junior Secondary School						Senior Secondary School					
	Public			Private			Public			Private			Public			Private		
	1997	2000	Change	1997	2000	Change	1997	2000	Change	1997	2000	Change	1997	2000	Change	1997	2000	Change
Education	13.7	14.5	0.7 **	13.8	14.4	0.5 *	14.9	15.4	0.5 **	14.8	15.2	0.4 **	15.7	15.8	0.1 **	15.6	15.8	0.2 **
(years)	(0.07)	(0.05)	(0.09)	(0.16)	(0.16)	(0.22)	(0.04)	(0.03)	(0.05)	(0.08)	(0.06)	(0.10)	(0.03)	(0.02)	(0.04)	(0.04)	(0.04)	(0.06)
– 7–12 years	42.2	20.0	–22.2 **	34.9	24.4	–10.4	1.9	0.5	–1.4 *	10.2	6.8	–3.4	0.4	0.0	–0.4	0.8	1.0	0.2
(percentage)	(2.12)	(1.55)	(2.63)	(4.42)	(4.16)	(6.07)	(0.59)	(0.30)	(0.66)	(1.95)	(1.42)	(2.41)	(0.39)	–	(0.39)	(0.56)	(0.57)	(0.80)
– 12+ years	57.8	80.0	22.2 **	65.1	75.6	10.4	98.1	99.5	1.4 *	89.8	93.2	3.4	99.6	100.0	0.4	99.2	99.0	–0.2
(percentage)	(2.12)	(1.55)	(2.63)	(4.42)	(4.16)	(6.07)	(0.59)	(0.30)	(0.66)	(1.95)	(1.42)	(2.41)	(0.39)	–	(0.39)	(0.56)	(0.57)	(0.80)
Teaching experience	17.1	18.3	1.2 **	15.4	16.1	0.8	13.6	14.5	0.9 *	11.0	12.5	1.5 *	11.6	13.6	2.0 **	10.2	10.9	0.7
(years)	(0.30)	(0.28)	(0.41)	(0.97)	(0.97)	(1.37)	(0.32)	(0.34)	(0.47)	(0.45)	(0.48)	(0.65)	(0.51)	(0.50)	(0.71)	(0.51)	(0.44)	(0.67)
Hours/week	32.8	34.1	1.3 **	30.1	30.3	0.2	22.6	24.2	1.6 **	21.0	21.8	0.8	22.7	24.4	1.7 *	20.8	21.3	0.4
	(0.42)	(0.29)	(0.51)	(1.19)	(1.05)	(1.58)	(0.33)	(0.42)	(0.53)	(0.61)	(0.58)	(0.84)	(0.46)	(0.57)	(0.73)	(0.73)	(0.63)	(0.97)
Having second	19.4	15.9	–3.5	32.1	35.1	3.0	28.0	25.4	–2.6	54.5	55.7	1.2	30.9	30.4	–0.5	59.8	67.7	7.9
job (percentage)	(1.71)	(1.40)	(2.21)	(4.39)	(4.44)	(6.24)	(2.14)	(1.83)	(2.82)	(3.25)	(2.98)	(4.41)	(2.88)	(2.86)	(4.05)	(3.15)	(2.72)	(4.16)
Hours/week on second job	17.0	17.0	0.0	16.9	22.3	5.5	14.4	16.3	2.0	19.4	20.6	1.3	13.0	15.8	2.9	18.5	21.8	3.4 **
(if any)	(0.88)	(1.23)	(1.51)	(2.29)	(1.96)	(3.01)	(0.85)	(0.95)	(1.27)	(0.74)	(0.78)	(1.07)	(0.95)	(1.33)	(1.64)	(0.74)	(0.74)	(1.05)
Number of observations	716	784		109	131		522	579		303	336		259	276		251	300	

Source: IFLS2 and IFLS3.
Standard errors (in parentheses) are robust to clustering at the community level. Significance at 5% (*) and 1% (**) indicated.

TABLE 6.14
Classroom Infrastructure
(Percent of schools)

	Primary School						Junior Secondary School						Senior Secondary School					
	Public			Private			Public			Private			Public			Private		
	1997	2000	Change	1997	2000	Change	1997	2000	Change	1997	2000	Change	1997	2000	Change	1997	2000	Change
Has electricity	60.1	65.8	5.7	82.2	83.6	1.4	85.2	88.9	3.6	77.1	81.0	3.9	87.2	91.1	4.0	89.5	90.1	0.7
	(2.44)	(2.26)	(3.33)	(3.58)	(3.04)	(4.70)	(1.64)	(1.45)	(2.19)	(2.56)	(2.26)	(3.41)	(1.96)	(1.71)	(2.60)	(1.87)	(1.87)	(2.65)
Rainy season problem: leakage	32.3	30.1	–2.2	17.8	17.8	0.0	15.1	14.4	–0.7	19.9	15.7	–4.2	11.2	8.2	–3.0	15.7	8.0	–7.6 **
	(1.82)	(1.86)	(2.60)	(3.61)	(3.17)	(4.80)	(1.60)	(1.61)	(2.28)	(2.32)	(2.10)	(3.13)	(1.82)	(1.54)	(2.39)	(2.05)	(1.59)	(2.59)
Rainy season problem: flooding	5.4	5.3	–0.1	3.9	2.7	–1.1	5.5	3.0	–2.4 *	4.4	3.6	–0.8	4.6	1.4	–3.2 *	2.6	2.8	0.2
	(0.87)	(0.86)	(1.22)	(1.72)	(1.35)	(2.19)	(0.99)	(0.73)	(1.23)	(1.13)	(0.97)	(1.49)	(1.35)	(0.67)	(1.50)	(0.88)	(0.90)	(1.26)
Rainy season problem: flash rain	28.3	25.3	–3.0	20.2	21.2	1.1	13.4	11.1	–2.2	19.1	17.4	–1.7	9.9	7.8	–2.0	15.7	12.7	–3.0
	(1.82)	(1.71)	(2.49)	(3.44)	(3.58)	(4.97)	(1.58)	(1.32)	(2.06)	(2.27)	(2.13)	(3.11)	(1.71)	(1.75)	(2.45)	(2.15)	(1.78)	(2.79)
Number of observations	834	815		129	146		583	592		362	357		304	293		313	324	

Source: IFLS2 and IFLS3.
Standard errors (in parentheses) are robust to clustering at the community level. Significance at 5% (*) and 1% (**) indicated.

TABLE 6.15
Primary School Charges
(Percent of schools charging)

	Public			Private		
	1997	**2000**	**Change**	**1997**	**2000**	**Change**
New students						
– registration	50.6	19.4	–31.1 **	86.4	76.4	–10.1 *
	(2.41)	(1.83)	(3.02)	(3.02)	(3.77)	(4.83)
– payment (SPP,	94.9	91.6	–3.4 *	99.2	97.2	–1.9
POMG/BP3, OSIS)	(0.90)	(1.35)	(1.63)	(0.84)	(1.37)	(1.61)
– evaluation/testing fees	52.3	38.4	–14.0 **	71.2	60.4	-10.8
	(2.36)	(2.31)	(3.30)	(4.92)	(4.74)	(6.83)
Continuing students						
– registration	1.6	1.5	–0.2	22.9	20.8	–2.0
	(0.48)	(0.42)	(0.64)	(3.90)	(3.86)	(5.49)
– payment (SPP,	93.2	90.5	–2.7	98.3	96.5	–1.8
POMG/BP3, OSIS)	(1.08)	(1.41)	(1.78)	(1.18)	(1.54)	(1.94)
– evaluation/testing fees	62.7	39.0	–23.7 **	79.7	60.4	–19.2 **
	(2.31)	(2.27)	(3.24)	(3.92)	(4.78)	(6.18)
All students						
– EBTANAS fees	41.0	38.1	–2.8	80.5	83.3	2.8
	(2.26)	(2.25)	(3.19)	(3.90)	(3.47)	(5.22)
– extracurricular activities	15.4	9.8	–5.6 **	31.4	18.1	–13.3 *
fees	(1.51)	(1.21)	(1.93)	(4.60)	(3.08)	(5.53)
Number of observations	791	808		118	144	

Source: IFLS2 and IFLS3.
Standard errors (in parentheses) are robust to clustering at the community level. Significance at 5% (*) and 1% (**) indicated.

TABLE 6.16
Junior Secondary School Charges
(Percent of schools charging)

	Public			Private		
	1997	**2000**	**Change**	**1997**	**2000**	**Change**
New students						
– registration	85.1	68.4	–16.7 **	93.5	86.2	–7.3 **
	(1.95)	(2.31)	(3.02)	(1.35)	(2.00)	(2.41)
– payment (SPP,	98.0	98.8	0.8	98.8	97.4	–1.4
POMG/BP3, OSIS)	(0.59)	(0.56)	(0.81)	(0.58)	(0.85)	(1.03)
– evaluation/testing fees	22.8	20.4	–2.4	85.6	70.4	–15.2 **
	(1.93)	(1.95)	(2.74)	(2.14)	(2.45)	(3.25)
Continuing students						
– registration	7.6	9.7	2.1	27.3	22.7	–4.6
	(1.17)	(1.36)	(1.79)	(2.67)	(2.32)	(3.53)
– payment (SPP,	95.7	97.6	1.9	99.1	97.7	–1.4
POMG/BP3, OSIS)	(0.84)	(0.70)	(1.09)	(0.50)	(0.80)	(0.95)
– evaluation/testing fees	28.6	20.1	–8.5 **	87.1	69.8	–17.3 **
	(2.17)	(1.91)	(2.89)	(1.94)	(2.56)	(3.21)
All students						
– EBTANAS fees	23.7	31.1	7.4 *	89.7	89.9	0.2
	(2.09)	(2.34)	(3.14)	(1.78)	(1.71)	(2.47)
– extracurricular activities	18.5	14.6	–3.9	21.1	16.7	–4.4
fees	(1.71)	(1.50)	(2.28)	(2.18)	(2.12)	(3.04)
Number of observations	556	588		341	348	

Source: IFLS2 and IFLS3.
Standard errors (in parentheses) are robust to clustering at the community level. Significance at 5% (*) and 1% (**) indicated.

TABLE 6.17
Senior Secondary School Charges
(Percent of schools charging)

	Public			Private		
	1997	**2000**	**Change**	**1997**	**2000**	**Change**
New students						
– registration	91.6	71.2	–20.4 **	96.6	92.1	–4.5 *
	(1.78)	(2.91)	(3.41)	(1.06)	(1.59)	(1.91)
– payment (SPP, POMG/BP3, OSIS)	98.9	99.0	0.0	98.3	97.8	–0.5
	(0.60)	(0.59)	(0.84)	(0.75)	(0.82)	(1.11)
– evaluation/testing fees	13.7	10.8	–2.9	76.1	69.4	–6.7
	(2.09)	(2.13)	(2.99)	(2.62)	(2.77)	(3.81)
Continuing students						
– registration	8.1	10.4	2.3	28.0	27.1	–0.9
	(1.58)	(1.88)	(2.45)	(2.67)	(2.60)	(3.73)
– payment (SPP, POMG/BP3, OSIS)	98.2	97.6	–0.7	96.9	97.8	0.9
	(0.77)	(1.03)	(1.28)	(1.00)	(0.82)	(1.30)
– evaluation/testing fees	22.1	10.8	–11.3 **	81.2	71.0	–10.3 **
	(2.58)	(2.14)	(3.35)	(2.42)	(2.78)	(3.68)
All students						
– EBTANAS fees	17.9	23.3	5.4	86.7	89.0	2.3
	(2.35)	(2.74)	(3.61)	(2.03)	(1.86)	(2.76)
– extracurricular activities fees	22.1	16.7	–5.4	21.8	20.8	–1.0
	(2.57)	(2.12)	(3.33)	(2.45)	(2.39)	(3.43)
Number of observations	285	288		293	317	

Source: IFLS2 and IFLS3.

Standard errors (in parentheses) are robust to clustering at the community level. Significance at 5% (*) and 1% (**) indicated.

In Table 6.15, we find that public primary schools are less likely to charge for services than private schools. Nevertheless, almost all primary schools required some sort of payment (SPP, POMG/BP3, OSIS). However, we do observe a significant decline in the percentage of public primary schools charging new students fees from 1997 to 2000. This is consistent with the government abolishing school entrance fees starting in the 1998/99 academic year. Filmer and Suwaryani 2001 made this note and also commented that enforcing this policy could be difficult since schools frequently re-name such fees. Interview comments in IFLS3 attest to this, where their notes conclude that the decline in the prevalence of the registration fees and testing has been in part due to the reassignment of these fees into the monthly fee category). In 2000 compared to 1997, fewer schools charged evaluation/testing fees to continuing students or had charges associated with extracurricular activities in both public and private primary schools.

The patterns of charges among junior and senior secondary schools is largely similar (Tables 6.16 and 6.17). Overall, secondary schools are much more likely to charge various fees than primary schools; of course real costs of providing schooling are much higher for secondary than for primary schools. Private secondary schools are more likely to charge for services than public schools. As in the case of primary schools, we observe a significant decline in the prevalence of registration fees for new students in public and private secondary schools. The decline is largest among public schools, which widens the gap in prevalence of registration fees between private and public schools. Likewise, we observe a decline in the percentage of schools that charge continuing students fees for evaluation and testing at both private and public secondary schools.

SUMMARY

Studies of the initial impact of the crisis showed some decrease in enrolment rates among poor children. The concern that the crisis would lead to decreases in enrolment rates after 1998 is one that is not borne out by IFLS and other data. Enrolment rates of primary school-aged children are slightly higher in 2000 than 1997, although the increase is not significant. However, this group average masks some important differences among sub-groups. For poor children 7–12 years, we do observe a significant increase in enrolment rates from 1997 to 2000, to 94%. Among junior secondary school-aged children the enrolment rates are about the same in the two years, at 76–80%, as are the rates for senior secondary-aged children, 47–50%.

Using data from IFLS school interviews, we find that there were few changes in school characteristics between 1997 and 2000. One change of note was a decline in the proportion of public schools that charge official entrance fees. Private schools are more likely to charge fees than are public schools, which is consistent with the observation that in certain dimensions of quality, such as student–teacher ratios, private schools are also better.

Notes

1 The IFLS3 records several government sources for scholarship, with a separate category for assistance from the JPS programme. Here we do not focus on the JPS programme exclusively. Note that for primary school children, the programme guidelines for JPS specify that only grades 4–6 are eligible for the scholarship although Sumarto et al. (2001) find in the SUSENAS that a significant portion of children in grades 1–3 did report receiving the scholarship, albeit slightly less than the portion of children in grades 4–6. Overall, the programme was intended to provide scholarships to (at most) 6% of primary school students, 17% among lower secondary and 10% among senior secondary. Sumarto et al. (2001) examine the incidence and income-targeting of the JPS programme based on the 1999 *SUSENAS*. This remains a topic of debate since they find that the incidence is lower than the programme targets and their calculations suggest substantial mis-targeting.

2 Other sections of this report include information on school characteristics related to decision-making (Chapter 13), and supplementary food programmes at primary schools, scholarship programmes and school budgets (Chapter 12).

3 The results for the Bahasa Indonesia teachers, many of whom also teach mathematics, are very close and so are not shown.

APPENDIX TABLE 6.1
School Type Among Children Currently Enrolled
(In percent)

	Children 7–12			Children 13–15			Children 16–18		
	1997	2000	Change	1997	2000	Change	1997	2000	Change
Boys									
– Government	87.2	87.6	0.4	72.8	71.9	–0.9	48.1	42.4	–5.7
	(1.52)	(1.36)	(2.04)	(1.94)	(2.09)	(2.86)	(2.91)	(2.72)	(3.98)
– Private, non-religious	2.7	1.4	–1.2 *	11.3	9.8	–1.4	30.3	32.2	1.9
	(0.49)	(0.32)	(0.59)	(1.26)	(1.36)	(1.85)	(2.79)	(2.81)	(3.96)
– Private, religious	10.1	11.0	0.8	16.0	18.3	2.3	21.6	25.4	3.8
	(1.48)	(1.31)	(1.97)	(1.69)	(1.84)	(2.50)	(2.38)	(2.46)	(3.42)
Number of observations	2,041	2,018		960	808		538	546	
Girls									
– Government	88.1	86.8	–1.3	70.1	66.6	–3.5	49.5	48.2	–1.3
	(1.42)	(1.36)	(1.97)	(2.16)	(2.30)	(3.15)	(2.66)	(2.62)	(3.73)
– Private, non-religious	1.4	2.0	0.6	11.9	12.3	0.5	28.7	27.6	–1.2
	(0.31)	(0.42)	(0.52)	(1.40)	(1.49)	(2.04)	(2.45)	(2.32)	(3.38)
– Private, religious	10.5	11.2	0.7	18.0	21.1	3.1	21.7	24.2	2.5
	(1.36)	(1.30)	(1.88)	(1.88)	(2.02)	(2.76)	(2.38)	(2.25)	(3.27)
Number of observations	2,007	1,878		952	802		540	563	

Source: IFLS2 and IFLS3.

Estimates were weighted using individual sampling weights. Standard errors (in parentheses) are robust to clustering at the community level. Significance at 5% (*) and 1% (**) indicated. Number of observations is in brackets.

7

Health Outcomes and Risk Factors

In this chapter we focus on health outcomes and risk factors as one key part of welfare. This has the advantage that there is no controversy about which price deflator to use, or which poverty line (although as we shall see there are health "thresholds" that we will employ in part of the analysis, and they have an arbitrariness about them just as do poverty lines). Further, it is outcomes, and not health inputs such as health care utilization, that are the final objects of concern if we want to assess individual welfare.

Health outcomes are multi-dimensional and IFLS contains a very rich array of data on many health outcomes, some physical health measures and some either self-reported or reported by a proxy household member (for adults) or a parent (for children). Self and proxy reports have known problems of systematic misreporting (see for example Strauss and Thomas 1995, for a discussion), although the biases are different for different measures and may vary in different surveys and countries. Not having systematic measurement error is an advantage of the physical health measures we report.

In this report, for children, we use data on age and sex standardized child heights and weight-for-height,[1] blood haemoglobin levels,[2] plus self- or parent-reported general health, and health as reported by one of the two nurses on the interviewing team that took the physical health measures. We stratify all tables and figures by gender and age. For the self-, parent- or nurse-assessed measures we distinguish age groups 0–59 months and 5–14 years. For height, weight-for-height and haemoglobin, it is important to stratify more finely by age. Thus for these measures we differentiate by age in months using as our groups: 3–17, 18–35, and 36–59.

For adults, defined to be 15 years or older, our health outcomes include body mass index (BMI),[3] blood haemoglobin levels, blood pressure,[4] self-reported general health and nurse-assessed general health, and self-reported activities of daily living (ADLs).[5] For persons 40 years and older we also measure waist and hip circumference. Body mass, waist circumference and blood pressure are useful indicators for risk of coronary heart diseases. We report on a third important risk factor, smoking. In most of the tables, we distinguish adolescents, 15–19 years from prime-aged adults 20–59, from the elderly, defined as 60 years or older.

For standardized child heights and weights for height, we report z-scores, using the World Health Organization (WHO) and the U.S. Centers for Disease Control (CDC) standard.[6] In the tables, we report means and standard deviations, plus we also report fractions below certain thresholds. As is common in the child anthropometric literature, we use –2.0 as the cut-off for standardized height and weight-for-height.

For haemoglobin the standards used here are those of CDC (CDC 1998), except for the threshold for adult non-pregnant women, for which we use 11.5 as our cut-off, the threshold used by the Health Ministry of Indonesia (12.0 is the cut-off used for non-pregnant women by CDC).

For body mass index, the standards are those of the CDC, the U.S. National Institutes of Health (NIH), and WHO. Prime-aged adults or elderly whose BMI is under 18.5 are considered undernourished, those with BMI greater than or equal to 25.0 are classified as overweight and those at or over 30.0 as obese (National Institutes of Health 1998). Longitudinal studies in Norway and the United States have shown that adults who are overweight have a higher risk factor of subsequent mortality, especially from coronary heart disease and stroke, and those who are obese have a much higher risk factor (National Institutes of Health 1998). Pathways include a greater likelihood of hypertension, in part from a greater likelihood of having high blood pressure, and also a greater chance of having high cholesterol and diabetes. For people who are overweight or obese, their risk of future mortality increases still more if their waist circumference is greater than 102 cm for men or 88 cm for women (National Institutes of Health 1998). Waist circumference, holding BMI constant, is a measure of a person's abdominal fat content, which is the pathway that is related to higher mortality. In IFLS3 we added waist circumference to our health measures, so for the year 2000 we can calculate the fraction being both overweight (or obese) and with large waists. For blood pressure we use as cut-offs the thresholds commonly used to define Level I hypertension: 140 or above for systolic and 90 or above for diastolic (National Institutes of Health 1997).

The thresholds used do not all have strong scientific backing, and particularly so for low income countries. For instance, there is not a substantial literature showing that children aged 3–17 months who have z-scores at or less than –2.0 for height or weight-for-height face a markedly higher risk of certain negative functional consequences. Maybe –2.25 is a better threshold, or maybe –1.50. Furthermore, much is still unknown about the consequences, particularly socioeconomic consequences, of being below these thresholds. As a different example, the BMI thresholds are based on studies from industrial countries with different risk factors and much different medical establishments. Perhaps having more available blood pressure medications in the United States lowers the risk in overweight persons of certain heart diseases, such as stroke, relative to what is found among the overweight in lower income countries such as Indonesia. On the other hand, the lower fat intakes of most diets in Indonesia compared to the United States may reduce other associated risks for the overweight, reversing the previous argument. In this sense the thresholds have both arbitrariness and uncertainty to them, much as do poverty lines. As another example, the CDC cut-offs for haemoglobin levels are based on the 5th percentile from NHANES III (CDC 1998). There does not seem to be a strong scientific justification for choosing this particular percentile. For these reasons, examining the entire distribution of outcomes makes more sense than looking only at fractions below a somewhat arbitrary cut-off point.

To this end, for each age/sex group, we compare the cumulative distribution functions (CDFs) for 1997 and 2000. As is the case for *pce*, if we do choose to take the thresholds seriously, we can examine whether one curve first-order stochastically dominates the other at points below the threshold, in the sense of one curve lying completely below the other at all points less than the cut-off. We again use the Davidson and Duclos results to test for differences between the curves in the relevant ranges. If first-order dominance is not found we test for second-order dominance.

CHILD HEIGHT-FOR-AGE

We begin by looking at standardized child height-for-age. Child height has for some time been viewed as a very useful summary indicator of child health (Martorell and Habicht 1986). It is a stock measure that reflects all of the health events since birth. It may not be immediately responsive to sudden events, such as an economic crisis, but may well respond over time, particularly if the shock is large. Child height will be strongly related to final adult height, which has been increasingly used as a useful summary indicator of health of a population (for instance Fogel 1994). Figure 7.1 shows for Indonesia attained adult height by birth cohort, from those born in 1900 to those born in 1980. The pattern demonstrates that heights of men and women grew steadily over the 20th century, reflecting improvements in health and nutrition. Mean adult heights for men increased by 9 centimetres over the 80-year period 1900–1980 (a little over 1 centimetre per decade). Men born in 1980 averaged nearly 164 centimetres. For women growth in average height over the same period was approximately 11 centimetres, to a level of nearly 152 centimetres for women born in 1980.[7]

FIGURE 7.1
Adult Height by Birth Cohorts 1900–1980

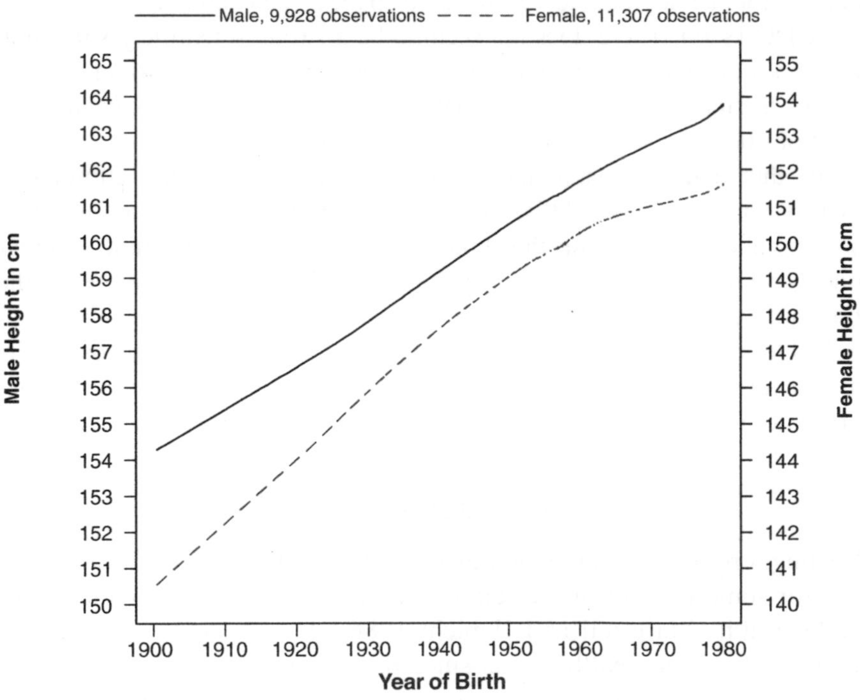
Male, 9,928 observations
Female, 11,307 observations
165
164
163
162
161
160
159
158
157
156
155
154
153
152
151
150
155
154
153
152
151
150
149
148
147
146
145
144
143
142
141
140
Male Height in cm
Female Height in cm
1900
1910
1920
1930
1940
1950
1960
1970
1980
Year of Birth

Source: IFLS3.
Lowess, bandwidth=0.8.

In late 2000 it had been nearly three years since the onset of the crisis in Indonesia, long enough perhaps to see crisis impacts on child heights if there were any. On the other hand in late 1998, when IFLS2+ was in the field, it may have been too early to pick up impacts on height-for-age; indeed, Frankenberg et al. (1999) found none. We would especially expect to see any crisis impacts, if they exist, on very young children since they would have lived their short lives since the crisis began. For this reason, in part, we stratify our age groups into narrow ranges.

We start in Figure 7.2 by showing the pattern between mean height-for-age z-scores and child age in months, for boys and girls aged 3–108 months in both 1997 and 2000.[8, 9] We see the typical age pattern for cross-sections in low income countries (see Martorell and Habicht 1986). The z-scores begin to decline at 3 months, faster at first and then slowing until the z-scores stabilize, for 36-month-old children in our sample.[10] This decline, which varies by socioeconomic factors, is widely attributed to the introduction of water and solid foods into the diet, which will tend to introduce impurities such as bacteria into the child's digestive system, inducing illness (Martorell and Habicht 1986). It is clear from this figure that mean z-scores in 2000 are higher than in 1997 for both boys and girls across the age distribution.

This pattern is mirrored in Table 7.1, which reports means and the percent at or below –2.0 for ages 3–17, 18–35 and 36–59 months. There is a clear increase in mean z-scores, in most cases statistically significant at 5 or at least 10%, and declines in the fraction with z-scores less than or equal to –2.0 (called stunting), significant at 10% for all three age groups for boys and two out of three age groups for girls. This pattern shows a clear improvement in child health.[11]

One must be careful, however, not to lose the forest for the trees. While there is a clear improvement in means and the fraction less than the threshold, stunting, the degree of improvement may be less than what would have occurred absent the crisis. Furthermore, the *levels* of stunting are high, in 1997, being in the mid-40 percent range, declining to the mid-to-high 30 percent range in 2000. In sub-Saharan Africa by comparison, stunting levels are in the 30 to mid-40 percent range for many countries according to data from the WHO Global Database on Child Growth and Malnutrition, although in South Asia levels are higher. Thus even with a strong decline in stunting, levels are still high in the IFLS sample.

Figure 7.2 displays smoothed means at different ages, but our interest is more in what is occurring at the bottom of the distribution. Did the z-scores at the bottom of the height distribution decline during the crisis?

FIGURE 7.2
Child Standardized Height-for-Age, 3–108 Months

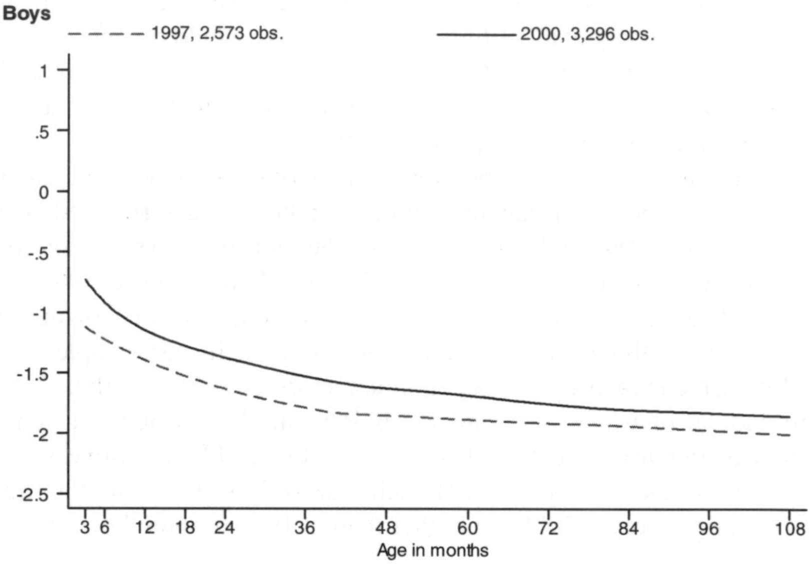
Boys
1997, 2,573 obs.
2000, 3,296 obs.
1
.5
0
-.5
-1
-1.5
-2
-2.5
3 6 12 18 24 36 48 60 72 84 96 108
Age in months

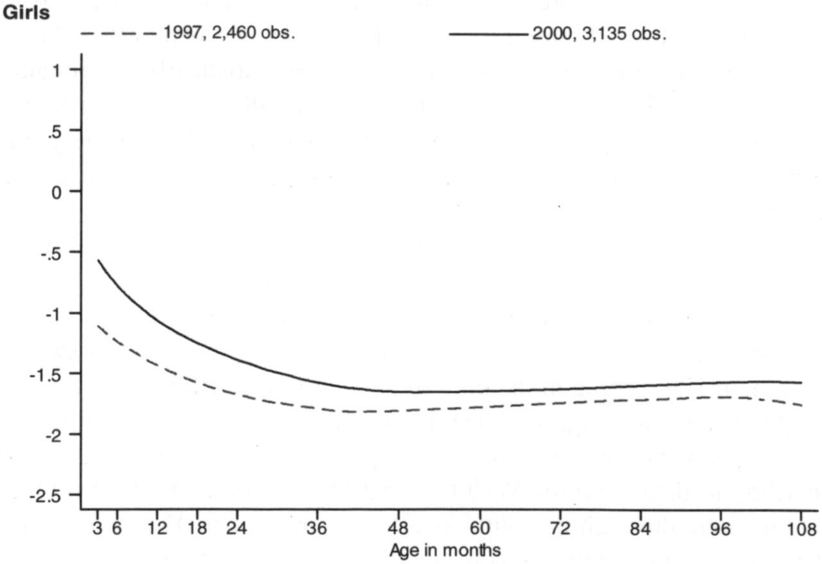
Girls
1997, 2,460 obs.
2000, 3,135 obs.
1
.5
0
-.5
-1
-1.5
-2
-2.5
3 6 12 18 24 36 48 60 72 84 96 108
Age in months

Source: IFLS2 and IFLS3.
Lowess, bandwidth=0.8.

TABLE 7.1
Child Standardized Height-for-Age

	Boys			Girls		
	1997	**2000**	**Change**	**1997**	**2000**	**Change**
Age 3–17 months						
Mean	–1.24	–1.00	0.24	–1.34	–0.95	0.39 *
	(0.134)	(0.088)	(0.160)	(0.134)	(0.090)	(0.161)
% z-score ≤ –2	33.8	26.7	–7.1	31.0	23.4	–7.6
	(3.28)	(1.88)	(3.78)	(3.52)	(1.86)	(3.98)
Number of observations	[302]	[597]		[305]	[534]	
Age 18–35 months						
Mean	–1.81	–1.53	0.28*	–1.81	–1.55	0.26
	(0.115)	(0.079)	(0.140)	(0.118)	(0.100)	(0.155)
% z-score ≤ –2	45.6	38.4	–7.2	45.1	39.5	–5.5
	(3.08)	(2.49)	(3.96)	(2.77)	(2.48)	(3.72)
Number of observations	[367]	[540]		[374]	[487]	
Age 36–59 months						
Mean	–1.90	–1.53	0.37**	–1.78	–1.53	0.25 *
	(0.069)	(0.060)	(0.091)	(0.072)	(0.065)	(0.097)
% z-score ≤ –2	46.7	34.6	–12.2 **	41.0	35.2 **	
	(2.33)	(1.99)	(3.07)	(2.49)	(2.08)	(3.25)
Number of observations	[569]	[710]		[543]	[726]	

Source: IFLS2 and IFLS3.
Estimates were weighted using individual sampling weights. Standard errors (in parentheses) are robust to clustering at the community level. Significance at 5% (*) and 1% (**) indicated.

To examine that question we display the cumulative distribution functions for 1997 and 2000 and look for stochastic dominance below –1.5. It is clear from Figure 7.2 that the mean of z-scores is changing over age, hence it seems better to disaggregate child age when presenting the curves, into more homogeneous age groups in order to gauge the time/cohort effect. We use 3–17 months, 18–35 months and 36–59 months as our groupings. The first group corresponds to ages over which mean z-scores are declining rapidly, the second to ages over which the z-scores are declining, but more slowly, and the third to an age group over which z-scores have stabilized.

Figures 7.3–7.5 show the results. For the 3–17 months group (Figure 7.3), the curves cross for boys but not for girls, and the male crossing point is well above –2.0. Below and somewhat above –2.0, the 2000 curve lies

FIGURE 7.3
CDF of Child Standardized Height-for-Age for 3–17 Months

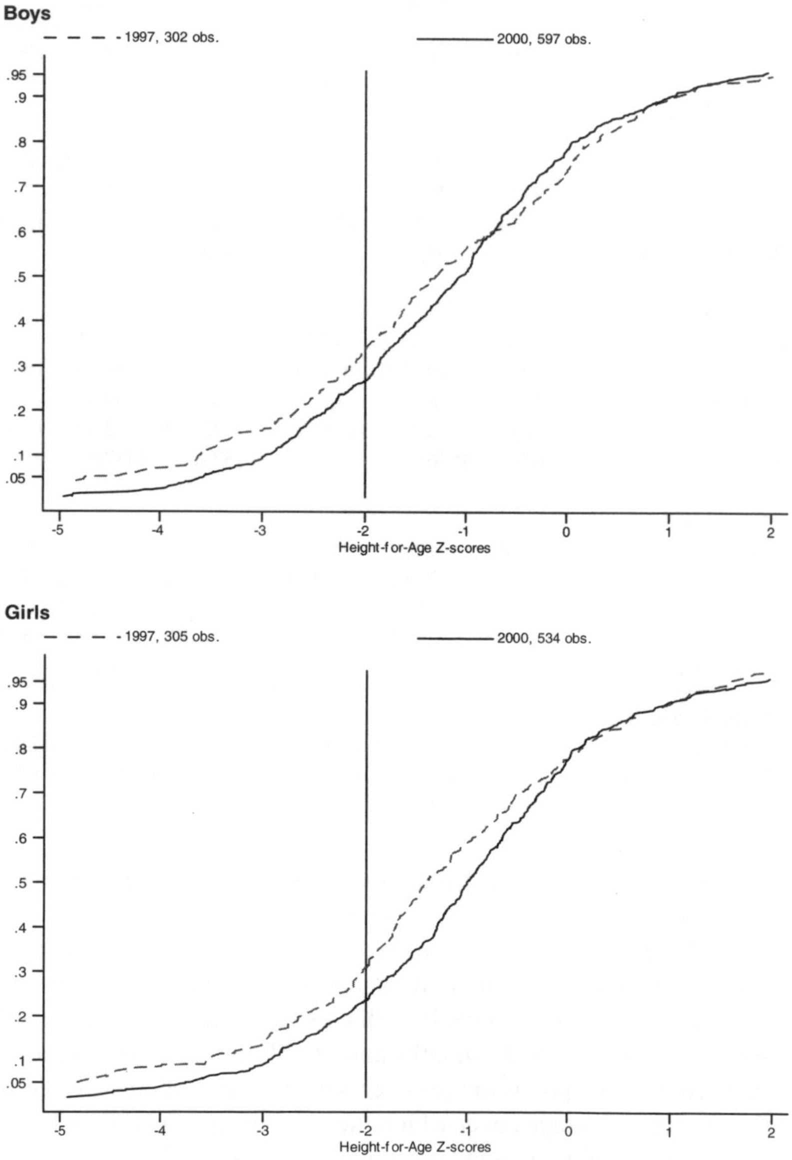
Boys
1997, 302 obs.
2000, 597 obs.
.95
.9
.8
.7
.6
.5
.4
.3
.2
.1
.05
-5
-4
-3
-2
-1
0
1
2
Height-for-Age Z-scores
Girls
1997, 305 obs.
2000, 534 obs.
Height-for-Age Z-scores

Source: IFLS2 and IFLS3.
Observations were weighted using individual sampling weights.

FIGURE 7.4
CDF of Child Standardized Height-for-Age for 18–35 Months

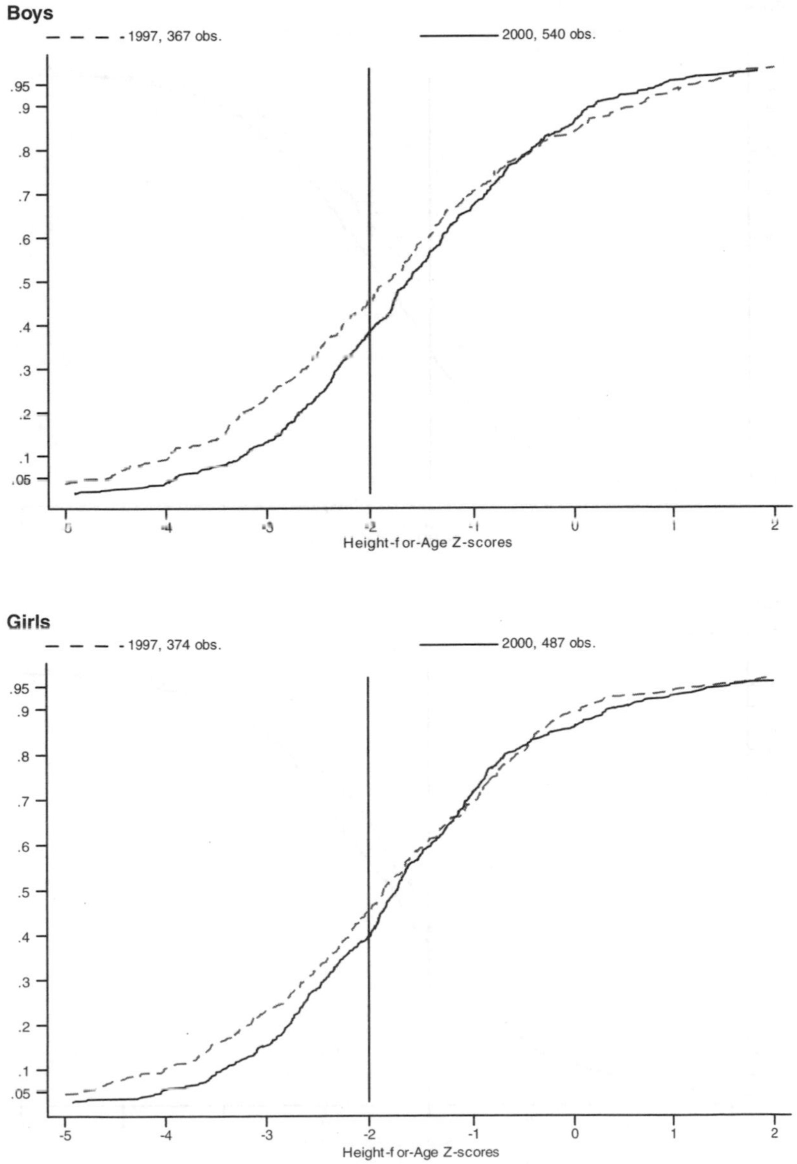
Boys
1997, 367 obs.
2000, 540 obs.
.95
.9
.8
.7
.6
.5
.4
.3
.2
.1
.05
-5
-4
-3
-2
-1
0
1
2
Height-for-Age Z-scores
Girls
1997, 374 obs.
2000, 487 obs.
.95
.9
.8
.7
.6
.5
.4
.3
.2
.1
.05
-5
-4
-3
-2
-1
0
1
2
Height-for-Age Z-scores

Source: IFLS2 and IFLS3.
Observations were weighted using individual sampling weights.

FIGURE 7.5
CDF of Child Standardized Height-for-Age for 36–59 Months

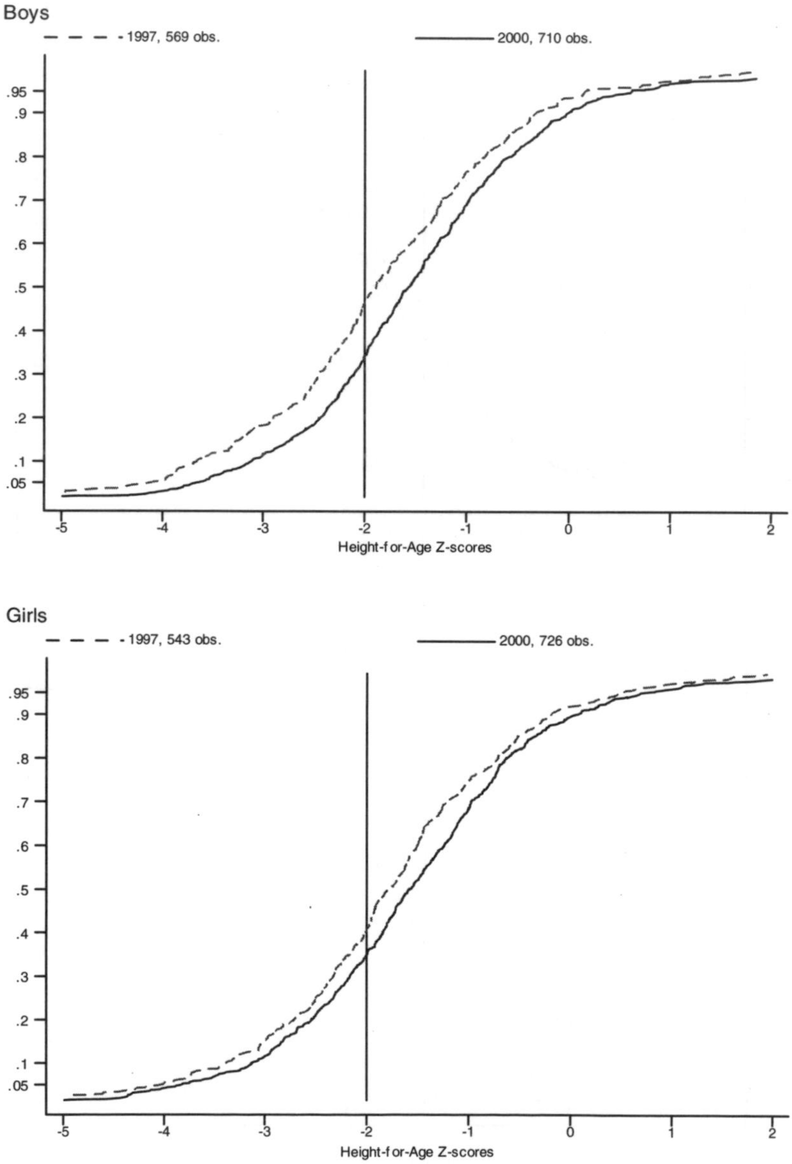
Boys
1997, 569 obs.
2000, 710 obs.
.95
.9
.8
.7
.6
.5
.4
.3
.2
.1
.05
-5
-4
-3
-2
-1
0
1
2
Height-for-Age Z-scores
Girls
1997, 543 obs.
2000, 726 obs.
.95
.9
.8
.7
.6
.5
.4
.3
.2
.1
.05
-5
-4
-3
-2
-1
0
1
2
Height-for-Age Z-scores

Source: IFLS2 and IFLS3.
Observations were weighted using individual sampling weights.

completely below the 1997 curve indicating that for any threshold point in this range, a smaller fraction of children are stunted in 2000 than in 1997. Using Davidson and Duclos' derivation we can calculate the standard errors for these crossing points and as well test for the significance of the vertical distances between the two curves. Appendix Table 7.1 shows these results. For boys aged 3–17 months, taking two standard errors less than the crossing point, –0.73, we obtain –1.16. That is well above –2.0 so one can conclude with 97.5% confidence (a one-sided confidence interval seems appropriate in this case), that there is first-order dominance of the 2000 distribution below the threshold, –2.0. Testing for differences between the curves also shows significant differences at many, though not all, points chosen.[12] This could be taken that the distributions are not different at a 5% level. On the other hand, tests for second-order stochastic dominance in the same way does show significant differences at all points tested. So the statistical evidence seems pretty strong that there is dominance, at least second-order and arguably first-order, for young boys. For girls 3–17 months the pattern is almost the same as for boys.

For the 18–35 months group, there are crossings of the 1997 and 2000 distributions for both boys and girls (see Figure 7.4). Two standard errors less than the crossing point is above –2.0 for boys (Appendix Table 7.1), but below for girls, indicating first-order dominance in the relevant range for boys but not for girls. Points tested below –2.0 also show significant differences at 10% for boys, although at points at and above –2.0, this is not the case. For both boys and girls, there is second-order dominance in 2000.

At the older toddler ages of 36–59 months, there are no crossings, the 2000 curves lie completely underneath the 1997 curves (Figure 7.4). For boys at all points tested at or below –1.5, the 2000 curve is significantly different from the 1997 curve at 10%, although not for girls (Appendix Table 7.1).

One potential reason why this dimension of child health may have improved over this crisis period is that the comparison base of the second half of 1997 was in fact a crisis period in rural areas, because of a major drought and because of serious smoke from forest fires in Sumatra and Kalimantan. Sastry (2002) has shown that these fires are responsible for higher infant mortality rates in Malaysia during that period. It may be that these difficulties resulted in lower child heights as well. If that explanation is the case then we might expect to see improvements in 2000 mainly in rural areas. However from Appendix Figures 7.1–7.3, it can be seen that while substantial improvement did occur in rural areas, improvement also occurred in urban areas.

Another potential explanation for the improvement has to do with birth and/or mortality selection. Suppose that poor households decided to delay childbirth in the face of the crisis, and that their children would have been in the lower tail of the height-for-age distribution. Then one would observe an improvement of the lower tail of the distribution, as we do, but the improvement would not have been caused by an improvement in living standards, rather the reverse. Such a demographic response to a sharp economic decline has been observed in several African countries for example (see National Research Council 1993). However, it is not enough that families delay childbirths for this explanation to be valid. Rather it must be that those who delay are the families whose children would have been in poor health. In contrast, it might be that it is the higher income urban households who delayed childbirth, and their children would have been in good health. In that case we would be understating the improvement in the upper tail of the distribution. The fact that the height distribution also improved for children 36–59 months argues against the birth selection story, since those children would have already been born by late 1997.

A related explanation has to do with the possibility that infant mortality rose during the crisis and that it was the more frail infants who died, thus improving the lower tail of the distribution of heights among the living. The fact, as we shall see, that the shifts in the weight-for-height distributions are quite different from what we see for height-for-age also weakly suggests that both birth and mortality selection stories may not be the principle ones responsible for the pattern of results observed. Still, these are avenues open to future research.

We explore the differences in levels and changes in child height-for-age z-scores by regressing the z-score for boys and girls aged 3–59 months on a similar set of co-variates to those we used when looking at poverty, again pooling the 1997 and 2000 data. Guided by Figure 7.2, we allow our linear spline for child age to have different slopes between 3 and 17, 18 and 35, and 36 and 59 months. In addition to controls for years of education of the mother and the father if they live in the household, we examine the impact of percapita household expenditure (*pce*) by including a linear spline in log *pce*, as we do in Chapter 6, again using the log of Rp 150,000 per month as our "knot point", that demarcates the segments. As discussed in Chapter 3, Rp 150,000 is above any reasonable poverty line that one might set. So this allows *pce* to have a different impact among the poor and the non-poor.

Table 7.2 presents the results; we focus on the 1997 co-efficients first. Higher schooling for mothers in the household is associated with higher

TABLE 7.2
Child Standardized Height-for-Age Regressions

	Boys		Girls	
	1997	Change in 2000	1997	Change in 2000
Age (spline): 3–17 months	–0.092 **	0.003	–0.085 **	–0.022
	(4.94)	(0.12)	(3.86)	(0.82)
18–35 months	0.007	0.015	0.018	–0.009
	(0.65)	(1.11)	(1.51)	(0.60)
36–59 months	–0.005	–0.013	–0.007	0.006
	(0.58)	(1.23)	(0.83)	(0.54)
Mother's education if in household (years)	0.009	0.022	0.054 **	–0.005
	(0.50)	(0.97)	(3.36)	(0.19)
Father's education if in household (years)	0.044 **	–0.018	0.003	–0.009
	(2.82)	(0.82)	(0.16)	(0.35)
log *pce* (spline): 0- log Rp 150,000	–0.053	–0.191	0.182	–0.111
	(0.25)	(0.50)	(0.88)	(0.41)
> log Rp 150,000	0.329 **	0.046	0.271 *	0.071
	(3.06)	(0.32)	(2.57)	(0.50)
Rural	–0.359 **	0.119	–0.232	0.034
	(2.92)	(0.75)	(1.91)	(0.22)
North Sumatra	–0.435 *	–0.136	–0.528 *	0.372
	(2.31)	(0.53)	(2.44)	(1.32)
West Sumatra	0.070	–0.232	–0.668 **	0.667 *
	(0.24)	(0.67)	(2.72)	(2.08)
South Sumatra	–0.254	0.171	–0.498 *	0.389
	(0.79)	(0.46)	(2.08)	(1.17)
Lampung	–0.208	0.285	–0.069	0.322
	(0.81)	(0.91)	(0.26)	(0.98)

continued on next page

TABLE 7.2 – cont'd

	Boys		Girls	
	1997	Change in 2000	1997	Change in 2000
West Java	–0.331	0.471	–0.298	0.700 **
	(1.72)	(1.91)	(1.53)	(2.73)
Central Java	0.176	–0.166	0.150	0.072
	(0.95)	(0.66)	(0.70)	(0.28)
Yogyakarta	–0.072	–0.014	–0.122	0.238
	(0.33)	(0.05)	(0.46)	(0.72)
East Java	0.075	–0.097	–0.137	0.322
	(0.33)	(0.33)	(0.56)	(1.11)
Bali	0.275	–0.420	0.161	–0.206
	(1.39)	(1.54)	(0.56)	(0.58)
West Nusa Tenggara	–0.988 **	0.318	–1.225 **	0.491
	(3.71)	(0.99)	(5.21)	(1.66)
South Kalimantan	0.034	–0.040	–0.381	0.141
	(0.15)	(0.13)	(1.53)	(0.47)
South Sulawesi	0.371	–0.509	–0.529	0.526
	(1.15)	(1.37)	(1.91)	(1.58)
Constant	0.169	2.089	–2.671	1.570
	(0.07)	(0.47)	(1.07)	(0.49)
F-test (p-values):				
Interaction variables	0.2061		0.2771	
Education variables	0.0000		0.0001	
Expenditure variables	0.0000		0.0002	
Number of observations	3085		2969	
R-squared	0.13		0.12	

Source: IFLS2 and IFLS3.

Dummy variable for missing parental education or parent not in the household and dummy variable for missing per capita expenditures are included in the regressions but not reported in the table. The omitted category for province is Jakarta. Estimates were weighted using individual sampling weights. Standard errors are robust to clustering at the community level and to heteroscedasticity. Absolute t-statistics are in parentheses with significance at 5% (*) and 1% (**) indicated.

child z-scores for girls, though not boys, while father's education has an impact on boys and not girls. These gender-specific impacts of mother's and father's education are quite similar to results found by Thomas (1994) in Brazil, Ghana and the United States. Higher *pce* is also associated with higher z-scores, but only when *pce* is above Rp 150,000 per month. The reasons for this extreme non-linearity in the *pce* result are not clear. Not surprisingly, children in rural areas have lower z-scores, by an average of .36 less for boys and .23 less for girls. Boys in West Nusa Tenggara, North Sumatra and West Java are shorter than boys in Jakarta, while for girls we find negative province effects for West Nusa Tenggara, North, West and South Sumatra. An F-test of the hypothesis that there were no changes in co-efficients between 1997 and 2000 cannot be rejected for both girls and boys.

CHILD WEIGHT-FOR-HEIGHT

Weight-for-height is widely thought to be a more responsive measure of child health to shocks in the very short-run (see, for example, Foster 1995). Frankenberg et al. (1999) found that while no major differences were apparent between mean z-scores in 1997 and 1998, for very young children there was an indication of a decline in weight-for-height. However their sample sizes were too small to detect statistically significant differences.

Figure 7.6 shows the mean z-scores by age in months, for girls and boys, similar to Figure 7.2 for height. The same relationship appears, z-scores first declining at 3 months and then stabilizing by 36 months. For boys, the 1997 curve and the 2000 curve lie on top of each other, there are effectively no changes from 1997 to 2000. For girls, however, there does seem to be a worsening of z-scores in the first two and a half years of life.

Table 7.3 shows that the mean z-scores declined in 2000 for girls in the 3–17 and 18–36 months age groups, with significance at near the 5% level. For the fractions below –2.0, however, while they rise for these age groups, the changes are not significant at even 10%. Nevertheless, as is true for height, the fraction of children less than the threshold, –2.0, is high, at or over 10% for children under 36 months. This level of wasting is at or higher than levels in sub-Saharan Africa, although not as high as in South Asia (see the WHO Global Database on Child Growth and Malnutrition at www.who.org), usually considered the part of the world where wasting is most prevalent.

Figures 7.7–7.9 plot the cumulative distribution functions for the three age groups 3–17, 18–35 and 36–59 months (see Appendix Figures 7.4–7.6

FIGURE 7.6
Child Standardized Weight-for-Height for 3–108 Months

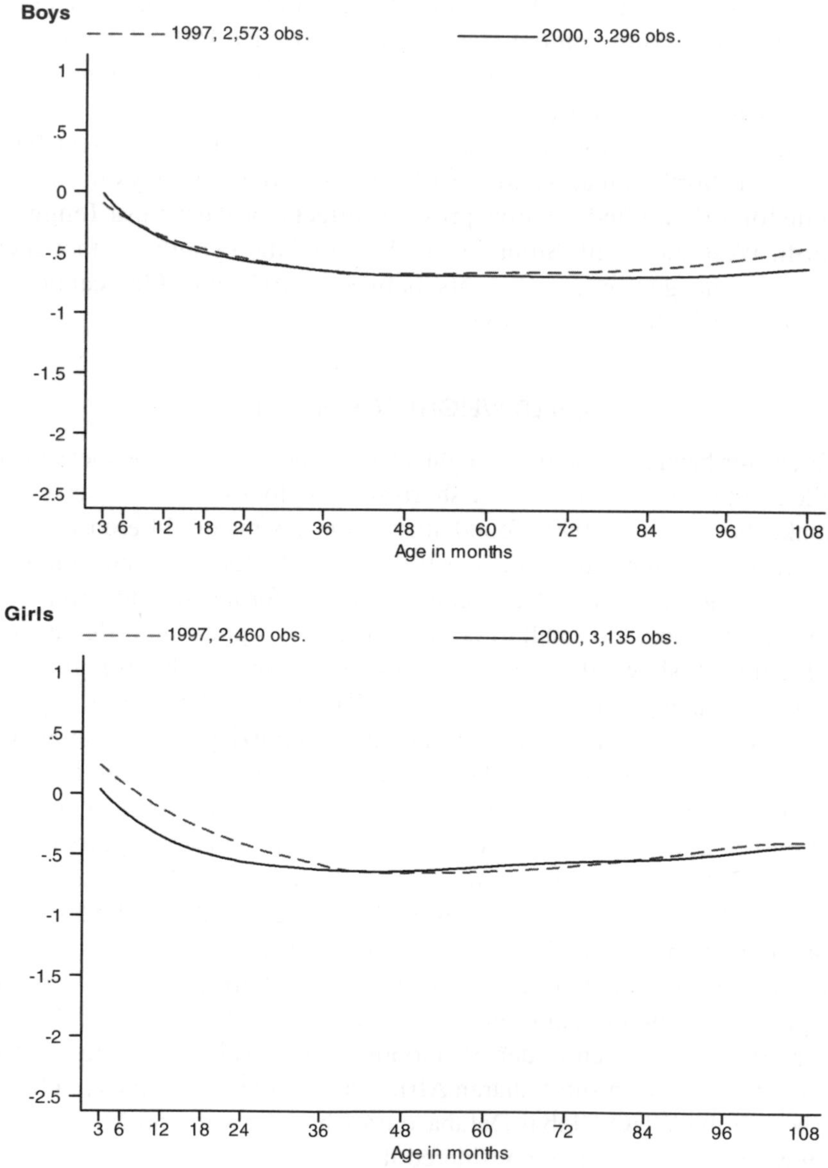
Boys
1997, 2,573 obs.
2000, 3,296 obs.
1
.5
0
-.5
-1
-1.5
-2
-2.5
3 6 12 18 24 36 48 60 72 84 96 108
Age in months
Girls
1997, 2,460 obs.
2000, 3,135 obs.
1
.5
0
-.5
-1
-1.5
-2
-2.5
3 6 12 18 24 36 48 60 72 84 96 108
Age in months

Source: IFLS2 and IFLS3.
Lowess, bandwidth=0.8.

TABLE 7.3
Child Standardized Weight-for-Height

	Boys			Girls		
	1997	**2000**	**Change**	**1997**	**2000**	**Change**
Age 3–17 months						
Mean	–0.28	–0.35	–0.08	0.05	–0.27	–0.33 *
	(0.127)	(0.094)	(0.158)	(0.144)	(0.082)	(0.166)
% z-score ≤ –2	13.4	12.5	–0.9	7.9	11.2	3.3
	(2.33)	(1.52)	(2.78)	(1.79)	(1.46)	(2.31)
Number of observations	[302]	[597]		[305]	[534]	
Age 18–35 months						
Mean	–0.72	–0.80	–0.07	–0.57	–0.85	–0.27 *
	(0.088)	(0.065)	(0.110)	(0.117)	(0.069)	(0.136)
% z-score ≤ –2	12.5	13.9	1.4	13.8	14.8	1.0
	(1.82)	(1.69)	(2.49)	(1.88)	(1.78)	(2.59)
Number of observations	[367]	[540]		[374]	[487]	
Age 36–59 months						
Mean	–0.58	–0.60	–0.02	–0.68	–0.61	0.07
	(0.085)	(0.058)	(0.103)	(0.071)	(0.051)	(0.087)
% z-score ≤ –2	8.8	7.3	–1.5	9.8	8.0	–1.9
	(1.46)	(1.08)	(1.82)	(1.46)	(1.06)	(1.81)
Number of observations	[569]	[710]		[543]	[726]	

Source: IFLS2 and IFLS3.
Estimates were weighted using individual sampling weights. Standard errors (in parentheses) are robust to clustering at the community level. Significance at 5% (*) and 1% (**) indicated.

for breakdowns by urban and rural areas). Similar to Figure 7.6, for boys 3–17 months (top panel, Figure 7.7) there seem to be very little difference in the curves, there are several crossings, before and just after –2.0. For girls 3–17 months (bottom panel, Figure 7.7), the 1997 curve is below the 2000 curve at and below –2.0 indicating a worsening in 2000 for the bottom tail of the distribution. This worsening is reversed for girls aged 36–59 months (Figure 7.9) and is not apparent for the 18–35 months group (Figure 7.8). Thus it is just for the youngest girls that this negative impact in 2000 appears.

Appendix Table 7.2 shows the Davidson-Duclos tests of significance between these curves. Note that two standard errors below the crossing

FIGURE 7.7
CDF of Child Standardized Weight-for-Height for 3–17 Months

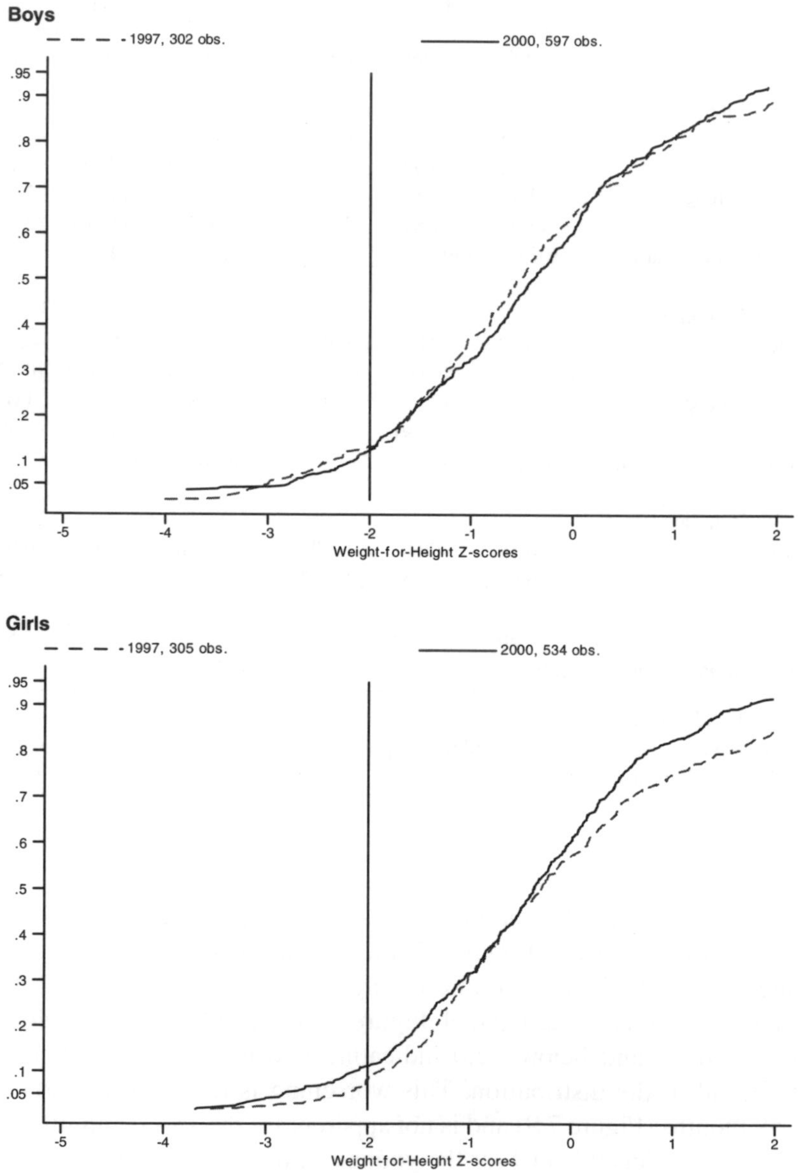
Boys
1997, 302 obs.
2000, 597 obs.
.95
.9
.8
.7
.6
.5
.4
.3
.2
.1
.05
-5
-4
-3
-2
-1
0
1
2
Weight-for-Height Z-scores
Girls
1997, 305 obs.
2000, 534 obs.
.95
.9
.8
.7
.6
.5
.4
.3
.2
.1
.05
-5
-4
-3
-2
-1
0
1
2
Weight-for-Height Z-scores

Source: IFLS2 and IFLS3.
Observations were weighted using individual sampling weights.

FIGURE 7.8
CDF of Child Standardized Weight-for-Height for 18–35 Months

Boys

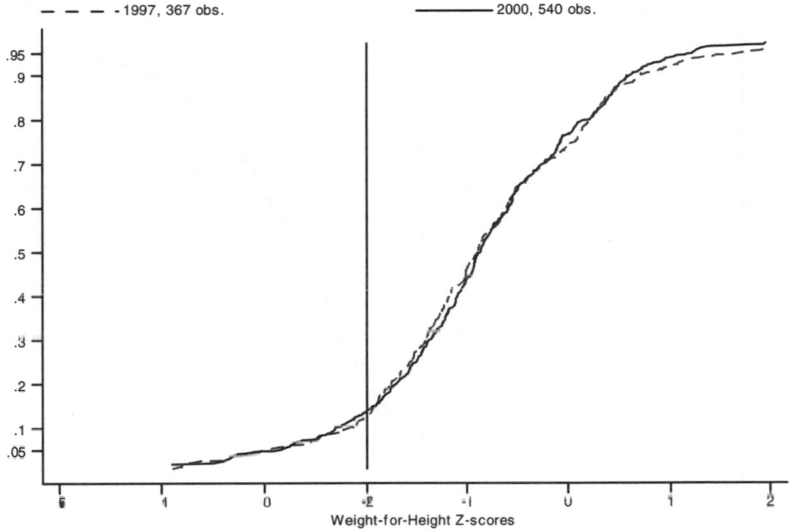
- - - - 1997, 367 obs.
——— 2000, 540 obs.
.95
.9
.8
.7
.6
.5
.4
.3
.2
.1
.05
Weight-for-Height Z-scores

Girls

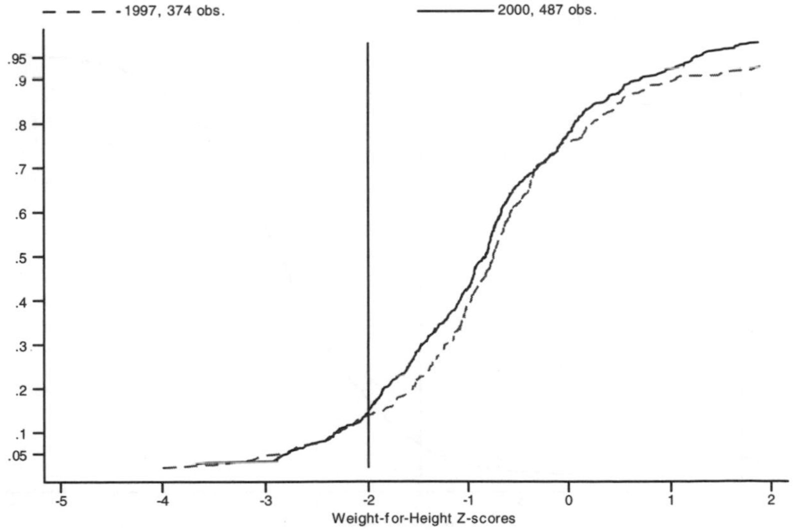
- - - - 1997, 374 obs.
——— 2000, 487 obs.
.95
.9
.8
.7
.6
.5
.4
.3
.2
.1
.05
-5
-4
-3
-2
-1
0
1
2
Weight-for-Height Z-scores

Source: IFLS2 and IFLS3.
Observations were weighted using individual sampling weights.

FIGURE 7.9
CDF of Child Standardized Weight-for-Height for 36–59 Months

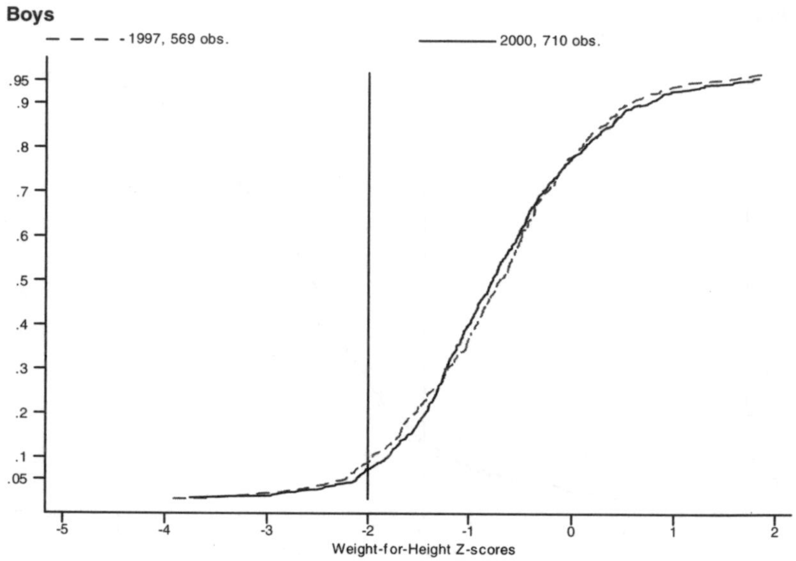
Boys
1997, 569 obs.
2000, 710 obs.
.95
.9
.8
.7
.6
.5
.4
.3
.2
.1
.05
-5
-4
-3
-2
-1
0
1
2
Weight-for-Height Z-scores

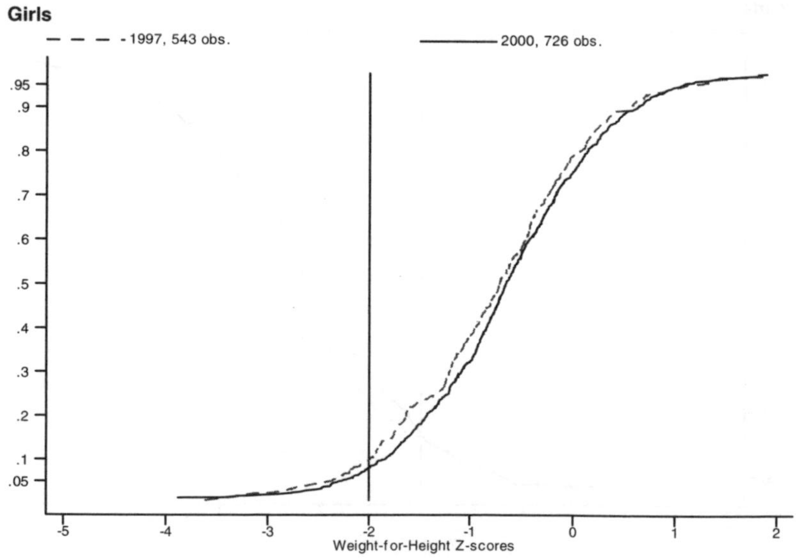
Girls
1997, 543 obs.
2000, 726 obs.
.95
.9
.8
.7
.6
.5
.4
.3
.2
.1
.05
-5
-4
-3
-2
-1
0
1
2
Weight-for-Height Z-scores

Source: IFLS2 and IFLS3.
Observations were weighted using individual sampling weights.

point (–0.98) for 3–17 months girls is –2.16, less than –2.0. Furthermore, direct tests of distances between the distributions also show high standard errors relative to the differences; the differences are not close to being significant at even 10%. The 1997 distribution cannot even be said to dominate at Order 2. So the worsening that is observed for 3–17 months girls is not statistically significant at standard levels.

Table 7.4 presents descriptive regression results for child weight-for-height z-scores using the same specification we used for height-for-age. As is typical in the literature, the explanatory power is considerably lower for weight-for-height than it is for height. Unlike for height, mother's education does not have a significant impact, while father's education has a positive impact on weight-for-height for girls, but only in 2000, and in 1997 actually has a negative association. *PCE* has a positive impact (not precisely estimated) for girls in 1997, but not in 2000. Unlike for height, there are no significant differences between children in rural and urban areas. Boys in Yogyakarta, East Java and Bali tend to be larger than boys in Jakarta, although this is not so for girls in these provinces, and many of these differences are lost though by 2000.

CHILD BLOOD HAEMOGLOBIN

Blood haemoglobin levels are of interest because low levels may indicate problems of anaemia, folic acid and other micronutrient deficiencies, which can have various negative functional consequences, including consequences on physical activity and on learning. However low haemoglobin levels do not tell us the cause. For instance, low haemoglobin levels may not necessarily reflect low iron intakes, as is often assumed. Haemoglobin counts can be low if a person has an infection, or for various other reasons. Table 7.5 shows levels and changes in mean haemoglobin levels and fractions of children and adults below commonly used thresholds. Here we discuss the results for children. The first point to note is that mean levels are very low and fractions below the thresholds very high (remember that these thresholds are at approximately the 5th percentile in the US distribution). There clearly has been an increasing fraction of children under five years below threshold levels, especially for boys, although not for older children.

The cumulative distribution functions, shown in Figures 7.10 and 7.11 are consistent. They show a worsening in 2000 for 12–59 months old, but not for older children. However, there is some ambiguity even for the 12–59 months group, since the curves cross below the thresholds for both

TABLE 7.4
Child Standardized Weight-for-Height Regressions

	Boys		Girls	
	1997	Change in 2000	1997	Change in 2000
Age (spline): 3–17 months	–0.092**	0.017	–0.095**	0.019
	(5.56)	(0.78)	(5.33)	(0.82)
18–35 months	0.030**	–0.008	0.001	0.004
	(2.70)	(0.53)	(0.11)	(0.30)
36–59 months	–0.010	0.007	0.001	0.014
	(1.39)	(0.73)	(0.13)	(1.16)
Mother's education if in household (years)	0.024	0.000	0.023	–0.030
	(1.25)	(0.01)	(1.38)	(1.47)
Father's education if in household (years)	–0.030	0.029	–0.039**	0.072 **
	(1.85)	(1.42)	(2.85)	(3.85)
log *pce* (spline) : 0- log Rp 150,000	0.073	0.168	0.304	–0.432
	(0.22)	(0.38)	(1.50)	(1.75)
> log Rp 150,000	0.071	0.008	–0.044	0.083
	(0.64)	(0.05)	(0.57)	(0.77)
Rural	0.154	–0.110	–0.003	0.153
	(1.20)	(0.70)	(0.02)	(0.97)
North Sumatra	0.078	–0.169	–0.385	0.421
	(0.36)	(0.59)	(1.51)	(1.27)
West Sumatra	0.125	–0.375	–0.623**	0.707*
	(0.50)	(1.15)	(2.79)	(2.36)
South Sumatra	0.121	–0.173	–0.349	0.493
	(0.40)	(0.43)	(1.12)	(1.06)
Lampung	0.167	–0.488	–0.613	0.489
	(0.58)	(1.35)	(1.90)	(1.26)

West Java	0.329	−0.467	0.225	−0.247
	(1.39)	(1.55)	(0.95)	(0.89)
Central Java	−0.141	0.054	−0.453*	0.492
	(0.67)	(0.18)	(2.03)	(1.81)
Yogyakarta	0.611*	−0.650	−0.310	0.331
	(2.16)	(1.67)	(1.48)	(1.13)
East Java	0.343	−0.299	−0.101	−0.016
	(1.41)	(0.91)	(0.42)	(0.06)
Bali	0.374	−0.271	−0.253	0.537
	(1.21)	(0.74)	(0.93)	(1.66)
West Nusa Tenggara	0.082	0.164	0.031	0.255
	(0.29)	(0.46)	(0.12)	(0.79)
South Kalimantan	−0.144	−0.276	−0.573*	0.272
	(0.60)	(0.87)	(2.48)	(0.96)
South Sulawesi	−0.088	0.179	−0.470*	0.513
	(0.37)	(0.58)	(1.98)	(1.74)
Constant	−0.449	−2.150	−2.189	3.849
	(0.12)	(0.42)	(0.92)	(1.33)
F-test (p-values):				
Interaction variables	0.3392		0.0012	
Education variables	0.1062		0.0034	
Expenditure variables	0.5598		0.5348	
Number of observations	3085		2969	
R-squared	0.05		0.08	

Source: IFLS2 and IFLS3.

Dummy variable for missing parental education or parent not in the household and dummy variable for missing per capita expenditures are included in the regressions but not reported in the table. The omitted category for province is Jakarta. Estimates were weighted using individual sampling weights. Standard errors are robust to clustering at the community level and to heteroscedasticity. Absolute t-statistics are in parentheses with significance at 5% (*) and 1% (**) indicated.

TABLE 7.5
Haemoglobin Level

	Boys/Men			Girls/Women		
	1997	2000	Change	1997	2000	Change
Age 12–59 months						
Mean	10.85	10.72	–0.13	10.91	10.87	–0.04
	(0.060)	(0.047)	(0.076)	(0.072)	(0.044)	(0.085)
% < 11.1	51.9	57.4	5.5 *	48.8	52.7	3.9
	(1.86)	(1.66)	(2.49)	(2.15)	(1.66)	(2.72)
Number of observations	[967]	[1,368]	[894]	[1,310]		
Age 5–14 years						
Mean	12.23	12.17	–0.07	12.13	12.11	–0.02
	(0.045)	(0.037)	(0.058)	(0.043)	(0.035)	(0.055)
% < 11.9	38.8	40.7	1.9	41.2	39.6	–1.6
	(1.29)	(1.19)	(1.76)	(1.33)	(1.20)	(1.79)
Number of observations	[3,307]	[3,578]	[3,216]	[3,434]		
Age 15–59 years (for women, excluding those who were pregnant)						
Mean	14.09	14.32	0.23 **	12.38	12.28	–0.10 *
	(0.050)	(0.036)	(0.062)	(0.038)	(0.027)	(0.047)
% < 13.5 (male), 11.5 (female)	33.6	26.5	–7.1 **	24.6	24.6	0.0
	(1.19)	(0.80)	(1.44)	(0.91)	(0.66)	(1.12)
Number of observations	[7,447]	[10,283]	[8,854]	[11,048]		
Age 15–59 years, pregnant women						
Mean	–	–	–	10.99	11.08	0.09
	–	–	–	(0.103)	(0.072)	(0.125)
% < 11 (female)	–	–	–	43.4	46.9	3.4
	–	–	–	(3.08)	(2.57)	(4.01)
Number of observations	–	–	–	[287]	[497]	
Age > 60 years						
Mean	12.77	12.98	0.20	11.97	11.88	–0.09
	(0.089)	(0.067)	(0.111)	(0.081)	(0.059)	(0.100)
% < 13.5 (male), 11.5 (female)	61.1	55.5	–5.6 *	33.6	35.1	1.4
	(1.88)	(1.59)	(2.46)	(1.86)	(1.55)	(2.42)
Number of observations	[1,139]	[1,387]		[1,302]	[1,679]	

Source: IFLS2 and IFLS3.
Test using hemocue. Units are in g/dL. Estimates were weighted using individual sampling weights. Standard errors (in parentheses) are robust to clustering at the community level. Significance at 5% (*) and 1% (**) indicated.

FIGURE 7.10
CDF of Haemoglobin Level for Children 12–59 Months

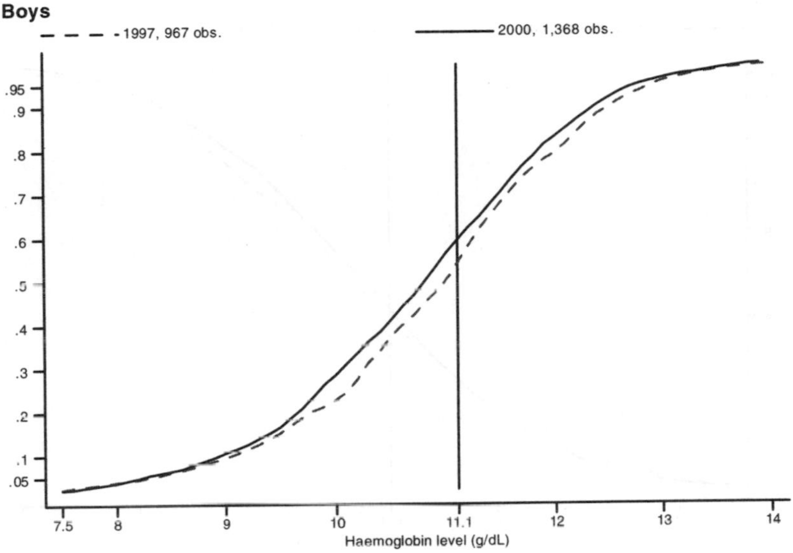
Boys
1997, 967 obs.
2000, 1,368 obs.
.95
.9
.8
.7
.6
.5
.4
.3
.2
.1
.05
7.5
8
9
10
11.1
12
13
14
Haemoglobin level (g/dL)

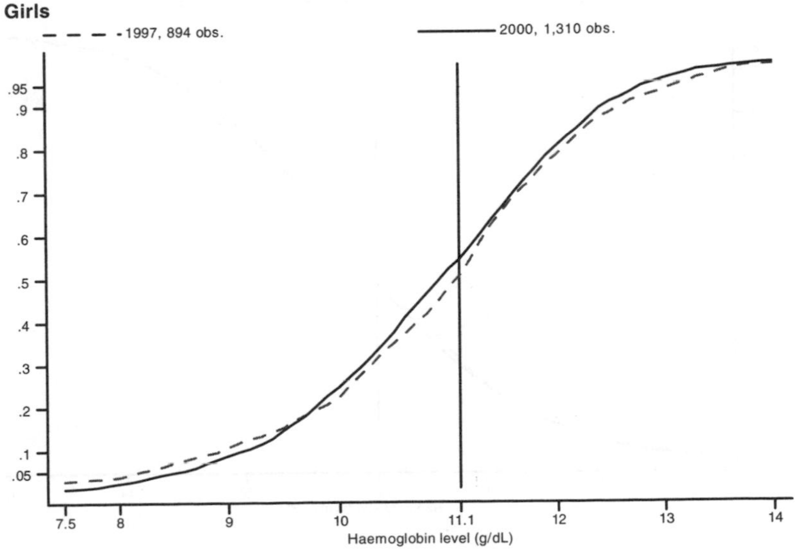
Girls
1997, 894 obs.
2000, 1,310 obs.
.95
.9
.8
.7
.6
.5
.4
.3
.2
.1
.05
7.5
8
9
10
11.1
12
13
14
Haemoglobin level (g/dL)

Source: IFLS2 and IFLS3.
Observations were weighted using individual sampling weights.

FIGURE 7.11
CDF of Haemoglobin Level for Children 5–14 Years

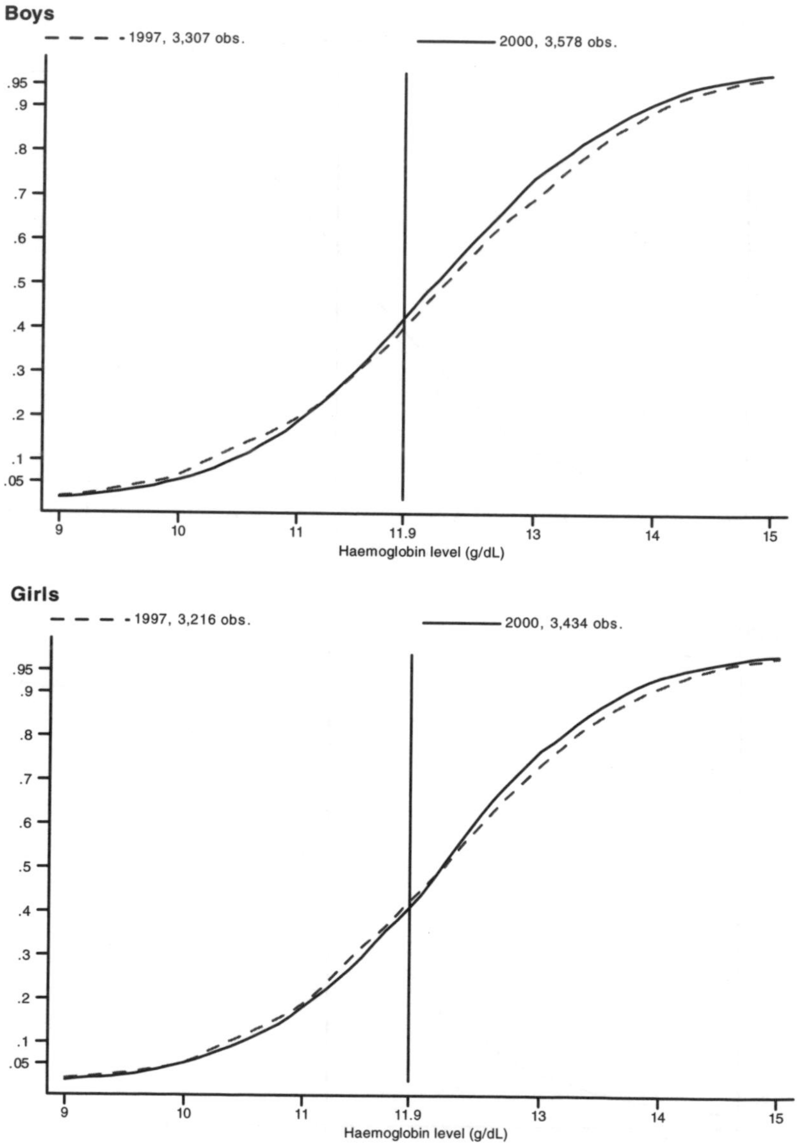
Boys
1997, 3,307 obs.
2000, 3,578 obs.
.95
.9
.8
.7
.6
.5
.4
.3
.2
.1
.05
9
10
11
11.9
13
14
15
Haemoglobin level (g/dL)
Girls
1997, 3,216 obs.
2000, 3,434 obs.
.95
.9
.8
.7
.6
.5
.4
.3
.2
.1
.05
9
10
11
11.9
13
14
15
Haemoglobin level (g/dL)

Source: IFLS2 and IFLS3.
Observations were weighted using individual sampling weights.

boys and girls. Furthermore, tests using the Davidson-Duclos asymptotic distributions (Appendix Table 7.3), show that none of these pairs of curves is significantly different, for boys or girls. Differences at the threshold point is significant for boys, but this is a different statement than saying that the entire lower tail of the 2000 distribution is worse than for 1997.

Table 7.6 presents our descriptive regressions for children 12–59 months. Parental education is jointly significant at 5% for both boys and girls, with mother's education being associated with modestly higher blood haemoglobin levels for girls, more so in 2000. Higher household *pce* is also associated with higher haemoglobin levels for children in poor households, especially for girls. There do not seem to be strong province effects for boys, relative to living in Jakarta, except for boys in West Sumatra who have higher levels, and boys in South Sulawesi who have lower levels. For girls, the province differences are stronger, with girls living in Jakarta tending to have lower haemoglobin levels in 1997. Most of these provincial differences, however, disappear by 2000.

SELF- AND PARENT-REPORTED CHILD HEALTH MEASURES

Other health measures were collected on children. Usually this information was asked of one of the parents (sometimes from another proxy respondent), although older children sometimes answered on their own. Here we use a standard general health question, which we categorize into being poor health or not being in poor health. In addition, as discussed above, a trained nurse assessed the child's health on an ordinal scale of 1–9, 9 being the best health. We look at the proportion with scores less than or equal to 5 as an indicator of poor health. We use 5 or below as a threshold since the fractions less than or equal to 4 are quite small. We stratify our ages in this case by 0–59 months and 5–14 years, and by gender.

Table 7.7 indicates that for most of these indicators, there was a worsening between 1997 and 2000 for both boys and girls. Many of these changes are statistically significant at 5 or 10%. The means of the nurse assessments did not change very much, although the changes were significant at 5%. However, the fraction of children with nurse assessments from 1–5 on the 1–9 scale increased by between 20% and 30%. It is not clear how to evaluate this compared to the improvement in heights or the other changes in physical measures.

Table 7.8 presents the descriptive regression results for parent- or self-reported and nurse-assessed general health. These two indicators behave very differently with respect to socioeconomic factors. A poor nurse

TABLE 7.6
Child Haemoglobin Level Regressions

	Boys		Girls	
	1997	Change in 2000	1997	Change in 2000
Age (spline): 12–17 months	–0.051	0.153**	0.112	–0.010
	(1.34)	(2.93)	(1.82)	(0.13)
18–35 months	0.046**	–0.004	0.031**	–0.003
	(4.70)	(0.33)	(2.67)	(0.22)
36–59 months	0.016*	–0.004	0.015*	–0.009
	(2.23)	(0.39)	(1.98)	(0.84)
Mother's education if in household (years)	0.022	0.010	0.031	0.006
	(1.37)	(0.48)	(1.54)	(0.25)
Father's education if in household (years)	–0.020	0.018	0.005	–0.009
	(1.46)	(0.97)	(0.29)	(0.39)
log *pce* (spline) : 0 - log Rp 150,000	0.263	–0.083	0.400*	–0.044
	(1.51)	(0.35)	(2.15)	(0.19)
> log Rp 150,000	0.167	0.047	0.030	–0.035
	(1.53)	(0.33)	(0.33)	(0.29)
Rural	0.001	0.120	–0.208	0.337*
	(0.01)	(0.82)	(1.43)	(1.97)
North Sumatra	0.055	0.191	0.773**	–0.772*
	(0.20)	(0.54)	(2.77)	(2.24)
West Sumatra	0.874**	–0.735	0.964**	–0.890*
	(3.22)	(1.91)	(3.22)	(2.43)
South Sumatra	–0.473	–0.237	0.178	–1.006
	(1.15)	(0.49)	(0.38)	(1.79)
Lampung	–0.457	0.148	–0.081	–0.274
	(1.75)	(0.42)	(0.23)	(0.70)

West Java	–0.231	0.180	0.250	–0.384
	(1.00)	(0.59)	(0.93)	(1.23)
Central Java	–0.137	0.349	0.488	–0.565
	(0.59)	(1.13)	(1.66)	(1.64)
Yogyakarta	0.273	–0.359	1.245**	–1.382**
	(1.01)	(1.02)	(5.00)	(3.78)
East Java	0.069	–0.281	0.582*	–0.830**
	(0.29)	(0.91)	(2.35)	(2.74)
Bali	–0.028	0.210	0.706*	–0.743
	(0.10)	(0.57)	(2.04)	(1.86)
West Nusa Tenggara	0.226	–0.468	1.085**	–1.470**
	(1.01)	(1.53)	(4.23)	(4.29)
South Kalimantan	–0.225	0.397	0.506	–0.491
	(0.60)	(0.83)	(1.68)	(1.31)
South Sulawesi	–0.920**	1.156**	0.555	–0.702
	(3.31)	(3.23)	(1.35)	(1.42)
Constant	8.050**	–2.164	3.125	1.160
	(3.85)	(0.75)	(1.30)	(0.39)
F-test (p-values):				
Interaction variables	0.0000		0.0003	
Education variables	0.0479		0.0066	
Expenditure variables	0.0068		0.0127	
Number of observations	2311		2173	
R-squared	0.15		0.13	

Source: IFLS2 and IFLS3.

Dummy variable for missing parental education or parent not in the household and dummy variable for missing per capita expenditures are included in the regressions but not reported in the table. The omitted category for province is Jakarta. Estimates were weighted using individual sampling weights. Standard errors are robust to clustering at the community level and to heteroscedasticity. Absolute t-statistics are in parentheses with significance at 5% (*) and 1% (**) indicated.

TABLE 7.7
Health Conditions of Children

	0–59 months						5–14 years					
	Boys			Girls			Boys			Girls		
	1997	2000	Change	1997	2000	Change	1997	2000	Change	1997	2000	Change
% self-reported in poor health now	10.3	14.6	4.3 **	10.6	12.9	2.3	5.0	6.8	1.7 *	5.1	7.5	2.4 **
	(0.98)	(1.03)	(1.42)	(1.07)	(0.84)	(1.36)	(0.45)	(0.49)	(0.66)	(0.51)	(0.52)	(0.73)
Nurse evalution: [a]												
– mean	6.0	5.9	–0.2 *	6.0	5.8	–0.2 **	6.2	6.0	–0.2 *	6.2	6.0	–0.2 *
	(0.06)	(0.05)	(0.08)	(0.05)	(0.05)	(0.07)	(0.05)	(0.05)	(0.07)	(0.05)	(0.05)	(0.07)
– % with evaluation score <=5	29.7	36.4	6.8	30.0	39.3	9.4 **	27.9	32.6	4.7	27.0	34.7	7.7 *
	(2.65)	(2.29)	(3.50)	(2.56)	(2.21)	(3.39)	(2.58)	(2.30)	(3.46)	(2.46)	(2.36)	(3.41)
Number of observations	1,343	2,042		1,318	1,931		3,405	3,732		3,313	3,587	

Source: IFLS2 and IFLS3.

[a] Nurse evaluation is reported by nurse who collects physical assessment. The scale is from 1 (the most unhealthy) to 9 (the most healthy).

Estimates were weighted using individual sampling weights. Standard errors (in parentheses) are robust to clustering at the community level. Significance at 5% (*) and 1% (**) indicated.

TABLE 7.8
Parent- and Nurse-reported General Health: Linear Probability Models for Poor Health Children, aged 0–14 years

		Boys				Girls			
		Parent- or self-reported		Nurse evaluation		Parent- or self-reported		Nurse evaluation	
		1997	Change in 2000	1997	Change in 2000	1997	Change in 2000	1997	Change in 2000
Age (spline, × 10^{-2}):									
	0–17 months	0.430	0.002	0.214	0.418	0.537*	–0.260	0.759*	–0.281
		(1.77)	(0.01)	(0.73)	(1.06)	(2.35)	(0.87)	(2.32)	(0.64)
	18–35 months	–0.233	–0.235	0.202	–0.558	–0.195	–0.074	–0.478*	0.522
		(1.24)	(0.94)	(0.93)	(1.73)	(1.00)	(0.28)	(2.19)	(1.59)
	36–59 months	–0.132	–0.039	–0.091	0.148	–0.220*	0.088	0.004	–0.304
		(1.45)	(0.30)	(0.71)	(0.82)	(2.29)	(0.67)	(0.04)	(1.71)
	5–14 years	–0.037**	0.003	–0.064**	–0.049	–0.019	–0.014	–0.039*	–0.012
		(3.26)	(0.19)	(3.03)	(1.59)	(1.42)	(0.75)	(2.15)	(0.40)
Mother's education if in household (yr.)		0.139	–0.466*	–0.876**	–0.261	0.008	–0.109	–0.739**	–0.256
		(0.96)	(2.24)	(3.03)	(0.66)	(0.06)	(0.61)	(2.59)	(0.59)
Father's education if in household (yr.)		–0.133	0.180	–0.497*	0.149	–0.117	0.024	–0.715**	0.208
		(1.06)	(0.94)	(2.23)	(0.43)	(0.90)	(0.12)	(2.64)	(0.53)
log *pce* (spline)	0- log Rp 150,000	–0.650	–0.649	–15.577**	11.259	–0.654	–1.228	–18.601**	12.556
		(0.44)	(0.29)	(3.56)	(1.90)	(0.37)	(0.44)	(3.97)	(2.08)
	> log Rp 150,000	0.063	1.354	–4.916**	0.301	–0.254	1.170	–4.962**	0.979
		(0.07)	(1.07)	(2.86)	(0.12)	(0.29)	(0.83)	(3.10)	(0.39)
Rural (× 10^{-1})		–0.132	0.143	–0.523	0.408	–0.079	0.152	–0.752	0.647
		(1.34)	(1.03)	(1.31)	(0.73)	(0.76)	(1.04)	(1.94)	(1.14)
North Sumatra		–0.039*	–0.006	–0.418**	0.685**	–0.047*	–0.003	–0.492**	0.793**
		(2.00)	(0.18)	(4.99)	(6.23)	(2.33)	(0.11)	(5.96)	(6.88)
West Sumatra		–0.051*	0.062	–0.351**	1.158**	–0.021	0.005	–0.407**	1.212**
		(2.40)	(1.71)	(4.08)	(11.37)	(0.67)	(0.12)	(4.77)	(11.98)
South Sumatra		–0.037	0.013	0.404**	–0.434**	–0.038	0.003	0.222	–0.238
		(1.58)	(0.34)	(4.15)	(4.23)	(1.79)	(0.08)	(2.14)	(2.20)

continued on next page

TABLE 7.8 – cont'd

	Boys				Girls			
	Parent- or self-reported		Nurse evaluation		Parent- or self-reported		Nurse evaluation	
	1997	Change in 2000	1997	Change in 2000	1997	Change in 2000	1997	Change in 2000
Lampung	0.005	–0.050	–0.372**	0.826**	0.006	–0.058	–0.415**	0.949**
	(0.16)	(1.16)	(4.10)	(7.58)	(0.21)	(1.49)	(4.71)	(9.05)
West Java	0.008	–0.022	–0.177	0.574**	–0.003	–0.035	–0.270**	0.714**
	(0.43)	(0.71)	(1.87)	(5.41)	(0.14)	(1.16)	(2.91)	(6.80)
Central Java	–0.003	–0.003	0.080	0.261*	–0.049**	–0.012	0.001	0.333**
	(0.12)	(0.08)	(0.75)	(2.05)	(2.68)	(0.38)	(0.01)	(2.70)
Yogyakarta	–0.028	–0.023	–0.392**	0.667**	–0.003	–0.058	–0.456**	0.763**
	(1.26)	(0.66)	(4.69)	(6.40)	(0.09)	(1.39)	(5.48)	(7.20)
East Java	–0.050**	0.003	–0.243**	0.469**	–0.057**	–0.000	–0.327**	0.625**
	(2.75)	(0.09)	(2.59)	(4.53)	(2.98)	(0.02)	(3.62)	(6.14)
Bali	–0.043	–0.043	–0.419**	0.391**	–0.049*	–0.063	–0.516**	0.477**
	(1.84)	(1.25)	(4.91)	(4.31)	(2.06)	(1.90)	(6.15)	(5.40)
West Nusa Tenggara	0.002	–0.050	0.413**	0.097	–0.017	–0.061	0.378**	0.151
	(0.07)	(1.33)	(4.43)	(0.81)	(0.66)	(1.75)	(4.15)	(1.29)
South Kalimantan	–0.034	–0.028	–0.348**	0.383**	–0.012	–0.101**	–0.417**	0.442**
	(1.72)	(0.83)	(4.00)	(4.01)	(0.41)	(2.67)	(4.78)	(4.56)
South Sulawesi	–0.029	–0.032	0.104	–0.171	–0.022	–0.065*	0.091	–0.134
	(1.14)	(0.88)	(0.76)	(1.22)	(1.03)	(2.05)	(0.71)	(1.02)
Constant	0.385	0.022	3.264**	–0.805**	0.487	0.064	3.816**	–0.647**
	(1.43)	(0.30)	(4.58)	(4.92)	(1.49)	(1.29)	(5.26)	(4.54)
F-test (p-values):								
Interaction variables	0.060		0.000		0.120		0.000	
Education variables	0.122		0.000		0.622		0.000	
Expenditure variables	0.627		0.000		0.863		0.000	
Number of observations	10,522		10,522		10,149		10,149	
R-squared	0.03		0.24		0.02		0.24	

Source: IFLS2 and IFLS3.

Dummy variable for missing parental education or parent not in household and dummy variable for missing per capita expenditure are included in the regressions but not reported in the table. The omitted category for province is Jakarta. Estimates were weighted using individual sampling weights. Standard errors are robust to clustering at the community level and to heteroscedasticity. Absolute t-statistics are in parentheses with significance at 5% (*) and 1% (**) indicated.

evaluation is negatively associated with mother's and father's education and with household *pce*, all being statistically significant at 5%. Notice that in 1997 the *pce* impact is quite non-linear, being much stronger at low levels of *pce*, while in 2000 the impact is much closer to linear. However, the parent- or self-reported health variable is not associated with these variables at all. Strauss and Thomas (1995), among others, argue that self-reported health measures of poor health are often positively associated with better schooling and higher income of parents. This is in part because those groups are more likely to go to modern sector health practitioners, and are consequently better informed of their maladies. This interpretation is consistent with what we see here.

Also of note is the heterogeneity by province in assessed poor health by nurses. In 1997, children in Jakarta were more likely to be assigned a lower health rating by nurses. This differential was reduced considerably in 2000; in Jakarta the likelihood of a 5 or below fell, but it rose in most of the other provinces.[13]

ADULT BODY MASS INDEX

One of the ways in which the health of children might have been protected was by sacrificing the health of adults. Indeed Frankenberg et al. (1999) show that the BMI of the elderly declined in the first year of the crisis, with a significant increase in the fraction by less than 18.5. By 2000, however, that situation had changed. Table 7.9 reports mean BMI and the fractions undernourished (less than 18.5), overweight (greater than or equal to 25.0) and obese (greater than or equal to 30.0) for different groups of men and women.[14] Figures 7.12–7.15 plot the cumulative distributions of BMI for male and female adolescents, 20–39 year olds, 40–59 year olds and those over 60 years.

There are no clear patterns between 1997 and 2000 relative to undernutrition (low BMI). In terms of prevalence of low BMI, there is some worsening for men 20–39, but not for women in that age range (Figure 7.13). On the other hand, there is an improvement in undernutrition for men and women aged 40–59 (not significant; see Figure 7.14 and Appendix Table 7.4), and no change for the elderly (Figure 7.15). Hence, apparently older Indonesians lost weight in the first year after the crisis, when food prices skyrocketed, but re-gained it over the subsequent two years.

Strong cross-sectional age patterns exist for undernutrition: the incidence falls with age after adolescents, but then rises dramatically among the elderly.

TABLE 7.9
Adult Body Mass Index

	Men			Women		
	1997	2000	Change	1997	2000	Change
Age 15–19 years						
Mean	19.28	19.16	–0.12	20.19	20.29	0.10
	(0.067)	(0.061)	(0.091)	(0.085)	(0.072)	(0.111)
% Undernourished (<18.5)	37.9	40.8	2.9	26.0	26.1	0.1
	(1.43)	(1.25)	(1.90)	(1.38)	(1.21)	(1.84)
% Overweight (≥ 25)	1.8	2.0	0.1	4.1	5.1	1.0
	(0.35)	(0.34)	(0.49)	(0.55)	(0.52)	(0.76)
% Obese (≥ 30)	0.6	0.5	–0.1	0.7	0.5	–0.2
	(0.20)	(0.16)	(0.26)	(0.23)	(0.16)	(0.28)
Number of observations	[1,509]	[1,872]	[1,611]	[2,017]		
Age 20–39 years						
Mean	21.03	21.12	0.09	21.99	22.21	0.22 *
	(0.061)	(0.054)	(0.082)	(0.078)	(0.068)	(0.103)
% Undernourished (<18.5)	14.5	16.7	2.2 *	12.8	13.0	0.2
	(0.83)	(0.65)	(1.05)	(0.62)	(0.54)	(0.83)
% Overweight (≥ 25)	7.6	10.0	2.4 **	17.3	19.6	2.3 *
	(0.51)	(0.49)	(0.71)	(0.80)	(0.67)	(1.05)
% Obese (≥ 30)	0.8	1.2	0.3	2.9	3.5	0.5
	(0.15)	(0.15)	(0.22)	(0.28)	(0.26)	(0.38)
Number of observations	[3,592]	[5,508]	[4,480]	[5,816]		
Age 40–59 years						
Mean	21.41	21.77	0.35 **	22.43	23.02	0.59 **
	(0.092)	(0.093)	(0.131)	(0.128)	(0.131)	(0.183)
% Undernourished (<18.5)	16.1	13.9	–2.2	16.3	14.3	–2.1
	(0.92)	(0.76)	(1.19)	(0.90)	(0.82)	(1.22)

% Overweight (≥ 25)	13.4	16.3	2.9 *	24.6	30.3	5.8 **
	(0.89)	(0.97)	(1.32)	(1.18)	(1.21)	(1.69)
% Overweight with high abdominal fat	–	1.5	–	–	15.3	–
	–	(0.25)	–	–	(0.88)	–
% Obese (≥ 30)	1.5	1.6	0.1	5.4	7.3	1.9
	(0.29)	(0.25)	(0.39)	(0.50)	(0.57)	(0.76)
% Obese with high abdominal fat	–	0.7	–	–	6.1	–
	–	(0.16)	–	–	(0.51)	–
Number of observations	[2,453]	[2,957]	[2,939]	[3,298]		
Age > 60 years						
Mean	19.75	19.92	0.17	20.47	20.52	0.05
	(0.120)	(0.113)	(0.165)	(0.162)	(0.150)	(0.220)
% Undernourished (<18.5)	38.5	34.8	–3.8	35.0	35.3	0.3
	(1.86)	(1.44)	(2.35)	(1.78)	(1.51)	(2.34)
% Overweight (≥ 25)	6.1	7.1	1.0	13.5	14.4	0.9
	(0.81)	(0.80)	(1.13)	(1.19)	(1.11)	(1.63)
% Overweight with high abdominal fat	–	1.3	–	–	9.3	–
	–	(0.33)	–	–	(0.97)	–
% Obese (≥ 30)	0.6	0.7	0.2	2.9	2.7	–0.2
	(0.21)	(0.34)	(0.40)	(0.47)	(0.42)	(0.63)
% Obese with high abdominal fat	–	0.4	–	–	2.4	–
	–	(0.18)	–	–	(0.40)	–
Number of observations	[1,140]	[1,376]	[1,315]	[1,638]		

Source: IFLS2 and IFLS3.

Observations exclude women who were pregnant. Having high abdominal fat is defined as having waist circumference > 102 cm for male or >88 cm for female. In 2000, data on waist circumference were collected for those 40 or above. Data on waist circumference were not collected in 1997. Estimates were weighted using individual sampling weights. Standard errors (in parentheses) are robust to clustering at the community level. Significance at 5% (*) and 1% (**) indicated.

FIGURE 7.12
CDF of Adult BMI for 15–19 Years

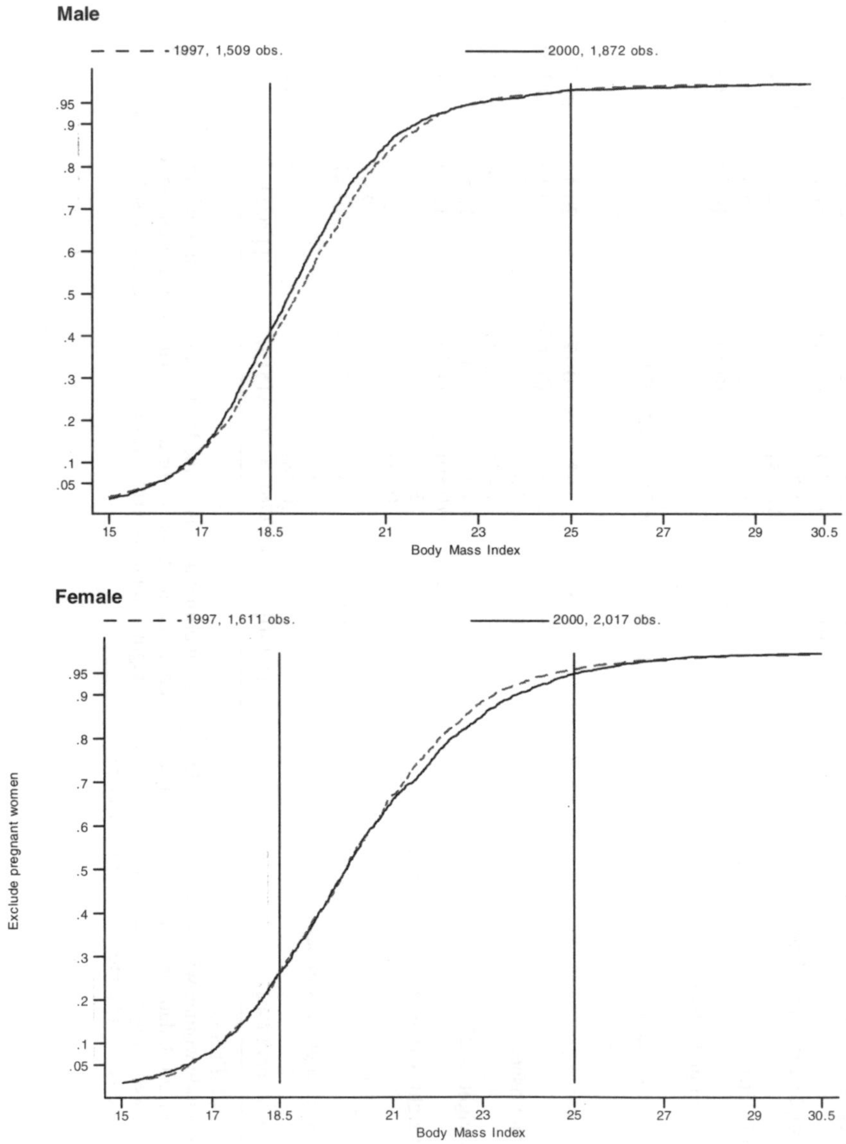
Male
- - - 1997, 1,509 obs.
2000, 1,872 obs.
.95
.9
.8
.7
.6
.5
.4
.3
.2
.1
.05
15
17
18.5
21
23
25
27
29
30.5
Body Mass Index
Female
- - - 1997, 1,611 obs.
2000, 2,017 obs.
Exclude pregnant women
.95
.9
.8
.7
.6
.5
.4
.3
.2
.1
.05
15
17
18.5
21
23
25
27
29
30.5
Body Mass Index

Source: IFLS2 and IFLS3.
Observations were weighted using individual sampling weights.

FIGURE 7.13
CDF of Adult BMI for 20–39 Years

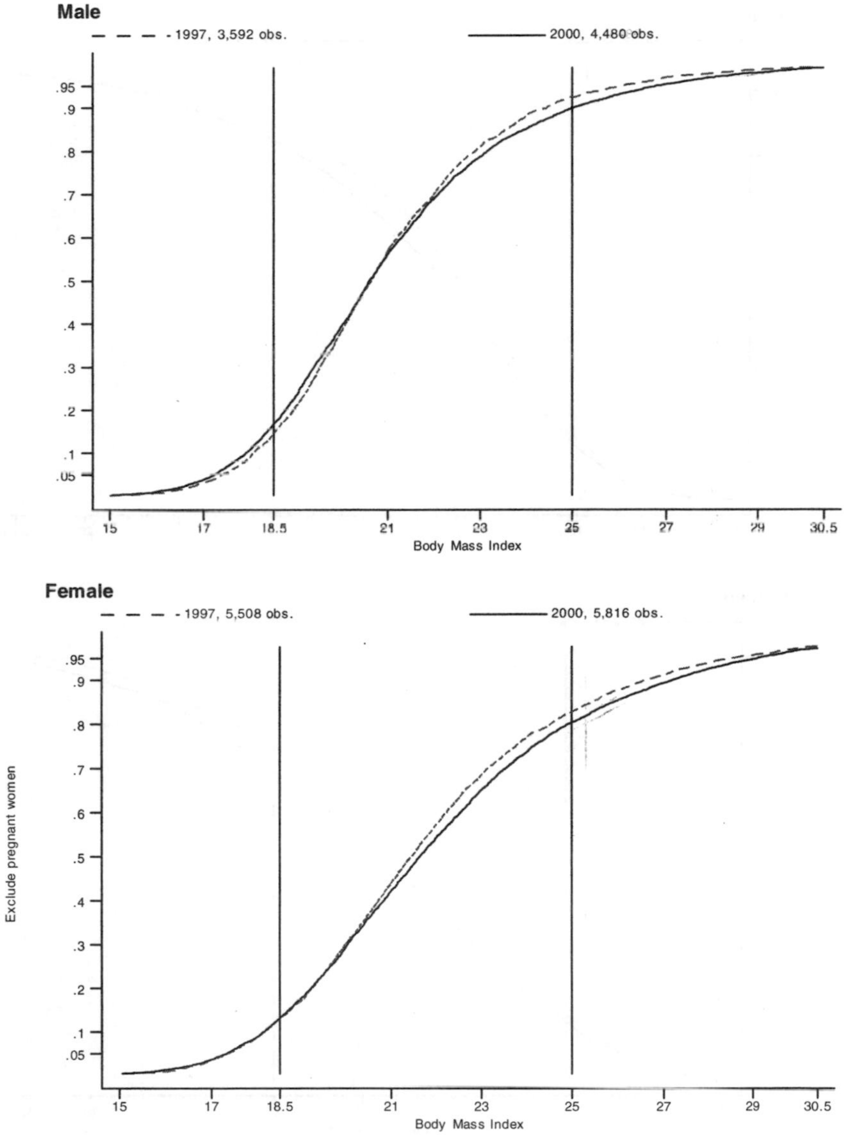
Male
1997, 3,592 obs.
2000, 4,480 obs.
.95
.9
.8
.7
.6
.5
.4
.3
.2
.1
.05
15
17
18.5
21
23
25
27
29
30.5
Body Mass Index
Female
1997, 5,508 obs.
2000, 5,816 obs.
Exclude pregnant women
Body Mass Index

Source: IFLS2 and IFLS3.
Observations were weighted using individual sampling weights.

FIGURE 7.14
CDF of Adult BMI for 40–59 Years

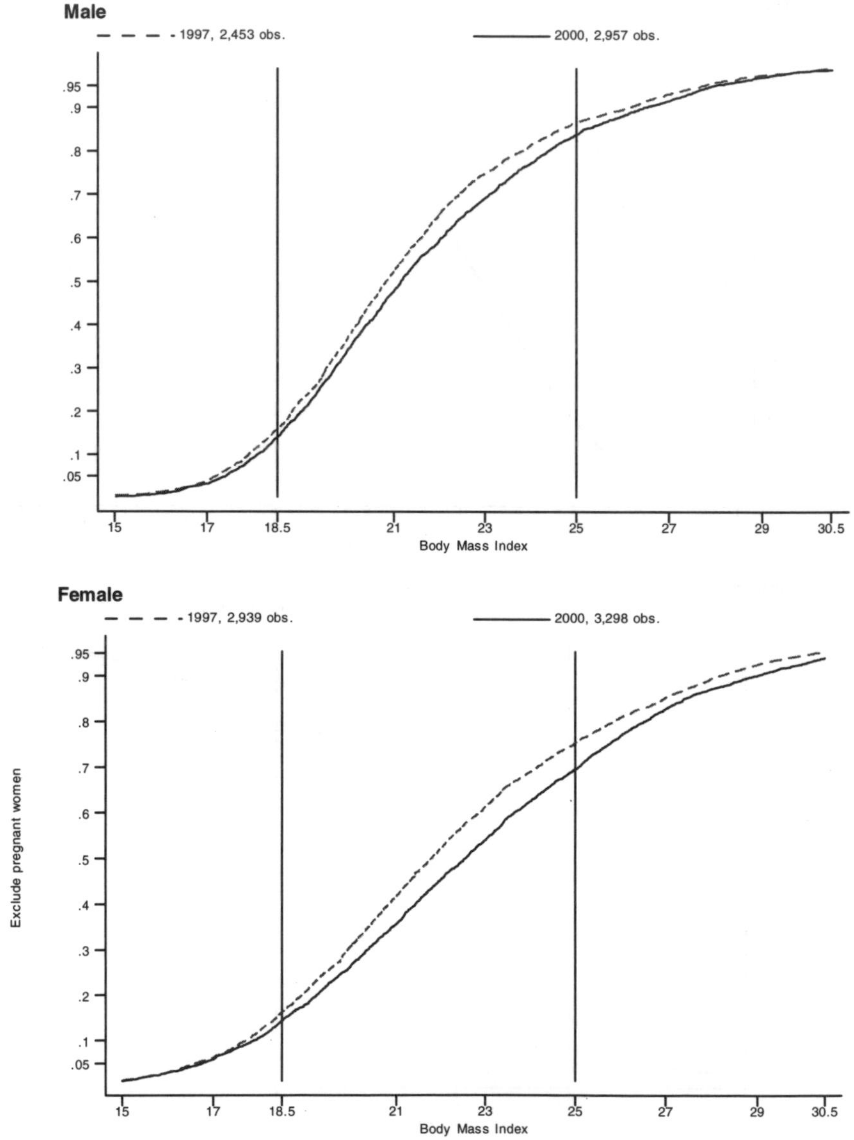
Male
1997, 2,453 obs.
2000, 2,957 obs.
.95
.9
.8
.7
.6
.5
.4
.3
.2
.1
.05
15
17
18.5
21
23
25
27
29
30.5
Body Mass Index
Female
1997, 2,939 obs.
2000, 3,298 obs.
Exclude pregnant women
Body Mass Index

Source: IFLS2 and IFLS3.
Observations were weighted using individual sampling weights.

FIGURE 7.15
CDF of Adult BMI for 60 Years and Above

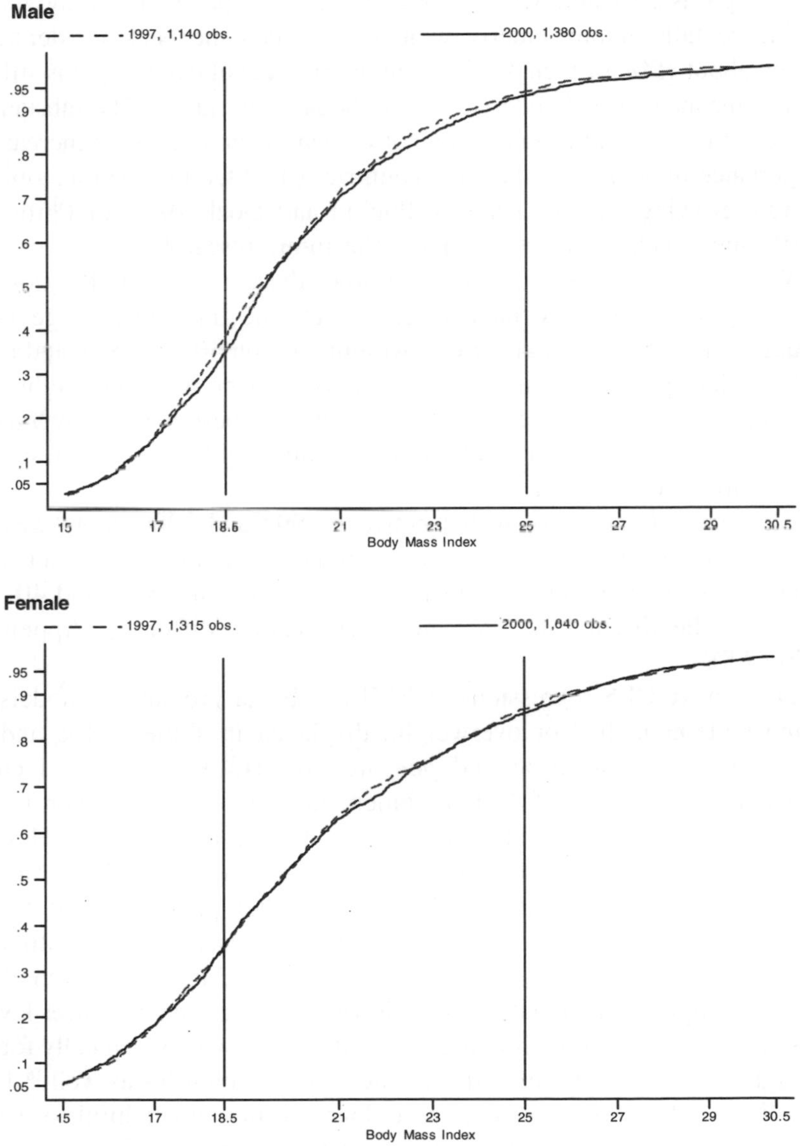
Male
1997, 1,140 obs.
2000, 1,380 obs.
.95
.9
.8
.7
.6
.5
.4
.3
.2
.1
.05
15
17
18.5
21
23
25
27
29
30.5
Body Mass Index
Female
1997, 1,315 obs.
2000, 1,640 obs.
.95
.9
.8
.7
.6
.5
.4
.3
.2
.1
.05
15
17
18.5
21
23
25
27
29
30.5
Body Mass Index

Source: IFLS2 and IFLS3.
Observations were weighted using individual sampling weights.

What is at least as interesting about this table has to do with overnutrition. A relatively high fraction of adults are overweight, especially among women. Among non-pregnant women aged 40–59, the incidence of being overweight is 25% and 30% in 1997 and 2000 respectively, although the incidence falls among elderly women. For men the peak incidence is lower, about 15% for men 40–59, though this level of overweight is still as high as the incidence of underweight for the same age group. The substantial degree of overweight is an example of a phenomenon that is of increasing importance in poor as well as rich countries (the literature on this topic is rapidly growing, see for instance Popkin and Doak 1998, or Philipson 2001) and which needs to be explored in future research.

While levels of obesity are still low, there is a high fraction of overweight women who have large waists, and thus on average high abdominal fat content: half of overweight women 40–59 years and over half of elderly overweight women. Individuals who are overweight, but not obese, raise their risk factors to the levels of obese persons by having a high level of abdominal fat (National Institutes of Health 1998), so this interaction is of concern.

Moreover, it can be seen that between 1997 and 2000, there was an increase in the incidence of overweight people among both men and women above adolescence, especially among women 20–39 and 40–59, although the distributions are not significantly different (Appendix Table 7.5).

Descriptive OLS regressions of BMI and linear probability models of being undernourished or overweight, displayed in Tables 7.10a and b, show that own education and *pce* are powerful explanatory factors explaining higher adult BMI. For women, education has a very non-linear relationship with BMI and with being under- or overweight.[15] Having some schooling for women is associated with higher BMIs, a lower probability of being underweight and a higher probability of being overweight. The impact of education on BMI rises slightly until one achieves completion of primary school. Completing senior secondary school or higher is associated with a lower BMI than having lower levels of schooling (except no schooling), consistent with what is typically found in higher income countries and some developing countries as well.[16] This non-linear effect for women suggests learning in ways helpful to better managing one's health. For men, however, the impact of schooling is much closer to linear, with BMI rising as schooling levels rise, even for completing secondary school or beyond.

The effect of *pce* is also strong for both men and women. Higher *pce* is associated with higher BMIs, both among the poor and the non-poor. Likewise, being in a rural area is associated with lower BMIs. People who live in Jakarta are heavier on average, although the co-efficients tend not to be significant, unlike for the rural co-efficient. Age also has a non-linear effect, with BMIs rising until adults reach their 40s, and then falling as people enter into middle and older ages.

ADULT BLOOD PRESSURE

High blood pressure, or hypertension, is a serious problem for middle-aged and elderly Indonesians, as shown in Table 7.11. There are very strong age effects on having high blood pressure, with the rates of Stage 1 hypertension for systolic pressure rising from 25% to 33% for 40–59 year olds and to 50–65% for the elderly. The incidence of diastolic hypertension tends to be lower. At young ages high systolic readings are a little higher among men, but that changes by age 40, and thereafter it is higher for women. Shifts in the distributions between 1997 and 2000 are small, as suggested in Figures 7.16–7.18, and tests show no significant shifts in the upper tails (Appendix Tables 7.6a and b).

The descriptive regressions shown in Tables 7.12a and b demonstrate that socioeconomic factors such as education and *pce* have only a small effect on high blood pressure. There is a hint at a non-linear relationship of female schooling on systolic pressure, with those having some primary schooling having somewhat higher systolic readings than women with no schooling, whereas women who completed senior secondary or above having lower readings. This lack of an education or *pce* impact is interesting because to the extent that being overweight increases the likelihood of having hypertension, the impacts of underlying factors should be similar, but they don't seem to be strongly related in this instance. It is aging which is the dominant factor raising blood pressure, as the regressions demonstrate. Living in Jakarta is also associated with lower blood pressure in 1997, but the advantage disappears in 2000. While it may be tempting to point to the impact of the crisis in Jakarta to explain this result, that would be a stretch, as there is no corroborating evidence.

SMOKING

A third risk factor for cardiovascular disease is smoking. Table 7.13 displays the incidence of ever and current smoking by age and gender.

TABLE 7.10a
Adult Female Body Mass Index Regressions

	BMI		Undernourished		Overweight	
	1997	Change in 2000	1997	Change in 2000	1997	Change in 2000
Age (spline, × 10^{-1}): 15–19 years	2.540**	–0.189	–0.302**	0.003	0.089*	–0.005
	(5.81)	(0.34)	(4.40)	(0.04)	(2.48)	(0.11)
20–29 years	1.566**	0.110	–0.097**	0.011	0.149**	–0.012
	(8.31)	(0.45)	(4.88)	(0.40)	(7.76)	(0.46)
30–39 years	1.187**	0.255	–0.025	–0.029	0.099**	0.055
	(5.89)	(0.93)	(1.40)	(1.31)	(4.75)	(1.84)
40–49 years	–0.692**	0.302	0.076**	–0.022	–0.020	–0.005
	(3.62)	(1.06)	(3.57)	(0.86)	(0.97)	(0.16)
50–59 years	–1.100**	–0.392	0.105**	0.031	–0.063**	–0.021
	(4.75)	(1.21)	(4.27)	(0.97)	(2.75)	(0.64)
≥ 60 years	–0.545**	–0.058	0.063**	–0.013	–0.025*	–0.008
	(4.83)	(0.35)	(4.17)	(0.62)	(2.52)	(0.61)
Education: 1–5 years	1.040**	0.152	–0.065**	–0.012	0.078**	0.012
	(7.63)	(0.71)	(4.61)	(0.59)	(5.39)	(0.57)
6–8 years	1.183**	0.186	–0.064**	–0.016	0.100**	0.005
	(7.58)	(0.80)	(4.46)	(0.72)	(6.78)	(0.23)
9–11 years	1.039**	0.163	–0.058**	–0.019	0.082**	0.015
	(5.76)	(0.64)	(3.14)	(0.73)	(4.91)	(0.65)
12+ years	0.612**	0.189	–0.032*	–0.024	0.054**	0.013
	(3.40)	(0.72)	(2.12)	(1.00)	(3.06)	(0.52)
log *pce* (spline, × 10^{-2}): 0 – log Rp 150,000	40.700*	17.944	–2.201	–1.365	4.309**	0.428
	(2.53)	(0.78)	(1.16)	(0.53)	(2.88)	(0.20)
> log Rp 150,000	49.521**	11.480	–2.515**	–1.111	3.567**	1.148
	(7.20)	(1.11)	(3.74)	(1.17)	(4.64)	(1.00)
Rural	–0.952**	0.009	0.039**	0.003	–0.097**	0.008
	(7.17)	(0.05)	(3.57)	(0.19)	(8.45)	(0.54)
North Sumatra	0.188	–0.311	–0.049*	–0.007	–0.014	0.008
	(0.71)	(0.91)	(2.52)	(0.27)	(0.58)	(0.25)

West Sumatra	0.195	–0.099	–0.043	–0.012	0.021	–0.001
	(0.56)	(0.22)	(1.94)	(0.41)	(0.62)	(0.01)
South Sumatra	–0.577	0.058	0.011	–0.004	–0.061*	0.028
	(1.82)	(0.14)	(0.45)	(0.10)	(2.43)	(0.81)
Lampung	–0.380	–0.050	–0.010	–0.042	–0.057*	0.015
	(1.27)	(0.12)	(0.33)	(1.15)	(2.56)	(0.43)
West Java	–0.207	–0.275	–0.025	0.000	–0.042*	0.011
	(0.92)	(0.91)	(1.49)	(0.00)	(2.24)	(0.43)
Central Java	–0.331	–0.145	–0.016	0.014	–0.039	0.015
	(1.24)	(0.40)	(0.85)	(0.52)	(1.71)	(0.50)
Yogyakarta	–0.556*	–0.283	–0.006	0.025	–0.074**	0.019
	(2.25)	(0.84)	(0.34)	(1.04)	(3.23)	(0.59)
East Java	–0.142	–0.067	–0.005	–0.008	–0.025	0.024
	(0.60)	(0.21)	(0.29)	(0.33)	(1.27)	(0.87)
Bali	–0.193	–0.223	–0.017	–0.002	–0.054*	0.007
	(0.72)	(0.61)	(0.74)	(0.05)	(2.25)	(0.20)
West Nusa Tenggara	–0.424	–0.063	0.002	–0.019	–0.054*	0.017
	(1.56)	(0.17)	(0.10)	(0.60)	(2.47)	(0.58)
South Kalimantan	–0.622*	–0.108	0.059	–0.028	–0.023	–0.016
	(2.07)	(0.27)	(1.83)	(0.67)	(0.93)	(0.51)
South Sulawesi	–0.161	–0.557	–0.017	0.027	–0.026	–0.031
	(0.46)	(1.29)	(0.61)	(0.78)	(0.94)	(0.92)
Constant	10.376**	–1.828	1.117**	0.184	–0.641**	–0.065
	(4.83)	(0.62)	(4.29)	(0.53)	(3.35)	(0.24)
F-test (p-values):						
Interaction variables	0.7523		0.8189		0.7619	
Education variables	0.0000		0.0000		0.0000	
Expenditure variables	0.0000		0.0000		0.0000	
Number of observations	23,114		23,114		23,114	
R-squared	0.14		0.07		0.09	

Source: IFLS2 and IFLS3.
Observations exclude women who were pregnant. The first regression uses BMI (a continuous variable) as the dependent variable. Dummy variables for being undernourished and overweight are used as dependent variables in the second and third regressions, respectively, and estimated by linear probability models. Dummy variable for missing education and dummy variable for missing per capita expenditures are included in the regressions but not reported in the table. The omitted category for education is no schooling, and for province is Jakarta. Estimates were weighted using individual sampling weights. Standard errors are robust to clustering at the community level and to heteroscedasticity. Absolute t-statistics are in parentheses with significance at 5% (*) and 1% (**) indicated.

TABLE 7.10b
Adult Male Body Mass Index Regressions

	BMI		Undernourished		Overweight	
	1997	Change in 2000	1997	Change in 2000	1997	Change in 2000
Age (spline, × 10^{-1}): 15–19 years	3.040**	–0.369	–0.793**	0.049	–0.065**	0.021
	(9.34)	(0.85)	(11.98)	(0.55)	(3.00)	(0.68)
20–29 years	1.128**	0.200	–0.048*	–0.023	0.077**	0.007
	(7.92)	(1.04)	(2.02)	(0.80)	(6.18)	(0.39)
30–39 years	0.828**	0.071	–0.035	–0.020	0.080**	0.006
	(5.45)	(0.34)	(1.85)	(0.77)	(4.76)	(0.25)
40–49 years	–0.375*	0.426	0.041*	–0.033	–0.006	0.016
	(2.08)	(1.74)	(2.07)	(1.21)	(0.29)	(0.58)
50–59 years	–0.782**	–0.313	0.145**	–0.002	–0.036	–0.022
	(4.32)	(1.26)	(5.57)	(0.05)	(1.92)	(0.82)
≥ 60 years	–0.649**	–0.081	0.093**	–0.003	–0.014	–0.005
	(5.47)	(0.51)	(4.76)	(0.12)	(1.28)	(0.38)
Education: 1–5 years	0.427**	0.078	–0.060**	0.016	0.020*	0.010
	(4.09)	(0.51)	(3.34)	(0.60)	(2.39)	(0.90)
6–8 years	0.788**	0.008	–0.071**	0.012	0.051**	0.003
	(6.89)	(0.05)	(4.08)	(0.45)	(4.91)	(0.21)
9–11 years	0.993**	–0.002	–0.065**	0.001	0.068**	0.013
	(7.04)	(0.01)	(2.94)	(0.02)	(5.82)	(0.81)
12+ years	1.280**	0.310	–0.049*	–0.019	0.115**	0.013
	(9.21)	(1.61)	(2.50)	(0.70)	(9.15)	(0.76)
log *pce* (spline, × 10^{-2}): 0 – log Rp 150,000	31.977**	2.589	–3.467	0.842	1.955*	–0.274
	(2.59)	(0.15)	(1.75)	(0.30)	(1.98)	(0.20)
> log Rp 150,000	46.022**	16.698	–3.783**	–0.253	3.884**	1.454
	(5.97)	(1.66)	(4.15)	(0.22)	(5.52)	(1.47)
Rural	–0.580**	0.138	0.042**	–0.036*	–0.041**	0.003
	(6.83)	(1.20)	(3.66)	(2.41)*	(5.55)	(0.29)
North Sumatra	0.435*	–0.326	–0.113**	0.012	–0.034	–0.012
	(2.03)	(1.09)	(4.52)	(0.36)	(1.57)	(0.42)

West Sumatra	–0.225	–0.165	–0.061*	0.056	–0.058**	0.022
	(1.08)	(0.55)	(2.15)*	(1.44)	(2.84)	(0.77)
South Sumatra	–0.242	0.160	–0.048	0.010	–0.045*	0.012
	(1.09)	(0.50)	(1.62)	(0.23)	(2.36)	(0.46)
Lampung	–0.123	–0.025	–0.061*	0.030	–0.046**	0.015
	(0.59)	(0.08)	(1.90)	(0.72)	(2.70)	(0.60)
West Java	–0.108	–0.213	–0.079**	0.052	–0.054**	0.007
	(0.65)	(0.96)	(3.70)	(1.82)	(3.38)	(0.33)
Central Java	0.080	–0.143	–0.113**	0.037	–0.059**	0.008
	(0.49)	(0.64)	(5.12)	(1.24)	(3.59)	(0.35)
Yogyakarta	–0.319	–0.084	–0.057*	0.044	–0.058**	0.010
	(1.65)	(0.31)	(2.54)	(1.37)	(2.95)	(0.35)
East Java	–0.010	0.032	–0.093**	0.026	–0.041*	0.014
	(0.05)	(0.13)	(3.98)	(0.86)	(2.50)	(0.62)
Bali	0.889**	–0.078	–0.163**	0.036	0.038	0.005
	(2.91)	(0.20)	(5.70)	(0.97)	(1.24)	(0.12)
West Nusa Tenggara	–0.187	0.043	–0.095**	0.028	–0.063**	0.020
	(0.87)	(0.15)	(3.47)	(0.78)	(3.33)	(0.75)
South Kalimantan	–0.272	0.136	–0.006	–0.029	–0.030	0.018
	(1.10)	(0.4[illegible])	(0.20)	(0.78)	(1.35)	(0.56)
South Sulawesi	0.380	–0.270	–0.163**	0.076	–0.031	–0.007
	(1.26)	(0.76)	(4.53)	(1.69)	(1.24)	(0.25)
Constant	9.432**	0.051	2.312**	–0.163	–0.117	–0.029
	(6.19)	(0.02)	(9.02)	(0.44)	(0.95)	(0.17)
F-test (p-values):						
Interaction variables		0.3520		0.0891		0.8822
Education variables	0.0000		0.0001		0.0000	
Expenditure variables		0.0000		0.0000		0.0000
Number of observations	20,407		20,407		20,407	
R-squared	0.17		0.10		0.09	

Source: IFLS2 and IFLS3.

The first regression uses BMI (a continuous variable) as the dependent variable. Dummy variables for being undernourished and overweight are used as dependent variables in the second and third regressions, respectively, and estimated by linear probability models. Dummy variable for missing education and dummy variable for missing per capita expenditures are included in the regressions but not reported in the table. The omitted category for education is no schooling, and for province is Jakarta. Estimates were weighted using individual sampling weights. Standard errors are robust to clustering at the community level and to heteroscedasticity. Absolute t-statistics are in parentheses with significance at 5% (*) and 1% (**) indicated.

TABLE 7.11
Adult Blood Pressure and Levels of Hypertension

	Men			Women		
	1997	2000	Change	1997	2000	Change
Age 15–19 years						
Systolic						
Mean	119.7	118.4	−1.3 *	112.2	111.0	−1.3 *
	(0.44)	(0.37)	(0.58)	(0.44)	(0.34)	(0.56)
% ≥140	7.9	5.7	−2.2 *	2.4	1.7	−0.7
	(0.82)	(0.60)	(1.02)	(0.41)	(0.31)	(0.51)
Diastolic						
Mean	74.1	75.2	1.1 **	73.6	76.0	2.4 **
	(0.32)	(0.26)	(0.41)	(0.31)	(0.26)	(0.40)
% ≥ 90	7.6	6.9	−0.7	5.6	8.0	2.4 *
	(0.78)	(0.65)	(1.02)	(0.71)	(0.68)	(0.98)
% systolic ≥140 and diastolic ≥ 90	2.7	2.0	−0.7	1.1	0.9	−0.2
	(0.50)	(0.33)	(0.60)	(0.28)	(0.23)	(0.36)
Number of observations	[1,480]	[1,875]	[1,591]	[2,012]		
Age 20–39 years						
Systolic						
Mean	123.4	121.7	−1.7 **	118.0	115.9	−2.1 **
	(0.39)	(0.25)	(0.46)	(0.39)	(0.30)	(0.49)
% ≥140	11.1	9.4	−1.7	9.7	7.5	−2.3 **
	(0.72)	(0.48)	(0.86)	(0.56)	(0.40)	(0.67)
Diastolic						
Mean	77.8	78.9	1.1 **	76.8	78.3	1.6 **
	(0.29)	(0.17)	(0.34)	(0.24)	(0.17)	(0.30)
% ≥ 90	11.9	13.4	1.5	11.9	13.6	1.7 *
	(0.72)	(0.56)	(0.91)	(0.58)	(0.54)	(0.80)
% systolic ≥140 and diastolic ≥ 90	5.1	5.1	0.0	5.8	4.9	−0.9
	(0.47)	(0.36)	(0.59)	(0.42)	(0.33)	(0.54)
Number of observations	[3,592]	[5,538]	[4,471]	[5,858]		

Age 40–59 years						
Systolic						
Mean	131.7	130.1	–1.5 *	133.5	131.6	–1.9 *
	(0.53)	(0.45)	(0.70)	(0.67)	(0.56)	(0.87)
% ≥140	29.3	25.7	–3.5 *	33.5	30.7	–2.8
	(1.11)	(0.95)	(1.46)	(1.05)	(0.99)	(1.44)
Diastolic						
Mean	81.6	83.1	1.5 **	81.3	82.6	1.2 **
	(0.33)	(0.27)	(0.43)	(0.34)	(0.27)	(0.44)
% ≥ 90	22.7	25.1	2.4	23.3	24.3	1.0
	(1.12)	(0.99)	(1.49)	(0.95)	(0.93)	(1.33)
% systolic ≥140 and diastolic ≥ 90	16.5	17.3	0.8	18.4	18.4	0.0
	(0.94)	(0.85)	(1.27)	(0.84)	(0.83)	(1.18)
Number of observations	[2,460]	[3,015]	[2,939]	[3,355]		
Age > 60 years						
Systolic						
Mean	144.5	144.4	–0.1	153.5	151.2	–2.3
	(0.79)	(0.79)	(1.12)	(1.17)	(0.93)	(1.49)
% ≥140	51.3	52.1	0.8	64.6	61.2	–3.4
	(1.60)	(1.51)	(2.20)	(1.70)	(1.50)	(2.27)
Diastolic						
Mean	82.6	83.0	0.5	84.1	84.3	0.2
	(0.43)	(0.45)	(0.62)	(0.54)	(0.45)	(0.71)
% ≥ 90	28.9	28.4	–0.5	32.7	31.8	–0.9
	(1.44)	(1.26)	(1.92)	(1.63)	(1.40)	(2.15)
% systolic ≥140 and diastolic ≥ 90	25.7	25.5	–0.2	31.0	29.1	–1.9
	(1.39)	(1.26)	(1.87)	(1.60)	(1.40)	(2.13)
Number of observations	[1,152]	[1,401]	[1,333]	[1,706]		

Source: IFLS2 and IFLS3.
Observations exclude women who were pregnant. Estimates were weighted using individual sampling weights. Standard errors (in parentheses) are robust to clustering at the community level. Significance at 5% (*) and 1% (**) indicated.

FIGURE 7.16
CDF of Blood Pressure Levels for Adult 20–39 Years

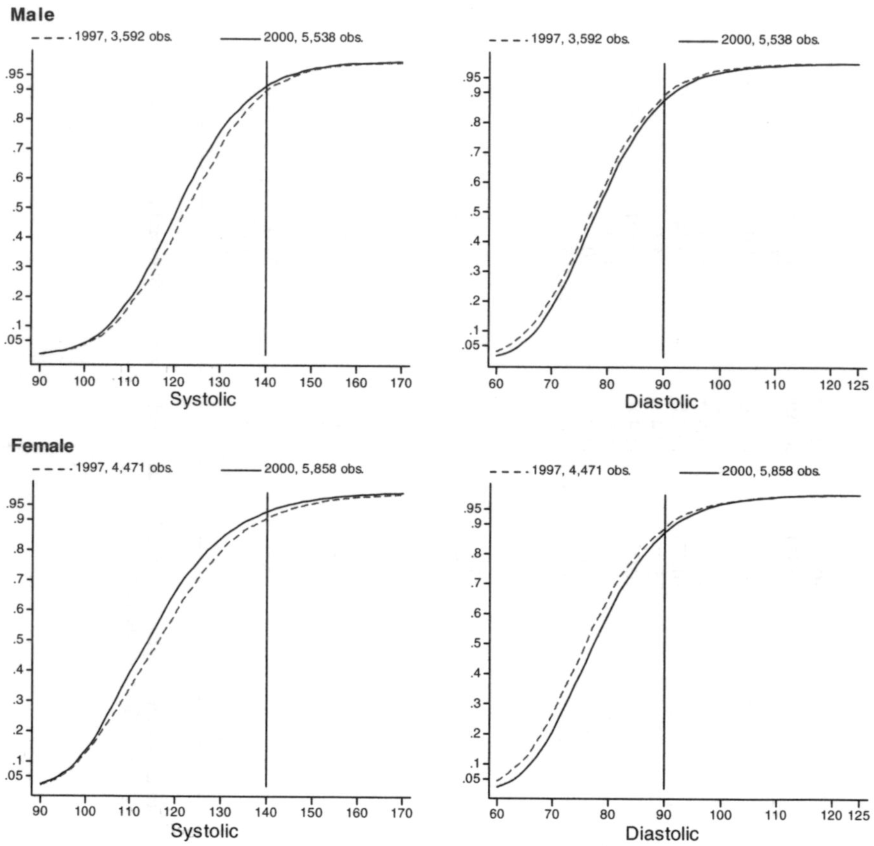
Male
1997, 3,592 obs.
2000, 5,538 obs.
.95
.9
.8
.7
.6
.5
.4
.3
.2
.1
.05
90 100 110 120 130 140 150 160 170
Systolic
60 70 80 90 100 110 120 125
Diastolic
Female
1997, 4,471 obs.
2000, 5,858 obs.
Systolic
Diastolic

Source: IFLS2 and IFLS3.
Observations were weighted using individual sampling weights.

FIGURE 7.17
CDF of Blood Pressure Levels for Adult 40–59 Years

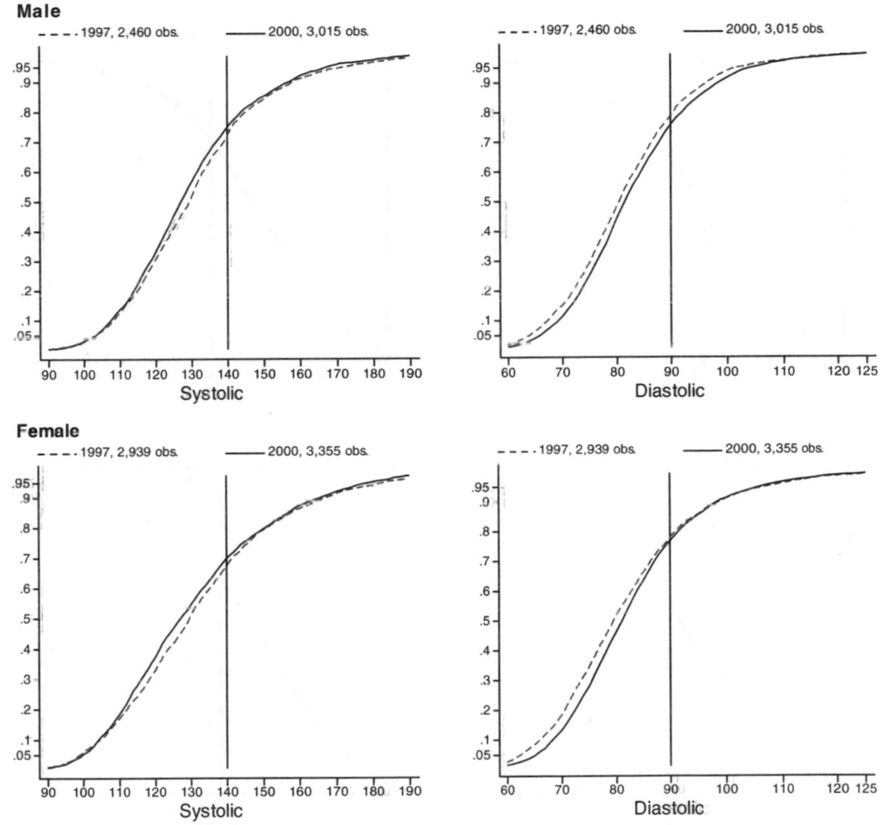
Male
1997, 2,460 obs.
2000, 3,015 obs.
.05
.1
.2
.3
.4
.5
.6
.7
.8
.9
.95
90 100 110 120 130 140 150 160 170 180 190
Systolic
60 70 80 90 100 110 120 125
Diastolic
Female
1997, 2,939 obs.
2000, 3,355 obs.
Systolic
Diastolic

Source: IFLS2 and IFLS3.
Observations were weighted using individual sampling weights.

FIGURE 7.18
CDF of Blood Pressure Levels for Adult 60 Years and Above

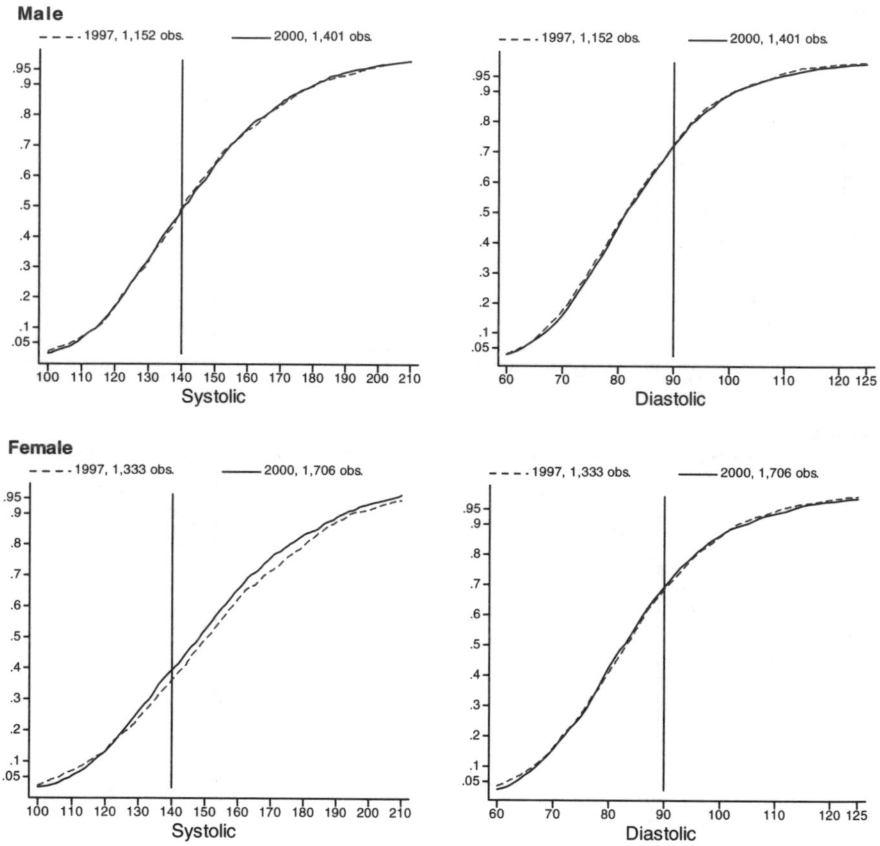
Male
1997, 1,152 obs.
2000, 1,401 obs.
.95
.9
.8
.7
.6
.5
.4
.3
.2
.1
.05
100 110 120 130 140 150 160 170 180 190 200 210
Systolic
60 70 80 90 100 110 120 125
Diastolic
Female
1997, 1,333 obs.
2000, 1,706 obs.
Systolic
Diastolic

Source: IFLS2 and IFLS3.
Observations were weighted using individual sampling weights.

TABLE 7.12a
Female Blood Pressure and Levels of Hypertension Regressions

	Systolic		Diastolic		High Systolic		High Diastolic		High Systolic and Diastolic	
	1997	Change in 2000	1997	Change in 2000	1997	Change in 2000	1997	Change in 2000	1997	Change in 2000
Age (spline, × 10^{-1}): 15–19 years	3.387	2.331	–0.418	3.061	0.046	–0.030	–0.003	0.047	0.010	–0.014
	(1.62)	(0.86)	(0.29)	(1.62)	(1.67)	(0.88)	(0.09)	(0.96)	(0.56)	(0.55)
20–29 years	5.143**	–2.395*	4.531**	–3.261**	0.055**	–0.023	0.077**	–0.048*	0.050**	–0.020
	(5.78)	(2.17)	(7.59)	(4.38)	(3.94)	(1.38)	(4.72)	(2.25)	(4.55)	(1.52)
30–39 years	5.897**	2.018	1.728**	2.693**	0.102**	0.018	0.052**	0.055*	0.067**	0.011
	(6.14)	(1.57)	(3.03)	(3.64)	(6.09)	(0.77)	(2.98)	(2.33)	(4.74)	(0.59)
40–49 years	9.603**	–0.342	2.989**	–2.573**	0.156**	–0.022	0.089**	–0.063	0.094**	–0.002
	(6.70)	(0.18)	(4.23)	(2.69)	(6.42)	(0.67)	(3.73)	(1.96)	(4.46)	(0.08)
50–59 years	11.961**	–0.604	0.892	0.966	0.199**	–0.005	0.015	0.042	0.049*	0.017
	(7.01)	(0.29)	(1.08)	(0.89)	(7.20)	(0.14)	(0.57)	(1.20)	(2.04)	(0.53)
≥ 60 years	7.229**	–1.014	1.281*	–1.451*	0.103**	–0.010	0.056**	–0.037	0.062**	–0.043*
	(6.79)	(0.73)	(2.54)	(2.30)	(7.04)	(0.51)	(3.44)	(1.82)	(3.97)	(2.16)
Education: 1–5 years	2.097*	–1.576	1.356**	–0.002	0.036*	–0.025	0.033*	0.015	0.039**	0.001
	(2.53)	(1.34)	(3.03)	(0.00)	(2.31)	(1.14)	(2.14)	(0.71)	(2.84)	(0.05)
6–8 years	0.779	–0.944	1.232**	–0.250	0.018	–0.032	0.030*	0.003	0.035**	–0.016
	(0.98)	(0.80)	(2.93)	(0.42)	(1.30)	(1.57)	(2.14)	(0.15)	(2.89)	(0.88)
9–11 years	–1.134	–0.977	1.015	–0.713	0.009	–0.033	0.028	–0.016	0.033*	–0.022
	(1.23)	(0.75)	(1.84)	(0.97)	(0.56)	(1.48)	(1.67)	(0.71)	(2.56)	(1.18)
12+ years	–3.555**	–1.536	–0.369	–0.393	–0.024	–0.021	–0.007	0.015	0.008	–0.008
	(3.74)	(1.16)	(0.74)	(0.58)	(1.53)	(0.96)	(0.46)	(0.68)	(0.61)	(0.45)
log *pce* (spline, × 10^{-3}): 0-log Rp 150,000	11.255	–729.322	–25.094	–178.772	–1.753	–3.056	–2.409	–19.803	2.927	–15.439
	(0.01)	(0.53)	(0.04)	(0.22)	(0.11)	(0.13)	(0.13)	(0.76)	(0.20)	(0.73)
> log Rp 150,000	–75.160	–46.379	342.004	–2.913	0.483	8.663	11.738	–4.119	2.445	2.690
	(0.16)	(0.08)	(1.21)	(0.01)	(0.06)	(0.83)	(1.77)	(0.43)	(0.47)	(0.36)
Rural	–0.654	–0.146	–0.370	–0.074	–0.010	–0.014	–0.011	–0.013	–0.002	–0.015
	(0.95)	(0.16)	(0.96)	(0.15)	(0.97)	(1.07)	(1.12)	(0.97)	(0.20)	(1.37)
North Sumatra × 10^{-1}	30.493*	–49.246**	22.507**	–31.775**	–0.024	–0.078	0.159	–0.512	0.025	–0.251
	(2.56)	(3.17)	(2.54)	(3.03)	(0.12)	(0.32)	(0.78)	(1.84)	(0.15)	(1.22)
West Sumatra × 10^{-1}	59.321**	–65.023**	33.857**	–9.543	0.288	–0.196	0.636**	–0.104	0.329	–0.059
	(3.85)	(3.35)	(3.49)	(0.76)	(1.07)	(0.62)	(3.06)	(0.34)	(1.88)	(0.27)

continued on next page

TABLE 7.12a – cont'd

	Systolic		Diastolic		High Systolic		High Diastolic		High Systolic and Diastolic	
	1997	Change in 2000	1997	Change in 2000	1997	Change in 2000	1997	Change in 2000	1997	Change in 2000
South Sumatra × 10^{-1}	90.706**	–83.948**	38.731**	-53.933**	0.583*	–0.310	0.454*	–0.811**	0.185	–0.286
	(6.33)	(4.71)	(4.26)	(4.73)	(2.35)	(1.05)	(2.18)	(2.65)	(1.04)	(1.27)
Lampung × 10^{-1}	60.501**	-57.196**	41.583**	-59.192**	0.388	–0.146	0.441*	–0.793*	0.276	–0.231
	(4.01)	(2.92)	(4.50)	(4.89)	(1.87)	(0.47)	(2.06)	(2.45)	(1.43)	(0.88)
West Java × 10^{-1}	58.199**	-53.742**	34.076**	–44.184**	0.313	–0.169	0.296	–0.608**	0.240*	–0.282
	(5.49)	(4.05)	(4.46)	(4.85)	(1.96)	(0.84)	(1.89)	(2.69)	(2.11)	(1.83)
Central Java × 10^{-1}	26.713*	-58.785**	12.463	-3.298	0.054	–0.214	–0.022	–0.012	–0.063	–0.087
	(2.25)	(3.92)	(1.45)	(0.32)	(0.30)	(0.94)	(0.13)	(0.05)	(0.45)	(0.46)
Yogyakarta × 10^{-1}	55.458**	–112.869**	35.844**	–40.614**	0.284	–0.706**	0.248	–0.493*	0.028	–0.347
	(4.81)	(6.71)	(4.93)	(4.58)	(1.51)	(2.87)	(1.50)	(2.00)	(0.20)	(1.91)
East Java × 10 –1	48.212**	-56.062**	33.669**	–44.479**	0.162	–0.079	0.269	–0.689**	0.057	–0.211
	(4.51)	(4.09)	(4.39)	(4.77)	(1.00)	(0.38)	(1.66)	(2.85)	(0.49)	(1.31)
Bali × 10^{-1}	–12.141	–70.404**	17.661*	-32.029**	–0.632**	–0.157	–0.241	–0.273	–0.502**	–0.015
	(0.85)	(3.76)	(2.34)	(3.18)	(2.96)	(0.58)	(1.37)	(1.01)	(3.10)	(0.08)
West Nusa Tenggara × 10^{-1}	57.726**	–41.223*	45.884**	–41.955**	0.204	0.079	0.429	–0.624*	0.218	–0.277
	(4.10)	(2.13)	(5.22)	(3.89)	(0.83)	(0.24)	(1.87)	(2.04)	(1.14)	(1.14)
South Kalimantan × 10^{-1}	97.230**	-54.402*	57.407**	-35.810**	1.083**	–0.479	1.110**	–0.587	0.881**	–0.420
	(5.38)	(2.54)	(4.78)	(2.62)	(3.37)	(1.26)	(3.97)	(1.58)	(4.49)	(1.62)
South Sulawesi × 10^{-1}	23.761	1.565	21.640*	-20.717	–0.206	0.680*	0.309	–0.363	0.010	0.056
	(1.69)	(0.08)	(2.11)	(1.67)	(0.92)	(2.28)	(1.07)	(1.00)	(0.06)	(0.23)
Constant	102.163**	9.976	70.584**	2.960	–0.062	0.131	0.039	0.230	–0.087	0.249
	(8.56)	(0.58)	(8.78)	(0.28)	(0.33)	(0.46)	(0.17)	(0.70)	(0.50)	(0.97)
F-test (p-values):										
Interaction variables	0.0000		0.0000		0.0050		0.0009		0.3381	
Education variables	0.0000		0.0000		0.0000		0.0001		0.0000	
Expenditure variables	0.9346		0.3905		0.7571		0.2654		0.8307	
Number of observations	23,265		23,265		23,265		23,265		23,265	
R-squared	0.31		0.09		0.25		0.06		0.10	

Source: IFLS2 and IFLS3. Observations exclude women who were pregnant. The first two regressions use systolic and diastolic levels (continuous variables) as the dependent variables. The next three regressions are linear probability models using dummy variables for having high systolic level (140 and above), high diastolic level (90 and above), and high systolic and diastolic as the dependent variables. Dummy variable for missing education and dummy variable for missing per capita expenditures are included in the regressions but not reported in the table. The omitted category for education is no schooling, and for province is Jakarta. Estimates were weighted using individual sampling weights. Standard errors are robust to clustering at the community level and to heteroscedasticity. Absolute t-statistics are in parentheses with significance at 5% (*) and 1% (**) indicated.

TABLE 7.12b
Male Blood Pressure and Levels of Hypertension Regressions

	Systolic		Diastolic		High Systolic		High Diastolic		High Systolic and Diastolic	
	1997	Change in 2000	1997	Change in 2000	1997	Change in 2000	1997	Change in 2000	1997	Change in 2000
Age (spline, × 10^{-1}): 15–19 years	15.927**	–5.663*	5.740**	–0.816	0.112**	–0.048	–0.002	0.053	0.043	–0.035
	(7.73)	(2.11)	(3.68)	(0.42)	(2.66)	(0.95)	(0.05)	(0.98)	(1.63)	(1.12)
20–29 years	–1.266	1.377	2.254**	–0.147	–0.018	0.025	0.055**	–0.019	0.011	0.011
	(1.55)	(1.31)	(3.67)	(0.20)	(0.91)	(1.09)	(2.99)	(0.80)	(0.88)	(0.74)
30–39 years	2.256*	1.100	1.922**	1.341	0.069**	–0.006	0.045*	0.048	0.052**	0.016
	(2.51)	(0.94)	(3.19)	(1.73)	(3.75)	(0.24)	(2.42)	(1.89)	(3.90)	(0.85)
40–49 years	7.317**	–0.079	2.577**	–0.111	0.153**	–0.005	0.074**	0.007	0.098**	–0.002
	(5.78)	(0.05)	(3.64)	(0.12)	(6.04)	(0.13)	(3.16)	(0.20)	(4.56)	(0.07)
50–59 years	6.951**	1.847	0.835	–0.671	0.121**	0.034	0.048	–0.028	0.050*	0.015
	(4.72)	(0.91)	(1.03)	(0.62)	(4.23)	(0.86)	(1.74)	(0.74)	(1.96)	(0.44)
≥ 60 years	5.229**	–0.409	–0.469	–0.494	0.086**	0.007	0.006	–0.013	0.020	–0.018
	(5.72)	(0.32)	(0.92)	(0.73)	(5.10)	(0.30)	(0.31)	(0.54)	(1.16)	(0.82)
Education: 1–5 years	0.638	0.379	0.127	0.627	0.027	–0.016	0.001	0.037	0.002	0.033
	(0.66)	(0.30)	(0.27)	(0.90)	(1.40)	(0.61)	(0.07)	(1.63)	(0.11)	(1.62)
6–8 years	0.320	1.739	0.611	0.809	0.028	0.007	0.032	0.030	0.030*	0.028
	(0.32)	(1.36)	(1.22)	(1.11)	(1.43)	(0.28)	(1.92)	(1.31)	(2.06)	(1.44)
9–11 years	–0.511	1.774	0.958	0.893	0.008	0.025	0.032	0.046	0.025	0.031
	(0.43)	(1.24)	(1.49)	(1.06)	(0.38)	(0.90)	(1.62)	(1.79)	(1.61)	(1.51)
12+ years	–0.511	2.324	1.684**	1.022	0.026	0.021	0.038*	0.061*	0.027	0.042
	(0.47)	(1.71)	(2.86)	(1.27)	(1.25)	(0.76)	(1.98)	(2.30)	(1.69)	0.033
log *pce* (spline, × 10^{-3}): 0-log Rp 150,000	850.637	–463.222	832.369	–889.502	9.668	–25.228	22.213	–27.312	12.626	–18.421
	(0.86)	(0.34)	(1.70)	(1.14)	(0.47)	(0.96)	(1.38)	(1.14)	(0.93)	(0.99)
> log Rp 150,000	46.639	146.024	331.243	380.451	0.343	0.481	13.650	1.730	7.642	–1.578
	(0.12)	(0.28)	(1.41)	(1.16)	(0.04)	(0.05)	(1.70)	(0.16)	(1.21)	(0.19)
Rural	–1.825**	1.500*	–1.292**	0.503	–0.020	0.010	–0.036**	0.016	–0.021*	0.003
	(2.88)	(1.97)	(3.21)	(1.00)	(1.66)	(0.64)	(3.19)	(1.06)	(2.39)	(0.25)
North Sumatra × 10^{-1}	16.437	–35.658	16.742	–27.483*	–0.062	–0.307	0.362	–0.578	0.028	–0.269
	(1.23)	(1.93)	(1.60)	(2.04)	(0.28)	(0.99)	(1.38)	(1.67)	(0.15)	(1.06)
West Sumatra × 10^{-1}	70.168**	–75.458**	43.190**	–31.521*	0.723	–0.909*	1.057**	–0.689	0.421	–0.426
	(5.08)	(3.95)	(4.46)	(2.30)	(2.44)	(2.46)	(3.23)	(1.67)	(1.75)	(1.43)

continued on next page

TABLE 7.12b – cont'd

	Systolic		Diastolic		High Systolic		High Diastolic		High Systolic and Diastolic	
	1997	Change in 2000	1997	Change in 2000	1997	Change in 2000	1997	Change in 2000	1997	Change in 2000
South Sumatra × 10^{-1}	30.629*	–14.987	5.555	–13.736	0.366	–0.058	–0.111	0.197	0.025	–0.004
	(2.31)	(0.91)	(0.57)	(1.13)	(1.59)	(0.18)	(0.50)	(0.67)	(0.14)	(0.02)
Lampung × 10^{-1}	45.108**	–52.000**	33.964**	–48.094*	0.355	–0.376	0.473*	–0.650*	0.251	–0.220
	(3.78)	(3.36)	(4.02)	(4.51)	(1.38)	(1.09)	(2.09)	(2.16)	(1.22)	(0.83)
West Java × 10^{-1}	39.047**	–43.750**	25.099**	–34.836**	0.338*	–0.492*	0.320	–0.520*	0.172	–0.322
	(4.29)	(3.78)	(3.57)	(3.96)	(2.02)	(2.14)	(1.82)	(2.27)	(1.22)	(1.75)
Central Java × 10^{-1}	21.533*	–50.195**	7.406	–5.013	0.218	–0.706**	–0.006	–0.063	0.002	–0.276
	(2.03)	(3.84)	(0.83)	(0.47)	(1.20)	(2.86)	(0.04)	(0.25)	(0.01)	(1.44)
Yogyakarta × 10^{-1}	47.633**	–84.074**	26.706**	–24.284*	0.312	–0.895**	0.265	–0.333	0.149	–0.416
	(3.69)	(5.47)	(3.22)	(2.41)	(1.28)	(2.94)	(1.16)	(1.10)	(0.73)	(1.64)
East Java × 10^{-1}	42.483**	–44.058**	32.330**	–39.384**	0.376	–0.471	0.438*	–0.580*	0.105	–0.265
	(4.18)	(3.53)	(4.22)	(4.13)	(1.88)	(1.83)	(2.17)	(2.25)	(0.67)	(1.33)
Bali × 10^{-1}	11.779	–56.427**	23.254*	–39.893**	–0.086	–0.766*	0.125	–0.523	–0.194	–0.437
	(0.95)	(3.39)	(2.40)	(3.26)	(0.34)	(2.30)	(0.52)	(1.60)	(1.06)	(1.82)
West Nusa Tenggara × 10^{-1}	5.641	–12.937	8.558	–14.228	0.121	–0.101	–0.024	–0.141	–0.143	0.057
	(0.46)	(0.79)	(0.87)	(1.22)	(0.53)	(0.33)	(0.11)	(0.46)	(1.00)	(0.28)
South Kalimantan × 10^{-1}	69.609**	–41.864*	43.147**	–22.977	0.806**	–0.247	0.912**	–0.132	0.655**	–0.121
	(5.03)	(2.40)	(4.38)	(1.91)	(3.24)	(0.66)	(3.79)	(0.40)	(3.13)	(0.38)
South Sulawesi × 10^{-1}	41.390**	–7.031	30.773**	–22.468	0.292	0.548	0.580*	–0.040	0.216	0.336
	(3.13)	(0.38)	(2.94)	(1.74)	(1.29)	(1.58)	(2.09)	(0.11)	(1.16)	(1.25)
Constant	79.666**	15.341	51.804**	14.206	–0.269	0.383	–0.230	0.209	–0.228	0.263
	(6.53)	(0.90)	(8.06)	(1.44)	(1.08)	(1.19)	(1.06)	(0.69)	(1.35)	(1.16)
F-test (p-values):										
Interaction variables	0.0000		0.0000		0.0027		0.0037		0.2681	
Education variables	0.1303		0.0000		0.0395		0.0000		0.0000	
Expenditure variables	0.7690		0.0012		0.8667		0.0152		0.2881	
Number of observations	20,513		20,513		20,513		20,513		20,513	
R-squared	0.18		0.08		0.15		0.05		0.08	

Source: IFLS2 and IFLS3. The first two regressions use systolic and diastolic levels (continuous variables) as the dependent variables. The next three regressions are linear probability models using dummy variables for having high systolic level (140 and above), high diastolic level (90 and above), and high systolic and diastolic as the dependent variables. Dummy variable for missing education and dummy variable for missing per capita expenditures are included in the regressions but not reported in the table. The omitted category for education is no schooling, and for province is Jakarta. Estimates were weighted using individual sampling weights. Standard errors are robust to clustering at the community level and to heteroscedasticity. Absolute t-statistics are in parentheses with significance at 5% (*) and 1% (**) indicated.

TABLE 7.13
Frequency of Smoking

	15 and above						15–19 years					
	Men			Women			Men			Women		
	1997	2000	Change	1997	2000	Change	1997	2000	Change	1997	2000	Change
% ever smoked	70.9	71.1	0.2	6.4	5.8	–0.6	38.2	43.7	5.4 *	0.3	0.4	0.2
	(0.85)	(0.65)	(1.07)	(0.44)	(0.38)	(0.58)	(1.72)	(1.36)	(2.19)	(0.12)	(0.15)	(0.19)
% currently smoke [a)]	66.1	65.6	–0.5	2.6	2.7	0.1	36.8	42.6	5.8 **	0.0	0.3	0.3
	(0.89)	(0.70)	(1.14)	(0.26)	(0.25)	(0.36)	(1.69)	(1.40)	(2.19)	(0.04)	(0.13)	(0.14)
% currently smoke tobacco	9.4	7.5	–1.9 *	0.4	0.3	0.2	6.2	8.7	2.5 *	0.0	0.1	0.0
	(0.64)	(0.45)	(0.78)	(0.08)	(0.05)	(0.09)	(0.76)	(0.80)	(1.10)	(0.04)	(0.08)	(0.09)
% currently smoke cloves	55.9	58.2	2.2	2.2	2.4	0.2	30.2	33.9	3.7	0.0	0.2	0.2
	(1.05)	(0.82)	(1.33)	(0.24)	(0.24)	(0.34)	(1.73)	(1.40)	(2.22)	(0.00)	(0.11)	(0.11)
Total observations	9,086	12,056	10,734	13,401	1,581	1,925	1,703	2,136				

	20–29 years						30–39 years					
	Men			Women			Men			Women		
	1997	2000	Change	1997	2000	Change	1997	2000	Change	1997	2000	Change
% ever smoked	69.9	72.3	2.4	0.8	1.0	0.2	77.9	75.6	–2.3	3.4	2.8	–0.6
	(1.48)	(1.02)	(1.80)	(0.19)	(0.18)	(0.26)	(1.15)	(1.08)	(1.57)	(0.50)	(0.40)	(0.64)
% currently smoke [a)]	68.0	69.7	1.7	0.4	0.8	0.4	74.7	71.1	–3.6 *	2.6	2.2	–0.4
	(1.51)	(1.04)	(1.83)	(0.15)	(0.16)	(0.22)	(1.20)	(1.15)	(1.66)	(0.47)	(0.31)	(0.56)
% currently smoke tobacco	11.1	10.9	–0.1	0.2	0.3	0.1	8.5	6.8	–1.7	0.4	0.2	–0.2
	(0.87)	(0.75)	(1.15)	(0.09)	(0.09)	(0.13)	(0.79)	(0.58)	(0.98)	(0.15)	(0.09)	(0.17)
% currently smoke cloves	56.4	58.7	2.3	0.2	0.5	0.3	65.7	64.3	–1.4	2.1	2.0	–0.1
	(1.60)	(1.15)	(1.97)	(0.12)	(0.13)	(0.17)	(1.38)	(1.26)	(1.87)	(0.42)	(0.30)	(0.52)
Total observations	1,855	3,171	2,397	3,489	1,974	2,552	2,451	2,851				

continued on next page

TABLE 7.13 – cont'd

	40–49 years						50–59 years					
	Men			Women			Men			Women		
	1997	2000	Change	1997	2000	Change	1997	2000	Change	1997	2000	Change
% ever smoked	76.4	76.9	0.4	5.3	5.1	–0.1	83.6	79.2	–4.5 *	16.7	12.5	–4.2 *
	(1.40)	(1.33)	(1.93)	(0.86)	(0.70)	(1.11)	(1.43)	(1.45)	(2.03)	(1.67)	(1.15)	(2.03)
% currently smoke [a)]	71.0	70.6	–0.4	3.6	3.7	0.1	76.3	70.1	–6.2 **	6.6	5.9	–0.7
	(1.47)	(1.35)	(1.99)	(0.64)	(0.59)	(0.87)	(1.66)	(1.63)	(2.33)	(0.96)	(0.78)	(1.24)
% currently smoke tobacco	7.9	4.7	–3.2 **	0.4	0.3	–0.1	11.7	4.8	–7.0 **	1.0	0.4	–0.6
	(0.96)	(0.59)	(1.12)	(0.17)	(0.12)	(0.21)	(1.62)	(0.72)	(1.77)	(0.30)	(0.17)	(0.35)
% currently smoke cloves	61.8	65.9	4.1	3.2	3.4	0.3	63.4	65.3	1.9	5.6	5.5	–0.1
	(1.67)	(1.38)	(2.16)	(0.63)	(0.54)	(0.83)	(2.03)	(1.73)	(2.67)	(0.90)	(0.76)	(1.18)
Total observations	1,488	1,884	1,678	2,050	1,065	1,181	1,292	1,332				

	60 and above					
	Men			Women		
	1997	2000	Change	1997	2000	Change
% ever smoked	83.4	82.3	–1.0	29.2	26.2	–3.0
	(1.37)	(1.23)	(1.84)	(2.22)	(2.03)	(3.01)
% currently smoke [a)]	68.6	65.9	–2.6	6.7	6.5	–0.3
	(1.82)	(1.57)	(2.40)	(0.99)	(0.90)	(1.34)
% currently smoke tobacco	12.1	6.1	–6.1 **	1.1	0.4	–0.6
	(1.59)	(0.84)	(1.80)	(0.36)	(0.17)	(0.40)
% currently smoke cloves	54.7	59.9	5.2	5.5	6.0	0.5
	(2.31)	(1.68)	(2.85)	(0.85)	(0.88)	(1.22)
Total observations	1,123	1,343	1,213	1,543		

Source: IFLS2 and IFLS3
[a)] Currently smoke cigarettes/cigars. Estimates were weighted using individual sampling weights. Standard errors (in parentheses) are robust to clustering at the community level. Significance at 5% (*) and 1% (**) indicated.

Smokers include those smoking tobacco or clove cigarettes, or cigars. Pipe smokers and tobacco chewing are excluded. Among men, smoking rates are high, over 67% for men 15 years old and over. Current rates are lower for adolescents, 40%, but rise to over 70% for men 20 years and older. Current smoking rates are somewhat higher for rural men, 70%, with the rural–urban gap larger for older men (Appendix Table 7.7). The overwhelming majority of male smokers smoke clove cigarettes, over 90%, rather than tobacco.

Among women, smoking is rare. Just over 2.5% of women 15 and over currently smoke, although the rate rises with age, to just over 5% among elderly women. As for men, rural women are more likely to smoke, with the probability at 7–8% for rural women over 60 years.

Table 7.14 indicates that prime-aged men who smoke consume about one pack (12 cigarettes) per day, while younger and older men consume a little less. Women who smoke consume less, between 6 and 9 cigarettes per day. Quantities smoked are approximately equal in rural and urban areas for those who smoke (Appendix Table 7.8).

The time between 1997 and 2000 saw few changes in current smoking propensities in the aggregate, however we do see some (offsetting) patterns across specific age-groups. Young men 15–19 increased their smoking rates significantly, however, for men over 30, current rates declined, significantly for some groups.

We don't have information on how long a person has been continuously smoking, but we do have information on the age of first smoking. In Table 7.15 we present information on the percent of each age group who smoked by age 15, 18, 21, and 24. A rising fraction of younger age cohorts are starting to smoke at younger ages. Only 19% of men 50–59 first smoked before age 15, but among current teens aged 15–19 that fraction has risen to nearly 25%. A similar trend can be observed for smoking by age 18, 21 and 24. Current rural residents begin smoking at earlier ages than men currently living in urban areas (Appendix Table 7.9). The trend towards starting to smoke at earlier ages is apparent among both urban and rural men.

We present descriptive regressions for the probability of currently smoking and for the quantity consumed daily among those who smoke, in Tables 7.16a and b. We do so for male teenagers and male and female adults (20 and over) separately. For teenagers, the level of schooling dummies are jointly, but not individually, significant in deterring smoking. The impacts become negative starting with completion of primary school, and are stronger in 2000 than in 1997. Higher *pce* is associated with smoking more cigarettes.

TABLE 7.14
Average Number of Cigarettes Smoked Per Day (for Current Smokers)

Age/ Gender		Average		
		1997	2000	Change
15–19				
	Men	8.3	8.1	–0.3
		(0.32)	(0.24)	(0.39)
	Women	5.0	5.2	0.2
		(0.00)	(2.53)	(2.53)
20–29				
	Men	10.9	10.8	–0.1
		(0.27)	(0.18)	(0.33)
	Women	9.5	6.3	–3.3 *
		(0.91)	(1.14)	(1.46)
30–39				
	Men	12.4	12.2	–0.3
		(0.24)	(0.22)	(0.32)
	Women	7.0	7.9	0.9
		(0.85)	(1.19)	(1.46)
40–49				
	Men	12.5	12.1	–0.3
		(0.32)	(0.24)	(0.40)
	Women	7.4	7.5	0.1
		(0.75)	(0.71)	(1.04)
50–59				
	Men	11.4	11.4	0.0
		(0.36)	(0.32)	(0.48)
	Women	6.9	6.3	–0.6
		(0.67)	(0.54)	(0.86)
60 or above				
	Men	10.0	9.8	–0.2
		(0.28)	0.27	(0.39)
	Women	6.2	6.4	0.2
		(0.79)	(0.51)	(0.94)

Source: IFLS2 and IFLS3.
Estimates were weighted using individual sampling weights. Standard errors (in parentheses) are robust to clustering at the community level. Significance at 5% (*) and 1% (**) indicated.

TABLE 7.15
Age When Start Smoking

Age/Gender		% Age Start Smoking				Avg Age Start
		<=15	<=18	<=21	<=24	
15–19						
	Men	24.7	...	...	...	15.1
		(1.23)	...	...	...	(0.09)
	Women	0.2	...	...	...	14.5
		(0.11)	...	...	...	(1.00)
20–29						
	Men	21.3	48.9	...	...	17.2
		(0.97)	(1.16)	...	...	(0.09)
	Women	0.0	0.4	...	...	20.2
		(0.03)	(0.11)	...	...	(0.58)
30–39						
	Men	19.5	41.1	60.0	65.5	18.7
		(0.93)	(1.25)	(1.27)	(1.23)	(0.14)
	Women	0.5	0.9	1.1	1.4	23.6
		(0.14)	(0.20)	(0.23)	(0.26)	(0.96)
40–49						
	Men	19.6	32.5	52.8	59.7	20.3
		(1.18)	(1.48)	(1.57)	(1.48)	(0.20)
	Women	1.0	1.9	2.5	2.9	25.8
		(0.25)	(0.37)	(0.44)	(0.48)	(1.15)
50–59						
	Men	18.9	32.9	52.5	57.3	21.2
		(1.48)	(1.59)	(1.80)	(1.77)	(0.33)
	Women	2.7	3.5	5.4	6.0	27.2
		(0.51)	(0.57)	(0.78)	(0.81)	(1.15)
60 or above						
	Men	26.7	36.0	54.6	58.7	21.2
		(1.45)	(1.52)	(1.56)	(1.53)	(0.34)
	Women	5.6	7.5	13.2	13.9	26.8
		(0.82)	(0.97)	(1.34)	(1.41)	(0.79)

Source: IFLS3.

Estimates were weighted using individual sampling weights. Standard errors (in parentheses) are robust to clustering at the community level. Significance at 5% (*) and 1% (**) indicated.

TABLE 7.16a
Linear Probability Model of Current Smoking, Men 15–19

	Currently smoking		Cigarette consumption	
	1997	Change in 2000	1997	Change in 2000
Education: 1–5 years	0.184	–0.095	–0.845	0.408
	(1.55)	(0.62)	(0.28)	(0.12)
6–8 years	–0.062	–0.047	–2.890	2.462
	(0.53)	(0.33)	(0.93)	(0.72)
9–11 years	–0.075	–0.081	–4.106	2.096
	(0.65)	(0.57)	(1.38)	(0.63)
12+ years	–0.055	–0.060	–3.512	1.950
	(0.45)	(0.41)	(1.14)	(0.56)
log *pce* (spline): 0- log Rp 150,000	0.084	–0.065	1.926	–2.212
	(1.55)	(0.86)	(1.64)	(1.69)
> log Rp 150,000	–0.027	0.039	0.382	0.522
	(1.14)	(1.25)	(0.65)	(0.75)
Rural	0.027	0.043	0.787	–0.309
	(0.92)	(1.22)	(1.16)	(0.38)
North Sumatra	–0.230**	0.109	7.292**	–5.197*
	(4.10)	(1.31)	(3.24)	(2.12)
West Sumatra	0.070	–0.181*	0.980	–1.594
	(0.93)	(2.17)	(0.63)	(0.86)
South Sumatra	–0.047	–0.008	–1.616	1.892
	(0.62)	(0.09)	(1.30)	(0.98)
Lampung	0.136	–0.256*	0.817	–1.094
	(1.58)	(2.38)	(0.55)	(0.57)

West Java	0.070	–0.148*	–0.011	–0.349
	(1.29)	(2.21)	(0.01)	(0.29)
Central Java	0.049	–0.128	–1.556	0.588
	(0.81)	(1.74)	(1.42)	(0.45)
Yogyakarta	–0.212	0.162	–0.325	–1.956
	(3.74)**	(1.60)	(0.15)	(0.85)
East Java	–0.096	0.025	1.044	–1.509
	(1.53)	(0.34)	(0.88)	(1.10)
Bali	–0.098	–0.037	0.365	0.414
	(1.30)	(0.43)	(0.23)	(0.20)
West Nusa Tenggara	0.001	–0.175*	–0.604	1.133
	(0.01)	(2.27)	(0.46)	(0.61)
South Kalimantan	–0.079	–0.115	1.935	0.965
	(1.00)	(1.24)	(1.37)	(0.56)
South Sulawesi	–0.150*	0.064	2.253	0.551
	(2.07)	(0.72)	(1.51)	(0.38)
Constant	–0.651	1.320	–8.689	–21.266
	(1.00)	(1.44)	(0.65)	(1.40)
F-test (p-values):				
Interaction variables	0.0000	–0.0000*		
Education variables	0.0000	0.0018		
Expenditure variables	0.4817	0.0495		
Number of observations	3,506		1,354	
R-squared	0.05		0.10	

Source: IFLS2 and IFLS3. The regression for currently smoking is a linear probability model using a dummy variable for currently smoking as the dependent variable. The cigarette consumption regression uses the number of cigarettes smoked per day (a continuous variable) for those who smoke as the dependent variable. Dummy variable for missing education and dummy variable for missing per capita expenditures are included in the regression but not reported in the table. The omitted category for education is no schooling, and for province is Jakarta. Estimates are weighted using individual sampling weights. Standard errors are robust to clustering at the community level and to heteroscedasticity. Absolute t-statistics are in parentheses with significance at 5% (*) and 1% (**) indicated.

TABLE 7.16b
Linear Probability Model of Current Smoking, Men and Women 20 and Above

	Men				Women			
	Currently Smoking		Cigarette Consumption		Currently Smoking		Cigarette Consumption	
	1997	Change in 2000	1997	Change in 2000	1997	Change in 2000	1997	Change in 2000
Age 30–39	0.039*	–0.040*	1.415**	–0.139	0.022**	–0.011	–3.466**	5.398**
	(2.41)	(2.38)	(4.87)	(0.39)	(4.55)	(1.93)	(3.03)	(2.78)
Age 40–49	–0.008	–0.030	1.477**	–0.171	0.030**	–0.009	–2.097	3.240
	(0.43)	(1.57)	(4.12)	(0.46)	(4.48)	(1.25)	(1.74)	(1.86)
Age 50–59	0.033	–0.087**	0.804*	–0.158	0.061**	–0.019*	–2.749*	3.255
	(1.58)	(4.11)	(2.17)	(0.36)	(6.58)	(2.13)	(2.31)	(1.82)
Age > 60	–0.058*	–0.057*	–0.501	–0.297	0.063**	–0.018	–2.934*	3.190
	(2.55)	(2.56)	(1.37)	(0.70)	(6.50)	(1.70)	(2.08)	(1.55)
Education: 1–5 years	0.034	–0.046*	–0.240	0.890*	–0.013	0.002	–0.377	0.020
	(1.68)	(2.14)	(0.68)	(2.17)	(1.73)	(0.29)	(0.47)	(0.02)
6–8 years	0.003	–0.056**	–0.308	0.157	–0.012	–0.016*	0.374	–1.189
	(0.12)	(2.63)	(0.84)	(0.41)	(1.62)	(2.45)	(0.36)	(0.98)
9–11 years	–0.085**	–0.014	0.605	–0.268	–0.007	–0.018*	4.626*	–3.979
	(3.31)	(0.53)	(1.18)	(0.50)	(0.84)	(2.20)	(2.23)	(1.72)
12+ years	–0.138**	–0.069**	0.046	0.080	–0.012	–0.016	0.386	–1.452
	(6.06)	(3.02)	(0.10)	(0.15)	(1.45)	(1.94)	(0.25)	(0.63)
log *pce* (spline): 0- log Rp 150,000	0.038	–0.037	1.518**	–0.025	0.010	–0.013	0.292	–1.102
	(1.39)	(1.03)	(3.08)	(0.04)	(1.37)	(1.35)	(0.20)	(0.61)
> log Rp 150,000	–0.012	0.011	1.170**	0.454	0.005	0.013*	0.315	1.774
	(1.22)	(0.84)	(4.98)	(1.56)	(1.14)	(2.08)	(0.57)	(1.46)
Rural	0.069**	–0.013	–0.475	0.159	0.008	–0.005	0.414	–1.369
	(4.57)	(0.96)	(1.64)	(0.57)	(1.48)	(1.26)	(0.46)	(1.11)
North Sumatra	–0.031	0.118**	4.679**	–0.374	–0.017	0.012	1.656	–2.923
	(0.73)	(3.74)	(6.84)	(0.43)	(1.79)	(1.13)	(0.76)	(1.28)
West Sumatra	0.065	0.019	2.862**	0.221	0.013	0.004	1.207	0.596
	(1.90)	(0.54)	(4.00)	(0.26)	(0.82)	(0.26)	(0.39)	(0.22)

South Sumatra	0.048	0.007	–0.589	0.495	–0.007	–0.018	–4.059	4.871
	(1.39)	(0.20)	(0.81)	(0.64)	(0.58)	(1.95)	(1.82)	(1.81)
Lampung	0.065	–0.013	–2.156*	0.196	–0.007	–0.017	–1.676	1.753
	(1.68)	(0.38)	(2.52)	(0.31)	(0.61)	(1.73)	(0.77)	(0.70)
West Java	0.062*	–0.049*	–0.895	–0.230	0.020	–0.019*	–3.624*	1.393
	(2.43)	(2.13)	(1.81)	(0.43)	(1.66)	(2.09)	(2.02)	(0.77)
Central Java	0.044	–0.041	–3.381**	1.819**	–0.028**	–0.008	–4.678*	2.695
	(1.38)	(1.57)	(6.57)	(3.47)	(3.05)	(1.08)	(2.44)	(1.35)
Yogyakarta	–0.036	–0.019	–2.229**	0.380	–0.048**	–0.001	–2.480	0.000
	(1.16)	(0.71)	(3.55)	(0.59)	(5.66)	(0.15)	(0.70)	(.)
East Java	–0.031	0.015	–1.811**	1.216*	–0.034**	–0.004	–4.833*	5.364
	(1.06)	(0.59)	(3.49)	(2.22)	(3.85)	(0.60)	(2.29)	(1.89)
Bali	–0.247**	0.036	–2.518**	2.104**	–0.028*	–0.010	–4.278*	8.193**
	(5.84)	(1.30)	(3.33)	(2.71)	(2.57)	(1.24)	(2.31)	(3.57)
West Nusa Tenggara	0.052	–0.027	–1.380*	0.875	–0.037**	–0.009	–4.607*	4.271
	(1.41)	(0.82)	(2.06)	(1.32)	(3.33)	(0.83)	(2.28)	(1.78)
South Kalimantan	–0.092**	0.015	2.742**	0.123	0.041	–0.016	0.986	1.751
	(2.69)	(0.51)	(3.92)	(0.19)	(1.67)	(1.31)	(0.51)	(0.83)
South Sulawesi	–0.077*	0.047	2.174**	–0.473	–0.010	–0.007	0.707	1.603
	(2.29)	(1.47)	(3.21)	(0.71)	(0.81)	(0.78)	(0.34)	(0.71)
Constant	0.454	0.434	–4.302	–2.165	–0.135	0.213	–8.025	13.404
	(1.36)	(1.02)	(0.72)	(0.31)	(1.47)	(1.79)	(0.44)	(0.51)
F-test (p-values):								
Interaction variables	0.0000		0.0000		0.0931		0.0014	
Education variables	0.0000		0.0407		0.0464		0.4456	
Expenditure variables	0.6255		0.0000		0.0007		0.4049	
Number of observations	17636		12115		20296		630	
R-squared	0.06		0.10		0.04		0.19	

Source: IFLS2 and IFLS3. The regression for currently smoking is a linear probability model using a dummy variable for currently smoking as the dependent variable. The cigarette consumption regression uses the number of cigarettes smoked per day (a continuous variable) for those who smoke as the dependent variable. Dummy variable for missing education and dummy variable for missing per capita expenditures are included in the regression but not reported in the table. The omitted category for education is no schooling, and for province is Jakarta. Estimates were weighted using individual sampling weights. Standard errors are robust to clustering at the community level and to heteroscedasticity. Absolute t-statistics are in parentheses with significance at 5% (*) and 1% (**) indicated.

For adult men the results are stronger. Schooling does have an inhibiting effect on smoking for those who complete junior secondary school or higher in 1997 and by 2000 even completion of primary school or more has an negative effect. A man who has completed primary school is 5.3% less likely to be smoking in 2000 than a man with no schooling, a man with junior secondary school 10% less, and a man with senior secondary school over 20% less. For women, schooling seems a weaker deterrent, though the negative effects are still there. Men who have higher *pce* on the other hand, are not less likely to smoke, but will consume more, presumably through an income effect. As was true for BMI, higher education is associated with better health behaviours, while greater income alone, is not. Men living in rural areas are 7% more likely to smoke, while Balinese men are 25% less likely than men in Jakarta. Women in Central and East Java, Yogyakarta, Bali and West Nusa Tenggara are also somewhat less likely to smoke than women in Jakarta.

ADULT BLOOD HAEMOGLOBIN

As discussed for children, low haemoglobin levels have several causes, iron deficiency being only one. For adults the incidence of low haemoglobin (see Table 7.5) is distinctly higher for the elderly, especially for men. It is higher for men than women, although that is a function of the lower female standards used in this report. Among women, the incidence of low levels rises substantially for pregnant women.

Between 1997 and 2000 there was an improvement for men in terms of the proportion under the CDC threshold of 13.5 g/dL, in contrast to the higher rates observed for young children. For women, there were no significant changes between 1997 and 2000. However, examining the entire cumulative distribution functions (Figures 7.19–7.21) shows that even for men, the 1997 and 2000 curves cross at levels below the threshold. Tests of the differences (Appendix Table 7.10) do not show any significant first- or second-order domination. Hence looking only at the proportions would be misleading in this case.

Descriptive regressions, Table 7.17, show that both higher education and *pce* are associated with an increase in haemoglobin levels, especially for men. Higher levels of completed schooling is associated uniformly with higher haemoglobin levels for men, while for women the effect hits a plateau after completion of primary school. The impacts may come both in the composition and amount of foods eaten, as well as in the many health-related factors that affect having infections and other influences on blood haemoglobin levels. Living in rural areas is associated with lower

FIGURE 7.19
CDF of Haemoglobin Level for Adult 15–19 Years

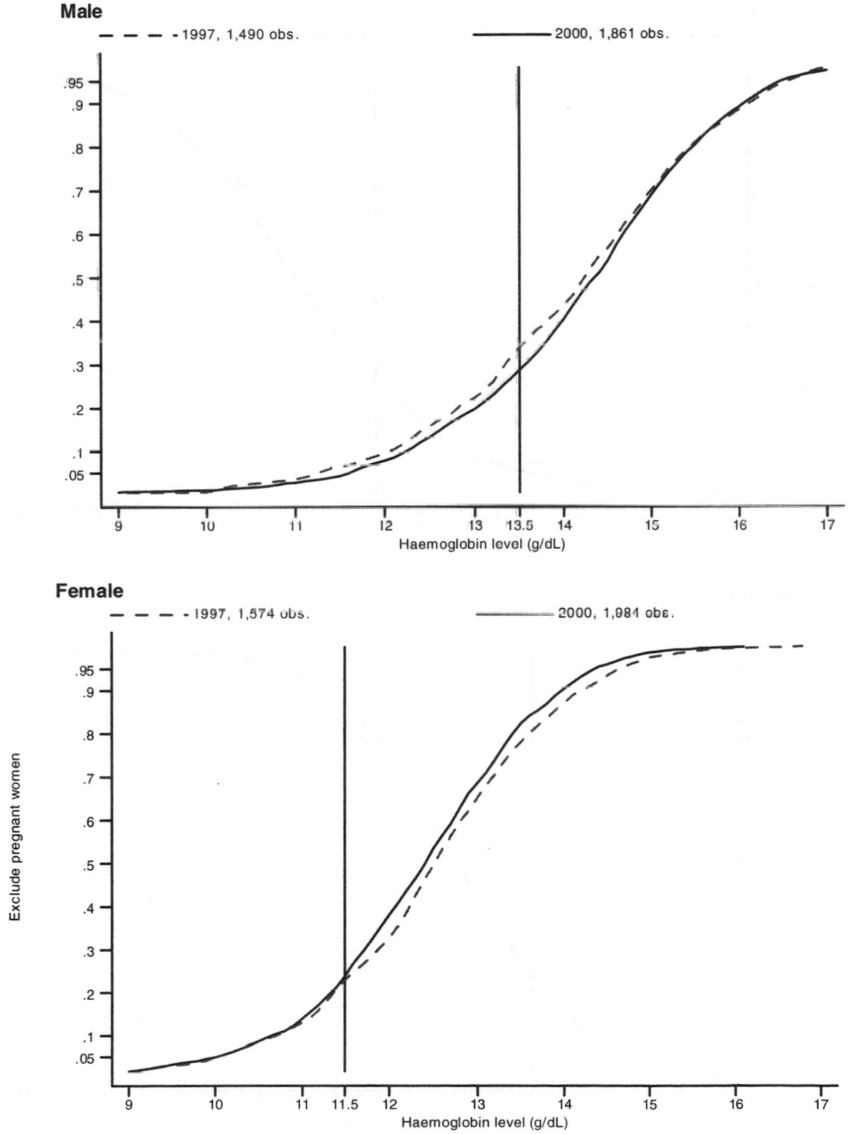
Male
1997, 1,490 obs.
2000, 1,861 obs.
.95
.9
.8
.7
.6
.5
.4
.3
.2
.1
.05
9
10
11
12
13
13.5
14
15
16
17
Haemoglobin level (g/dL)
Female
1997, 1,574 obs.
2000, 1,984 obs.
Exclude pregnant women
.95
.9
.8
.7
.6
.5
.4
.3
.2
.1
.05
9
10
11
11.5
12
13
14
15
16
17
Haemoglobin level (g/dL)

Source: IFLS2 and IFLS3.
Observations were weighted using individual sampling weights.

FIGURE 7.20
CDF of Haemoglobin Level for Adult 20–59 Years

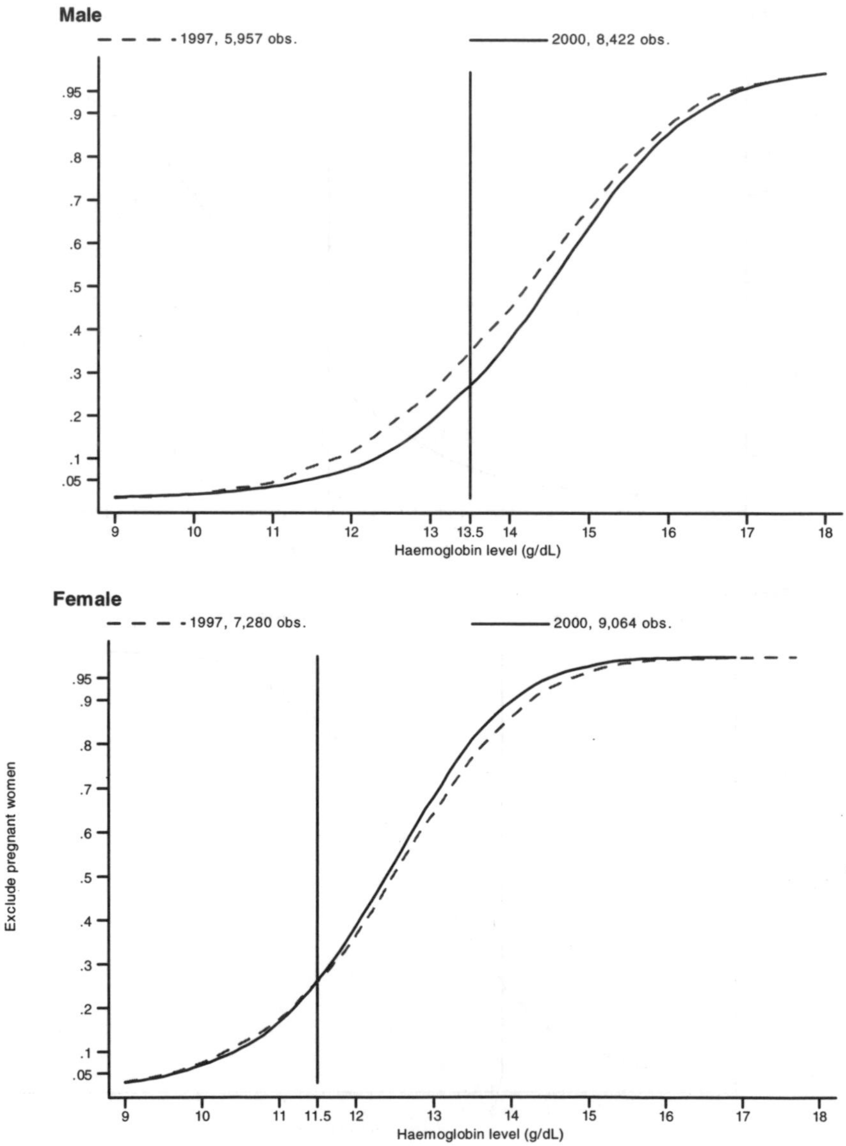
Male
1997, 5,957 obs.
2000, 8,422 obs.
.95
.9
.8
.7
.6
.5
.4
.3
.2
.1
.05
9
10
11
12
13
13.5
14
15
16
17
18
Haemoglobin level (g/dL)
Female
1997, 7,280 obs.
2000, 9,064 obs.
Exclude pregnant women
.95
.9
.8
.7
.6
.5
.4
.3
.2
.1
.05
9
10
11
11.5
12
13
14
15
16
17
18
Haemoglobin level (g/dL)

Source: IFLS2 and IFLS3.
Observations were weighted using individual sampling weights.

FIGURE 7.21
CDF of Haemoglobin Level for Adult 60 Years amd Above

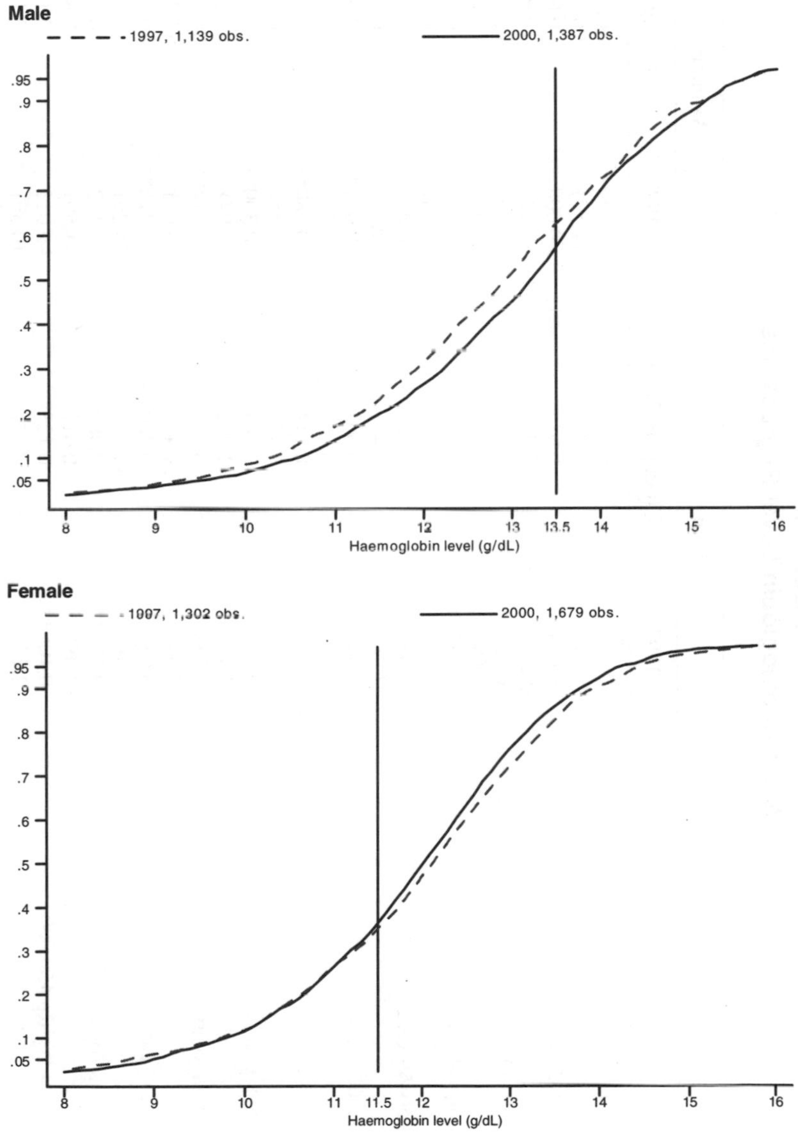
Male
1997, 1,139 obs.
2000, 1,387 obs.
.95
.9
.8
.7
.6
.5
.4
.3
.2
.1
.05
8
9
10
11
12
13
13.5
14
15
16
Haemoglobin level (g/dL)
Female
1997, 1,302 obs.
2000, 1,679 obs.
.95
.9
.8
.7
.6
.5
.4
.3
.2
.1
.05
8
9
10
11
11.5
12
13
14
15
16
Haemoglobin level (g/dL)

Source: IFLS2 and IFLS3.
Observations were weighted using individual sampling weights.

TABLE 7.17
Adult Haemoglobin Level Regressions

		Men		Women	
		1997	Change in 2000	1997	Change in 2000
Age (spline):	15–19 years	0.137**	0.074*	0.030	–0.014
		(5.17)	(2.23)*	(1.57)	(0.52)
	20–29 years	–0.004	–0.017	–0.008	0.009
		(0.40)	(1.28)	(1.02)	(0.94)
	30–39 years	–0.031**	0.017	–0.007	–0.003
		(2.69)	(1.20)	(0.97)	(0.24)
	40–49 years	–0.031**	–0.009	–0.015	0.003
		(2.65)	(0.65)	(1.53)	(0.23)
	50–59 years	–0.049**	–0.007	0.017	–0.011
		(3.98)	(0.42)	(1.51)	(0.75)
	≥ 60 years	–0.032**	–0.007	–0.029**	0.005
		(4.21)	(0.66)	(5.17)	(0.66)
Education:	1–5 years	0.292**	–0.114	0.180**	–0.076
		(3.15)	(0.92)	(2.65)	(0.80)
	6–8 years	0.384**	–0.144	0.300**	–0.124
		(4.47)	(1.20)	(4.04)	(1.28)
	9–11 years	0.569**	–0.203	0.314**	–0.155
		(5.08)	(1.43)	(3.63)	(1.37)
	12+ years	0.680**	–0.230	0.276**	–0.116
		(6.48)	(1.67)	(3.25)	(1.03)
log *pce* (spline):	0- log Rp 150,000	0.219*	0.080	0.132	–0.069
		(2.08)	(0.61)	(1.59)	(0.60)
	> log Rp 150,000	0.105*	0.128*	–0.012	0.138**
		(2.17)	(2.13)	(0.39)	(3.10)
Rural		–0.216*	0.014	–0.020	–0.013
		(2.46)	(0.13)	(0.28)	(0.15)
North Sumatra		0.401	–0.452	0.654**	–0.283
		(1.95)	(1.78)	(5.57)	(1.76)

West Sumatra	0.582**	–0.902**	0.846**	–0.562 **
	(3.45)	(4.01)	(5.95)	(3.34)
South Sumatra	0.064	–1.063**	0.289	–0.861**
	(0.26)	(3.26)	(1.66)	(3.99)
Lampung	–0.451**	–0.219	–0.212	0.039
	(2.97)	(1.08)	(1.56)	(0.22)
West Java	–0.100	–0.338*	0.179	–0.138
	(0.75)	(2.14)	(1.87)	(1.12)
Central Java	0.280	–0.419*	0.576**	–0.225
	(1.75)	(2.23)	(4.29)	(1.40)
Yogyakarta	–0.064	–0.211	0.004	0.001
	(0.49)	(1.28)	(0.04)	(0.01)
East Java	–0.015	–0.203	0.345**	–0.180
	(0.10)	(1.16)	(3.01)	(1.28)
Bali	0.130	–0.197	0.511**	–0.563**
	(0.91)	(1.13)	(3.64)	(3.14)
West Nusa Tenggara	0.095	–0.373*	0.373**	–0.090
	(0.65)	(2.07)	(3.51)	(0.66)
South Kalimantan	0.153	–0.266	0.110	0.103
	(1.13)	(1.58)	(0.78)	(0.59)
South Sulawesi	0.289	–0.443*	0.465**	–0.342
	(1.44)	(1.99)	(2.83)	(1.80)
Constant	8.676**	–1.737	9.829**	1.132
	(6.65)	(1.04)	(9.74)	(0.80)
F-test (p-values):				
Interaction variables	0.0009		0.0000	
Education variables	0.0000		0.0015	
Expenditure variables	0.0000		0.0001	
Number of observations	20,256		22,883	
R-squared	0.14		0.04	

Source: IFLS2 and IFLS3. Observations exclude women who were pregnant. The omitted category for education is no schooling, and for province is Jakarta. Dummy variable for missing education and dummy variable for missing per capita expenditures are included in the regression but not reported in the table. Estimates were weighted using individual sampling weights. Standard errors are robust to clustering at the community level and to heteroscedasticity. Absolute t-statistics are in parentheses with significance at 5% (*) and 1% (**) indicated.

haemoglobin levels for men, but not for women. The age pattern is also a little different between men and women. For men, haemoglobin levels begin to decline by the 30s, while for women it is at older ages that levels become appreciably lower.

GENERAL HEALTH AND PHYSICAL FUNCTIONING

Self- and nurse-assessed general health measures are reported in Table 7.18, along with whether any difficulty is reported in doing any of the nine activities of daily living, plus the number of activities for which difficulty is reported. Strong age patterns appear for self-reported poor health and measures of physical functioning, though not as strong for the nurse-reported scores.[17] As is usual, women report worse general health than do men and women are far more likely to report having difficulties with various dimensions of physical functioning (Strauss et al. 1993). It is interesting, though, to note that nurses also report a higher probability that women have worse health.

There is a small increase in the fraction of people reporting being in poor health from 1997 to 2000 among prime-aged adults, but not among the elderly. On the other hand, elderly women in 2000 are much more likely to receive low health evaluations by the nurses. Little change is observed in the rates of difficulty with ADLs.

Descriptive regressions, reported in Table 7.19, show education and *pce* to be important factors in determining poor health, especially as assessed by nurses. It is interesting that the education dummies are jointly and individually significant and negatively related to the probability of reporting oneself to be in poor health. As for children, the *pce* effects are highly non-linear for the nurse evaluations, with far greater impact among those with low *pce* than those with high *pce*.

For activities of daily living (ADL) for both men and women (Table 7.20), there is only a very weak negative impact of education on having difficulty with at least one measure of physical functioning; but a stronger impact on the number. Percapita expenditure has a very small, if any, effect on reporting difficulties with ADLs for men, a somewhat larger effect on women, at low levels of *pce*. Age is the major factor that affects these outcomes.

SUMMARY

Looking at the broad picture of levels of child health and changes in the IFLS sample between 1997 and 2000, the results are nuanced rather than

TABLE 7.18
Health Conditions of Adults

	15–59 years						60+ years					
	Men			Women			Men			Women		
	1997	2000	Change	1997	2000	Change	1997	2000	Change	1997	2000	Change
% self-reported in poor health now	7.7	9.6	1.9 **	9.3	12.2	2.8 **	28.1	27.6	–0.5	28.5	29.9	1.4
	(0.39)	(0.41)	(0.57)	(0.43)	(0.42)	(0.60)	(1.66)	(1.38)	(2.16)	(1.37)	(1.38)	(1.95)
Nurse evalution: [a]												
– mean	6.4	6.3	–0.1	6.1	6.0	–0.2 **	5.9	5.7	–0.2 *	5.7	5.4	–0.3 **
	(0.05)	(0.04)	(0.06)	(0.05)	(0.04)	(0.06)		(0.06)	(0.05)	(0.08)	(0.05)	(0.05)
	(0.07)											
– % with evaluation score <=5	22.6	23.7	1.1	28.6	34.2	5.6 *	37.1	41.9	4.8	40.8	54.3	13.5 **
	(2.15)	(1.50)	(2.62)	(2.23)	(1.74)	(2.83)	(2.97)	(2.50)	(3.88)	(2.96)	(2.27)	(3.73)
Number of observations	7,399	10,417		9,157	11,727		1,137	1,397		1,310	1,704	
	40–59 years											
Physical ability in daily activity: [b]												
– % with any activity done uneasily	14.7	14.2	–0.5	41.4	43.9	2.5	54.1	51.6	–2.5	78.0	78.4	0.3
	(0.81)	(0.73)	(1.09)	(1.36)	(1.16)	(1.79)	(1.76)	(1.50)	(2.31)	(1.43)	(1.28)	(1.92)
– number of activities done uneasily	0.3	0.3	–0.1 *	0.8	0.7	–0.1	1.8	1.6	–0.2 *	2.9	2.7	–0.2
	(0.02)	(0.02)	(0.03)	(0.04)	(0.03)	(0.05)	(0.08)	(0.07)	(0.10)	(0.08)	(0.08)	(0.11)
Number of observations	2,788	3,215		3,087	3,459		1,273	1,468		1,483	1,823	

Source: IFLS2 and IFLS3.

[a] Nurse evaluation is reported by nurse who collects physical assessment. The scale is from 1 (the most unhealthy) to 9 (the most healthy).

[b] Activities include: to carry a heavy load for 20 metres, to walk for 5 kilometres, to bow, squat or kneel, to sweep the house floor yard, to draw a pail of water from a well, to stand up from sitting position on the floor without help, to stand up from sitting position in a chair without help, to go the bathroom without help, and to dress without help.

Estimates were weighted using individual sampling weights. Standard errors (in parentheses) are robust to clustering at the community level. Significance at 5% (*) and 1% (**) indicated.

TABLE 7.19
Self- and Nurse-reported General Health: Linear Probability Models for Poor Health Adults, Aged 15+

	Men				Women			
	Self-reported		Nurse evaluation		Self-reported		Nurse evaluation	
	1997	Change in 2000	1997	Change in 2000	1997	Change in 2000	1997	Change in 2000
Age (spline, × 10^{-2})								
15–29 years	–0.000	–0.007	–0.022*	–0.005	0.002	–0.005	–0.011	–0.008
	(0.07)	(0.78)	(2.24)	(0.35)	(0.35)	(0.56)	(1.19)	(0.57)
30–59 years	0.037**	–0.010	0.026**	0.022**	0.035**	–0.002	0.019*	0.003
	(8.25)	(1.63)	(4.48)	(2.64)	(9.14)	(0.39)	(2.56)	(0.37)
60+ years	0.082**	0.005	0.045**	–0.013	0.089**	–0.029	0.016	0.024
	(6.37)	(0.30)	(2.92)	(0.64)	(8.51)	(1.95)	(1.40)	(1.48)
Education: 1–5 years	–0.006	0.003	–0.085**	0.064	0.020	–0.016	–0.052	0.005
	(0.40)	(0.14)	(3.14)	(1.69)	(1.78)	(0.89)	(2.02)	(0.13)
6–8 years	–0.010	0.005	–0.114**	0.074	–0.006	–0.007	–0.124**	0.019
	(0.67)	(0.21)	(3.83)	(1.79)	(0.51)	(0.40)	(4.08)	(0.48)
9–11 years	–0.018	0.005	–0.155**	0.106*	–0.012	–0.004	–0.129**	–0.002
	(1.10)	(0.21)	(4.32)	(2.22)	(0.92)	(0.18)	(3.65)	(0.05)
12+ years	–0.021	–0.014	–0.176**	0.096*	–0.021	–0.013	–0.164**	0.008
	(1.34)	(0.61)	(5.16)	(1.99)	(1.56)	(0.64)	(4.86)	(0.17)
log *pce* (spline): 0 - log Rp 150,000	-2.400	-2.519	-12.256**	5.492	0.475	-1.817	-13.956**	9.557*
	(1.66)	(0.96)	(3.59)	(1.24)	(0.37)	(0.84)	(4.07)	(2.19)
> log Rp 150,000	0.618	–0.930	–4.020**	1.993	0.105	1.297	-3.979**	1.567
	(1.03)	(1.12)	(3.62)	(1.30)	(0.17)	(1.46)	(3.50)	(0.99)
Rural (× 10^{-1})	0.154	–0.030	–0.195	0.094	–0.090	0.034	–0.127	–0.109
	(1.91)	(0.27)	(0.58)	(0.21)	(1.03)	(0.27)	(0.35)	(0.23)
North Sumatra	–0.077**	0.029	–0.376**	0.477**	–0.097**	0.027	–0.461**	0.662**
	(3.98)	(1.06)	(5.15)	(5.96)	(5.18)	(1.00)	(5.89)	(7.27)

West Sumatra	–0.012	0.054	–0.341**	0.933**	–0.028	0.096*	–0.416**	1.204**
	(0.55)	(1.44)	(4.55)	(11.25)	(0.95)	(2.51)	(5.14)	(13.43)
South Sumatra	–0.065**	–0.006	0.240**	–0.267**	–0.054**	0.053	0.290**	–0.317**
	(2.95)	(0.19)	(2.59)	(2.81)	(2.87)	(1.67)	(3.11)	(3.31)
Lampung	–0.056*	–0.043	–0.342**	0.545**	–0.086**	0.016	–0.428**	0.925**
	(2.03)	(1.27)	(4.35)	(6.24)	(3.96)	(0.46)	(5.09)	(9.43)
West Java	–0.044**	–0.005	–0.194*	0.427**	–0.071**	0.031	–0.238**	0.596**
	(2.60)	(0.24)	(2.38)	(4.87)	(4.15)	(1.30)	(2.69)	(6.17)
Central Java	–0.072**	–0.028	0.049	0.237*	–0.057**	–0.024	0.035	0.332**
	(4.00)	(1.20)	(0.50)	(2.08)	(3.23)	(0.99)	(0.35)	(2.82)
Yogyakarta	–0.084**	0.003	–0.328**	0.525**	–0.064**	–0.015	–0.405**	0.695**
	(4.13)	(0.12)	(4.44)	(6.04)	(3.17)	(0.56)	(5.11)	(6.86)
East Java	–0.113**	0.001	–0.204	0.489**	–0.126**	0.038	–0.226**	0.617**
	(6.54)	(0.06)	(2.48)	(5.62)	(7.90)	(1.61)	(2.62)	(6.71)
Bali	–0.086**	–0.017	–0.399**	0.369**	–0.061**	–0.042	–0.490**	0.455**
	(3.94)	(0.64)	(5.29)	(4.76)	(2.99)	(1.46)	(6.09)	(5.40)
West Nusa Tenggara	0.032	–0.112**	0.027	0.359**	0.004	–0.043	0.162	0.348**
	(1.11)	(3.12)	(0.32)	(3.57)	(0.13)	(1.20)	(1.91)	(3.52)
South Kalimantan	–0.021	–0.090**	–0.368	0.419**	0.003	–0.056	–0.378**	0.488**
	(0.97)	(3.20)	(4.87)	(5.20)	(0.10)	(1.37)	(4.59)	(5.54)
South Sulawesi	–0.066**	–0.002	0.095	–0.147	–0.054*	0.008	0.074	–0.135
	(2.62)	(0.05)	(0.80)	(1.22)	(2.26)	(0.24)	(0.57)	(1.03)*
Constant	0.915**	0.042	2.788	–0.338*	0.185	0.118	2.825**	–0.334
	(2.94)	(0.42)	(5.23)	(2.31)	(0.70)	(1.27)	(5.26)	(2.23)
F-test (p-values)								
Interaction variables	0.000		0.000		0.000		0.000	
Education variables	0.013		0.000		0.002		0.000	
Expenditure variables	0.031		0.000		0.270		0.000	
Number of observations	20,350		20,350		23,898		23,898	
R-squared	0.07		0.16		0.06		0.20	

Source: IFLS2 and IFLS3.

Dummy variable for missing education and dummy variable for missing per capita expenditure are included in the regressions but not reported in the table. The omitted category for education is no schooling, and for province is Jakarta. Estimates were weighted using individual sampling weights. Standard errors are robust to clustering at the community level and to heteroscedasticity. Absolute t-statistics are in parentheses with significance at 5% (*)

TABLE 7.20
Physical Ability in Daily Activity: Linear Probability Model of Having Any Activity and OLS of Number of Activities Done Uneasily, Adults Aged 40+

	Men				Women			
	Any Activity		Number of Activities		Any Activity		Number of Activities	
	1997	Change in 2000	1997	Change in 2000	1997	Change in 2000	1997	Change in 2000
Age (spline, × 10^{-2}):								
40–49 years	0.013	0.000	–0.003	0.001	0.106**	–0.000	0.237**	–0.001
	(0.70)	(0.72)	(0.05)	(0.70)	(3.92)	(0.69)	(3.25)	(1.02)
50–59 years	0.205**	–0.001	0.478**	–0.003	0.224**	–0.000	0.696**	–0.001
	(9.71)	(1.82)	(6.20)	(2.52)	(9.19)	(0.35)	(8.39)	(0.56)
60+ years	0.163**	0.000	0.952**	0.001	0.106**	–0.000	1.161**	–0.000
	(11.75)	(1.11)	(12.75)	(0.93)	(11.06)	(0.22)	(18.69)	(0.20)
Education: 1–5 years	0.009	–0.056	–0.060	–0.110	–0.010	0.025	–0.070	0.031
	(0.47)	(1.82)	(0.74)	(0.95)	(0.44)	(0.86)	(0.93)	(0.30)
6–8 years	–0.026	–0.029	–0.172*	–0.004	–0.040	0.060	–0.138*	0.039
	(1.17)	(0.94)	(2.07)	(0.04)	(1.65)	(1.83)	(1.99)	(0.40)
9–11 years	–0.055*	–0.008	–0.240*	0.074	0.019	0.032	0.025	–0.062
	(2.11)	(0.19)	(2.43)	(0.52)	(0.51)	(0.63)	(0.22)	(0.42)
12+ years	–0.029	–0.014	–0.099	0.017	–0.055	0.027	–0.269**	–0.019
	(1.05)	(0.35)	(0.91)	(0.12)	(1.55)	(0.59)	(3.26)	(0.15)
log *pce* (spline): 0- log Rp 150,000	–0.932	–2.729	–9.780	–14.588	–1.855	0.334	–24.301*	–2.680
	(0.33)	(0.69)	(0.96)	(0.97)	(0.54)	(0.07)	(2.01)	(0.16)
> log Rp 150,000	1.993	–0.904	5.494	0.205	2.531*	–2.236	3.653	8.413
	(1.61)	(0.54)	(1.14)	(0.03)	(1.98)	(1.17)	(0.87)	(1.31)
Rural	–0.011	–0.134	–0.097	–0.269	–0.309	–0.205	0.026	–1.754
	(0.07)	(0.64)	(0.16)	(0.36)	(1.56)	(0.74)	(0.04)	(1.90)
North Sumatra	0.165**	–0.080	0.366**	0.056	0.091*	–0.012	–0.138	0.337
	(4.43)	(1.47)	(3.05)	(0.32)	(2.20)	(0.19)	(0.93)	(1.57)

West Sumatra	0.101**	–0.063	0.420*	–0.250	0.100*	–0.045	0.171	0.191
	(2.97)	(1.24)	(2.52)	(1.17)	(2.03)	(0.67)	(0.91)	(0.73)
South Sumatra	0.087	–0.065	0.154	–0.208	0.118**	0.032	0.115	–0.165
	(2.50)	(1.35)	(1.27)	(1.30)	(2.77)	(0.52)	(0.64)	(0.74)
Lampung	0.048	0.112*	0.109	–0.051	–0.051	0.259**	–0.569**	0.489*
	(1.19)	(2.08)	(0.58)	(0.23)	(1.13)	(4.04)	(3.36)	(2.12)
West Java	0.049	–0.094*	0.151	–0.224	–0.006	–0.016	–0.185	0.198
	(1.84)	(2.57)	(1.57)	(1.81)	(0.16)	(0.32)	(1.28)	(1.04)
Central Java	–0.043	–0.018	–0.103	–0.066	–0.156**	0.087	–0.643**	0.410*
	(1.53)	(0.44)	(0.91)	(0.46)	(4.45)	(1.71)	(4.51)	(2.14)
Yogyakarta	–0.056	–0.053	–0.298**	0.057	–0.200**	0.056	–0.928**	0.380
	(1.77)	(1.26)	(2.74)	(0.40)	(5.10)	(0.83)	(6.12)	(1.73)
East Java	–0.043	–0.027	–0.141	–0.014	–0.143**	0.097	–0.607**	0.341
	(1.55)	(0.71)	(1.44)	(0.11)	(3.65)	(1.80)	(3.96)	(1.71)
Bali	0.220**	–0.143	0.692**	–0.558**	0.134**	–0.029	0.622**	–0.371
	(6.30)	(2.37)	(5.46)	(3.37)	(3.29)	(0.46)	(3.03)	(1.46)
West Nusa Tenggara	0.084*	–0.059	0.126	–0.158	0.173**	–0.060	0.132	–0.057
	(2.22)	(1.19)	(0.96)	(0.85)	(3.24)	(0.82)	(0.61)	(0.23)
South Kalimantan	0.09	–0.112	–0.041	–0.050	0.064	0.002	–0.180	0.365
	(1.75)	(1.71)	(0.32)	(0.29)	(1.44)	(0.02)	(0.80)	(1.33)
South Sulawesi	0.096*	–0.144	0.267	–0.547**	0.065	–0.050	–0.143	–0.050
	(2.46)	(2.81)	(1.66)	(2.98)	(1.30)	(0.74)	(0.69)	(0.20)
Constant	0.329	0.197	3.234	1.058	0.265	0.186	4.984*	1.205
	(0.67)	(1.05)	(1.76)	(1.31)	(0.47)	(0.66)	(2.36)	(1.51)
F-test (p-values)								
Interaction variables	0.004		0.003			0.000	0.002	
Education variables	0.064		0.039		0.207		0.000	
Expenditure variables	0.325		0.128		0.383		0.019	
Number of observations	8,744		8,744		9,852		9,852	
R-squared	0.23		0.25		0.18		0.34	

Source: IFLS2 and IFLS3.
Dummy variable for missing education and dummy variable for missing per capita expenditure are included in the regressions but not reported in the table. The omitted category for education is no schooling, and for province is Jakarta. Estimates were weighted using individual sampling weights. Standard errors are robust to clustering at the community level and to heteroscedasticity. Absolute t-statistics are in parentheses with significance at 5% (*) and 1% (**) indicated.

straightforward. Height-for-age is often considered the single most important measure of child health. The fraction of pre-school-aged children who have very low heights for their age and sex dropped between 1997 and 2000, from 43% to 33% for boys, and 40% to 33% for girls. This is a very favourable development. However, even with the decline in the incidence of stunting, the levels are still very high by international standards, being comparable to many sub-Saharan African countries. Weight-for-height, which can respond more quickly to economic dislocations and can also rebound quickly, showed essentially no changes between 1997 and 2000. There was a slight worsening for girls 3–17 months, but this is not statistically significant. However, on a negative note, the fraction of boys 12–59 months with blood haemoglobin levels less than threshold levels (considered bad for health) increased to 57%. There is some question how to interpret this because a more formal test of whether the entire lower tail of the distribution worsened does not find statistically significant differences. Moreover, for older children even the fraction beneath the threshold did not change significantly.

As with children, the picture of changes in adult health between 1997 and 2000 is mixed. The fraction with low body mass index, related to undernutrition, did not worsen between 1997 and 2000. Since there is evidence the BMIs of the elderly declined significantly between 1997 and 1998 (Frankenberg et al. 1999), this indicates a recovery by 2000 by this sub-group.

While health analysts typically focus on problems of undernutrition in developing economies, and those problems do indeed exist in Indonesia, problems of overnutrition and health risks from behavioural factors usually associated with industrial countries are also a problem. Levels are high for three risk-factors underlying cardiovascular disease: overweight, high blood pressure and smoking. Overweight and high blood pressure seem to be more of a problem for women, especially high blood pressure, while smoking is predominately observed among men. We find that overweight among women 40 years and older is 25% in 2000 (for women aged 40–59 it is higher, 30%), with male rates half that. Rates of Stage 1 hypertension for systolic are 33% for men over 40 and 40% for women. Moreover, these rates rise with age to over 50% for men over 60 years and 60% for women over 60. Over 70% of men aged 20 and older currently smoke cigarettes, on average 1 pack of 12 clove cigarettes daily. For women over 20, smoking rates are only 5%. There is weak evidence that between 1997 and 2000 that the incidence of overweight increased among prime-aged women and the rate of smoking increased for teenage boys. We find evidence that the age at which men begin smoking has been declining.

For some aspects such as being overweight and smoking, it appears that levels rise with higher incomes.[18] On the other hand, as education levels increase to completing secondary school or more, some risky behaviours are moderated, such as being overweight in the case of women, or smoking in the case of men.

Overall, this is not a pattern of health catastrophe that one might have worried about given the economic crisis, although the trajectory of historical health improvements very likely was interrupted. This suggests that in the medium-run either the crisis did not hit hard at many of the IFLS households, or that its impacts occurred only in the very short-run, or that households had ways with which they were able to smooth these child health outcomes in the medium-run. The results of Frankenberg et al. (1999) show that most measured health outcomes did not suffer in the very short-run, but that many IFLS households did suffer serious losses in *pce*. This suggests that it is thc last possibility, smoothing mechanisms, which was important.

Notes

1 Heights were taken by trained nurses, two per field team, using wood child/adult height boards made by Irwin Shorr. Standard field procedures were followed; recumbent length was measured for children under 24 months and standing height for all those older. Weights were measured using electronic mother/child scales, model 881, made by Seca. Heights were measured to the nearest millimetre and weights to the nearest tenth of a kilogram.

2 Finger pricks for all persons 12 months and older were taken by one of the trained nurses on the team. HEMOCUE was used to measure the blood haemoglobin level. Haemoglobin levels are measured to the nearest g/dL.

3 Body mass index is defined as weight, in kilograms, divided by the square of height, in metres.

4 Heights, weights and haemoglobin counts were taken using the same equipment as for children. Blood pressures were taken using Omron, model 711, digital blood pressure machines.

5 ADLs include nine categories for which respondents assess their capacity to: carry a heavy load for 20 meters; walk for 5 kilometres; bow, squat or kneel; sweep the house floor yard; draw a pail of water from a well;

stand from sitting on the floor without help; stand from a sitting position without help; go to the bathroom without help; and dress without help.

[6] A z-score for height subtracts from the child's height, the median height in the reference population, for a child of the same gender and age in months, and divides by the standard deviation of height in the reference population, also for a child of the same gender and age in months. A weight-for-height z-score is defined in an analogous manner, except that the standardization is done using the reference population median and standard deviation of weight for children of a given gender and height. The WHO-CDC standards use a U.S. reference population.

[7] Shrinkage at old age will result in heights of older birth cohorts being somewhat understated.

[8] We omit infants less than 3 months because it is usual that measurement error is higher for them; for example, it is difficult to completely flatten and straighten their legs.

[9] These and our other bivariate non-parametric figures are estimated using locally weighted smoothed scatterplots (LOWESS), with a bandwidth of .8. Individual weights were used.

[10] Of course any cohort and time effects, if they exist, are also embodied in this pattern.

[11] Results from a longitudinal survey in central Java by the Helen Keller Foundation find the same results for pre-school child height, weight-for-height and haemoglobin (Alatas and Pradhan 2002).

[12] Testing differences between curve ordinates below the threshold and testing based on crossing points should be asymptotically identical, since the test statistics are based on distributions which are correct asymptotically. However in small samples the two tests may not agree, as in this case.

[13] It is possible that some of these provincial differences result from individual nurses working in Jakarta in 1997 being more likely to give low scores.

[14] Pregnant women are not included in the statistics on BMI.

[15] These regressions are specified in dummy variables for levels of schooling rather than years, in order to better capture these non-linearities.

[16] See Thomas et al. (1996) for example.

[17] This may be because nurses are implicitly standardizing for age when they make their assessments.

[18] In addition to our evidence, Erwidodo et al. (2002) estimate an income elasticity for tobacco expenditure of 0.67 nationally. They also estimate an own price elasticity of –1.0.

APPENDIX FIGURE 7.1
CDF of Standardized Height-for-Age for Children Age 3–17 Months in Urban and Rural Areas

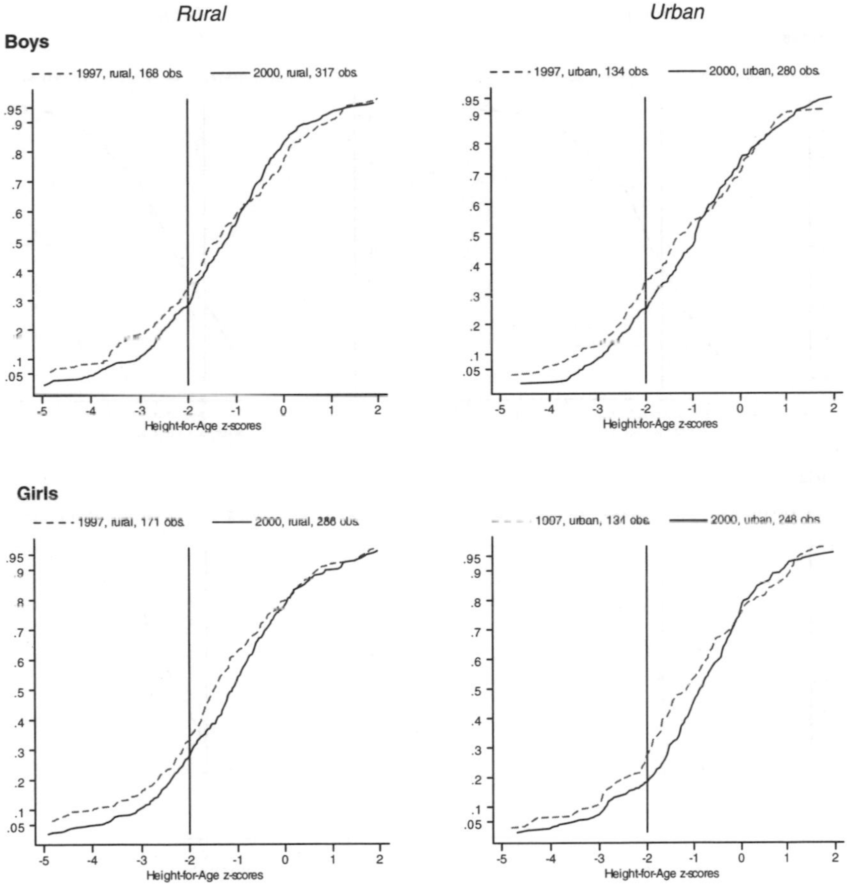
Rural
Urban
Boys
1997, rural, 168 obs
2000, rural, 317 obs
1997, urban, 134 obs
2000, urban, 280 obs
Girls
Height-for-Age z-scores

Source: IFLS2 and IFLS3.

Observations were weighted using individual sampling weights.

APPENDIX FIGURE 7.2
CDF of Standardized Height-for-Age for Children Age 18–35 Months in Urban and Rural Areas

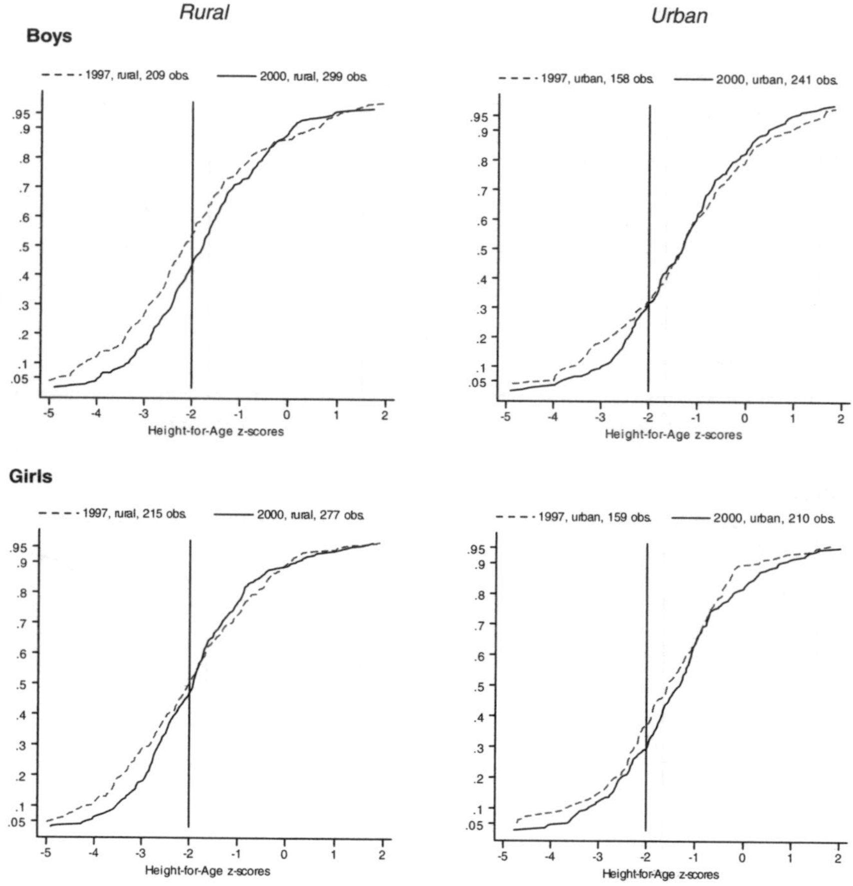
Rural
Urban
Boys
1997, rural, 209 obs.
2000, rural, 299 obs.
1997, urban, 158 obs.
2000, urban, 241 obs.
Height-for-Age z-scores
Girls
1997, rural, 215 obs.
2000, rural, 277 obs.
1997, urban, 159 obs.
2000, urban, 210 obs.
Height-for-Age z-scores

Source: IFLS2 and IFLS3.

Observations were weighted using individual sampling weights.

APPENDIX FIGURE 7.3
CDF of Standardized Height-for-Age for Children Age 36–59 Months in Urban and Rural Areas

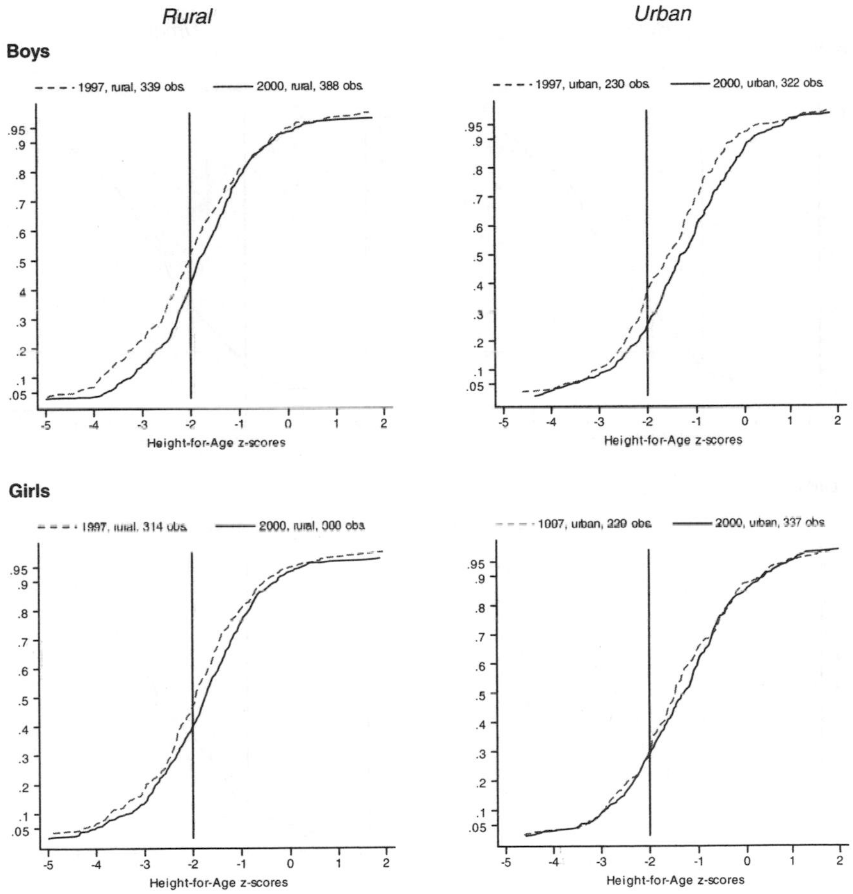
Rural
Urban
Boys
1997, rural, 339 obs
2000, rural, 388 obs
1997, urban, 230 obs
2000, urban, 322 obs
Height-for-Age z-scores
Girls
Height-for-Age z-scores

Source: IFLS2 and IFLS3.
Observations were weighted using individual sampling weights.

APPENDIX FIGURE 7.4
CDF of Standardized Weight-for-Height for Children Age 3–17 Months in Urban and Rural Areas

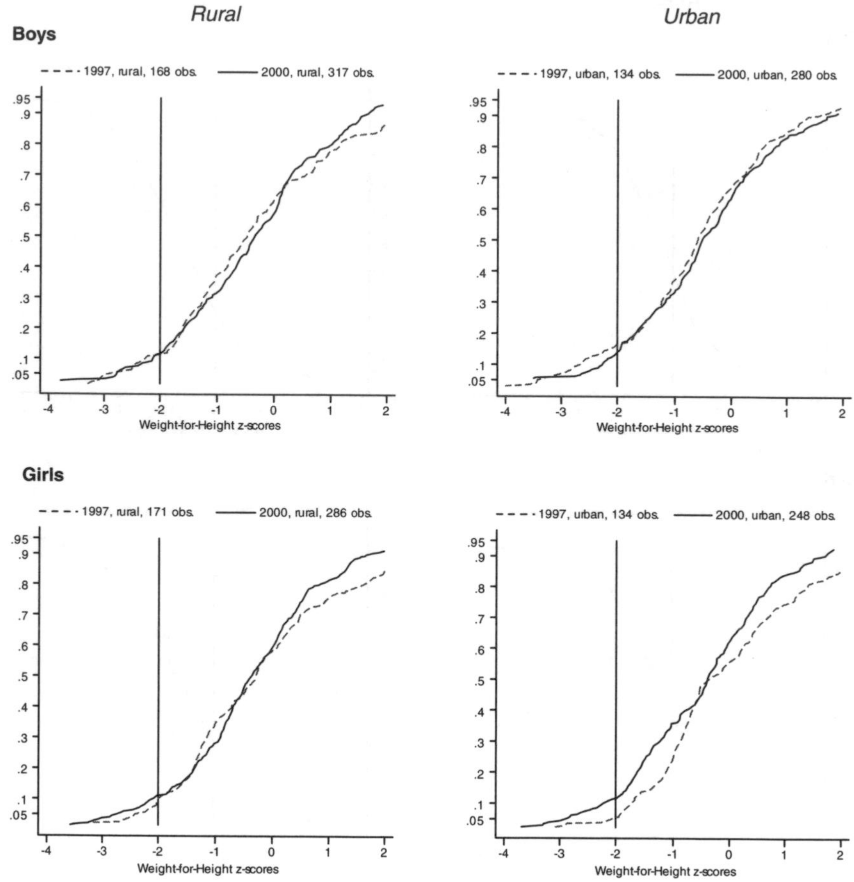
Rural
Urban
Boys
1997, rural, 168 obs.
2000, rural, 317 obs.
1997, urban, 134 obs.
2000, urban, 280 obs.
Girls
1997, rural, 171 obs.
2000, rural, 286 obs.
1997, urban, 134 obs.
2000, urban, 248 obs.
Weight-for-Height z-scores

Source: IFLS2 and IFLS3.
Observations were weighted using individual sampling weights.

APPENDIX FIGURE 7.5
CDF of Standardized Weight-for-Height for Children Age 18–35 Months in Urban and Rural Areas

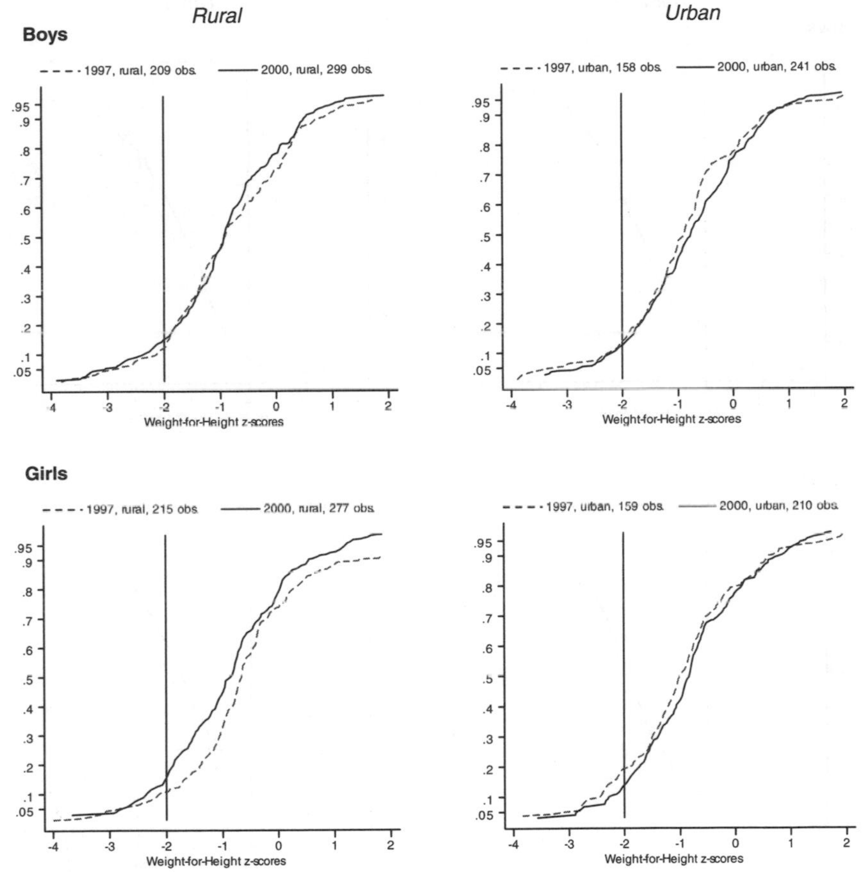
Rural
Urban
Boys
1997, rural, 209 obs.
2000, rural, 299 obs.
1997, urban, 158 obs.
2000, urban, 241 obs.
Girls
1997, rural, 215 obs.
2000, rural, 277 obs.
1997, urban, 159 obs.
2000, urban, 210 obs.
Weight-for-Height z-scores

Source: IFLS2 and IFLS3.
Observations were weighted using individual sampling weights.

APPENDIX FIGURE 7.6
CDF of Standardized Weight-for-Height for Children Age 36–59 Months in Urban and Rural Areas

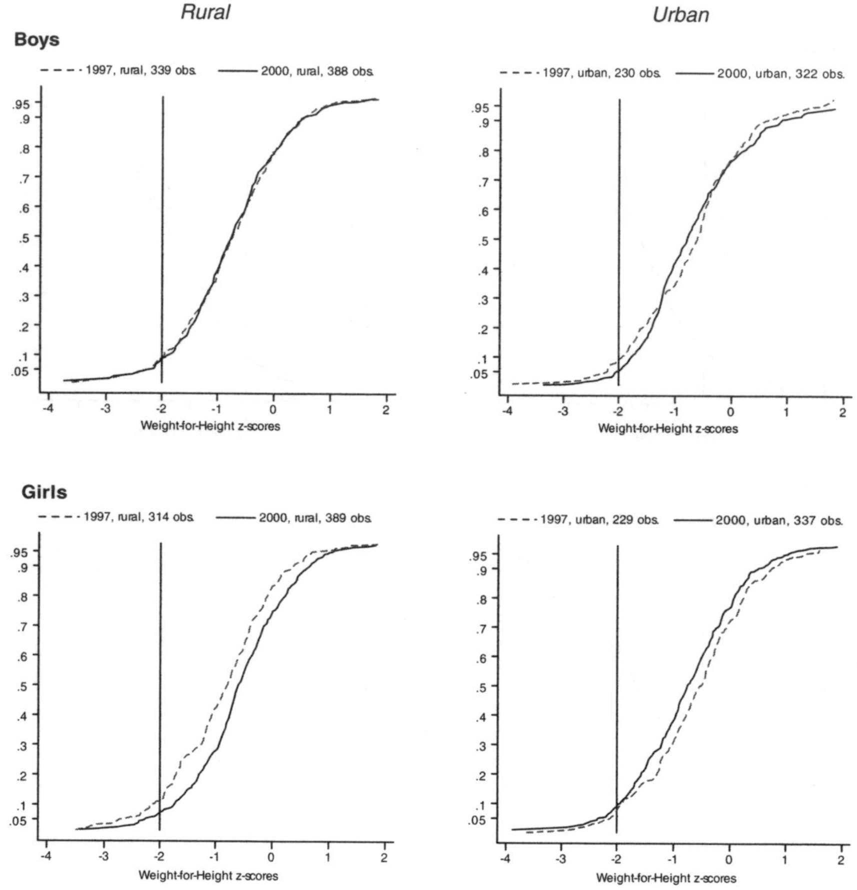
Rural
Urban
Boys
1997, rural, 339 obs.
2000, rural, 388 obs.
1997, urban, 230 obs.
2000, urban, 322 obs.
Girls
1997, rural, 314 obs.
2000, rural, 389 obs.
1997, urban, 229 obs.
2000, urban, 337 obs.
Weight-for-Height z-scores

Source: IFLS2 and IFLS3.
Observations were weighted using individual sampling weights.

APPENDIX TABLE 7.1
Child Height-for-Age: Test for Stochastic Dominance

	First crossing point and the difference between curves (2000 – 1997)							
	Boys				Girls			
	First-Order Dominance	Standard Errors	Second-Order Dominance	Standard Errors	First-Order Dominance	Standard Errors	Second-Order Dominance	Standard Errors
Age 3–17 months								
First crossing point	–0.732	(0.213)	–	–	–	–	–	–
Points of testing								
–4.0	–0.046	(0.019)	–0.056	(0.027)	–0.044	(0.022)	–0.064	(0.031)
–3.5	–0.057	(0.025)	–0.078	(0.035)	–0.041	(0.027)	–0.085	(0.041)
–3.0	–0.059	(0.029)	–0.111	(0.046)	–0.053	(0.030)	–0.108	(0.053)
–2.5	–0.045	(0.034)	–0.138	(0.057)	–0.056	(0.036)	–0.135	(0.067)
–2.0	–0.071	(0.038)	–0.163	(0.070)	–0.076	(0.040)	–0.162	(0.082)
–1.5	–0.060	(0.038)	–0.191	(0.083)	–0.121	(0.042)	–0.210	(0.097)
Number of observations								
1997	302		302		305		305	
2000	597		597		534		534	
Age 18–35 months								
First crossing point	–0.485	(0.478)	–		–1.171	(0.564)	–	
Points of testing								
–4.0	–0.052	(0.018)	–0.090	(0.038)	–0.048	(0.021)	–0.054	(0.032)
–3.5	–0.065	(0.024)	–0.121	(0.045)	–0.066	(0.026)	–0.082	(0.040)
–3.0	–0.102	(0.030)	–0.165	(0.053)	–0.079	(0.030)	–0.117	(0.051
–2.5	–0.101	(0.036)	–0.214	(0.064)	–0.045	(0.034)	–0.146	(0.062)
–2.0	–0.072	(0.040)	–0.258	(0.077)	–0.055	(0.037)	–0.168	(0.074)
–1.5	–0.051	(0.039)	–0.288	(0.090)	–0.013	(0.039)	–0.183	(0.086)
Number of observations								
1997	367		367		374		374	
2000	540		540		487		487	

continued on next page

APPENDIX TABLE 7.1 – cont'd

	First crossing point and the difference between curves (2000 – 1997)							
	Boys				Girls			
	First-Order Dominance	Standard Errors	Second-Order Dominance	Standard Errors	First-Order Dominance	Standard Errors	Second-Order Dominance	Standard Errors
Age 36–59 months								
First crossing point	–		–			–		–
Points of testing								
–4.0	–0.025	(0.013)	–0.030	(0.021)	–0.013	(0.014)	–0.023	(0.018)
–3.5	–0.052	(0.018)	–0.053	(0.027)	–0.017	(0.018)	–0.032	(0.024)
–3.0	–0.065	(0.023)	–0.083	(0.033)	–0.034	(0.023)	–0.045	(0.031)
–2.5	–0.098	(0.027)	–0.121	(0.042)	–0.039	(0.029)	–0.062	(0.040)
–2.0	–0.122	(0.031)	–0.174	(0.051)	–0.058	(0.033)	–0.086	(0.051)
–1.5	–0.089	(0.030)	–0.228	(0.060)	–0.083	(0.033)	–0.122	(0.062)
Number of observations								
1997	569		569		543		543	
2000	710		710		726		726	

Source: IFLS2 and IFLS3. Dash (–) indicates that the curves do not cross. Formulae for the standard errors are from Russel Davidson and Jean-Yves Duclos (2000), "Statistical Inference for Stochastic Dominance and for the Measurement of Poverty and Inequality", *Econometrica* v86 n6. Computation for the table above was performed using "DAD: A Software for Distributive Analysis/Analyse Distributive", version 4.2, copyrighted by Jean-Yves Duclos, Abdelkrim Araar, and Carl Fortin. Standard errors are robust to clustering at the community level. Estimates were weighted using individual sampling weights.

APPENDIX TABLE 7.2
Child Weight-for-Height: Test for Stochastic Dominance

	First crossing point and the difference between curves (2000 – 1997)							
	Boys				Girls			
	First-Order Dominance	Standard Errors	Second-Order Dominance	Standard Errors	First-Order Dominance	Standard Errors	Second-Order Dominance	Standard Errors
Age 3–17 months								
First crossing point	–3.058	(0.151)	–0.068	(2.064)	–0.981	(0.589)	–2.815	(1.115)
Points of testing								
–4.0	0.020	(0.012)	0.042	(0.024)	0.002	(0.009)	–0.009	(0.018)
–3.5	0.020	(0.013)	0.052	(0.028)	0.002	(0.011)	–0.008	(0.022)
–3.0	–0.006	(0.017)	0.058	(0.034)	0.018	(0.013)	–0.003	(0.026)
–2.5	–0.013	(0.023)	0.053	(0.040)	0.034	(0.016)	0.010	(0.032)
–2.0	–0.009	(0.028)	0.044	(0.048)	0.033	(0.023)	0.028	(0.038)
–1.5	–0.008	(0.032)	0.047	(0.058)	0.051	(0.030)	0.044	(0.046)
Number of observations								
1997	302		302		305		305	
2000	597		597		534		534	
Age 18–35 months								
First crossing point	–3.69	(0.166)	–1.221	(1.309)		–3.311	(0.372)	–
Points of testing								
–4.0	0.009	(0.007)	0.005	(0.006)	0.010	(0.010)	0.015	(0.010)
–3.5	–0.008	(0.011)	0.005	(0.010)	0.005	(0.012)	0.018	(0.014)
–3.0	–0.002	(0.015)	0.005	(0.015)	–0.014	(0.015)	0.017	(0.019)
–2.5	0.003	(0.019)	0.006	(0.022)	0.003	(0.020)	0.015	(0.025)
–2.0	0.014	(0.025)	0.011	(0.030)	0.010	(0.026)	0.015	(0.033)
–1.5	–0.017	(0.032)	0.006	(0.039)	0.065	(0.031)	0.039	(0.043)
Number of observations								
1997	367		367		374		374	
2000	540		540		487		487	

continued on next page

APPENDIX TABLE 7.2 – cont'd

	First crossing point and the difference between curves (2000 – 1997)							
	Boys				Girls			
	First-Order Dominance	Standard Errors	Second-Order Dominance	Standard Errors	First-Order Dominance	Standard Errors	Second-Order Dominance	Standard Errors
Age 36–59 months								
First crossing point	–3.553	(5.416)	–2.717	(3.380)	–3.332	(0.399)	–2.183	(1.017)
Points of testing								
–4.0	0.002	(0.004)	0.001	(0.003)	0.005	(0.005)	0.005	(0.007)
–3.5	0.000	(0.005)	0.002	(0.005)	0.002	(0.006)	0.008	(0.009)
–3.0	–0.007	(0.007)	0.001	(0.007)	–0.004	(0.009)	0.008	(0.012)
–2.5	–0.008	(0.011)	–0.001	(0.010)	–0.014	(0.012)	0.004	(0.015)
–2.0	–0.015	(0.018)	–0.007	(0.015)	–0.019	(0.018)	–0.003	(0.020)
–1.5	–0.035	(0.026)	–0.020	(0.023)	–0.051	(0.028)	–0.025	(0.027)
Number of observations								
1997	569		569		543		543	
2000	710		710		726		726	

Source: IFLS2 and IFLS3. Dash (–) indicates that the curves do not cross. Formulae for the standard errors are from Russel Davidson and Jean-Yves Duclos (2000), "Statistical Inference for Stochastic Dominance and for the Measurement of Poverty and Inequality", *Econometrica* v86 n6. Computation for the table above was performed using "DAD: A Software for Distributive Analysis/Analyse Distributive", version 4.2, copyrighted by Jean-Yves Duclos, Abdelkrim Araar, and Carl Fortin. Standard errors are robust to clustering at the community level. Estimates were weighted using individual sampling weights.

APPENDIX TABLE 7.3
Child Haemoglobin Level: Test for Stochastic Dominance

	First crossing point and the difference between curves (2000 – 1997)							
	Boys				Girls			
	First-Order Dominance	Standard Errors	Second-Order Dominance	Standard Errors	First-Order Dominance	Standard Errors	Second-Order Dominance	Standard Errors
Age 12–59 months								
First crossing point	7.996	(0.202)	8.975	(2.019)	9.495	(0.111)	11.797	(3.591)
Points of testing								
8.0	0.001	(0.009)	–0.004	(0.010)	–0.015	(0.015)	–0.021	(0.012)
8.5	0.001	(0.012)	–0.003	(0.014)	–0.026	(0.013)	–0.03	(0.016)
9.0	0.014	(0.015)	0.000	(0.019)	–0.02	(0.017)	–0.041	(0.022)
9.5	0.017	(0.019)	0.006	(0.025)	0.001	(0.021)	–0.051	(0.029)
10.0	0.063	(0.022)	0.022	(0.033)	0.017	(0.025)	–0.047	(0.038)
10.5	0.036	(0.025)	0.049	(0.041)	0.035	(0.027)	–0.037	(0.048)
11.0	0.055	(0.025)	0.073	(0.051)	0.039	(0.027)	–0.016	(0.057)
11.5	0.028	(0.023)	0.093	(0.059)	0.01	(0.025)	–0.004	(0.067)
12.0	0.039	(0.019)	0.107	(0.065)	0.021	(0.021)	0.003	(0.074)
Number of observations								
1997	967		967		894		894	
2000	1,368		1,368		1,310		1,310	

continued on next page

APPENDIX TABLE 7.3 – cont'd

	First crossing point and the difference between curves (2000 – 1997)							
	Boys				Girls			
	First-Order Dominance	Standard Errors	Second-Order Dominance	Standard Errors	First-Order Dominance	Standard Errors	Second-Order Dominance	Standard Errors
Age 5–14 years								
First crossing point	11.254	(0.189)	9.759	(0.705)	12.089	(0.117)	–	–
Points of testing								
9.0	–0.003	(0.004)	0.005	(0.005)	–0.004	(0.004)	–0.005	(0.007)
9.5	–0.009	(0.006)	0.002	(0.007)	–0.004	(0.006)	–0.007	(0.008)
10.0	–0.011	(0.008)	–0.002	(0.009)	–0.001	(0.008)	–0.009	(0.010)
10.5	–0.028	(0.011)	–0.013	(0.012)	–0.015	(0.012)	–0.013	(0.014)
11.0	–0.005	(0.015)	–0.023	(0.017)	–0.007	(0.014)	–0.02	(0.018)
11.5	0.003	(0.017)	–0.023	(0.024)	–0.02	(0.017)	–0.028	(0.024)
12.0	0.024	(0.018)	–0.015	(0.031)	–0.01	(0.018)	–0.035	(0.031)
12.5	0.028	(0.018)	–0.003	(0.038)	0.028	(0.017)	–0.031	(0.038)
Number of observations								
1997	3,307				3,216			
2000	3,578				3,434			

Source: IFLS2 and IFLS3. Dash (–) indicates that the curves do not cross. Formulae for the standard errors are from Russel Davidson and Jean-Yves Duclos (2000), "Statistical Inference for Stochastic Dominance and for the Measurement of Poverty and Inequality", *Econometrica* v86 n6. Computation for the table above was performed using "DAD: A Software for Distributive Analysis/Analyse Distributive", version 4.2, copyrighted by Jean-Yves Duclos, Abdelkrim Araar, and Carl Fortin. Standard errors are robust to clustering at the community level. Estimates were weighted using individual sampling weights.

APPENDIX TABLE 7.4
Adult Body Mass Index: Test for Stochastic Dominance for Undernourishment

	First crossing point and the difference between curves (2000 – 1997)							
	Men				Women			
	First-Order Dominance	Standard Errors	Second-Order Dominance	Standard Errors	First-Order Dominance	Standard Errors	Second-Order Dominance	Standard Errors
Age 15–19 years								
First crossing point	16.087	(0.312)	17.451	(1.370)	15.198	(0.422)	–	–
Points of testing:								
16.0	–0.003	(0.008)	–0.007	(0.009)	0.008	(0.006)	0.006	(0.006)
16.5	0.003	(0.010)	–0.007	(0.012)	0.003	(0.008)	0.009	(0.009)
17.0	0.001	(0.013)	–0.004	(0.016)	0.002	(0.011)	0.01	(0.012)
17.5	0.024	(0.016)	0.001	(0.022)	–0.009	(0.014)	0.009	(0.017)
18.0	0.032	(0.018)	0.015	(0.028)	–0.002	(0.016)	0.008	(0.023)
18.5	0.027	(0.019)	0.031	(0.035)	–0.001	(0.018)	0.009	(0.030)
19.0	0.038	(0.020)	0.046	(0.042)	–0.002	(0.020)	0.007	(0.037)
19.5	0.039	(0.020)	0.067	(0.049)	–0.001	(0.021)	0.005	(0.045)
Number of observations		1997	1,509			1997	1,611	
		2000	1,872			2000	2,017	
Age 20–39 years								
First crossing point	–	–	–	–		–	–	–
Points of testing:								
16.0	0.004	(0.002)	0.004	(0.003)	0.004	(0.002)	0.005	(0.004)
16.5	0.005	(0.003)	0.007	(0.004)	0.002	(0.003)	0.005	(0.005)
17.0	0.008	(0.005)	0.01	(0.005)	0.000	(0.004)	0.007	(0.006)
17.5	0.014	(0.007)	0.015	(0.007)	0.003	(0.005)	0.008	(0.007)
18.0	0.017	(0.007)	0.023	(0.010)	0.000	(0.007)	0.009	(0.009)
18.5	0.022	(0.009)	0.033	(0.010)	0.003	(0.008)	0.009	(0.012)
19.0	0.025	(0.011)	0.044	(0.019)	0.007	(0.009)	0.010	(0.016)
19.5	0.018	(0.014)	0.058	(0.024)	0.001	(0.011)	0.012	(0.020)
Number of observations		1997	3,592			1997	4,480	
		2000	5,508			2000	5,816	

continued on next page

APPENDIX TABLE 7.4 – cont'd

	First crossing point and the difference between curves (2000 – 1997)							
	Men				Women			
	First-Order Dominance	Standard Errors	Second-Order Dominance	Standard Errors	First-Order Dominance	Standard Errors	Second-Order Dominance	Standard Errors
Age 40–59 years								
First crossing point	–	–	–	–	16.018	*(0.925)*	–	–
Points of testing:								
16.0	–0.004	(0.003)	–0.004	(0.005)	0.000	(0.005)	–0.002	(0.007)
16.5	–0.002	(0.004)	–0.006	(0.006)	–0.004	(0.006)	–0.004	(0.009)
17.0	–0.006	(0.006)	–0.007	(0.008)	–0.004	(0.008)	–0.006	(0.012)
17.5	–0.01	(0.008)	–0.012	(0.010)	–0.006	(0.009)	–0.007	(0.015)
18.0	–0.017	(0.009)	–0.020	(0.013)	–0.015	(0.009)	–0.012	(0.019)
18.5	–0.021	(0.012)	–0.029	(0.017)	–0.020	(0.012)	–0.021	(0.024)
19.0	–0.026	(0.014)	–0.040	(0.022)	–0.028	(0.014)	–0.032	(0.029)
19.5	–0.025	(0.016)	–0.051	(0.028)	–0.030	(0.016)	–0.048	(0.035)
Number of observations	1997	2,453			1997	2,939		
	2000	2,957			2000	3,298		
Age 60 years and above								
First crossing point	15.39	(0.602)	17.534	(1.853)	16.965	(0.358)	15.18	(5.796)
Points of testing:								
16.0	–0.002	(0.011)	0.006	(0.012)	0.006	(0.014)	0.003	(0.020)
16.5	0.003	(0.014)	0.007	(0.017)	0.004	(0.017)	0.006	(0.026)
17.0	–0.009	(0.017)	0.007	(0.023)	–0.001	(0.019)	0.009	(0.034)
17.5	–0.011	(0.020)	0.001	(0.029)	–0.007	(0.022)	0.007	(0.028)
18.0	–0.031	(0.022)	–0.011	(0.038)	–0.013	(0.023)	0.001	(0.051)
18.5	–0.039	(0.024)	–0.028	(0.046)	0.006	(0.023)	–0.001	(0.061)
19.0	–0.035	(0.025)	–0.046	(0.056)	0.001	(0.025)	0.001	(0.070)
19.5	–0.009	(0.027)	–0.056	(0.066)	–0.003	(0.025)	0.001	(0.080)
Number of observations	1997	1,140			1997	1,315		
	2000	1,376			2000	1638		

Source: IFLS2 and IFLS3. Dash (–) indicates that the curves do not cross. Formulae for the standard errors are from Russel Davidson and Jean-Yves Duclos (2000), "Statistical Inference for Stochastic Dominance and for the Measurement of Poverty and Inequality", *Econometrica* v86 n6. Computation for the table above was performed using "DAD: A Software for Distributive Analysis/Analyse Distributive", version 4.2, copyrighted by Jean-Yves Duclos, Abdelkrim Araar, and Carl Fortin. Standard errors are robust to clustering at the community level. Estimates were weighted using individual sampling weights.

APPENDIX TABLE 7.5
Adult Body Mass Index: Test for Stochastic Dominance for Overweight

	Last crossing point and the difference between curves (2000 – 1997)			
	Men		Women	
	First-Order Dominance	Standard Errors	First-Order Dominance	Standard Errors
Age 15–19 years				
Last crossing point	30.636	(2.411)	32.227	(1.754)
Points of testing:				
24.5	–0.003	(0.006)	–0.019	(0.009)
25.5	–0.001	(0.005)	–0.009	(0.007)
26.5	–0.004	(0.004)	–0.003	(0.005)
27.5	–0.004	(0.003)	0.001	(0.004)
28.5	–0.001	(0.003)	0.002	(0.004)
29.5	0.001	(0.003)	0.001	(0.003)
30.5	0.000	(0.002)	0.001	(0.002)
Number of observations	1997: 1,509 2000: 1,872		1997: 1,611 2000: 2,017	
Age 20–39 years				
Last crossing point	20.79	(0.628)	19.574	(0.803)
Points of testing:				
24.5	–0.027	(0.008)	–0.023	(0.011)
25.5	–0.022	(0.006)	–0.023	(0.010)
26.5	–0.016	(0.005)	–0.022	(0.008)
27.5	–0.013	(0.004)	–0.017	(0.006)
28.5	–0.007	(0.003)	–0.013	(0.005)
29.5	–0.005	(0.003)	–0.005	(0.004)
30.5	–0.001	(0.002)	–0.005	(0.003)
Number of observations	1997: 3,592 2000: 5,508		1997: 4,480 2000: 5,816	
Age 40–59 years				
Last crossing point	36.84	(3.657)	16.018	(2.189)
Points of testing:				
24.5	–0.034	(0.015)	–0.060	(0.018)
25.5	–0.020	(0.012)	–0.047	(0.016)
26.5	–0.015	(0.009)	–0.030	(0.014)
27.5	–0.010	(0.008)	–0.020	(0.012)
28.5	–0.008	(0.006)	–0.024	(0.010)
29.5	0.000	(0.005)	–0.020	(0.008)
30.5	–0.003	(0.003)	–0.013	(0.007)
Number of observations	1997: 2,453 2000: 2,957		1997: 2,939 2000: 3,298	
Age 60 years and above				
Last crossing point	30.27	(2.103)	34.338	(1.183)
Points of testing:				
24.5	–0.008	(0.013)	–0.011	(0.013)
25.5	–0.010	(0.010)	–0.009	(0.015)
26.5	–0.007	(0.008)	–0.003	(0.013)
27.5	0.009	(0.007)	0.004	(0.011)
28.5	–0.007	(0.005)	0.004	(0.009)
29.5	–0.003	(0.004)	–0.001	(0.007)
30.5	0.000	(0.003)	0.001	(0.006)
Number of observations	1997: 1,140 2000: 1,376		1997: 1,315 2000: 1,638	

Source: IFLS2 and IFLS3. Dash (–) indicates that the curves do not cross. Formulae for the standard errors are from Russel Davidson and Jean-Yves Duclos (2000), "Statistical Inference for Stochastic Dominance and for the Measurement of Poverty and Inequality", *Econometrica* v86 n6. Computation for the table above was performed using "DAD: A Software for Distributive Analysis/Analyse Distributive", version 4.2, copyrighted by Jean-Yves Duclos, Abdelkrim Araar, and Carl Fortin. Standard errors are robust to clustering at the community level. Estimates were weighted using individual sampling weights.

APPENDIX TABLE 7.6a
Systolic Levels: Test for Stochastic Dominance

	Last crossing point and the difference between curves (2000 – 1997)			
	Men		Women	
	First-Order Dominance	Standard Errors	First-Order Dominance	Standard Errors
Age 15–39 years				
Last crossing point	–	–	–	–
Points of testing:				
138	0.018	(0.008)	0.02	(0.006)
140	0.014	(0.006)	0.019	(0.005)
142	0.013	(0.006)	0.016	(0.005)
144	0.012	(0.005)	0.013	(0.004)
146	0.006	(0.005)	0.011	(0.004)
148	0.006	(0.004)	0.01	(0.004)
150	0.003	(0.003)	0.009	(0.003)
152	0.002	(0.003)	0.008	(0.003)
154	0.002	(0.003)	0.007	(0.003)
156	0.003	(0.002)	0.006	(0.003)
158	0.004	(0.002)	0.006	(0.002)
160	0.002	(0.002)	0.005	(0.002)
Number of observations:	1997: 5,072 2000: 7,413		1997: 6,062 2000: 7,870	
Age 40–59 years				
Last crossing point	–	–	–	–
Points of testing:				
138	0.033	(0.015)	0.026	(0.015)
140	0.024	(0.014)	0.022	(0.014)
142	0.013	(0.013)	0.015	(0.013)
144	0.016	(0.013)	0.016	(0.013)
146	0.01	(0.012)	0.008	(0.013)
148	0.014	(0.012)	0.003	(0.013)
150	0.006	(0.011)	0.006	(0.012)
152	0.007	(0.011)	0.004	(0.012)
154	0.009	(0.010)	0.004	(0.012)
156	0.008	(0.010)	0.005	(0.011)
158	0.005	(0.009)	0.006	(0.011)
160	0.01	(0.008)	0.011	(0.011)
Number of observations:	1997: 2,460 2000: 3,015		1997: 2,939 2000: 3,355	

continued on next page

APPENDIX TABLE 7.6a – cont'd

	Last crossing point and the difference between curves (2000 – 1997)			
	Men		Women	
	First-Order Dominance	Standard Errors	First-Order Dominance	Standard Errors
Age 60 years and above				
Last crossing point	213.94	(7.820)	–	–
Points of testing:				
138	–0.002	(0.023)	0.038	(0.023)
140	–0.008	(0.022)	0.032	(0.022)
142	–0.022	(0.022)	0.027	(0.023)
144	–0.003	(0.022)	0.035	(0.023)
146	–0.014	(0.022)	0.025	(0.023)
148	–0.010	(0.021)	0.031	(0.023)
150	–0.002	(0.020)	0.032	(0.023)
152	–0.012	(0.020)	0.038	(0.023)
154	–0.001	(0.019)	0.036	(0.023)
156	0.001	(0.019)	0.032	(0.022)
158	0.003	(0.018)	0.035	(0.022)
160	0.012	(0.017)	0.03	(0.021)
Number of observations:	1997: 1,152 2000: 1,401		1997: 1,333 2000: 1,706	

Source: IFLS2 and IFLS3. Dash (–) indicates that the curves do not cross. Formulae for the standard errors are from Russel Davidson and Jean-Yves Duclos (2000), "Statistical Inference for Stochastic Dominance and for the Measurement of Poverty and Inequality", *Econometrica* v86 n6. Computation for the table above was performed using "DAD: A Software for Distributive Analysis/Analyse Distributive", version 4.2, copyrighted by Jean-Yves Duclos, Abdelkrim Araar, and Carl Fortin. Standard errors are robust to clustering at the community level. Estimates were weighted using individual sampling weights.

APPENDIX TABLE 7.6b
Diastolic Levels: Test for Stochastic Dominance

	Last crossing point and the difference between curves (2000 – 1997)			
	Men		Women	
	First-Order Dominance	Standard Errors	First-Order Dominance	Standard Errors
Age 15–39 years				
Last crossing point	–	–	–	–
Points of testing:				
88	–0.012	(0.008)	–0.023	(0.007)
90	–0.015	(0.007)	–0.017	(0.006)
92	–0.012	(0.006)	–0.014	(0.006)
94	–0.006	(0.005)	–0.012	(0.004)
96	–0.005	(0.004)	–0.008	(0.004)
98	–0.007	(0.003)	–0.004	(0.003)
100	–0.005	(0.003)	–0.002	(0.003)
102	–0.004	(0.003)	–0.001	(0.003)
104	–0.002	(0.002)	–0.002	(0.002)
106	–0.002	(0.002)	–0.001	(0.002)
108	–0.002	(0.002)	–0.001	(0.002)
110	–0.002	(0.001)	–0.001	(0.001)
Number of observations:	1997: 5,072 2000: 7,413		1997: 6,062 2000: 7,870	
Age 40–59 years				
Last crossing point	–	–	97.09	*(4.193)*
Points of testing:				
88	–0.037	(0.015)	–0.012	(0.014)
90	–0.033	(0.014)	–0.013	(0.013)
92	–0.035	(0.012)	–0.009	(0.012)
94	–0.028	(0.011)	–0.002	(0.011)
96	–0.03	(0.010)	–0.005	(0.010)
98	–0.026	(0.009)	0.004	(0.009)
100	–0.023	(0.007)	0.001	(0.008)
102	–0.013	(0.007)	0.002	(0.007)
104	–0.008	(0.006)	0.002	(0.007)
106	–0.007	(0.006)	0.003	(0.006)
108	–0.004	(0.005)	0.005	(0.006)
110	–0.002	(0.005)	0.005	(0.005)
Number of observations:	1997: 2,460 2000: 3,015		1997: 2,939 2000: 3,355	

continued on next page

APPENDIX TABLE 7.6b – cont'd

	Last crossing point and the difference between curves (2000 – 1997)			
	Men		Women	
	First-Order Dominance	Standard Errors	First-Order Dominance	Standard Errors
Age 60 years and above				
Last crossing point	–	–	102.04	–1.521
Points of testing:				
88	0.004	(0.020)	0.010	(0.022)
90	–0.006	(0.019)	0.006	(0.021)
92	–0.007	(0.017)	0.013	(0.019)
94	–0.005	(0.016)	0.004	(0.018)
96	–0.009	(0.015)	0.003	(0.016)
98	–0.001	(0.014)	0.008	(0.015)
100	–0.003	(0.013)	–0.001	(0.015)
102	0.001	(0.013)	–0.002	(0.014)
104	–0.003	(0.012)	–0.01	(0.013)
106	0.000	(0.011)	–0.011	(0.011)
108	–0.002	(0.010)	–0.003	(0.010)
110	–0.009	(0.009)	–0.011	(0.010)
Number of observations:	1997: 1,152 2000: 1,401		1997: 1,333 2000: 1,706	

Source: IFLS2 and IFLS3. Dash (–) indicates that the curves do not cross. Formulae for the standard errors are from Russel Davidson and Jean-Yves Duclos (2000), "Statistical Inference for Stochastic Dominance and for the Measurement of Poverty and Inequality", *Econometrica* v86 n6. Computation for the table above was performed using "DAD: A Software for Distributive Analysis/Analyse Distributive", version 4.2, copyrighted by Jean-Yves Duclos, Abdelkrim Araar, and Carl Fortin. Standard errors are robust to clustering at the community level. Estimates were weighted using individual sampling weights.

APPENDIX TABLE 7.7
Frequency of Smoking: Rural and Urban

	15 and above											
	Men						Women					
	Rural			Urban			Rural			Urban		
	1997	2000	Change	1997	2000	Change	1997	2000	Change	1997	2000	Change
% ever smoked	74.2	75.2	1.0	65.8	66.2	0.4	7.9	7.0	–0.9	4.2	4.4	0.1
	(0.12)	(0.00)	(1.47)	(0.97)	(0.82)	(1.27)	(0.67)	(0.82)	(0.91)	(0.40)	(0.35)	(0.53)
% currently smoke a)	70.6	70.6	0.0	59.5	59.7	0.2	2.9	2.7	–0.2	2.3	2.6	0.3
	(1.23)	(0.91)	(1.53)	(0.99)	(0.83)	(1.29)	(0.38)	(0.40)	(0.55)	(0.33)	(0.28)	(0.43)
% currently smoke tobacco	9.7	6.9	–2.8 *	8.9	8.1	–0.8	0.5	0.3	–0.3	0.3	0.3	0.0
	(0.99)	(0.69)	(1.20)	(0.58)	(0.54)	(0.79)	(0.12)	(0.08)	(0.14)	(0.08)	(0.07)	(0.10)
% currently smoke cloves	59.9	63.7	3.8	49.9	51.6	1.7	2.3	2.4	0.1	1.9	2.3	0.4
	(1.49)	(1.10)	(1.85)	(1.11)	(0.91)	(1.43)	(0.35)	(0.38)	(0.51)	(0.30)	(0.27)	(0.40)
Number of observations	4,746	6,081	4,340	5,975	5,551	6,754	5,183	6,647				
	15–19 years											
	Men						Women					
	Rural			Urban			Rural			Urban		
	1997	2000	Change	1997	2000	Change	1997	2000	Change	1997	2000	Change
% ever smoked	40.9	46.6	5.7	34.6	40.4	5.8 *	0.1	0.1	0.0	0.5	0.8	0.3
	(2.54)	(2.05)	(3.26)	(2.02)	(1.65)	(2.61)	(0.09)	(0.08)	(0.12)	(0.25)	(0.29)	(0.39)
% currently smoke [a)]	39.1	45.7	6.6 *	33.6	39.0	5.5 *	0.0	0.0	0.0	0.1	0.6	0.5
	(2.49)	(2.10)	(3.25)	(2.01)	(1.69)	(2.62)	(0.00)	(0.00)	(0.00)	(0.08)	(0.27)	(0.28)
% currently smoke tobacco	5.4	7.5	2.1	7.4	10.0	2.6	0.0	0.0	0.0	0.1	0.2	0.1
	(1.03)	(1.14)	(1.53)	(1.09)	(1.09)	(1.55)	(0.00)	(0.00)	(0.00)	(0.08)	(0.16)	(0.18)
% currently smoke cloves	33.3	38.2	5.0	25.9	29.1	3.2	0.0	0.0	0.0	0.0	0.5	0.5 *
	(2.55)	(2.09)	(3.30)	(1.99)	(1.65)	(2.58)	(0.00)	(0.00)	(0.00)	(0.00)	(0.22)	(0.22)
Number of observations	749	896	832	1,029	782	1,019	921	1,117				

	20–29 years											
	Men						Women					
	Rural			Urban			Rural			Urban		
	1997	2000	Change	1997	2000	Change	1997	2000	Change	1997	2000	Change
% ever smoked	72.2	76.5	4.3	67.1	68.1	1.0	0.6	0.5	–0.1	1.0	1.5	0.5
	(2.19)	(1.35)	(2.57)	(1.89)	(1.45)	(2.38)	(0.21)	(0.18)	(0.28)	(0.33)	(0.30)	(0.45)
% currently smoke [a)]	71.0	74.4	3.4	64.3	65.0	0.6	0.4	0.4	0.0	0.4	1.2	0.8
	(2.20)	(1.37)	(2.59)	(1.96)	(1.47)	(2.45)	(0.18)	(0.17)	(0.25)	(0.25)	(0.27)	(0.36)
% currently smoke tobacco	8.9	9.2	0.3	13.7	12.7	–1.0	0.2	0.2	0.0	0.2	0.4	0.2
	(1.19)	(1.04)	(1.58)	(1.21)	(1.07)	(1.62)	(0.13)	(0.11)	(0.18)	(0.12)	(0.15)	(0.19)
% currently smoke cloves	61.8	65.2	3.4	49.9	52.3	2.4	0.2	0.3	0.0	0.3	0.8	0.5
	(2.30)	(1.48)	(2.74)	(1.94)	(1.62)	(2.53)	(0.12)	(0.13)	(0.18)	(0.22)	(0.23)	(0.31)
Number of observations	905	1,500	950	1,671	1,221	1,670	1176	1,819				

	30–39 years											
	Men						Women					
	Rural			Urban			Rural			Urban		
	1997	2000	Change	1997	2000	Change	1997	2000	Change	1997	2000	Change
% ever smoked	79.6	77.8	–1.8	75.3	72.9	–2.3	3.0	2.5	–0.6	4.0	3.1	–0.9
	(1.59)	(1.57)	(2.24)	(1.53)	(1.45)	(2.11)	(0.65)	(0.55)	(0.85)	(0.78)	(0.58)	(0.97)
% currently smoke [a)]	76.9	74.1	–2.8	71.3	67.6	–3.7	2.3	1.9	–0.4	3.0	2.6	–0.5
	(1.63)	(1.67)	(2.33)	(1.66)	(1.52)	(2.25)	(0.61)	(0.39)	(0.72)	(0.72)	(0.51)	(0.88)
% currently smoke tobacco	8.8	6.3	–2.5	8.1	7.4	–0.7	0.4	0.2	–0.2	0.4	0.2	–0.2
	(1.15)	(0.82)	(1.41)	(0.98)	(0.81)	(1.27)	(0.19)	(0.13)	(0.23)	(0.22)	(0.10)	(0.25)
% currently smoke cloves	67.6	67.8	0.2	62.7	60.2	–2.5	1.9	1.8	–0.1	2.5	2.3	–0.1
	(1.89)	(1.82)	(2.62)	(1.87)	(1.64)	(2.49)	(0.58)	(0.37)	(0.68)	(0.61)	(0.49)	(0.79)
Number of observations	1,063	1,278		911	1,457		1,286	1,274		1,165	1,394	

continued on next page

APPENDIX TABLE 7.7 – cont'd

	40–49 years											
	Men						Women					
	Rural			Urban			Rural			Urban		
	1997	2000	Change	1997	2000	Change	1997	2000	Change	1997	2000	Change
% ever smoked	79.7	80.7	1.0	71.2	72.2	0.9	5.3	5.8	0.5	5.2	4.3	−1.0
	(1.85)	(1.67)	(2.49)	(2.04)	(2.01)	(2.86)	(1.21)	(1.09)	(0.53)	(1.15)	(0.82)	(1.41)
% currently smoke [a)]	75.4	75.5	0.1	64.1	64.5	0.5	3.0	3.6	0.6	4.5	3.9	–0.6
	(1.91)	(1.74)	(2.58)	(2.10)	(1.92)	(2.84)	(0.88)	(0.88)	(1.25)	(0.90)	(0.74)	(1.17)
% currently smoke tobacco	9.2	5.2	–4.1 *	5.9	4.2	−1.7	0.4	0.3	–0.1	0.4	0.2	–0.1
	(1.42)	(0.92)	(1.69)	(1.03)	(0.67)	(1.23)	(0.24)	(0.18)	(0.30)	(0.24)	(0.15)	(0.28)
% currently smoke cloves	64.4	70.3	5.9*	57.6	60.4	2.8	2.5	3.2	0.7	4.1	3.6	–0.5
	(2.29)	(1.84)	(2.94)	(2.18)	(1.90)	(2.89)	(0.86)	(0.78)	(1.16)	(0.88)	(0.73)	(1.15)
Number of observations	772	964		716	920		835	1,016		843	1,034	

	50–59 years											
	Men						Women					
	Rural			Urban			Rural			Urban		
	1997	2000	Change	1997	2000	Change	1997	2000	Change	1997	2000	Change
% ever smoked	89.2	85.4	−3.8	74.3	70.3	−3.9	21.4	16.0	−5.4	7.9	7.7	–0.2
	(1.53)	(1.56)	(2.18)	(2.44)	(2.42)	(3.44)	(2.34)	(1.71)	(2.90)	(1.27)	(1.17)	(1.72)
% currently smoke [a)]	84.4	77.8	–6.6 *	62.6	59.2	−3.4	7.8	6.7	−1.1	4.4	4.8	0.4
	(1.73)	(1.85)	(2.53)	(2.67)	(2.43)	(3.61)	(1.37)	(1.16)	(1.80)	(0.99)	(0.92)	(1.35)
% currently smoke tobacco	14.2	4.9	−9.3	7.5	4.6	−2.9	1.5	0.5	−1.0	0.2	0.3	0.1
	(2.36)	(1.01)	(2.56)**	(1.71)	(0.98)	(1.97)	(0.46)	(0.27)	(0.53)	(0.14)	(0.17)	(0.22)
% currently smoke cloves	68.7	72.9	4.2	54.5	54.6	0.1	6.4	6.2	–0.1	4.2	4.5	0.3
	(2.66)	(2.03)	(3.35)	(2.72)	(2.50)	(3.70)	(1.28)	(1.12)	(1.70)	(0.98)	(0.91)	(1.34)

Number of observations	579	637		486	544		744	715		548	617	

	60 and above											
	Men						Women					
	Rural			Urban			Rural			Urban		
	1997	2000	Change	1997	2000	Change	1997	2000	Change	1997	2000	Change
% ever smoked	87.0	87.4	0.4	76.1	74.6	–1.5	35.1	31.0	–4.1	17.9	18.9	1.0
	(1.62)	(1.35)	(2.11)	(2.31)	(2.11)	(3.13)	(3.03)	(2.94)	(4.22)	(2.02)	(2.23)	(3.01)
% currently smoke a)	76.8	74.5	–2.3	52.2	52.8	0.6	8.1	7.3	–0.8	4.2	5.3	1.1
	(1.98)	(1.80)	(2.67)	(2.77)	(2.29)	(3.59)	(1.42)	(1.33)	(1.95)	(0.94)	(1.02)	(1.38)
% currently smoke tobacco	14.5	7.2	–7.2 **	7.5	4.3	–3.2	1.3	0.7	–0.6	0.6	0.1	–0.5
	(2.24)	(1.26)	(2.57)	(1.59)	(0.92)	(1.84)	(0.53)	(0.28)	(0.60)	(0.33)	(0.09)	(0.34)
% currently smoke cloves	60.4	67.3	6.9	43.3	48.5	5.2	6.6	6.6	0.0	3.4	5.2	1.8
	(2.99)	(2.09)	(3.65)	(2.86)	(2.34)	(3.69)	(1.20)	(1.30)	(1.77)	(0.89)	(1.02)	(1.35)
Number of observations	678	806		445	537		683	877	530	666		

Source: IFLS2 and IFLS3.

a) Currently smoke cigarettes/cigars. Estimates were weighted using individual sampling weights. Standard errors (in parentheses) are robust to clustering at the community level. Significance at 5% (*) and 1% (**) indicated.

APPENDIX TABLE 7.8
Average Number of Cigarettes Smoked Per Day (for Current Smokers): Rural and Urban

Age/ Gender		Rural			Urban		
		1997	2000	Change	1997	2000	Change
15–19							
	Male	8.5	8.3	–0.2	8.1	7.8	–0.3
		(0.41)	(0.33)	(0.53)	(0.50)	(0.33)	(0.59)
	Female	0.0	0.0	0.0	5.0	5.2	0.2
		(0.00)	(0.00)	(0.00)	(0.00)	(2.53)	(2.53)
20–29							
	Male	9.9	10.5	0.6	12.2	11.2	–1.0
		(0.34)	(0.26)	(0.43)	(0.40)	(0.26)	(0.47)
	Female	10.4	5.6	–4.8 *	8.5	6.5	–1.9
		(0.83)	(1.77)	(1.95)	(1.53)	(1.44)	(2.10)
30–39							
	Male	12.2	11.8	–0.4	12.9	12.7	–0.2
		(0.32)	(0.29)	(0.43)	(0.32)	(0.31)	(0.45)
	Female	7.4	5.5	–1.9	6.6	10.1	3.5
		(1.24)	(0.69)	(1.42)	(1.14)	(2.10)	(2.38)
40–49							
	Male	11.7	12.0	0.2	13.9	12.4	–1.5 *
		(0.39)	(0.32)	(0.51)	(0.49)	(0.37)	(0.61)
	Female	7.0	6.5	–0.5	7.9	8.6	
		(0.93)	(0.87)	(1.27)	(1.24)	(1.68)	
50–59							
	Male	11.3	11.2	–0.1	11.8	11.9	0.1
		(0.47)	(0.41)	(0.62)	(0.53)	(0.51)	(0.74)
	Female	6.5	6.6	0.1	8.2	5.7	–2.6
		(0.61)	(0.68)	(0.91)	(2.26)	(0.82)	(2.41)
60 or above							
	Male	10.1	9.7	–0.5	9.5	10.0	0.5
		(0.35)	0.33	(0.48)	(0.46)	0.46	(0.65)
	Female	6.0	6.9	0.9	7.2	5.4	–1.8
		(0.93)	(0.68)	(1.15)	(1.48)	(0.77)	(1.67)

Source: IFLS2 and IFLS3.

Estimates were weighted using individual sampling weights. Standard errors (in parentheses) are robust to clustering at the community level. Significance at 5% (*) and 1% (**) indicated.

APPENDIX TABLE 7.9
Age When Start Smoking: Rural and Urban

Age/Gender		Rural					Urban				
		% Age Start Smoking				Avg Age Start	% Age Start Smoking				Avg Age Start
		<=15	<=18	<=21	<=24		<=15	<=18	<=21	<=24	
15–19											
	Male	27.4	...	...	...	15.0	21.8	...	...	...	15.2
		(1.82)	...	...	...	(0.13)	(1.53)	...	...	...	(0.10)
	Female	0.1	...	...	...	9.0	0.4	...	...	...	15.2
		(0.08)	...	...	...	(0.00)	(0.21)	...	...	...	(0.83)
20–29											
	Male	23.6	52.3	...	...	17.1	19.1	45.4	...	...	17.3
		(1.55)	(1.64)	...	...	(0.14)	(1.12)	(1.56)	...	...	(0.10)
	Female	0.1	0.2	...	...	21.0	0.0	0.7	...	...	19.9
		(0.07)	(0.10)	...	...	(1.59)	(0.00)	(0.21)	...	...	(0.54)
30–39											
	Male	22.9	43.0	62.5	67.6	18.5	15.6	38.9	57.1	63.1	19.0
		(1.40)	(1.88)	(1.91)	(1.81)	(0.20)	(1.06)	(1.57)	(1.61)	(1.66)	(0.17)
	Female	0.4	0.6	0.8	0.9	24.8	0.6	1.3	1.5	2.0	22.5
		(0.16)	(0.20)	(0.27)	(0.28)	(1.53)	(0.24)	(0.37)	(0.38)	(0.47)	(1.11)
40–49											
	Male	22.6	34.9	55.7	62.2	20.2	16.0	29.7	49.2	56.6	20.5
		(1.80)	(2.18)	(2.06)	(1.97)	(0.29)	(1.28)	(1.84)	(2.31)	(2.15)	(0.27)
	Female	1.1	1.9	2.5	2.9	27.4	0.7	1.9	2.4	2.8	23.2
		(0.38)	(0.49)	(0.61)	(0.67)	(1.49)	(0.30)	(0.55)	(0.65)	(0.68)	(1.49)
50–59											
	Male	24.3	38.8	59.0	63.3	20.7	11.2	24.7	43.4	48.7	22.1
		(2.06)	(2.05)	(2.32)	(2.33)	(0.42)	(1.64)	(2.08)	(2.50)	(2.38)	(0.48)
	Female	3.8	5.0	7.3	8.1	25.7	1.1	1.4	2.5	3.1	31.4
		(0.80)	(0.88)	(1.20)	(1.23)	(1.21)	(0.43)	(0.49)	(0.68)	(0.76)	(2.43)
60 or above											
	Male	30.7	39.8	58.3	61.9	21.2	20.5	30.4	48.9	53.8	21.3
		(2.03)	(2.10)	(2.07)	(2.01)	(0.46)	(1.78)	(2.02)	(2.21)	(2.25)	(0.48)
	Female	6.5	8.5	15.6	16.3	26.9	4.3	5.9	9.7	10.3	26.7
		(1.22)	(1.44)	(1.99)	(2.08)	(0.98)	(0.87)	(1.06)	(1.38)	(1.49)	(1.32)

Source: IFLS3.
Estimates were weighted using individual sampling weights. Standard errors (in parentheses) are robust to clustering at the community level. Significance at 5% (*) and 1% (**) indicated.

APPENDIX TABLE 7.10
Adult Haemoglobin Level: Test for Stochastic Dominance

	First crossing point and the difference between curves (2000 – 1997)							
	Men				Women			
	First-Order Dominance	Standard Errors	Second-Order Dominance	Standard Errors	First-Order Dominance	Standard Errors	Second-Order Dominance	Standard Errors
Age 15–19 years								
First crossing point	10.079	(0.240)	10.912	(2.217)	9.138	(0.689)	9.819	(2.361)
Points of testing								
9.0	0.002	(0.003)	0.002	(0.008)	0.001	(0.005)	–0.001	(0.007)
9.5	0.003	(0.003)	0.004	(0.009)	0.003	(0.007)	–0.001	(0.009)
10.0	0.003	(0.003)	0.005	(0.010)	–0.002	(0.008)	0.001	(0.011)
10.5	–0.010	(0.006)	0.003	(0.012)	0.002	(0.011)	0.000	(0.015)
11.0	–0.009	(0.007)	–0.001	(0.014)	0.008	(0.014)	0.002	(0.019)
11.5	–0.022	(0.009)	–0.008	(0.016)	0.014	(0.018)	0.007	(0.025)
12.0	–0.017	(0.012)	–0.016	(0.019)	0.054	(0.022)	0.023	(0.032)
12.5	–0.028	(0.015)	–0.028	(0.024)	0.033	(0.027)	0.045	(0.040)
13.0	–0.024	(0.018)	–0.040	(0.029)	0.029	(0.030)	0.061	(0.051)
13.5	–0.051	(0.022)	–0.058	(0.036)	0.044	(0.033)	0.079	(0.063)
14.0	–0.027	(0.025)	–0.081	(0.044)	0.032	(0.034)	0.097	(0.077)
Number of observations:								
1997	1,490		1,490		1,574		1,574	
2000	1,861		1,861		1,984		1,984	
Age 20–59 years								
First crossing point	9.951	(0.694)	11.440	(0.311)	11.410	(0.092)	9.258	(1.521)
Points of testing								
9.0	0.002	(0.002)	0.011	(0.004)	–0.003	(0.003)	0.001	(0.004)
9.5	0.002	(0.002)	0.012	(0.005)	–0.002	(0.004)	–0.001	(0.005)
10.0	–0.001	(0.003)	0.013	(0.006)	–0.005	(0.005)	–0.002	(0.007)
10.5	–0.007	(0.003)	0.012	(0.006)	–0.011	(0.006)	–0.006	(0.009)

11.0	–0.011	(0.004)	0.008	(0.008)	–0.006	(0.007)	–0.011	(0.011)
11.5	–0.032	(0.005)	–0.002	(0.009)	0.004	(0.009)	–0.013	(0.014)
12.0	–0.040	(0.006)	–0.019	(0.011)	0.023	(0.010)	–0.007	(0.017)
12.5	–0.064	(0.007)	–0.044	(0.013)	0.024	(0.011)	0.006	(0.021)
13.0	–0.064	(0.009)	–0.077	(0.016)	0.039	(0.013)	0.021	(0.025)
13.5	–0.080	(0.010)	–0.112	(0.019)	0.041	(0.013)	0.041	(0.030)
14.0	–0.069	(0.011)	–0.151	(0.022)	0.036	(0.014)	0.061	(0.035)
Number of observations:								
1997	5,957		5,957		7,280		7,280	
2000	8,422		8,422		9,064		9,064	
Age 60 years and above								
First crossing point	–	–	–	–	10.017	(0.240)	11.998	(1.759)
Points of testing								
9.0	–0.006	(0.009)	–0.008	(0.019)	–0.009	(0.010)	–0.009	(0.015)
9.5	–0.008	(0.010)	–0.011	(0.023)	–0.005	(0.012)	–0.012	(0.019)
10.0	–0.016	(0.013)	–0.018	(0.027)	0.000	(0.014)	–0.013	(0.024)
10.5	–0.032	(0.015)	–0.027	(0.032)	–0.007	(0.017)	–0.014	(0.029)
11.0	–0.032	(0.018)	–0.042	(0.037)	0.003	(0.021)	–0.015	(0.036)
11.5	–0.036	(0.021)	–0.057	(0.044)	0.010	(0.024)	–0.011	(0.044)
12.0	–0.049	(0.024)	–0.079	(0.051)	0.026	(0.028)	0.000	(0.054)
12.5	–0.059	(0.027)	–0.108	(0.060)	0.031	(0.031)	0.014	(0.065)
13.0	–0.066	(0.030)	–0.137	(0.070)	0.042	(0.034)	0.032	(0.077)
13.5	–0.049	(0.033)	–0.169	(0.082)	0.029	(0.037)	0.052	(0.091)
14.0	–0.020	(0.036)	–0.187	(0.095)	0.024	(0.038)	0.062	(0.106)
Number of observations:								
1997	1,139		1,139		1,302		1,302	
2000	1,387		1,387		1,680		1,680	

Source: IFLS2 and IFLS3. Dash (–) indicates that the curves do not cross. Formulae for the standard errors are from Russel Davidson and Jean-Yves Duclos (2000), "Statistical Inference for Stochastic Dominance and for the Measurement of Poverty and Inequality", *Econometrica* v86 n6. Computation for the table above was performed using "DAD: A Software for Distributive Analysis/Analyse Distributive", version 4.2, copyrighted by Jean-Yves Duclos, Abdelkrim Araar, and Carl Fortin. Estimates were weighted using individual sampling weights.

8

Health Input Utilization

Changes in health outcomes are caused by changes in health inputs, some chosen by households given the information and constraints that they face, and some purely external to household decision-making. In this chapter, we examine changes in three such inputs: outpatient health care utilization separately for children and adults, and for young children, receipt of immunizations and supplemental vitamin A.[1] For outpatient utilization, we distinguish by type, including by public or private sector.

In our comparison of public and private services, we note the ambiguities that sometimes arise. For instance, doctors who work at *puskesmas* or hospitals may also have a private practice. In principal, the private practice will not be held at the public facility, but sometimes it is. Even then, however, the hours are often distinct, making it possible for respondents to distinguish whether they are seeing a doctor in his or her public or private practice. For village midwives, however, this differentiation can be much more difficult. Virtually all village midwives have important public roles, such as being the coordinator of the village *posyandu* or co-ordinating the distribution of *Kartu Sehat*.[2] However, many of them also act as private midwives, making it impossible to distinguish. In this report, we treat village and private midwives together and call them private, but one must treat that distinction with caution.

Table 8.1 shows utilization rates in the previous four weeks by type of outpatient facility by boys and girls, aged 0–59 months and 5–14 years.[3] Overall, the large change that has occurred between 1997 and 2000 is the major drop in utilization of *posyandu* by young children (*posyandu* child services are targeted only at children from birth to 5 years).[4] This result was also found in 1998 (Frankenberg et al. 1999). The decline in *posyandu* utilization has occurred both in urban and rural areas, but with a larger percentage point drop in rural areas (Appendix Table 8.1).

TABLE 8.1
Use of Outpatient Healthcare Facilities by Children in Last Four Weeks (In percent)

	0–59 months						5–14 years					
	Boys			Girls			Boys			Girls		
	1997	2000	Change	1997	2000	Change	1997	2000	Change	1997	2000	Change
Use any health services	61.3	56.0	–5.3 *	62.9	55.4	–7.5 **	12.5	12.6	0.2	11.8	13.2	1.4
	(1.74)	(1.42)	(2.25)	(1.95)	(1.53)	(2.47)	(0.69)	(0.67)	(0.96)	(0.71)	(0.69)	(0.99)
Public services:	55.6	46.3	–9.3 **	57.2	45.4	–11.8 **	6.0	5.4	–0.7	6	6.3	0.4
	(1.77)	(1.51)	(2.33)	(2.02)	(1.57)	(2.56)	(0.49)	(0.43)	(0.65)	(0.49)	(0.49)	(0.70)
– Government hospitals	0.7	1.0	0.3	0.8	0.9	0.1	0.6	0.4	–0.2	0.3	0.4	0.1
	(0.24)	(0.27)	(0.36)	(0.25)	(0.22)	(0.33)	(0.15)	(0.12)	(0.20)	(0.09)	(0.12)	(0.15)
– *puskesmas/pustu*	10.2	9.7	-0.5	9.1	10.8	1.7	5.4	5.0	–0.4	5.7	6	0.2
	(0.91)	(0.74)	(1.17)	(0.94)	(0.83)	(1.25)	(0.47)	(0.41)	(0.62)	(0.49)	(0.48)	(0.68)
– *Posyandu*	52.0	40.2	–11.7 **	53.5	40.1	–13.4 **						
	(1.77)	(1.54)	(2.35)	(1.93)	(1.63)	(2.52)						
Private services:	12.4	18.9	6.4 **	13.7	18.1	4.4 **	6.7	7.5	0.8	6.3	6.8	0.4
	(0.96)	(1.03)	(1.41)	(1.09)	(1.05)	(1.52)	(0.55)	(0.56)	(0.79)	(0.51)	(0.51)	(0.73)
– Private hospitals	0.7	0.8	0.0	0.7	1.0	0.4	0.3	0.3	–0.1	0.3	0.3	0
	(0.28)	(0.21)	(0.35)	(0.21)	(0.25)	(0.32)	(0.09)	(0.10)	(0.13)	(0.09)	(0.10)	(0.14)
– Polyclinic and private doctor	5.6	8.7	3.1 **	6.5	8.0	1.4	3.6	4.3	0.7	3.3	3.6	0.3
	(0.64)	(0.73)	(0.97)	(0.73)	(0.68)	(1.00)	(0.40)	(0.43)	(0.59)	(0.37)	(0.41)	(0.55)
– Nurse, midwife and paramedic	6.5	9.7	3.2 **	7.1	9.4	2.3	3.1	3.1	0.1	2.9	2.9	0
	(0.75)	(0.84)	(1.13)	(0.92)	(0.85)	(1.25)	(0.36)	(0.37)	(0.51)	(0.38)	(0.31)	(0.48)
Traditional health services	0.5	0.7	0.1	0.6	0.7	0.0	0.3	0.2	-0.1	0.3	0.2	-0.1
	(0.18)	(0.19)	(0.27)	(0.23)	(0.21)	(0.32)	(0.09)	(0.07)	(0.11)	(0.12)	(0.07)	(0.14)
Other services	0.2	0.1	0.0	0.3	0.3	0.0	0.1	0.0	0.0	0.0	0.1	0.0
	(0.08)	(0.09)	(0.12)	(0.15)	(0.13)	(0.20)	(0.04)	(0.03)	(0.05)	(0.03)	(0.05)	(0.05)
Number of observations	1,537	2,115		1,518	1,999		3,686	3,858		3,590	3,705	

Source: IFLS2 and IFLS3.
Estimates were weighted using individual sampling weights. Standard errors (in parentheses) are robust to clustering at the community level. Significance at 5% (*) and 1% (**) indicated.

There is also an increase in utilization of private health services by young children, particularly of private nurses and midwives and, to a lesser extent, of polyclinics and private doctors. Almost no change in utilization is observed for older children, aged 5–14 years. Also little change in utilization by children of *puskesmas* or *puskesmas/pembantu* services is observed. This is important because it is arguably the *puskesmas* level that is the major point of contact with the health system of most people, older than 5 years.

For adults, outpatient utilization in the last four weeks has not changed significantly between 1997 and 2000 (Table 8.2). There is a small increase in utilization of private practitioners by the elderly, but the change is not significant. Utilization by adults of *puskesmas* is slightly higher in rural areas, whereas hospitals are used slightly more in urban areas, as are private doctors and clinics (Appendix Table 8.2). These results are different from the results of Frankenberg et al. (1999), who did find a 10% decline in *puskesmas* use between 1997 and 1998. Evidently, then, *puskesmas* use by adults has recovered in the interim.

Table 8.3a examines immunization and vitamin A supplementation among children 12–59 months from a combination of vaccination (KMS) cards and mother reports. It is interesting to see a substantial increase in the fraction of children who have received their completed cycles of polio and DPT vaccinations, as well as large increases in hepatitis B vaccinations. Overall, this has led to 50% increase of the proportion of children receiving all vaccinations (including hepatitis B) to just under 55% of children 12–59 months.[5] The main source of the increase is an improvement in hepatitis B coverage. This massive increase has occurred in both rural and urban areas (Appendix Table 8.3). In urban areas, complete vaccinations are up to 65% in 2000, while in rural areas the rate is at 45%. As we will see below, there is evidence from facilities that is consistent with these changes. One worrisome trend is a decline in the fraction of children who have had one or more, or two or more, polio vaccines.

Table 8.3b provides immunization information only from the vaccination KMS cards. Only 25% of the children had cards at home that could be shown by the parents. The rest either had their cards at the *puskesmas* or with the *bidan desa*, or did not have them. The probability of being able to show the card is highly related to many socioeconomic variables that also affect immunization rates, so that these rates almost certainly suffer from selection bias. Nevertheless, one can see clearly here that the fraction receiving polio at birth went up substantially, as it did for hepatitis B. The increase in polio at birth is probably due both to an increasing number of

TABLE 8.2
Use of Outpatient Healthcare Facilities by Adults in Last Four Weeks
(In percent)

	Age 15–59 years						Age 60+ years					
	Men			Women			Men			Women		
	1997	2000	Change	1997	2000	Change	1997	2000	Change	1997	2000	Change
Use any health services	10.5	10.7	0.2	16.9	16.8	–0.1	18.0	19.1	1.1	21.4	21.9	0.5
	(0.42)	(0.38)	(0.57)	(0.48)	(0.45)	(0.66)	(1.33)	(1.20)	(1.79)	(1.31)	(1.21)	(1.78)
Public services:	4.0	3.6	–0.4	7.5	7.1	–0.4	9.0	7.9	–1.1	9.6	8.6	–1
	(0.28)	(0.22)	(0.35)	(0.37)	(0.32)	(0.49)	(0.94)	(0.83)	(1.25)	(0.97)	(0.83)	(1.27)
- Government hospitals	0.7	0.7	0.0	0.9	1.0	0.2	1.5	1.6	0.0	0.7	1.1	0.4
	(0.11)	(0.09)	(0.14)	(0.10)	(0.12)	(0.16)	(0.36)	(0.37)	(0.51)	(0.19)	(0.29)	(0.35)
- Puskesmas/Pustu	3.4	3.0	–0.4	6.7	6.1	–0.6	7.5	6.5	–1.0	9.1	7.6	–1.5
	(0.25)	(0.20)	(0.33)	(0.35)	(0.30)	(0.46)	(0.38)	(0.75)	(1.16)	(0.95)	(0.76)	(1.22)
Private services:	6.7	7.2	0.5	10.0	10.2	0.2	9.9	11.8	1.9	12.2	14.3	2.1
	(0.32)	(0.31)	(0.45)	(0.42)	(0.37)	(0.56)	(0.98)	(0.99)	(1.39)	(1.12)	(1.00)	(1.50)
- Private hospitals	0.5	0.6	0.1	0.7	0.7	0.0	0.3	1.0	0.8 *	0.4	1.1	0.7 *
	(0.09)	(0.10)	(0.13)	(0.10)	(0.09)	(0.13)	(0.15)	(0.29)	(0.32)	(0.13)	(0.25)	(0.29)
- Polyclinic and private doctor	3.9	4.5	0.6	4.8	5.1	0.3	5.3	6.4	0.7	6	6.7	0.7
	(0.25)	(0.27)	(0.37)	(0.29)	(0.28)	(0.40)	(0.79)	(0.72)	(1.07)	(0.69)	(0.66)	(0.95)
- Nurse, midwife and paramedic	2.5	2.2	–0.3	4.9	4.8	–0.1	4.1	4.9	0.8	6.1	6.8	0.7
	(0.24)	(0.20)	(0.31)	(0.34)	(0.28)	(0.44)	(0.57)	(0.70)	(0.97)	(0.87)	(0.76)	(1.15)
Traditional health services	0.3	0.3	–0.1	0.3	0.4	0.1	0.5	0.7	0.1	0.6	0.3	–0.3
	(0.07)	(0.05)	(0.09)	(0.06)	(0.07)	(0.09)	(0.22)	(0.27)	(0.35)	(0.24)	(0.13)	(0.27)
Other services	0.0	0.0	0.0	0.0	0.2	0.2 **	0.0	0.1	0.1	0.3	0.1	–0.2
	(0.02)	(0.02)	(0.03)	(0.02)	(0.05)	(0.06)	–	(0.06)	(0.06)	(0.18)	(0.07)	(0.19)
Number of observations	8,813	11,303		9,879	12,094		1,272	1.468		1,481	1,824	

Source: IFLS2 and IFLS3.
Estimates were weighted using individual sampling weights. Standard errors (in parentheses) are robust to clustering at the community level. Significance at 5% (*) and 1% (**) indicated.

TABLE 8.3a
Immunization Uptake for Children, aged 12–59 months
(In percent)

	Boys			Girls		
	1997	2000	Change	1997	2000	Change
Child received Vitamin A in 6 months before the survey	67.4	57.0	–10.3 **	69.4	56.0	–13.4 **
	(2.13)	(1.65)	(2.70)	(1.88)	(1.76)	(2.58)
Type of vaccination received:						
– BCG	84.6	86.1	1.5	83.3	85.3	2.0
	(1.91)	(1.35)	(2.34)	(1.66)	(1.59)	(2.30)
– Polio, 1+ times	94.9	89.0	–6.0 **	94.0	88.3	–5.8 **
	(1.07)	(1.19)	(1.60)	(1.13)	(1.53)	(1.91)
– Polio, 2+ times	87.4	80.2	–7.2 **	86.3	80.4	–5.9 *
	(1.57)	(1.40)	(2.10)	(1.76)	(1.73)	(2.47)
– Polio, 3+ times	67.1	67.6	0.6	64.7	68.7	4.1
	(1.97)	(1.65)	(2.57)	(1.99)	(1.81)	(2.69)
– Polio, 4+ times	22.4	36.1	13.7 **	23.0	34.9	11.8 **
	(1.46)	(1.78)	(2.30)	(1.47)	(1.79)	(2.31)
– DPT, 1+ times	83.3	85.1	1.8	82.1	84.7	2.6
	(1.82)	(1.37)	(2.28)	(1.79)	(1.66)	(2.44)
– DPT, 2+ times	70.4	74.7	4.3	69.6	75.8	6.2 *
	(2.11)	(1.65)	(2.68)	(2.11)	(1.77)	(2.75)
– DPT, 3+ times	55.8	63.3	7.5 **	55.1	64.4	9.4 **
	(2.13)	(1.74)	(2.75)	(2.24)	(1.88)	(2.92)
– Measles	77.9	77.1	–0.8	74.6	78.3	3.6
	(1.90)	(1.64)	(2.51)	(1.99)	(1.68)	(2.60)
– Hepatitis B	56.0	73.7	17.6 **	54.8	72.2	17.4 **
	(2.24)	(1.66)	(2.79)	(2.36)	(1.82)	(2.97)
– All vaccinations	35.4	53.3	17.9 **	35.5	55.1	19.6 **
	(1.86)	(1.76)	(2.56)	(2.07)	(1.80)	(2.74)
Children able to show KMS	24.4	24.4	–0.1	24.7	21.4	–3.3
	(1.57)	(1.39)	(2.10)	(1.63)	(1.27)	(2.07)
Number of observations	1,130	1,494		1,106	1,419	

Source: IFLS2 and IFLS3.

Estimates were weighted using individual sampling weights. Standard errors (in parentheses) are robust to clustering at the community level. Significance at 5% (*) and 1% (**) indicated.

TABLE 8.3b
Immunization Uptake for Children, aged 12–59 months From Viewed KMS Cards (In percent)

	Boys			Girls		
	1997	2000	Change	1997	2000	Change
Child received Vitamin A in 6 months before the survey	74.2	76.8	2.6	76.7	72.3	–4.4
	(3.31)	(2.44)	(4.11)	(2.74)	(2.92)	(4.00)
Type of vaccination received:						
– BCG	95.4	94.3	–1.2	93.1	93.2	0.1
	(1.28)	(1.30)	(1.82)	(1.89)	(1.69)	(2.54)
– Polio at birth	46.8	76.1	29.3 **	46.2	72.7	26.5 **
	(3.38)	(2.47)	(4.18)	(3.49)	(2.96)	(4.58)
– Polio 1	95.7	96.2	0.4	93.7	94.3	0.6
	(1.37)	(1.01)	(1.70)	(1.86)	(1.61)	(2.46)
– Polio 2	95.0	92.3	–2.7	91.6	91.4	–0.2
	(1.45)	(1.82)	(2.32)	(1.98)	(1.93)	(2.76)
– Polio 3	88.9	85.9	–3.0	83.5	86.2	2.7
	(1.94)	(2.30)	(3.01)	(2.50)	(2.28)	(3.38)
– DPT 1	94.6	94.4	–0.2	94.2	94.9	0.7
	(1.37)	(1.41)	(1.96)	(1.77)	(1.43)	(2.27)
– DPT 2	89.8	90.9	1.1	89.4	91.8	2.3
	(2.10)	(1.82)	(2.78)	(2.19)	(1.81)	(2.84)
– DPT 3	86.3	85.5	–0.8	86.3	84.8	–1.5
	(2.14)	(2.44)	(3.25)	(2.36)	(2.36)	(3.34)
– Measles	85.6	83.8	–1.9	82.4	87.0	4.6
	(2.16)	(2.40)	(3.23)	(2.45)	(2.14)	(3.26)
– Hepatitis B	60.1	84.8	24.7 **	62.8	83.6	20.8 **
	(3.54)	(2.25)	(4.20)	(3.90)	(2.45)	(4.61)
– All vaccinations	51.6	73.6	22.0 **	53.2	73.8	20.6 **
	(3.27)	(2.79)	(4.29)	(3.64)	(2.94)	(4.68)
Number of observations	276	364		273	303	

Source: IFLS2 and IFLS3.
Estimates were weighted using individual sampling weights. Standard errors (in parentheses) are robust to clustering at the community level. Significance at 5% (*) and 1% (**) indicated.

births taking place at modern health facilities where polio vaccines are given, as opposed to at home, and to an increasing fraction of births at home attended by midwives who have the capacity to provide polio vaccines. Note that for the children with KMS cards available, the fraction with only polio 1 did not decline, and the small declines in the fraction with polio 2 and 3 are not statistically significant.

For supplemental vitamin A uptake, rates have declined substantially, by over 10%, perhaps because much of the vitamin A distribution had been through *posyandu*, which as we have seen, have had major declines in use. Over 55% received supplemental vitamin A in the six months before the interview in 2000, which is down from about 69% in 1997 (Table 8.3a).

Tables 8.4a and b present the descriptive regressions for child and outpatient utilization of some modern service, and then broken into public/*puskesmas* and private.[6] Tables 8.5a and b present these regressions for adult usage and Table 8.6 presents regressions for use of *posyandu* by children under 5 years. Table 8.7 presents the results for children 12–59 months having received a complete set of vaccinations.

Higher *pce* among children from low income households is associated with a large increase in the probability that both boys and girls receive some outpatient care (Tables 8.4a and b). This income effect declines some in magnitude in 2000 compared to 1997, consistent with an easing of resource constraints by 2000. The mother's higher education has small, positive impacts. Older children are less likely to visit an outpatient facility. Children in rural areas are also less likely to utilize outpatient facilities. Within Java, children living outside of Jakarta were much more likely to utilize care in 1997. However, for girls much of this positive differential relative to Jakarta disappears by 2000. By 2000, utilization of services by girls declined by especially large proportions in the eastern islands of Bali, West Nusa Tenggara, South Kalimantan and South Sulawesi. For boys, the declines in these provinces were a little more moderate.

The positive association of *pce* and parental education with utilization of private facilities is strong across the income distribution, similar to what is found in many other health studies. Mother's education has a stronger effect on girls' utilization than boys, again similar to the results found by Thomas (1994) and others.

For *puskesmas*, higher *pce* is associated with more utilization if *pce* is low, while for higher levels of *pce* the impact on *puskesmas* utilization is negative. Thus at low levels of income, higher *pce* helps households to afford more public and private care for children, while at higher levels, *pce* enables children to seek private care. Mother's and father's education have

TABLE 8.4a
Usage of Health Care Facilities in the Last Four Weeks: Linear Probability Models of Usage by Boys, Aged 0–14 years

	Any health services		*Puskesmes/Pustu*		Private services	
	1997	Change in 2000	1997	Change in 2000	1997	Change in 2000
Age (spline, × 10^{-3}): 0–17 months	7.871*	–3.494	–0.528	6.192*	9.825**	–8.504*
	(2.29)	(0.79)	(0.25)	(2.35)	(3.94)	(2.45)
18–35 months	–8.063**	–4.105	–1.084	–1.970	–10.004**	2.291
	(3.11)	(1.21)	(0.61)	(0.85)	(5.28)	(0.88)
36–59 months	–13.880**	1.528	–1.142	0.159	1.440	–1.484
	(9.17)	(0.76)	(1.23)	(0.13)	(1.71)	(1.17)
5–14 years	–2.057**	0.912**	–0.315**	–0.008	–0.508**	–0.091
	(11.59)	(3.62)	(2.63)	(0.05)	(4.23)	(0.50)
Mother's education, if in household (years, × 10^{-2})	0.495*	–0.265	–0.035	–0.183	0.243	0.025
	(2.30)	(0.89)	(0.28)	(0.08)	(1.49)	(0.11)
Father's education, if in household (years, × 10^{-2})	0.004	0.405	–0.123	0.139	0.205	0.012
	(0.02)	(1.41)	(0.88)	(0.73)	(1.50)	(0.06)
log *pce* (spline, × 10^{-2}) 0– log Rp 150,000	10.236**	–5.782*	4.479**	–1.304	3.028**	–1.998
	(5.12)	(2.04)	(3.82)	(0.76)	(2.79)	(1.09)
> log Rp 150,000	0.777	–2.073	–2.210**	–0.807	4.342**	1.057
	(0.56)	(1.09)	(2.72)	(0.75)	(3.97)	(0.65)
Rural (× 10^{-1})	–0.347*	–0.121	–0.356**	0.120	–0.199	0.103
	(2.27)	(0.60)	(3.35)	(0.87)	(1.85)	(0.67)
North Sumatra	–0.097**	0.036	–0.040*	–0.008	–0.064**	0.045
	(3.25)	(0.83)	(2.29)	(0.34)	(3.08)	(1.45)

continued on next page

TABLE 8.4a – cont'd

	Any health services		*Puskesmas/Pustu*		Private services	
	1997	Change in 2000	1997	Change in 2000	1997	Change in 2000
West Sumatra	0.051	–0.064	0.027	–0.059	–0.038	–0.018
	(1.40)	(1.21)	(1.01)	(1.79)	(1.59)	(0.55)
South Sumatra	0.026	–0.089	0.027	–0.069*	–0.013	–0.013
	(0.73)	(1.87)	(1.22)	(2.40)	(0.57)	(0.38)
Lampung	0.049	–0.041	–0.002	–0.006	–0.000	–0.005
	(1.31)	(0.79)	(0.08)	(0.19)	(0.00)	(0.14)
West Java	0.061*	–0.024	0.014	–0.019	–0.018	0.006
	(2.19)	(0.61)	(0.72)	(0.74)	(0.88)	(0.20)
Central Java	0.088**	0.022	0.027	–0.032	0.018	0.038
	(3.00)	(0.52)	(1.26)	(1.12)	(0.77)	(1.10)
Yogyakarta	0.166**	–0.021	0.065*	–0.050	0.031	0.026
	(3.92)	(0.39)	(2.30)	(1.28)	(0.97)	(0.55)
East Java	0.066*	–0.022	0.010	–0.029	–0.008	0.028
	(2.11)	(0.50)	(0.51)	(1.07)	(0.40)	(0.92)
Bali	0.065	–0.049	0.035	–0.021	0.015	–0.041
	(1.92)	(0.82)	(1.31)	(0.55)	(0.60)	(1.17)
West Nusa Tenggara	0.059	–0.094*	0.042	–0.059*	–0.038	–0.039
	(1.87)	(2.12)	(1.87)	(1.98)	(1.63)	(1.25)
South Kalimantan	0.027	–0.075	0.011	–0.007	–0.038	–0.023
	(0.68)	(1.47)	(0.43)	(0.21)	(1.40)	(0.64)
South Sulawesi	0.008	–0.065	0.035	–0.041	–0.066**	–0.007
	(0.23)	(1.42)	(1.47)	(1.21)	(3.41)	(0.24)
Constant	–0.671*	0.799*	–0.446**	0.187	–0.360*	0.373
	(2.53)*	(2.15)	(2.58)	(0.82)	(2.41)	(1.52)
F-test (p-values)						
Interaction variables	0.0001		0.2277		0.0077	
Education variables	0.0008		0.7695		0.0007	
Expenditure variables	0.0000		0.0000		0.0000	
Number of observations	11,196		11,196		11,196	
R-squared	0.26		0.02		0.07	

Source: IFLS2 and IFLS3.

Dummy variable for missing parental education or parent not in household and dummy variable for missing per capita expenditure are included in the regressions but not reported in the table. The omitted category for province is Jakarta. Estimates were weighted using individual sampling weights. Standard errors are robust to clustering at the community level and to heteroscedasticity. Absolute t-statistics are in parentheses with significance at 5% (*) and 1% (**) indicated.

TABLE 8.4b
Usage of Health Care Facilities in the Last Four Weeks: Linear Probability Models of Usage by Girls, Aged 0–14 years

	Any health services		*Puskesmas/Pustu*		Private services	
	1997	Change in 2000	1997	Change in 2000	1997	Change in 2000
Age (spline, × 10^{-3}): 0–17 months	5.529	–6.019	0.834	–0.230	2.719	2.568
	(1.46)	(1.23)	(0.31)	(0.07)	(0.92)	(0.67)
18–35 months	–2.215	–4.076	–3.517*	3.849	–7.166**	1.738
	(0.94)	(1.23)	(2.17)	(1.74)	(4.16)	(0.68)
36–59 months	–18.438**	5.995**	1.469	–3.057**	–0.002	–1.934
	(12.88)	(3.11)	(1.94)	(2.70)	(0.00)	(1.59)
5–14 years	–1.880**	0.487*	–0.534**	0.165	–0.362**	–0.229
	(10.80)	(1.97)	(4.38)	(1.00)	(3.18)	(1.34)
Mother's education, if in household (years, × 10^{-2})	0.322	0.429	–0.121	0.159	0.387*	0.089
	(1.35)	(1.35)	(0.91)	(0.82)	(2.25)	(0.37)
Father's education, if in household (years, × 10^{-2})	0.047	–0.221	0.097	–0.247	0.097	–0.026
	(0.21)	(0.74)	(0.62)	(1.17)	(0.64)	(0.12)
log *pce* (spline, × 10^{-2}) 0– log Rp 150,000	8.669**	–4.123	2.908*	–0.900	2.728**	0.135
	(3.72)	(1.28)	(2.08)	(0.44)	(2.01)	(0.07)
> log Rp 150,000	2.978*	–1.638	–0.170	–2.216	4.678**	1.274
	(2.31)	(0.86)	(0.14)	(1.46)	(4.02)	(0.77)
Rural (× 10^{-1})	–0.244	0.043	–0.254*	0.051	–0.024	–0.047
	(1.59)	(0.21)	(2.24)	(0.33)	(0.20)	(0.28)
North Sumatra	–0.091**	–0.043	–0.021	–0.030	–0.048	0.018
	(2.79)	(0.97)	(1.32)	(1.32)	(1.95)	(0.52)
West Sumatra	0.045	–0.080	0.038	–0.044	–0.038	–0.030
	(1.07)	(1.39)	(1.29)	(1.20)	(1.50)	(0.86)
South Sumatra	0.023	–0.065	0.020	–0.055*	–0.010	0.002
	(0.62)	(1.32)	(1.09)	(2.12)	(0.33)	(0.05)

continued on next page

TABLE 8.4b – cont'd

	Any health services		*Puskesmas/Pustu*		Private services	
	1997	Change in 2000	1997	Change in 2000	1997	Change in 2000
Lampung	0.042	–0.110*	0.010	–0.045	–0.007	–0.008
	(1.19)	(2.29)	(0.48)	(1.53)	(0.23)	(0.18)
West Java	0.053	–0.067	0.026	–0.039	–0.015	–0.007
	(1.96)	(1.74)	(1.49)	(1.64)	(0.68)	(0.22)
Central Java	0.065*	–0.030	0.009	–0.027	–0.011	0.020
	(2.28)*	(0.73)	(0.57)	(1.11)	(0.46)	(0.59)
Yogyakarta	0.183**	–0.103*	0.092**	–0.066	0.051	–0.034
	(5.21)	(2.02)	(3.33)	(1.60)	(1.85)	(0.76)
East Java	0.062*	–0.052	0.047*	–0.035	–0.019	0.019
	(2.04)	(1.18)	(2.28)	(1.22)	(0.80)	(0.57)
Bali	0.074	–0.193**	0.016	–0.067*	0.016	–0.085*
	(1.87)	(3.39)	(0.64)	(2.19)	(0.50)	(2.05)
West Nusa Tenggara	0.059*	–0.126**	0.060**	–0.083**	–0.059**	–0.007
	(2.11)	(2.93)	(2.72)	(2.67)	(2.63)	(0.22)
South Kalimantan	0.035	–0.147**	0.055*	–0.081*	–0.073**	0.026
	(0.89)	(2.72)	(2.07)	(2.34)	(3.13)	(0.72)
South Sulawesi	0.026	–0.156**	0.027	–0.063*	–0.038	–0.049
	(0.70)	(3.09)	(1.38)	(1.98)	(1.50)	(1.45)
Constant	–0.379	0.524	–0.190	0.127	–0.165	–0.113
	(1.29)	(1.28)	(1.20)	(0.52)	(0.96)	(0.45)
F-test (p-values)						
Interaction variables	0.0000		0.0762		0.1350	
Education variables	0.0019		0.7135		0.0003	
Expenditure variables	0.0000		0.0178		0.0000	
Number of observations	10,812		10,812		10,812	
R-squared	0.26		0.02		0.07	

Source: IFLS2 and IFLS3.

Dummy variable for missing parental education or parent not in household and dummy variable for missing per capita expenditure are included in the regressions but not reported in the table. The omitted category for province is Jakarta. Estimates were weighted using individual sampling weights. Standard errors are robust to clustering at the community level and to heteroscedasticity. Absolute t-statistics are in parentheses with significance at 5% (*) and 1% (**) indicated.

insignificant impacts on *puskesmas* utilization. Mother's schooling does have a significant, positive impact on private sector utilization for girls.

For adults, the factors raising *puskesmas* and private utilization, are quite similar to those for children (Tables 8.5a and b). Education and *pce* are especially correlated with use of any facility and in particular utilizing private sector facilities for both men and women. For women, education is positively correlated with *puskesmas* utilization, although in a non-linear manner, with the largest impact for those who completed primary school and smaller effects for women with higher levels. The association of *pce* with *puskesmas* utilization for women has an inverted-U shape, just as it does for children. There are no strong urban/rural differences and there are weak provincial effects.

Posyandu utilization is not strongly associated with parental schooling (Table 8.6). In 1997 posyandu usage had an inverted U-shape with respect to *pce*. *Posyandu* use in 1997 was strongly increasing with low *pce*, but weakly negative for those with high *pce*. However, this pattern changed by 2000. The impact of higher *pce* for children from low *pce* households was cut nearly in half for boys and disappeared for girls. On the other side, the negative impact of higher *pce* greatly strengthened among households with higher *pce*. Hence much of the flight from *posyandu* was of children of the non-poor.

For getting complete immunizations (Table 8.7), mother's education has important positive effects even higher in 2000. A boy of a mother who completes primary school (six years) has an 18% better chance of having received a complete set of vaccinations in 2000 (the mean percent in 2000 being about 53%) than a boy of an illiterate mother. Impacts of mother's schooling are similar on girls' immunization uptake. *PCE* has no impact, leading one to conclude that the impact of mother's education is not through raising income, but probably through better knowledge and information. Across provinces, children in Bali and Yogyakarta began with a substantial advantage in complete immunization rates over children Jakarta in 1997. By 2000 there were substantial increases in most provinces, but more so in provinces outside of Jakarta and Bali.

SUMMARY

For adults, little change has occurred in health care utilization between 1997 and 2000, while for young children, there has been a sharp decline in the usage of *posyandu* services in the last one month, from 52% to 40% for both boys and girls. Use of *puskesmas* services did not change much,

TABLE 8.5a
Usage of Healthcare Facilities in the Last Four Weeks: Linear Probability Models of Usage by Men, Aged 15+

		Any health services		*Puskesmas/Pustu*		Private services	
		1997	Change in 2000	1997	Change in 2000	1997	Change in 2000
Age (spline, × 10^{-3}):	15–29 years	0.090	0.090	0.010	0.004	0.113*	0.036
		(1.42)	(1.00)	(0.26)	(0.08)	(2.14)	(0.49)
	30–59 years	0.217**	–0.060	0.114**	–0.041	0.080*	–0.008
		(5.59)	(1.11)	(4.58)	(1.23)	(2.36)	(0.18)
	60+ years	0.171	0.221	0.087	–0.002	0.090	0.204
		(1.66)	(1.58)	(1.19)	(0.02)	(1.31)	(1.93)
Education (× 10^{-2}):	1–5 years	2.491	–0.407	0.367	0.422	1.921	–0.248
		(1.68)	(0.20)	(0.41)	(0.32)	(1.81)	(0.17)
	6–8 years	2.666	0.354	0.253	0.298	2.135*	0.419
		(1.84)	(0.18)	(0.28)	(0.24)	(2.10)	(0.30)
	9–11 years	4.331**	–1.433	0.805	–1.065	3.282**	–0.384
		(2.63)	(0.68)	(0.76)	(0.78)	(2.63)	(0.24)
12+ years	3.798*	1.576	0.993	–0.808	2.346*	2.448	
		(2.39)	(0.72)	(1.07)	(0.62)	(2.00)	(1.45)
log *pce* (spline, × 10^{-2}):	0 – log Rp 150,000	1.764	0.393	0.528	0.833	1.398	–0.250
		(1.47)	(0.22)	(0.72)	(0.75)	(1.42)	(0.18)
	> log Rp 150,000	2.434**	0.286	0.045	–0.970	2.253**	0.927
		(3.50)	(0.30)	(0.11)	(1.89)	(3.53)	(1.10)
Rural (× 10^{-1})		0.059	0.024	0.117*	–0.079	0.019	0.060
		(0.68)	(0.21)	(2.04)	(1.08)	(0.27)	(0.62)
North Sumatra		–0.068**	0.053*	–0.021**	0.015	–0.050**	0.040*
		(4.76)	(2.48)	(2.76)	(1.23)	(4.11)	(2.38)
West Sumatra		0.001	0.011	0.012	0.008	–0.021	0.012
		(0.06)	(0.45)	(0.93)	(0.43)	(1.45)	(0.57)
South Sumatra		–0.023	–0.010	0.007	–0.029*	–0.030*	0.009
		(1.20)	(0.38)	(0.54)	(1.98)	(2.05)	(0.45)

Lampung	–0.006	0.035	0.008	0.010	–0.018	0.028
	(0.36)	(1.38)	(0.68)	(0.52)	(1.21)	(1.32)
West Java	0.016	–0.009	0.011	–0.009	0.001	0.006
	(1.03)	(0.43)	(1.21)	(0.71)	(0.08)	(0.35)
Central Java	–0.016	0.019	0.004	–0.007	–0.019	0.024
	(0.96)	(0.83)	(0.41)	(0.57)	(1.44)	(1.39)
Yogyakarta	0.016	0.004	0.008	–0.001	0.004	0.013
	(0.79)	(0.17)	(0.72)	(0.05)	(0.27)	(0.64)
East Java	–0.029	0.040	–0.004	0.009	–0.028*	0.034*
	(1.96)	(1.91)	(0.50)	(0.78)	(2.30)	(2.06)
Bali	0.075**	–0.056	0.020	–0.001	0.043*	–0.040
	(3.12)	(1.79)	(1.94)	(0.07)	(2.12)	(1.55)
West Nusa Tenggara	0.045	–0.037	0.072**	–0.043	–0.032*	0.008
	(1.56)	(1.08)	(2.71)	(1.48)	(2.19)	(0.40)
South Kalimantan	0.005	–0.014	0.022	–0.008	–0.018	0.002
	(0.25)	(0.47)	(1.52)	(0.42)	(0.95)	(0.10)
South Sulawesi	–0.013	–0.008	0.026	–0.034	–0.055**	0.024
	(0.56)	(0.25)	(1.68)	(1.86)	(4.67)	(1.48)
Constant	–0.250	–0.027	–0.050	–0.073	–0.166	–0.044
	(1.65)	(0.12)	(0.57)	(0.56)	(1.31)	(0.24)
F-test (p-values)						
Interaction variables	0.0207		0.1233		0.1057	
Education variables	0.0029		0.6688		0.0020	
Expenditure variables	0.0000		0.0259		0.0000	
Number of observations	22,856		22,856		22,856	
R-squared	0.02		0.01		0.02	

Source: IFLS2 and IFLS3.

Dummy variable for missing education and dummy variable for missing per capita expenditure are included in the regressions but not reported in the table. The omitted category for education is no schooling, and for province is Jakarta. Estimates were weighted using individual sampling weights. Standard errors are robust to clustering at the community level and to heteroscedasticity. Absolute t-statistics are in parentheses with significance at 5% (*) and 1% (**) indicated.

TABLE 8.5b
Usage of Healthcare Facilities in the Last Four Weeks: Linear Probability Models of Usage by Women, Aged 15+

	Any health services		*Puskesmas/Pustu*		Private services	
	1997	Change in 2000	1997	Change in 2000	1997	Change in 2000
Age (spline, × 10^{-3}): 15–29 years	0.298**	0.125	0.121*	0.112	0.137*	0.028
	(3.88)	(1.20)	(2.44)	(1.70)	(2.14)	(0.32)
30–59 years	0.149**	–0.084	0.119**	–0.095*	0.030	0.002
	(3.47)	(1.36)	(3.82)	(2.20)	(0.83)	(0.05)
60+ years	0.085	0.018	–0.126*	0.067	0.190*	–0.020
	(1.02)	(0.15)	(2.04)	(0.82)	(2.54)	(0.19)
Education (× 10^{-2}): 1–5 years	2.679*	–3.403	1.637*	–1.296	0.443	–1.745
	(2.11)	(1.87)	(1.96)	(1.05)	(0.45)	(1.19)
6–8 years	5.055**	–4.689*	2.087*	–1.577	2.746*	–3.404*
	(3.73)	(2.51)	(2.55)	(1.25)	(2.32)	(2.13)
9–11 years	3.564*	–1.299	1.655	–2.097	1.417	–0.429
	(2.41)	(0.59)	(1.68)	(1.45)	(1.08)	(0.22)
12+ years	5.228**	–5.288*	1.227	–2.760	3.398*	–2.964
	(3.29)	(2.35)	(1.28)	(1.88)	(2.46)	(1.52)
log *pce* (spline, × 10^{-2}): 0 – log Rp 150,000	7.866**	–1.818	4.689**	–2.022	3.733**	–1.475
	(5.87)	(0.83)	(5.21)	(1.54)	(3.72)	(0.85)
> log Rp 150,000	2.337**	1.305	–1.941**	1.043	3.511**	1.288
	(3.17)	(1.26)	(4.96)	(1.84)	(4.94)	(1.37)
Rural (× 10^{-1})	0.055	–0.320*	0.110	–0.162	–0.016	–0.122
	(0.59)	(2.41)	(1.53)	(1.68)	(0.17)	(1.02)
North Sumatra	–0.098**	0.080**	–0.029*	–0.002	–0.060**	0.075**
	(4.97)	(2.81)	(2.49)*	(0.11)	(3.50)	(3.14)
West Sumatra	0.013	0.013	0.019	–0.005	–0.016	0.010
	(0.71)	(0.48)	(1.52)	(0.25)	(0.73)	(0.36)
South Sumatra	–0.036	0.062*	0.013	–0.030	–0.040*	0.072**
	(1.70)	(1.98)	(0.87)	(1.40)	(2.34)	(2.71)

Lampung	–0.003	0.028	0.018	–0.009	–0.012	0.030
	(0.12)	(0.75)	(0.90)	(0.30)	(0.67)	(1.09)
West Java	0.003	0.002	0.008	–0.004	0.005	–0.002
	(0.18)	(0.11)	(0.77)	(0.27)	(0.32)	(0.13)
Central Java	–0.031	0.039	0.006	–0.020	–0.026	0.049*
	(1.77)	(1.47)	(0.47)	(1.24)	(1.75)	(2.21)
Yogyakarta	0.031	–0.003	0.049**	–0.029	–0.007	0.018
	(1.60)	(0.11)	(3.61)	(1.56)	(0.35)	(0.65)
East Java	–0.026	0.032	0.008	–0.008	–0.028	0.033
	(1.55)	(1.27)	(0.67)	(0.49)	(1.84)	(1.60)
Bali	0.074**	–0.052	0.037**	–0.042*	0.042	–0.019
	(2.95)	(1.56)	(2.67)	(2.09)	(1.85)	(0.69)
West Nusa Tenggara	0.019	–0.041	0.054**	–0.049*	–0.038*	0.011
	(0.81)	(1.32)	(3.18)	(2.22)	(2.10)	(0.45)
South Kalimantan	0.013	0.011	0.035	–0.032	–0.005	0.025
	(0.59)	(0.35)	(1.93)	(1.40)	(0.24)	(0.89)
South Sulawesi	–0.025	0.012	0.013	–0.000	–0.048*	0.007
	(1.17)	(0.38)	(0.92)	(0.02)	(2.48)	(0.27)
Constant	–0.918**	0.225	–0.587**	0.293	–0.362**	0.120
	(5.25)	(0.83)	(4.73)	(1.70)	(2.93)	(0.57)
F-test (p-values)						
Interaction variables	0.0005		0.0804		0.0181	
Education variables	0.0080		0.0408		0.0510	
Expenditure variables	0.0000		0.0000		0.0000	
Number of observations	25,278		25,278		25,278	
R-squared	0.02		0.01		0.02	

Source: IFLS2 and IFLS3.
Dummy variable for missing education and dummy variable for missing per capita expenditure are included in the regressions but not reported in the table. The omitted category for education is no schooling, and for province is Jakarta. Estimates were weighted using individual sampling weights. Standard errors are robust to clustering at the community level and to heteroscedasticity. Absolute t-statistics are in parentheses with significance at 5% (*) and 1% (**) indicated.

TABLE 8.6
Posyandu Usage in the Last Four Weeks: Linear Probability Models of Usage by Children, Aged 0–59 months

	Boys		Girls	
	1997	Change in 2000	1997	Change in 2000
Age (spline, × 10^{-3}): 0–17 months	9.440**	–7.805	6.669	–4.411
	(2.58)	(1.67)	(1.63)	(0.84)
18–35 months	–12.086**	2.041	–1.992	–11.332**
	(4.03)	(0.53)	(0.71)	(3.03)
36–59 months	–0.847	–7.060*	–10.410**	9.309**
	(0.33)	(2.18)	(4.45)	(3.02)
Mother's education, if in household (years, × 10^{-2})	0.626	–0.692	0.353	0.721
	(1.31)	(1.13)	(0.67)	(1.08)
Father's education, if in household (years, × 10^{-2})	–0.166	0.940	–0.174	–0.176
	(0.40)	(1.77)	(0.37)	(0.29)
log *pce* (spline, × 10^{-2}): 0 – log Rp 150,000	15.419**	–6.500	14.705**	–12.077
	(2.90)	(0.94)	(2.64)	(1.71)
> log Rp 150,000	–2.612	–12.130**	–3.663	–6.756
	(0.83)	(3.07)	(1.31)	(1.76)
Rural (× 10^{-1})	0.298	–1.029*	0.161	–0.030
	(0.84)	(2.23)	(0.45)	(0.07)
North Sumatra	–0.049	–0.114	–0.132	–0.189
	(0.74)	(1.28)	(1.57)	(1.91)
West Sumatra	0.109	–0.104	0.189	–0.199
	(1.25)	(0.91)	(1.91)	(1.53)
South Sumatra	0.085	–0.233*	0.034	–0.183
	(1.00)	(2.16)	(0.42)	(1.78)

Lampung	0.210*	–0.282*	0.109	–0.240*
	(2.51)	(2.51)	(1.21)	(2.09)
West Java	0.234**	–0.126	0.223**	–0.150
	(4.18)	(1.57)	(3.51)	(1.80)
Central Java	0.236**	–0.023	0.220**	–0.082
	(3.22)	(0.23)	(2.88)	(0.82)
Yogyakarta	0.309**	–0.006	0.453**	–0.228*
	(4.02)	(0.06)	(5.36)	(2.08)
East Java	0.212**	–0.127	0.156*	–0.134
	(3.17)	(1.36)	(2.11)	(1.36)
Bali	0.090	–0.151	0.166	–0.320*
	(1.03)	(1.19)	(1.46)	(2.36)
West Nusa Tenggara	0.095	–0.104	0.155	–0.251*
	(1.09)	(0.93)	(1.73)	(2.25)
South Kalimantan	0.181	–0.297*	0.063	–0.268*
	(1.95)	(2.49)	(0.68)	(2.31)
South Sulawesi	0.137	–0.201	0.060	–0.232*
	(1.71)	(1.89)	(0.69)	(2.09)
Constant	–1.289*	1.122	–1.456	2.013*
	(1.99)	(1.31)	(1.95)	(2.18)
F-test (p-values)				
Interaction variables	0.0000		0.0012	
Education variables	0.0705		0.1142	
Expenditure variables	0.0000		0.0001	
Number of observations	3,652		3,517	
R-squared	0.13		0.13	

Source: IFLS2 and IFLS3.

Dummy variable for missing parental education or parent not in household and dummy variable for missing per capita expenditure are included in the regressions but not reported in the table. The omitted category for province is Jakarta. Estimates were weighted using individual sampling weights. Standard errors are robust to clustering at the community level and to heteroscedasticity. Absolute t-statistics are in parentheses with significance at 5% (*) and 1% (**) indicated.

TABLE 8.7
Immunizations Uptake for Children One to Five Years Old: Linear Probability Models of Children with Completed Immunization Uptake

	Boys		Girls	
	1997	Change in 2000	1997	Change in 2000
Age (spline, × 10^{-3}): 12–17 months	–9.907	14.895	7.820	–28.793
	(0.61)	(0.71)	(0.59)	(1.49)
18–35 months	–1.740	3.749	1.475	2.839
	(0.55)	(0.89)	(0.46)	(0.62)
36–59 months	0.004	–0.008*	0.002	–0.002
	(1.62)	(2.20)	(0.73)	(0.58)
Mother's education, if in household (years, × 10^{-2})	1.063*	1.967**	1.435**	0.736
	(2.07)	(2.83)	(2.72)	(1.03)
Father's education, if in household (years, × 10^{-2})	0.619	0.251	1.149*	0.534
	(1.18)	(0.36)	(2.43)	(0.86)
log *pce* (spline, × 10^{-2}): 0 – log Rp 150,000	5.363	–2.809	5.964	–7.770
	(0.92)	(0.33)	(1.42)	(1.17)
> log Rp 150,000	2.196	–6.364	0.203	–4.288
	(0.65)	(1.34)	(0.08)	(1.06)
Rural (× 10^{-1})	–0.617	–0.547	–0.591	–0.112
	(1.72)	(1.13)	(1.48)	(0.21)
North Sumatra	–0.130	–0.113	–0.238**	0.061
	(1.87)	(1.14)	(3.10)	(0.55)
West Sumatra	–0.038	0.135	–0.187*	0.252*
	(0.48)	(1.28)	(2.21)	(2.12)
South Sumatra	–0.200**	0.146	–0.320**	0.266*
	(2.75)	(1.43)	(4.33)	(2.44)

Lampung	0.168*	–0.220*	–0.082	0.074
	(2.35)*	(2.20)	(0.89)	(0.63)
West Java	–0.013	0.133	0.048	0.087
	(0.20)	(1.58)	(0.69)	(0.93)
Central Java	–0.107	0.294**	–0.019	0.191
	(1.64)	(3.00)	(0.24)	(1.76)
Yogyakarta	0.234**	0.025	0.253**	0.031
	(2.71)	(0.23)	(2.91)	(0.26)
East Java	0.032	0.113	0.038	0.091
	(0.47)	(1.24)	(0.50)	(0.85)
Bali	0.386**	–0.240*	0.508**	–0.421**
	(4.55)	(2.09)	(7.08)	(4.07)
West Nusa Tenggara	–0.138	0.447**	–0.086	0.276*
	(1.90)	(3.99)	(1.09)	(2.34)
South Kalimantan	0.078	0.025	–0.246**	0.364**
	(0.77)	(0.19)	(3.39)	(2.98)
South Sulawesi	–0.131	0.249*	–0.175*	0.162
	(1.60)	(2.33)	(2.34)	(1.43)
Constant	–0.166	–0.424	–0.617	1.074
	(0.23)	(0.39)	(1.11)	(1.25)
F-test (p-values)				
Interaction variables	0.0000		0.0000	
Education variables	0.0000		0.0000	
Expenditure variables	0.5104		0.3286	
Number of observations	2,624		2,525	
R-squared	0.17		0.18	

Source: IFLS2 and IFLS3.

Dummy variable for missing parental education or parent not in household and dummy variable for missing per capita expenditure are included in the regressions but not reported in the table. The omitted category for province is Jakarta. Estimates were weighted using individual sampling weights. Standard errors are robust to clustering at the community level and to heteroscedasticity. Absolute t-statistics are in parentheses with significance at 5% (*) and 1% (**) indicated.

staying constant at 10% for children under 5 years, and at 5% for older children. There has also been a small increase in child use of private and village midwives to about 10%. A significant increase in total immunization coverage occurred between 1997 and 2000. In 2000 about 53% of children had a complete set of immunizations. The major increases have come in hepatitis B vaccinations. On the other hand, there has been a significant decline in the receipt of Vitamin A pills, from 67% to 55%, perhaps because the *posyandu* had played an important role in its distribution.

In this report we do not connect use of health services directly with health outcomes, but it is quite interesting to note that a major indicator of child health, height, improved over this period, while *posyandu* use was declining so dramatically. The declines in pre-school child haemoglobin levels are probably not a result of declining *posyandu* use, disease and diet are much more likely reasons, except perhaps through not receiving as much nutrition and health information. This is suggestive that *posyandus* have not been effective in improving child health outcomes, although more analytical research is needed to rigorously establish that.

Notes

1 Data on child immunizations are taken from immunization (KMS) cards in the possession of the mother, one for each child, on which a record of immunizations and dates are kept. When the card is not available, we use recall data only when the mother is quite sure about the record.

2 Frankenberg and Thomas (2001) explore the impacts the village midwives have had on health outcomes related to pregnancy, demonstrating that they have had positive impacts.

3 The questionnaire allows for multiple visits and to multiple types of facilities. Hence visits to each sub-group such as *puskesmas* and *posyandu* will not add up to visit rates for the group, public clinics.

4 *Posyandu* are monthly local mother-child health clinics which are run by the local community out of their own resources, usually with support from the local *puskesmas* and the local village midwife (*bidan desa*). A typical *posyandu* offers services once per month. During this time, a meal is provided to children under 5 years, their heights and weights are taken, and monitored over time, immunizations and vitamin A tablets are given, and mother/child nutrition and health advice is provided. Some *posyandu* also provide family planning counselling, and in a few cases, supplies.

[5] Having a complete set of vaccinations is defined as having three or more polio, three DPT, BCG, measles and at least one hepatitis B. If we define complete vaccinations not including hepatitis B, as the 1997 Demographic and Health Survey (DHS) did, then our complete completion rates for 1997 are 48% (rising to 58% in 2000), compared with 57% reported in the 1997 DHS (CBS et al. 1998). Among children who could show kms cards, our completion rates for 1997 (minus hepatitis B) are almost identical, at 75%, to those reported in DHS.

[6] Since multiple types of facilities could have been visited, we do not use a multinomial logit or a similar estimator, but simply use linear probability models to estimate use.

APPENDIX TABLE 8.1
Use of Outpatient Healthcare Facilities by Children in Last Four Weeks: Urban and Rural Areas (In percent)

	Age 0–59 months						Age 5–14 years					
	Boys			Girls			Boys			Girls		
	1997	2000	Change	1997	2000	Change	1997	2000	Change	1997	2000	Change
Urban												
Use any health services	62.4	61.9	–0.6	65.4	57.9	–7.6 *	16.6	15.8	–0.8	14.6	16.2	1.5
	(2.24)	(2.04)	(3.04)	(2.37)	(2.12)	(3.18)	(1.07)	(1.12)	(1.55)	(1.21)	(1.13)	(1.66)
Public services:	54.1	50.9	–3.2	56.9	46.0	–11.0 **	8.0	7.1	–0.8	7.2	7.8	0.6
	(2.39)	(2.26)	(3.29)	(2.53)	(2.22)	(3.37)	(0.84)	(0.74)	(1.12)	(0.90)	(0.84)	(1.23)
– Government hospitals	1.1	1.8	0.8	1.3	1.1	–0.2	1.0	0.8	–0.2	0.5	0.5	0.0
	(0.42)	(0.56)	(0.70)	(0.49)	(0.35)	(0.60)	(0.33)	(0.28)	(0.44)	(0.19)	(0.19)	(0.27)
– *Puskesmas/Pustu*	12.4	10.6	–1.8	11.8	11.0	–0.8	7.0	6.3	–0.7	6.7	7.3	0.6
	(1.47)	(1.13)	(1.85)	(1.48)	(1.26)	(1.94)	(0.81)	(0.68)	(1.06)	(0.90)	(0.83)	(1.22)
– *Posyandu*	49.9	44.9	–4.9	52.3	40.2	–12.0 **						
	(2.47)	(2.31)	(3.38)	(2.58)	(2.26)	(3.43)						
Private services:	15.9	22.1	6.2 **	17.2	21.3	4.1	9.1	9.4	0.3	7.9	8.6	0.6
	(1.50)	(1.55)	(2.16)	(1.67)	(1.60)	(2.31)	(0.95)	(0.91)	(1.31)	(0.85)	(0.80)	(1.17)
– Private hospitals	1.5	1.1	–0.4	1.4	1.3	–0.1	0.6	0.4	–0.1	0.6	0.6	–0.1
	(0.63)	(0.37)	(0.73)	(0.48)	(0.42)	(0.64)	(0.17)	(0.21)	(0.27)	(0.22)	(0.22)	(0.31)
– Polyclinic and private doctor	8.6	13.5	4.9 **	9.9	12.6	2.8	6.1	7.4	1.2	5.8	5.8	0.1
	(1.16)	(1.29)	(1.74)	(1.37)	(1.18)	(1.81)	(0.76)	(0.81)	(1.11)	(0.74)	(0.69)	(1.02)
– Nurse, midwife and paramedic	6.3	8.0	1.8	6.5	7.5	1.0	2.9	1.8	–1.1	1.7	2.3	0.6
	(1.09)	(1.12)	(1.56)	(1.15)	(1.03)	(1.55)	(0.61)	(0.44)	(0.75)	(0.34)	(0.41)	(0.54)
Traditional health services	0.3	0.3	0.0	0.5	0.3	–0.2	0.3	0.1	–0.1	0.2	0.1	–0.1
	(0.18)	(0.15)	(0.23)	(0.30)	(0.16)	(0.34)	(0.14)	(0.07)	(0.16)	(0.12)	(0.07)	(0.14)
Other services	0.2	0.1	–0.1	0.2	0.4	0.2	0.1	0.1	–0.1	0.1	0.1	0.0
	(0.15)	(0.14)	(0.20)	(0.16)	(0.22)	(0.27)	(0.10)	(0.07)	(0.12)	(0.07)	(0.07)	(0.10)
Number of observations	646	965		660	899		1,570	1,626		1,485	1,561	

Rural												
Use any health services	60.6	51.5	−9.1 **	51.4	53.5	−7.9 *	10.1	10.5	0.4	10.2	11.1	0.9
	(2.43)	(1.86)	(3.06)	(2.74)	(2.13)	(3.47)	(0.83)	(0.79)	(1.15)	(0.86)	(0.82)	(1.19)
Public services:	56.6	42.7	−13.9 **	57.4	45.0	−12.4 **	4.9	4.2	−0.7	5.3	5.4	0.1
	(2.45)	(1.96)	(3.14)	(2.83)	(2.18)	(3.58)	(0.58)	(0.50)	(0.77)	(0.57)	(0.59)	(0.82)
– Government hospitals	0.6	0.4	−0.2	0.6	0.7	0.2	0.4	0.1	−0.3	0.2	0.3	0.2
	(0.29)	(0.19)	(0.34)	(0.27)	(0.27)	(0.38)	(0.14)	(0.08)	(0.17)	(0.09)	(0.16)	(0.19)
– *Puskesmas/Pustu*	8.8	9.0	0.2	7.5	10.6	3.1	4.5	4.1	−0.4	5.1	5.0	−0.1
	(1.15)	(0.97)	(1.50)	(1.18)	(1.10)	(1.62)	(0.55)	(0.50)	(0.74)	(0.55)	(0.57)	(0.80)
– *Posyandu*	53.3	36.6	−16.7 **	54.2	39.9	−14.2 **						
	(2.43)	(2.00)	(3.14)	(2.66)	(2.30)	(3.52)						
Private services:	10.4	16.4	6.0 **	11.6	15.7	4.0 *	5.3	6.3	1.0	5.4	5.5	0.1
	(1.20)	(1.35)	(1.80)	(1.43)	(1.37)	(1.98)	(0.65)	(0.70)	(0.96)	(0.63)	(0.65)	(0.91)
– Private hospitals	0.3	0.5	0.2	0.2	0.8	0.6	0.2	0.1	−0.1	0.1	0.1	0.1
	(0.22)	(0.24)	(0.33)	(0.16)	(0.30)	(0.34)	(0.10)	(0.08)	(0.13)	(0.06)	(0.08)	(0.10)
– Polyclinic and private doctor	3.8	5.1	1.2	4.6	4.3	−0.2	2.1	2.2	0.1	1.8	2.1	0.2
	(0.69)	(0.72)	(1.00)	(0.80)	(0.71)	(1.07)	(0.41)	(0.39)	(0.57)	(0.34)	(0.47)	(0.58)
– Nurse, midwife and paramedic	6.6	10.9	4.3 **	7.5	10.9	3.4	3.2	4.0	0.9	3.6	3.4	−0.3
	(1.02)	(1.22)	(1.59)	(1.29)	(1.26)	(1.30)	(0.44)	(0.54)	(0.70)	(0.55)	(0.43)	(0.70)
Traditional health services	0.7	1.0	0.3	0.7	1.0	0.2	0.3	0.2	−0.1	0.4	0.3	−0.1
	(0.28)	(0.32)	(0.43)	(0.33)	(0.36)	(0.48)	(0.11)	(0.10)	(0.15)	(0.17)	(0.11)	(0.20)
Other services	0.1	0.1	0.0	0.4	0.2	−0.2	0.0	0.0	0.0	0.0	0.1	0.1
	(0.09)	(0.11)	(0.14)	(0.22)	(0.16)	(0.27)	–	–	–	–	(0.06)	(0.06)
Number of observations	890	1,150		858	1,100		2,116	2,232		2,103	2,144	

Source: IFLS2 and IFLS3.
Estimates were weighted using individual sampling weights. Standard errors (in parentheses) are robust to clustering at the community level. Significance at 5% (*) and 1% (**) indicated.

APPENDIX TABLE 8.2
Use of Outpatient Healthcare Facilities by Adults in Last Four Weeks: Urban and Rural Areas
(In percent)

	Age 15–59 years						Age 60+ years					
	Men			Women			Men			Women		
	1997	2000	Change	1997	2000	Change	1997	2000	Change	1997	2000	Change
Urban												
Use any health services	10.9	11.0	0.1	17.6	18.7	1.1	19.1	20.4	1.3	23.7	25.4	1.7
	(0.58)	(0.54)	(0.79)	(0.61)	(0.66)	(0.90)	(1.97)	(1.96)	(2.78)	(1.67)	(1.83)	(2.48)
Public services:	3.8	3.4	–0.4	7.0	7.6	0.6	9.1	8.6	–0.5	9.7	10.5	0.8
	(0.40)	(0.29)	(0.49)	(0.48)	(0.43)	(0.65)	(1.44)	(1.38)	(2.00)	(1.27)	(1.34)	(1.85)
– Government hospitals	1.1	0.8	–0.2	1.5	1.6	0.1	3.0	2.8	–0.2	1.4	2.3	0.9
	(0.19)	(0.14)	(0.23)	(0.20)	(0.21)	(0.29)	(0.79)	(0.78)	(1.11)	(0.45)	(0.67)	(0.81)
– *Puskesmas/Pustu*	2.8	2.6	–0.2	5.8	6.1	0.3	6.1	6.0	0.0	8.3	8.5	0.1
	(0.31)	(0.26)	(0.41)	(0.44)	(0.38)	(0.58)	(1.12)	(1.10)	(1.57)	(1.20)	(1.19)	(1.69)
Private services:	7.5	7.7	0.2	11.2	11.7	0.5	10.2	13.0	2.8	14.7	15.5	0.8
	(0.46)	(0.46)	(0.65)	(0.51)	(0.52)	(0.73)	(1.50)	(1.62)	(2.21)	(1.31)	(1.54)	(2.02)
– Private hospitals	0.8	0.8	–0.1	1.4	1.1	–0.2	0.4	1.8	1.4 *	1.0	1.8	0.8
	(0.18)	(0.16)	(0.24)	(0.21)	(0.15)	(0.26)	(0.27)	(0.62)	(0.67)	(0.35)	(0.47)	(0.59)
– Polyclinic and private doctor	5.3	6.1	0.8	7.3	7.4	0.2	7.7	9.1	1.4	10.2	8.8	–1.3
	(0.40)	(0.42)	(0.58)	(0.42)	(0.44)	(0.61)	(1.33)	(1.28)	(1.84)	(1.15)	(1.15)	(1.62)
– Nurse, midwife and paramedic	1.6	1.0	–0.6 *	3.1	3.6	0.4	2.1	2.7	0.6	3.9	5.1	1.2
	(0.28)	(0.17)	(0.33)	(0.35)	(0.30)	(0.46)	(0.61)	(0.72)	(0.94)	(0.75)	(1.06)	(1.30)
Traditional health services	0.2	0.3	0.0	0.2	0.3	0.1	0.6	0.6	–0.1	0.1	0.3	0.2
	(0.08)	(0.09)	(0.12)	(0.07)	(0.08)	(0.11)	(0.38)	(0.28)	(0.47)	(0.06)	(0.17)	(0.18)
Other services	0.1	0.1	0.0	0.0	0.2	0.2 *	0.0	0.1	0.1	0.1	0.2	0.1
	(0.04)	(0.03)	(0.05)	(0.02)	(0.06)	(0.06)	–	(0.14)	(0.14)	(0.10)	(0.16)	(0.19)
Number of observations	4,336	5,732		4,847	6,106		513	610		652	811	

Rural												
Use any health services	10.2	10.5	0.2	16.4	15.2	–1.2	17.4	18.1	0.8	20.2	19.5	–0.7
	(0.58)	(0.55)	(0.80)	(0.69)	(0.59)	(0.91)	(1.73)	(1.52)	(2.30)	(1.79)	(1.58)	(2.39)
Public services:	4.2	3.8	–0.4	7.8	6.6	–1.2	8.9	7.4	–1.5	9.5	7.2	–2.3
	(0.39)	(0.32)	(0.50)	(0.52)	(0.46)	(0.70)	(1.22)	(1.02)	(1.59)	(1.32)	(1.04)	(1.68)
– Government hospitals	0.4	0.6	0.1	0.4	0.5	0.1	0.9	0.8	–0.1	0.3	0.2	0.0
	(0.12)	(0.11)	(0.16)	(0.09)	(0.11)	(0.14)	(0.34)	(0.29)	(0.45)	(0.17)	(0.17)	(0.24)
– *Puskesmas/Pustu*	3.9	3.4	–0.5	7.4	6.2	–1.2	8.2	6.8	–1.4	9.4	7.0	–2.5
	(0.37)	(0.31)	(0.48)	(0.51)	(0.45)	(0.68)	(1.20)	(1.01)	(1.57)	(1.31)	(0.98)	(1.64)
Private services:	6.2	6.8	0.6	9.1	8.9	–0.2	9.7	11.0	1.2	10.8	13.5	2.6
	(0.44)	(0.43)	(0.61)	(0.60)	(0.50)	(0.78)	(1.27)	(1.24)	(1.78)	(1.56)	(1.31)	(2.04)
– Private hospitals	0.2	0.5	0.3 *	0.3	0.3	0.0	0.2	0.5	0.3	0.1	0.6	0.5
	(0.08)	(0.11)	(0.14)	(0.08)	(0.08)	(0.11)	(0.17)	(0.24)	(0.30)	(0.07)	(0.27)	(0.28)
– Polyclinic and private doctor	3.0	3.2	0.2	3.0	3.0	0.1	4.8	4.6	–0.2	3.8	5.2	1.5
	(0.30)	(0.31)	(0.43)	(0.33)	(0.30)	(0.45)	(0.97)	(0.83)	(1.27)	(0.82)	(0.77)	(1.12)
– Nurse, midwife and paramedic	3.1	3.3	0.1	6.1	5.8	–0.3	5.2	6.5	1.3	7.2	8.0	0.8
	(0.36)	(0.32)	(0.48)	(0.50)	(0.43)	(0.66)	(0.96)	(1.04)	(1.42)	(1.25)	(1.05)	(1.63)
Traditional health services	0.4	0.2	–0.1	0.4	0.5	0.1	0.7	0.9	0.2	0.9	0.4	–0.5
	(0.10)	(0.07)	(0.12)	(0.10)	(0.11)	(0.15)	(0.27)	(0.42)	(0.50)	(0.36)	(0.18)	(0.40)
Other services	0.0	0.0	0.0	0.1	0.3	0.2 *	0.0	0.0	0.0	0.4	0.0	–0.4
	–	(0.03)	(0.03)	(0.03)	(0.09)	(0.09)	–	–	–	(0.27)	–	(0.27)
Number of observations	4,477	5,571		5,031	5,988		759	858		829	1,013	

Source: IFLS2 and IFLS3.
Estimates were weighted using individual sampling weights. Standard errors (in parentheses) are robust to clustering at the community level. Significance at 5% (*) and 1% (**) indicated.

APPENDIX TABLE 8.3
Immunization Uptake for Children, aged 12–59 months: Urban and Rural Areas
(In percent)

	Urban						Rural					
	Boys			Girls			Boys			Girls		
	1997	2000	Change	1997	2000	Change	1997	2000	Change	1997	2000	Change
Child received Vitamin A in	69.5	62.6	–6.9 *	72.6	61.6	–11.1 **	66.1	52.6	–13.5 **	67.5	51.4	–16.0 **
6 months before the survey	(2.42)	(2.14)	(3.23)	(2.42)	(2.25)	(3.30)	(3.07)	(2.36)	(3.87)	(2.62)	(2.57)	(3.67)
Type of vaccination received:												
– BCG	88.5	94.1	5.5 *	89.9	91.5	1.6	82.3	79.9	–2.4	79.4	80.2	0.8
	(2.00)	(1.06)	(2.26)	(1.76)	(1.55)	(2.35)	(2.79)	(2.13)	(3.51)	(2.35)	(2.51)	(3.44)
– Polio, 1+ times	96.8	94.5	–2.2	96.2	93.1	–3.1	93.8	84.6	–9.2 **	92.8	84.3	–8.5 **
	(0.84)	(0.97)	(1.28)	(1.25)	(1.52)	(1.97)	(1.62)	(1.92)	(2.51)	(1.64)	(2.44)	(2.94)
– Polio, 2+ times	91.4	88.2	–3.2	89.7	86.3	–3.4	85.0	73.9	–11.1 **	84.2	75.4	–8.8 *
	(1.35)	(1.41)	(1.95)	(1.82)	(1.93)	(2.65)	(2.36)	(2.10)	(3.16)	(2.57)	(2.65)	(3.69)
– Polio, 3+ times	71.6	77.9	6.4 *	74.9	77.8	2.9	64.3	59.4	–4.9	58.5	61.2	2.7
	(2.28)	(1.92)	(2.98)	(2.44)	(2.06)	(3.20)	(2.82)	(2.34)	(3.66)	(2.65)	(2.64)	(3.74)
– Polio, 4+ times	26.9	42.2	15.3 **	26.6	41.4	14.7 **	19.7	31.3	11.6 **	20.9	29.4	8.6 **
	(2.17)	(2.81)	(3.55)	(2.33)	(2.59)	(3.48)	(1.88)	(2.24)	(2.92)	(1.86)	(2.31)	(2.97)
– DPT, 1+ times	88.1	93.5	5.4 *	89.5	91.5	1.9	80.5	78.6	–1.9	77.5	79.0	1.5
	(1.94)	(1.01)	(2.19)	(1.83)	(1.78)	(2.55)	(2.64)	(2.18)	(3.42)	(2.53)	(2.54)	(3.59)
– DPT, 2+ times	77.9	85.7	7.8 **	77.5	84.4	6.9 *	65.8	66.0	0.1	64.9	68.6	3.8
	(2.28)	(1.54)	(2.75)	(2.41)	(1.95)	(3.11)	(3.01)	(2.47)	(3.90)	(2.93)	(2.64)	(3.94)
– DPT, 3+ times	64.6	76.1	11.4 **	66.9	75.0	8.2 *	50.4	53.1	2.7	47.9	55.6	7.7
	(2.49)	(2.05)	(3.22)	(2.97)	(2.15)	(3.67)	(2.95)	(2.34)	(3.77)	(2.91)	(2.69)	(3.96)

– Measles	80.1	84.1	4.0	81.4	84.4	3.1	76.6	71.6	–5.0	70.6	73.2	2.6
	(2.25)	(1.92)	(2.95)	(2.15)	(1.94)	(2.90)	(2.71)	(2.42)	(3.63)	(2.83)	(2.54)	(3.80)
– Hepatitis B	64.6	83.5	18.8 **	65.2	80.3	15.1 **	50.8	65.9	15.1 **	48.5	65.4	16.9 **
	(3.03)	(1.72)	(3.49)	(3.01)	(2.04)	(3.63)	(2.96)	(2.47)	(3.86)	(3.14)	(2.72)	(4.15)
– All vaccinations	42.9	64.9	22.0 **	45.5	63.8	18.3 **	30.9	44.2	13.3 **	29.5	47.9	18.3 **
	(2.88)	(2.26)	(3.66)	(3.17)	(2.28)	(3.90)	(2.32)	(2.31)	(3.27)	(2.53)	(2.49)	(3.55)
Children able to show KMS	28.7	28.2	–0.6	28.1	21.9	–6.3 *	21.2	21.2	0.0	22.0	20.9	–1.0
	(2.20)	(2.03)	(3.00)	(2.31)	(1.87)	(2.97)	(2.13)	(1.87)	(2.83)	(2.26)	(1.73)	(2.85)
Number of observations	484	682		487	659		646	812		619	760	

Source: IFLS2 and IFLS3.

Estimates were weighted using individual sampling weights. Standard errors (in parentheses) are robust to clustering at the community level. Significance at 5% (*) and 1% (**) indicated.

9

Health Service Delivery

Complementary to examining utilization by individuals, it is also possible with IFLS to monitor the levels and changes in availability and quality of health services. It is plausible that services offered may have deteriorated during the crisis, since real central government expenditures were cut, with the health budget cut by 20%. On the other hand, an inflow of foreign assistance partly made up for the difference (Lieberman et al. 2001).

This chapter examines the availability, quality and cost of services provided by public clinics and sub-clinics (*puskesmas* and *puskesmas pembantu*), *posyandu* and private providers: private physicians and clinics, private paramedics and nurses, and private and village midwives. We measure the quality of health service delivery from inputs and cost of inputs provided. We do not have data that ascertains the patients' view of the service that they have got, or of the process of service delivery. Further, in this report we do not try to statistically link inputs to health outcomes of individuals. We begin by looking at public clinics and private facilities and then turn to *posyandu*, which serve a very targeted clientele and offer unique services. We measure general services, including whether there are or have been stock outages for these services, then turn to drug availability, laboratory services, and the availability of supplies and instruments. We then analyse data on the costs of these services. In the discussions, we emphasize both the current year situation and the changes from 1997 to 2000.

SERVICE DELIVERY AND FEES AT *PUSKESMAS* AND PRIVATE PRACTITIONERS

Provision of general services

Data on some of the basic services provided by government and private health facilities is shown in Table 9.1.[1] The data show the percentage of

TABLE 9.1
Provision of General Services by Type of Facilities (in percent)

	Puskesmas and Pustu			Private Physician and Clinic			Midwife and Village Midwife			Paramedic and Nurse		
	1997	2000	Change	1997	2000	Change	1997	2000	Change	1997	2000	Change
Check-up + injection + medicine	99.5	98.7	–0.7	75.0	78.2	3.2	85.4	90.4	5.0 *	91.9	94.2	2.3
	(0.24)	(0.36)	(0.43)	(2.33)	(1.93)	(3.02)	(1.52)	(1.35)	(2.03)	(1.39)	(1.21)	(1.84)
Medical treatment of tuberculosis	79.1	77.1	–2.0	52.7	53.0	0.3	8.3	5.5	–2.8	17.4	16.6	–0.9
	(1.50)	(1.50)	(2.12)	(2.22)	(1.87)	(2.90)	(1.14)	(0.89)	(1.45)	(1.87)	(1.80)	(2.59)
Dental exam [a]	65.4	68.8	3.4									
	(1.71)	(1.67)	(2.38)									
Pre-natal care	95.1	95.0	–0.1	55.7	56.3	0.6	98.0	98.1	0.1	17.2	19.8	2.6
	(0.82)	(0.79)	(1.14)	(2.09)	(2.11)	(2.97)	(0.57)	(0.50)	(0.75)	(1.70)	(1.97)	(2.60)
Delivery	24.7	30.9	6.2 *	15.5	16.2	0.7	91.3	93.8	2.5	11.1	12.3	1.2
	(1.71)	(1.72)	(2.43)	(1.41)	(1.49)	(2.05)	(1.20)	(0.90)	(1.50)	(1.54)	(1.70)	(2.30)
Immunization:												
– BCG	82.5	86.1	3.6	30.6	26.4	–4.2	54.1	50.9	–3.2	7.2	4.7	–2.5
	(1.46)	(1.24)	(1.91)	(2.37)	(1.96)	(3.08)	(2.45)	(2.39)	(3.42)	(1.23)	(1.05)	(1.62)
– DPT	82.6	86.3	3.7 *	32.4	28.7	–3.7	55.7	52.7	–3.0	7.7	4.5	–3.1
	(1.46)	(1.23)	(1.91)	(2.41)	(2.03)	(3.16)	(2.45)	(2.38)	(3.42)	(1.25)	(1.03)	(1.62)
– Anti polio	82.5	86.4	4.0 *	32.2	28.4	–3.9	55.4	52.8	–2.5	7.7	5.0	–2.7
	(1.45)	(1.22)	(1.90)	(2.42)	(2.04)	(3.16)	(2.45)	(2.36)	(3.40)	(1.25)	(1.10)	(1.67)
– Measles	82.7	86.3	3.6	31.6	27.2	–4.4	55.2	51.4	–3.9	7.4	4.5	–2.9
	(1.45)	(1.23)	(1.90)	(2.43)	(1.99)	(3.14)	(2.46)	(2.38)	(3.42)	(1.24)	(1.03)	(1.61)
– Tetanus Toxoid for pregnant women	88.4	89.6	1.3	33.3	30.2	–3.1	76.9	71.2	–5.7 *	10.2	7.1	–3.1
	(1.20)	(1.06)	(1.60)	(2.21)	(1.93)	(2.94)	(1.87)	(1.98)	(2.73)	(1.45)	(1.17)	(1.86)
– Hepatitis B	78.9	84.6	5.7 **	34.6	34.2	–0.4	45.4	50.4	5.0	5.1	5.0	–0.1
	(1.51)	(1.20)	(1.92)	(2.15)	(2.15)	(3.04)	(2.30)	(2.30)	(3.25)	(1.01)	(1.09)	(1.49)
Number of observations	919	944		673	698		663	740		470	464	

Source: IFLS2 and IFLS3.
[a] Information on dental exam is collected only at *Puskesmas* and *Pustu*.
Standard errors (in parentheses) are robust to clustering at the community level. Significance at 5% (*) and 1% (**) indicated.

facilities that offer each service in each year. Such services encompass a basic check-up (called check-up +injection + medicine) medical treatment of tuberculoses, dental examination, pre-natal care, and delivery, in addition to the provision of immunizations. Excluding immunizations, there has not been much change in services offered in the government clinics. The only statistically significant change is an increase in the proportion of *puskesmas* that offer delivery services, although the fraction is still under one-third. In the private sector the provision of basic check-ups increased significantly for midwives.

For immunization, availability rose in the public sector, with especially large increases in the provision of hepatitis B vaccine, of almost 6%. There was a significant increase in the availability of DPT and polio vaccines, by 4% respectively. Only about one-third of private physicians and clinics supply vaccinations and over half of midwives do, but almost no paramedics and private nurses supply them. There was a decline in vaccines offered at private facilities, except for hepatitis B, which saw an increase among private and village midwives (although none of these changes are statistically significant). This increase in the number of clinics offering immunizations is clearly consistent with the increase in immunization uptake at the child level, discussed in Chapter 8. However, given the size of the increase at the child level, it is likely that more intensive immunization services in clinics already providing vaccines also played a role.

A different measure of problem, or success, in providing vaccinations is whether a clinic has had a stock outage of vaccines and for how long. The problem with this measure is that an outage could result from supply problems or from excess demand. The former interpretation would be considered as bad, whereas the latter would be considered good. In fact, we cannot distinguish between these two explanations.

With this caveat in mind, we count facilities that provide vaccination services in examining outages and examine the incidence and severity of outages over a six-month reference period. Table 9.2 presents the results. There is no evidence of a large percentage of facilities with shortages of vaccines, both in government and privately run health facilities. A comparison between 1997 and 2000 shows that the stock outages of vaccines at both government and private physicians and clinics experienced significant declines. Stock outages also declined among midwives during this period, though by a smaller amount.

TABLE 9.2
Stock Outages of Vaccines During the Last Six Months Among Those Providing, by Type of Facilities (in percent)

	Puskesmas and Pustu			Private Physician and Clinic			Midwife and Village Midwife		
	1997	2000	Change	1997	2000	Change	1997	2000	Change
BCG	7.1	2.7	–4.4 **	15.6	10.1	–5.4	11.1	7.1	–4.0
	(1.20)	(0.66)	(1.37)	(2.94)	(2.13)	(3.64)	(2.04)	(1.35)	(2.45)
	[621]	[707]	[180]	[178]	[279]	[338]			
DPT	6.6	3.0	–3.6 **	9.7	3.7	–6.0 *	8.3	5.8	–2.6
	(1.16)	(0.69)	(1.34)	(2.19)	(1.36)	(2.58)	(1.84)	(1.28)	(2.24)
	[621]	[708]	[186]	[190]	[288]	[347]			
Anti polio	7.1	3.5	–3.5 **	10.2	4.8	–5.4 *	7.7	6.9	–0.8
	(1.13)	(0.70)	(1.33)	(2.24)	(1.50)	(2.70)	(1.80)	(1.32)	(2.23)
	[622]	[708]	[186]	[188]	[285]	[349]			
Measles	6.4	2.8	–3.6 **	12.4	5.9	–6.5 *	8.8	5.0	–3.7
	(1.10)	(0.65)	(1.27)	(2.39)	(1.68)	(2.92)	(1.89)	(1.17)	(2.22)
	[622]	[707]	[185]	[185]	[285]	[337]			
Tetanus toxoid	6.5	1.9	–4.6 **	12.8	5.2	–7.6 **	11.6	5.8	–5.8 **
	(1.12)	(0.58)	(1.26)	(2.50)	(1.50)	(2.92)	(1.80)	(1.06)	(2.09)
	[629]	[719]	[195]	[212]	[371]	[449]			
Hepatitis B	9.7	5.4	–4.3 *	12.1	8.6	–3.5	9.4	8.4	–1.0
	(1.45)	(0.97)	(1.74)	(2.32)	(1.79)	(2.93)	(2.19)	(1.44)	(2.62)
	[608]	[708]		[198]	[221]		[235]	[345]	

Source: IFLS2 and IFLS3.

Stock outages by paramedics and nurses are not reported due to small cell size. Standard errors (in parentheses) are robust to clustering at the community level. Significance at 5% (*) and 1% (**) indicated. Number of observations is in brackets.

Drug availability

The availability of drugs, or the lack of it, for outpatient care in health facilities is not necessarily good or bad. After all, pharmacies can be used to purchase medications just as well. As a practical matter, having drugs available in the outpatient facilities may be useful for at least two reasons. First, drugs will often be needed to treat emergencies in the facility. In addition, it should be the case that a patient is more likely to purchase a recommended medication if its price is lower. Having drugs available in health facilities enables the subsidization of prices. Private facilities will need to be reimbursed in order to do this, which is probably why it is easier to subsidize through public facilities. Ideally one would want the subsidy linked to need. If drugs are being subsidized primarily in public facilities and if it is the poor who tend to go to public facilities, while the non-poor go to private doctors, then a certain amount of targeting will be achieved. As we saw in Chapter 8, while it is not true that only the poor go to *puskesmas* and only the non-poor go to private doctors, there is a positive income effect on private sector utilization.

In that light, Table 9.3 provides information on whether the facility generally has available certain specific drugs. Data indicates that the percentage of facilities with drugs of all categories was higher in public than that in private health facilities.

Looking at changes, there is some improvement of supplies of antibiotics, with large increases among private providers. On the other hand, there is a large decline in availability of Vitamin A in both public and private sectors. This suggests a cutback in the Vitamin A programme, consistent with individual level information that children in particular were much less likely to receive Vitamin A in the last six months in 2000 than in 1997. For other drugs most changes are small, with some increasing and some declining availability.

Table 9.4a shows whether the drugs were in stock on the day of the IFLS team visit.[2] The picture on current stock outages looks uniformly positive for the private sector: the incidence of stock outages declined for many drugs, between 1997 and 2000, especially for private doctors and clinics. For *puskesmas*, the picture for current outages is less clear; there are few statistically significant differences, although the signs of the differences are negative.

If one examines stock outages over the most recent six-month period, instead of today, the picture is a bit different (Table 9.4b). There are more indications of a decline in the incidence of stock outages in the public

TABLE 9.3
Provision of Drugs by Type of Facilities
(in percent)

	Puskesmas and *Pustu*			Private Physician and Clinic			Midwife and Village Midwife			Paramedic and Nurse		
	1997	2000	Change	1997	2000	Change	1997	2000	Change	1997	2000	Change
Antibiotics:												
– Penicilin	37.6	32.7	–4.9	23.8	18.9	–4.9 *	21.7	18.9	–2.8	24.1	22.8	–1.3
	(2.03)	(1.87)	(2.76)	(1.85)	(1.65)	(2.48)	(1.86)	(1.68)	(2.51)	(2.24)	(2.18)	(3.12)
– Ampicilin	95.3	95.7	0.3	64.1	65.5	1.4	81.0	88.8	7.7 **	78.2	84.3	6.1 *
	(0.79)	(0.78)	(1.11)	(2.43)	(2.27)	(3.33)	(1.73)	(1.21)	(2.11)	(2.05)	(1.82)	(2.74)
– Tetraciclin	97.5	97.9	0.4	58.7	59.3	0.6	72.8	74.1	1.3	84.0	87.3	3.3
	(0.55)	(0.48)	(0.73)	(2.42)	(2.22)	(3.29)	(1.97)	(1.92)	(2.75)	(1.69)	(1.52)	(2.27)
– Chloramphenicol	93.8	97.5	3.7 **	57.3	64.3	7.0 *	58.0	63.2	5.3	70.3	73.5	3.2
	(0.99)	(0.52)	(1.12)	(2.49)	(2.04)	(3.22)	(2.29)	(2.16)	(3.15)	(2.32)	(2.23)	(3.22)
– Cotrimoxazole	82.7	96.9	14.2 **	48.0	63.8	15.8 **	46.9	68.8	21.8 **	48.9	67.5	18.5 **
	(1.47)	(0.58)	(1.58)	(2.42)	(2.17)	(3.25)	(2.42)	(2.03)	(3.16)	(2.49)	(2.23)	(3.34)
– Ciprofloxacin	2.2	4.3	2.2 *	14.3	36.7	22.3 **	2.3	4.6	2.3 *	1.3	5.8	4.5 **
	(0.56)	(0.74)	(0.93)	(1.78)	(2.03)	(2.70)	(0.75)	(0.80)	(1.09)	(0.52)	(1.19)	(1.30)
– Acyclovir	1.1	1.5	0.4	4.2	14.9	10.7 **	0.5	1.5	1.0 *	0.4	3.2	2.8 **
	(0.37)	(0.42)	(0.56)	(1.03)	(1.47)	(1.79)	(0.26)	(0.44)	(0.51)	(0.30)	(0.84)	(0.89)
Analgetic:												
– Antalgin	98.2	99.4	1.2 *	67.1	67.3	0.2	85.0	83.9	–1.1	88.2	89.2	1.0
	(0.44)	(0.26)	(0.51)	(2.38)	(2.03)	(3.13)	(1.69)	(1.48)	(2.25)	(1.54)	(1.55)	(2.18)
Antipiretic:												
– Acetosal	46.9	43.0	–3.9	32.7	26.5	–6.2 *	20.5	16.2	–4.3	18.4	15.7	–2.6
	(2.05)	(1.99)	(2.86)	(2.27)	(1.83)	(2.92)	(1.76)	(1.49)	(2.31)	(1.77)	(1.82)	(2.54)
– Paracetamol	98.5	99.6	1.1 *	70.3	78.2	7.9 **	88.7	94.3	5.6 **	90.8	94.0	3.2
	(0.40)	(0.21)	(0.45)	(2.28)	(1.93)	(2.98)	(1.46)	(0.91)	(1.72)	(1.32)	(1.20)	(1.78)

continued on next page

TABLE 9.3 – cont'd

	Puskesmas and *Pustu*			Private Physician and Clinic			Midwife and Village Midwife			Paramedic and Nurse		
	1997	2000	Change	1997	2000	Change	1997	2000	Change	1997	2000	Change
Anti fungi:												
– Nystatin	37.2	45.7	8.4 **	21.6	22.6	1.1	19.6	22.0	2.5	12.0	11.6	–0.3
	(2.00)	(2.07)	(2.88)	(1.91)	(1.78)	(2.61)	(1.65)	(1.61)	(2.30)	(1.59)	(1.50)	(2.18)
Anti TBC (short-term):												
– INH	76.9	73.2	–3.7	34.5	32.2	–2.3	11.5	5.3	–6.2 **	19.0	16.6	–2.4
	(1.60)	(1.60)	(2.26)	(2.41)	(1.93)	(3.08)	(1.40)	(0.91)	(1.67)	(1.95)	(2.01)	(2.80)
– Rifampicin	53.9	61.0	7.2 **	29.4	26.9	–2.5	5.4	2.8	–2.5 *	10.5	11.4	1.0
	(1.99)	(1.76)	(2.66)	(2.16)	(1.82)	(2.82)	(0.95)	(0.68)	(1.17)	(1.39)	(1.62)	(2.14)
– Ethambutol	69.0	65.9	–3.1	28.8	27.1	–1.7	7.0	3.8	–3.2 *	12.0	12.1	0.1
	(1.76)	(1.75)	(2.48)	(2.10)	(1.81)	(2.78)	(1.17)	(0.80)	(1.41)	(1.70)	(1.67)	(2.39)
– Streptomicyne	30.3	26.6	–3.7	11.0	7.2	–3.8	3.4	1.9	–1.5	6.8	5.8	–1.0
	(1.89)	(1.70)	(2.54)	(1.63)	(1.17)	(2.01)	(0.78)	(0.53)	(0.94)	(1.29)	(1.15)	(1.73)
Anti malaria	44.1	44.1	0.0	22.8	22.6	–0.1	17.4	19.2	1.8	30.3	40.1	9.7 *
	(2.33)	(2.22)	(3.22)	(2.07)	(2.04)	(2.91)	(1.85)	(1.93)	(2.68)	(2.61)	(2.83)	(3.85)
Skin disease medicines	97.2	98.0	0.8	63.7	68.1	4.4	65.7	68.5	2.8	74.4	75.9	1.5
	(0.60)	(0.47)	(0.76)	(2.50)	(2.09)	(3.26)	(2.07)	(1.97)	(2.86)	(2.17)	(2.15)	(3.06)
Cough medicines	98.2	99.2	1.0	69.7	74.8	5.1	78.7	84.3	5.6 *	89.1	89.4	0.3
	(0.46)	(0.30)	(0.55)	(2.34)	(1.99)	(3.07)	(1.78)	(1.57)	(2.37)	(1.50)	(1.59)	(2.18)
Oralit	97.4	98.3	0.9	59.1	54.6	–4.5	79.5	80.8	1.3	77.6	71.8	–5.8 *
	(0.56)	(0.44)	(0.71)	(2.46)	(2.05)	(3.20)	(1.69)	(1.51)	(2.27)	(1.97)	(2.18)	(2.94)
Iron tablets	93.3	95.1	1.9	50.5	45.0	–5.5	84.9	82.0	–2.8	45.3	41.6	–3.7
	(1.00)	(0.76)	(1.26)	(2.44)	(2.22)	(3.30)	(1.70)	(1.51)	(2.28)	(2.46)	(2.55)	(3.54)
Vitamin A	88.5	61.7	–26.8 **	44.9	23.5	–21.5 **	72.3	45.5	–26.8 **	39.1	15.3	–23.8 **
	(1.21)	(1.87)	(2.23)	(2.47)	(1.90)	(3.11)	(1.89)	(2.13)	(2.85)	(2.47)	(1.89)	(3.12)
Number of observations	919	944		663	698		654	740		468	464	

Source: IFLS2 and IFLS3.
Standard errors (in parentheses) are robust to clustering at the community level. Significance at 5% (*) and 1% (**) indicated.

TABLE 9.4a
Stock Outages of Drugs at Present Among Those Providing, by Type of Facilities
(In percent)

	Puskesmas and *Pustu*			Private Physician and Clinic			Midwife and Village Midwife			Paramedic and Nurse		
	1997	2000	Change	1997	2000	Change	1997	2000	Change	1997	2000	Change
Antibiotics:												
– Penicilin	4.3	6.1	1.8	3.2	5.3	2.1	11.3	8.6	–2.7	13.3	7.5	–5.7
	(1.14)	(1.44)	(1.84)	(1.39)	(1.95)	(2.40)	(2.64)	(2.27)	(3.48)	(3.61)	(2.39)	(4.33)
– Ampicilin	5.7	8.4	2.7 *	4.5	1.8	–2.7 *	5.8	3.3	–2.5 *	8.7	5.9	–2.9
	(0.81)	(0.97)	(1.26)	(1.12)	(0.67)	(1.31)	(1.04)	(0.71)	(1.26)	(1.58)	(1.14)	(1.95)
– Tetraciclin	3.2	2.9	–0.3	2.3	1.4	–0.9	3.4	1.6	–1.7	3.8	4.0	0.1
	(0.57)	(0.60)	(0.83)	(0.73)	(0.58)	(0.93)	(0.87)	(0.53)	(1.02)	(1.06)	(0.94)	(1.42)
– Chloramphenicol	3.2	3.6	0.3	4.2	1.8	–2.4 *	5.3	3.6	–1.6	6.4	4.4	–2.0
	(0.61)	(0.65)	(0.89)	(1.06)	(0.62)	(1.22)	(1.18)	(0.84)	(1.45)	(1.42)	(1.23)	(1.88)
– Cotrimoxazole	4.7	4.3	–0.5	4.1	1.1	–3.0 *	7.5	1.8	–5.7 **	7.4	5.8	–1.7
	(0.82)	(0.69)	(1.07)	(1.39)	(0.49)	(1.47)	(1.46)	(0.70)	(1.62)	(1.71)	(1.40)	(2.21)
– Ciprofloxacin	–	–	–	3.2	2.3	–0.8	–	–	–	–	–	–
				(1.73)	(0.93)	(1.96)						
– Acyclovir	–	–	–	10.7	4.8	–5.9	–	–	–	–	–	–
				(6.16)	(2.09)	(6.51)						
Analgetic:												
– Antalgin	3.7	2.8	–0.9	3.6	0.6	–3.0 **	2.0	1.3	–0.7	2.4	2.4	0.0
	(0.63)	(0.54)	(0.83)	(0.90)	(0.36)	(0.97)	(0.59)	(0.45)	(0.74)	(0.74)	(0.74)	(1.05)
Antipiretic:												
– Acetosal	4.9	4.9	0.1	2.3	3.8	1.5	0.7	2.5	1.8	4.7	1.4	–3.3
	(1.15)	(1.06)	(1.56)	(1.01)	(1.39)	(1.72)	(0.75)	(1.44)	(1.62)	(2.26)	(1.37)	(2.64)
– Paracetamol	3.8	1.7	–2.1 **	2.8	1.5	–1.3	2.4	1.9	–0.6	3.8	2.1	–1.7
	(0.65)	(0.44)	(0.79)	(0.74)	(0.57)	(0.94)	(0.67)	(0.54)	(0.87)	(1.00)	(0.67)	(1.20)

continued on next page

TABLE 9.4a – cont'd

	Puskesmas and *Pustu*			Private Physician and Clinic			Midwife and Village Midwife			Paramedic and Nurse		
	1997	2000	Change	1997	2000	Change	1997	2000	Change	1997	2000	Change
Anti fungi:												
– Nystatin	4.1	6.3	2.2	9.1	4.4	–4.7	10.9	11.0	0.1	10.7	5.6	–5.2
	(1.06)	(1.27)	(1.66)	(2.28)	(1.57)	(2.77)	(2.95)	(2.42)	(3.82)	(4.05)	(3.14)	(5.13)
Anti TBC (short–term):												
– INH	5.9	4.5	–1.5	6.1	1.3	–4.8 **	6.7	0.0	–6.7 *	7.9	7.8	–0.1
	(0.97)	(0.83)	(1.27)	(1.51)	(0.76)	(1.69)	(2.93)	–	(2.93)	(2.83)	(3.41)	(4.43)
– Rifampicin	9.1	5.6	–3.5 *	7.2	2.1	–5.1 *	–	–	–	10.2	7.5	–2.7
	(1.43)	(1.04)	(1.77)	(1.82)	(1.03)	(2.09)	(4.36)	(3.54)	(5.62)			
– Ethambutol	7.1	6.9	–0.2	7.3	0.5	–6.8 **	6.7	7.1	0.5	14.3	7.1	–7.1
	(1.14)	(1.11)	(1.60)	(1.81)	(0.52)	(1.89)	(3.78)	(4.94)	(6.22)	(4.65)	(3.37)	(5.74)
– Streptomicyne	12.2	4.0	–8.2 **	4.1	4.0	–0.1	–	–	–	6.3	3.7	–2.5
	(2.10)	(1.24)	(2.44)	(2.84)	(2.82)	(4.00)	(4.19)	(3.66)	(5.57)			
Anti malaria	6.2	5.0	–1.1	5.4	3.8	–1.6	4.4	5.6	1.2	7.9	2.7	–5.2 *
	(1.15)	(1.13)	(1.61)	(1.88)	(1.52)	(2.42)	(1.92)	(2.03)	(2.79)	(2.27)	(1.18)	(2.55)
Skin disease medicines	6.5	4.4	–2.1	3.3	0.8	–2.5 *	3.5	3.4	–0.1	6.0	6.8	0.8
	(0.86)	(0.71)	(1.12)	(0.98)	(0.42)	(1.06)	(0.98)	(0.83)	(1.29)	(1.42)	(1.52)	(2.08)
Cough medicines	6.5	2.5	–4.1 **	3.5	0.8	–2.7 **	2.5	1.3	–1.2	3.4	5.1	1.7
	(0.89)	(0.54)	(1.04)	(0.93)	(0.46)	(1.04)	(0.73)	(0.45)	(0.86)	(0.87)	(1.05)	(1.36)
Oralit	6.0	3.2	–2.8 **	6.1	2.4	–3.8 **	6.5	5.0	–1.5	9.1	6.6	–2.5
	(0.83)	(0.65)	(1.05)	(1.24)	(0.77)	(1.46)	(1.23)	(0.93)	(1.54)	(1.60)	(1.44)	(2.15)
Iron tablets	1.5	3.7	2.2 **	7.2	3.2	–4.0 *	4.3	5.4	1.1	12.7	5.2	–7.6 **
	(0.41)	(0.60)	(0.73)	(1.46)	(0.97)	(1.75)	(0.90)	(0.96)	(1.32)	(2.41)	(1.56)	(2.87)
Vitamin A	4.6	4.0	–0.6	11.4	4.3	–7.1 **	8.0	5.6	–2.4	14.2	7.0	–7.2
	(0.81)	(0.79)	(1.13)	(1.98)	(1.57)	(2.53)	(1.33)	(1.24)	(1.81)	(2.86)	(2.95)	(4.11)
Number of observations	919	944		663	698		654	740		468	464	

Source: IFLS2 and IFLS3.

Number of observations varies per cell, and is equal to the number of facilities that provides the drugs (see Table 9.3). Dash (–) indicates that the estimates are not reported due to small cell size. Standard errors (in parentheses) are robust to clustering at the community level. Significance at 5% (*) and 1% (**) indicated.

TABLE 9.4b
Stock Outages of Drugs During Last Six Months Among Those Providing, by Type of Facilities
(In percent)

	Puskesmas and *Pustu*			Private Physician and Clinic			Midwife and Village Midwife			Paramedic and Nurse		
	1997	2000	Change	1997	2000	Change	1997	2000	Change	1997	2000	Change
Antibiotics:												
– Penicilin	19.1	18.2	–0.9	8.7	3.9	–4.8	17.6	20.7	3.2	34.3	18.9	–15.4 *
	(2.47)	(2.40)	(3.45)	(2.56)	(1.69)	(3.07)	(3.61)	(3.96)	(5.36)	(5.51)	(3.68)	(6.63)
– Ampicilin	26.4	22.8	–3.7	7.8	3.8	–4.1 *	12.0	8.1	–3.9	15.0	11.3	–3.7
	(2.09)	(1.53)	(2.59)	(1.38)	(0.99)	(1.70)	(1.66)	(1.20)	(2.05)	(2.14)	(1.86)	(2.84)
– Tetraciclin	16.8	9.8	–7.1 **	6.6	3.2	–3.5 *	6.9	5.7	–1.2	12.4	9.7	–2.7
	(1.81)	(1.08)	(2.11)	(1.39)	(0.85)	(1.63)	(1.45)	(1.06)	(1.80)	(1.94)	(1.56)	(2.49)
– Chloramphenicol	17.6	10.3	–7.3 **	7.4	2.7	–4.7 **	9.1	7.1	–2.0	11.4	7.1	–4.3
	(1.85)	(1.10)	(2.15)	(1.50)	(0.82)	(1.71)	(1.82)	(1.18)	(2.17)	(1.88)	(1.57)	(2.45)
– Cotrimoxazole	18.4	10.4	–8.0 **	5.2	1.8	–3.4 *	9.0	5.9	–3.0	11.8	9.6	–2.2
	(1.98)	(1.12)	(2.28)	(1.44)	(0.63)	(1.57)	(1.91)	(1.27)	(2.29)	(2.43)	(2.12)	(3.22)
– Ciprofloxacin	–	–	–	5.9	3.5	–2.4	–	–	–	–	–	–
				(2.58)	(1.15)	(2.83)						
– Acyclovir	–	–	–	8.7	9.7	1.0	–	–	–	–	–	–
				(6.19)	(2.94)	(6.85)						
Analgetic:												
– Antalgin	10.8	8.9	–1.9	4.3	1.7	–2.6 *	6.5	2.3	–4.2 **	8.4	5.6	–2.8
	(1.39)	(1.07)	(1.75)	(1.08)	(0.59)	(1.23)	(1.24)	(0.63)	(1.39)	(1.56)	(1.22)	(1.98)
Antipiretic:												
– Acetosal	8.5	8.7	0.3	3.9	4.9	1.1	7.2	1.7	–5.5 *	10.7	2.7	–8.0 *
	(1.73)	(1.50)	(2.29)	(1.45)	(1.59)	(2.16)	(2.30)	(1.19)	(2.59)	(3.34)	(1.92)	(3.86)
– Paracetamol	12.4	9.5	–2.9	4.1	2.0	–2.0	5.3	3.0	–2.3	7.0	5.7	–1.2
	(1.50)	(1.03)	(1.82)	(1.03)	(0.65)	(1.21)	(1.13)	(0.67)	(1.32)	(1.40)	(1.22)	(1.86)

continued on next page

TABLE 9.4b – cont'd

	Puskesmas and *Pustu*			Private Physician and Clinic			Midwife and Village Midwife			Paramedic and Nurse		
	1997	2000	Change	1997	2000	Change	1997	2000	Change	1997	2000	Change
Anti fungi:												
– Nystatin	4.8	7.1	2.3	6.6	5.8	–0.8	13.9	9.9	–4.0	10.2	11.1	0.9
	(1.35)	(1.25)	(1.84)	(2.23)	(1.88)	(2.92)	(3.36)	(2.51)	(4.19)	(4.30)	(4.34)	(6.11)
Anti TBC (short–term):												
– INH	7.4	5.3	–2.1	8.0	1.8	–6.2 **	10.3	12.8	2.5	9.6	9.5	–0.2
	(1.41)	(0.89)	(1.67)	(2.08)	(1.09)	(2.35)	(3.72)	(5.32)	(6.49)	(3.26)	(3.72)	(4.95)
– Rifampicin	13.8	8.5	–5.4 *	10.5	4.8	–5.6	–	–	–	11.1	8.0	–3.1
	(1.94)	(1.27)	(2.31)	(2.46)	(1.73)	(3.01)				(5.49)	(3.82)	(6.68)
– Ethambutol	11.9	8.8	–3.1	7.9	3.7	–4.2	11.9	10.7	–1.2	9.6	9.3	–0.4
	(1.84)	(1.22)	(2.20)	(2.26)	(1.36)	(2.64)	(5.15)	(5.98)	(7.89)	(4.02)	(3.78)	(5.52)
– Streptomicyne	15.4	7.6	–7.8 *	9.0	6.0	–3.0	–	–	–	13.8	14.8	1.0
	(2.77)	(1.75)	(3.27)	(3.66)	(3.37)	(4.97)				(6.35)	(6.99)	(9.44)
Anti malaria	6.7	5.4	–1.3	7.9	4.5	–3.4	12.1	9.4	–2.8	14.3	11.8	–2.5
	(1.53)	(1.22)	(1.95)	(2.42)	(1.65)	(2.93)	(3.39)	(2.82)	(4.41)	(3.06)	(2.98)	(4.27)
Skin disease medicines	16.0	9.8	–6.2 **	4.5	2.5	–2.0	8.3	7.7	–0.6	9.3	12.0	2.7
	(1.73)	(1.10)	(2.05)	(1.12)	(0.72)	(1.33)	(1.62)	(1.32)	(2.09)	(1.86)	(2.02)	(2.75)
Cough medicines	13.0	5.2	–7.8 **	4.2	1.3	–2.8 *	5.7	4.2	–1.5	7.1	6.4	–0.7
	(1.64)	(0.74)	(1.80)	(1.03)	(0.51)	(1.15)	(1.24)	(0.84)	(1.50)	(1.41)	(1.29)	(1.91)
Oralit	6.6	3.6	–2.9 *	6.0	2.9	–3.1 *	7.5	5.9	–1.6	10.4	7.9	–2.5
	(1.09)	(0.71)	(1.30)	(1.29)	(0.86)	(1.55)	(1.41)	(1.04)	(1.75)	(1.89)	(1.65)	(2.51)
Iron tablets	7.7	4.1	–3.6 *	5.2	4.5	–0.7	5.2	4.6	–0.7	14.0	6.8	–7.1 *
	(1.21)	(0.72)	(1.41)	(1.30)	(1.24)	(1.80)	(1.19)	(0.96)	(1.53)	(2.62)	(2.05)	(3.33)
Vitamin A	9.5	5.9	–3.6 *	6.7	4.3	–2.4	6.7	4.0	–2.7	12.4	10.1	–2.3
	(1.40)	(0.99)	(1.72)	(1.59)	(1.59)	(2.24)	(1.44)	(1.16)	(1.85)	(2.76)	(3.66)	(4.59)
Number of observations	919	944		663	698		654	740		468	464	

Source: IFLS2 and IFLS3.

Number of observations varies per cell, and is equal to the number of facilities that provides the drugs (see Table 9.3). Dash (–) indicates that the estimates are not reported due to small cell size. Standard errors (in parentheses) are robust to clustering at the community level. Significance at 5% (*) and 1% (**) indicated.

sector, especially for antibiotics. This is very good because it is antibiotics that have the highest incidence of stock outages over the past six months. The same trend is true for antibiotics among private sector providers, except that the differences are not always significant, except for doctors and clinics.

Provision of services at the laboratory

One of the indicators of good health service delivery is the availability of laboratories for in-house testing. This may be especially important in more remote areas, where sending samples to centralized laboratories may involve sample degradation or contamination, not to mention time. Data collected by IFLS in 1997 and 2000 on laboratory facilities covered eight types of tests, as appears in Table 9.5. Based on the results of the two surveys, there is a general indication of a small, though not significant, increase in laboratory tests provided by *puskesmas* and *pustu*. The major change was a large increase in the ability to conduct pregnancy tests, which was also found among private providers.

In terms of levels, it is interesting that for *puskesmas*, the tests they most frequently had capabilities to conduct were for pregnancy and for haemoglobin and it is not clear what haemoglobin tests were available. Other blood, urine and faeces tests are much less common, only one-third or fewer *puskesmas* have the laboratory facilities to conduct these sorts of tests. Evidently then hospitals are relied upon for more complicated tests, which may make sense from an efficiency point of view. Private facilities have a much lower incidence of being able to perform laboratory tests. Again the presumption is that laboratory tests are usually referred/sent to higher level health facilities.

Availability of supplies and instruments

The availability of various other supplies and instruments which support health service delivery is presented in Table 9.6. The availability of health supplies and instruments is higher in public than in private facilities. Supplies having to do with cleanliness — antiseptics, bandages, gloves — are nearly universally available. Surgical instruments, and equipment needed to do tests, such as microscopes, centrifuges and refrigeration, are much more likely to be available in a *puskesmas* than in a private facility. Moreover, the availability of such instruments in government run units increased significantly between 1997 and 2000, unlike for the private sector.

TABLE 9.5
Provision of Services at the Laboratory by Type of Facilities
(In percent)

	Puskesmas and *Pustu*			Private Physician and Clinic			Midwife and Village Midwife			Paramedic and Nurse		
	1997	2000	Change	1997	2000	Change	1997	2000	Change	1997	2000	Change
Haemoglobin test	67.5	65.8	–1.7	11.3	16.0	4.8 *	28.1	26.1	–2.0	3.8	2.8	–1.0
	(1.58)	(1.67)	(2.30)	(1.20)	(1.48)	(1.91)	(1.95)	(1.67)	(2.57)	(0.90)	(0.75)	(1.18)
Leukocyte calculation	30.4	30.9	0.6	5.8	7.2	1.4	0.2	0.1	0.0	0.0	0.2	0.2
	(1.55)	(1.54)	(2.19)	(0.95)	(1.09)	(1.44)	(0.15)	(0.13)	(0.20)	–	(0.22)	(0.22)
Blood type calculation	26.3	29.0	2.7	5.5	5.9	0.4	0.2	0.1	0.0	0.2	0.2	0.0
	(1.48)	(1.57)	(2.16)	(0.86)	(0.94)	(1.28)	(0.15)	(0.13)	(0.20)	(0.21)	(0.22)	(0.30)
Erythrocyte calculation	26.6	28.8	2.3	5.3	6.0	0.7	0.3	0.0	–0.3	0.0	0.2	0.2
	(1.49)	(1.56)	(2.16)	(0.90)	(0.95)	(1.31)	(0.21)	–	(0.21)	–	(0.22)	(0.22)
Urinanalysis	36.2	40.0	3.8	8.2	10.7	2.6	5.7	3.8	–1.9	0.9	1.5	0.7
	(1.56)	(1.61)	(2.24)	(1.06)	(1.33)	(1.70)	(0.95)	(0.80)	(1.24)	(0.42)	(0.56)	(0.70)
Pregnancy test	61.0	73.3	12.3 **	25.9	46.0	20.1 **	50.1	79.3	29.2 **	6.8	16.8	10.0 **
	(1.78)	(1.53)	(2.34)	(1.96)	(2.19)	(2.94)	(2.40)	(1.67)	(2.92)	(1.21)	(1.97)	(2.31)
Faeces examination	34.2	33.3	–0.9	3.9	6.0	2.2	0.5	0.3	–0.2	0.0	0.0	0.0
	(1.55)	(1.60)	(2.22)	(0.77)	(1.02)	(1.27)	(0.26)	(0.19)	(0.32)	–	–	–
Sputum examination	38.5	44.6	6.1 **	4.0	5.3	1.3	0.5	0.1	–0.3	0.0	0.0	0.0
	(1.55)	(1.61)	(2.24)	(0.78)	(1.00)	(1.27)	(0.26)	(0.13)	(0.29)	–	–	–
Number of observations	919	944		673	698		663	740		470	464	

Source: IFLS2 and IFLS3.

Standard errors (in parentheses) are robust to clustering at the community level. Significance at 5% (*) and 1% (**) indicated.

TABLE 9.6
Availability of Supplies and Instruments by Type of Facilities
(In percent)

	Puskesmas and *Pustu*			Private Physician and Clinic			Midwife and Village Midwife			Paramedic and Nurse		
	1997	2000	Change	1997	2000	Change	1997	2000	Change	1997	2000	Change
Antiseptic:												
– Alcohol	98.4	98.8	0.5	97.8	99.0	1.2	98.5	99.7	1.2 *	97.5	98.7	1.2
	(0.41)	(0.34)	(0.54)	(0.66)	(0.37)	(0.75)	(0.46)	(0.19)	(0.50)	(0.71)	(0.60)	(0.93)
– Betadine	96.8	98.4	1.6 *	97.2	98.4	1.2	98.5	99.9	1.4 **	96.8	98.7	1.9
	(0.60)	(0.43)	(0.73)	(0.73)	(0.50)	(0.89)	(0.46)	(0.13)	(0.48)	(0.79)	(0.60)	(0.99)
Bandages	99.1	99.3	0.1	97.5	96.0	–1.5	97.7	98.4	0.6	97.2	97.4	0.2
	(0.30)	(0.28)	(0.41)	(0.65)	(0.80)	(1.03)	(0.57)	(0.46)	(0.73)	(0.74)	(0.78)	(1.08)
Giemsa solution	43.6	44.2	0.5	9.0	8.9	–0.1	4.7	2.7	–2.0	1.5	1.1	–0.4
	(1.55)	(1.60)	(2.23)	(1.47)	(1.22)	(1.91)	(0.80)	(0.62)	(1.01)	(0.55)	(0.48)	(0.72)
Benedict solution	40.8	42.1	1.2	8.7	9.7	1.0	3.6	2.3	–1.3	1.7	1.1	–0.6
	(1.55)	(1.59)	(2.22)	(1.39)	(1.18)	(1.82)	(0.74)	(0.61)	(0.96)	(0.66)	(0.48)	(0.81)
Wright solution	25.0	26.5	1.5	6.4	8.0	1.7	2.1	0.7	–1.4 *	0.4	0.4	0.0
	(1.48)	(1.47)	(2.09)	(1.10)	(1.12)	(1.57)	(0.59)	(0.30)	(0.66)	(0.30)	(0.30)	(0.43)
Pregnancy test (strip)	55.4	69.3	13.9 **	32.7	51.1	18.5 **	62.4	85.0	22.6 **	7.6	19.6	12.0 **
	(1.78)	(1.66)	(2.43)	(2.05)	(2.15)	(2.98)	(2.21)	(1.51)	(2.68)	(1.29)	(2.00)	(2.38)
Protein test (strip)	32.2	36.7	4.4 *	9.8	12.6	2.8	5.1	6.6	1.5	0.0	1.1	1.1 *
	(1.54)	(1.65)	(2.26)	(1.38)	(1.36)	(1.94)	(0.89)	(0.96)	(1.31)	–	(0.47)	(0.47)
Glucose test (strip)	31.4	35.8	4.4	12.4	19.2	6.8 **	5.1	4.7	–0.4	0.8	2.2	1.3
	(1.53)	(1.61)	(2.22)	(1.42)	(1.70)	(2.21)	(0.88)	(0.87)	(1.24)	(0.42)	(0.72)	(0.84)
Gloves	95.8	93.0	–2.7 *	93.8	94.0	0.2	97.6	98.8	1.2	76.9	83.6	6.7 *
	(0.72)	(0.88)	(1.14)	(0.95)	(0.89)	(1.30)	(0.58)	(0.44)	(0.73)	(2.10)	(1.86)	(2.80)

continued on next page

TABLE 9.6 – cont'd

	Puskesmas and *Pustu*			Private Physician and Clinic			Midwife and Village Midwife			Paramedic and Nurse		
	1997	2000	Change	1997	2000	Change	1997	2000	Change	1997	2000	Change
Instruments:												
– Minor surgical instruments	42.1	51.3	9.2 **	62.3	69.2	6.9 *	20.6	29.7	9.1 **	28.6	45.7	17.1 **
	(1.70)	(1.84)	(2.51)	(2.09)	(1.98)	(2.88)	(1.66)	(1.85)	(2.49)	(2.20)	(2.50)	(3.33)
– Other surgical instruments	75.5	99.2	23.6 **	98.4	99.0	0.6	98.6	99.9	1.2 **	97.7	98.1	0.4
	(1.66)	(0.30)	(1.69)	(0.52)	(0.37)	(0.64)	(0.44)	(0.13)	(0.46)	(0.68)	(0.70)	(0.98)
– Oxygen tank	15.8	24.4	8.6 **	22.2	25.5	3.3	11.9	12.0	0.1	3.0	1.9	–1.0
	(1.30)	(1.48)	(1.97)	(1.86)	(1.66)	(2.50)	(1.51)	(1.42)	(2.07)	(0.83)	(0.71)	(1.09)
– Incubator	10.9	13.7	2.8	11.7	10.5	–1.2	9.2	10.9	1.8	1.3	1.1	–0.2
	(1.10)	(1.19)	(1.62)	(1.70)	(1.23)	(2.10)	(1.24)	(1.33)	(1.82)	(0.51)	(0.56)	(0.76)
– Microscope	49.6	54.7	5.0 *	12.7	13.9	1.2	2.4	1.1	–1.3	1.1	0.6	–0.4
	(1.48)	(1.56)	(2.15)	(1.49)	(1.38)	(2.03)	(0.62)	(0.38)	(0.72)	(0.47)	(0.37)	(0.60)
– Centrifuge	33.6	40.8	7.2 **	8.4	9.6	1.2	2.6	0.5	–2.0 **	0.2	0.4	0.2
	(1.48)	(1.62)	(2.19)	(1.22)	(1.18)	(1.70)	(0.60)	(0.27)	(0.65)	(0.21)	(0.30)	(0.37)
– Gyneacology table	79.5	78.0	–1.6	20.9	21.8	0.9	42.4	43.2	0.8	3.8	2.2	–1.7
	(1.37)	(1.51)	(2.04)	(1.75)	(1.77)	(2.48)	(2.22)	(2.10)	(3.06)	(0.90)	(0.66)	(1.12)
– Refrigerator/cold storage	69.0	76.1	7.1 **	43.8	46.4	2.6	49.8	54.6	4.8	15.0	15.9	0.9
	(1.58)	(1.45)	(2.14)	(2.34)	(2.14)	(3.17)	(2.25)	(2.31)	(3.23)	(1.71)	(1.94)	(2.58)
Number of observations	919	944		676	698		665	740		472	464	

Source: IFLS2 and IFLS3.

Standard errors (in parentheses) are robust to clustering at the community level. Significance at 5% (*) and 1% (**) indicated.

Service charges by *puskesmas* and private practitioners

Service charges that we examine encompass the cost of basic services, provision of medicines/drugs, and laboratory services. They are shown in Tables 9.7–9.9. All values have been deflated to December 2000 values, so that they may be compared between 1997 and 2000.[3] Because of possible gross outliers we report median prices and the interquartile range instead of standard errors.[4] The basic service charges in government health facilities include registration costs. There is a question, however, of how closely these charges, which are reported by representatives in the facilities, correspond to the actual prices that individuals pay. We do not explore that issue in this report, except for family planning services, in the next chapter.

A major result which comes out of these tables is that charges for virtually all services, drugs and tests are far lower in public than in private health facilities. In turn, prices charged by paramedics, nurses and midwives, are substantially lower than those charged by doctors and clinics. This mostly reflects the large subsidy component to users of the public sector; *Kartu Sehat* users have further subsidies. Thus, there will be much leakage of subsidies to the non-poor unless there is a high degree of self-selection by the poor into public facilities. As we have seen in Chapter 8, there is some self-selection by the poor away from the private sector, but it is far from universal. On the other hand, the price differentials are such to make one wonder why demand for private sector services is as high as it is. Presumably strong quality differentials in favour of private providers is part of the answer. Possible differentials of waiting times, probably shorter when using private practitioners, may be another. It may be too that for some services public providers are used heavily, whereas for other services they are not. Finally, it may also be that actual prices paid are different than those reported by facilities. All these explanations will need to be further explored in future work.

A second major finding that comes out of these tables is that in general, real prices stay remarkably constant over this period. There are some exceptions. Services provided in public health facilities for treatment of tuberculosis (TBC) experienced a decrease in price. The charges for delivery, on the contrary, experienced quite a substantial increase. Real prices at private facilities also changed very little. There were slight declines in prices of some services, and slight increases in some drug prices.

SERVICE DELIVERY AND FEES AT *POSYANDU*

As discussed in Chapter 8, the *posyandu* serve pre-school-aged children plus mothers and pregnant women. The *posyandu* also provides services

TABLE 9.7
Median Charges for the Provision of General Services by Type of Facilities

	Puskesmas and *Pustu*		Private Physician and Clinic		Midwife and Village Midwife		Paramedic and Nurse	
	1997	2000	1997	2000	1997	2000	1997	2000
Check-up + injection + medicine	1,234	1,190	15,455	15,710	8,836	10,272	7,796	10,141
	(990)	(1,128)	(11,285)	(12,668)	(4,029)	(5,047)	(4,363)	(5,124)
	[909]	[931]	[497]	[540]	[562]	[667]	[428]	[434]
Medical treatment of tuberculosis	1,049	311	15,847	16,708	8,480	3,164	7,521	15,319
	(1,131)	(1,041)	(17,275)	(20,636)	(7,493)	(8,050)	(6,738)	(15,069)
	[715]	[727]	[330]	[364]	[54]	[41]	[77]	[76]
Dental exam [a)]	1,368	1,511						
	(1,048)	(1,135)						
	[593]	[648]						
Pre-natal care	1,136	1,041	11,243	10,318	7,586	7,416	6,755	5,239
	(795)	(1,037)	(8,695)	(10,093)	(4,145)	(5,144)	(4,013)	(7,943)
	[861]	[896]	[363]	[388]	[643]	[721]	[80]	[92]
Delivery	38,819	51,411	147,480	154,263	114,387	129,389	89,388	83,229
	(54,120)	(52,181)	(221,944)	(156,502)	(74,988)	(123,610)	(52,615)	(54,513)
	[206]	[286]	[98]	[109]	[593]	[691]	[51]	[57]
Immunization:								
– BCG	913	929	9,775	10,359	5,320	5,186	–	–
	(1,464)	(1,550)	(10,764)	(10,413)	(6,806)	(4,705)		
	[748]	[812]	[204]	[182]	[355]	[376]		

– DPT [b]	929 (1,549) [813]	9,775 (9,551) [214]	10,318 (10,342) [198]	5,252 (6,705) [364]	5,184 (4,696) [389]	–	–	–
– Anti polio [b]	624 (1,537) [814]	9,620 (9,502) [210]	10,122 (11,336) [196]	5,222 (6,723) [359]	5,162 (5,700) [390]	–	–	–
– Measles [b]	929 (1,549) [813]	9,698 (11,768) [208]	10,318 (10,422) [188]	5,385 (6,707) [361]	5,183 (4,684) [379]	–	–	–
– Tetanus Toxoid for pregnant women	1,033 (1,148) [802]	939 (1,563) [845]	10,051 (8,905) [217]	8,653 (10,352) [208]	5,163 (7,007) [496]	5,167 (6,908) [526]	–	–
– Hepatitis B	991 (1,687) [719]	939 (1,565) [796]	21,118 (36,863) [227]	20,967 (43,208) [235]	6,756 (9,606) [295]	5,202 (7,182) [372]	–	–

Source: IFLS2 and IFLS3.

[a] Information on dental exam is collected only at *puskesmas* and *pustu*.

[b] Information on prices for DPT, anti polio and measles immunizations at the public facilities is not collected in IFLS2, 1997.

Dash (–) indicates that the estimates are not reported due to small cell size. Charges are in December 2000 Rupiahs. Differences between 75th and 25th percentiles are in parentheses. Number of observations is in brackets.

TABLE 9.8
Median Charges for the Provision of Drugs by Type of Facilities

	Puskesmas and *Pustu*		Private Physician and Clinic		Midwife and Village Midwife		Paramedic and Nurse	
	1997	2000	1997	2000	1997	2000	1997	2000
Antibiotics:								
– Penicilin	1,044	1,047	12,214	11,378	8,379	7,235	6,152	7,625
	(902)	(1,116)	(11,183)	(10,209)	(5,477)	(5,248)	(5,220)	(5,219)
	[321]	[303]	[153]	[101]	[134]	[126]	[111]	[102]
– Ampicilin	1,033	1,041	12,961	15,451	8,942	8,291	7,758	7,855
	(953)	(1,209)	(9,340)	(10,339)	(4,079)	(5,258)	(4,127)	(5,202)
	[843]	[887]	[408]	[348]	[516]	[574]	[359]	[351]
– Tetraciclin	1,033	1,041	12,173	15,111	7,892	7,890	6,974	7,736
	(913)	(999)	(9,296)	(10,220)	(4,766)	(5,226)	(4,329)	(5,188)
	[858]	[905]	[379]	[318]	[463]	[485]	[388]	[363]
– Chloramphenicol	1,033	1,041	12,878	15,451	8,488	8,316	7,139	8,237
	(950)	(1,009)	(8,953)	(10,374)	(4,335)	(5,229)	(4,489)	(5,213)
	[825]	[904]	[368]	[340]	[365]	[415]	[324]	[308]
– Cotrimoxazole	1,033	1,041	12,690	15,378	8,007	8,003	7,139	7,253
	(938)	(1,085)	(9,182)	(10,058)	(4,702)	(5,212)	(4,424)	(5,189)
	[722]	[892]	[306]	[338]	[297]	[446]	[225]	[289]
– Ciprofloxacin	–	–	19,526	18,396	–	–	–	–
			(17,772)	(10,565)				
			[90]	[188]				
– Acyclovir	–	–	27,153	15,646	–	–	–	–
			(36,552)	(12,017)				
			[27]	[71]				
Analgetic:								
– Antalgin	1,032	1,041	10,610	14,492	7,090	7,221	6,195	5,644
	(890)	(845)	(9,795)	(7,396)	(5,204)	(7,075)	(4,814)	(5,159)
	[856]	[920]	[427]	[365]	[540]	[543]	[404]	[373]

Antipiretic:								
– Acetosal	1,044	1,042	11,880	15,423	7,967	7,643	6,324	5,989
	(1,013)	(663)	(9,359)	(10,540)	(4,725)	(5,182)	(5,678)	(5,270)
	[407]	[402]	[208]	[139]	[129]	[115]	[86]	[65]
– Paracetamol	1,033	1,041	10,717	15,167	7,139	7,416	6,244	5,683
	(890)	(845)	(9,648)	(11,406)	(5,279)	(6,694)	(4,812)	(5,208)
	[856]	[925]	[446]	[415]	[559]	[603]	[412]	[392]
Anti fungi:								
– Nystatin	1,033	1,041	15,220	15,493	8,802	8,358	7,020	8,029
	(886)	(769)	(13,348)	(10,297)	(5,231)	(7,028)	(4,580)	(5,163)
	[323]	[422]	[132]	[113]	[123]	[134]	[55]	[50]
Anti TBC (short-term):								
– INH	826	705	13,912	20,636	7,448	5,709	6,974	7,714
	(1,353)	(1,542)	(14,521)	(18,683)	(7,139)	(8,850)	(6,190)	(8,771)
	[665]	[676]	[216]	[173]	[71]	[38]	[87]	[68]
– Rifampicin	622	518	15,811	15,380	–	–	8,550	8,291
	(1,166)	(1,043)	(19,682)	(21,010)			(6,991)	(10,181)
	[459]	[559]	[178]	[140]			[49]	[44]
– Ethambutol	759	524	14,657	15,254	–	–	6,974	5,808
	(1,390)	(1,048)	(19,207)	(21,848)			(6,206)	(9,816)
	[594]	[607]	[173]	[141]			[53]	[48]
– Streptomicyne	799	311	14,301	15,212	–	–	–	–
	(1,391)	(1,039)	(10,761)	(23,194)				
	[252]	[243]	[70]	[41]				
Anti malaria	983	1,042	10,946	15,111	7,031	5,244	6,235	5,378
	(658)	(1,022)	(9,586)	(8,420)	(5,919)	(6,956)	(5,388)	(5,560)
	[362]	[394]	[140]	[129]	[111]	[136]	[135]	[179]

continued on next page

TABLE 9.8 – cont'd

	Puskesmas and *Pustu*		Private Physician and Clinic		Midwife and Village Midwife		Paramedic and Nurse	
	1997	2000	1997	2000	1997	2000	1997	2000
Skin disease medicines	1,033	1,041	11,833	15,476	7,452	7,314	6,955	7,882
	(938)	(1,014)	(9,391)	(10,064)	(5,970)	(5,212)	(4,804)	(5,196)
	[832]	[905]	[405]	[349]	[416]	[418]	[340]	[298]
Cough medicines	1,033	1,041	11,341	15,189	7,503	7,316	6,611	7,182
	(953)	(947)	(9,474)	(10,207)	(5,269)	(5,308)	(4,200)	(5,148)
	[842]	[916]	[441]	[394]	[499]	[537]	[410]	[371]
Oralit	1,033	1,036	9,698	10,335	5,622	5,000	5,289	5,158
	(946)	(927)	(10,275)	(10,484)	(6,907)	(7,380)	(6,257)	(6,209)
	[824]	[893]	[369]	[268]	[495]	[495]	[350]	[283]
Iron tablets [a]		1,035		10,484		5,378		5,216
		(968)		(8,402)		(7,730)		(7,123)
		[863]		[243]		[522]		[173]
Vitamin A [a]		1,021		10,318		3,106		5,193
		(1,044)		(14,947)		(7,814)		(7,133)
		[558]		[127]		[279]		[63]

Source: IFLS2 and IFLS3.

[a] Information on prices for iron tables and vitamin A is not collected in IFLS2, 1997.

Dash (–) indicates that the estimates are not reported due to small cell size. Charges are in December 2000 Rupiahs. Differences between 75th and 25th percentiles are in parentheses. Number of observations is in brackets.

TABLE 9.9
Median Charges for the Provision of Services at the Laboratory by Type of Facilities

	Puskesmas and *Pustu*		Private Physician and Clinic		Midwife and Village Midwife	
	1997	**2000**	**1997**	**2000**	**1997**	**2000**
Haemoglobin test	1,044 (980) [613]	1,042 (1,442) [618]	5,753 (7,158) [73]	5,183 (7,107) [110]	3,259 (5,811) [178]	3,070 (5,209) [192]
Leukocyte calculation	1,033 (1,159) [271]	1,041 (1,563) [291]	6,804 (6,361) [37]	5,159 (7,644) [48]	–	–
Blood type calculation	1,044 (1,063) [233]	1,046 (1,546) [272]	7,496 (7,097) [35]	5,159 (5,703) [39]	–	–
Erythrocyte calculation	1,033 (1,101) [236]	1,041 (1,551) [270]	7,070 (6,361) [34]	5,171 (6,388) [40]	–	–
Urinanalysis	1,139 (1,310) [321]	1,549 (2,026) [374]	9,936 (11,754) [51]	10,338 (9,526) [73]	9,830 (4,903) [36]	10,365 (3,221) [26]
Pregnancy test	5,205 (8,220) [546]	7,369 (7,844) [691]	13,827 (8,413) [170]	10,484 (5,446) [316]	10,719 (4,417) [328]	10,350 (2,608) [580]
Faeces examination	1,056 (1,095) [303]	1,066 (1,451) [311]	10,761 (8,919) [24]	10,208 (10,454) [41]	–	–
Sputum examination	1,030 (1,307) [345]	1,026 (2,066) [415]	10,761 (8,861) [25]	10,263 (10,278) [36]	–	–

Source: IFLS2 and IFLS3.
Median charges by paramedic and nurse are not reported due to small cell size. Dash (–) indicates that the estimates are not reported due to small cell size. Charges are in December 2000 Rupiah. Differences between 75th and 25th percentiles are in parentheses. Number of observations is in brackets.

for family planning, in addition to the services provided to children and mothers. Family planning services will be discussed in Chapter 11. Some details of service provision are shown in Table 9.10.

Over the three-year period, there is evidence of a change in service provision at *posyandus*. The provision of almost all services experienced decreases, many of them statistically significant. The provision of child monitoring services suffered the highest decline of 14%, from 50% to 36% from 1997 to 2000. Other *posyandu* services that increased include the provision of supplementary food (a 7% increase from 88% in 1997) and maternal and child health services (to 46% in 2000).

In carrying out its service delivery, *posyandu* use a variety of supplies and instruments, which include: the KMS card to provide a record of

TABLE 9.10
Provision of Services by *Posyandu*

	1997	2000	Change
Provision of supplementary food	87.8	94.9	7.1 **
	(1.45)	(0.94)	(1.73)
Provision of oralit	92.4	83.0	–9.4 **
	(1.17)	(1.68)	(2.05)
Provision of iron and vitamin supplement	75.4	72.3	–3.0
	(2.00)	(2.03)	(2.85)
Treatment of patients	30.5	27.0	–3.4
	(2.26)	(2.11)	(3.10)
Immunization service	90.3	87.1	–3.2
	(1.45)	(1.76)	(2.28)
Pregnancy examination	61.3	63.0	1.7
	(2.37)	(2.41)	(3.38)
Child growth monitoring	49.8	35.6	–14.1 **
	(2.28)	(2.09)	(3.09)
Maternal and child health	37.3	45.8	8.5 **
	(2.26)	(2.17)	(3.13)
Number of observations	617	629	

Source: IFLS2 and IFLS3.

Standard errors (in parentheses) are robust to clustering at the community level. Significance at 5% (*) and 1% (**) indicated.

immunizations, medicines such as Oralit, iron tablets, and Vitamin A, contraceptives, books, and other items. Table 9.11 provides information on the supplies and instruments available at *posyandus*. It is apparent that all manners of facilities and tools available at *posyandus* suffered large and statistically significant decreases. Supplies pertaining to KMS cards declined from 95% to 71%. A large proportion of drugs also experienced significant declines. Oralit prevalence declined from 73% to 46% and Vitamin A availability from 81% to 54%. Demonstration tools/books were available in 44% of *posyandu* in 1997, but in only 32% in 2000.

Charges for services by *posyandu* are reported in Table 9.12. We first examine the fraction of *posyandu* that report any charge for the particular service. For those that do charge, we report the median charge. Between 1997 and 2000 there has been a decline in the proportion of *posyandu* that charge for treatment of patients, as well as for some other services. Median prices in those *posyandu* that charge have tended not to change much.

In contrast to what we see for *puskesmas* and private practitioners, service availability and service quality at *posyandus* seems to have declined over this period, consistent with the large decline in *posyandu* usage. However, this decline in availability may be following the decline in *posyandu* usage, so that one has to be somewhat careful in interpreting these results.

SUMMARY

Between 1997 and 2000 there have been some small improvements in the quality of services at *puskesmas*, for instance in the availability of vaccines, antibiotics, and some equipment. Health service prices at *puskesmas* and *pustu* remain quite low compared to the private sector. Among private sector providers, few changes have been observed. There has been a decline in the fraction of providers who supply vaccines, but among those that do, fewer stock outages are observed in 2000 compared to 1997. Stock outages have also declined in both private and public sectors for drug supply, although the welfare interpretation of that fact is unclear. In general, the provision of tests and services by *puskesmas* is higher than by private providers.

Posyandu quality has dropped considerably, which is consistent with the large decline in use. This is perhaps alarming since there does exist a *posyandu* revitalization programme, under which funds are available from the central government.

TABLE 9.11
Availability of Supplies and Instruments by *Posyandu*
(In percent)

	1997	2000	Change
Cards:			
– KMS cards	94.7	71.1	–23.6 **
	(0.93)	(1.95)	(2.16)
– Pregnant mother cards	53.3	32.8	–20.6 **
	(2.36)	(2.09)	(3.15)
Drugs:			
– Oralit	83.5	59.8	–23.7 **
	(1.61)	(2.18)	(2.71)
– Iron tablets	65.8	43.4	–22.4 **
	(2.17)	(2.26)	(3.14)
– Vitamin A	80.7	53.6	–27.1 **
	(1.75)	(2.20)	(2.81)
– Other drugs	9.6	13.2	3.6
	(1.24)	(1.51)	(1.96)
Contraceptives:			
– Oral contraceptives	72.9	36.4	–36.5 **
	(2.09)	(2.16)	(3.00)
– Condom	28.0	16.1	–12.0 **
	(2.24)	(1.65)	(2.78)
Books and other instruments:			
– Demonstration tools/books	43.6	32.1	–11.5 **
	(2.20)	(1.95)	(2.94)
– Instruction books for the BKB program	57.1	52.1	–4.9
	(2.22)	(2.18)	(3.12)
– Children's toys	32.1	24.0	–8.1 **
	(2.09)	(1.87)	(2.81)
– Baby scales	95.5	95.4	–0.1
	(0.94)	(0.89)	(1.29)
– Height measuring devices	26.4	27.0	0.6
	(1.99)	(1.92)	(2.76)
Number of observations	617	629	

Source: IFLS2 and IFLS3.
Standard errors (in parentheses) are robust to clustering at the community level. Significance at 5% (*) and 1% (**) indicated.

TABLE 9.12
Median Charges for the Provision of Services by *Posyandu*

	Any charge (percent)		Median charges	
	1997	2000	1997	2000
Provision of supplementary food [a)]		15.6		314
		[553]		(313)
				[86]
Provision of oralit [a)]		4.2		–
		[473]		
Provision of iron and vitamin supplement	9.4	7.6	950	525
	[416]	[421]	(700)	(524)
			[39]	[32]
Treatment of patients	65.7	49.7	1,136	1,053
	[172]	[157]	(1,182)	(1,439)
			[113]	[78]
Immunization service [a)]		28.6		1,040
		[528]		(943)
				[151]
Pregnancy examination	22.6	13.9	1,126	1,049
	[359]	[380]	(1,103)	(1,433)
			[81]	[53]
Maternal and child health [a)]		10.0		1,497
		[269]		(1,435)
				[27]

Source: IFLS2 and IFLS3.
[a)] Information on charges for these services is not collected in IFLS2, 1997.
Dash (–) indicates that the estimates are not reported due to small cell size. Charges are in December 2000 Rupiah. Differences between 75th and 25th percentiles are in parentheses. Number of observation is in brackets.

Notes

1. For the tables using facility and other community information, we do not use facility weights as we have not yet calculated those.
2. A physical exam was made of the room where drugs were kept.
3. We used the same constructed Tornquist-based CPI for each of 34 cities represented in the IFLS data and for each rural province area.
4. The interquartile range is the difference between the 75th and the 25th percentiles.

10

Family Planning

TRENDS AND PATTERNS IN CONTRACEPTIVE USE

Indonesia's family planning programme before the crisis has long been associated with success, based on a dramatic increase of current contraceptive users in the period 1976–97. Based on the 1976 Indonesia Fertility Survey, only 26% of currently married women use contraceptives. Two decades later, in 1997, this figure more than doubled to 57% (CBS et al. 1998). This change has had a significant impact on the declining fertility rate in Indonesia during this period.

Several people have projected that the economic crisis in Indonesia would affect the performance of the family planning programme. The 1997 and 2000 IFLS data show that the level of contraceptive use stayed roughly constant (Table 10.1). There was a very small drop in the prevalence rate of current use from 58% to 56%, similar to what is found in the 1997 and 2000 SUSENAS, but the difference in IFLS is not statistically significant. Use of modern methods shows essentially the same result because use of traditional methods is so little, only 2% of currently married women 15–49 in 2000. This relative constancy of use is also what was found between 1997 and 1998, at the height of the crisis, by Frankenberg et al. (1999). The result is different from the worried projections made by so many people that the economic crisis would decrease the prevalence substantially. On the other hand, as with other outcomes, it is entirely possible that had the crisis not occurred that utilization would have continued to rise, as in the past.

There is little change in the composition of contraceptive use by type in the period 1997–2000, as shown in Table 10.1. The most commonly used contraceptives in 1997 were injection (24%), the pill (16%), IUD (8%), implants (4%), and female sterilization (4%). In 2000, there was a small decline in pill use, significant at 10%, but little change in use of other forms. The small decrease in pill use may be due to the decline in availability

TABLE 10.1
Use of Contraceptives by Currently Married Women Aged 15–49, by Age Group
(In percent)

	All age groups			15–19 years			20–24 years			25–34 years			35–49 years		
	1997	2000	Change	1997	2000	Change	1997	2000	Change	1997	2000	Change	1997	2000	Change
Ever used any method	76.4	76.9	0.5	60.7	53.8	–7.0	74.8	72.0	–2.9	81.4	82.5	1.1	73.7	76.4	2.7
	(1.17)	(0.82)	(1.43)	(4.37)	(3.13)	(5.37)	(2.26)	(1.57)	(2.75)	(1.41)	(1.03)	(1.74)	(1.36)	(1.17)	(1.79)
Currently using any method	57.5	56.4	–1.1	48.3	43.1	–5.2	58.6	56.7	–1.8	62.8	60.6	–2.2	52.9	54.0	1.1
	(1.17)	(0.87)	(1.45)	(4.55)	(3.00)	(5.45)	(2.61)	(1.70)	(3.11)	(1.60)	(1.15)	(1.97)	(1.45)	(1.35)	(1.98)
Currently using modern methods:	56.3	54.7	–1.5	47.6	42.0	–5.6	58.2	56.4	–1.8	61.8	59.1	–2.6	51.1	51.6	0.5
	(1.16)	(0.87)	(1.45)	(4.38)	(3.02)	(5.32)	(2.50)	(1.71)	(3.12)	(1.58)	(1.17)	(1.96)	(1.46)	(1.35)	(1.98)
– pill	15.7	13.8	–1.9	14.1	13.7	–0.3	16.0	14.1	–1.8	17.4	14.5	–2.9	14.0	13.0	–1.0
	(0.83)	(0.69)	(1.08)	(2.97)	(2.35)	(3.79)	(1.89)	(1.39)	(2.34)	(1.19)	(0.93)	(1.51)	(0.98)	(0.90)	(1.33)
– injection	24.4	24.3	–0.1	31.4	22.9	–8.5 *	34.4	34.6	0.3	30.1	30.5	0.5	14.5	14.8	0.3
	(0.97)	(0.79)	(1.25)	(3.50)	(2.02)	(4.04)	(2.55)	(1.75)	(3.09)	(1.28)	(1.24)	(1.79)	(1.02)	(0.85)	(1.33)
– condom	0.5	0.9	0.4 *	0.0	0.0	0.0	0.0	0.0	0.0	0.3	1.0	0.8 **	0.9	1.1	0.2
	(0.11)	(0.14)	(0.18)	–	–	–	–	–	–	(0.12)	(0.22)	(0.25)	(0.21)	(0.25)	(0.33)
– IUD	7.6	7.2	–0.4	0.4	1.7	1.3	3.0	3.3	0.2	7.2	6.0	–1.1	10.3	10.4	0.1
	(0.61)	(0.52)	(0.80)	(0.27)	(0.69)	(0.74)	(0.77)	(0.59)	(0.97)	(0.73)	(0.54)	(0.91)	(0.89)	(0.90)	(1.27)
– implant	4.2	4.6	0.5	1.7	3.7	1.9	4.8	4.1	–0.8	5.0	5.5	0.5	3.4	4.1	0.8
	(0.48)	(0.39)	(0.62)	(0.97)	(0.99)	(1.39)	(1.03)	(0.66)	(1.22)	(0.75)	(0.59)	(0.95)	(0.55)	(0.50)	(0.74)
– female sterilization	3.7	3.6	–0.1	0.0	0.0	0.0	0.0	0.2	0.2	1.7	1.4	–0.3	7.4	7.5	0.1
	(0.34)	(0.30)	(0.46)	–	–	–	–	(0.13)	(0.13)	(0.35)	(0.28)	(0.45)	(0.65)	(0.62)	(0.90)

continued onnext page

TABLE 10.1 – cont'd

	All age groups			15–19 years			20–24 years			25–34 years			35–49 years		
	1997	2000	Change	1997	2000	Change	1997	2000	Change	1997	2000	Change	1997	2000	Change
– male sterilization	0.2	0.3	0.1	0.0	0.0	0.0	0.0	0.0	0.0	0.1	0.1	0.0	0.5	0.6	0.1
	(0.08)	(0.08)	(0.11)	–	–	–	–	–	–	(0.07)	(0.07)	(0.10)	(0.18)	(0.17)	(0.25)
– intra vaginal (diaphragm, foam, jelly)	0.1	0.0	0.0	0.0	0.0	0.0	0.0	0.1	0.1	0.0	0.0	0.0	0.2	0.0	–0.1
	(0.04)	(0.03)	(0.05)	–	–	–	–	(0.14)	(0.14)	(0.03)	(0.02)	(0.04)	(0.09)	(0.04)	(0.10)
Currently using traditional methods	1.2	1.6	0.4	0.0	0.7	0.7	0.4	0.3	0.0	1.0	1.4	0.4	1.7	2.4	0.6
	(0.19)	(0.18)	(0.27)	–	(0.43)	(0.43)	(0.22)	(0.16)	(0.27)	(0.27)	(0.24)	(0.37)	(0.30)	(0.33)	(0.45)
Number of observations	5,260	6,913		223	403		609	1,119		2,114	2,600		2,314	2,791	

Source: IFLS2 and IFLS3.

Estimates were weighted using individual sampling weights. Standard errors (in parentheses) are robust to clustering at the community level. Significance at 5% (*) and 1% (**) indicated.

of the pill in public service centres. After the crisis struck the country in late 1997, the stock of pills usually available in community health centres, *puskesmas* and *posyandu*, declined (see Chapter 11).

Across age groups, there was a relatively large decline in any use among teens 15–19, mainly in the use of injections. Levels of contraceptive use increase with age, until women become older, typically 25–34, and then it declines. This age pattern is comparable to what is found in other surveys such as the DHS. The composition of contraceptive use varies across age groups. Injection is the most popular contraceptive for all age groups with the exception of the age group 35–49, and the pill is the second most commonly used contraceptive across age groups.

Table 10.2 shows usage rates among currently married women aged 15–49 by area of residence. In general, prevalence in urban areas is higher than that in rural areas and in Java/Bali than in the other provinces. In 2000, about 59% of urban women are using a method compared to 54% of rural women. There is a small 3% decline in prevalence among urban women and no change among rural women, from 1997 to 2000.

The composition of contraceptive use among types is almost the same between urban and rural areas. Injection, followed by the pill, are the most extensively used methods. However IUD use is higher among urban women, while implants are higher in rural areas. Over this crisis period, pill use declined, though not significantly, in both urban and rural areas. At the same time, injection use decreased in urban and increased in rural areas.

Between Java–Bali and other regions, composition switched between 1997 and 2000. Injection was the most preferred method in Java–Bali both in 1997 and 2000, but in other regions the most prevalent method was the pill in 1997, switching to injection by 2000. These figures indicate that in terms of composition, other regions are less stable than Java–Bali.

Contraceptive use rises with the respondents' level of education and levels off (or decreases slightly) for those with nine years of schooling and over (Table 10.3). This finding is common around the world, and in other Indonesian surveys such as the 1997 DHS. Changes in prevalence between 1997 and 2000 are similar across education groups with little change in composition between 1997 and 2000.

Table 10.4 displays the results of a linear probability model of current contraceptive use for any method — the pill, injection and IUD. Education does have a significantly positive impact on current use. For any method, a woman with some primary schooling is 16% more likely to be a user and someone with 9–11 years of schooling is 21% more likely to use a contraceptive. Women with senior secondary school education or more

TABLE 10.2
Use of Contraceptives by Currently Married Women Aged 15–49, by Regions (In percent)

	Urban			Rural			Java–Bali			Other Regions		
	1997	2000	Change	1997	2000	Change	1997	2000	Change	1997	2000	Change
Ever used any method	80.8	79.9	–0.9	73.9	74.8	0.9	78.2	78.4	0.2	70.8	72.4	1.6
	(1.05)	(0.83)	(1.34)	(1.70)	(1.26)	(2.12)	(1.41)	(0.96)	(1.71)	(1.89)	(1.54)	(2.44)
Currently using any method	62.4	59.1	–3.3 *	54.7	54.5	–0.2	59.1	57.6	–1.5	52.9	52.9	0.0
	(1.09)	(1.10)	(1.54)	(1.69)	(1.24)	(2.10)	(1.43)	(1.04)	(1.76)	(1.80)	(1.49)	(2.34)
Currently using modern methods:	60.4	56.9	–3.5 *	53.9	53.2	–0.7	57.6	56.1	–1.5	52.3	50.6	–1.7
	(1.14)	(1.11)	(1.59)	(1.67)	(1.25)	(2.09)	(1.41)	(1.04)	(1.75)	(1.81)	(1.48)	(2.34)
– pill	16.3	14.9	–1.4	15.4	13.0	–2.3	14.4	13.4	–0.9	19.7	14.9	–4.8 **
	(1.01)	(0.98)	(1.41)	(1.16)	(0.95)	(1.50)	(0.98)	(0.85)	(1.30)	(1.43)	(1.09)	(1.80)
– injection	24.2	22.3	–1.9	24.5	25.7	1.2	26.2	25.5	–0.7	19.0	20.5	1.6
	(1.29)	(1.13)	(1.71)	(1.33)	(1.06)	(1.70)	(1.19)	(0.95)	(1.52)	(1.34)	(1.22)	(1.82)
– condom	1.0	1.6	0.6	0.2	0.3	0.1	0.5	1.0	0.5 *	0.4	0.5	0.1
	(0.22)	(0.29)	(0.36)	(0.10)	(0.11)	(0.15)	(0.14)	(0.18)	(0.22)	(0.13)	(0.14)	(0.19)
– IUD	11.6	10.6	–1.0	5.3	4.8	–0.5	8.5	8.3	–0.2	4.5	3.8	–0.7
	(1.04)	(0.89)	(1.37)	(0.69)	(0.54)	(0.87)	(0.79)	(0.66)	(1.03)	(0.68)	(0.57)	(0.89)
– implant	2.0	2.6	0.6	5.4	6.2	0.8	3.8	3.8	0.0	5.3	7.3	2.1
	(0.36)	(0.36)	(0.51)	(0.71)	(0.59)	(0.92)	(0.55)	(0.42)	(0.69)	(1.03)	(0.91)	(1.38)
– female sterilization	5.0	4.6	–0.4	2.9	2.9	0.0	3.8	3.7	–0.1	3.4	3.4	0.0
	(0.51)	(0.44)	(0.67)	(0.44)	(0.40)	(0.59)	(0.41)	(0.35)	(0.54)	(0.57)	(0.56)	(0.80)
– male sterilization	0.2	0.3	0.1	0.2	0.3	0.0	0.3	0.4	0.1	0.0	0.0	0.0
	(0.10)	(0.10)	(0.14)	(0.11)	(0.11)	(0.15)	(0.10)	(0.10)	(0.14)	–	–	–
– intra vaginal (diaphragm, foam, jelly)	0.1	0.0	–0.1	0.1	0.1	0.0	0.1	0.0	–0.1	0.0	0.1	0.1
	(0.05)	(0.02)	(0.05)	(0.05)	(0.05)	(0.07)	(0.05)	(0.02)	(0.06)	(0.03)	(0.09)	(0.09)
Currently using traditional methods	2.0	2.2	0.2	0.7	1.2	0.5	1.4	1.4	0.0	0.5	2.2	1.7 **
	(0.31)	(0.28)	(0.42)	(0.24)	(0.24)	(0.34)	(0.25)	(0.22)	(0.33)	(0.14)	(0.33)	(0.36)
Number of observations	2,355	3,153		2,905	3,760		3,395	4,412		1,865	2,501	

Source: IFLS2 and IFLS3.

Estimates were weighted using individual sampling weights. Standard errors (in parentheses) are robust to clustering at the community level. Significance at 5% (*) and 1% (**) indicated.

TABLE 10.3
Use of Contraceptives by Currently Married Women Aged 15–49, by Years of Schooling
(In percent)

	No Schooling			1–5 years			6–8 years			9+ years		
	1997	2000	Change	1997	2000	Change	1997	2000	Change	1997	2000	Change
Ever used any method	59.6	59.5	–0.1	76.3	77.2	0.9	80.4	80.4	0.0	80.5	78.3	–2.3
	(3.86)	(3.51)	(5.22)	(1.53)	(1.38)	(2.06)	(1.36)	(1.08)	(1.74)	(1.22)	(0.96)	(1.55)
Currently using any method	41.6	38.6	–3.0	56.8	54.0	–2.8	61.9	60.3	–1.6	61.2	59.1	–2.1
	(3.05)	(2.87)	(4.19)	(1.79)	(1.82)	(2.56)	(1.59)	(1.33)	(2.07)	(1.51)	(1.12)	(1.88)
Currently using modern methods:	40.7	37.7	–3.0	56.4	52.6	–3.8	61.0	58.9	–2.1	58.7	56.9	–1.8
	(3.02)	(2.84)	(4.14)	(1.79)	(1.81)	(2.55)	(1.60)	(1.34)	(2.09)	(1.49)	(1.16)	(1.89)
– pill	11.9	9.5	–2.5	18.6	15.5	–3.1	16.9	14.8	–2.1	13.7	13.0	–0.6
	(1.93)	(1.88)	(2.70)	(1.57)	(1.37)	(2.08)	(1.20)	(0.99)	(1.56)	(0.98)	(0.88)	(1.32)
– injection	15.8	14.8	–1.0	21.6	20.2	–1.5	29.7	28.7	–1.0	24.8	25.2	0.3
	(2.12)	(1.42)	(2.55)	(1.58)	(1.55)	(2.21)	(1.62)	(1.30)	(2.07)	(1.29)	(1.07)	(1.68)
– condom	0.0	0.0	0.0	0.2	0.3	0.1	0.1	0.2	0.1	1.4	2.0	0.6 **
	–	–	–	(0.11)	(0.15)	(0.18)	(0.09)	(0.11)	(0.14)	(0.30)	(0.32)	(0.43)
–IUD	4.6	5.1	0.5	5.6	4.8	–0.7	6.2	5.8	–0.4	12.4	10.4	–2.0
	(1.08)	(1.04)	(1.50)	(0.85)	(0.78)	(1.16)	(0.77)	(0.68)	(1.03)	(1.05)	(0.84)	(1.34)
– implant	5.4	5.0	–0.4	6.2	6.8	0.6	3.7	5.4	1.8 *	2.5	2.7	0.2
	(1.12)	(1.13)	(1.58)	(0.99)	(0.80)	(1.28)	(0.60)	(0.64)	(0.88)	(0.51)	(0.37)	(0.63)
– female sterilization	2.9	2.8	–0.1	4.1	4.6	0.5	4.0	3.6	–0.4	3.5	3.4	–0.1
	(0.76)	(0.84)	(1.13)	(0.69)	(0.64)	(0.94)	(0.54)	(0.48)	(0.72)	(0.51)	(0.42)	(0.66)
– male sterilization	0.1	0.5	0.4	0.2	0.3	0.1	0.3	0.4	0.0	0.2	0.2	0.0
	(0.08)	(0.34)	(0.35)	(0.12)	(0.15)	(0.19)	(0.15)	(0.14)	(0.21)	(0.13)	(0.09)	(0.15)
– intra vaginal (diaphragm, foam, jelly)	0.0	0.0	0.0	0.0	0.0	0.0	0.1	0.1	0.0	0.2	0.0	–0.1
	–	–	–	–	(0.05)	(0.05)	(0.07)	(0.04)	(0.08)	(0.10)	(0.05)	(0.11)
Currently using traditional methods	0.9	0.9	0.0	0.3	1.4	1.1 **	0.9	1.4	0.5	2.4	2.1	–0.3
	(0.33)	(0.36)	(0.49)	(0.15)	(0.36)	(0.39)	(0.23)	(0.29)	(0.37)	(0.45)	(0.28)	(0.53)
Number of observations	775	662		1,211	1,465		1,667	2,077		1,591	2,648	

Source: IFLS2 and IFLS3.
Estimates were weighted using individual sampling weights. Standard errors (in parentheses) are robust to clustering at the community level. Significance at 5% (*) and 1% (**) indicated.

TABLE 10.4
Use of Contraceptives by Currently Married Women Aged 15–49 Years: Linear Probability Models of the Use of Contraceptives

	Use any method		Pill		Injection		IUD	
	1997	Change in 2000	1997	Change in 2000	1997	Change in 2000	1997	Change in 2000
Age: 20–24 years	0.045	0.023	0.012	–0.004	0.024	0.075	–0.014	0.005
	(1.52)	(0.62)	(0.51)	(0.14)	(0.75)	(1.89)	(1.60)	(0.43)
25–34 years	0.174**	0.058	0.044	–0.023	–0.003	0.097**	0.026**	–0.012
	(5.57)	(1.48)	(1.87)	(0.75)	(0.12)	(2.75)	(3.16)	(1.05)
35–49 years	0.124**	0.089*	0.009	–0.003	–0.146**	0.100**	0.067**	0.007
	(3.70)	(2.09)	(0.39)	(0.08)	(4.74)	(2.66)	(6.47)	(0.45)
Education ($\times 10^{-2}$): 1–5 years	0.159**	0.020	0.054*	0.001	0.046	–0.003	0.018	–0.013
	(4.97)	(0.42)	(2.52)	(0.05)	(1.91)	(0.09)	(1.79)	(0.88)
6–8 years	0.208**	0.025	0.048*	0.003	0.100**	–0.008	0.029*	–0.001
	(6.25)	(0.50)	(2.17)	(0.09)	(3.98)	(0.24)	(2.47)	(0.07)
9–11 years	0.209**	0.035	0.014	0.047	0.080**	0.016	0.030*	0.001
	(5.94)	(0.66)	(0.57)	(1.33)	(3.07)	(0.46)	(2.15)	(0.05)
12+ years	0.170**	0.025	0.000	0.014	0.045	0.022	0.107**	–0.027
	(4.94)	(0.47)	(0.00)	(0.42)	(1.60)	(0.61)	(5.94)	(1.15)
log *pce* ($\times 10^{-2}$): 0–log Rp 150,000	9.807*	–4.530	–0.664	2.965	4.337	4.348	–1.234	0.286
	(2.10)	(0.85)	(0.24)	(0.84)	(1.53)	(1.21)	(1.05)	(0.17)
> log Rp 150,000	–1.035	–4.954**	–0.052	–2.462	–4.441**	–3.498*	1.235	0.131
	(0.87)	(2.92)	(0.05)	(1.82)	(3.79)	(2.19)	(1.69)	(0.13)
Rural	–0.046*	0.016	–0.024	–0.007	–0.002	0.036	–0.035**	0.006
	(2.55)	(0.71)	(1.52)	(0.31)	(0.12)	(1.41)	(3.00)	(0.38)
North Sumatra	–0.248**	0.051	–0.009	–0.021	–0.127**	–0.022	–0.019	0.007
	(5.20)	(0.81)	(0.31)	(0.51)	(3.76)	(0.48)	(0.68)	(0.19)
West Sumatra	–0.028	–0.001	–0.027	–0.012	0.014	–0.034	0.038	–0.001
	(0.69)	(0.02)	(0.96)	(0.32)	(0.41)	(0.71)	(1.39)	(0.02)
South Sumatra	0.004	0.001	0.074*	–0.059	–0.090*	0.028	–0.045*	0.013
	(0.09)	(0.01)	(2.14)	(1.31)	(2.00)	(0.48)	(2.24)	(0.50)

Lampung	0.066	–0.079	0.069*	–0.057	–0.013	–0.029	0.007	–0.028
	(1.64)	(1.34)	(2.05)	(1.16)	(0.39)	(0.46)	(0.25)	(0.85)
West Java	0.048	–0.032	0.031	–0.033	0.028	–0.035	0.010	0.013
	(1.81)	(0.89)	(1.23)	(0.95)	(0.97)	(0.87)	(0.49)	(0.44)
Central Java	0.020	–0.037	–0.001	–0.035	–0.019	0.019	0.011	–0.008
	(0.62)	(0.85)	(0.02)	(0.99)	(0.56)	(0.42)	(0.46)	(0.29)
Yogyakarta	–0.002	–0.049	–0.035	–0.024	–0.087*	–0.002	0.131**	–0.008
	(0.07)	(1.06)	(1.19)	(0.65)	(2.32)	(0.04)	(3.74)	(0.19)
East Java	0.001	–0.025	0.007	0.014	–0.021	–0.030	0.004	0.008
	(0.03)	(0.59)	(0.27)	(0.37)	(0.68)	(0.71)	(0.16)	(0.25)
Bali	0.104**	–0.085	–0.098**	–0.002	–0.079*	–0.000	0.289**	–0.057
	(2.63)	(1.58)	(3.25)	(0.05)	(2.12)	(0.01)	(5.12)	(0.82)
West Nusa Tenggara	–0.020	–0.007	–0.012	–0.035	–0.039	–0.029	–0.000	0.010
	(0.54)	(0.14)	(0.33)	(0.81)	(0.94)	(0.50)	(0.01)	(0.29)
South Kalimantan	0.091**	–0.034	0.300**	–0.164**	–0.154**	0.083	–0.027	0.007
	(2.85)	(0.79)	(7.63)	-3.03	(3.91)	(1.49)	(1.18)	(0.22)
South Sulawesi	–0.152**	–0.061	0.051	–0.024	–0.109**	–0.031	–0.043*	0.009
	(3.11)	(0.86)	(1.41)	(0.49)	(3.04)	(0.58)	(2.04)	(0.31)
Constant	–1.089	–0.146	0.060	–0.133	–1.130*	–0.064	0.313	–0.028
	(1.68)	(0.83)	(0.15)	(1.44)	(2.58)	(0.46)	(1.54)	(0.52)
F-test (p-values)								
Interaction variables	0.324		0.087		0.367		0.768	
Education variables	0.000		0.000		0.000		0.000	
Expenditure variables	0.000		0.114		0.000		0.161	
Number of observations	12,173		12,173		12,173		12,173	
R-squared	0.07		0.03		0.06		0.07	

Source: IFLS2 and IFLS3.

Dummy variable for missing education and dummy variable for missing per capita expenditure are included in the regressions but not reported in the table. The omitted category for age is 15–29 years, for education is no schooling, and for province is Jakarta. Estimates were weighted using individual sampling weights. Standard errors are robust to clustering at the community level and to heteroscedasticity. Absolute t-statistics are in parentheses with significance at 5% (*) and 1% (**) indicated.

have a slightly lower probability of using any contraceptive than women who have completed junior secondary school, though still much higher than women with no schooling. Higher *pce* is associated with a higher likelihood of use of any method for low income women, however the impact flattens out and becomes slightly negative compared to the apex, for women from higher income households. Women in rural areas are slightly less likely to use contraceptives, controlling for other factors. Also, women in North Sumatra and South Sulawesi are much less likely to be users compared to women in Jakarta, while women in Bali and South Kalimantan are more likely to be users.

Across types of contraception the results vary in interesting ways. The impact of education has a very non-linear pattern. Incomplete primary schooling has its biggest impact on pill use, while completed primary and junior secondary schooling raises use of injections most. Completed senior secondary schooling seems to tilt women towards IUD. Higher *pce* among the non-poor is associated with a higher likelihood of using IUD and lower probabilities of using injection or pills. Across age groups, it is the older women who are more likely to currently use IUD and less likely to use injection.

SOURCES OF CONTRACEPTIVE SUPPLIES

One major change that has taken place since 1997 is a switch in the source of supplies for contraceptives. These results are shown in Table 10.5, which displays data on source of supply from individuals, for pills and injection. There are large and statistically significant declines from 1997 to 2000 in the fraction of both pill and injection users who obtained their supplies in public facilities, especially from *puskesmas* and *posyandu*. Pill users have switched in part to pharmacies and injection users to private midwives, and to a lesser extent, private doctors and clinics, as their source. This has occurred in both urban and rural areas (Appendix Table 10.1a), although in rural areas pharmacies are a less important source for pills than in urban areas, community services are more prevalent in rural areas. It has also occurred both in Java–Bali and in outside provinces (Appendix Table 10.1b), although there are some interesting differences. Private midwives are a more important source of injections in Java and Bali, whereas village midwives serve this role in other provinces. This source switching is a potentially important development, yet, as we have seen, this has occurred without a major change in overall prevalence.

TABLE 10.5
Source of Contraceptive Supplies Among Pill and Injection Users Currently Married Women Aged 15–49

	Pills			Injection		
	1997	2000	Change	1997	2000	Change
Public and private hospitals	1.9	0.9	–1.0	1.0	1.6	0.6
	(0.55)	(0.35)	(0.65)	(0.27)	(0.37)	(0.45)
Puskesmas and *Pustu*	25.8	15.8	–10.0 **	29.9	15.7	–14.2 **
	(2.21)	(1.71)	(2.80)	(2.25)	(1.54)	(2.73)
Private physician and clinic	3.1	3.2	0.2	2.8	9.8	7.0 **
	(0.71)	(0.65)	(0.96)	(0.54)	(1.03)	(1.16)
Midwife	25.9	23.9	–2.0	25.5	57.0	31.5 **
	(2.20)	(2.00)	(2.97)	(1.91)	(2.09)	(2.83)
Village midwife	3.1	3.9	0.8	1.3	6.3	5.0 **
	(0.93)	(0.80)	(1.23)	(0.36)	(0.93)	(1.00)
Paramedic and nurse	1.2	1.7	0.5	0.9	4.6	3.7 **
	(0.43)	(0.51)	(0.66)	(0.32)	(0.70)	(0.76)
Posyandu	17.4	11.0	–6.4 *	14.9	0.9	–13.9 **
	(2.09)	(1.35)	(2.49)	(1.21)	(0.34)	(1.29)
Community services (PLKB, fieldworker, etc) [a]	11.3	10.1	–1.2	9.4	0.5	–8.9 **
	(1.68)	(1.64)	(2.35)	(1.45)	(0.18)	(1.46)
Pharmacy	7.0	21.5	14.5 **	2.7	0.0	–2.7 **
	(1.09)	(1.93)	(2.22)	(0.53)	–	(0.53)
Number of observations	823	889		1,185	1,568	

Source: IFLS2 and IFLS3.

[a] PLKB does not provide injections.

Estimates were weighted using individual sampling weights. Standard errors (in parentheses) are robust to clustering at the community level. Significance at 5% (*) and 1% (**) indicate.

One reason for the switching may have to do with what has been happening to relative real prices at each of these types of providers. Table 10.6 presents median real charges, by source, from individual data on charges paid. For pills, the relative price between pharmacies and *puskesmas* declined from double in 1997 to just under 40% in 2000. Private physicians and private midwives have comparable prices to pharmacies. For injections, the relative prices were close between private midwives and puskesmas in 1997, only a 6% relative difference, and by 2000 prices were actually *lower* among private midwives. Village midwives, paramedics and nurses have even lower injection prices in 2000. Comparisons across urban and

TABLE 10.6
Median Charges of Contraceptive Services Among Pill and Injection Users Currently Married Women Aged 15–49

	Pills		Injection	
	1997	2000	1997	2000
Puskesmas and *Pustu*	1,205 (1,316) [227]	2,617 (1,499) [150]	8,550 (2,681) [371]	9,558 (2,774) [271]
Private physician and clinic	2,443 (5,796) [26]	3,578 (6,251) [29]	9,588 (4,934) [37]	10,341 (5,929) [154]
Midwife	2,082 (2,096) [205]	3,549 (2,601) [211]	9,073 (2,809) [298]	9,353 (2,188) [845]
Village midwife	–	3,023 (3,038) [43]	–	8,841 (2,524) [109]
Paramedic and nurse	–	–	–	8,373 (2,710) [77]
Posyandu	1,221 (1,553) [142]	2,585 (2,581) [95]	8,550 (2,966) [169]	–
Community services (PLKB, fieldworker, etc)	1,072 (1,727) [86]	2,093 (1,612) [84]	8,136 (2,684) [99]	–
Pharmacy	2,493 (3,476) [53]	3,634 (3,441) [184]	9,445 (5,636) [32]	–

Source: IFLS2 and IFLS3.
Dash (–) indicates that the estimates are not reported due to small cell size. Charges included pills/injections, services and other related costs, and are in December 2000 Rupiah. Differences between 75th and 25th percentiles are in parentheses. Number of observations is in brackets.

rural areas (Appendix Table 10.2a) and Java–Bali and outside provinces (Appendix Table 10.2b) show very similar results. It is interesting and perhaps surprising to note that injection prices in the private sector are actually lower than *puskesmas*' prices in rural areas. Injection prices outside of Java and Bali are somewhat higher, which is consistent with transportation cost differentials for these areas.

SUMMARY

Between 1997 and 2000, there has been very little change in the use of modern contraceptives, overall and by type, among married women in the IFLS sample, contrary to the expectations of some. On the other hand, usage has been flat over this period, not rising as it had been in earlier years. About 55% of currently married women aged 15–49 currently use a modern method, with injections (24%) and pills (14%) having the highest use. However, there has been a large decline in the fraction of women who get their supplies (of pills and injections) from *puskesmas* and *posyandu*, and a corresponding increase in the use of private providers: pharmacies for pills and private midwives for injections. Part of the switch in providers may stem from a convergence in relative prices charged, which is observed.

APPENDIX TABLE 10.1a
Source of Contraceptive Supplies Among Pill and Injection Users Currently Married Women Aged 15–49, by Residence
(In percent)

	Urban						Rural					
	Pills			Injection			Pills			Injection		
	1997	2000	Change	1997	2000	Change	1997	2000	Change	1997	2000	Change
Public and private hospitals	3.5	0.9	–2.6 *	2.5	3.0	0.5	0.9	1.0	0.0	0.2	0.8	0.6
	(1.17)	(0.47)	(1.26)	(0.66)	(0.80)	(1.04)	(0.50)	(0.51)	(0.72)	(0.13)	(0.31)	(0.34)
Puskesmas and *Pustu*	25.4	16.0	–9.4 *	29.8	12.2	–17.6 **	26.0	15.7	–10.3 **	30.0	17.9	–12.1 **
	(3.04)	(2.56)	(3.98)	(2.52)	(1.62)	(3.00)	(3.04)	(2.28)	(3.80)	(3.22)	(2.31)	(3.96)
Private physician and clinic	4.8	5.4	0.6	6.1	15.4	9.3 **	2.0	1.4	–0.6	1.0	6.2	5.3 **
	(1.25)	(1.06)	(1.64)	(1.21)	(1.95)	(2.29)	(0.85)	(0.68)	(1.09)	(0.39)	(1.10)	(1.16)
Midwife	26.6	23.7	–2.9	25.1	59.8	34.7 **	25.5	24.1	–1.4	25.7	55.2	29.5 **
	(3.34)	(2.96)	(4.46)	(2.06)	(2.58)	(3.31)	(2.89)	(2.70)	(3.96)	(2.75)	(3.02)	(4.08)
Village midwife	1.9	1.5	–0.4	1.0	2.4	1.4	3.8	5.9	2.1	1.5	8.8	7.3 **
	(0.74)	(0.64)	(0.98)	(0.50)	(0.69)	(0.85)	(1.41)	(1.37)	(1.97)	(0.49)	(1.43)	(1.51)
Paramedic and nurse	1.1	1.6	0.5	0.4	2.2	1.9 **	1.3	1.8	0.5	1.2	6.0	4.9 **
	(0.65)	(0.68)	(0.94)	(0.26)	(0.66)	(0.71)	(0.57)	(0.73)	(0.93)	(0.47)	(1.04)	(1.14)
Posyandu	16.3	10.3	–6.0	15.7	0.8	–14.9 **	18.0	11.5	–6.5	14.4	1.0	–13.4 **
	(2.75)	(1.78)	(3.27)	(1.90)	(0.64)	(2.01)	(2.91)	(1.99)	(3.53)	(1.60)	(0.38)	(1.65)
Community services (PLKB, fieldworker, etc) [a)]	5.7	5.4	–0.3	5.0	1.1	–3.9 *	14.8	14.1	–0.7	11.9	0.2	–11.7 **
	(1.49)	(1.08)	(1.84)	(1.46)	(0.41)	(1.52)	(2.48)	(2.73)	(3.69)	(2.08)	(0.12)	(2.08)
Pharmacy	13.2	29.3	16.1 **	5.8	0.0	–5.8 **	3.3	15.0	11.7 **	0.9	0.0	–0.9 *
	(2.15)	(3.01)	(3.70)	(1.19)	–	(1.19)	(1.00)	(2.27)	(2.48)	(0.39)	–	(0.39)
Number of observations	380	444		521	662		443	445		664	906	

Source: IFLS2 and IFLS3.

a) PLKB does not provide injections.

Estimates were weighted using individual sampling weights. Standard errors (in parentheses) are robust to clustering at the community level. Significance at 5% (*) and 1% (**) indicated.

APPENDIX TABLE 10.1b
Source of Contraceptive Supplies Among Pill and Injection Users Currently Married Women Aged 15–49, by Regions
(In percent)

	Java–Bali						Other Regions					
	Pills			Injection			Pills			Injection		
	1997	2000	Change	1997	2000	Change	1997	2000	Change	1997	2000	Change
Public and private hospitals	1.9	0.8	–1.2	0.8	1.5	0.7	1.9	1.4	–0.5	2.1	2.2	0.0
	(0.74)	(0.36)	(0.82)	(0.28)	(0.43)	(0.51)	(0.66)	(0.86)	(1.09)	(0.77)	(0.67)	(1.02)
Puskesmas and *Pustu*	21.2	13.8	–7.4 *	28.4	13.2	–15.2 **	36.1	21.6	–14.5 **	36.3	25.2	–11.0 *
	(2.62)	(1.98)	(3.29)	(2.67)	(1.66)	(3.14)	(3.51)	(3.20)	(4.75)	(3.47)	(3.52)	(4.95)
Private physician and clinic	3.4	3.4	0.0	3.0	10.7	7.7 **	2.4	2.7	0.3	2.0	6.3	4.3 *
	(0.95)	(0.80)	(1.24)	(0.63)	(1.25)	(1.40)	(0.86)	(0.99)	(1.31)	(0.93)	(1.49)	(1.76)
Midwife	25.3	23.9	–1.4	25.2	61.2	36.0 **	27.2	23.9	–3.4	26.8	40.9	14.1 **
	(2.73)	(2.41)	(3.65)	(2.20)	(2.33)	(3.20)	(3.63)	(3.42)	(4.99)	(3.55)	(3.71)	(5.14)
Village midwife	4.1	1.9	–2.2	1.5	5.3	3.8 **	0.9	9.6	8.7 **	0.4	10.2	9.8 **
	(1.30)	(0.60)	(1.43)	(0.44)	(0.98)	(1.08)	(0.53)	(2.36)	(2.42)	(0.38)	(2.37)	(2.40)
Paramedic and nurse	1.1	1.4	0.3	0.6	3.3	2.7 **	1.5	2.6	1.1	1.9	9.5	7.5 **
	(0.50)	(0.60)	(0.78)	(0.29)	(0.65)	(0.71)	(0.81)	(0.90)	(1.22)	(1.05)	(2.13)	(2.38)
Posyandu	18.7	12.1	–6.6 *	15.7	0.8	–14.9 **	14.3	7.7	–6.6	11.4	1.5	–9.9 **
	(2.66)	(1.71)	(3.16)	(1.44)	(0.40)	(1.50)	(3.13)	(1.64)	(3.53)	(2.10)	(0.55)	(2.18)
Community services (PLKB, fieldworker, etc) [a]	11.9	10.2	–1.6	9.6	0.5	–9.1 **	10.2	9.8	–0.4	8.7	0.9	–7.8 **
	(2.29)	(2.03)	(3.06)	(1.68)	(0.20)	(1.70)	(1.82)	(2.47)	(3.07)	(2.61)	(0.43)	(2.64)
Pharmacy	8.8	23.4	14.6 **	3.0	0.0	–3.0 **	3.1	16.1	13.0 **	1.2	0.0	–1.2 *
	(1.48)	(2.45)	(2.86)	(0.64)	–	(0.64)	(1.16)	(2.53)	(2.78)	(0.59)	–	(0.59)
Number of observations	464	546		845	1,080		359	343		340	488	

Source: IFLS2 and IFLS3.

[a] PLKB does not provide injections.

Estimates were weighted using individual sampling weights. Standard errors (in parentheses) are robust to clustering at the community level. Significance at 5% (*) and 1% (**) indicated.

APPENDIX TABLE 10.2a
Median Charges of Contraceptive Services Among Pill and Injection Users Currently Married Women Aged 15–49, by Residence

	Urban				Rural			
	Pills		Injection		Pills		Injection	
	1997	2000	1997	2000	1997	2000	1997	2000
Puskesmas and *Pustu*	1,483 (1,080) [98]	2,584 (1,532) [78]	8,355 (3,702) [156]	9,286 (3,120) [90]	1,162 (1,613) [129]	3,057 (1,561) [72]	8,550 (2,540) [215]	10,055 (2,581) [181]
Private physician and clinic	–	–	9,932 (5,543) [30]	10,534 (6,710) [100]	–	–	–	8,373 (2,892) [54]
Midwife	2,147 (3,278) [100]	3,658 (2,570) [111]	9,509 (3,604) [137]	10,318 (2,109) [385]	1,859 (1,257) [105]	3,121 (2,614) [100]	8,924 (2,255) [161]	9,015 (2,325) [460]
Village midwife	–	–	–	–	–	2,650 (3,027) [32]	–	8,841 (2,524) [90]
Paramedic and nurse	–	–	–	–	–	–	–	8,373 (2,981) [61]
Posyandu	1,113 (1,455) [65]	2,102 (2,018) [44]	8,402 (2,954) [79]	–	1,221 (1,277) [77]	2,601 (2,609) [51]	8,575 (2,800) [90]	–
Community services (PLKB, fieldworker, etc)	–	–	–	–	1,072 (1,671) [64]	2,081 (1,620) [58]	8,365 (2,682) [77]	–
Pharmacy	3,510 (3,440) [40]	4,147 (3,091) [117]	–	–	–	3,161 (2,602) [67]	–	–

Source: IFLS2 and IFLS3.
Dash (–) indicates that the estimates are not reported due to small cell size. Charges included pills/injections, services and other related costs, and are in December 2000 Rupiah. Differences between 75th and 25th percentiles are in parentheses. Number of observations is in brackets.

APPENDIX TABLE 10.2b
Median Charges of Contraceptive Services Among Pill and Injection Users Currently Married Women Aged 15–49, by Region

	Java–Bali				Other Regions			
	Pills		Injection		Pills		Injection	
	1997	2000	1997	2000	1997	2000	1997	2000
Puskesmas and *Pustu*	1,662 (1,159) [103]	2,598 (1,518) [77]	8,550 (2,543) [244]	9,316 (2,641) [149]	1,030 (1,879) [124]	2,654 (1,499) [73]	8,924 (3,642) [127]	10,354 (2,545) [122]
Private physician and clinic	–	–	9,588 (6,340) [30]	10,301 (5,161) [123]	–	–	–	10,494 (6,000) [31]
Midwife	2,201 (2,696) [115]	3,628 (3,546) [132]	9,073 (2,870) [214]	9,288 (2,180) [648]	1,191 (1,295) [90]	3,062 (2,008) [79]	8,896 (3,156) [84]	10,215 (2,155) [197]
Village midwife	–	–	–	8,328 (1,825) [54]	–	3,023 (3,069) [33]	–	10,141 (1,308) [55]
Paramedic and nurse	–	–	–	8,254 (741) [34]	–	–	–	10,191 (2,231) [43]
Posyandu	1,249 (1,206) [80]	2,121 (2,070) [63]	8,575 (2,798) [127]	–	939 (2,059) [62]	2,621 (3,021) [32]	7,480 (3,886) [42]	–
Community services (PLKB, fieldworker, etc)	1,074 (1,476) [53]	2,103 (1,606) [52]	7,951 (2,684) [75]	–	879 (1,575) [33]	2,065 (2,006) [32]	–	–
Pharmacy	4,013 (3,743) [42]	3,635 (3,105) [128]	9,037 (5,749) [28]	–	–	3,203 (2,657) [56]	–	–

Source: IFLS2 and IFLS3.
Dash (–) indicates that the estimates are not reported due to small cell size. Charges included pills/injections, services and other related costs, and are in December 2000 Rupiah. Differences between 75th and 25th percentiles are in parentheses. Number of observations is in brackets.

11

Family Planning Services

PROVISION OF FAMILY PLANNING SERVICES IN PUBLIC AND PRIVATE FACILITIES

In this chapter, we examine data from facilities to explore changes in family planning service provision. Table 11.1 shows the provision of contraceptive supplies at *puskesmas* and private health practitioners. Among *puskesmas*, we see results consistent with the individual use data. The fraction of facilities that supply pills declined substantially from 1997 to 2000. Part of this is a substitution into new types of pills that were not supplied before such as Planotab and Microdiol, but not all of the decline can be accounted for in that way.

The same phenomenon can be found among private and village midwives, where there is also a decrease in the provision of Microgynon and Marvelon, but an increase in other types of pills such as Planotab and Microdiol.

There is a very significant decrease in public facilities in the provision of removal of IUD plastic services, while there tends to be no change in this type of service in private facilities. A very significant decrease from 1997 to 2000 is seen in the provision of Noristerat, an injectable contraceptive, at both public and private providers. This may be due to the fact that this type of contraceptive only lasts for two instead of three months, and because the needle required for injection is much larger than for other methods. On the other hand, the provision of Depo Progestin, which is another type of injection, has increased enormously and significantly in private facilities; in public facilities it was already very high in 1997. Thus among all types of private providers: midwives, doctors and nurse/paramedics, there has been a major increase in supplies of injectable contraceptives. This is consistent with the finding that women switched their source of injections from public to private providers (Table 10.5).

TABLE 11.1
Provision of Family Planning Services, By Type of Providers
(In percent)

	Puskesmas and *Pustu*			Private physician and clinic			Midwife and village midwife			Paramedic and nurse		
	1997	2000	Change	1997	2000	Change	1997	2000	Change	1997	2000	Change
Supply of oral contraceptive:												
– Microgynon	76.0	52.0	–23.9 **	41.0	38.1	–2.9	76.3	63.6	–12.7 **	17.4	18.5	1.1
	(1.67)	(1.85)	(2.49)	(2.28)	(2.20)	(3.17)	(1.83)	(1.90)	(2.64)	(1.81)	(1.92)	(2.64)
– Marvelon	65.0	41.5	–23.4 **	27.5	19.1	–8.4 **	51.3	35.8	–15.5 **	12.3	10.1	–2.2
	(1.95)	(1.86)	(2.69)	(2.21)	(1.74)	(2.81)	(2.22)	(2.07)	(3.03)	(1.62)	(1.38)	(2.13)
– Excluton	69.9	61.8	–8.1 **	27.2	24.5	–2.7	58.4	55.4	–3.0	10.6	12.5	1.9
	(1.80)	(1.74)	(2.50)	(2.12)	(1.86)	(2.82)	(2.18)	(2.13)	(3.05)	(1.55)	(1.69)	(2.29)
– Nordette	69.0	55.8	–13.2 **	21.8	17.2	–4.7	40.9	41.2	0.3	7.4	12.1	4.6 *
	(1.79)	(1.81)	(2.55)	(2.09)	(1.62)	(2.65)	(2.25)	(2.10)	(3.08)	(1.32)	(1.61)	(2.08)
– Other pills	32.1	46.8	14.7 **	10.0	11.7	1.8	28.5	40.4	11.9 **	7.4	8.6	1.2
	(1.90)	(1.98)	(2.74)	(1.25)	(1.24)	(1.75)	(2.06)	(2.07)	(2.92)	(1.30)	(1.44)	(1.94)
IUD:												
– Insertion of IUD plastic [a]	70.9			13.7			46.2			2.1		
	(1.82)			(1.55)			(2.10)			(0.65)		
– Removal of IUD plastic	70.6	63.5	–7.2 **	15.5	14.9	–0.6	46.9	45.8	–1.1	1.9	2.4	0.5
	(1.82)	(1.66)	(2.46)	(1.72)	(1.28)	(2.14)	(2.17)	(2.07)	(3.00)	(0.62)	(0.69)	(0.93)
– Insertion of IUD copper T	71.2	71.9	0.8	18.6	18.8	0.2	58.5	61.2	2.7	3.2	2.4	–0.8
	(1.76)	(1.68)	(2.43)	(1.66)	(1.62)	(2.32)	(2.18)	(2.12)	(3.04)	(0.79)	(0.69)	(1.05)
– Removal of IUD copper T	71.4	73.8	2.5	20.5	19.2	–1.3	58.5	63.0	4.5	3.2	2.6	–0.6
	(1.75)	(1.66)	(2.41)	(1.79)	(1.62)	(2.42)	(2.19)	(2.12)	(3.05)	(0.79)	(0.71)	(1.07)

continued on next page

TABLE 11.1 – cont'd

	Puskesmas and *Pustu*			Private physician and clinic			Midwife and village midwife			Paramedic and nurse		
	1997	2000	Change	1997	2000	Change	1997	2000	Change	1997	2000	Change
Injectable contraceptive:												
– Depo-provera	70.3	66.3	–4.0	62.7	66.5	3.8	82.5	79.9	–2.6	27.4	36.9	9.4 **
	(1.80)	(1.72)	(2.49)	(2.06)	(2.05)	(2.91)	(1.56)	(1.59)	(2.23)	(2.05)	(2.37)	(3.13)
– Depo-progestin	79.1	81.5	2.4	27.2	57.0	29.8 **	43.4	89.5	46.0 **	5.5	40.9	35.4 **
	(1.39)	(1.39)	(1.96)	(2.12)	(1.95)	(2.88)	(2.50)	(1.23)	(2.78)	(1.12)	(2.42)	(2.67)
– Noristerat	16.8	6.5	–10.3 **	17.8	6.0	–11.8 **	19.6	5.1	–14.5 **	4.9	2.2	–2.7 *
	(1.52)	(0.89)	(1.76)	(1.85)	(0.83)	(2.03)	(1.64)	(0.82)	(1.84)	(1.04)	(0.66)	(1.23)
– Cyclofeem	25.8	28.6	2.8	34.2	55.9	21.7 **	60.8	70.7	9.9 **	19.4	15.3	–4.1
	(1.72)	(1.76)	(2.46)	(2.31)	(2.23)	(3.22)	(2.34)	(2.13)	(3.16)	(1.92)	(1.75)	(2.60)
Implants:												
– Insertion of Norplant	52.3	50.3	–2.0	11.7	10.3	–1.4	21.9	30.1	8.3 **	3.0	3.9	0.9
	(1.79)	(1.78)	(2.52)	(1.41)	(1.31)	(1.92)	(2.04)	(2.11)	(2.93)	(0.82)	(0.96)	(1.27)
– Removal of Norplant	50.9	52.4	1.5	14.6	14.9	0.3	22.6	33.5	10.9 **	3.0	4.5	1.5
	(1.78)	(1.74)	(2.49)	(1.64)	(1.44)	(2.19)	(2.08)	(2.12)	(2.97)	(0.82)	(1.02)	(1.31)
– Insertion of Implanon [b]		34.7			11.0			26.4			1.7	
		(1.80)			(1.24)			(1.91)			(0.60)	
– Removal of Implanon [b]		35.8			13.2			24.1			2.6	
		(1.79)			(1.34)			(1.79)			(0.73)	
Treatment of contraceptive side effects	86.3	88.8	2.5	51.3	54.2	2.9	79.8	86.4	6.6 **	19.1	22.8	3.7
	(1.38)	(1.13)	(1.79)	(2.19)	(1.96)	(2.94)	(1.90)	(1.34)	(2.32)	(1.89)	(2.04)	(2.78)
Family planning check-up/ counselling	89.6	92.2	2.6	47.3	65.0	17.8 **	78.9	93.6	14.8 **	16.8	30.8	14.0 **
	(1.17)	(0.92)	(1.49)	(2.10)	(1.99)	(2.89)	(1.91)	(0.94)	(2.13)	(1.77)	(2.41)	(2.99)
Number of observations	919	944		673	698		663	740		470	464	

Source: IFLS2 and IFLS3.

[a] Information on insertion of IUD plastic is not collected in IFLS3, 2000.

[b] Information on Implanon is not collected in IFLS2, 1997.

Standard errors (in parentheses) are robust to clustering at the community level. Significance at 5% (*) and 1% (**) indicated.

The fraction of midwives, private and village, who provide treatment of contraceptive side effects has also increased. As will be seen below, the number of *posyandu* providing this service has declined, possibly creating spillover effects to doctors or private midwives.

The provision of family planning check ups and counselling services in private facilities has increased in all of the private provider types. Midwives are now as likely to provide this service as are *puskesmas*. Again, this is consistent with a switch in use of family planning services from the public to the private sector.

FEES FOR THE PROVISION OF FAMILY PLANNING SERVICES

The real prices of contraceptives supplied in public and private facilities, as reported by facility staff, are reported in Table 11.2 and show a somewhat different pattern than the prices reported by individuals in Table 10.6. In principle, these prices are supposed to be comparable, for example, both are supposed to include *puskesmas* registration and exam fees pro-rated. Of course doing so is difficult and so it seems likely that the staff reported prices which were only for the individual contraceptive. The evidence is consistent with that hypothesis. If one compares prices for pills or injections at *puskesmas* between Tables 10.6 and 11.2, it is apparent that the prices reported by individuals are higher. Since the individual prices represent the total cost of service, including all charges, this makes sense. It is also the more relevant charge to compare.[1] A comparison of individual and facility reports of prices charged by private providers shows that they are not too different. Prices are somewhat higher among private providers than public. This may mean that *puskesmas*' prices are systematically understated in Table 11.2, relative to prices of private providers.

Looking at changes in staff reported prices, they have tended to increase between 1997 and 2000, but not across the board. For oral contraceptives, in public facilities prices have remained roughly constant for Microgynon, Marvelon and Excluton, while increasing for Nordette, and other types of oral contraceptives such as Planotab and Microdiol. Among private providers, price increases have occurred across the board for pills.

The median real price for treatment of contraceptive side effects has been relatively stable in public and private facilities. The same tendency can be seen for the median real price of family planning check-ups and counselling in public facilities. However, at private facilities there was a large decline in the relative price of this type of service from almost 600% higher in 1997 to 150% in 2000, making private providers more competitive with public providers for this service.

TABLE 11.2
Median Charges for the Provision of Family Planning Services, By Type of Providers

	Puskesmas and *Pustu*		Private physician and clinic		Midwife and village midwife		Paramedic and nurse	
	1997	2000	1997	2000	1997	2000	1997	2000
Supply of oral contraceptive:								
– Microgynon	1,049 (1,186) [695]	1,076 (1,766) [489]	5,850 (6,546) [269]	6,793 (5,078) [262]	3,247 (4,114) [501]	5,159 (3,720) [471]	2,212 (5,054) [82]	3,645 (4,039) [85]
– Marvelon	1,033 (1,141) [592]	1,056 (1,461) [390]	5,622 (7,361) [179]	5,169 (7,113) [130]	2,136 (3,665) [336]	3,500 (2,574) [265]	1,544 (2,066) [57]	3,123 (2,083) [46]
– Excluton	1,035 (1,170) [638]	1,067 (1,463) [580]	5,199 (7,225) [176]	5,169 (5,209) [167]	2,152 (3,913) [379]	3,152 (2,572) [410]	1,499 (1,308) [50]	3,057 (2,048) [57]
– Nordette	1,039 (1,141) [628]	1,422 (1,477) [524]	5,853 (7,246) [141]	4,211 (4,775) [118]	2,062 (2,811) [266]	3,120 (1,635) [305]	1,205 (2,088) [35]	3,032 (1,610) [56]
– Other pills	994 (1,123) [290]	1,511 (1,929) [441]	3,661 (5,382) [64]	4,688 (4,159) [81]	2,066 (2,759) [186]	3,629 (2,506) [299]	1,205 (1,322) [34]	3,121 (2,583) [40]
IUD:								
– Insertion of IUD plastic [a)]	1,275 (3,151) [646]		30,977 (30,195) [91]		21,221 (25,102) [301]		–	
– Removal of IUD plastic	1,205 (2,140) [620]	2,050 (4,340) [596]	18,739 (16,985) [101]	20,636 (16,143) [101]	10,444 (9,911) [305]	10,744 (10,509) [338]	–	–
– Insertion of IUD copper T	1,390 (4,566) [639]	2,556 (6,972) [674]	46,412 (46,298) [124]	46,883 (49,320) [129]	37,603 (35,078) [382]	41,284 (31,180) [452]	–	–
– Removal of IUD copper T	1,246 (2,735) [611]	2,070 (4,379) [692]	18,890 (18,780) [137]	15,677 (15,639) [131]	11,210 (10,234) [380]	10,484 (8,584) [463]	–	–

Injectable contraceptive:								
– Depo-provera	5,938	7,747	11,334	12,382	9,698	10,363	8,809	10,192
	(7,316)	(8,542)	(5,475)	(5,346)	(2,613)	(656)	(2,601)	(2,167)
	[642]	[626]	[414]	[458]	[545]	[588]	[128]	[171]
– Depo-progestin	6,431	7,500	12,391	10,367	10,444	10,076	10,299	9,687
	(6,899)	(7,595)	(5,510)	(6,268)	(3,033)	(2,098)	(2,753)	(2,184)
	[720]	[769]	[179]	[393]	[287]	[661]	[26]	[190]
– Noristerat	1,951	1,658	12,052	10,387	9,588	10,301	–	–
	(6,165)	(9,336)	(7,634)	(5,628)	(3,975)	(1,235)		
	[151]	[61]	[115]	[42]	[128]	[38]		
– Cyclofeem	7,800	10,074	10,631	13,098	8,824	10,418	8,260	10,367
	(8,911)	(4,228)	(5,701)	(5,265)	(2,955)	(2,296)	(2,740)	(2,204)
	[235]	[270]	[226]	[385]	[400]	[521]	[91]	[71]
Implants:								
– Insertion of Norplant	4,120	6,383	31,084	51,702	26,743	41,974	–	–
	(9,884)	(14,960)	(37,940)	(51,368)	(31,139)	(36,598)		
	[475]	[474]	[76]	[70]	[144]	[223]		
– Removal of Norplant	2,346	5,378	26,597	26,400	20,625	20,823	–	–
	(10,552)	(14,390)	(25,771)	(20,931)	(21,339)	(14,421)		
	[462]	[493]	[92]	[102]	[146]	[248]		
– Insertion of Implanon [b)]		5,782		76,737		76,435		–
		(19,737)		(55,769)		(52,447)		
		[327]		[76]		[194]		
– Removal of Implanon [b)]		5,183		26,017		20,837		–
		(14,581)		(19,848)		(10,693)		
		[335]		[89]		[177]		
Treatment of contraceptive side effects	1,074	1,039	11,681	12,450	7,802	7,416	6,659	5,340
	(957)	(1,045)	(7,731)	(9,875)	(4,485)	(5,248)	(4,544)	(7,070)
	[784]	[836]	[335]	[374]	[514]	[637]	[88]	[106]
Family planning check-up/ counselling	1,045	1,032	9,652	6,151	6,215	0	4,130	0
	(993)	(1,036)	(8,521)	(10,456)	(6,853)	(5,209)	(7,328)	–
	[811]	[870]	[308]	[450]	[504]	[691]	[77]	[143]

Source: IFLS2 and IFLS3.

a) Information on insertion of IUD plastic is not collected in IFLS3, 2000.

b) Information on Implanon is not collected in IFLS2, 1997.

Dash (–) indicates that the estimates are not reported due to small cell size. Charges are in December 2000 Rupiah. Differences between 75th and 25th percentiles are in parentheses. Number of observations is in brackets.

PROVISION OF FAMILY PLANNING SERVICES BY *POSYANDU*

Table 11.3 displays various data on the family planning service provision by *poyandu*. *Posyandu* had been an important source of family planning. In the top panel of the table we see the provision of various contraceptive services offered by *posyandu* decreased in 2000 compared to 1997. A significant decline can be found in the provision of oral contraceptives and injectables, corresponding again to the decline in individual use of *posyandu* reported in Table 10.5. The decrease may be due to the decline of provision of those contraceptives from BKKBN, which are usually given to health centres (*puskesmas*). It is the *puskesmas* that then pass on some of the contraceptives to the *posyandu*.

From 1997 to 2000, the number of *posyandu* that offer treatment for contraceptive side effects has decreased significantly. On the other hand, there was also a significant increase in the provision of family planning counselling during this period.

The services provided by the *posyandu* are not always given for free (right panel, Table 11.3). Many *posyandu* charge users for services. Compared to 1997, there was an increase in the fraction of *posyandu* that charged users for oral contraceptive services and condoms, but a decline in the fraction charging for injections and treatment of side effects. Median charges for all of these supplies and services increased between 1997 and 2000, but remain lower than prices charged by private providers.

SUMMARY

The facility data by and large confirms the picture that the individual use data portrays, that family planning service availability has tended to decline in *puskesmas* and especially in *posyandu*, except for counselling and treatment of side effects. This decline may have helped to cause the shift in source of supplies, or may simply reflect that shift; from these results it is not possible to distinguish.

Note

1 On the other hand, the prices reported by staff are for a specific contraceptive, whereas the individual reported prices data is for an aggregated group of items, such as all injectables.

TABLE 11.3
Provision and Median Charges of Family Planning Services by *Posyandu*

	Provision of services [a] (in percent)			Any charge (in percent)		Median charges [b]	
	1997	2000	Change	1997	2000	1997	2000
Provision of oral contraceptive	74.0 (2.11) [619]	49.6 (2.20) [631]	–24.4 ** (3.05)	76.2 [445]	84.5 [310]	1,074 (1,061) [339]	1,573 (1,568) [262]
Provision of condom	29.6 (2.19) [619]	28.4 (2.05) [631]	–1.2 (3.00)	82.5 [171]	92.2 [179]	7,503 (3,278) [141]	8,361 (3,156) [165]
Provision of injectable contraceptive	29.6 (2.30) [619]	17.1 (1.67) [631]	–12.4 ** (2.84)	42.9 [170]	34.6 [104]	962 (982) [73]	1,028 (530) [36]
Treatment of contraceptive side effects	18.3 (1.76) [619]	11.7 (1.37) [631]	–6.5 ** (2.23)	33.0 [94]	25.7 [74]	1,785 (1,556) [31]	–
Family planning check-up/counselling	47.7 (2.40) [619]	66.7 (2.01) [631]	19.1 ** (3.13)				

Source: IFLS2 and IFLS3.
[a] Standard errors (in parentheses) are robust to clustering at the community level. Significance at 5% (*) and 1% (**) indicated.
[b] Information on charge for family planning check-up/counseling is not collected in IFLS2, 1997 and IFLS3, 2000. Dash (–) indicates that the estimates are not reported due to small cell size. Charges are in December 2000 Rupiah. Differences between 75th and 25th percentiles are in parentheses. Number of observations is in brackets.

12

Social Safety Net Programmes

PROGRAMME DESCRIPTIONS

In an effort to cushion the effect of the crisis and to prevent a further economic decline, the Indonesian government embarked on a set of Social Safety Net programmes (JPS) at the beginning of the 1998/1999 budget year (BAPPENAS 1999). In general, the Social Safety Net programmes could be categorized into four major groups:

1. Food Security, aimed at guaranteeing the availability of food at an affordable price.
2. Employment creation through labour-intensive projects targeted to reduce the rate of unemployment and to encourage and maintain the sustainability of productive economic activities.
3. Social protection programmes, designed to maintain accessibility to social, health and educational services.
4. Development and support for small and medium enterprises, in terms of training, supervision, guidance, counselling, promotion assistance and partnership

These programmes are implemented in various specific programmes and activities as listed in Table 12.1.

In IFLS3 there are various parts in both the household and community sections that collect information on some of these social safety net programmes. Not all the programmes listed in Table12.1 are included in the survey; in this chapter we review the description of the programmes that are included in IFLS.

Special market operation for rice (OPK rice)

In response to the sharp price increase for food, especially rice, due to the economic crisis, the government in the middle of 1998 embarked on a

TABLE 12.1
Various Activities/Programmes under Social Safety Net Programme

Food Security	Social Safety in Education	Social Safety in Health	Employment Creation	Community Development Fund
• Special Market Operation (OPK) (includes OPK rice) • Seed development and cultivation of local chicken • Development of people ponds	• Scholarship and Operational Assistance Fund (DBO) for Primary and Secondary School • Scholarship and Operational Assistance Fund (DBO) for Higher Education • Operational funds and Maintenance of Primary School	• Social Safety Net for Health (JPS-BK) (*Kartu Sehat*) • Food Supplementation Programme for children (PMT-AS)	• Labour Intensive Program of Ministry of Public Works (PKSPU-CK) (Padat Karya) • Special Programme for Unemployed Women (PKPP)	• Regional empowerement to overcome the effect of economic crisis (PDMDKE)

Source: BAPPENAS, 1999

special programme, "OPK beras", or special market operation for rice (OPK rice). It is a subsidized (not free) food distribution programme, which concentrates on rice, hence OPK rice.[1] The rice is not distributed in the general market, but directly to the targeted receivers.

OPK rice is organized by the Logistic Board of the government (BULOG/DOLOG) in collaboration with the Family Coordinating Board (BKKBN) and the village office throughout Indonesia. In principal, target households are identified by using listings of low income families, collected and maintained by BKKBN. Initially, the programme was targeted at very low income families (Keluarga Pra sejahtera, Pra KS), but later extended to upper low income families (Keluarga Sejahtera 1, KS 1). In addition, other households who are not listed by BKKBN (particularly in urban areas), are also included in principal if they satisfied one of the following criteria:

- Unable to feed twice a day;
- Unable to afford medical treatment from the health facilities;
- Unable to consume protein once a week;
- Have children who drop-out of school for economic reason;
- Workers affected by mass retrenchment.

The amount of assistance that was supposed to be provided by the programme in 2000 was 10 kilograms of medium quality rice per month for each target household. This was supposed to be purchased at a subsidized price of Rp 1,000 per kilogram. Given that median market prices for rice in late 2000 were Rp 2,300 per kilogram, this would amount to a subsidy of roughly, Rp 1,300 per kilogram, or Rp 13,000 per month per household.

Employment creation programme (programme Padat Karya)

The objective of this programme is to provide employment opportunity to low income households and improve the quality of community infrastructure. The target group is low income households that had members who lost their jobs, are unskilled and unable to maintain themselves. These individuals are mostly secondary school drop-outs aged 15–55 years who registered at the Job Seekers Registration Unit and are willing to be paid at a minimum wage rate. The activities of Padat Karya programme are executed through labour-intensive development projects, aimed at operating and improving various community infrastructure.

Programme Padat Karya Desa (PKD) is aimed at creating a temporary source of income in areas affected by drought in 1997. These areas are:

Central Sulawesi, South East Sulawesi, West and East Nusa Tenggara. Approximately 1,957 villages were covered by this programme, out of which 323 villages are located in West Nusa Tenggara. The programme provides assistance of Rp 50 million to each targeted village to finance labour-intensive projects such as road repair, or construction of other infrastructure. In principal, at least 70% of the funds is allocated to payment of wages, not more than 26% for purchase of materials or rental equipment and not more than 4% for administration and honorariums. This programme was implemented by BAPPENAS.

PKSPU-CK is implemented by directorate General Cipta Karya–Ministry of Public Works and aimed at improving the quality of infrastructures in urban areas. The geographical coverage of the programme is urban areas throughout Indonesia (including metropolitan cities, capitals of provinces and big and medium size cities). The programme is targeted to cover 4 million poor unemployed, with a target of at least 20% women.

Regional empowerment to overcome the effect of the economic crisis (PDMDKE)

The objectives of the programme are: to increase the purchasing power of the poor, both urban and rural, through creation of employment and business opportunities; to foster local economies by development of infrastructure to support the system of production and distribution of goods and services and to effectively increase the function of socioeconomic infrastructure capable of maintaining environmental functions.

The target group for the programme is the poor who have lost their jobs, or those who are not capable of maintaining themselves, most especially with regards to food, education and health.

The activities of PDMDKE consist of public employment programmes and economic loans determined by the communities themselves. The public employment programmes are similar to Padat Karya (except that Padat Karya is not community-determined), and involves construction or maintenance of labour-intensive socioeconomic, environmental and health infrastructure such as roads, irrigation systems, sewage systems, and flood prevention systems. The wage paid is supposed to be at the minimum wage.

The economic loans come from a revolving capital fund at the village-level, for businesses that are affected by the crisis or for individual or groups starting new businesses. The central government makes allocations to receiving villages for the revolving credit fund, with a minimum amount of Rp 10 million per village. Loans are supposed to be made in amounts of Rp 2.5 million per person, with the interest rate subsidized.

The PDMDKE programme was planned by BAPENAS and began in June 1999. The amount of funds allocated to each village is between Rp 10 million, for villages with small populations and relatively prosperous, to Rp 1,000 million for village with large populations of poor or unemployed.

Social safety net programmes in education: scholarship and operational assistance funds (DBO)

Under the schools social safety net programme, primary and secondary school students from poor households can obtain scholarships. The scholarship programme is aimed at preventing school drop-out due to the economic crisis. The programme ensures that students from poor households are given a chance to remain enrolled in school and continue to the next level, and for female students, to complete at least junior secondary school. The scholarships can be used for payment of tuition, fees, books, uniforms and other school equipment, transportation and other living expenses related to attending school.

In principle, student recipients in primary school receive Rp 120,000 per student per year, junior secondary school students receive Rp 240,000 per student and senior secondary school students get Rp 300,000 per student per year.

In addition, operational assistance funds (DBO) were implemented to cushion the effect of the crisis on school operational expenses. DBO was given to primary, junior high and senior secondary schools, covering government as well as private schools that are considered needing assistance. The criteria for getting the assistance is that the school is not an expensive school, in the sense that it must be school that enrols students from poor households, and has a minimum enrolment of 90 students for primary schools, and 60 for secondary schools.

DBO funds are targeted for expenditure on teaching material supplies, such as books, demonstration materials, and consumables. DBO funds are not supposed to be used for payment of salaries or honorariums, or for construction of buildings or other capital. The amount of assistance given by the programme is Rp 2 million for primary schools, Rp 4 million for junior secondary schools and Rp 10 million for secondary schools.

Social safety net programmes in health (JPS–BK)

The JPS–BK programme is designed to prevent the decline of health and nutritional status as a result of the economic crisis. The community health centres (*puskesmas*) and the village midwives are the key actors of the programme, which was started in 1998. The JPS–BK provides access to health services to the programme beneficiaries by the use of a special health card (*Kartu Sehat*). In principle, the services are supposed to be free of charge. JPS–BK also provides funds to local clinics and to specially chosen village midwives to improve local health services.

In general, the target of the programme is the poor. A team at the village level, consisting of village staff, family planning workers, village midwives, and community activists, identify the beneficiaries using criteria, such as:

- Unable to have two meals a day;
- Unable to afford health services;
- The head of the household lost his job due to retrenchment;
- Households with school drop-outs due to the crisis.

The identified poor households are given health cards signed by the head of the community health post and the head of the village. This card is valid for one year and can be extended as long as the households meet the criteria.

The types of services covered by the JPS–BK funds include:

a. Basic health services, medical attention as first treatment or referrals, family planning services, immunization and other basic health services.
b. Basic maternal health care and referrals for pregnant mother, delivery care, post- and neonatal care.
c. Nutritional improvement through food supplementation to undernourished poor families. The target is children aged 6–59 months, pregnant mothers, and post-partum women from poor families who are undernourished.
d. Eradication of communicable diseases such as malaria, tuberculosis and diseases that could be prevented through immunization. The target are persons infected by the diseases and for immunization the target are babies aged less than 12 months, pregnant women, primary school children, women of reproductive age and persons who are getting married.

e. Revitalization of *posyandu* (integrated health post), a health post improvement programme to mitigate negative effects of the crisis on the nutrition and health status of mothers and young children.

Food supplementation programme for school children (PMT-AS)

The food supplementation programme is a component of Community Empowerment programme of the Social Safety Net Programme (PJPS-PM). The goal is to improve nutritional and health status of students in poor urban and rural areas. School supplementary feeding programmes existed before 1998, supported by both government and private sector resources, as we shall see. The JPS programme took over what had previously existed and made some changes.

The target group is poor students of primary school age (7–12 years). Beneficiaries should live in a poor neighbourhood or in areas that are considered to be the worst affected by the economic crisis. The food assistance is given at least three times a week or 108 times in a school year.

INCIDENCE, VALUES AND TARGETING OF JPS ASSISTANCE

IFLS3 contains numerous questions regarding the JPS and other social safety net programmes, at the individual, household and community levels. We discuss the evidence on the incidence, values and targeting of programme assistance by programme, beginning with an overview.

Table 12.2 displays the proportion of communities (or schools for the scholarship programme) that received each of these programmes at least some time since 1998. Some of the programmes have near universal reach across the IFLS *desas* and *kelurahans* (or schools): OPK rice, the scholarship programme at public schools and *Kartu Sehat*. Since there are poor in most areas, this is not necessarily inconsistent with targeting to the poor, although it indicates that geographical targeting of programme incidence is not being used (geographical targeting of the flow of funds still might be used, however). Other programmes have more limited reach: Padat Karya and PDMDKE. Some of these programmes, such as Padat Karya and PDMDKE have substantially declined in their village coverage to under 5% by 2000, compared to village coverage of 40% and 50% respectively, in 1998. OPK coverage expanded in 1999 and shrunk a little in 2000, but still at levels above the coverage in 1998.

Since these programmes are supposed to be targeted it is interesting to explore what eligibility criteria are claimed to be used within communities. The communities had the choice of using general criteria for all programmes

TABLE 12.2
Prevalence of Social Safety Net Programmes in IFLS3 Communities

	Social Safety Net in Communities					Scholarship in Schools					
						Public			Private		
	OPK Beras	Padat Karya	PDMDKE	*Kartu Sehat*	*Posyandu* Revitalization	Primary	Junior high	Senior high	Primary	Junior high	Senior high
% of communities with programme											
– since 1998	97.4	54.3	73.0	98.1	83.6						
	(0.90)	(2.83)	(2.52)	(0.78)	(2.10)						
	[311]	[311]	[311]	[311]	[311]						
– since April 2000 [1)]	87.8	5.8	4.8	66.2	50.8						
	(1.86)	(1.33)	(1.22)	(2.69)	(2.84)						
	[311]	[311]	[311]	[311]	[311]						
– during FY 1999/2000	94.5	14.8	21.9	66.9	48.2	96.3	98.6	97.1	79.2	90.7	93.3
	(1.29)	(2.02)	(2.35)	(2.67)	(2.84)	(0.70)	(0.55)	(1.00)	(3.80)	(1.81)	(1.43)
	[311]	[311]	[311]	[311]	[311]	[782]	[572]	[278]	[144]	[344]	[314]
– during FY 1998/1999	78.5	39.9	54.0	59.8	19.0						
	(2.34)	(2.78)	(2.83)	(2.78)	(2.23)						
	[311]	[311]	[311]	[311]	[311]						

continued on next page

TABLE 12.2 – cont'd

	Social Safety Net in Communities					Scholarship in Schools					
						Public			Private		
	OPK Beras	Padat Karya	PDMDKE	*Kartu Sehat*	*Posyandu* Revitalization	Primary	Junior high	Senior high	Primary	Junior high	Senior high
% of urban communities with programme											
– since 1998	99.4	61.3	81.8	98.3	86.6						
	(0.55)	(3.63)	(2.87)	(0.95)	(2.51)						
	[181]	[181]	[181]	[181]	[186]						
– since April 2000 [1)]	89.5	7.7	3.3	68.5	54.8						
	(2.28)	(1.99)	(1.33)	(3.46)	(3.65)						
	[181]	[181]	[181]	[181]	[186]						
– during FY 1999/2000	95.0	17.1	26.0	68.0	56.5	96.0	99.1	97.2	76.2	88.8	93.5
	(1.62)	(2.80)	(3.26)	(3.47)	(3.64)	(1.02)	(0.51)	(1.21)	(4.81)	(2.40)	(1.62)
	[181]	[181]	[181]	[181]	[186]	[429]	[338]	[181]	[101]	[241]	[245]
– during FY 1998/1999	76.8	44.2	60.8	61.3	21.0						
	(3.14)	(3.70)	(3.64)	(3.63)	(2.99)						
	[181]	[181]	[181]	[181]	[186]						
% of rural communities with programme											
– since 1998	94.6	44.6	60.8	97.7	79.2						
	(1.98)	(4.37)	(4.29)	(1.32)	(3.64)						
	[130]	[130]	[130]	[130]	[125]						
– since April 2000 1)	85.4	3.1	6.9	63.1	44.8						
	(3.10)	(1.52)	(2.23)	(4.24)	(4.46)						
	[130]	[130]	[130]	[130]	[125]						
– during FY 1999/2000	93.8	11.5	16.2	65.4	36.0	96.6	97.9	96.9	86.0	95.1	92.8
	(2.11)	(2.81)	(3.23)	(4.18)	(4.30)	(0.94)	(1.11)	(1.78)	(5.47)	(2.08)	(3.02)
	[130]	[130]	[130]	[130]	[125]	[353]	[234]	[96]	[43]	[103]	[69]
– during FY 1998/1999	80.8	33.8	44.6	57.7	16.0						
	(3.46)	(4.16)	(4.37)	(4.34)	(3.28)						
	[130]	[130]	[130]	[130]	[125]						

Source: IFLS3.
[1)] This covers the period from April 2000 to the IFLS interview in the fall of 2000.
Standard errors (in parentheses) are robust to clustering at the community level. Significance at 5% (*) and 1% (**) indicated. Number of observations is in brackets.

or programme-specific criteria. Table 12.3 shows the percentage of *desas* and *kelurahans* that report using general versus specific criteria and which criteria are reported to be used. General criteria tend to be used for OPK rice and for *Kartu Sehat*, whereas other programmes are split between general and specific criteria.

Among the general criteria used, the most frequently used are the poverty classifications developed by BKKBN: being a *pra KS* family, followed by being a *KS 1* family. For Padat Karya, having a head who became unemployed or does not have a permanent source of income are common criteria.

Table 12.4 shows who the local programme decision-makers are for the purpose of setting local eligibility criteria. The village head and staff, and head of the RT/RW are most frequently mentioned for all of these programmes. For *Kartu Sehat*, the PLKB is also important, as are the village midwife and *puskesmas* staff. PLKB, PKK women's group members and LKMD staff also play a role in setting OPK rice criteria. This level of local involvement suggests that local voices are important in deciding who gets access to these programmes within the community.

Of course, what is true in theory does not necessarily correspond to what occurs on the ground. Table 12.5 displays data at the individual level, showing the percentage of recipients (or were in recipient households) of five programmes that can easily be traced at the household or individual level. Two of these are JPS programmes: OPK and *Kartu Sehat*. In addition, we track whether any free assistance, typically rice, was received from a government or non-governmental source that is not connected with the JPS programmes, or whether any cash assistance was received from a community assistance organization. Finally, we also include whether the household of the individual possesses a Letter of Non-affordability, which is similar to the *Kartu Sehat*, but predates the JPS programme and applies to several publicly-provided services: health, education, and transportation. Whether a household receives aid is the combination of three separate decisions: which communities receive assistance, how much they receive and who in the community are recipients given that a community is chosen (see Jayne et al. 2002 for such an analysis of receipt of food aid in Ethiopia).

Of these, the OPK programme is the most common, covering 40% of individuals in the last 12 months. Almost all of that comes from the rice subsidy. OPK is national, but coverage is higher in rural areas and more generally among the poor. Among the poor, OPK coverage is nearly 60% for the last 12 months. *Kartu Sehat* covers just under 20% of the general population; again slightly higher among rural households (21%) and among

TABLE 12.3
Community Criteria for Targeted Households in Social Safety Net Programme

	General Criteria	Specific Criteria				
		Kartu Sehat				
		Village Staff	*Puskesmas* Staff/Village Midwife	OPK Beras	Padat Karya	PDMDKE
% of communities						
Had general criteria for some/all programmes	96.1					
	(1.10)					
	[310]					
Used specific criteria if had programme		22.0		18.5	47.3	40.4
		(2.37)		(2.23)	(3.85)	(3.29)
		[305]		[303]	[169]	[223]
Type of criteria [1)]						
– less than two meals a day	42.3	22.4	76.3	14.3	6.3	2.2
	(2.87)	(5.13)	(2.50)	(4.72)	(2.72)	(1.56)
– cannot obtain health services	25.2	23.9	58.1	3.6	1.3	1.1
	(2.52)	(5.25)	(2.90)	(2.50)	(1.25)	(1.11)
– head of household became unemployed	48.7	23.9	63.9	21.4	68.8	37.8
	(2.90)	(5.25)	(2.82)	(5.53)	(5.21)	(5.14)
– children dropped out of school	19.5	11.9	51.9	5.4	23.8	4.4
	(2.30)	(3.99)	(2.93)	(3.04)	(4.79)	(2.18)
– *keluarga pra sejahtera* (pre-welfare family)	95.6	82.1	74.9	80.4	38.8	36.7
	(1.19)	(4.72)	(2.55)	(5.36)	(5.48)	(5.11)
– *keluarga sejahtera 1* (welfare 1 family)	71.1	49.3	50.5	50.0	22.5	27.8
	(2.63)	(6.15)	(2.94)	(6.74)	(4.70)	(4.75)

– IDT households	13.1	4.5	16.2	3.6	2.5	2.2
	(1.96)	(2.55)	(2.16)	(2.50)	(1.76)	(1.56)
– low health status	27.2	19.4	33.3	3.6	1.3	1.1
	(2.58)	(4.87)	(2.77)	(2.50)	(1.25)	(1.11)
– widow/widower	19.1	17.9	17.9	16.1	3.8	3.3
	(2.28)	(4.72)	(2.25)	(4.95)	(2.14)	(1.90)
– do not have permanent income	47.3	32.8	47.4	25.0	50.0	31.1
	(2.90)	(5.78)	(2.93)	(5.84)	(5.63)	(4.91)
– do not have assistance	19.1	13.4	28.9	10.7	3.8	7.8
	(2.28)	(4.20)	(2.66)	(4.17)	(2.14)	(2.84)
– other	17.4	17.9	16.8	28.6	46.3	70.0
	(2.20)	(4.72)	(2.20)	(6.09)	(5.61)	(4.86)
Total community for general/specific criteria	298	67	291	56	80	90

Source: IFLS3.

[1)] Responses are not mutually exclusive.

Standard errors (in parentheses) are robust to clustering at the community level. Number of observations is in brackets.

TABLE 12.4
Decision Makers for Beneficiaries of Social Safety Net Programmes

	General	*Kartu Sehat*	OPK Beras	Padat Karya	PDMDKE
Village head	50.6	42.0	47.5	50.9	41.4
	(2.84)	(2.83)	(2.87)	(3.86)	(3.28)
Village official/staff	56.1	44.3	61.4	60.9	50.7
	(2.82)	(2.85)	(2.80)	(3.76)	(3.33)
PLKB	58.4	58.4	45.5	10.7	13.2
	(2.80)	(2.83)	(2.87)	(2.38)	(2.25)
Village midwife	27.7	49.2	11.6	4.1	3.1
	(2.55)	(2.87)	(1.84)	(1.54)	(1.15)
Puskesmas staff	24.2	39.0	6.3	2.4	3.5
	(2.44)	(2.80)	(1.40)	(1.17)	(1.23)
Community figure	39.7	20.3	30.7	33.1	38.8
	(2.78)	(2.31)	(2.65)	(3.63)	(3.24)
Activist	6.1	2.6	30.7	7.1	5.3
	(1.36)	(0.92)	(2.65)	(1.98)	(1.49)
PKK	6.1	2.6	23.4	7.1	5.3
	(1.36)	(0.92)	(2.44)	(1.98)	(1.49)
NGO	2.6	1.6	1.7	3.0	2.6
	(0.90)	(0.73)	(0.73)	(1.31)	(1.07)
LKMD	40.6	18.4	27.7	56.8	65.2
	(2.79)	(2.22)	(2.58)	(3.82)	(3.17)
Head of RT/RW	68.4	51.5	69.0	74.0	64.8
	(2.65)	(2.87)	(2.66)	(3.39)	(3.18)
Other	22.9	25.2	20.8	21.3	17.2
	(2.39)	(2.49)	(2.34)	(3.16)	(2.51)
Number of observations	310	305	303	169	227

Source: IFLS3.
Responses are not mutually exclusive. Standard errors (in parentheses) are robust to clustering at the community level.

the poor (25%). Other forms of assistance covered in this table are quite small in coverage.

We now discuss more detailed information by programme.

OPK

Table 12.6 shows the prevalence of OPK rice in the IFLS3 communities. Over 97% of communities have had the programme since 1998; the prevalence of the programme is equally high in urban and rural areas. However, rice distribution is not given out regularly every month. In the table it can be observed that in the year 1999, when the programme fully

TABLE 12.5
Assistance and Subsidies Received by Individuals, by Type
(In percent)

	All	Urban	Rural	Poor	Non-poor
Assistance from government and NGO	3.5	4.4	2.8	4.4	3.3
(cash, rice, and other goods) past 12 months	(0.34)	(0.50)	(0.47)	(0.78)	(0.35)
– money	0.6	0.9	0.4	1.1	0.5
	(0.10)	(0.17)	(0.11)	(0.39)	(0.09)
– rice	2.4	3.3	1.8	3	2.3
	(0.24)	(0.43)	(0.27)	(0.65)	(0.25)
– other food	1.2	1.5	1	1.5	1.1
	(0.22)	(0.28)	(0.33)	(0.46)	(0.23)
– other goods	0.3	0.5	0.2	0.5	0.3
	(0.07)	(0.12)	(0.08)	(0.25)	(0.07)
Number of individuals	[42,712]	[2,0713]	[21,999]	[6,473]	[36,239]
Number of households	[10,219]	[4,902]	[5,317]	[1,223]	[8,996]
Purchased in OPK subsidized market	40.7	32.7	46.9	56.6	37.6
(rice and other goods) past 12 months	(1.73)	(1.91)	(2.58)	(2.61)	(1.69)
– rice	39.3	30.3	46.4	56.1	36.2
	(1.76)	(1.98)	(2.58)	(2.61)	(1.72)
– sugar	0.9	1.4	0.5	0.6	0.9
	(0.18)	(0.36)	(0.14)	(0.28)	(0.18)
– oil	0.8	1.4	0.3	0.6	0.8
	(0.18)	(0.35)	(0.13)	(0.27)	(0.17)
– other	2.7	4.4	1.2	1.5	2.9
	(0.31)	(0.56)	(0.30)	(0.41)	(0.33)

continued on next page

TABLE 12.5 – cont'd

	All	Urban	Rural	Poor	Non-poor
Number of individuals	[42,730]	[20,732]	[21,998]	[6,472]	[36,258]
Number of households	[10,221]	[4,905]	[5,316]	[1,222]	[8,999]
Cash assistance from community group past 12 months	2.5	2.9	2.2	2.9	2.4
	(0.22)	(0.34)	(0.27)	(0.64)	(0.22)
Number of individuals	[42,559]	[20,732]	[21,827]	[6,425]	[36,134]
Number of households	[10,186]	[4,905]	[5,281]	[1,213]	[8,973]
Health Card	18.9	16.9	20.5	24.5	17.8
	(0.83)	(1.03)	(1.24)	(1.67)	(0.86)
Number of individuals	[42,559]	[20,732]	[21,827]	[6,425]	[36,134]
Number of households	[10,186]	[4,905]	[5,281]	[1,213]	[8,973]
Letter of Non-affordability	5.6	6.1	5.2	7.7	5.2
	(0.35)	(0.56)	(0.45)	(0.98)	(0.35)
Number of individuals	[42,559]	[20,732]	[21,827]	[6,425]	[36,134]
Number of households	[10,186]	[4,905]	[5,281]	[1,213]	[8,973]

Source: IFLS3.

Estimates are from household data weighted using household sampling weights multiplied by the number of household members. Standard errors (in parentheses) are robust to clustering at the community level. Significance at 5% (*) and 1% (**) indicated.

TABLE 12.6
Prevalence of OPK Rice Programme in IFLS3 Communities

	Have Programme In			
	Ever Have Programme Since 1998	**Since April 2000**	**FY 1999/2000**	**FY 1998/1999**
% of communities with programme	97.4 (0.90) [311]	87.8 (1.86) [311]	94.5 (1.29) [311]	78.5 (2.34) [311]
% of urban communities with programme	99.4 (0.55) [181]	89.5 (2.28) [181]	95.0 (1.62) [181]	76.8 (3.14) [181]
% of rural communities with programme	94.6 (1.98) [130]	85.4 (3.10) [130]	93.8 (2.11) [130]	80.8 (3.46) [130]
% of months getting programme, among communities with programme [a]		86.3 (1.47) [273]	85.3 (1.53) [294]	53.6 (1.95) [238]
% of household that received rice [a]		29.1 (1.92) [231]	31.8 (1.95) [231]	29.9 (1.93) [231]

Source: IFLS3.
[a] The percentage of months receiving programme is calculated from the number of months in a year (12 months) the programme was received. For 2000, the percentage is calculated out of the number of months before the interview data. Data is missing in some communities. Standard errors (in parentheses) are robust to clustering at the community level. Number of observations is in brackets.

existed for the entire year, OPK rice assistance was received for an average of only 85% of the months.

Table 12.3 shows that for OPK rice, general criteria were used to determine eligibility in 80% of communities. For those who reported using specific criteria, the criteria turned out to be very similar, "*pra sejahtera* households and *KS1* households getting priority. With respect to who plays the role of selecting the beneficiaries of OPK rice, it appears that the village head and his staff are primarily responsible for selecting targeted households within villages (Table 12.4).

More details of individual coverage of OPK are shown in Table 12.7. This includes OPK rice as well as other foods in the OPK programme. Clearly OPK coverage is considerably greater than is free assistance (as noted, usually rice) from government organizations or NGOs. Although 40% of individuals lived in households that received some OPK subsidy (on all foods covered by OPK) during past year, only 24% received any during the past one month. Part of the reason for this may be due to the village receipt of OPK assistance not coming in all months, as noted above. However, it may also be the case that not every household received assistance in each month, even when the village did.

A potential reason for this is easy to see; the amount of the subsidy per household is very small. Only Rp 7,874 in subsidies for all foods was received during the last month for those households that received some.[2] This suggests that the quantities received were correspondingly small.

IFLS does not collect quantity information directly on receipt of OPK rice, but it can be estimated. As noted above, the stated OPK price for rice was Rp 1,000 per kilogram during this period,[3] and the median market price Rp 2,300,[4] hence the subsidy was approximately Rp 1,300 per kilogram. Assuming that all of the subsidy was in rice (approximately true; see Table 12.2), this implies that each receiving household obtained 6 kilograms monthly on average, just over half the 10 kilograms targeted by the programme's guidelines (BAPPENAS 1999). As an alternative way to estimate quantities, we can take the estimated market value of the OPK rice received last month and divide by 2,300, the median market price/kilogram. The median estimated market value of rice received is Rp 14,200, which suggests just under 6.2 kilograms per receiving household. So these different methods provide similar estimates of quantities obtained by receiving households, all substantially less than the goal of 10 kilograms per household per month.

The value of the subsidy received by receiving households, Rp 7,874, amounts to only Rp 1,891 per capita in those households, on average only 1.2% of monthly per capita expenditures (*pce*). Averaging over all

TABLE 12.7
Prevalence and Value of Assistance and Subsidy Received by Individuals

	Percent Receiving in Past 12 Months	Percent Receiving in Past 4 Weeks	Mean Per Capita Value in Past 4 Weeks [a)]	Among Individuals Receiving		
				Mean Household Value in Past 4 Weeks [a)]	Mean Per Capita Value in Past 4 Weeks [a)]	Percent of Per Capita Consumption
All individuals						
Assistance from government and NGO	3.5	1.1	132	57,353	11,743	6.2
(cash, rice and other goods)	(0.34)	(0.14)	(34)	(14,373)	(2,780)	(1.15)
No. of individuals	[42,712]	[42,712]	[42,712]	[527]	[527]	[527]
No. of households	[10,219]	[10,219]	[10,219]	[122]	[122]	[122]
Purchased in OPK subsidized market	40.7	24	453	7,874	1,891	1.2
(rice and other goods)	(1.73)	(1.62)	(37)	(399)	(101)	(0.07)
No. of individuals	[42,730]	[42,730]	[42,730]	[8,657]	[8,657]	[8,657]
No. of households	[10,221]	[10,221]	[10,221]	[2,061]	[2,061]	[2,061]
Urban						
Assistance from government and NGO	4.4	1.6	145	39,209	8,813	4.5
(cash, rice and other goods)	(0.50)	(0.26)	(32)	(7,824)	(1,745)	(1.00)
No. of individuals	[20,713]	[20,713]	[20,713]	[355]	[355]	[355]
Purchased in OPK subsidized market	32.7	19.1	342	8,000	1,791	1.2
(rice and other goods)	(1.91)	(1.65)	(43)	(668)	(164)	(0.11)
No. of individuals	[20,732]	[20,732]	[20,732]	[3,333]	[3,333]	[3,333]
Rural						
Assistance from government and NGO	2.8	0.7	122	90,012	17,017	9.4
(cash, rice and other goods)	(0.47)	(0.14)	(55)	(35,976)	(6,916)	(2.42)
No. of individuals	[21,999]	[21,999]	[21,999]	[172]	[172]	[172]
Purchased in OPK subsidized market	46.9	27.8	541	7,805	1,945	1.2
(rice and other goods)	(2.58)	(2.55)	(56)	(495)	(128)	(0.09)
No. of individuals	[21,998]	[21,998]	[21,998]	[5,324]	[5,324]	[5,324]

continued on next page

TABLE 12.7 – cont'd

	Percent Receiving in Past 12 Months	Percent Receiving in Past 4 Weeks	Mean Per Capita Value in Past 4 Weeks [a)]	Among Individuals Receiving		
				Mean Household Value in Past 4 Weeks [a)]	Mean Per Capita Value in Past 4 Weeks [a)]	Percent of Per Capita Consumption
Poor						
Assistance from government and NGO	4.4	1.6	131	61,290	8,245	9.9
(cash, rice and other goods)	(0.78)	(0.45)	(63)	(24,647)	(3,024)	(3.26)
No. of individuals	[6,473]	[6,473]	[6,473]	[95]	[95]	[95]
Purchased in OPK subsidized market	56.6	33.3	527	8,018	1,581	2.1
(rice and other goods)	(2.61)	(2.69)	(54)	(493)	(110)	(0.14)
No. of individuals	[6,472]	[6,472]	[6,472]	[1,925]	[1,925]	[1,925]
Non-poor						
Assistance from government and NGO	3.3	1.0	132	56,211	12,758	5.1
(cash, rice and other goods)	(0.35)	(0.14)	(39)	(16,954)	(3,448)	(1.04)
No. of individuals	[36,239]	[36,239]	[36,239]	[432]	[432]	[432]
Purchased in OPK subsidized market	37.6	22.2	439	7,833	1,979	1.0
(rice and other goods)	(1.69)	(1.56)	(39)	(470)	(120)	(0.06)
No. of individuals	[36,258]	[36,258]	[36,258]	[6,732]	[6,732]	[6,732]

Source: IFLS3.

Subsidy in past four weeks is defined as difference between the expenditure that would have been paid in regular market and the expenditure in the subsidized market where commodities were bought. Estimates were from household data weighted using household sampling weights multiplied by the number of household members. Standard errors (in parentheses) are robust to clustering at the community level. Significance at 5% (*) and 1% (**) indicated.

households, the subsidy amounts to only Rp 453 per capita per month, which is only 0.3% of *pce*.

Critics of the Social Safety Net Programme considered the programme to be hurriedly conceived and implemented and claim that the programme does not reach the targeted beneficiaries (for example, Sumarto et al. 2001). OPK rice, in particular, was criticized for the poor quality and low quantity of rice given to households, and for leakage away from the poor in its distribution.

IFLS3 data shows that the amounts given per household are indeed low, as just explained. However, there has been clear targeting towards the poor in the distribution, though with leakage. Coverage is higher in rural than in urban areas and among poor households than the non-poor. Still, among the non-poor (as measured by our criteria, not the criteria of BKKBN), as many as 22% of individuals received some subsidy during the last month and 38% during the last year. By comparison, among the poor 33% received some subsidy last month and 57% last year. These differences do suggest targeting on *pce*. The degree of targeting can be seen more clearly in Figure 12.1a, which shows a nonparametric, smoothed, graph of the probability of an individual's receiving any OPK subsidy during the last 12 months, and other forms of aid, against the household's *pce*.[5] For the poorest individuals, the probability of receiving an OPK subsidy in the last 12 months is just over 55%, although it is still as high as 25% for households with monthly *pce* of Rp 300,000, (just over $1 per day at the market exchange rate prevailing in December 2000) and nearly 20% at a monthly *pce* of Rp 500,000. The shape of the curve clearly shows targeting of OPK subsidies by household *pce*.[6] On the other hand two other points can be made. First, coverage among the poor is far from complete and second, a non-trivial number of non-poor is covered as well.

In terms of values the amounts are still very small, even among the poor (Table 12.7, Figure 12.1b). As a percent of *pce* among poor recipient individuals, the total OPK subsidy (on all foods) amounted to only 2% (Table 12.7), and only 0.7% among all poor individuals (not just recipients). Even at the level of the poorest of the poor, the OPK subsidy in the last month amounts to only 0.8% of *pce* among all such persons (Figure 12.1b). To compare, remember that the mean budget share of rice among the poor was 18% in 2000 (Table 3.2). Another way of looking at this question is to ask how much more rice could have been purchased if all of the subsidy was spent on extra rice (which would not be the case). The Rp 7,874 per receiving household would have bought 3.4 kilograms per month, or 0.8 kilograms per person. Averaged among all households this would amount to 0.8 kilograms per household per month or 0.16 kilograms per person extra, at the maximum.

FIGURE 12.1a
Probability of Receiving Aid by Per Capita Expenditure 2000

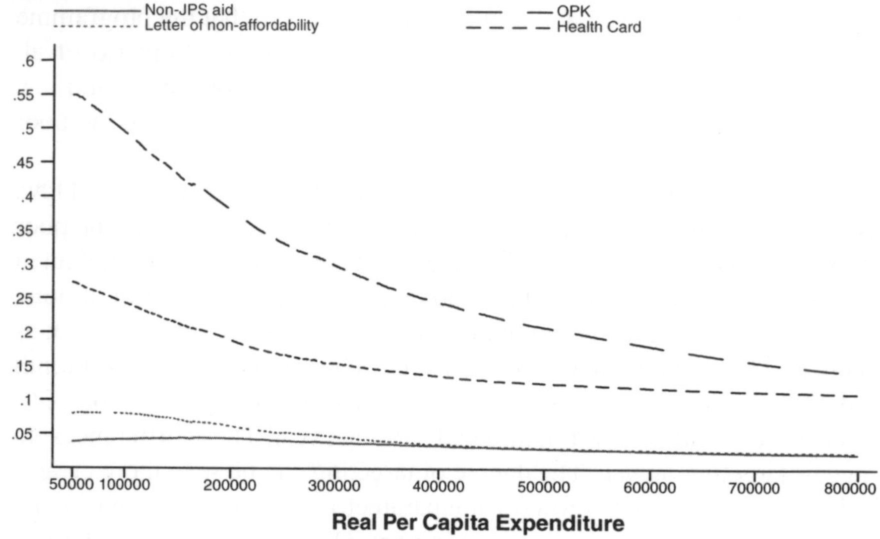
Non-JPS aid
Letter of non-affordability
OPK
Health Card
.6
.55
.5
.45
.4
.35
.3
.25
.2
.15
.1
.05
50000 100000
200000
300000
400000
500000
600000
700000
800000
Real Per Capita Expenditure

FIGURE 12.1b
OPK Subsidy as Percent of Per Capita Expenditure by Per Capita Expenditure 2000

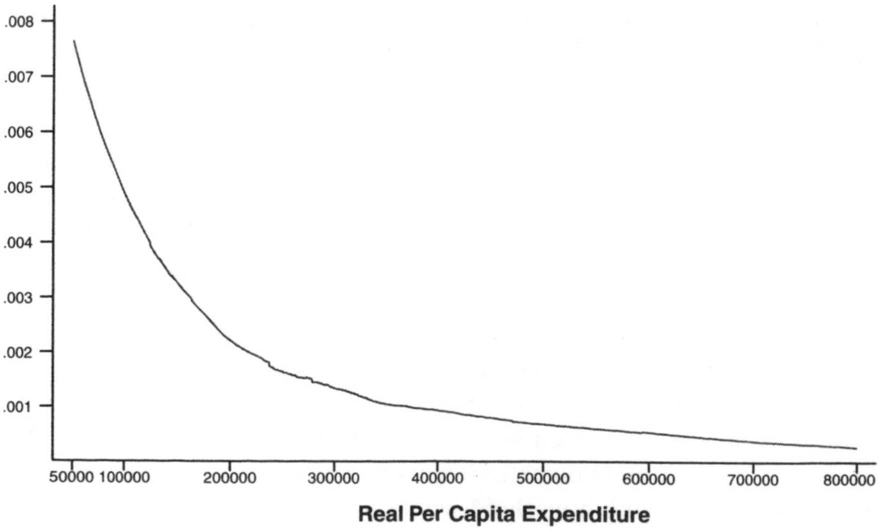
.008
.007
.006
.005
.004
.003
.002
.001
50000 100000
200000
300000
400000
500000
600000
700000
800000
Real Per Capita Expenditure

Source: IFLS3.
Observations are individuals. Lowess, bandwidth = 0.7.

Breaking down individuals by urban and rural status, the targeting is strongest among urban households and less so among rural ones (Appendix Figures 12.1a and 12.2a). However the values as a percentage of *pce* drops sharply for both urban and rural households (Appendix Figures 12.1b and 12.2b).

Using multivariate analysis, we estimate a linear probability model of individual receipt of an OPK subsidy (Table 12.8).[7] Results show that *pce* is indeed strongly negatively related to receipt of subsidy, as is education of the household head, especially if the head completed junior or senior secondary school. Since we control for province and urban/rural location, this is targeting on *pce* within provinces.[8] Being a young child, under 5 years, raises the likelihood of being in a receiving household. Being a rural versus urban resident raises the probability by a substantial amount, but is not significant. The regional variations are interesting. Relative to living in Jakarta, people in IFLS provinces in Sumatra (except Lampung), Bali, South Kalimantan and South Sulawesi have significantly lower probabilities of receiving OPK subsidies, while people living in Lampung, Central Java, Yogyakarta, East Java have higher probabilities of OPK assistance.

Among recipients of OPK subsidy, we examine factors that are correlated with the amount of subsidy per capita in the household (Table 12.9). The dependent variable for these regressions is the log of the per capita subsidy, so the co-efficients on the splined log of *pce* are elasticities along the line segments. Notice that the co-efficients on log *pce* are positive, so that a person from a household with higher *pce* receives more per capita than someone from a poorer household. However, since the co-efficients are less than one, the value of the subsidy as a percent of *pce*, falls with *pce*.

Thus the IFLS3 data seems to indicate there are still loopholes in the implementation of OPK in general and OPK rice in particular. Although the main criteria in selecting the beneficiaries seem to be consistent with the stipulated criteria, there are indications that the amounts and the targeted households have not been implemented, as it was originally intended.

However, we must be very clear that this limited analysis is not an evaluation of how well the programme has worked, for example in terms of improving child health, or more broadly whether this programme is the best use of public funds in order to provide a social safety net. While impact evaluation on actual outcomes related to welfare would be one important part of an economic analysis of the programme's net benefits, it would be only one element; costs would have to be considered, as well as factors such as whether market failures truly justify a public subsidy on food at all. These are questions that we are not answering here.

TABLE 12.8
Linear Probability Models for Receiving Assistance and OPK Subsidy

		Any Assistance Last Year	Any OPK Subsidy Last Year	Cash from Community Last Year	Health Card	Letter of Non-Affordability
Age (spline, × 10^{-4}):	0–59 months	–0.020	7.432**	2.384**	8.497**	3.899**
		(0.02)	(2.95)	(2.55)	(3.59)	(3.07)
	5–14 years	–0.495	–3.039**	–0.865**	–3.350**	0.225
		(1.81)	(3.78)	(3.00)	(4.58)	(0.54)
	15–59 years	0.033	0.509**	0.048	0.248	–0.245**
		(0.53)	(3.30)	(1.08)	(1.94)	(3.35)
	60+ years	0.241	0.037	–0.187	–0.589	0.052
		(1.00)	(0.06)	(0.91)	(1.21)	(0.17)
Female (× 10^{-2})		0.039	0.567	–0.213	0.086	–0.207
		(0.28)	(1.74)	(1.93)	(0.28)	(1.15)
Household head's education (× 10^{-1}):						
	1–5 years	0.056	0.083	0.116*	0.174	0.123
		(0.72)	(0.39)	(2.03)	(0.91)	(1.01)
	6–8 years	–0.068	–0.332	0.090	0.242	–0.046
		(0.89)	(1.46)	(1.58)	(1.25)	(0.40)
	9–11 years	–0.039	–1.142**	0.147	0.103	–0.151
		(0.41)	(4.58)	(1.72)	(0.47)	(1.18)
	12+ years	–0.144	–2.191**	–0.033	–0.486*	–0.358**
		(1.69)	(9.06)	(0.54)	(2.40)	(3.25)
log *pce* (spline):	0– log Rp150,000	–0.003	–0.078**	0.001	–0.057*	–0.002
		(0.31)	(2.90)	(0.14)	(2.22)	(0.17)
	> log Rp 150,000	–0.013**	–0.130**	–0.003	–0.053**	–0.028**
		(2.77)	(11.34)	(0.75)	(6.03)	(5.59)
Rural (× 10^{-2})		–0.922	3.378	–0.607	0.337	–2.445**
		(1.34)	(1.42)	(1.26)	(0.22)	(3.16)
North Sumatra		–0.115**	–0.297**	–0.035**	–0.065**	–0.066**
		(6.05)	(10.22)	(2.76)	(2.80)	(4.21)

West Sumatra	–0.097**	–0.296**	–0.041**	0.004	–0.014
	(4.75)	(8.59)	(3.18)	(0.15)	(0.73)
South Sumatra	–0.105	–0.153**	–0.021	–0.047	–0.036
	(5.13)	(3.52)	(1.10)	(1.57)	(1.67)**
Lampung	–0.111**	0.190**	–0.042**	0.005	–0.061
	(4.74)	(3.31)	(3.22)	(0.09)	(3.26)
West Java	–0.110**	–0.003	–0.032**	–0.028	–0.048**
	(5.85)	(0.10)	(2.68)	(1.49)	(3.07)
Central Java	–0.101**	0.318**	–0.031	0.116**	–0.001
	(5.02)	(9.24)	(2.46)	(4.02)	(0.04)
Yogyakarta	–0.083**	0.158**	0.036	0.197**	0.009
	(3.90)	(3.24)	(2.05)	(5.49)	(0.46)
East Java	–0.098**	0.148**	–0.036	0.074**	–0.002
	(4.85)	(4.22)	(2.91)	(3.01)	(0.11)
Bali	–0.107**	–0.246**	–0.041	–0.074*	–0.027
	(5.23)	(6.69)	(3.34)	(2.30)	(1.51)
West Nusa Tenggara	–0.111**	0.086	–0.041	0.036	–0.015
	(5.25)	(1.43)	(3.07)	(1.06)	(0.68)
South Kalimantan	–0.093**	–0.145**	–0.040	0.006	–0.057**
	(3.79)	(3.14)	(2.84)	(0.21)	(3.17)
South Sulawesi	–0.111**	–0.265**	–0.006	0.008	–0.041*
	(5.22)	(4.86)	(0.38)	(0.29)	(2.21)
Constant	0.195	1.378**	0.032	0.840**	0.127
	(1.51)	(4.36)	(0.26)	(2.76)	(0.75)
F-test (p-values)					
Education variables	0.113	0.000	0.017	0.000	0.000
Expenditure variables	0.009	0.000	0.755	0.000	0.000
Number of observations	42,709	42,730	42,559	42,559	42,559
R-squared	0.02	0.25	0.01	0.05	0.03

Source: IFLS3.
Dummy variable for missing household head's education is included in the regressions but not reported in the table. The omitted category for education is no schooling, and for province is Jakarta. Estimates are weighted using individual sampling weights. Standard errors are robust to clustering at the community level and to heteroscedasticity. Absolute t-statistics are in parentheses with significance at 5% (*) and 1% (**) indicated.

TABLE 12.9
Linear Regressions for Value of Log Per Capita Assistance and OPK Subsidy During Last Four Weeks, Among Those Receiving

		Total Assistance	Total OPK Subsidy
Age (spline, × 10^{-2}):	0–59 months	–0.765	–0.109
		(1.62)	(1.01)
	5–14 years	0.180	–0.035
		(0.96)	(1.34)
	15–59 years	–0.064	0.036**
		(1.88)	(6.94)
	60+ years	0.292*	0.063**
		(2.54)	(2.60)
Female (× 10^{-1})		–0.422	0.220
		(0.63)	(1.55)
Household head's education:	1–5 years	0.314	–0.128
		(0.92)	(1.63)
	6–8 years	0.282	–0.211*
		(0.87)	(2.48)
	9–11 years	–0.127	–0.057
		(0.35)	(0.63)
	12+ years	–0.258	–0.135
		(0.69)	(1.31)
log *pce* (spline):	0– log Rp 150,000	0.298	0.284**
		(0.76)	(3.26)
	> log Rp 150,000	0.481	0.222**
		(1.70)	(3.86)
Rural (× 10^{-1})		0.365	–0.222
		(0.11)	(0.27)
North Sumatra		1.005*	1.201**
		(2.01)	(5.18)
West Sumatra		1.416**	1.895**
		(2.68)	(9.33)
South Sumatra		–0.243	0.728**
		(0.88)	(3.65)
Lampung		–0.428	0.980**
		(0.50)	(4.46)
West Java		–0.425	0.371
		(0.92)	(1.93)
Central Java		0.024	0.385*
		(0.06)	(2.10)
Yogyakarta		1.442	0.211
		(1.76)	(0.90)

continued on next page

TABLE 12.9 – cont'd

	Total Assistance	Total OPK Subsidy
East Java	0.227	0.792**
	(0.56)	(4.21)
Bali	0.446	0.251
	(0.67)	(0.95)
West Nusa Tenggara	–0.263	0.467
	(0.49)	(2.06)
South Kalimantan	0.799	0.435
	(1.61)	(1.89)
South Sulawesi	1.508*	–0.057
	(2.49)	(0.25)
Constant	4.849	3.385**
	(1.06)	(3.30)
F-test (p-values)		
Education variables	0.321	0.109
Expenditure variables	0.022	0.000
Number of observations	527	8445
R-squared	0.23	0.15

Source: IFLS3.
Dummy variable for missing household head's education is included in the regressions but not reported in the table. The omitted category for education is no schooling, and for province is Jakarta. Estimates were weighted using individual sampling weights. Standard errors are robust to clustering at the community level and to heteroscedasticity. Absolute t-statistics are in parentheses with significance at 5% (*) and 1% (**) indicated.

Labour-intensive programme (Padat Karya)

The prevalence of a labour-intensive programme in IFLS communities is not as high as the prevalence of OPK rice programme. Just over half of the IFLS3 communities have had the programme since 1998 (Table 12.10). The prevalence of the programme is more prominent in the urban areas than in the rural areas (61% and 45%). However the table also shows that the programme was effectively phased down, and almost out, by 2000; only 6% of communities report having this programme in 2000 and this decline is observed in both rural and urban areas. The reasons for the decline are unclear. It may be that the government perceived that unemployment had not increased dramatically as had been feared (see

TABLE 12.10
Prevalence of Padat Karya Programme in IFLS3 Communities

	Ever Have Programme Since 1998	Have Programme in		
		Since April 2000	FY 1999/2000	FY 1998/1999
% of communities with programme	54.3	5.8	14.8	39.9
	(2.83)	(1.33)	(2.02)	(2.78)
	[311]	[311]	[311]	[311]
% of urban communities with programme	61.3	7.7	17.1	44.2
	(3.63)	(1.99)	(2.80)	(3.70)
	[181]	[181]	[181]	[181]
% of rural communities with programme	44.6	3.1	11.5	33.8
	(4.37)	(1.52)	(2.81)	(4.16)
	[130]	[130]	[130]	[130]
Daily wage for men [a]				
– mean		11,218	8,124	11,548
– standard error		(848)	(1,747)	(401)
– median		9,808	8,031	10,691
		[17]	[7]	[120]
Daily wage for women [a]				
– mean		10,541	8,235	10,268
– standard error		(891)	(2,063)	(688)
– median		9,682	8,585	10,625
		[13]	[6]	[47]

Source: IFLS3.

[a] Among communities with programme. Data are missing in some communities. Values are in real terms set to December 2000. Standard errors (in parentheses) are robust to clustering at the community level. Number of observations is in brackets.

Chapter 5), and thus the need for this programme was not large. It may also be that the programme as implemented was not successful.

Table 12.3 shows the criteria used for determining the target population of the Padat Karya programme. Those who lost their jobs and those who do not have permanent income are the main criteria for the beneficiaries of the programme. The LKMD and the head of neighbourhood (RW/RT) play a prominent role in drawing the list of beneficiaries, followed by the head of the village and his staff (Table 12.4).

Data from the community side of IFLS3 demonstrates that an average of only 50% of total Padat Karya funds were allocated to wages, less than the 70% target. Given a smaller effective wage bill, the issue of what level to set wages becomes particularly important. Paying low wages has several advantages for these types of programmes, a larger number of persons can be employed with a fixed budget and low wages will lead to self-targeting of the poor. The median real wage in 2000 for those few communities that still had Padat Karya, Rp 9,800 per day, is large relative to the market (means are even larger). Compared to market wages, the median Padat Karya wage is at the 40th percentile of individual market wages. This comparison group is comprised of all men and women, irrespective of their skill level. Since Padat Karya jobs are largely unskilled, it is more appropriate to compare those wages to the wage distribution of the unskilled, in which case it would compare even more favourably. In 1998, when Padat Karya had its biggest penetration, median real wages for Padat Karya workers were even higher than in 2000 (Rp 10,700 per day), yet market wages were lower (Frankenberg et al. 1999). This means that Padat Karya wages compared even more favourably to market wages in 1998 than in 2000. Distorting of market wages by Padat Karya also extends to gender differences. As can be seen from Table 12.10, men and women are paid roughly the same in Padat Karya, in contrast to the market.

PDMDKE

The prevalence of PDMDKE is presented in Table 12.11. Almost 75% of the IFLS3 communities had experienced the programme since 1998. The prevalence of the programme is higher in the urban areas than in rural areas by 20% (80% versus 60%). This programme also declines drastically over the three-year period, to under 5% in 2000. Not only does the prevalence decline, but the flow of funds into the villages that do receive loans has been sharply declining as well, to under half its starting level.

TABLE 12.11
Prevalence of PDMDKE Programme in IFLS3 Communities

	Ever Have Programme Since 1998	Have Programme in		
		Since April 2000	FY 1999/2000	FY 1998/1999
% of communities with programme	73.0 (2.52) [311]	4.8 (1.22) [311]	21.9 (2.35) [311]	54.0 (2.83) [311]
% of urban communities with programme	81.8 (2.87) [181]	3.3 (1.33) [181]	26.0 (3.26) [181]	60.8 (3.64) [181]
% of rural communities with programme	60.8 (4.29) [130]	6.9 (2.23) [130]	16.2 (3.23) [130]	44.6 (4.37) [130]
Number of household getting loan [a)]		160.4 (68.75) [10]	274.2 (51.25) [55]	338.1 (45.36) [139]
Average loan per household [a)]				
– mean		504,406	880,307	846,653
– standard error		(113,966)	(293,435)	(202,323)
– median		488,177 [10]	286,952 [58]	318,539 [144]

Monthly rate of interest [a]	1.1	0.6	1.1
	(0.52)	(0.10)	(0.15)
	[9]	[54]	[140]
Average funds for the programme [a]			
– mean	54,717,796	117,911,621	149,983,749
– standard error	(32,657,444)	(22,567,747)	(21,371,156)
– median	26,817,748	54,143,236	67,188,533
	[14]	[65]	[160]
% of funds for loan	83.8	62.7	58.8
	(8.28)	(3.57)	(2.47)
	[13]	[64]	[159]
% of funds for infrastructure	16.2	32.7	37.6
	(8.28)	(3.50)	(2.43)
	[13]	[64]	[159]

Source: IFLS3.

[a] Among communities with programme. Data is missing in some communities. Values of loan and fund are in real terms set to December 2000. Standard errors (in parentheses) are robust to clustering at the community level. Number of observations is in brackets.

The purpose of the funds has also been changing, going more into loans relative to public employment.

A rapid appraisal of the programme conducted early in its implementation found several flaws in programme implementation (SMERU 1999). First, the objectives and the implementation rules of the programme were not well understood by the implementers at the village level. Secondly, the programme did not reach the targets in the sense that the selection of the projects or activities were conducted by village staff with very little input from the poor members of the communities. Thirdly, the activities were not targeted at the poor. The loans were directed to already established businesses while the public employment only involved very small proportions of the unskilled (probably in part because the high wages that we discuss for Padat Karya attract higher skilled workers to apply). The lack of penalties for defaulters of loans from the revolving funds was also observed as a programme flaw. A large number of defaulters may cause the dwindling of the funds and hence the decline in the number of beneficiaries.

The median loan received, just under Rp 500,000 is below the amount of Rp 2.5 million per loan, stipulated in the programme guidelines (Table 12.11). This should allow for more people to obtain loans, given the budget available, although the mean fraction of households getting loans is not large. On the other hand, the average amount of funds available for a community was declining from 1998 to 2000. The rate of interest, 1% per month, is highly subsidized. Few other programme details are available in the data, so that it is not possible to say from IFLS, for example, what the incentive structure is to repay, or whether the programme suffers from problems of adverse selection.

Scholarship and operational assistance funds (DBO)

Compared to other social safety net programmes, the scholarship programme reached a high percent of IFLS3 communities. In Tables 12.2 and 12.12 it can be seen that among public schools, 96% of primary schools, 99% of junior secondary schools and 97% of senior secondary schools reported their students receiving scholarships from the JPS programme. These high incidences are higher than scholarships received from any other sources. A smaller, though still large, fraction of private primary schools receive JPS scholarship funds. For junior and senior secondary schools the receipt is just a little less than government schools.

The next most prevalent programme comprises scholarships given on merit. This programme is more prevalent in public post-primary schools.

The programme incidence among students is low, although it is not far from the targets set by the government. Table 12.13 shows that among enrolled students in the 2000/2001 school year, 2% of boys and 3% of girls aged 7–12 received some government assistance (which includes JPS but may also include funds from other government sources). For junior secondary aged children (13–15) the receipt was higher, 7% of boys and 8% of girls. For senior secondary school aged children, 16–18, the rates fall off again. These fractions of coverage for any government aid is somewhat lower than the JPS programme goals of reaching 6% of primary, 17% of junior secondary and 10% of senior secondary students.

The fraction of students who report receiving JPS scholarships is even lower, by nearly half in many cases. It may be that scholarship assistance is under-reported or that recipients had a scholarship but don't know that the source was JPS. Note that a higher fraction of girls get government scholarships, especially at the junior secondary level, consistent with programme design.

Government scholarships are weakly targeted to the poor, as seen in Table 12.13. There is clear targeting towards rural areas, however, especially at the junior secondary level. However this is evidently not strongly pro-poor. More pro-poor targeting is apparent in Figure 12.2a, where we can see how the probability of scholarship receipt by students varies continuously with household *pce*. For junior secondary school aged children, as much as 11% of students from households with *pce* of only Rp 50,000 per month receive scholarships, which falls to around 6% for students from households with Rp 450,000 monthly *pce*. For students from households with even lower monthly *pce* than RP 50,000 receipt incidence falls, for reasons that are unclear. So even among students from poor households the coverage rate is small, and as is the case for other JPS programmes, there is leakage to the non-poor.

From a quite different point of view one can ask how much targeting exists if we consider all children, not just those enrolled. On the one hand, this is a student programme and one designed to enable low income students to continue their education. On the other hand, one can ask if this type of programme is likely to be a good vehicle for providing income supplements to the poor during a crisis. This is a relevant consideration since this programme was part of a broader crisis-related social safety net programme, and social safety nets are usually thought of as mechanisms to

TABLE 12.12
Prevalence of Scholarship Programmes Among Schools

	Public			Private		
	Primary	Junior High	Senior High	Primary	Junior High	Senior High
% schools where its students got any scholarship	98.7 (0.40)	99.1 (0.46)	99.3 (0.51)	92.4 (2.41)	95.9 (1.11)	97.5 (0.98)
Type of scholarship (%)						
1. JPS scholarship	96.3 (0.70)	98.6 (0.55)	97.1 (1.00)	79.2 (3.80)	90.7 (1.81)	93.3 (1.43)
2. Non-JPS scholarship:						
– talent and merit	25.3 (1.95)	66.3 (2.21)	75.2 (2.47)	26.4 (4.01)	33.1 (2.72)	45.5 (2.85)
– GNOTA (national foster parents action)	19.4 (1.63)	17.3 (1.62)	2.9 (1.00)	12.5 (2.91)	12.8 (1.86)	3.2 (0.98)
– POMG (parents teachers association)	11.1 (1.42)	12.4 (1.47)	16.9 (2.24)	13.2 (2.74)	9.9 (1.63)	10.8 (1.73)
– specific programme non-GNOTA/POMG	6.5 (1.02)	7.0 (1.11)	11.2 (1.82)	12.5 (3.01)	9.0 (1.52)	14.0 (1.96)
– other scholarship from government	5.1 (0.90)	6.6 (1.12)	20.5 (2.58)	4.9 (1.77)	5.2 (1.17)	7.3 (1.45)
– scholarship from community group	5.1 (0.85)	7.3 (1.21)	13.3 (1.98)	5.6 (2.12)	6.7 (1.51)	8.0 (1.54)
– scholarship from religious group	7.7 (1.14)	9.4 (1.32)	7.6 (1.84)	15.3 (3.10)	13.1 (2.01)	9.2 (1.74)
– other	10.5 (1.24)	18.5 (1.79)	25.5 (2.73)	13.9 (2.93)	16.6 (2.03)	24.2 (2.62)
Number of observations	782	572	278	144	344	314

Source: IFLS3.
Standard errors (in parentheses) are robust to clustering at the community level. Number of observations is in brackets.

TABLE 12.13
Receipt of Assistance for School Among Enrolled Students, School Year 2000/2001
(In percent)

	Children, 7–12		Children, 13–15		Children, 16–18	
	Any Government Aid	JPS Aid	Any Government Aid	JPS Aid	Any Government Aid	JPS Aid
Male	2.3	1.0	6.6	3.4	2.0	1.0
	(0.39)	(0.24)	(1.01)	(0.68)	(0.73)	(0.53)
Female	3.1	1.2	8.2	4.9	1.7	1.4
	(0.49)	(0.28)	(1.16)	(0.96)	(0.55)	(0.53)
Poor	3.4	1.4	8.2	3.2	2.7	2.7
	(0.76)	(0.45)	(1.90)	(1.14)	(2.00)	(2.00)
Non-poor	2.4	1.0	7.2	4.3	1.7	1.1
	(0.35)	(0.21)	(0.85)	(0.68)	(0.47)	(0.36)
Urban	2.8	1.2	3.9	2.6	1.6	0.9
	(0.53)	(0.33)	(0.85)	(0.66)	(0.56)	(0.40)
Rural	2.5	1.0	10.4	5.5	2.1	1.7
	(0.42)	(0.21)	(1.26)	(0.96)	(0.79)	(0.69)
Number of observations	3,850		1.567		1,032	

Source: IFLS3.

Estimates were weighted using individual sampling weights. Standard errors (in parentheses) are robust to clustering at the community level. Number of observations is in brackets.

distribute income supplements to groups designated as needy during a short-run crisis. As we saw in Chapter 6, children are more likely to be enrolled if they are from higher income households, especially for older children. If we examine how receipt of scholarship varies by log of *pce* for *all* children (Figure 12.2b), then targeting is almost non-existent, ranging from just under 6% to 4% for children aged 13–15.

Table 12.14 shows estimates from a linear probability model of scholarship receipt among enrolled children, by age group. With linear splines in log of *pce* at Rp 50,000 and Rp 150,000, the *pce* variables are not jointly significant for any of the age groups. Mother's education is significantly, negatively related to scholarship receipt for primary age students, but parental education is not related to receipt for other age groups.

For junior secondary aged children, who have the highest prevalence of receipt, the largest differences are by geographic location. Those children living in rural areas are more likely to be recipients than are urban children. Likewise, children living in Lampung, Central Java, West Nusa Tenggara and South Sulawesi are more likely to be recipients than are children in Jakarta. This geographical targeting is evidently responsible for the negative bivariate relationship with *pce* that we see in Figure 12.2a.

We have only analysed the receipt and targeting of the scholarships, not their impact, if any, on school attendance or progression. A recent study by Cameron (2002) using data from the 100 Village Study finds an effect of receiving scholarships in lowering drop-out rates for junior secondary students, but not for others. The methods used in this study, however, rely on very strong assumptions, ones which seem implausible, and so should be treated with caution. Nevertheless, Cameron's study raises the issue that the JPS scholarship programme might have had on impact on behaviour even though it had limited reach and had considerable leakage.

Operational assistance to schools is another form of JPS programme in education. The prevalence of this programme is lower than the scholarship programme. The percentage of schools that received operational assistance funds is 70%, 63% and 80% for government primary schools, junior secondary schools and senior secondary schools respectively (Table 12.15). These percentages are 8% to 10% lower for private schools. The second panel of Table 12.15 shows the percentage of schools receiving assistance from the maintenance fund. These results indicate that operational assistance is more prominent for secondary schools, while at the primary school the incidence levels are virtually identical.

FIGURE 12.2a
Government Scholarship Receipt by Log *pce* by Age of Enrolled Children

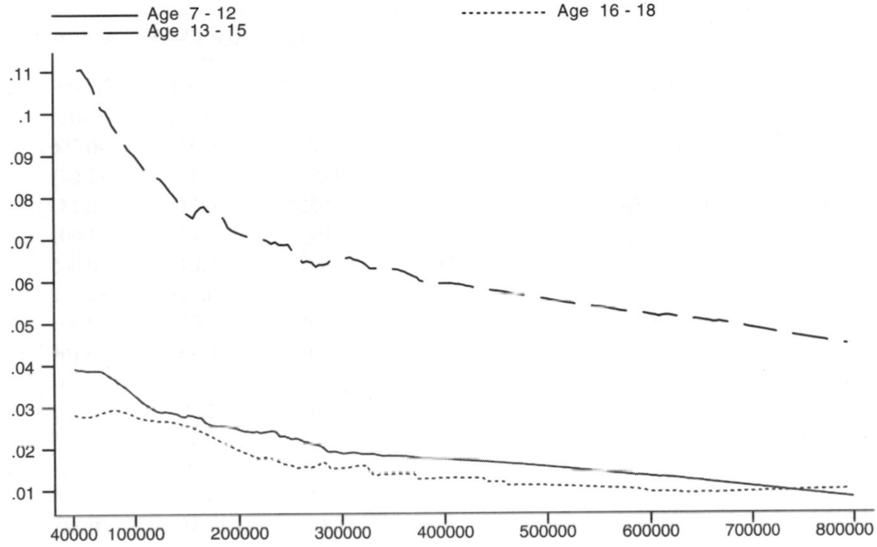
Age 7 - 12
Age 13 - 15
Age 16 - 18
.11
.1
.09
.08
.07
.06
.05
.04
.03
.02
.01
40000
100000
200000
300000
400000
500000
600000
700000
800000

FIGURE 12.2b
Government Scholarship Receipt by Log *pce* by Age for All Children

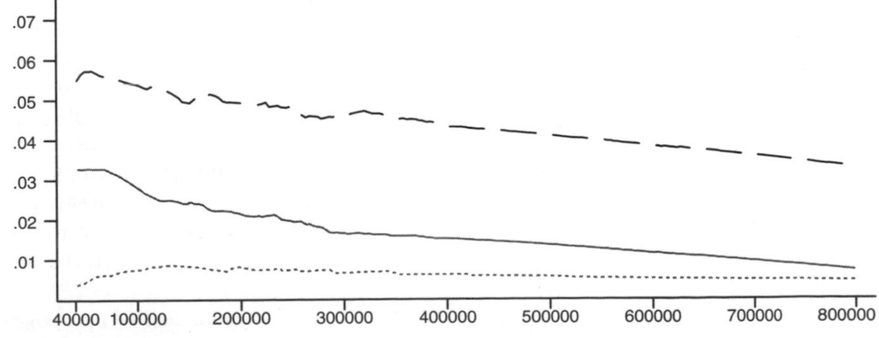
Age 7 - 12
Age 13 - 15
Age 16 - 18
.11
.1
.09
.08
.07
.06
.05
.04
.03
.02
.01
40000
100000
200000
300000
400000
500000
600000
700000
800000

Source: IFLS3.
Lowess, bandwidth = 8.5.

TABLE 12.14
Linear Probability Models of Student Receipt of Government Scholarship by Age Group, 2000/2001

	Age 7–12	Age 13–15	Age 16–18
Mother's education if in household ($\times 10^{-2}$)	–0.247**	–0.020	–0.003
	(2.75)	(0.07)	(0.02)
Father's education if in household ($\times 10^{-2}$)	0.009	–0.367	–0.306
	(0.09)	(1.45)	(1.64)
log *pce* (spline): 0 – log Rp 50,000	0.055*	0.114	0.137
	(2.09)	(1.83)	(1.60)
log Rp 50,000 – log Rp 150,000	–0.022	–0.015	0.005
	(1.50)	(0.42)	(0.26)
> log Rp 150,000	–0.005	0.014	–0.001
	(0.80)	(0.83)	(0.16)
Rural	–0.015*	0.042**	0.002
	(2.09)	(2.70)	(0.16)
North Sumatra	0.007	0.033	–0.013
	(0.70)	(1.19)	(1.04)
West Sumatra	0.042*	0.038	0.009
	(2.47)	(1.35)	(0.44)
South Sumatra	0.007	0.038	–0.016
	(0.64)	(1.48)	(1.28)
Lampung	0.028	0.076*	–0.019
	(1.83)	(1.99)	(1.40)
West Java	0.009	0.012	0.007
	(0.94)	(0.61)	(0.42)
Central Java	0.030*	0.106**	0.024
	(2.41)	(4.13)	(1.27)
Yogyakarta	0.026	–0.001	–0.012
	(1.62)	(0.07)	(1.00)
East Java	0.026*	0.036	0.006
	(2.32)	(1.65)	(0.36)
Bali	0.006	–0.026	0.006
	(0.41)	(1.86)	(0.29)
West Nusa Tenggara	0.028*	0.077*	0.033
	(2.10)	(2.31)	(1.30)
South Kalimantan	0.009	0.046	0.016
	(0.72)	(0.87)	(0.51)
South Sulawesi	–0.009	0.114**	0.025
	(1.04)	(2.86)	(0.64)
Constant	–0.544*	–1.193	–1.446
	(1.98)	(1.82)	(1.60)

continued on next page

TABLE 12.14 – cont'd

	Age 7–12	Age 13–15	Age 16–18
F-test (p-values):			
Education variables	0.012	0.190	0.134
Expenditure variables	0.149	0.182	0.102
Number of observations	3,850	1,567	1,032
R-squared	0.01	0.04	0.02

Source: IFLS3.

Dummy variable for missing parental education or parent not in the household is included in the regressions but not reported in the table. The omitted category for education is no schooling, and for province is Jakarta. Estimates were weighted using individual sampling weights. Standard errors are robust to clustering at the community level and to heteroscedasticity. Absolute t-statistics are in parentheses with significance at 5% (*) and 1% (**) indicated.

Social safety net programmes in health (*Kartu Sehat*)

The JPS–BK programme covered almost all IFLS3 communities. Approximately 98% of IFLS3 communities have had the programme since 1998, with little difference between urban and rural areas (Table 12.2).

The family planning workers (PLKB) and the head of the neighbourhood organization (RW/RT) play a prominent role (Table 12.4) in selecting the beneficiaries of the programme. They draw the list of poor households that are eligible for getting the health card (*Kartu Sehat*) with input from the head of the village and his staff. About 78% of the communities reported that they used general criteria for selecting the targeted households (Table 12.3). Communities that do not use general criteria still use *pra sejahtera* and *KS1* as the main specific criteria.

IFLS collects information about the criteria for selecting the beneficiaries of the health card from both the village staff and the person responsible for administering the JPS–BK funds nominated by the community health centre (*puskesmas*). In Table 12.3, the responses from both sources are recorded. Interestingly, the village staff report using *pra sejahtera* and *KS1* as the main criteria, while the persons in charge of administering the JPS–BK funds cite inability to have two meals a day and unemployed head of the household as the main criteria along with *pra sejahtera*. Apart from economic based criteria, they also used accessibility to health services and health status as an important criteria.

TABLE 12.15
Prevalence of Operational Funds Assistance (DBO) and Operational and Maintenance Funds for Schools

	Public			Private		
	Primary	**Junior High**	**Senior High**	**Primary**	**Junior High**	**Senior High**
% Ever received DBO since 1998	69.7 (2.01) [814]	70.5 (2.32) [593]	79.8 (2.60) [292]	59.6 (4.50) [146]	62.7 (2.85) [357]	70.1 (2.87) [324]
– since April 2000	10.2 (1.38) [806]	12.6 (1.61) [587]	15.0 (2.22) [286]	10.3 (2.82) [145]	11.6 (1.81) [354]	14.0 (2.25) [322]
– during FY 1999/2000	60.3 (2.17) [812]	56.1 (2.50) [592]	71.5 (2.84) [291]	51.4 (4.54) [146]	50.4 (2.98) [357]	60.5 (2.99) [324]
– during FY 1998/1999	42.0 (2.14) [809]	49.7 (2.50) [592]	63.6 (3.01) [291]	30.1 (4.08) [146]	35.9 (2.86) [357]	44.8 (3.01) [324]
% Ever received operational and maintenance funds since 1998	72.2 (2.08) [813]	28.6 (2.10) [591]	27.3 (2.98) [286]	61.6 (4.18) [146]	19.3 (2.41) [357]	1.2 (0.61) [324]
– since April 2000	10.3 (1.32) [804]	11.1 (1.44) [584]	11.2 (2.08) [285]	11.7 (2.63) [145]	6.2 (1.41) [356]	0.3 (0.31) [324]
– during FY 1999/2000	69.5 (2.10) [810]	26.2 (2.06) [587]	25.7 (2.88) [284]	55.5 (4.28) [146]	16.5 (2.28) [357]	0.9 (0.53) [324]
– during FY 1998/1999	46.2 (2.21) [807]	22.0 (1.87) [587]	20.7 (2.68) [285]	31.5 (3.80) [146]	12.4 (2.06) [355]	0.9 (0.53) [324]

Source: IFLS3.
Standard errors (in parentheses) are robust to clustering at the community level. Number of observations is in brackets.

With regards to the utilization of the health card, IFLS3 asked about the type of services for which the holder of the health card could use the health card. Such services include general examination, pre-natal care, delivery services, child immunization, oral contraception and injection (Table 12.16). It appears that the holders of health cards can obtain any of these types of services from *puskesmas* or *puskesmas pembantu* (*pustu*). However, the private sector tends to accept *Kartu Sehat* less frequently.

The last row of Table 12.16 presents data from *puskesmas* recording the percentage of patients who visited the health facility during the last week and had health cards. The data is taken from patient registration records. Some 17%–19% of patients at *puskesmas* or *pustu* are reported to have had

TABLE 12.16
***Kartu Sehat* Services and Coverage by Type of Provider**

	Puskesmas	*Pustu*	Midwife	Village Midwife
% of providers:				
Health services covered:				
– General check-up	99.2	97.7	85.0	94.9
	(0.36)	(0.85)	(4.58)	(2.60)
	[617]	[306]	[60]	[99]
– Pre-natal care	99.0	97.4	85.5	91.5
	(0.41)	(0.97)	(4.61)	(2.75)
	[591]	[269]	[69]	[106]
– Delivery	99.4	99.5	96.7	93.8
	(0.35)	(0.54)	(1.87)	(2.31)
	[487]	[186]	[90]	[113]
– Immunization for children	97.3	97.1	83.8	100.0
	(0.65)	(1.06)	(7.01)	–
	[598]	[243]	[37]	[39]
– Oral contraception	92.8	88.1	77.8	83.3
	(1.09)	(2.31)	(6.95)	(4.54)
	[559]	[218]	[45]	[78]
– Injection contraception	92.8	88.1	76.3	82.0
	(1.09)	(2.31)	(6.39)	(4.94)
	[559]	[218]	[59]	[89]
Patients covered	17.3	19.6	5.8	16.4
	(0.66)	(1.17)	(1.34)	(2.43)
	[591]	[273]	[80]	[81]

Source: IFLS3.
Standard errors (in parentheses) are robust to clustering at the community level. Number of observations is in brackets.

Kartu Sehat, while smaller percentages had it among the private sector patients. This matches closely with the percent of the population covered by *Kartu Sehat*, 19.4% (Table 12.5).

For each visit made during the last month, respondents report whether they used the *Kartu Sehat* to help pay their *puskesmas* bills. Only 12% claim doing so (Table 12.17). Very few report using *Kartu Sehat* for private providers and just over 4% of inpatients to public hospitals report doing so. The reason(s) for this discrepancy is unclear. It may be that individuals underreport *Kartu Sehat* use. However it may also be that the

TABLE 12.17
Usage of Health Card and Letter of Non-affordability in Outpatient and Inpatient Care Visits by Type of Provider

	Outpatient Care Visits		Inpatient Care Visits	
	Health Card	Letter of Non-affordability	Health Card	Letter of Non-affordability
% of visits used:				
All type of providers	4.5 (0.49) [8,159]	0.3 (0.10) [8,159]	3.2 (0.73) [838]	1.4 (0.51) [838]
Puskesmas* and *Pustu				
All individuals	12.0 (1.35) [2,794]	0.6 (0.26) [2,794]		
Urban residence	14.7 (2.22) [1,336]	0.6 (0.35) [1,336]		
Rural residence	9.7 (1.58) [1,458]	0.7 (0.39) [1,458]		
Poor individuals	23.0 (5.21) [409]	0.9 (0.71) [409]		
Non-poor individuals	10.0 (1.10) [2,385]	0.6 (0.26) [2,385]		

continued on next page

TABLE 12.17 – cont'd

	Outpatient Care Visits		Inpatient Care Visits	
	Health Card	Letter of Non-affordability	Health Card	Letter of Non-affordability
Public hospitals				
All individuals	1.7	0.5	4.1	2.9
	(0.72)	(0.46)	(1.16)	(1.11)
	[409]	[409]	[380]	[380]
Urban residence	1.6	0.7	2.9	0.0
	(0.87)	(0.72)	(1.36)	–
	[257]	[257]	[207]	[207]
Rural residence	1.8	0.0	5.4	5.9
	(1.31)	–	(1.90)	(2.12)
	[152]	[152]	[173]	[173]
Poor individuals	0.0	0.0	19.9	12.7
	–	–	(10.02)	(7.38)
	[12]	[12]	[29]	[29]
Non-poor individuals	1.7	0.5	2.9	2.1
	(0.75)	(0.48)	(0.89)	(0.90)
	[397]	[397]	[351]	[351]
Private facilities				
All individuals	0.6	0.1	1.0	0.2
	(0.23)	(0.04)	(0.58)	(0.20)
	[4,956]	[4,956]	[401]	[401]
Urban residence	1.0	0.1	0.7	0.0
	(0.44)	(0.06)	(0.68)	–
	[2,610]	[2,610]	[266]	[266]
Rural residence	0.3	0.1	1.5	0.6
	(0.13)	(0.06)	(1.07)	(0.57)
	[2,346]	[2,346]	[135]	[135]
Poor individuals	1.4	0.4	4.1	0.0
	(0.81)	(0.36)	(4.05)	–
	[407]	[407]	[28]	[28]
Non-poor individuals	0.5	0.0	0.7	0.2
	(0.21)	(0.03)	(0.52)	(0.22)
	[4,549]	[4,549]	[373]	[373]

Source: IFLS3.

Estimates were for visits in the last four weeks. Estimates for inpatient care visits at *puskesmas/pustu* were not reported due to small sample size. Standard errors (in parentheses) are robust to clustering at the community level. Number of observations is in brackets.

puskesmas have in their registration records whether a patient possessed a card, but not whether it was used. Remember that there are some services for which *puskesmas* do not accept *Kartu Sehat*.

Clearly *Kartu Sehat* is now the dominant way to subsidize health care for the poor, as compared to the Letter of Non-affordability, which is very limited in coverage and has effectively been replaced by *Kartu Sehat*. It is interesting that among individuals who report using the *Kartu Sehat* for visits to a *puskesmas*, 25% report paying a positive amount for their visit. *Kartu Sehat* is supposed to entitle one to free service for services covered. It may be that these visits involved several services, some covered by *Kartu Sehat* and some not. It could also reflect physicians charging prices differently from stated programme policy.

In Table 12.5 it can be seen that the having *Kartu Sehat* is more prevalent among the poor (25% versus 18%). Figure 12.1a shows the same, with the probability of having a *Kartu Sehat* ranging from nearly 30% amongst the very poor, to over 10% among the rich. Table 12.17 shows that self-reported use at *puskesmas* is 23% among the poor and 10% among the non-poor. Thus as is true for OPK subsidies, there is targeting, but the fraction of the poor who are covered is relatively small and there is some non-trivial leakage to the non-poor. Table 12.8 shows linear probability model estimates for the probability of having a *Kartu Sehat*. The co-efficients on log *pce* are consistent with the picture in Figure 12.1a, showing some targeting, but much less than for OPK subsidies. On the other hand, higher schooling of the household head is only negatively associated with having a *Kartu Sehat* for those who completed senior secondary level or higher. People in Central Java, Yogyakarta and East Java are much more likely to have *Kartu Sehat* compared to people in Jakarta, while those in Bali and North Sumatra are less likely.

Posyandu revitalization and food supplementation to pre-school and school children

Revitalization of integrated health services post (*posyandu*) and food supplementation programme are programmes within the JPS–BK aimed at improving the nutritional status of targeted individuals. Table 12.2 shows that 84% of IFLS3 communities have had funds injected to revitalize their posyandu. Surprisingly, the prevalence of the programme is higher in urban than rural areas (87% and 79% respectively). Despite this, coupled with the results from Chapters 9 and 11, which show that *posyandu*

TABLE 12.18
Supplementary Distribution Programme (PMT) in IFLS3 Communities

	Percent
% of communities:	
PMT covers:	
– Infant, 6–11 months	94.4
	(1.32)
	[303]
– Children, 12–23 months	96.0
	(1.12)
	[303]
– Children, 24–59 months	87.8
	(1.88)
	[303]
– Pregnant and postpartum mother	88.8
	(1.82)
	[303]
– Other (children, 5–14 years, women at reproductive age, adults)	3.7
	(1.08)
	[301]

Source: IFLS3.
Standard errors (in parentheses) are robust to clustering at the community level. Number of observations is in brackets.

services declined drastically in quality from 1997 to 2000, it is questionable if this programme had an important impact on *posyandu* services offered.

The child food supplementation programme is run through both the posyandu and the schools. Table 12.18 shows the prevalence of the food supplementation in the *posyandu*. The programme exists in most of IFLS3 communities. On the other hand, the same type of programme run through the schools has a lower prevalence rate as shown in Table 12.19. Just over 25% of public primary schools and under 20% of private primary school reported having the programme in 2000. This represented an increase since 1997 in the incidence of schools having feeding programmes where public schools saw a 5% increase but private schools suffered a decline of

TABLE 12.19
Supplementary Food Programmes at Primary School

	Public			Private		
	1997	2000	Change	1997	2000	Change
% school with programme	19.8	25.5	5.7 *	19.4	16.4	–2.9
	(2.02)	(2.02)	(2.86)	(3.85)	(3.29)	(5.06)
	[834]	[815]	[129]	[146]		
Support sources among schools with programme (%) [a]						
– government	84.8	88.0	3.1	48.0	87.5	39.5 **
	(3.47)	(2.53)	(4.30)	(11.18)	(6.85)	(13.11)
– private sector	4.8	1.4	–3.4	20.0	0.0	–20.0 *
	(1.90)	(0.83)	(2.07)	(8.25)	–	(8.25)
– institution/non-government organization	1.2	2.4	1.2	24.0	12.5	–11.5
	(0.86)	(1.05)	(1.36)	(9.77)	(6.85)	(11.93)
– parents/schools/community	11.5	9.1	–2.4	24.0	8.3	–15.7
	(2.79)	(2.29)	(3.61)	(8.43)	(5.70)	(10.18)
– others	0.0	5.3	5.3 **	4.0	0.0	–4.0
	–	(1.55)	(1.55)	(3.78)	–	(3.78)
	[165]	[208]		[25]	[24]	

Source: IFLS2 and IFLS3.

[a] Responses are not mutually exclusive.

Standard errors (in parentheses) are robust to clustering at the community level. Number of observations is in brackets.

3%. This programme is clearly a government-supported programme for public schools. For private schools, there had been a large measure of private sector and NGO support in 1997, which shrank enormously by 2000 as the government took over much of the support of feeding programmes in private schools.

SUMMARY

Using data from IFLS, we explore the incidence, magnitude and targeting of assistance from a variety of social safety net programmes, JPS, most of which were implemented, or broadened, in 1998. We assess the programmes in the context of the stated programme goals where possible, but also more broadly, in terms of how well they address the short-term problems caused by the crisis. In this report, we do not attempt any causal analyses of possible programme impacts on welfare outcomes.

As argued, a major cause of the dislocations to the poor during this crisis was the sharply rising relative food prices, especially for rice. This suggests that a potentially effective way for a safety net programme to get income supplements to the poor would be through targeted rice subsidies. In fact this was part of the JPS response: the OPK rice subsidy programme. However the JPS programmes were far broader than the rice subsidy; including a public employment programme, a rotating credit programme, a health subsidy programme and a school scholarship programme. It is not clear that this set of programmes represented the best mix for the 1998 crisis or for potential future ones; some of these were probably not a very good use of resources in 1998. Of course, it is much easier in hindsight to make this point. For example, high unemployment was not a major problem during the 1998 crisis. Falling wages were, but wages fell largely due to rising food prices. Access to credit may have been a problem for some, but it is not clear that the poor fared so much worse during the crisis as before with regards to credit. In fact, for most communities, neither the public employment nor the credit programme were operational by 2000, whereas they were in 1998.

In the OPK programme, 57% of the poor received some subsidized rice (or other food) from OPK during the last year, although this assistance is not monthly; only 33% of the poor were recipients in the last month. On the one hand, while there was targeting of this programme, a large fraction of the poor received no OPK subsidized foods, while many non-poor were recipients. Further, the amount of rice given to the targeted households was very low, around 6 kilograms per household per month, so that the value of the subsidy was correspondingly low. Even among the poor, the value of the subsidy represented only 0.7% of *pce* averaged over all poor households, and only 2% among those poor households that received some OPK rice in the last month.

The public employment programme (Padat Karya) has been discontinued in most communities. One potential problem observed with this programme was that mean wage rates were quite high relative to the market. The mean wage paid in 2000 was at the 40th percentile of the private sector wage distribution. This is probably too high to serve as a screening device to attract only the poor into the programme.

The prevalence of PDMDKE among communities also declined substantially over the three-year period 1998–2000. There are also indications that the amount of revolving funds available declined within the communities that kept the programme.

The scholarship and school fund assistance programme has reached almost every school in the IFLS3 sample. The JPS scholarship programme is more prevalent than any other scholarship programme. The student coverage is low, just over 10% among poor junior secondary students, but close to the programme's target coverage rate. Poor students are more likely to receive scholarships than non-poor students, but among all children (whether or not a child is a student), the poor are no more likely to receive these scholarships than children of the non-poor. This result stems from children of the poor being less likely to be enrolled in school. The programme is designed to target students, not the general child population. This raises the question of the effectiveness of this safety net programme if the main goal is to provide short-term income assistance to those poor dislocated by the crisis. On the other hand, scholarships to the poor may make sense as a long-run programme, if it can be shown that it raises school completion rates of poor children.

The prevalence of JPS–BK is almost universal among IFLS3 communities. Among individuals, just under 20% have cards and the percentage is a little higher among the poor (25%). A beneficiary holder a of health card could obtain most of the services available in public as well private health facilities. However its utilization in the private facilities is much lower than in public health centres.

Notes

1 Sugar and cooking oils are also covered and a small number of foods aggregated into the category "other".

2 IFLS3 collects data on the value that households actually paid for each OPK distributed food (rice, sugar, etc.) at the last purchase, on the household's estimate of the local market value of that purchase, and on the number of times during the last one month that an OPK purchase was made. Subsidy values are constructed by subtracting the value actually paid from the estimated market value multiplying by the number of times it was received within the last one month and summing over the food types. This was then converted to December 2000 Jakarta prices by using our deflators.

3 IFLS3 community data indicate that Rp 1,000 was the price that was claimed by Kepala Desa staff to be charged for rice bought under the OPK rice programme. There is very little variation in the data on

reported prices charged. Programme records show that Rp 1,000/kilogram was the price that was charged to communities by BULOG. It may be that communities had to charge somewhat higher prices to households to cover distribution costs.

4 This price is the median price of medium quality rice as measured in the IFLS3 household data. Respondents were asked the amount they purchased, the units and its value, for the last purchase within the last month. These quantities and unit prices are only available for a small number of commodities. In general, all expenditure information in IFLS is for values only, not quantities.

5 These Lowess plots are not weighted.

6 In contrast, note that there is no targeting of free assistance.

7 These regressions combine decisions on which communities receive and how much, with who is chosen within the communities.

8 We do not control for community in these results. Targeting within communities is another important question.

APPENDIX FIGURE 12.1a
Probability of Receiving Aid by Per Capita Expenditure 2000: Urban

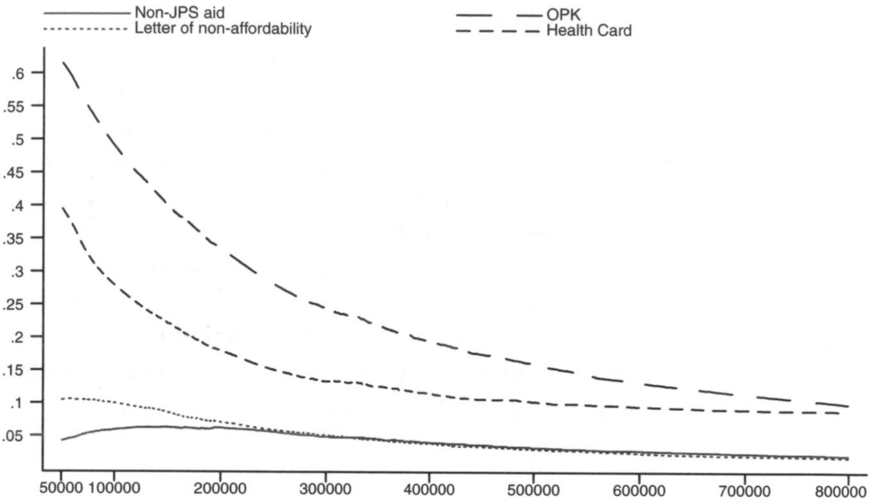
Non-JPS aid
Letter of non-affordability
OPK
Health Card
.6
.55
.5
.45
.4
.35
.3
.25
.2
.15
.1
.05
50000 100000
200000
300000
400000
500000
600000
700000
800000
Real Per Capita Expenditure

APPENDIX FIGURE 12.1b
OPK Subsidiary as Percent of Per Capita Expenditure by Per Capita Expenditure: Urban

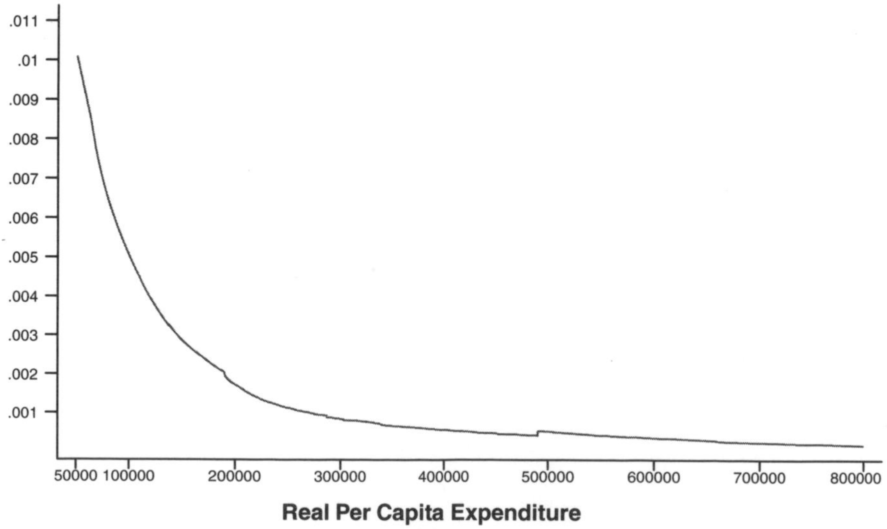
.011
.01
.009
.008
.007
.006
.005
.004
.003
.002
.001
50000 100000
200000
300000
400000
500000
600000
700000
800000
Real Per Capita Expenditure

Source: IFLS3.
Observations are individuals. Lowess, bandwidth = 0.7.

APPENDIX FIGURE 12.2a
Probability of Receiving Aid by Per Capita Expenditure 2000: Rural

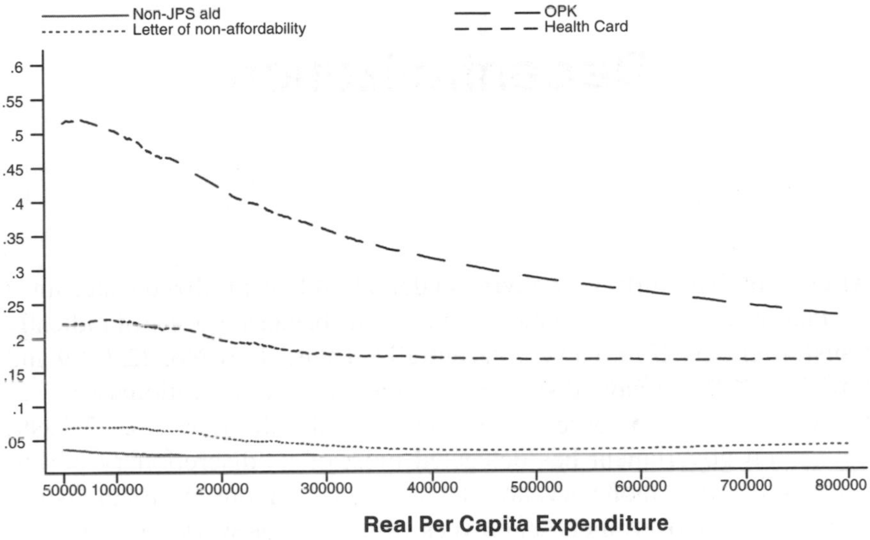
Non-JPS aid
Letter of non-affordability
OPK
Health Card
.6
.55
.5
.45
.4
.35
.3
.25
.2
.15
.1
.05
50000 100000
200000
300000
400000
500000
600000
700000
800000
Real Per Capita Expenditure

APPENDIX FIGURE 12.2b
OPK Subsidiary as Percent of Per Capita Expenditure by Per Capita Expenditure: Rural

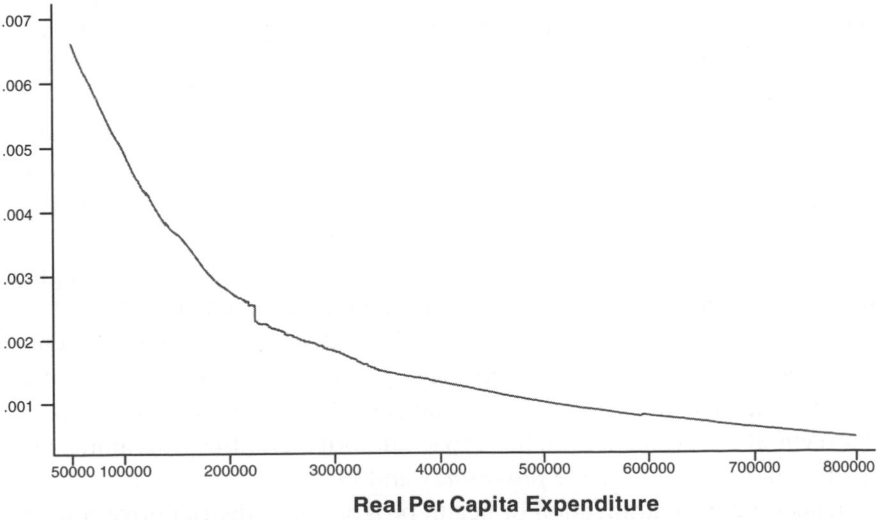
.007
.006
.005
.004
.003
.002
.001
50000 100000
200000
300000
400000
500000
600000
700000
800000
Real Per Capita Expenditure

Source: IFLS3.
Observations are individuals. Lowess, bandwidth = 0.7

13

Decentralization

After more than thirty years living under a highly centralized state, since 1st January 2001 the government of Indonesia began a process of radically transforming itself into a very decentralized state. Law No. 22/1999 and Law No. 25/1999 gave district governments more discretionary power and better access to sources of revenues. Under the Law No. 22/1999, the central government has delegated most of its discretionary power, except on justice, monetary, law, defence, and religious affairs to district governments. Government employees who had been working locally for the central government, have now been put under district jurisdiction. This new system of government provides provincial governments unclear and limited roles such as the management of issues related to cross-district affairs.

The implementation of regional autonomy has provided much room for district governments to formulate their own policies and programmes, including health and educational programmes. For health programmes, district governments have the right to decide what programme and services to be delivered by their *puskesmas* and *puskesmas pembantu* (*pustu*) and how these programmes and services are to be carried out. District governments have also been given budgetary power and authority to decide the amount of user fees for their own *puskesmas* and *pustu* and how the fees are distributed and managed.

In the past, the district governments had very limited role in managing health programmes and services. The central government decided on health policies and programmes to be implemented by district governments. The personnel of the *puskesmas* and *pustu* belonged to the central government and thus, were fully controlled by the central government. The central government even had broad authority over the programme and operational activities of the *puskesmas* and *pustu*.

Under the decentralization of health programmes, district governments have the right to decide what programmes and services will be delivered by their *puskesmas* and *pustu* and how these programmes and services are to be carried out. District governments have also been given budgetary power including authority to decide the amount of user fees for their *puskesmas* and *pustu* and how the revenues from those fees are distributed and managed.

During the centralized era, district educational agencies (education *dinas*) only had authority to manage primary schools. Their influence on even personnel matters was limited. The central government decided the salary, curricula, and other logistic needs, such as choice of reading books, office supplies, etc. With the new system, district governments have a mandatory role to manage educational services from primary schools to senior secondary schools. Now, district governments have the right to decide personnel matters, salary levels, school programmes, and other matters related to the operational activities of their schools.

Thus, health and educational programmes and services may vary across districts, depending on factors such as local politics and needs. The quality and quantity of health and educational services are very much influenced by local political processes. District governments now have more access to revenues and greater concern for education and health may result in the allocation of more resources to these sectors and thus, provide more and better health and educational services. On the contrary, if district governments have less fiscal capacity, they may not be able to provide improved health and educational services.

Since the operational activities of health and educational services are fully managed by the district governments, it will be interesting to see how the methods employed by district governments to manage schools, *puskesmas*, and *pustu* vary and how outcomes respond, or not, to that variation. It is expected that district governments will employ different approaches to manage their health facilities and schools. Some district governments may provide more authority to their schools and *puskesmas* to decide their operational activities but others may provide the authority to the head of Education and Health Agencies. In several districts, Bupati and head of the Planning Agency (BAPPEDA) may play dominant roles in decision-making regarding budget allocation, procurement, and development plan of schools and *puskesmas*.

Since IFLS3 was fielded in the months prior to enactment of the decentralization laws, we present the practice of decision-making on various matters related to health and educational services at that time, which will serve as a baseline for later comparisons. IFLS3 contains a limited amount of information on village and facility budgets, budgetary discretion at the local level, and the degree to which *puskesmas*, *pustu* and school staff participate in decision-making. On the other hand, IFLS does not collect information at the district level, which limits its use to assess decentralization issues.

BUDGET AND REVENUES

Table 13.1 displays budget information for the *desa* or *kelurahan*, providing the real December 2000 value of the budgets and the fraction that comes from different sources.[1] It is important to note that not all localities had complete budget data even for the current budget year. For fiscal year 1999/2000 urban localities were more likely than rural localities to have complete data (80% vs. 72%). This is an indication of a potential transitional problem as decentralization unfolds, localities may not always have the staff or capability to maintain and work with their budgets.

Examining the budget totals, one can see the crisis impact; budgets were cut by 30% or more in 1998/99, with a substantial but incomplete recovery in 1999/2000. Rural per capita village budgets were higher than urban budgets. There are interesting differences between villages in Java and Bali and in other provinces (Appendix Tables 13.1a and 13.1b). The percentage of communities that had complete budget data for our enumerators to examine, is far lower outside of Java and Bali; 25% lower in rural communities and 20% in urban ones. There was a huge improvement in records in urban areas outside of Java–Bali for the 1999/2000 fiscal year. Total and per capita urban budgets were larger in Java–Bali but the reverse was true for rural budgets. During 1998/99 budgets were cut everywhere, but percentage cuts were largest, 42%, in rural areas in Java–Bali.

Turning to the sources of budget revenues, the village was the source for almost 50% in rural communities and 30% in urban ones. There was an increase in the share coming from local sources in the 1998/1999 fiscal year, presumably because less money was available from central and provincial government sources because of the crisis. In the year following, 1999/2000, the share from the central government increased substantially. In urban areas, the central and provincial governments have a nearly equal role in supporting local budgets, with the role of the central government having become marginally more important over the crisis period. District government and municipality contributions represent a small share, between 10%–15%. In rural areas the shares are distributed somewhat differently, with the central government playing a strong supporting role to the locality,

TABLE 13.1
Desa/Kelurahan Finance

	Urban			Rural		
Fiscal Years:	**1999/2000**	**1998/1999**	**1997/1998**	**1999/2000**	**1998/1999**	**1997/1998**
Total APPKD/PAK (Rps) [a]	131,697,482 (17,117,470)	117,083,368 (15,607,170)	167,641,539 (30,546,271)	96,415,432 (16,444,572)	72,407,032 (11,834,671)	113,303,422 (20,065,290)
Total APPKD/PAK per capita (Rps)	12,020 (1,284)	10,681 (1,154)	13,926 (1,489)	19,801 (2,331)	17,534 (2,103)	25,816 (2,915)
Percentage of sources of revenue to total APPKD/APK						
– balance from previous year	1.4 (0.45)	1.8 (0.61)	1.5 (0.42)	1.1 (0.50)	1.1 (0.61)	0.5 (0.15)
– revenue originated from the village	30.2 (2.86)	32.9 (3.08)	30.5 (2.96)	48.4 (3.28)	51.8 (3.33)	43.9 (3.27)
– central government contribution	28.1 (4.62)	22.1 (4.39)	19.3 (3.24)	31.6 (3.19)	28.6 (2.83)	27.9 (2.63)
– provincial government contribution	20.9 (3.04)	20.8 (3.22)	23.7 (3.37)	4.9 (1.18)	5.1 (1.04)	5.5 (1.23)
– district/municipality contribution	10.7 (1.69)	12.2 (1.99)	11.9 (1.89)	3.6 (0.87)	4.2 (0.89)	3.9 (0.89)
% communities with data [b]	80.2	71.4	68.7	72.3	71.5	71.5
Number of communities	182			130		

Source: IFLS3.

[a] APPKD = village revenue and expenditure budget (for rural area); PAK = village budget management (for urban area).

[b] Percentage of communities with complete APPKD/PAK and revenue information.

Total APPKD/PAK and revenue and their corresponding per capita values are in real terms and set to December 2000. Percentage of sources will not necessarily add up to 100. Standard errors (in parentheses) are robust to clustering at the community level.

and other levels of government having much smaller roles. Village resources are a more important source of revenues in Java–Bali than in the other provinces, especially in rural areas where almost 60% of village budgets come from own resources in Java-Bali, compared to 31% does in other provinces. Support from the central government is especially important outside of Java–Bali, especially in urban areas, where the fraction of budget coming from the central government is 60%. Provincial government support is high in urban Java–Bali. Support from district governments is only around 10% in urban areas and under 5% in rural ones. As decentralization unfolds, the role of support from the district government should rise considerably at the expense of the central government's role.

Table 13.2 displays budgets, their sources and issues of autonomy at the *puskesmas* and *pustu* levels. Nearly 10% of *puskesmas* do not have their own budgets, probably because the health *dinas* directly controls it. Most *pustus* have their budgets controlled by the *puskesmas*. Of those *puskesmas* that do have budgets, nearly 60% of funds in 2000 came from JPS funds, and 17% from patients. The rest came from central government non-JPS funds or from the *dinas*. *Pustus* with their own budgets largely get their resources from patients.

One critical question is whether facilities are allowed to keep patient revenues for their own use. Before decentralization began only 35% of patient revenues were kept by *puskesmas*, 46% went to the health *dinas* and 22.5% to the district government.

The *dinas* are reported to have control over the *puskesmas*' budget in 69% of the cases. The district government has control for just under 20% of *puskesmas*. *Puskesmas* themselves control their budget in 12% of cases. Even without "control", 34% of all *puskesmas* report being able to re-allocate at least some funds without *dinas*' approval.

DECISION-MAKING

Health

In general, before decentralization, facility staff had very little authority over key decisions. Tables 13.3 and 13.4 present results on the participation of various groups in *puskesmas* and *pustu* decision-making. In the sphere of service provision, about 40% of *puskesmas* and *pustu* made decisions. About 20% made decisions regarding medical supplies and equipment provision. In regards to charges for services and medicines, staffing and payroll and building maintenance, very few decisions were made at the

TABLE 13.2
Budget and Budget Authority of *Puskesmas/Puskesmas Pembantu*

	Total		Urban		Rural	
	Puskesmas	*Pustu*	*Puskesmas*	*Pustu*	*Puskesmas*	*Pustu*
% facilities without own budget	9.5	56.8	13.2	53.8	2.7	58.9
	(1.82)	(3.45)	(2.67)	(5.26)	(1.10)	(4.27)
	[622]	[322]	[402]	[130]	[220]	[192]
Budget FY 1999/2000 (Rupiah) [a]						
– mean	74,775,982	4,320,176	74,720,386	5,775,227	74,867,517	3,240,623
– standard error	(3,885,336)	(602,544)	(5,561,806)	(1,168,937)	(4,161,242)	(513,292)
– median	54,942,624	2,483,125	50,855,963	2,883,050	65,900,000	2,013,000
	[479]	[108]	[298]	[46]	[181]	[62]
Source of budget (%)						
– patients	17.3	66.9	19.0	65.5	14.6	67.9
	(0.95)	(5.06)	(1.25)	(7.98)	(1.33)	(5.55)
– JPS	59.4	21.1	57.0	28.6	63.3	15.6
	(1.31)	(4.60)	(1.50)	(7.85)	(2.07)	(3.68)
– assistance from the regional government (*Dinas*) office	5.3	4.4	4.7	2.7	6.4	5.7
	(0.64)	(1.61)	(0.78)	(1.82)	(1.10)	(2.44)
– assistance from central government	8.4	0.2	8.0	0.5	9.0	0.0
	(0.80)	(0.22)	(0.95)	(0.52)	(1.32)	–
	[479]	[108]	[298]	[46]	[181]	[62]

continued on next page

TABLE 13.2 – cont'd

	Total		Urban		Rural	
	Puskesmas	*Pustu*	*Puskesmas*	*Pustu*	*Puskesmas*	*Pustu*
Allocation of revenue from patients (%)						
– for *puskesmas* expenditures	35.0	21.8	34.9	26.6	35.2	18.0
	(1.24)	(2.50)	(1.41)	(3.89)	(1.95)	(2.87)
– remitted to the regional government (*Dinas*) office	45.9	44.4	44.3	39.3	48.6	48.3
	(2.10)	(4.52)	(2.51)	(6.04)	(3.30)	(5.85)
– for general budget of the Kabupaten	22.5	13.4	23.4	15.2	21.0	12.1
	(1.61)	(2.69)	(2.07)	(4.28)	(2.17)	(3.28)
– other uses	1.6	20.2	1.1	17.1	2.4	22.6
	(0.40)	(4.47)	(0.32)	(6.94)	(0.93)	(5.15)
	[495]	[131]	[309]	[57]	[186]	[74]
Institution currently determines the budget (%)						
– *Puskesmas*	12.0	55.8	11.8	53.9	12.3	57.1
	(1.48)	(3.03)	(1.88)	(4.51)	(2.17)	(3.92)
– *Dinas*	68.6	29.2	69.3	28.1	67.3	29.8
	(2.01)	(2.83)	(2.54)	(4.11)	(3.09)	(3.72)
– Kabupaten Planning Unit	18.4	4.4	17.8	4.7	19.5	4.2
	(1.66)	(1.22)	(2.04)	(2.13)	(2.65)	(1.43)
– others	1.0	10.7	1.0	13.3	0.9	8.9
	(0.39)	(2.17)	(0.49)	(3.36)	(0.64)	(2.31)
	[618]	[319]	[398]	[128]	[220]	[191]
Authority to reallocate between posts of expenditure without approval from *Dinas* or any other parties (%)	33.7	12.2	32.4	7.8	35.9	15.2
	(2.26)	(1.99)	(2.71)	(2.35)	(3.60)	(2.79)
	[618]	[319]	[398]	[128]	[220]	[191]

Source: IFLS3.

a) Values are in real terms set to December 2000.

Standard errors (in parentheses) are robust to clustering at the community level. Number of observations is in brackets.

facility-level. At most, facility staff were able to offer suggestions to the real decision-makers, and then only for some types of decisions such as the types of medicines and medical equipment to be purchased, or staff to be hired. Rather, it was the health *dinas* and the central government that dominated the decision-making processes in all types of decisions regarding health service delivery at *puskesmas* and *pustu*. In staff recruitment, for example, the health *dinas* plays the biggest role (83% of *puskesmas* report the health *dinas* playing the largest role), followed by the central government (68%) and District Planning Agency (BAPPEDA) (17%). *Puskesmas* however have the right to give suggestions to the health *dinas*. The central government still has significant influence on *puskesmas*, still being involved in most types of decisions, especially regarding hiring of staff and payroll. As regional autonomy progresses, it is expected that the role of the central government will diminish.

In the procurement of medicines and medical equipment, the role of health *dinas* is larger, though still relegated largely to making suggestions, not final decisions. The decision is still mostly in the hands of the health *dinas*. The central government however maintains a significant role on these matters. There are some urban–rural differences in the degree of *puskesmas* control, with more decision-making involvement by the *puskesmas* on service provision decisions in rural areas. The central government had significant influence on *puskesmas*, being involved in most types of decisions, especially regarding hiring of staff and payroll. As regional autonomy progresses, it is expected that the role of the central government will diminish.

It is clear that the *puskesmas*, as the health service organizational unit, did not have much discretion regarding its operational activities. Most of the decisions on various issues related to health service delivery are made by other institutions, particularly by the health *dinas*. A key question is whether the implementation of regional autonomy will provide more power to the *puskesmas* to manage their own affairs, particularly in delivering health services. A related issue is whether *puskesmas* as well as *dinas* staff will be able to make such decisions efficiently and equitably.

Education

The main objective of regional autonomy policy is to shift power from the central government to district government to manage their own fate. This means that the district governments will have the authority to formulate their own policies and programmes to respond their own needs. It is

TABLE 13.3
Degree of Decision-making Authority at *Puskesmas* and *Puskesmas Pembantu* (*Pustu*)
(In percent)

	Total		Urban		Rural	
	Puskesmas	*Pustu*	*Puskesmas*	*Pustu*	*Puskesmas*	*Pustu*
Service provision						
– making decisions	39.3	38.2	35.6	39.2	46.1	37.4
	(2.35)	(3.12)	(2.81)	(4.70)	(3.72)	(3.87)
– abide by decisions	34.5	49.2	36.9	47.7	30.1	50.3
	(2.09)	(3.07)	(2.64)	(4.68)	(3.30)	(3.93)
– give suggestions	25.7	12.0	27.0	12.3	23.3	11.8
	(1.97)	(1.88)	(2.48)	(2.72)	(3.09)	(2.59)
– others	0.5	0.6	0.5	0.8	0.5	0.5
	(0.28)	(0.45)	(0.36)	(0.77)	(0.46)	(0.53)
	[615]	[317]	[396]	[130]	[219]	[187]
Charge of services						
– making decisions	4.0	9.2	2.8	8.7	6.1	9.6
	(0.87)	(1.86)	(0.82)	(2.94)	(1.75)	(2.30)
– abide by decisions	86.0	87.3	87.6	87.4	83.0	87.2
	(1.54)	(2.18)	(1.75)	(3.34)	(2.81)	(2.72)
– give suggestions	9.9	3.5	9.4	3.9	10.8	3.2
	(1.30)	(1.12)	(1.54)	(1.73)	(2.24)	(1.26)
– others	0.2	0.0	0.3	0.0	0.0	0.0
	(0.17)	–	(0.25)	–	–	–
	[606]	[315]	[394]	[127]	[212]	[188]
Hiring and firing of staff						
– making decisions	0.8	3.8	0.8	5.4	0.9	2.7
	(0.36)	(1.09)	(0.43)	(2.01)	(0.65)	(1.19)
– abide by decisions	58.0	74.9	58.0	72.1	58.1	76.9
	(2.34)	(2.69)	(2.91)	(4.42)	(3.59)	(3.38)

– give suggestions	40.8	21.3	41.0	22.5	40.6	20.4
	(2.31)	(2.52)	(2.87)	(4.08)	(3.57)	(3.21)
– others	0.3	0.0	0.3	0.0	0.5	0.0
	(0.23)	–	(0.25)	–	(0.46)	–
	[612]	[315]	[395]	[129]	[217]	[186]
Levels and procedures for payroll						
– making decisions	0.7	1.0	0.8	1.6	0.5	0.5
	(0.33)	(0.55)	(0.44)	(1.11)	(0.46)	(0.53)
– abide by decisions	91.8	92.7	93.1	91.3	89.4	93.6
	(1.24)	(1.51)	(1.46)	(2.48)	(2.10)	(1.77)
– give suggestions	7.5	6.3	6.1	7.1	10.1	5.9
	(1.19)	(1.42)	(1.40)	(2.25)	(2.07)	(1.71)
– others	0.0	0.0	0.0	0.0	0.0	0.0
	–	–	–	–	–	–
	[610]	[315]	[393]	[127]	[217]	[188]
Kinds of medicine to be purchased and time of purchase						
– making decisions	21.1	18.3	19.3	16.5	24.4	19.6
	(1.75)	(2.40)	(2.25)	(3.44)	(2.85)	(3.15)
– abide by decisions	21.3	42.8	21.1	43.3	21.7	42.4
	(1.81)	(3.10)	(2.29)	(4.84)	(2.75)	(3.90)
– give suggestions	57.3	38.3	59.1	39.4	53.9	37.5
	(2.23)	(3.11)	(2.84)	(4.79)	(3.42)	(3.84)
– others	0.3	0.6	0.5	0.8	0.0	0.5
	(0.23)	(0.45)	(0.36)	(0.79)	–	(0.54)
	[611]	[311]	[394]	[127]	[217]	[184]
Price of medicine						
– making decisions	4.1	8.4	3.1	8.5	6.0	8.2
	(0.79)	(1.77)	(0.87)	(2.90)	(1.58)	(2.08)
– abide by decisions	89.3	87.5	91.1	88.4	86.1	86.8
	(1.32)	(2.15)	(1.49)	(3.21)	(2.55)	(2.78)

continued on next page

TABLE 13.3 – cont'd

	Total		Urban		Rural	
	Puskesmas	*Pustu*	*Puskesmas*	*Pustu*	*Puskesmas*	*Pustu*
– give suggestions	5.9	3.2	5.1	2.3	7.4	3.8
	(1.03)	(1.00)	(1.14)	(1.34)	(1.94)	(1.41)
– others	0.7	1.0	0.8	0.8	0.5	1.1
	(0.33)	(0.55)	(0.44)	(0.77)	(0.46)	(0.77)
	[609]	[311]	[393]	[129]	[216]	[182]
Kinds of medical equipment to be purchaed and time of purchase						
– making decisions	16.1	9.2	12.2	10.2	23.1	8.6
	(1.51)	(1.85)	(1.65)	(2.91)	(2.83)	(2.28)
– abide by decisions	20.0	43.5	19.3	39.1	21.3	46.5
	(1.69)	(3.09)	(2.09)	(5.07)	(2.76)	(3.84)
– give suggestions	63.2	47.0	67.4	50.8	55.6	44.4
	(2.13)	(3.14)	(2.65)	(5.13)	(3.20)	(3.85)
– others	0.7	0.3	1.0	0.0	0.0	0.5
	(0.33)	(0.32)	(0.51)	–	–	(0.53)
	[609]	[315]	[393]	[128]	[216]	[187]
Building maintenance and expansion						
– making decisions	4.6	6.4	5.8	10.2	2.3	3.8
	(0.98)	(1.45)	(1.43)	(2.69)	(1.01)	(1.59)
– abide by decisions	19.0	34.7	19.2	32.0	18.6	36.6
	(1.71)	(2.89)	(2.19)	(4.20)	(2.67)	(3.86)
– give suggestions	76.1	58.8	74.5	57.8	79.1	59.6
	(1.81)	(2.99)	(2.36)	(4.69)	(2.79)	(3.82)
– others	0.3	0.0	0.5	0.0	0.0	0.0
	(0.23)	–	(0.36)	–	–	–
	[611]	[311]	[396]	[128]	[215]	[183]

Source: IFLS3.
Standard errors (in parentheses) are robust to clustering at the community level. Number of observations is in brackets.

TABLE 13.4
Degree of Decision-making Authority by Institution at *Puskesmas* and *Puskesmas Pembantu*

	Total				Urban				Rural			
	Puskes-mas	Dinas	Kabupaten Planning Unit	Central Govt	*Puskes-mas*	Dinas	Kabupaten Planning Unit	Central Govt	*Puskes-mas*	Dinas	Kabupaten Planning Unit	Central Govt
(% of facilities)												
Puskesmas												
Service provision	39.3	82.3	21.5	34.8	35.6	82.3	20.5	36.4	46.1	82.2	23.3	32.0
	(2.35)	(1.65)	(1.89)	(2.08)	(2.81)	(1.93)	(2.32)	(2.67)	(3.72)	(2.83)	(2.99)	(3.19)
	[615]	[615]	[615]	[615]	[396]	[396]	[396]	[396]	[219]	[219]	[219]	[219]
Charge of services	4.0	72.1	65.7	25.7	2.8	73.6	62.4	23.9	6.1	69.3	71.7	29.2
	(0.87)	(1.95)	(2.43)	(1.88)	(0.82)	(2.29)	(3.09)	(2.26)	(1.75)	(3.36)	(3.31)	(3.20)
	[606]	[606]	[606]	[606]	[394]	[394]	[394]	[394]	[212]	[212]	[212]	[212]
Hiring and firing of staff	0.8	82.8	16.8	67.8	0.8	83.0	17.7	68.9	0.9	82.5	15.2	65.9
	(0.36)	(1.67)	(1.68)	(2.12)	(0.43)	(2.07)	(2.16)	(2.58)	(0.65)	(2.58)	(2.52)	(3.39)
	[612]	[612]	[612]	[612]	[395]	[395]	[395]	[395]	[217]	[217]	[217]	[217]
Levels and procedures for payroll	0.7	66.6	28.0	73.8	0.8	65.1	28.5	75.3	0.5	69.1	27.2	71.0
	(0.33)	(2.10)	(1.96)	(1.94)	(0.44)	(2.75)	(2.37)	(2.35)	(0.46)	(3.04)	(3.07)	(3.10)
	[610]	[610]	[610]	[610]	[393]	[393]	[393]	[393]	[217]	[217]	[217]	[217]

continued on next page

TABLE 13.4 – cont'd

	Total				Urban				Rural			
	Puskes-mas	Dinas	Kabupaten Planning Unit	Central Govt	*Puskes-mas*	Dinas	Kabupaten Planning Unit	Central Govt	*Puskes-mas*	Dinas	Kabupaten Planning Unit	Central Govt
Kinds of medicine to be purchased and time of purchase	21.1 (1.75) [611]	88.4 (1.38) [611]	15.7 (1.57) [611]	30.4 (2.11) [611]	19.3 (2.25) [394]	87.3 (1.81) [394]	17.8 (2.02) [394]	32.5 (2.64) [394]	24.4 (2.85) [217]	90.3 (1.96) [217]	12.0 (2.25) [217]	26.7 (3.23) [217]
Price of medicine	4.1 (0.79) [609]	74.9 (1.89) [609]	28.9 (2.01) [609]	44.0 (2.11) [609]	3.1 (0.87) [393]	73.5 (2.42) [393]	28.5 (2.55) [393]	43.3 (2.64) [393]	6.0 (1.58) [216]	77.3 (2.97) [216]	29.6 (3.14) [216]	45.4 (3.40) [216]
Kinds of medical equipment to be purchased and time of purchase	16.1 (1.51) [609]	89.3 (1.37) [609]	20.9 (1.77) [609]	35.3 (2.21) [609]	12.2 (1.65) [393]	89.1 (1.67) [393]	21.9 (2.21) [393]	38.4 (2.72) [393]	23.1 (2.83) [216]	89.8 (2.35) [216]	19.0 (2.74) [216]	29.6 (3.44) [216]
Building maintenance and expansion	4.6 (0.98) [611]	81.8 (1.83) [611]	73.2 (2.06) [611]	34.0 (2.08) [611]	5.8 (1.43) [396]	79.3 (2.38) [396]	75.0 (2.40) [396]	34.8 (2.54) [396]	2.3 (1.01) [215]	86.5 (2.59) [215]	69.8 (3.55) [215]	32.6 (3.24) [215]
Puskesmas Pembantu												
Service provision	38.2 (3.12) [317]	79.5 (2.60) [317]	13.9 (2.09) [317]	27.4 (2.67) [317]	39.2 (4.70) [130]	76.2 (4.32) [130]	10.0 (2.51) [130]	28.5 (4.11) [130]	37.4 (3.87) [187]	81.8 (2.82) [187]	16.6 (2.86) [187]	26.7 (3.33) [187]
Charge of services	9.2 (1.86) [315]	76.2 (2.72) [315]	55.9 (3.07) [315]	32.1 (2.77) [315]	8.7 (2.94) [127]	73.2 (4.31) [127]	54.3 (4.78) [127]	37.0 (4.43) [127]	9.6 (2.30) [188]	78.2 (3.20) [188]	56.9 (3.72) [188]	28.7 (3.39) [188]

Hiring and firing of staff	3.8 (1.09) [315]	84.4 (2.16) [315]	10.8 (1.73) [315]	66.7 (2.82) [315]	5.4 (2.01) [129]	83.7 (3.29) [129]	8.5 (2.38) [129]	67.4 (4.18) [129]	2.7 (1.19) [186]	84.9 (2.58) [186]	12.4 (2.33) [186]	66.1 (3.64) [186]
Levels and procedures for payroll	1.0 (0.55) [315]	78.4 (2.41) [315]	20.3 (2.37) [315]	72.4 (2.73) [315]	1.6 (1.11) [127]	78.0 (3.93) [127]	21.3 (3.61) [127]	73.2 (4.22) [127]	0.5 (0.53) [188]	78.7 (2.95) [188]	19.7 (3.02) [188]	71.8 (3.35) [188]
Kinds of medicine to be purchased and time of purchase	18.3 (2.40) [311]	89.7 (1.78) [311]	9.6 (1.77) [311]	24.4 (2.68) [311]	16.5 (3.44) [127]	90.6 (2.54) [127]	9.4 (2.73) [127]	27.6 (4.14) [127]	19.6 (3.15) [184]	89.1 (2.25) [184]	9.8 (2.18) [184]	22.3 (3.29) [184]
Price of medicine	8.4 (1.77) [311]	82.6 (2.17) [311]	20.6 (2.44) [311]	35.7 (2.94) [311]	8.5 (2.90) [129]	82.2 (3.38) [129]	18.6 (3.87) [129]	36.4 (4.57) [129]	8.2 (2.08) [182]	83.0 (2.89) [182]	22.0 (3.01) [182]	35.2 (3.68) [182]
Kinds of medical equipment to be purchaed and time of purchase	9.2 (1.85) [315]	90.2 (1.74) [315]	13.7 (2.09) [315]	27.6 (2.70) [315]	10.2 (2.91) [128]	90.6 (2.57) [128]	16.4 (3.61) [128]	26.6 (3.99) [128]	8.6 (2.28) [187]	89.8 (2.26) [187]	11.8 (2.33) [187]	28.3 (3.45) [187]
Building maintenance and expansion	6.4 (1.45) [311]	90.0 (1.77) [311]	55.3 (3.07) [311]	36.3 (2.99) [311]	10.2 (2.69) [128]	90.6 (2.73) [128]	53.1 (4.59) [128]	35.2 (4.40) [128]	3.8 (1.59) [183]	89.6 (2.36) [183]	56.8 (3.97) [183]	37.2 (3.98) [183]

Source: IFLS3.

Answers can be at multiple levels, so percents do not add up to 100. Standard errors (in parentheses) are robust to clustering at the community level. Number of observations is in brackets.

expected that, with the implementation of regional autonomy, the education *dinas* and its schools will be more responsive to local needs.

Baseline results indicate that before decentralization began, school management had very limited participation in decision-making (Table 13.5). In hiring teachers, for example, school principals mostly are not involved in deciding on the right staff to be hired for their schools. The education *dinas* makes decisions on teacher recruitment, particularly for primary schools. For private schools, private foundations have a dominant role in teacher recruitment. The private schools themselves have some role in recruitment, though to only a limited extent.

The same pattern holds for decisions regarding teacher salary. Junior and senior secondary schools have very limited involvement in deciding teacher salaries. The education *dinas* and private foundations dominated the decision-making on this dimension. Private foundations tend to make salary decisions for private schools at the primary and senior secondary school levels. Curricula decisions have been even more centralized, although for book purchases the schools do have more say.

The fact that the school management has very limited access to decision-making processes regarding their own fate raises some issues about the future effects of regional autonomy on educational development in the country. As the implementation of regional autonomy progresses, it is expected that schools will have greater participation in the management of their own affairs and will have more ability to respond to needs. However, if the shift of power stops at the education *dinas*, schools will still struggle for power to respond to needs. Therefore, the effects of implementation of regional autonomy on increases in educational responsiveness are still unclear. The domination of education *dinas* in decision-making does not create a conducive environment for the implementation of school-based management. The government of Indonesia has initiated the introduction of school-based management for its schools at all levels, from primary to senior secondary schools. This policy will require the district governments to shift the power to manage schools from education *dinas* to the schools themselves.

Note

1 The percentages do not add to 100 because the categories of support are not necessarily exhaustive.

TABLE 13.5
Schools: Decision-making Authority

Issues	% of schools	Public school			Private school		
		Primary	Junior high	Senior high	Primary	Junior high	Senior high
Books:	Makes decision alone	4.7	5.2	8.8	13.7	14.8	23.8
		(0.84)	(1.04)	(1.72)	(2.94)	(1.96)	(2.46)
	Does not make decision	63.9	56.1	51.7	56.2	55.2	39.8
		(2.12)	(2.21)	(3.33)	(4.49)	(2.79)	(2.97)
	Makes decision with others	31.4	38.7	39.5	30.1	30.0	36.4
		(2.01)	(2.13)	(3.20)	(4.10)	(2.60)	(2.88)
		[815]	[594]	[294]	[146]	[357]	[324]
	Institution participates in making decision: [1]						
	– government	95.6	95.6	92.2	84.9	85.5	85.4
		(0.77)	(1.06)	(1.71)	(3.61)	(2.16)	(2.41)
	– private foundation	0.5	0.9	0.4	28.6	23.7	26.7
		(0.26)	(0.39)	(0.37)	(3.94)	(2.53)	(2.87)
	– other	5.3	8.3	13.1	12.7	11.8	13.4
		(0.97)	(1.41)	(2.16)	(3.44)	(2.13)	(2.37)
		[777]	[563]	[268]	[126]	[304]	[247]

continued on next page

TABLE 13.5 – cont'd

Issues	% of schools	Public school			Private school		
		Primary	Junior high	Senior high	Primary	Junior high	Senior high
Curriculum:	Makes decision alone	0.4	0.0	0.0	4.1	0.8	2.5
		(0.21)	–	–	(1.62)	(0.48)	(0.85)
	Does not make decision	96.9	93.3	93.5	88.4	91.0	88.6
		(0.72)	(1.05)	(1.61)	(2.59)	(1.52)	(1.77)
	Makes decision with others	2.7	6.7	6.5	7.5	8.1	9.0
		(0.70)	(1.05)	(1.61)	(2.17)	(1.42)	(1.62)
		[815]	[594]	[294]	[146]	[357]	[324]
	Institution participates in making decision: [1]						
	– government	95.8	94.9	94.2	94.3	92.7	91.8
		(0.80)	(1.25)	(1.51)	(1.97)	(1.62)	(1.85)
	– private foundation	0.2	0.2	0.7	18.6	15.3	13.9
		(0.17)	(0.17)	(0.48)	(3.57)	(2.03)	(2.11)
	– other	3.6	4.7	6.1	2.9	4.5	6.6
		(0.78)	(1.23)	(1.55)	(1.40)	(1.50)	(1.71)
		[812]	[594]	[294]	[140]	[354]	[316]
Hiring teacher:	Makes decision alone	0.1	1.0	0.7	2.7	10.1	10.2
		(0.12)	(0.47)	(0.48)	(1.34)	(1.74)	(1.61)
	Does not make decision	93.6	75.8	74.5	76.0	69.5	63.3
		(0.99)	(2.07)	(2.85)	(3.64)	(2.63)	(2.76)
	Makes decision with others	6.3	23.2	24.8	21.2	20.4	26.5
		(0.98)	(2.04)	(2.81)	(3.56)	(2.22)	(2.40)
		[815]	[594]	[294]	[146]	[357]	[324]
	Institution participates in making decision: [1]						
	– government	93.2	94.0	92.8	25.4	12.1	14.4
		(1.03)	(1.28)	(1.64)	(4.27)	(1.97)	(2.31)
	– private foundation	0.5	2.0	1.7	91.5	95.6	94.8
		(0.24)	(0.57)	(0.76)	(2.29)	(1.21)	(1.29)

	– other	6.9	5.3	6.8	1.4	2.8	6.2
		(1.16)	(1.26)	(1.67)	(0.98)	(0.92)	(1.40)
		[814]	[588]	[292]	[142]	[321]	[291]
Teacher's salary	Makes decision alone	0.1	1.0	1.4	5.5	9.0	7.1
		(0.12)	(0.47)	(0.67)	(1.90)	(1.62)	(1.44)
	Does not make decision	94.8	78.1	74.8	80.1	74.5	74.4
		(0.91)	(1.97)	(2.73)	(3.56)	(2.56)	(2.46)
	Makes decision with others	5.0	20.9	23.8	14.4	16.5	18.5
		(0.90)	(1.93)	(2.72)	(3.06)	(2.12)	(2.19)
		[815]	[594]	[294]	[146]	[357]	[324]
	Institution participates in making decision: [1]						
	– government	91.5	91.3	90.0	23.9	11.4	14.3
		(1.18)	(1.41)	(1.91)	(4.21)	(1.90)	(2.23)
	– private foundation	0.6	2.2	2.1	89.1	96.0	96.7
		(0.27)	(0.60)	(0.83)	(2.92)	(1.08)	(1.12)
	– other	9.2	8.5	9.0	1.4	2.5	4.7
		(1.32)	(1.40)	(1.88)	(1.01)	(0.86)	(1.29)
		[814]	[588]	[290]	[138]	[325]	[301]
Number of schools		815	594	294	146	357	324

Source: IFLS3.

[1] Among schools that do not make decision and those making decision with others. Multiple levels are possible so percents do not add up to 100.

Standard errors (in parentheses) are robust to clustering at the community level. Number of observations is in brackets.

APPENDIX TABLE 13.1a
Kelurahan Urban Finance by Region

	Java–Bali			Other Regions		
Fiscal Years:	**1999/2000**	**1998/1999**	**1997/1998**	**1999/2000**	**1998/1999**	**1997/1998**
Total PAK (Rps) [a]	149,863,818	131,975,147	193,227,884	71,855,433	57,516,252	47,850,922
	(19,994,566)	(18,575,787)	(36,509,445)	(30,445,050)	(19,931,853)	(10,488,538)
Total PAK per capita (Rps)	12,588	11,450	15,171	10,146	7,605	8,096
	(1,466)	(1,394)	(1,768)	(2,636)	(1,325)	(1,076)
Percentage of sources of revenue to total PAK						
– balance from previous year	1.6	2.2	1.8	0.7	0.6	0.2
	(0.55)	(0.75)	(0.51)	(0.56)	(0.50)	(0.11)
– revenue originated from the village	31.3	34.1	31.5	26.5	28.0	26.0
	(3.39)	(3.60)	(3.38)	(5.00)	(5.30)	(5.57)
– central government contribution	18.5	14.7	13.1	60.8	51.4	48.4
	(2.14)	(2.15)	(1.76)	(17.83)	(19.17)	(14.94)
– provincial government contribution	25.2	24.7	27.8	6.0	5.0	4.4
	(3.81)	(3.91)	(3.96)	(1.38)	(1.67)	(1.51)
– district/municipality contribution	10.2	13.2	12.8	12.4	8.1	7.4
	(1.89)	(2.45)	(2.26)	(3.69)	(1.59)	(1.67)
% communities with data [b]	86.7	82.0	81.3	64.8	48.1	40.7
Number of observations	128	128	128	54	54	54

Source: IFLS3.

[a] PAK = kelurahan budget management.

[b] Percentage of communities with complete PAK and revenue information.

Total PAK and its corresponding per capita value are in December 2000 Rupiah. Percentage of sources will not necessarily add up to 100. Standard errors (in parentheses) are robust to clustering at the community level.

APPENDIX TABLE 13.1b
Desa Rural Finance by Region

	Java–Bali			Other Regions		
Fiscal Years:	**1999/2000**	**1998/1999**	**1997/1998**	**1999/2000**	**1998/1999**	**1997/1998**
Total APPKD (Rps) [a]	91,836,392	73,119,141	126,805,937	104,496,092	71,279,527	91,924,439
	(16,226,039)	(8,908,109)	(28,319,593)	(35,271,943)	(27,123,923)	(25,603,197)
Total APPKD per capita (Rps)	17,694	17,066	24,380	23,519	18,276	28,090
	(1,609)	(2,686)	(3,748)	(5,728)	(3,377)	(4,612)
Percentage of sources of revenue to total APPKD						
– balance from previous year	1.7	1.7	0.8	0.0	0.1	0.0
	(0.77)	(0.99)	(0.23)	(0.01)	(0.13)	–
– revenue originated from the village	58.2	59.7	52.7	31.1	39.2	30.1
	(3.61)	(3.64)	(3.70)	(5.25)	(5.80)	(5.32)
– central government contribution	23.1	19.1	20.7	46.5	43.6	39.2
	(1.87)	(1.76)	(2.45)	(7.53)	(5.95)	(5.03)
– provincial government contribution	3.8	4.7	4.8	6.7	5.7	6.4
	(0.83)	(1.37)	(1.40)	(2.89)	(1.60)	(2.28)
– district/municipality contribution	2.9	4.0	4.1	4.9	4.6	3.5
	(1.14)	(1.30)	(1.36)	(1.29)	(1.04)	(0.84)
% communities with data [b]	84.9	78.1	78.1	59.6	63.2	63.2
Number of observations	73	73	73	57	57	57

Source: IFLS3.

[a] APPKD = village revenue and expenditure.

[b] Percentage of communities with complete APPKD and revenue information.

Total APPKD and its corresponding per capita value are in December 2000 Rupiah. Percentage of sources will not necessarily add up to 100. Standard errors (in parentheses) are robust to clustering at the community level.

14

Conclusions

As of late 2000, almost three years after the economic crisis began, individuals in the IFLS data do not appear to be substantially worse off compared to immediately before the crisis in late 1997, in terms various dimensions of their standard of living. Indeed, perhaps surprisingly, many people now seem a little better off, at least in terms of lowered levels of poverty and higher per capita expenditure. Of course, this masks the volatile changes that many had in the interim period. For example, poverty rates rose substantially and per capita expenditure fell between late 1997 and early 1999. Wages of self-employed workers and government workers have returned to their 1997 levels, after having fallen drastically just after the crisis began. Private sector wages are still 10% below what they were in late 1997, although they have rebounded from a 35% deficit in late 1998.

Focusing on the poor, it is interesting to note that levels of expenditure have recovered to pre-crisis levels. Moreover, we observe considerable movement into and out of poverty, with half the poor in 1997 moving out of poverty by 2000, and half the poor in 2000 were not in 1997.

One important lesson learnt from this experience is that it is incomplete to look only at incomes or expenditures. We see that labour supply has increased from 1997 and 2000, especially among women who are now much more likely to be self-employed or working as unpaid employees in family businesses. To the extent that leisure or time at home is substituted away from, this may represent a loss in welfare.

In terms of schooling of the young, despite initial declines in enrolment among the poor in 1998, by 2000, enrolment rates showed no marked decline compared to 1997. For child health, a key measure of child health in the long-run, child height, improved over this period. This strongly suggests that the long-run health of children did not deteriorate during the crisis. There is some suggestion that haemoglobin levels fell for young boys, which may indicate a decline in micronutrient intakes. Among adults, there is little indication of a major change in health status from 1997 to 2000, despite evidence finding some increase in undernutrition of the elderly from 1997 to 1998.

Health care utilization stayed roughly constant for adults. For children, utilization of *puskesmas* was unchanged, but use of *posyandu* fell dramatically. Consistent with this reduction in use, service availability in *posyandu* and various dimensions of service quality fell sharply over this period. Since health outcomes of children did not seem to suffer, and indeed improved in some dimensions, the role of the *posyandu* should be further evaluated. For *puskesmas*, there was not evidence of a decline in the availability of service or in service quality. If anything, there is evidence of some improvement, especially for immunizations, which rose sharply. Family planning supplies at public providers declined over this period, and there is evidence that women switched their source of supplies for contraceptives from the public to the private sector. Despite this, however, contraceptive use changed very little.

In response to the crisis, there were a series of publicly provided safety net programmes that were initiated or reconfigured. Some of these reached many communities and some were targeted towards the poor. On balance, the assistance received by the poor seems to have been extremely small, especially for the rice subsidy programme. In addition, many poor were not reached and there was considerable leakage to the non-poor.

We have also found, not surprisingly, that prior to the decentralization that begun in 2001, localities had very limited control over budgets, and key decisions made for public health facilities and schools were largely out of control of their staff. For public health facilities and schools, there is an issue that the full promise of decentralization may not be realized even if control becomes localized to district *dinas*, if the facilities themselves do not get control at least over some operational questions.

Taking a longer view, it is certainly the case that living conditions of people in Indonesia have improved substantially since 1960. The economic crisis has interrupted that progress, although in this examination of how individuals fared between 1997 and 2000, we do not quantify the crisis impact on longer term movements of welfare. This needs to be emphasized, because it is possible that failure to find strong overall negative impacts between 1997 and 2000 may be masking the possibility that the crisis had effects compared to the trend. Future research needs to address that possibility.

In addition, it needs to be emphasized that while we focused on the changes over the 1997–2000 period, that often masks serious issues related to continued low living standards for many Indonesians. A good example is the large chasm that remains in order to achieve the levels of child health set by international standards. As we have argued, child heights, weight-for-heights and haemoglobin levels are very low, both before and after the crisis. This reflects continued poor health outcomes, especially during the formative period before age 5 (though, again, clearly much better than in generations past). For adults, behaviours that greatly raise the risk of cardiovascular disease and other chronic diseases are highly prevalent and these problems are likely to become more pronounced in Indonesia as economic progress is restarted.

In sum, these results present a very heterogeneous picture of the economic and social environment. The last three years have shown a tremendous resiliency of the Indonesian population. Although predictions of catastrophic outcomes were not observed, there were some serious short-term dislocations to some people.

One important lesson that the Indonesian experience teaches us is the need for continual and relatively frequent monitoring of living standards. This is a point that is not sufficiently appreciated in the literature. Even the three years between waves of IFLS would have been too long to have measured important dislocations that occurred between late 1997 and early 1999. Fortunately the special IFLS2+ wave in 1998, plus the frequent rounds of SUSENAS, enables researchers to fill in many of the blanks for Indonesia. Most countries are not nearly so well-endowed with the necessary data.

References

Alatas, Vivi. 2002. "What Happened to Indonesia's Poverty: A Microsimulation Exercise Using Household Surveys". Jakarta: World Bank, mimeo.

Alatas, Vivi and Menno Pradhan. 2002. "Poverty Update". Jakarta: World Bank, mimeo.

Atkinson, Anthony B. 1987. "On the Measurement of Poverty". *Econometrica*, 55(4): 749–64.

BAPPENAS. 1999. "Pedoman Kerja, Jaring Pengaman Sosial (Guidleines JPS)". Jakarta: Pusat Informasi, Badan Perencanaan Pembangunan Nasional.

Basu, Kaushik. 1999. "Child Labor: Cause, Consequence and Cure, with Remarks on International Labor Standards". *Journal of Economic Literature*, 37(3): 1083–119.

Baulch, Robert and John Hoddinott. 2000. "Economic Mobility and Poverty Dynamics in Developing Coutries". *Journal of Development Studies*, 36(6): 1–24.

Bresciani, Fabrizio, Gerson Feder, Daniel Gilligan, Hanan Jacoby, Tongroj Onchan and Jaime Quizon. 2002. "Weathering the Storm: The Impact of the East Asian Crisis on Farm Households in Indonesia and Thailand". *World Bank Research Observer*, 17(1): 1–20.

Cameron, Lisa. 2002. "Did Social Safety Net Scholarships Reduce Drop-out Rates During the Indonesian Economic Crisis?". Department of Economics, University of Melbourne, mimeo.

Centers for Disease Control. 1998. *Recommendations to prevent and control iron deficiency in the United States*. Morbidity and Mortality Weekly Report: Recommendations and Reports, April 3, 1998, Vol 47, No. RR-3, Atlanta, Georgia.

Central Bureau of Statistics, National Family Planning Coordinating Board, Ministry of Health and Macro International. 1998. *Indonesia Demographic and Health Survey 1997*. Calverton, MD.

Davidson, Russell and Jean-Yves Duclos. 2000. "Statistical Inference for Stochastic Dominance and for the Measurement of Poverty and Inequality". *Econometrica*, 68(6): 1435–464.

Deaton, Angus and Margaret Grosh. 2000. "Consumption". In M. Grosh and P. Glewwe (eds.), *Designing Household Survey Questionnaires for Developing Countries: Lessons From 15 Years of the Living Standards Measurement Study*. Volume 1, Washington DC: World Bank.

Deaton, Angus and Alessandro Tarozzi. 2000. "Prices and Poverty in India". Department of Economics, Princeton University, mimeo.

Duclos, Jean_Yves, Abdelkrim Araar and Bernard Fortin. 2002. *DAD: A Software for Distributive Analysis/Analyse Distributive, Users Manual*. International Development Research Center, Ottawa, Canada, also at www.ecn.ulaval.ca/~jyves.

Erwidodo, Jack Molyneaux and Ning Pribaldi. 2002. "Household Food Demand: An Almost Ideal Demand System". Mimeo.

Filmer, Deon and Nanik Suwaryani. 2001. "Indonesia's Primary and Junior Secondary Schools in a Post-crisis Environment: Findings from a Follow-up Survey of 600 Schools". mimeo, World Bank.

Fogel, Robert. 1994. "Economic Growth, Population Theory and Physiology: The Bearing of Long-term Processes on the Making of Economic Policy". *American Economic Review*, 84(3): 369–95.

Foster, Andrew. 1995. "Rice Prices, Credit Markets and Child Growth in Rural Bangladesh". *Economic Journal*, 105(430): 551–70.

Foster, James, Joel Greer and Erik Thorbecke. 1984. "A Class of Decomposable Poverty Indices". *Econometrica*, 52(3): 761–66.

Fox, James. 2002. "The 1997–98 drought in Indonesia", Harvard University Asia Center, Natural Disasters and Policy Response in Asia: Implications for Food Security.

Frankenberg, Elizabeth and Lynn Karoly. 1995. "The 1993 Indonesian Family Life Survey: Overview and Field Report". Publication No. DRU-1195/1-NICHD/AID, RAND, Santa Monica, CA.

Frankenberg, Elizabeth and Duncan Thomas. 2000. "The Indonesia Family Life Survey (IFLS): Study Design and Results from Waves 1 and 2". Publication No. DRU-2238/Volume 1/NIA/NICHD, RAND, Santa Monica, CA.

Frankenberg, Elizabeth and Duncan Thomas. 2001. "Women's Health and Pregnancy Outcomes: Do Services Make a Difference?". *Demography*, 38: 253–66.

Frankenberg, Elizabeth, Duncan Thomas and Kathleen Beegle. 1999. "The Real Costs of Indonesia's Economic Crisis: Preliminary Findings from the Indonesia Family Life Surveys". RAND Labor and Population Program Working Paper Series 99-04, Santa Monica, CA.

Jayne, Thomas J., John Strauss, Takashi Yamano and Daniel Molla. 2002. "Targeting of Food Aid in Rural Ethiopia: Chronic Need or Inertia?". *Journal of Development Economics*, 68(2): 247–88.

Kaiser, Kai, Tubagus Choesni, Paul Gertler, David Levine, and Jack

Molyneaux. 2001. "The Cost of Living Over Time and Space in Indonesia". Mimeo.

Kapteyn, Arie, Peter Kooreman and Rob Willemse. 1988. "Some Methodological Issues in the Implementation of Subjective Poverty Definitions". *Journal of Human Resources*, 23(2): 222–42.

Lieberman, Sandy, Melanie Juwono and Puti Marzoeki. 2001. "Government Health Expenditures in Indonesia Through December 2000: An Update". *East Asia and Pacific Region Watching Brief*, October 15, 2001, Issue 6, World Bank.

Lokshin, Michael and Martin Ravallion. 2000. "Welfare Impacts of the 1998 Financial Crisis in Russia and the Response of the Public Safety Net". *Economics of Transition*, 8(2): 269–95.

Martorell, Reynaldo and Jean-Pierre Habicht. 1986. "Growth in Early Childhood in Developing Countries". In F. Falkner and J.M. Tanner (eds.), *Human Growth: A Comprehensive Treatise*, Volume 3, New York: Plenum Press.

National Institutes of Health. 1998. *Clinical Guidelines on the Identification, Evaluation and Treatment of Overweight and Obesity in Adults*. NIH Publication No. 98-4083, Bethesda, Md.

National Institutes of Health, 1997. *The Sixth Report of the Joint National Committee on Prevention, Detection, Evaluation and Treatment of High Blood Pressure*. NIH Publication No. 98-4080, Bethesda, Md.

National Research Council. 1993. *Demographic Effects of Economic Reversals in Sub-Saharan Africa*. Washington D.C.: National Academy Press.

Philipson, Tomas. 2001. "The World-wide Growth in Obesity: An Economic Research Agenda". *Health Economics*, 10: 1–7.

Popkin, Barry and Colleen Doak. 1998. "The Obesity Epidemic is a Worldwide Phenomenon". *Nutrition Reviews*, 56(4): 106–14.

Pradhan, Menno. 2001. "Basic Education Outcomes During Crisis: An Analysis Using the 1998–2000 Susenas". Mimeo, World Bank, Jakarta, Indonesia.

Pradhan, Menno and R. Sparrow. 2000. "Basic Education Outcomes During Crisis: An Analysis Using the 1995, 1997, 1998 and 1999 Susenas". Mimeo, World Bank, Jakarta, Indonesia.

Pradhan, Menno, Asep Suryahdi, Sudarno Sumarto, Lant Pritchett. 2001. "Eating like which 'Joneses?' An iterative solution to the choice of a poverty line 'reference group' ". *Review of Income and Wealth*, 47(4): 473–87.

Ravallion, Martin. 1994. *Poverty Comparisons*, Chur Switzerland: Harwood Academic Pubishers.

Ravallion, Martin and Benu Bidani. 1994. "How Robust is a Poverty Profile?". *World Bank Economic Review*, 8(1): 75–102.

Sastry, Narayan. 2002. "Forest Fires, Air Pollution, and Mortality in Southeast Asia". *Demography*, 39(1): 1–24.

Singh, Inderjit, Lyn Squire and John Strauss. 1986. *Agricultural Household Models: Extensions, Applications and Policy*. Baltimore: Johns Hopkins University Press.

SMERU Team. 1999. The result of intensive supervision of SMERU Team at the preparation for implementation of Region Empowerment to Overcome the Effect of Economic Crisis (PDMDKE), SMERU, Jakarta, Indonesia, mimeo.

Smith, James P., Duncan Thomas, Elizabeth Frankenberg, Kathleen Beegle and Graciela Teruel. 2002. "Wages, Employment and Economic Shocks: Evidence from Indonesia". *Journal of Population Economics*, 15: 161–93.

Sumarto, Sudarno, Asep Suryhadi and Wenefrida Widyanti. 2001. "Designs and Implementation of the Indonesian Social Safety Net Programs: Evidence from the JPS Module in the 1999 SUSENAS". SMERU Working Paper, March, Jakarta, Indonesia.

Suryahadi, Asep, Sudarno Sumarto, Yusuf Suharso, Lant Pritchett. 2000. "The Evolution of Poverty During the Crisis in Indonesia, 1996 to 1999". World Bank Staff Working Paper No. 2435, Washington D.C.

Strauss, John and Duncan Thomas. 1995. "Human Resources: Empirical Modeling of Household and Family Decisions". In J. Behrman and T.N. Srinivasan (eds.), *Handbook of Development Economics*, Volume 3A, Amsterdam: North Holland Press.

Strauss, John, Paul Gertler, Omar Rahman and Kristen Fox. 1993. "Gender and Life-cycle Differentials in the Patterns and Determinants of Adult Health". *Journal of Human Resources*, 28(4): 791–837.

Thomas, Duncan. 1994. "Like Father like Son; Like Mother, Daughter: Parental Resources and Child Height". *Journal of Human Resources*, 29(4): 950–88.

Thomas, Duncan., Kathleen Beegle, and Elizabeth Frankenberg. 2000. "Labor Market Transitions of Men and Women During an Economic Crisis: Evidence from Indonesia". DRU-2344-NICHD/NIA. Santa Monica, CA: RAND. IUSSP publication, forthcoming.

Thomas, Duncan, Elizabeth Frankenberg and James P. Smith. 2001. "Lost

But Not Forgotten: Attrition and Follow-up in the Indonesia Family Life Survey". *Journal of Human Resources*, 36(3): 556–92.

Thomas, Duncan, Victor Lavy and John Strauss. 1996. "Public Policy and Anthropometric Outcomes in the Cote d'Ivoire". *Journal of Public Economics*, 61: 155–92.

Thomas, Duncan, Kathleen Beegle, Elizabeth Frankenberg, Bondan Sikoki, John Strauss, and Graciela Teruel. 2001. "Education in a Crisis". Mimeo, UCLA Department of Economics.

Witoelar, Firman. 2002. "Income Pooling in Extended Households: Evidence from the Indonesia Family Life Survey". Mimeo, Department of Economics, Michigan State University, East Lansing, MI.

World Bank. 1997. *Everyone's Miracle? Revisiting Poverty and Inequality in East Asia*, Washington D.C.

World Bank. 1998. *East Asia: The Road to Recovery*, Washington DC.

Index